LEADING CASES AND MATERIALS ON THE COMMON MARKET

E.E.C.

EUROPA INSTITUTE
UNIVERSITY OF AMSTERDAM

# LEADING CASES AND MATERIALS ON THE COMPETITION LAW OF THE E.E.C.

D.J. GIJLSTRA AND D.F. MURPHY

THIRD EDITION

Edited by

D.J. Gijlstra

KLUWER LAW AND TAXATION PUBLISHERS
Deventer/Netherlands
Antwerp · Boston · London · Frankfurt

D/1984/2664/77

ISBN 90 6544 111 5

# PREFACE TO THIRD EDITION

The book is intended as an aid for students but presumes a reasonable knowledge of the general principles of Community Law. It is recommended that the Case Book is used in conjuntion with one of the text books on the subject.

This Case Book has been revised and up-dated to take into consideration the developments in EEC Competition Law since 1979. The basic structure has remained the same as in the First and Second Editions.

The many developments in EEC Competition Law since 1979, especially in the field of procedure and distribution, made it necessary however to change the structure of Chapter Five, now entitled "Procedural Aspects", and Chapter Six of this Case Book. The structure of Chapter Six has been especially adapted to the many new developments in the field of distribution.

As indicated in the Second Edition, the choice of materials to be included in the Case Book always presents a Hobson's choice as regards the size of the extracts from the cases and Decisions, as well as the amount of legislation to be included in the Case Book. We have opted for longer extracts of the cases and Decisions to make it easier for the reader to get a better grasp of what the cases and Decisions are about.

Again, as in the First and Second Editions, we have not included legislation on the application of EEC Rules of Competition to the transport sector. Requirements of space forces us to limit the amount of legislation to be included and since little is happening in the field of transportation, we believe this to be the most logical category of legislation to be left out. We have also not included the Revised Draft Regulation on Concentration as we have serious doubt about its future. Due to lack of space we have had to leave out the explanatory note of the Commission on Regulation 1983/83 and Regulation 1984/83.

We would like to thank Miss Mary Emms for her assistance in the typing of the manuscript and Francis Garlinck for revising the Tables of Decisions and Communications and Cases.

Amsterdam May 1984

Douwe Gijlstra

ABBREVIATIONS

| | |
|---|---|
| CCH | - Common Market Reports, published by Commerce Clearing House, Chicago |
| CMLR | - Common Market Law Reports |
| CML Rev. | - Common Market Law Review |
| Colum. J. Transnat. L. | - Columbia Journal of Transnational Law |
| Competition Law | - Competition Law in Western Europe and the United States, D.J. Gijlstra and D.F. Murphy, managing editors (loose leaf) |
| Competition Report | - Reports on Competition Policy annexed to the General Reports on the Activities of the Commission, published yearly by the European Commission |
| EAEC | - European Atomic Energy Community |
| EC | - European Communities |
| EL Rev | - European Law Review |
| ECR | - European Court Reports |
| ECSC | - European Coal and Steel Community |
| EEC | - European Economic Community |
| ICLQ | - International Comparative Law Quarterly |
| JBL | - Journal of Business Law |
| JO | - Journal Officiel des Communautés Européennes |
| JWTL | - Journal of World Trade Law |
| LIEI | - Legal Issues of European Integration |
| OJ | - Official Journal of the European Communities |
| MLR | - Modern Law Review |
| NLJ | - New Law Journal |
| NW. J. INT'L & Bus | - Northwestern Journal of International Law & Business |

TABLE OF CONTENTS

## Chapter One

# INTRODUCTION TO E.E.C. COMPETITION LAW

## 1. OBJECTIVES OF THE EUROPEAN ECONOMIC COMMUNITY

### A. Principles

a. Introduction

The objectives of the European Economic Community, the means by which to achieve these objectives and some basic general rules are laid down in Part 1 of the Treaty, entitled "Principles".

Article 2 mentions one long term, political objective: "Closer relations between the States belonging to the Community" and four economic objectives. These economic objectives are: the promotion throughout the Community of a harmonious development of economic activities; a continuous and balanced expansion; an increase in stability; and an accelerated raising of the standard of living. The objectives of Article 2 are of a dynamic nature and have their counterparts in the four more static objectives of Article 104. The latter article obliges each Member State to pursue the economic policy needed to ensure the equilibrium of its overall balance of payments and to maintain confidence in its currency, while taking care to ensure a high level of prices. Article 2 also provides the Community institutions with the economic instruments with which to achieve these differing objectives.
The first instrument is the establishment of a common market and the second instrument is the progressive approximation of the economic policies of the Member States.

Article 3 of the Treaty is a non exhaustive elaboration of Article 2 in as much as parts (a), (b), (c) and (f) of Article 3 are means by which to achieve the establishment of the Common Market, while parts (d), (e), (g), (i), (j) and (k) concern the progressive approximation of economic policies.
Part (h) of Article 3 concerns both the establishment of the Common Market and the progressive approximation of economic policies.

Article 4 of the Treaty provides an outline of the Institutional Structure of the Community; the institutions mentioned are an Assembly, a Council, a Commission and a Court of Justice.

Article 5 imposes a series of obligations on the Member States. Firstly, the Member States are required to take all appropriate measures whether general or particular, to ensure fulfilment of the obligations arising out of the Treaty or resulting from action taken by the institutions of the Community and to facilitate the achievement of the Community's task.

In the second place the Member States pledge to abstain from any measure which could jeopardise the attainment of the objectives of the Treaty.

Article 6 emphasises that the progressive approximation of economic policies is a matter of concern not only for the Member States but also for the Community.

A general prohibition of discrimination on grounds of nationality is contained in Article 7. It will be observed that more specific pro-

hibitions of discrimination are contained elsewhere in the Treaty.
Article 8 provides a timetable for the progressive establishment of the Common Market.

b. Cases

(1) Deutsche Grammophon Case

Deutsche Grammophon GmbH v. Metro-SB-Grossmärkte GmbH K.G., Case 78/80, Preliminary Ruling of 8 June 1971; (1971)ECR 487; CCH para, 8106; (1971) CMLR 656; Competition Law CM/M/III/22.

*Facts:* Deutsche Grammophon GmbH (DGG), the respondent company in the appellate proceedings in the action for an injunction, is a joint subsidiary of Philips Gloeilampen-Fabrieken, Eindhoven, and Siemens AG, Berlin/München. It produces grammophone records (for which it has certain artists under exclusive contracts) and markets its products under a number of marks. In the German Federal Republic the records are supplied to retailers and to two book-wholesalers which exclusively supply retail bookshops. The retail prices of the records are mostly controlled; in any event, all the numbers that are sold under the 'Polydor' mark are subject to a retail price-maintenance system. Retailers have to sign an appropriate form to this effect. The form in addition provides that the price-maintenance undertaking also applies to DGG records acquired from third parties and that such products can only be imported from abroad with the authorisation of DGG (and the consent is only given if the retailer also undertakes to observe the price maintenance system in this respect). DGG, on its part, is bound to supply solely to retailers who sign the undertaking. In addition, it has to ensure that the price-maintenance system is kept watertight and proceed against infringements. The records are marketed abroad through subsidiaries of DGG or Philips. This is the case in particular in France where Polydor S.A., Paris (99.55 per cent of the capital of which is held by DGG), supplies the market from its factories in Paris and Strasbourg. DGG has concluded a licensing agreement with it, whereby the licensee has inter alia the exclusive right in the territory of the agreement (i.e. France) to exploit DGG recordings through channels customary in the trade (i.e. through retailers) and to use the appropriate marks. For this purpose DGG supplies matrixes for reproduction against payment of licence fees. In special cases records manufactured in the Federal Republic are also supplied to Polydor Paris.
Metro-SB-Grossmärkte GmbH, Hamburg, the appellant company in the German court, bought Polydor records from DGG in the period from April to October 1969 but did not observe the retail price-maintenance system. Since Metro was not prepared to sign a retailer's undertaking, business relations were broken off at the end of October 1969. However, in January and February 1970 Metro succeeded in obtaining Polydor records manufactured by DGG in Germany from a Hamburg wholesaler. Apparently these records had been supplied by DGG to its Paris subsidiary. They had then reached the Hamburg wholesaler through the Strasbourg branch and a Swiss enterprise. Metro also sold these records to retail customers at a price below that fixed by DGG for the Federal Republic.
When DGG learnt of this it obtained a provisional injunction from the Landgericht Hamburg on 20 March 1970 prohibiting Metro from selling or distributing in any other way DGG records with certain serial

numbers under the Polydor mark. The application and the court's decision were based on the Gesetz über Urheberrecht und verwandte Schutzrechte (statute concerning Copyright and similar Protection Rights) of 9 September 1965, which came into force on 1 January 1966 and which, in accordance with the Convention concerning the Protection of Performing Artists, Manufacturers of Sound Recordings and Broadcasting Undertakings of 26 October 1961, created an original protection right, similar to copyright for manufacturers of sound recordings. (Incidentally, such a right only exists in the E.E.C. area in Italy - under Article 72 of the Statute of 22 April 1941 - while in the other Member States corresponding protection is ensured by the statutes concerning unfair competition or by the fact that the manufacturer acquired the original right of the artists). The Landgericht invoked sections 85 and 97 of the German Statute, which provide as follows:

Section 85: 'The manufacturer of a sound recording has the exclusive right to reproduce and to distribute the recording'.

Section 97: 'Any person who unlawfully infringes the copyright or any other right protected by this statute may, at the suit of the person whose rights are infringed, be ordered to abate the infringement, or, if there is a danger of repetition, be restrained by injunction, and if he is found to have acted with intent or negligence he may be ordered to pay damages'.

In addition, the court evidently found that the exclusive right attributed to DGG to distribute its records in Germany had not been exhausted by the delivery to Polydor Paris. Thus it held that there was no exhaustion of the right as provided in the appropriately applicable section 17 of the Copyright Statute in the following words: 'If the original or reproductions of the work have been brought into circulation with the consent of the person entitled to distribute them in the territory to which this statute applies by means of alienation their further distribution is permitted'. In the view of the court, this provision would only have applied if a distribution had occurred in the German Federal Republic. Otherwise the marketing of re-imported records in Germany had to be regarded as impermissable.

The protest lodged by Metro against the provisional injunction was unsuccessful. In a judgment of 22 May 1970 all the arguments submitted against the order of the court were held to be of no avail. Metro then lodged an appeal against this judgment and the matter thus came before the Hanseatische Oberlandesgericht. In support of the appeal it was submitted inter alia that DGG no longer had the distribution rights in the records in question as these rights had been extinguished by the delivery to the French subsidiary. In addition it was contended that the contractual relations between DGG and its French licensee constituted a division of the market and made inter-state trade more difficult, which, in conjunction with the price-maintenance system practised in the Federal Republic, justified the assertion that Articles 85 and 86 of the EEC Treaty were infringed.

In view of these arguments the Oberlandesgericht, by an order of 8 October 1970, suspended the proceedings and in accordance with Article 177 of the EEC Treaty submitted the following questions for a preliminary ruling:

1. Does an interpretation of Sections 97 and 85 of the Statute concerning Copyright and similar Protection Rights of 9 September 1965 (I BGBI, 1273), whereby a German manufacturer of sound recordings, by virtue of its distribution rights, can prohibit the marketing in the German Federal Republic of recordings which it has itself supplied to its subsidiary in France which is legally separate but economically

completely dependent, conflict with Article 5(2) or Article 85(1) of the EEC Treaty ?

2. Can the exercise of the distribution rights by the manufacturer of recordings be regarded as abusive if the tied selling price of the recordings is higher than the price of the same product re-imported from another Member State and at the same time the performers in question are bound by exclusive contracts to the manufacturer of the recordings (Article 86 of the EEC Treaty) ?

*The court held:*

.....

The first question

2. In the first question the Court is asked to rule whether it is contrary to the second paragraph of Article 5 or Article 85(1) of the EEC Treaty to interpret Articles 97 and 85 of the German Law of 9 September 1965 on copyright and related rights to mean that a German undertaking manufacturing sound recordings may rely on its exclusive right of distribution to prohibit the marketing in the Federal Republic of Germany of sound recordings which it has itself supplied to its French subsidiary which, although independent at law, is wholly subordinate to it commercially.

3. Under Article 177 the Court, when giving a preliminary ruling, is entitled only to pronounce on the interpretation of the Treaty and of acts of the institutions of the Community or on their validity but may not, on the basis of that Article, give judgment on the interpretation of a provision of national law. It may however extract from the wording of the questions formulated by the national court those matters only which pertain to the interpretation of the Treaty, taking into account the facts communicated by the said court.

4. It is clear from the facts recorded by the Hanseatisches Oberlandesgericht, Hamburg, that what it asks may be reduced in essentials to the question whether the exclusive right of distributing the protected articles which is conferred by a national law on the manufacturer of sound recordings may, without infringing Community provisions, prevent the marketing on national territory of products lawfully distributed by such manufacturer or with his consent on the territory of another Member State. The Court of Justice is asked to define the tenor and the scope of the relevant Community provisions, with particular reference to the second paragraph of Article 5 or Article 85(1).

5. According to the second paragraph of Article 5 of the Treaty, Member States 'shall abstain from any measure which could jeopardise the attainment of the objective of this Treaty'. The provision lays down a general duty for the Member States, the actual tenor of which depends in each individual case on the provisions of the Treaty or on the rules derived from its general scheme.

6. According to Article 85(1) of the Treaty 'The following shall be prohibited as incompatible with the common market: all agreements between undertakings, decisions by associations of undertakings and concerted practices which may affect trade between Member States and which have as their object or effect the prevention, restriction or distortion of competition within the Common Market'. The exercise of the exclusive right referred to in the question might fall under the prohi-

bition set out by this provision each time it manifests itself as the subject, the means or the result of an agreement which, by preventing imports from other Member States of products lawfully distributed there, has as its effect the partitioning of the market.

7. If, however, the exercise of the right does not exhibit those elements of contract or concerted practice referred to in Article 85(1) it is necessary, in order to answer the question referred, further to consider whether the exercise of the right in question is compatible with other provisions of the Treaty, in particular those relating to the free movement of goods.

8. The principles to be considered in the present case are those concerned with the attainment of a single market between the Member States, which are placed both in Part Two of the Treaty devoted to the foundations of the Community, under the free movement of goods, and in Article 3(g) of the Treaty which prescribes the institution of a system ensuring that competition in the common market is not distorted.

9. Moreover, where certain prohibitions or restrictions on trade between Member States are conceded in Article 36, the Treaty makes express reference to them, providing that such derogations shall not constitute 'a means of arbitrary discrimination or a disguised restriction on trade between Member States'.

10. It is thus in the light of those provisions, especially of Articles 36, 85 and 86, that an appraisal should be made as to how far the exercise of a national right related to copyright may impede the marketing of products from another Member State.

11. Amongst the prohibitions or restrictions on the free movement of goods which it concedes Article 36 refers to industrial and commercial property. On the assumption that those provisions may be relevant to a right related to copyright, it is nevertheless clear from that Article that, although the Treaty does not affect the existence of rights recognised by the legislation of a Member State with regard to industrial and commercial property, the exercise of such rights may nevertheless fall within the prohibitions laid down by the Treaty. Although it permits prohibitions or restrictions on the free movement of products, which are justified for the purpose of protecting industrial and commercial property, Article 36 only admits derogations from that freedom to the extent to which they are justified for the purpose of safeguarding rights which constitute the specific subject-matter of such property.

12. If a right related to copyright is relied upon to prevent the marketing in a Member State of products distributed by the holder of the right or with his consent on the territory of another Member State on the sole ground that such distribution did not take place on the national territory, such a prohibition, which would legitimise the isolation of national markets, would be repugnant to the essential purpose of the Treaty, which is to unite national markets into a single market.

That purpose could not be attained if, under the various legal systems of the Member States, nationals of those States were able to partition the market and bring about arbitrary discrimination or disguised restrictions on trade between Member States.

13. Consequently, it would be in conflict with the provisions prescribing the free movement of products within the common market for a manufacturer of sound recordings to exercise the exclusive right to distribute the protected articles, conferred upon him by the legislation of a Member State, in such a way as to prohibit the sale in that State of products placed on the market by him or with his consent in another Member State solely because such distribution did not occur within the territory of the first Member State.

.....

Having regard to the Treaty establishing the European Economic Community, especially Articles 3, 5, 36, 85, 86 and 177;
Having regard to the Protocol on the Statute of the Court of Justice of the EEC, especially Article 20;
Having regard to the Rules of Procedure of the Court of Justice of the European Communities,

THE COURT ruled

1. It is in conflict with the provisions prescribing the free movement of products within the common market for a manufacturer of sound recordings to exercise the exclusive right to distribute the protected articles, conferred upon him by the legislation of a Member State, in such a way as to prohibit the sale in that State of products placed on the market by him or with his consent in another Member State solely because such distribution did not occur within the territory of the first Member State.

2. (a) A manufacturer of sound recordings who holds an exclusive right of distribution under national legislation does not occupy a dominant position within the meaning of Article 86 of the Treaty merely by exercising that right. The position is different when having regard to the circumstances of the case he has the power to impede the maintenance of effective competition over a considerable part of the relevant market.

(b) The difference between the controlled price and the price of the product reimported from another Member State does not necessarily suffice to disclose an abuse of a dominant position; it may, however, if unjustified by any objective criteria and if it is particularly marked, be a determining factor in such abuse.

.....

Sequel

The Hanseatische Oberlandesgericht in its judgment of 28 October 1971, applying the ruling of the Court of Justice dismissed the application for an injunction brought by the Deutsche Grammophon Gesellschaft against the defendant, Metro-SB-Grossmärkte GmbH.

.....

(2) Walt Wilhelm Case

Walt Wilhelm a.o. v. Bundeskartellamt
Case 14/68, Preliminary Ruling of 13 February 1969; (1969) ECR 1;

(1969) CMLR 100; CCH para. 8506; Competition Law CM/M/III/10.

*Facts:* By an order of 28 November 1967 the Bundeskartellamt (Federal Cartel Bureau), Berlin, fined the applicants under head (i) of the first section of paragraph 38, jointly with paragraph 1, of the GWB (Gesetz gegen Wettbewerbsbeschränkungen - the German law against restraint of competition of 27 July 1957).
The Bundeskartellamt alleges that on 18 July 1967 these undertakings agreed amongst themselves, and with other manufacturers of dyestuffs from other Member States as well as from third countries, to raise the price of aniline by 8% from 16 October 1967. This decision is the subject of the cause pending before the Kammergericht (Kartellsenat), Berlin.
The Commission of the European Communities had on its own intiative commenced proceedings under Articles 9(3) and 3 of Regulation No 17 on 31 May 1967, against four of the German undertakings affected by the order of the Bundeskartellamt, as well as other aniline manufacturers from the Community and third countries. These proceedings may, according to Article 15(2) of Regulation No 17, result in the imposition of fines.
At first the Commission proceedings were concerned with verifying the compatibility with the EEC Treaty of the price increases for aniline of January 1964 and January 1965; subsequently the Commission also included the new increase of 16 October 1967 among the complaints made against the undertakings concerned in the proceedings, and they were informed of this by the Commission during October 1967 in accordance with Article 19(1) of Regulation No 17, in conjunction with Article 2 of Regulation No 99/63.

The Commission claims that these repeated and uniform price increases are evidence of concerted practices within the meaning of Article 85(1) of the EEC Treaty.

The undertakings concerned alleged before the Berlin Kammergericht, inter alia, that the Bundeskartellamt was not competent under German law to take proceedings against a breach of law which was simultaneously the subject of parallel proceedings before the Commission for infringement of Article 85 paragraph 1 of the EEC Treaty.

By an order of 18 July 1968, entered in the Court Registry on 25 July 1968, the Berlin Kammergericht asked the Court for a preliminary ruling under Article 177, first and second paragraphs, of the EEC Treaty on the following questions:
1. Is it in accordance with Article 85(1) and (3) of the EEC Treaty and Article 9 of Regulation No 17 of 6 February 1962, and with the prevailing general principles of Community law, to apply concurrently to a situation capable of fulfilling the conditions set out in Article 85(1) of the EEC Treaty not only the prohibition prescribed by that Article but also the restrictive provisions contained in the cartel law of a Member State, in this instance paragraph 1 together with paragraph 38(1)(i) of the GWB, when the Commission of the European Communities has already asserted its jurisdiction under Article 3 of the EEC Treaty through action taken under Article 14 of Regulation No. 17 ?
2. Or is this impossible because of the risk of its resulting in a double sanction imposed by the Commission of the European Communities and by the national authority with jurisdiction in cartel matters - in this case, the Bundeskartellamt ?
3. Does Article 5 of the EEC Treaty, in conjunction with Article 3(f) of the EEC Treaty and with Article 9 of Regulation No 17 make this impossible in particular because Member States must refrain from applying

their own law regarding competition when the uniform legal assessment of a case would otherwise be placed at risk and/or when there would thereby result a distortion of competition in the common market to the detriment of those subject to that law ?
4. Does Article 7 of the EEC Treaty make this impossible, in particular when the national authority with jurisdiction in cartel matters - in this case the Bundeskartellamt - addresses its measures exclusively to the nationals of its own state and thereby may place them at a disadvantage in comparison to the nationals of other Member States in a comparable situation ?

*The court held:*

The fourth question

12. Finally the national court asks whether, when a procedure has been initiated by the Commission against an agreement, it would be compatible with Article 7 of the EEC Treaty for the national authority to take punitive action in respect of the same agreement. This question envisages in particular cases in which the authorities of a state which have jurisdiction in cartel matters address their measures exclusively to the nationals of that state, thereby possibly placing the latter at a disadvantage in comparison with the nationals of other Member States who are in a comparable situation.
13. Article 7 of the EEC Treaty prohibits every Member State from applying its law on cartels differently on the ground of the nationality of the parties concerned. However, Article 7 is not concerned with any disparities in treatment or the distortions which may result, for the persons and undertakings subject to the jurisdiction of the Community, from divergencies existing between the laws of the various Member States, so long as the latter affect all persons subject to them, in accordance with objective criteria and without regard to their nationality.

*The court ruled:*

1. So long as a regulation adopted pursuant to Article 87(2)(e) of the Treaty has not provided otherwise, national authorities may take action against an agreement in accordance with their national law even when an examination of the position with regard to that agreement from the point of view of its compatibility with Community law is pending before the Commission, subject however to the condition that the application of national law must not prejudice the full and uniform application of Community law or the effects of measures taken or to be taken to implement it;

2. Article 7 of the EEC Treaty prohibits Member States from applying their laws on cartels differently on the ground of the nationality of the parties concerned, but it is not concerned with disparities in treatment resulting from divergences existing between the laws of Member States, so long as these affect all persons subject to them in accordance with objective criteria and without regard to nationality.
.....

Sequel

For the procedure in the dyestuffs case at Community level, see below page 41 for the Decision of the European Commission and below page 44 for the Judgment of the Court of Justice.

The German Bundesgerichtshof annulled the Decision of the Bundeskartellamt as regards the fines imposed on Wilhelm and the others. It considered that in this case, seen the fact that the Commission had also taken repressive measures against the companies involved, a double sanction would be discriminatory.

For the Opinion of the Court of Justice on the problem of parallel application of Community law and national law see below page 27 and for the question of double jeopardy see below Chapter Five.

## B. The Foundations and Policy of the Community

Part two of the Treaty - entitled "Foundations of the Community" - lays down rules aimed at securing the free movement of goods, persons, services and capital; it also provides common rules on agriculture and transport. The free movement of goods is based on a Customs Union, involving the elimination of customs duties between the Member States.

Part three of the Treaty - entitled "Policy of the Community" - is divided into four sections.

Title 1 provides common rules of economic policy for all the Member States. These consist of rules on competition, applicable both to public and private enterprises, anti-dumping rules and rules governing state-aids; common tax provisions; and finally, rules on approximation of laws.

Title 2 deals with short term economic policy and the balance of payments as well as providing for a common commercial policy.

Title 3 deals with social policy and the establishment of a European Social Fund.

Title 4 provides for the establishment of a European Investment Bank.

Part four of the Treaty provides for the association of the overseas countries and territories, part five lays down the rules governing the instructions (created by Art. 4 of the Treaty), and part 6 contains general and final provisions.

## II. THE PLACE AND ROLE OF THE COMPETITION RULES IN THE TREATY AND THE LEVEL OF COMPETITION REQUIRED.

### a. Introduction

The economic system embodied by the EEC Treaty is based on the principles of the free market economy: competition is accorded a central role in the operation of this system. The maintenance of adequate competition is a major consideration governing both the functioning of the common market and the approximation of the economies of the Member States.

Competition however, is not an end in itself. It is a means of ensuring the optimum division of labour, maximum productivity, the satisfaction of demand, and the preservation of private enterprise. Thus, Articles 85 and 86 of the Treaty prohibit artificial restrictions and distortions of competition.

The Treaty envisages a single market in which every participant should be free to invest, to produce, to work, to buy, to sell, or to obtain services, in undistorted conditions of competition, and wherever economic conditions are most favourable. The establishment of a customs union, the removal of customs barriers and the elimination of quotas, have, to a great extent, opened up the markets of the Member States. Nonetheless, practices, which restrict cross-frontier trade still exist. Examples of this can be seen in the maintenance of tax barriers and in the existence of different rules of business regulation.

The Treaty contains certain rules to cope with these distortions. Articles 95 - 99 deal with the elimination of tax frontiers. Article 100 lays down the procedure for the harmonisation of laws that directly affect the establishment or functioning of the Common Market. Articles 101 and 102 provide for the elimination of national rules or administrative practices that distort the conditions of competition in the Common Market. Competition can also be distorted by state participation in the economy: typical examples include state owned commercial monopolies; public works contracts; state procurement contracts; public enterprise; and assistance in the form of state aids. Article 37 of the Treaty aims at the progressive adjustment of state commercial monopolies. A Community-wide system has been worked out to allow enterprises from other Member States to tender for government contracts. Similarly, government procurements must be made on the basis of non-discrimination. Article 90 obliges governments not to treat public enterprises more favorably than private enterprises. Public enterprises entrusted with the operation of services of general economic interest are, however, exempt from this rule. Articles 92 - 94 establish a system of Community checks on the provision of state aids.

Articles 85 - 89 contain competition rules applicable to private enterprises. These rules are aimed at ensuring that the creation of effective conditions of competition in the common market is not hindered by the erection of private barriers or restrictions. The maintenance of competition is thus an essential canon of the Community's economic and legal order. Accordingly, the Court of Justice has held that Articles 85 and 86 must be interpreted and applied in the light of Articles 2 and 3(f) of the Treaty.

The court has ruled that the requirement contained in Articles 3 and 85 of the EEC Treaty that competition shall not be distorted, implies the existence on the market of workable competition.

b. Cases

(1) Continental Can Case

Europemballage and Continental Can v. Commission; Case 6/72, Judgment of 21 February 1973; (1973) ECR 215; (1973) CMLR 219; CCH para. 8171; Competition Law CM/M/III/38.

*Facts:* Continental Can Company Inc. (Continental) of New York (USA), a company manufacturing metal packages, packaging materials of paper and plastic and machines for manufacturing and using these packages, by successive purchases during the year 1969, brought its share in Schmalbach-Lubeca-Werke AG (SLW) of Brunswick (Germany) to 85.8% of the nominal capital.

During the same year, Continental contemplated the formation, with The Metal Box Company Ltd. (MB) of London, of a European holding company for packaging, in which the licensees of Continental in the Netherlands and in France, Thomassen & Drijver-Verblifa N.V. (TDV) of

Deventer and J.J. Carnaud and Forges de Basse-Indre (Carnaud) of Paris, would be invited to participate. However, Carnaud indicated, at the end of August 1969, that it could not participate in the contemplated holding company.

On 16 February 1970, an agreement was signed between Continental and TDV whereby it was agreed:

(a) that Continental would set up in Delaware (USA) a company (subsequently called Europemballage Corporation) to which it would transfer its interests in SLW;

(b) that Continental would induce Europemballage to offer to the shareholders of TDV other than MB and Carnaud, a sum of 140 florins cash for each TDV share of 20 florins nominal value. Each TDV shareholder offering his shares would also receive a certificate granting him a preferential right to purchase ordinary shares in Europemballage when these should be offered to the public. Continental would provide Europemballage with the necessary funds for such a purchase by acquiring additional shares in Europemballage.

In implementation of this agreement:

- on 20 February 1970, a company called Europemballage Corporation (Europemballage) was set up in Wilmington, under the legislation of the state of Delaware. This company opened an office in New York and another in Brussels;
- on 16 March 1970. TDV published the take-over bid made by Europemballage.

In March and April, the Commission drew the attention of the undertakings concerned to the possible incompatibility of the transaction contemplated with the provisions of Article 86 of the Treaty, and to the legal and financial consequences which might thereby arise for these companies. MB then indicated that it was postponing its contemplated transaction with Europemballage.

On 8 April 1970, Europemballage carried out the purchase of the shares and debentures of TDV offered up to that date, thus bringing the initial share of Continental in TDV to 91.07%.

On 9 April 1970, the Commission decided to open of its own motion a procedure, in application of Article 3(1) of Regulation No 17/62, against Continental and its subsidiary Europemballage concerning the acquisition by the latter of the majority of the shares of TDV.

On completion of that procedure the Commission made, on 9 December 1971, a decision under Article 86 of the Treaty which, having set out the reasons on which it was based concerning the characteristics of the undertakings in question, their mutual links on a personal, financial, contractual and technical level and, particularly as regards SLW and TDV, the characteristics of their production, their sales on their respective markets, the exports of one company into the territory of the other, their competitive situation, etc., provides as follows:

Article 1

It is found that Continental Can Company Inc. of New York, which holds through the medium of its subsidiary, Schmalbach-Lubeca-Werke AG of Brunswick, a dominant position over a substantial part of the Common Market on the market for light packaging for preserved meat, fish and crustacea and on the market in metal caps for glass jars, has abused this dominant position by the purchase made in April 1970 by its subsidiary Europemballage Corporation of approximately 80% of the shares and convertible debentures of the Dutch undertaking Thomassen & Drijver-

Verblifa N.V. of Deventer. This purchase has had the effect of practically eliminating competition in the above-mentioned packaging products over a substantial part of the Common Market.
Article 2
This Decision is addressed to Continental Can Company Inc. in New York'.

This decision - published in the Official Journal of the European Communities of 8 January 1972, No L 7, wherein it was stated that 'the French language version is the only authentic version' - was notified to Europemballage on 14 December 1971 and to Continental Can by post during the same month. The German version also was communicated to counsel for the applicants on 20 December 1971.

Europemballage and Continental Can appealed the Commission Decision, an appeal lodged with the registry of the Court on 9 February 1972.

In the application, and subsequently by a separate document lodged with the Registry of the Court on 23 February 1972, the applicants submitted, under Article 185 of the EEC Treaty, a request for suspension of execution of Article 2 of the contested decision. The President of the Court, after hearing the parties, rejected this request by order dated 21 March 1972.

*The court held:*

.....

*C. On Article 86 of the Treaty and abuse of a dominant position*

18. In Articles 1 and 2 of the Commission's decision of 9 December 1971 Continental Can is blamed for having infringed Article 86 of the EEC Treaty by abusing the dominant position which is alledgedly held through Schmalbach-Lubeca-Werke AG of Brunswick (hereinafter called SLW) in a substantial part of the Common Market in the market for light metal containers for meat, meat products, fish and crustacea as well as in the market for metal closures for glass jars. According to Article 1 the abuse consists in Continental having acquired in April 1970, through its subsidiary Europemballage, about 80% of the shares and debentures of TDV. By this acquisition competition in the containers mentioned was practically eliminated in a substantial part of the Common Market.

19. The applicants maintain that the Commission by its decision, based on an erroneous interpretation of Article 86 of the EEC Treaty, is trying to introduce a control of mergers of undertakings, thus exceeding its powers. Such an attempt runs contrary to the intention of the authors of the Treaty, which is clearly seen not only from a literal interpretation of Article 86, but also from a comparison of the EEC Treaty and the national legal provisions of the Member States. The examples given in Article 86 of abuse of a dominant position confirm this conclusion, for they show that the Treaty only refers to practices which have effects on the market and are to the detriment of consumers or trade partners. Further, Article 86 reveals that the use of economic power linked with a dominant position can be regarded as an abuse of this position only if it constitutes the means through which the abuse is effected. But structural measures of undertakings - such as strengthening a dominant position by way of a merger - do not amount to abuse of this position within the meaning of Article 86 of the Treaty. The decision contested is, therefore, said to be void as lacking the required legal basis.

20. Article 86 par. 1 of the Treaty says 'Any abuse by one or more undertakings of a dominant position within the common market or in a substantial part of it shall be prohibited as incompatible with the common market in so far as it may affect trade between Member States'. The question is whether the word 'abuse' in Article 86 refers only to practices of undertakings which may directly affect the market and are detrimental to production or sales, to purchasers or consumers, or whether this word refers also to changes in the structure of an undertaking, which lead to competition being seriously disturbed in a substantial part of the Common Market.
21. The distinction between measures which concern the structure of the undertaking and practices which affect the market cannot be decisive, for any structural measure may influence market conditions, if it increases the size and the economic power of the undertaking.
22. In order to answer this question, one has to go back to the spirit, general scheme and wording of Article 86, as well as to the system and objectives of the Treaty. These problems thus cannot be solved by comparing this Article with certain provisions of the ECSC Treaty.
23. Article 86 is part of the chapter devoted to the common rules on the Community's policy in the field of competition. This policy is based on Article 3(f) of the Treaty according to which the Community's activity shall include the institution of a system ensuring that competition in the Common Market is not distorted. The applicant's argument that this provision merely contains a general programme devoid of legal effect, ignores the fact that Article 3 considers the pursuit of the objectives which it lays down to be indispensable for the achievement of the Community's tasks. As regards in particular the aim mentioned in (f), the Treaty in several provisions contains more detailed regulations for the interpretation of which this aim is decisive.
24. But if Article 3(f) provides for the institution of a system ensuring that competition in the Common Market is not distorted, then it requires *a fortiori* that competition must not be eliminated. This requirement is so essential that without it numerous provisions of the Treaty would be pointless. Moreover, it corresponds to the precept of Article 2 of the Treaty according to which one of the tasks of the Community is 'to promote throughout the Community a harmonious development of economic activities'. Thus the restraints on competition which the Treaty allows under certain conditions because of the need to harmonise the various objectives of the Treaty, are limited by the requirements of Articles 2 and 3. Going beyond this limit involves the risk that the weakening of competition would conflict with the aims of the Common Market.
25. With a view to safeguarding the principles and attaining the objectives set out in Articles 2 and 3 of the Treaty, Articles 85 to 90 have laid down general rules applicable to undertakings. Article 85 concerns agreements between undertakings, decisions of associations of undertakings and concerted practices, while Article 86 concerns unilateral activity of one or more undertakings. Articles 85 and 86 seek to achieve the same aim on different levels, *viz.* the maintenance of effective competition within the Common Market. The restraint of competition which is prohibited if it is the result of behaviour falling under Article 85, cannot become permissible by the fact that such behaviour succeeds under the influence of a dominant undertaking and results in the merger of the undertakings concerned. In the absence of explicit provisions one cannot assume that the Treaty, which prohibits in Article 85 certain decisions of ordinary associations of undertakings

restricting competition without eliminating it, permits in Article 86 that undertakings, after merging into an organic unity, should reach such a dominant position that any serious chance of competition is practically rendered impossible. Such a diverse legal treatment would make a breach in the entire competition law which would jeopardise the proper functioning of the Common Market. If, in order to avoid the prohibitions in Article 85, it sufficed to establish such close connections between the undertakings that they escaped the prohibition of Article 85 without coming within the scope of that of Article 86, then, in contradiction to the basic principles of the Common Market, the partitioning of a substantial part of this market would be allowed. The endeavor of the authors of the Treaty to maintain in the market real or potential competition even in cases in which restraints on competition are permitted, was explicitly laid down in Article 85 par. 3(b) of the Treaty. Article 86 does not contain the same explicit provisions, but this can be explained by the fact that the system fixed there for dominant positions, unlike Article 85 par. 3, does not recognise any exemption from the prohibition. With such a system the obligation to observe the basic objectives of the Treaty, in particular that of Article 3(f), results from the obligatory force of these objectives. In any case Articles 85 and 86 cannot be interpreted in such a way that they contradict each other, because they serve to achieve the same aim.

26. It is in the light of these considerations that the condition imposed by Article 86 is to be interpreted whereby in order to come within the prohibition a dominant position must have been abused. The provision states a certain number of abusive practices which it prohibits. The list merely gives examples, not an exhaustive enumeration of the sort of abuses of a dominant position prohibited by the Treaty. As may further be seen from letters (c) and (d) of Article 86 par. 2, the provision is not only aimed at practices which may cause damage to consumers directly, but also at those which are detrimental to them through their impact on an effective competition structure, such as is mentioned in Article 3(f) of the Treaty. Abuse may therefore occur if an undertaking in a dominant position strengthens such position in such a way that the degree of dominance reached substantially fetters competition, i.e. that only undertakings remain in the market whose behaviour depends on the dominant one.

27. Such being the meaning and scope of Article 86 of the EEC Treaty, the question of the link of causality raised by the applicants which in their opinion has to question exist between the dominant position and its abuse, is of no consequence, for the strengthening of the position of an undertaking may be an abuse and prohibited under Article 86 of the Treaty, regardless of the means and procedure by which it is achieved, if it has the effects mentioned above.

<u>(2) Commercial Solvents Case</u>

Istituto Chemioterapico Italiano SpA and Commercial Solvents Corporation v. EEC Commission; Cases 6-7/73, Judgment of 6 March 1974; (1974) ECR 223; (1974) CMLR 309; CCH para. 8209; Competition Law CM/M/III/40.

*Facts:* Commercial Solvents Corporation (CSC) is a company incorporated under the law of the State of Maryland, having its principle office in the City and State of New York, United States of America. The company manufactures and sells among other things products based on nitroparaffines, inter alia 1. nitropropane ('nitropropane') and a derivative thereof 2. amino-1-butanol ('aminobutanol'). Both are intermediary products for the manufacture of ethambutol and ethambutol-based specialities, used as an anti-tuberculosis drug.

In 1962 CSC acquired a 51% of the voting stock in Istituto Chemioterapico Italiano SpA (Istituto), a company incorporated under Italian law - having its principle office in Milan. At present CSC has a 50 per cent representation in the 'Consiglio di amministrazione' - Board of Directors - (5 out of 10) and in the 'Comitato Esecutivo' - Executive Committee - (3 out of 6). The President of CSC is also Chairman of the Board of Directors, has an additional casting vote.

Until 1970 Istituto acted as a reseller of aminobutanol produced by CSC in the United States of America. A customer of Istituto for aminobutanol was Laboratorio Chemico Farmaceutico Giorgio Zoja SpA (Zoja), to whom Istituto began selling the products in 1966. Zoja used the products in the manufacture of ethambutol-based specialities. In 1968 Istituto started development of its own ethambutol-based specialities. It obtained governmental registration for the manufacture thereof in November 1969, and started production in 1970. Early in 1970 CSC decided that in principle it would no longer supply nitropropane and aminobutanol to the EEC, but instead would supply dextro-aminobutanol, an up-graded intermediate product, which Istituto would convert into bulk ethambutol for sale in the EEC and elsewhere, and for the manufacture of its own specialities. CSC informed its resellers, including Istituto, that thereafter nitropropane and aminobutanol would be available only in such quantities as had already been committed for resale.

In the spring of 1970 Zoja cancelled its order for 20,000 kg of aminobutanol prescribed by the then current agreement between Istituto and Zoja. This step was induced by the circumstances that a number of independent distributors were supplying large amounts of aminobutanol at lower prices than those provided by the aforesaid agreement.

Since early 1970 CSC has been supplying dextro-aminobutanol to Istituto, which processes it into bulk ethambutol. Most of this product is sold by Istituto to other producers of specialities, and the balance is used for the production of Istituto's own speciality.

At the end of 1970 Istituto informed CSC that Zoja had placed a new order for aminobutanol and asked whether this intermediary product could again be supplied for resale to Zoja. CSC replied that none was available.

After further attempts to obtain supplies of aminobutanol on the world market had failed as the search for the product inevitably led to one possible source of supply, namely CSC, Zoja, by letter dated 8 April 1972, applied to the Commission for the institution of proceedings against CSC and Istituto, under Article 3 of Regulation No. 17 for infringement of Article 86 of the Treaty.

By letter dated 25 April 1972 the Commission served the Notice of Objections on CSC ans Istituto. The enterprises were given two weeks in which to reply to the objections. On 15 May 1972 CSC and Istituto submitted their oral comments.

At its meeting of 14 December 1972 the Commission adopted a decision jointly and severally requiring the applicants in the present proceedings:

(a) under penalty of a fine of 1,000 units of account per day of delay, beginning 31 days after receipt of the Decision, to supply 60,000 kg of nitropropane or 30,000 of aminobutanol to Zoja, as its most urgent needs, at a price not exceeding the maximum price charged for those two products;

(b) under penalty of a second fine of 1,000 units of account per day, to submit to the Commission within two months after receipt of the Decision, proposals for the subsequent supply of Zoja.

(c) to pay a fine of 200,000 units of account.

*The court held:*

.....

(c) Abuse of a dominant position

23. The applicants state that they ought not to be held responsible for stopping supplies of aminobutanol to Zoja for this was due to the fact that in the spring of 1970 Zoja itself informed Istituto that it was cancelling the purchase of large quantities of aminobutanol which had been provided for in a contract then in force between Istituto and Zoja. When at the end of 1970 Zoja again contacted Istituto to obtain this product, the latter was obliged to reply, after consulting CSC, that in the meantime CSC had changed its commercial policy and that the product was no longer available. The change of policy by CSC was, they claim, inspired by a legitimate consideration of the advantage that would accrue to it of expanding its production to include the manufacture of finished products and not limiting itself to that of raw material or intermediate products. In pursuance of this policy it decided to improve its product nd no longer to supply aminobutanol save in respect of commitments already entered into by its distributors.
24. It appears from the documents and from the hearing that the suppliers of raw material are limited, as regards the EEC, to Istituto, which, as stated in the claim by CSC, started in 1968 to develop its own specialities based on ethambutol, and in November 1969 obtained the approvement of the Italian government necessary for the manufacture and in 1970 started manufacturing its own specialities. When Zoja sought to obtain further supplies of aminobutanol, it received a negative reply. CSC had decided to limit, if not completely to cease, the supply of nitropropane and aminobutanol to certain parties in order to facilitate its own access to the market for the derivatives.
25. However an undertaking being in a dominant position as regards the production of raw material and therefore able to control the supply to manufacturers of derivatives, cannot, just because it decides to start manufacturing those derivatives (in competition with its former customers) act in such a way as to eliminate their competition which in the case in question, would amount to eliminating one of the principal manufacturers of ethambutol in the Common Market. Since such conduct is contrary to the objectives expressed in Article 3(f) of the Treaty and set out in greater detail in Articles 85 and 86, it follows that an undertaking which has a dominant position in the market in raw materials and which, with the object of reserving such raw materials for manufacturing its own derivatives, refuses to supply a customer, which is itself a manufacturer of these derivatives and therefore risks eliminating all competition on the part of this customer, is abusing its dominant position within the meaning of Article 86. In this context it does not matter that the undertaking ceased to supply in the spring of 1970 because of the cancellation of the purchase by Zoja, because it appears from the applicant's own statement that, when the supplies provided for in the contract had been completed, the sale of aminobutanol would have stopped in any case.
26. It is also unnecessary to examine, as the applicants have asked, whether Zoja had an urgent need for aminobutanol in 1970 and 1971 or whether this company still had large quantities of this product which

would enable it to reorganise its production in good time, since that question is not relevant to the consideration of the conduct of the applicants.

27. Finally CSC states that its production of nitropropane and aminobutanol ought to be considered in the context of nitration of paraffin, of which nitropropane is only one of the derivatives, and that similarly aminobutanol is only one of the derivatives of nitropropane. Therefore the possibilities of producing the two products in question are not unlimited but depend in part on the possible sales outlets of the other derivatives.

28. However the applicants do not seriously dispute the statement in the Decision in question to the effect that 'in view of the production capacity of the CSC plant it can be confirmed that CSC can satisfy Zoja's needs, since Zoja represents a very small percentage (approximately 5-6%) of CSC's global production of nitropropane'. It must be concluded that the Commission was justified in considering that such statements could not be taken into account.

29. These submissions must therefore be rejected.

(d) The effect on trade between Member States

30. The applicants argue that in this case it is principally the world market which is affected, since Zoja sells 90% of its production outside the Common Market and in particular in the developing countries and that constitutes a much more important market for anti-tuberculosis drugs than the countries of the Community, where tuberculosis has largely disappeared. The sales outlets of Zoja in the Common Market are further reduced by the fact that in many Member States Zoja is blocked by the patents of other companies, in particular American Cyanamid, which prevent it from selling its specialities based on ethambutol. Therefore abuse of the dominant position, even if it were established, would not come within the ambit of Article 86, which prohibits such an abuse only 'in so far as it may affect trade between Member States'.

31. This expression is intended to define the sphere of application of Community rules in relation to national laws. It cannot therefore be interpreted as limiting the field of application of the prohibition which it contains to industrial and commercial activities supplying the Member States.

32. The prohibitions of Articles 85 and 86 must in fact be interpreted and applied in the light of Article 3(f) of the Treaty, which provides that the activities of the Community shall include the institution of a system ensuring that competition in the Common Market is not distorted, and Article 2 of the Treaty, which gives the Community the task of promoting 'throughout the Community harmonious development of economic activities'. By prohibiting the abuse of a dominant position within the market in so far as it may affect trade between Member States, Article 86 therefore covers abuse which may directly prejudice consumers as well as abuse which indirectly prejudices them by impairing the effective competitive structure as envisaged by Article 3(f) of the Treaty.

33. The Community authorities must therefore consider all the consequences of the conduct complained of for the competitive structure in the Common Market without distinguishing between production intended for sale within the market and that intended for export. When an undertaking in a dominant position with the Common Market abuses its position in such a way that a competitor in the Common Market is likely to be eliminated, it does not matter whether the conduct related to the latter's exports or its trade within the Common Market, once it has

been established that this elimination will have repercussions on the competitive structure within the Common Market.
34. Moreover the contrary argument would in practice mean that the control of Zoja's production and outlets would be in the hands of CSC and Istituto. Finally its cost prices would have been so affected that the ethambutol produced by it would possibly become unmarketable.
35. Moreover it emerged at the hearing that Zoja is at present able to export and does indeed export the products in question to at least two Member States. These exports are endangered by the difficulties caused to this company and by reason of this trade between Member States may be affected.
.....

Sequel

The Court of Justice rejected the application for annulment, but lowered the fine imposed jointly and severally on the applicants by the Commission to 100,000 units of account.

(3) Metro Case

Metro-SB-Grossmärkte GmbH & Co KG v. Commission; Case 26/76, Judgment of 25 October 1977; (1977) ECR 1875; (1978) 2 CMLR 1; CCH para. 8435; Competition Law CM/M/III/40.

*Facts:* The undertaking SABA whose head office is in Villingen-Schwenningen in the Federal Republic of Germany, manufactures electronic equipment for the leisure market (radios, televisions and tape recorders) and distributes it through a network of contracts and agreements between it and sole distributors, wholesalers and appointed retailers, all of which constitutes a selective distribution system. In a Decision of 15 December 1975 the Commission gave SABA negative clearance within the meaning of Article 2 of Regulation No 17 for certain specific features of that system and granted it exemption within the meaning of Article 85(3) of the EEC Treaty, to run until 21 July 1980 subject to certain conditions regarding the remaining parts of the system in question.

After the distribution system had been altered, following the intervention of the Commission, it constitutes a uniform distribution system for the entire territory of the Community and had the following salient features:

(1) cooperation between SABA and its sole distributors and wholesalers;

(2) restriction of the number of dealers; and

(3) the establishment by the manufacturer of distribution channels.

In the Federal Republic of Germany and West Berlin this represents a network of wholesalers and retailers, both categories being appointed and, in the other Member States except Ireland, sole distributors who appear in their turn to be connected with wholesalers and in any event with appointed retailers.

The contracts and agreements connecting SABA and the various distributors in its network may be described as follows:

(a) *German wholesalers* are appointed only if they agree to sign the three documents described beneath, and if they fulfil *in addition* the conditions set out under (4) below.

(1) A *so-called 'cooperation agreement'*, under which wholesalers undertake to conclude six-monthly supply contracts with SABA and to take delivery at the appropriate time of goods ordered, to stock the relevant products and to achieve a turnover considered by SABA to be adequate; SABA for its part is obliged to consult the wholesalers on the preparation of its production schedules.

(2) *A Distribution Agreement for SABA Wholesalers* which is in two parts. By the *first part* wholesalers are obliged to restrict supplies within the territory of the Federal Republic of Germany and West Berlin to other wholesalers and retailers appointed by SABA, which implies that they fulfil a certain number of qualitative conditions and are prepared to undertake to supply the services which are a condition of appointment by SABA to the status of a specialised wholesaler or retailer. The obligations described in this first part correspond in essentials to those which SABA imposes through the document described below at (3) upon its wholesalers throughout the EEC.

The *second part* of this agreement contains additional obligations specifically relating to distribution on the German market which must be related to the concepts of German legislation and case-law on the separation of the functions of wholesalers and retailers. In accordance with these concepts German wholesalers are prohibited from selling to *private customers* in the Federal Republic of Germany and West Berlin.

On the other hand, they are permitted to supply trade consumers, that is to say, industrial or commercial undertakings which employ the products purchased from wholesalers only for such commercial purposes as will promote the efficiency of the business and which agree to give a written undertaking to that effect in terms of a document known as 'SABA-Sonderverpflichtungsschein' (special undertaking). Provision is made for checks. However, wholesalers are prohibited from supplying institutional consumers (hospitals, schools and military establishments).

(3) *An agreement for SABA Wholesalers in the EEC*, which covers the marketing operations of such wholesalers within the Common Market as a whole.

The agreement repeats for the Common Market as a whole the undertaking to supply only other wholesalers or retailers who fulfil the conditions prescribed by SABA for their appointment and the obligation to carry out or permit checks. In this respect the document repeats the essential points of the above-mentioned obligations with regard to the Federal Republic of Germany contained in the first part of the document described above under (2).

(4) SABA has informed the Commission that ' in principle it is willing to supply any wholesaler in the Federal Republic of Germany or West Berlin who:

(a) keeps a specialised shop, i.e. one where over 50% of the turnover relates to the sale of radio, television, tape-recording or other electrical equipment, or
has set up a department specialising in the wholesale of radio, television and tape-recording equipment with a turnover comparable to that of a wholesaler specialising in electronic equipment for leisure purposes;

(b) participates in the creation and consolidation of the SABA sales network;
(c) participates in the service system'.

For its part, SABA gives an undertaking to each wholesaler that it will ensure that other wholesalers comply with its system of distribution. Furthermore, the system gives distributors freedom with regard to prices, freedom to undertake supplies throughout the Common Market as a whole and to undertake so-called 'cross' supplies (wholesaler to wholesaler, retailer to retailer) or return supplies (retailer to wholesaler).

(b) SABA *sole distributors* have been set up in each of the Member States, with the exception of Ireland. In France, the United Kingdom and Italy, these distributors are SABA subsidiaries. The sole distributors for Belgium, the Grand Duchy of Luxembourg, Denmark and the Netherlands have signed sole distributorship agreements which include the essential features of the cooperation agreements and the distribution agreements and in particular incorporate the undertaking to supply only appointed wholesalers and retailers.

(c) *Retailers both in the Federal Republic of Germany and in the other Member States* must, in order to become appointed dealers, sign a document named an Agreement for SABA Specialist Retailers in the EEC. By that agreement specialist retailers bind themselves to achieve an adequate turnover in SABA products, to keep a corresponding stock and to display SABA products in a representative manner, to maintain retail premises which are suitable for advertising and displaying SABA products, to maintain appropriate servicing facilities for customers and to supply other SABA resellers (wholesale or retail) only if they are appointed SABA distributors. All supplies to other appointed resellers must be registered so as to permit a check to be carried out.

*Inter alia*, Article 2 of that agreement also shows clearly, albeit indirectly, that in order to be appointed a specialist SABA retailer it is necessary for retailers, in addition, (a) to run a specialised business, that is to say one in which over 50% of the turnover relates to the sale of electronic products for leisure purposes or to the trade in other electronic articles or which has a special department for electronic leisure products; (b) to undertake that, if they are supplied directly by SABA (that is to say, without dealing through wholesalers), they will conclude long term supply contracts covering the entire range of SABA products.

Like the wholesalers, retailers are free with regard to prices, they may sell throughout the whole Community and they are entitled to distribute the equipment of competitors of SABA.

The system of distribution maintained thus has four essential features:
(1) Distribution is effected through selected and appointed wholesalers and retailers, and sole distributors;
(2) Those resellers undertake to supply within the Common Market only other resellers who are appointed distributors, and agree to carry out or permit stringent checks in order to ensure that this undertaking is fulfilled; German wholesalers undertake not to supply private customers in the Federal Republic of Germany;
(3) Such wholesalers, retailers and dealers undertake not to export SABA equipment from the Community or to import it from third countries;

(4) Such wholesalers and retailers undertake to achieve an adequate turnover and to keep a stock of SABA equipment.

In the Decision of 15 December 1975 the Commission considered that:

(1) The limiting of distribution of products exclusively to appointed distributors has as its object and effect appreciably to restrict competition within the common market;
(2) It is clear from the objective nature of the qualitative criteria applied that, in so far as all distributors fulfilling such criteria are in fact appointed no further restriction of competition within the meaning of Article 85(1) arises;
(3) Such a restriction nevertheless obtains in so far as selection does not depend exclusively on qualitative criteria ensuring sales under adequate conditions to consumers but is also subject to further specific conditions which cannot be justified by the requirements of the sale under adequate conditions of the products concerned (adequate turnover, maintenance of corresponding stocks);
(4) Furthermore, the obligations imposed upon distributors so that SABA can check that deliveries are not made to non-appointed dealers have as their object and effect the restriction and distortion of competition in that they are intended to ensure that distributors observe restrictions which are prohibited by Article 85(1). Such obligations reduce the freedom of choice both of consumers and of traders who, although capable of marketing electronic equipment for leisure purposes, have not been appointed by SABA;
(5) Finally, the last restriction on competition referred to in Article 85(1): the fact that SABA delivers only to national distributors, and the undertaking which sole distributors give in the sole distributorship agreement to respect each other's territories.

The contested decision adopts different procedures with regard to the various provisions which make up the said distribution system as a whole. Negative clearance was granted in respect of some when it had been established that they did not infringe the prohibition contained in Article 85(1), whilst in respect of others an exemption under Article 85(3) was granted.

*Negative clearance* was granted in respect of the 'Conditions of Sale for the Domestic Market' (Article 1 of the Decision). It appears that the clearance also relates to the provisions considered in paragraphs 34 (the prohibition imposed on SABA wholesalers in Germany preventing them from supplying private customers), 35 (the prohibition on exports from the Community) and 36 (the conditions of sale, covering most of the obligations undertaken by wholesalers and retailers in the so-called 'Distribution Agreements').

*Exemption under Article 85(3)* is principally reserved for cooperation agreements and for *certain* parts of the 'Distribution Agreements', namely the retailers' obligations to offer as complete a range of SABA equipment as possible, to achieve an adequate turnover and to maintain corresponding stocks (decision, paragraph 29), together with the obligation undertaken by distributors, wholesalers and retailers to verify, before supplying a reseller, whether he has been appointed by SABA.

The applicant runs a self-service wholesale business on a cash and carry basis. By cutting out a certain number of services which in traditional trading benefit the purchaser (the grant of credit, delivery and advice to customers) general expenses are cut and more favourable prices obtained. Access to Metro's premises is granted only to retailers (resellers or trade consumers) and to institutions which, owing to their structure, have considerable commercial needs in connection with their operation. The purchasers must hold a written licence to purchase. The general conditions of sale of the Metro undertaking bind customers *inter alia* to purchase goods from Metro only for the trade requirements of their business. However, an exception is made where commercial equipment intended specifically for an undertaking is subsequently used for private purposes.

Metro, to whom SABA refuses to supply products bearing its trade mark because Metro does not fulfil the conditions for appointment as a SABA wholesaler, lodged a complaint with the Commission by a telex message of 7 November 1973 and a written statement of 9 November 1973, pursuant to Article 3 of Regulation No 17, claiming that the system of distribution agreements in force infringed Articles 85 and 86 of the EEC Treaty and requested that such infringement be terminated.

At first, Metro chiefly disputed the prohibition, which resulted *at that time* from SABA's distribution system, on 'direct supplies', that is to say, supplies to trade consumers in Germany.

Following an intervention by the Commission SABA, in the course of the administrative procedure, amended the clause prohibiting direct supplies so that German wholesalers could thereafter, on certain conditions, supply SABA products to trade consumers and only supplies to 'institutions' such as military establishments, churches, hospitals and schools remained prohibited.

At the Commission's instigation SABA in addition extended the definition of 'wholesaler' to the self-service wholesale trade, so that Metro may be admitted to SABA's network provided that it fulfils the conditions for access thereto which are applied to other wholesalers. Moreover, SABA stated that its distributors are free either to provide after-sales service themselves or to subcontract such service.

Despite those modifications Metro continued to maintain that discrimination against the self-service wholesale trade still existed, in that various restrictions on competition were retained which were not necessary for the attainment of the objectives which justify an exemption under Article 85(3), namely:

(1) The prohibition on supplies to trade consumers by wholesalers;

(2) The requirement that products purchased by trade consumers from wholesalers must be such as will promote the efficiency of the business;

(3) The obligation on trade consumers to sign an undertaking, which cannot reasonably be required of them;

(4) The requirement that wholesalers with a special department must achieve a turnover comparable to that of a specialised wholesaler;

(5) The obligation to sign a cooperation agreement;

(6) The obligation on all wholesalers to participate in the consolidation of SABA's distribution network, which is unacceptable to a self-service wholesale trader.

Since the Commission considered that those objections were unfounded it adopted the contested decision on 15 December 1975 and notified it to the applicant by letter of 14 January 1976, at the same time dismissing its objections.

The application of 10 March 1976 was recorded at the Court Registry on 11 March 1976.

By an order of 5 May 1976 SABA was given leave to intervene in support of the conclusions of the defendant.

By an order of 23 July 1976 the Court dismissed an application lodged by Metro for the adoption of interim measures.

By an order of 30 November 1976 the Verband des SB-Grosshandels e.V. (Association of Self-Service Wholesale Traders) was given leave to intervene in support of the conclusions of the applicant.

*The court held:*

20. The requirement contained in Articles 3 and 85 of the EEC Treaty that competition shall not be distorted implies the existence on the market of workable competition, that is to say the degree of competition necessary to ensure the observance of the basic requirements and the attainment of the objectives of the Treaty, in particular the creation of a single market achieving conditions similar to those of a domestic market.

In accordance with this requirement the nature and intensiveness of competition may vary to an extent dictated by the products or services in question and the economic structure of the relevant market sectors.

In the sector covering the production of high quality and technically advanced consumer durables, where a relatively small number of large- and medium-scale producers offer a varied range of items which, or so consumers may consider, are readily interchangeable, the structure of the market does not preclude the existence of a variety of channels of distribution adapted to the peculiar characteristics of the various producers and to the requirements of the various categories of consumers.

On this view the Commission was justified in recognising that selective distribution systems constituted, together with others, an aspect of competition which accords with Article 85(1), provided that resellers are chosen on the basis of objective criteria of a qualitative nature relating to the technical qualifications of the reseller and his staff and the suitability of his trading premises and that such conditions are laid down uniformly for all potential resellers and are not applied in a discriminatory fashion.

21. It is true that in such systems of distribution price competition is not generally emphasised either as an exclusive or indeed as a principle factor.

This is particularly so when, as in the present case, access to the distribution network is subject to conditions exceeding the requirements of an appropriate distribution of the products.

However, although price competition is so important that it can never be eliminated it does not constitute the only effective form of competition or that to which absolute priority must in all circumstances be accorded.

The powers conferred upon the Commission under Article 85(3) show that the requirements for the maintenance of workable competition may be reconciled with the safeguarding of objectives of a different nature and that to this end certain restrictions on competition are permissable, provided that they are essential to the attainment of those objectives and that they do not result in the elimination of competition for a substantial part of the Common Market.

For specialist wholesalers and retailers the desire to maintain a certain price level, which corresponds to the desire to preserve, in the interests of consumers, the possibility of the continued existence of this channel of distribution in conjunction with new methods of distribution based on a different type of competition policy, forms one of the objectives which may be pursued without necessarily falling under the prohibition contained in Article 85(1), and, if it does fall thereunder, either wholly or in part, coming within the framework of Article 85(3).

This argument is strengthened if, in addition, such conditions promote improved competition inasmuch as it relates to factors other than prices.

22. Although the figures submitted by both sides concerning the existence of price competition amongst SABA distributors ultimately indicate that the price structure is somewhat rigid, they do not, especially in view of the existence at the same time of competition between products of the same brand (intra-brand competition) and the existence of effective competition between different brands, permit the conclusion that competition has been restricted or eliminated on the market in electronic equipment for leisure purposes.

Nevertheless, the Commission must ensure that this structural rigidity is not reinforced, as might happen if there were an increase in the number of selective distribution networks for marketing the same product.

Since the Commission granted the desired exemption only for a period expiring on 21 July 1980 it retains the possibility of reconsidering within a reasonable time the consequences of this aspect of its decision.

In those circumstances the submission based on the existence of a misuse of powers must be rejected.

## III. COMMUNITY LAW AND NATIONAL LAW

### A. Supremacy

#### (1) Costa-ENEL case

Costa v. ENEL, Case 6/64, Preliminary Ruling of 15 July 1964; (1964) ECR 585; (1964) CMLR 425; CCH para. 7390; Competition Law CM/M/III/2.

*Facts:* In a case before the Justice of Peace in Milano, Mr. Costa denied the validity of the Italian nationalisation law which led to the establishment of the ENEL Company. One of his submissions was that this law violated the EEC Treaty. The Justice of Peace sought a preliminary ruling on the compatibility of the nationalisation law with the Treaty. The Italian Government was of the opinion that the request for a preliminary ruling was inadmissable.

*The court held:*

On the submission that the Court was obliged to apply the national law

The Italian Governement submits that the request of the Giudice Conciliatore is 'absolutely inadmissable', inasmuch as a national court which is obliged to apply a national law cannot avail itself of Article 177.

By contrast with ordinary international treaties, the EEC Treaty has created its own legal system which, on the entry into force of the Treaty, became an integral part of the legal systems of the Member States and which their courts are bound to apply. By creating a Community of unlimited duration, having its own institutions, its own personality, its own legal capacity and capacity of representation on the international plane and, more particularly, real powers stemming from a limitation of sovereignty or a transfer of powers from the States to the Community, the Member States have limited their sovereign rights, albeit it within limited fields, and have thus created a body of law which binds both their nationals and themselves.

The integration into the law of each Member State of provisions which derive from the Community, and more generally the terms and the spirit of the Treaty, make it impossible for the States, as a corollary, to accord precedence to a unilateral and subsequent measue over a legal system accepted by them on a basis of reciprocity. Such a measure cannot therefore be inconsistent with that legal system. The executive force of Community law cannot vary from one State to another in deference to subsequent domestic laws, without jeopardising the attainment of the objectives of the Treaty set out in Article 5(2) and giving rise to the discrimination prohibited by Article 7.

The obligations undertaken under the Treaty establishing the Community would not be unconditional, but merely contingent, if they could be called in question by subsequent legislative acts of the signatories. Wherever the Treaty grants the States the right to act unilaterally, it does this by clear and precise provisions (for example Articles 15, 93 (3), 223, 224 and 225). Applications by Member States for authority to derogate from the Treaty are subject to a special authorisation procedure ( for example articles 8(4), 17(4), 25, 26, 73, the third subparagraph of Article 93(3), and 226) which would lose their purpose if the Member States could renounce their obligations by means of an ordinary law.

The precedence of Community law is confirmed by Article 189, whereby a regulation 'shall be binding' and 'directly applicable in all Member States'. This provision, which is subject to no reservation, would be quite meaningless if a State could unilaterally nullify its effects by means of a legislative measure which could prevail over Community law.

It follows from all these observations that the law stemming from the Treaty, an independent source of law, could not, because of its special and original nature, be overridden by domestic legal provisions, however framed, without being deprived of its character as Community law and without the legal basis of the Community itself being called into question.

The transfer by the States from their domestic legal system to the Community legal system of the rights and obligations arising under the Treaty carries with it a permanent limitation of their sovereign rights, against which a subsequent unilateral act incompatible with the concept of the Community cannot prevail.
Consequently Article 177 is to be applied regardless of any domestic law, whenever questions relating to the interpretation of the Treaty arise.

(2) Simmenthal Case II

Italian Minister for Finance v. Simmenthal SpA. Case 106/77, Preliminary Ruling of 9 March 1978; (1978) ECR p. 629; (1978) 3 CMLR 263; CCH para. 8476;

*Facts:* The Simmenthal Company had brought an action before the Pretore of Susa for repayment of certain veterinary and public health fees levied on imports of beef and veal. During these proceedings an application was made for a preliminary ruling (Case 35/76, Simmenthal Case I, (1976) ECR, p. 1871 et seq.). Having regard to the answers given by the Court of Justice in that judgment, the Pretore held that the levying of the fees in question was incompatible with the provisions of Community law and ordered the Italian Finance Administration to

repay the fees unlawfully charged. The fiscal authorities appealed against this order. They pointed out that the basis for charging fees under Italian law was to be found in a law of 30 December 1970. The issue before the Pretore therefore involved a conflict between certain directly applicable provisions of Community law and a subsequent national law. According to recently decided cases of the Italian constitutional Court, see the ICIC-Case, Cases Gen. p. 155, ordinary courts have no power to discard domestic provisions which are incompatible with Community law. On the contrary, as long as the legislature does not amend the national provisions, the national courts are required to bring the matter before the Constitutional Court which may then declare that the national law is unconstitutional under Article 11 of the Constitution.
In view of these arguments the Pretore requested the Court of Justice to give a preliminary ruling on the following question:
Since in accordance with Article 189 of the EEC Treaty and the established case-law of the Court of Justice of the European Communities, directly applicable Community provisions must, notwithstanding any internal rule or practice whatsoever of the Member States have full, complete and uniform effect in their legal systems in order to protect subjective legal rights created in favour of individuals, is the scope of the said provisions to be interpreted to the effect that any subsequent national measures which conflict with those provisions must be forthwith disregarded without waiting until those measures have been eliminated by action on the part of the national legislature concerned (repeal) or of other constitutional authorities (declaration that they are unconstitutional) especially, in the case of the latter alternative, where, since the national law continues to be fully effective pending such declaration, it is impossible to apply the Community provisions and, in consequence to ensure that they are fully, completely and uniformly applied and to protect the legal rights created in favour of individuals?

*The court held:*

....
13. The main purpose of the *first question* is to ascertain what consequences flow from the direct applicability of a provision of Community law in the event of incompatibility with a subsequent legislative provision of a Member State.
14. Direct applicability in such circumstances means that rules of Community law must be fully and uniformly applied in all the Member States from the date of their entry into force and for so long as they continue in force.
15. These provisions are therefore a direct source of rights and duties for all those affected thereby, whether Member States or individuals, who are parties to legal relationships under Community law.
16. This consequence also concerns any national court whose task it is as an organ of a Member State to protect, in a case within its jurisdiction, the rights conferred upon individuals by Community law.
17. Furthermore, in accordance with the principle of the precedence of Community law, the relationship between provisions of the Treaty and directly applicable measures of the institutions on the one hand and the national law of the Member States on the other is such that those provisions and measures not only by their entry into force render automatically inapplicable any conflicting provision of current national law but - in so far as they are an integral part of, and take precedence in, the legal order applicable in the territory of each of the Member States - also preclude the valid adoption of new

national legislative measures to the extent to which they would be incompatible with Community provisions.

18. Indeed any recognition that national legislative measures which encroach upon the field within which the Community exercises its legislative power or which are otherwise incompatible with the provisions of Community law had any legal effect would amount to a corresponding denial of the effectiveness of obligations undertaken unconditionally and irrevocably by Member States pursuant to the Treaty and would thus imperil the very foundations of the Community.

19. The same conclusion emerges from the construction of Article 177 of the Treaty which provides that any court or tribunal of a Member State is entitled to make a reference to the Court whenever it considers that a preliminary ruling on a question of interpretation or validity relating to Community law is necessary to enable it to give judgment.

20. The effectiveness of that provision would be impaired if the national court were prevented from forthwith applying Community law in accordance with the decision or the case-law of the Court.

21. It follows from the foregoing that every national court must, in a case within its jurisdiction, apply Community law in its entirety and protect rights which the latter confers on individuals and must accordingly set aside any provision of national law which may conflict with it, whether prior or subsequent to the Community rule.

22. Accordingly any provision of a national legal system and any legislative, administrative or judicial practice which might impair the effectiveness of Community law by witholding from the national court, having jurisdiction to apply such law, the power to do everything necessary at the moment of its application to set aside national legislative provisions which might prevent Community rules from having full force and effect are incompatible with those requirements which are the very essence of Community law.

23. This would be the case in the event of a conflict between a provision of Community law and a subsequent national law if the solution of the conflict were to be reserved for an authority with a discretion of its own, other than the court called upon to apply Community law, even if such an impediment to the full effectiveness of Community law were only temporary.

24. The first question should therefore be answered to the effect that a national court which is called upon, within the limits of its jurisdiction, to apply provisions of Community law is under a duty to give full effect to those provisions, if necessary refusing of its own motion to apply any conflicting provision of national legislation, even if adopted subsequently, and it is not necessary for the court to request or await the prior setting aside of such provisions by legislative or other constitutional means.

## B. Shared Competence

### (1) Walt Wilhelm Case

For facts and references see above, page 6.

*The court held:*

I - The first and third questions

2. In the first question the national court asks whether, when a procedure has already been initiated by the Commission under Article 14

of Regulation No 17 of 6 February 1962, it is compatible with the Treaty for the national authorities to apply to the same facts the prohibitions laid down by the national law on cartels. This request is elaborated in particular in the third question, relating to the risk of a different legal assessment of the same facts and to the possibility of distortions of competition in the common market to the detriment of those subject to the said national law. In this respect reference is made to Article 9 of Regulation No 17, to Articles 85 3(f) and 5 of the EEC Treaty and to the general principles of Community law.

3. Article 9(3) of Regulation No 17 is concerned with the competence of the authorities of the Member States only in so far as they are authorised to apply Articles 85(1) and 86 of the Treaty directly when the Commission has taken no action of its own. This provision does not apply where the said authorities are acting in pursuance not of the said articles but only of their internal law. Community and national law on cartels consider cartels from different points of view. Whereas Article 85 regards them in the light of the obstacles which may result for trade between Member States, each body of national legislation proceeds on the basis of the considerations peculiar to it and considers cartels only in that context. It is true that as the economic phenomena and legal situations under consideration may in individual cases be interdependent, the distinction between Community and national aspects could not serve in all cases as the decisive criterion for the delimination of jurisdiction. However, it implies that one and the same agreement may, in principle, be the object of two sets of parallel proceedings, one before the Community authorities under Article 85 of the EEC Treaty, the other before the national authorities under national law.

4. Moreover this interpretation is confirmed by the provision in Article 87(2)(e), which authorises the Council to determine the relationship between national laws and the Community rules on competition; it follows that in principle the national cartel authorities may take proceedings also with regard to situations likely to be the subject of a decision by the Commission. However, if the ultimate general aim of the Treaty is to be respected, this parallel application of the national system can only be allowed in so far as it does not prejudice the uniform application throughout the Common Market of the Community rules on cartels and of the full effect of the measures adopted in implementation of those rules.

5. Any other solution would be incompatible with the objectives of the Treaty and the character of its rules on competition. Article 85 of the Treaty applies to all the undertakings in the Community whose conduct it governs either by prohibitions or by means of exemptions, granted - subject to conditions which it specifies - in favour of agreements which contribute to improving the production or distribution of goods or to promoting technical or economic progress. While the Treaty's primary object is to eliminate by this means the obstacles to the free movement of goods within the common market and to confirm and safeguard the unity of that market, it also permits the Community authorities to carry out certain positive, though indirect, action with a view to promoting a harmonious development of economic activities within the whole Community, in accordance with Article 2 of the Treaty, Article 87(2)(e), in conferring on a Community institution the power to determine the relationship between national laws and the Community rules on competition, confirm the supremacy of Community law.

6. The EEC Treaty has established its own system of law, integrated into the legal systems of the Member States, and which must be applied

by their courts. It would be contrary to the nature of such a system to allow Member States to introduce or to retain measures capable of prejudicing the practical effectiveness of the Treaty. The binding force of the Treaty and of measures taken in application of it must not differ from one State to another as a result of internal measures, lest the functioning of the Community system should be impeded and the achievement of the aims of the Treaty placed in peril. Consequently, conflicts between the rules of the Community and national rules in the matter of the law on cartels must be resolved by applying the principle that Community law takes precedence.

7. It follows from the foregoing that should it prove that a decision of a national authority regarding an agreement would be incompatible with a decision adopted by the Commission at the culmination of the procedure initiated by it, the national authority is required to take proper account of the effects of the latter decision..

8. Where, during national proceedings, it appears possible that the decision to be taken by the Commission at the culmination of a procedure still in progress concerning the same agreement may conflict with the effects of the decision of the national authorities it is for the latter to take the appropriate measures.

9. Consequently, and so long as a regulation adopted pursuant to Article 87(2)(e) of the Treaty has not provided otherwise, national authorities may take action against an agreement in accordance with their national law, even when an examination of the agreement from the point of view of its compatibility with Community law is pending before the Commission, subject however to the condition that the application of national law may not prejudice the full and uniform application of Community law or the effects of measures taken or to be taken to implement it.

II - The second question

10. In the second question the Kammergericht asks whether 'the risk of its resulting in a double sanction imposed by the Commission of the European Communities and by the national authority with jurisdiction in cartel matters...' renders impossible the acceptance for one set of facts of two parallel procedures, the one Community and the other national.

11. The possibility of concurrent sanctions need not mean that the possibility of two parallel proceedings pursuing different ends is unacceptable. Without prejudice to the conditions and limits indicated in the answer to the first question, the acceptability of a dual procedure of this kind follows in fact from the special system of the sharing of jurisdiction between the Community and the Member States with regard to cartels. If, however, the possibility of two procedures being conducted separately were to lead to the imposition of consecutive sanctions, a general requirement of natural justice, such as that expressed at the end of the second paragraph of Article 90 of the ECSC Treaty, demands that any previous punitive decision must be taken into account in determining any sanction which is to be imposed. In any case, so long as no regulation has been issued under Article 87(2)(e), no means of avoiding such a possibility is to be found in the general principles of Community law; this leaves intact the reply given to the first question.

(2) Perfumes cases (Guerlain - Rochas - Lanvin - Nina Ricci)

Procureur de la République v. Guerlain - Rochas - Lanvin - Nina Ricci, joined cases 253/78 and 1 to 3/79, Preliminary Ruling of 10 July 1980; (1980) ECR 2327; (1981) CMLR 99; CCH para. 8712; Competition Law CM/M/III/86.

*Facts:* The defendants were ordered to appear before the Tribunal de Grande Instance, Paris, charged with having committed an offence, treated in the same way as the charging of illegal prices by refusing to fill an order for perfumers; from perfumers in Aix-en-Provence and Strasbourg respectively.
In order to justify their refusal the defendants claimed that their companies were connected with perfumers in Aix-en-Provence and Strasbourg respectively by authorised distributorship agreements and could not have any other distributors in those cities without causing harm to the first ones. They claimed, in addition, that in order to maintain the prestige of the trade mark and to ensure the protection of its customers, the four defendants practised a sales policy of selective distribution.

The defendants laid emphasis in particular on the fact that the marketing of the products in question is, both in France and the other Member States, organised by a system of selective distribution based on agreements notified to the Commission of the European Communities; they then claimed that the Commission authorised that selective distribution system by a decision of 26 March 1976 and by that decision on the basis of Article 85(3) ratified it as regards the Community rules of competition; in addition they claimed that that decision forms an integral part of Community law which cannot be called in question by national legislation, quoted in support of their arguments several judgments of the Court of Justice and in particular claimed that the national authorities are not authorised to prohibit restrictions on competition which the Commission has released from the prohibition pursuant to Article 85(3).

To justify their refusal, the defendants claimed in particular on the one hand that the premises of the perfumers did not exhibit the characteristics of a luxury business essential for the marketing of their prestige products and on the other that those products were marketed at enough sales points in Strasbourg and that a further sales point would have harmed their stockists by increasing advertising expenditure.

Taking the view that it was not sufficiently informed as regards Community law, the Tribunal de Grande Instance, Pris, ordered by four orders of 5 July 1978 that the exclusive dealing agreements entered into by Guerlain S.A., Parfums Rochas S.A., Lanvin-Parfum S.A. and Nina Ricci S.à r.l. and 'which are the outcome of a sales organisation based not only on qualitative but also on quantitative criteria of selection (should be submitted to the Court) so that that Court can decide whether certain luxury products whose brand image is important can benefit from the exemption provisions contained in Article 85(3) of the Treaty establishing the European Economic Community and whether in the present case (the companies concerned) benefit therefrom in Community law'.

During the procedure questions were raised about the nature of certain letters sent by the Commission to the defendants, the problem of provisional validity of old and new agreements and the relationship between Community law and national law.

1. By order of 16 January 1980 the Court decided to reopen the oral procedure in the present cases as well as in Cases 37/79 and 99/79 and

requested the parties in the main action, the Member States, the Council and the Commission to state their views on the following questions:

'If:

(a) the national court considers that the agreements concerned come within the scope of Article 85(1);

(b) the agreements at issue in Joined Cases 253/78 and 1 to 3/79 and in case 99/79 must be regarded as 'old agreements' protected by 'provisional validity';

(c) the letters sent by the various manufacturers to inform them that the files on their cases had been closed are not to be regarded as decisions of exemption under Article 8 of Regulation No 17 or negative clrarance certificates within the meaning of Article 2 of that regulation,

(d) it is improbable that such decisions will be adopted by the Commission in the foreseeable future;

1. Does the protection given to 'old agreements' duly notified or exempted from notification prevent the application to such agreements of provisions of the national law of a Member State which may in certain respects be more rigorous than Community law?

2. Do the grounds put forward hitherto in favour of the provisional protection given to 'old agreements' justify, in the circumstances mentioned above, maintaining indefinitely that protection against the application by a national court of the provisions of Article 85(1) and (2) of the Treaty?

3. How is the case of 'new agreements' notified or exempted from notification in the situations envisaged in Questions 1. and 2. above to be resolved?'

*The court held:*

1. By orders of 5 July 1978, which were received at the Court Registry on 14 November 1978 (Case 253/78) and 2 January 1979 (Cases 1 to 3/79), the Tribunal de Grande Instance, Paris, (31st Chamber), submitted to the Court of Justice for a preliminary ruling under Article 177 of the EEC Treaty questions on the interpretation of Article 85 of the Treaty.

2. Those questions were raised in the course of criminal proceedings brought against the managing directors of Guerlain S.A. (Case 253/78), Parfums Rochas S.A. (Case 1/79), Lanvin-Parfums S.A. (Case 2/79) and Nina Ricci S.à r.l. (Case 3/79), charging them with infringing Article 37(1)(a) of the French Order No 45-1483 of 30 June 1945 on prices, which makes it an offence for any producer, trader, industrialist or craftsman, "to refuse to fill to the best of his ability and on terms complying with the customs of the trade, orders by purchasers for products or requests for the performance of services where those orders or requests are in no way irregular, come from purchasers in good faith and the sale of the products or the performance of the services is not prohibited by law or by any regulation of any public authority." Those criminal proceedings were commenced following complaints with claims for damages lodged by retailers of perfumery products to whom the companies in question ahd refused to sell.

3. The accused maintained before the court making the reference that the refusals to sell giving rise to the dispute were justified in particular by the existence of selective distribution systems for the

products in question. They claimed furthermore that, as was shown by letters dated 28 October 1975 (Guerlain), 26 March 1976 (Parfums Rochas), 22 September 1976 (Lanvin-Parfums) and 20 January 1978 (Nina Ricci) sent to them by the Directorate-General for Competition, the agreements upon which those selective distribution systems were based had been authorised by the Commission of the European Communities. Those letters, which were worded in almost identical terms, informed the companies concerned that, in view of the small share held by each company in the market in perfumery, beauty products and toiletries and the presence in that market of a fairly large number of competing enterprises of comparable size, "the Commission considers that there is no longer any need, on the basis of the facts known to it, for it to take action in respect of the above-mentioned agreements under the provisions of Article 85(1) of the Treaty of Rome. The file on this case may therefore be closed."

4. Stating that those letters must be regarded as decisions applying Article 85(3), the accused maintained that by reason of the pre-eminence of Community rules the national authorities could not prohibit, by applying national law, restrictions on competition which had been recognised by the Commission as lawful from the point of view of Community law.

5. Considering that it did not have sufficient information regarding Community law, the Tribunal de Grande Instance ordered that there be submitted to the Court the exclusive dealing agreements entered into by the companies in question:
"which are the outcome of a sales organisation based not only on qualitative but also on quantitative criteria of selection so that the Court can decide whether certain luxury products whose brand image is important can benefit from the exemption provisions contained in Article 85(3) of the Treaty establishing the European Economic Community and whether in the present case (the companies concerned) benefit therefrom in Community law."

6. Within the framework of the task given it by Article 177 of the Treaty, the Court of Justice had no jurisdiction to decide the application of the Treaty to a given case but the need to reach a useful interpretation of Community law enables it to extract from the facts of the main dispute the details necessary for the understanding of the questions submitted and the formulation of an appropriate reply.

7. It appears from the orders making the references that the purpose of the questions submitted to this Court for a preliminary ruling is to allow the national court to decide whether, as the accused maintain, the view-point expressed in the letters sent to the companies concerned by the Directorate-General for Competition of the Commission prevents the application of the provisions of French legislation which prohibit a refusal to sell. The only explanation for the reference to Article 85(3) in the question put by the Tribunal de Grande Instance is the statement by the accused that the said letters constitute decisions granting exemption adopted in application of Article 85(3). In these circumstances the Court will confine itself to a consideration of the question of the extent to which, in circumstances such as these, Community law prevents the application of provisions of national competition law by national authorities.
.....

The application of national competition law

14. The central issue in these cases consists in determining the effect which such letters may have, on the assumption the national authorities apply not Articles 85 and 86 of the Treaty but their national law alone.

15. As the Court held in its judgment of 13 February 1969 in Case 14/68 *Walt Wilhelm and Others v. Bundeskartellamt* (1969) ECR 1, Community law and national law on competition consider restrictive practices from different points of view. Whereas Articles 85 and 86 regard them in the light of the obstacles which may result from trade between Member States, national law proceeds on the basis of the considerations peculiar to it and considers restrictive practices only in that context. It follows that national authorities may also take action in regard to situations which are capable of forming the subject-matter of a decision by the Commission.

16. However, in the above-mentioned judgment the Court stressed that parallel application of national competition law can only be permitted in so far as it does not prejudice the uniform application, throughout the common market, of the Community rules on cartels or the full effects of the measures adopted in implementation of those rules.

17. In that regard, it has been claimed that the application of national competition law may not be permitted where it would result in an exemption granted by a decision or a block exemption being called in question. It follows, however, from the observations set forth above that the agreements which form the subject-matter of the present cases do not benefit from any decision in application of Article 85(3). Moreover, it is not in dispute that the agreements concerned do not come within the scope of any regulation granting block exemption.

18. The contracts in question merely formed the subject-matter of a decision to close the file on the case taken by the Commission, which gave the opinion that there was no need for it to take action in respect of the contracts in question under the provisions of Article 85 (1). That fact cannot by itself have the result of preventing the national authorities from applying to those agreements provisions of national competition law which may be more rigorous than Community law in this respect. The fact that a practice has been held by the Commission not to fall within the ambit of the prohibition contained in Article 85(1) and (2), the scope of which is limited to agreements capable of affecting trade between Member States, in no way prevents that practice from being considered by the national authorities from the point of view of the restrictive effects which it may produce nationally.

19. Accordingly, the answer to the questions submitted must be that Community law does not prevent that application of national provisions prohibiting a refusal to sell even where the agreements relied upon for the purpose of justifying that refusal have formed the subject-matter of a decision by the Commission to close the file on the case.

## IV. DIRECT APPLICABILITY OF ARTICLES 85 AND 86

a. Introduction

In 1962, in the Van Gend & Loos case, (Case 26/62), the Tariefcommissie, (a tax tribunal), referred a question to the Court of Justice in Luxembourg seeking an interpretation of Article 12 EEC, which prohibits the introduction by the Member States of any new customs duties or charges of equivalent effect. The question asked whether Article 12 EEC had immediate effects on internal law in the sense that nationals of the Member States could, on the basis of such Article, claim rights which a national judge must safeguard. The court held

"...it must be concluded that the Community presents a new legal order in international law for the benefit of which the Member States have, albeit to a limited extent, surrendered their sovereign rights, and whose subjects are not only the Member States but individuals as well;
Thus, Community law, which is independent of the laws of the Member States, in the same way as it creates obligations for private parties independently of the legislation of the Member States, is also able to create rights which private parties can make applicable on their own behalf;
These rights are created, not only when they are explicitly stated by the Treaty, but also through obligations which the Treaty lays down in a very definite manner for individuals as well as for the Member States and the Community institutions;
The text of Article 12 lays down a clear and unconditional prohibition which involves a negative rather than positive duty.
In any case, such obligation does not carry with it the reservation that the States may subordinate its functioning to a positive act of internal law;
This prohibition by its very nature, lends itself perfectly to producing direct effects in legal relations between the Member States and persons under their jurisdiction".
Since the Van Gend & Loos case the Court of Justice has held that other Treaty provisions produce direct effects.

Article 189 EEC refers only to Regulations as "directly applicable", but the Court has held that provisions of directives and decisions can also produce direct effects in the national legal orders.

The conditions for direct applicability have been developed in the case law of the Court. In order to produce direct effects in the legal relationship between Member States and their subjects a Treaty provision, or a provision of Community secondary legislation, must:
i. be clear and precise; ii. be unconditional; iii. leave no latitude of action to the Member States.

Are Articles 85 and 86 EEC directly applicable? In the Bosch case, (Case 13/61) which was referred to the Court of Justice before the implementation of Regulation No 17, the Court was asked whether Article 85 was applicable from the time the Treaty took effect. The Court held:

"Articles 88 and 89 of the Treaty, conferring jurisdiction on national authorities and the Commission respectively, to apply Article 85, presuppose the applicability of this provision from the time the Treaty took effect.
Articles 88 and 89, however, are not of such a nature as to ensure a complete and full application of Article 85 so that their mere existence would permit the conclusion that Article 85, from the time the

Treaty entered into force, produces all its effects, in particular that the absolute nullity provided for in its paragraph 2 occurs in all those cases that come under the definition of paragraph 1 and in respect of which a declaration on the basis of paragraph (3) has not yet been made."

Although the Court confirmed the applicability of Article 85(1) during the period from the entry into force of the Treaty (1 January 1958) to the entry into force of Regulation No 17 (13 March), it did not refer to the creation of individual rights nor did it utilise the terminology of direct applicability.

In judgments issued after the entry into force of Regulation No 17 particularly in answers to requests for preliminary rulings under Article 177 EEC, the Court seems to have taken for granted the direct applicability of Articles 85 and 86 EEC. However, it was not until 1974, in the SABAM case, that the Court declared Articles 85(1) and 86 directly applicable.

b. Cases

(1) S.A.B.A.M. case (first judgement)

Belgische Radio en Televisie v. Société Belge des Auteurs, Compositeurs et Editeurs and NV Fonior; BRT v. NV Fonior; SABAM v. NV Fonior; Case 127/73, Preliminary Ruling of 30 January 1974; (1974) ECR 51; (1974) CMLR 238; CCH para. 8268; Competition Law CM/M/III/39.

*Facts:* The Belgian Association of Authors, Composers and Publishers (hereinafter referred to as SABAM), is a cooperative association governed by Belgian law with the object of exploiting, administering and managing, in the widest sense of those terms, all copyrights and kindred rights, ... on its own behalf, for its members and associates and for its clients and affiliated undertakings.

SABAM concluded standard form contracts with the composer, Mr. Davis, and with the songwriter, Mr. Rosenstraten, in 1963 and 1967; under these contracts they assigned and transferred to SABAM their copyrights in all present or future compositions of which they are or will be owners, and all present and future rights as performers and producers of grammophone records.

Under these contracts SABAM had the right, without having to account for its decision, to retain the rights which had been assigned to it and to exercise them for five years following the member's withdrawal from the association.

On 11 March 1969 the Belgische Radio en Televisie (BRT) concluded a separate contract with Mr. Davis and Mr. Rosenstraten by which they assigned to the BRT certain copyrights relating to the words and the music of a song. The special provisions of those contracts required in particular that the author assign exclusive to the BRT all his rights in the script, without any limitation, for a period of two years and, where the agreement was incompatible with contracts already concluded, the other parties to such prior contracts were to sign a declaration permitting him to enter into this transaction with the BRT.

Repeated broadcasts of the song took place on radio and television. A contract concluded between BIEM, the Bureau International d'Edition Mécanique (entrusted by SABAM with the task of managing the latter's repertoire as concerns the grant of permission for mechanical reproduction) and N.V. Fonior gave to the latter the non-exclusive right to exploit phonographically works from the repertoire of BIEM including the song in question.

N.V. Fonior recorded on tape the words of the song in question and marketed it in its own version on Decca records.

In March and April 1969 SABAM and the BRT attempted, in vain, to prohibit N.V. Fonior from publishing the song in issue. SABAM and the BRT both commenced actions in 1969 before the Tribunal de Première Instance of Brussels, seeking to have N.V. Fonior condemned for this alleged illegal reproduction.

On 3 June 1970 the Commission intiated, of its own motion, the procedure under Article 3 of Regulation No 17 in respect of GEMA (Germany), SACEM (France) and SABAM. By a letter of 8 June 1970 the Commission informed SABAM of its objections concerning especially the articles of the contracts dealing with the global assignment of copyrights and the duration of the period of management of the rights after withdrawal (five years). This procedure is still in progress. The main dispute relates inter alia, to the ownership of copyrights. SABAM and the BRT both claim title to the rights permitting the prohibition of reproduction of the records in question.

By its judgment of 4 April 1973 the Tribunal de Première Instance of Brussels decided to stay the proceedings and to ask the Court of Justice to give a preliminary ruling on the following questions:

1. Can the fact that an undertaking which enjoys a de facto monopoly in a Member State, for the management of copyrights requires the global assignment of all such rights without drawing any distinction between specific categories, be regarded as an abuse of a dominant position within the meaning of Article 86 of the EEC Treaty?

2. Can abuse of a dominant position also consist in the fact that such an undertaking stipulates that an author shall assign his present and future rights, and in particular in the fact that, without having to give an account of its action, that undertaking may continue to exercise the rights assigned for five of the association's years following the withdrawal of the member?

3. How should the expression 'undertaking entrusted with the operation of services of general economic interest' be understood? Is it necessary that such an undertaking should have definite privileges which are denied to other undertakings?

4. Can the provisions of Article 90(2) of the Treaty create rights in respect of private parties which national courts must safeguard?

*The court held:*

.....

1. By an order of 4 April 1973, filed at the Registry of the Court on 19 April 1973, the Tribunal de Première Instance of Brussels referred several questions under Article 177 of the Treaty on the interpretation of Articles 86 and 90(2) of the EEC Treaty.

2. The questions are put with the aim of enabling the national court to judge the conformity of certain articles of the statutes and standard form contracts of the Société Belge des Auteurs, Compositeurs et Editeurs (hereinafter referred to as SABAM) with the rules on competition in the EEC Treaty.

3. SABAM having brought an appeal against the order for reference, the Tribunal of Brussels informed the Court, by a letter of 18 September 1973, that it did not wish the examination of the preliminary questions before the Court to be suspended.

4 The appeal is based in particular on the alleged fact that, by virtue of Article 9(3) of Regulation No 17 of the Commission (OJ No 13 of 21 February 1962), the national court lacks competence.

5. It emerges from the preparatory enquiry into the case before the Court of Justice that the Commission decided on 3 June 1970 to initiate, of its own motion, the procedure under Article 3 of the said Regulation in respect of SABAM and informed the latter of this decision on 8 June 1970.

6. In the particular circumstances of this case it is necessary, before giving a ruling on the questions referred, first to examine the regularity of the reference to the Court.

As to the jurisdiction of the Court

7. The Court has jurisdiction to give judgment on a request for a preliminary ruling, within the meaning of Article 177, notified by a national court in accordance with Article 20 of the Protocol on the Statute of the Court of Justice.

8. The Treaty confers on national courts the right to judge whether a decision on a point of Community law is necessary for their judgments.

9. Consequently, the procedure under Article 20 of the Protocol on the Statute of the Court of Justice continues as long as the request of the national court has neither been withdrawn nor become devoid of object.

10. It has been maintained that the Court is not obliged to reply to the questions referred by the Tribunal of Brussels since the Commission has initiated, of its own motion, a procedure in respect of SABAM in pursuance of Article 3 of Regulation No 17.

11. According to SABAM, as the civil courts must be considered to be 'authorities of the Member States' within the meaning of Article 9(3) of the said Regulation, the Tribunal of Brussels ought to have stayed the proceedings as from 8 June until the Commission has given its decision.

12. Under Article 9(3) 'as long as the Commission has not initiated any procedure under Articles 2, 3 or 6, the authorities of the Member States shall remain competent to apply Article 85(1) and Article 86 in accordance with Article 88 of the Treaty.

13. Consequently, as soon as the Commission has initiated such a procedure the authorities of the Member States cease to be competent to proceed against the same practices or agreements under the same provisions.

14. It must thus be examined whether the national courts, before which the prohibitions contained in Articles 85 and 86 are invoked in a

dispute governed by private law, must be considered as 'authorities of Member States'.

15. The competence of those courts to apply the provisions of Community law, particularly in the case of such disputes, derives from the direct effect of those provisions.

16. As the prohibitions of Articles 85(1) and 86 tend, by their very nature, to produce direct effects in relations between individuals, these Articles create direct rights in respect of the individuals concerned which the national courts must safeguard.

17. To deny, by virtue of the afore-mentioned Article 9, the national courts' jurisdiction to afford this safeguard, would mean depriving individuals of rights which they hold under the Treaty itself.

18. The fact that Article 9(3) refers to 'the authorities of the Member States' competent to apply the provisions of Articles 85(1) and 86 'in accordance with Article 88' indicates that it refers solely to those national authorities whose competence derives from Article 88.

19. Under that Article the authorities of the Member States - including in certain Member States courts especially entrusted with the task of applying domestic legislation on competition or that of ensuring the legality of that application by the administrative authorities - are also rendered competent to apply the provisions of Articles 85 and 86 of the Treaty.

20. The fact that the expression 'authorities of the Member States', appearing in Article 9(3) of Regulation No 17, covers such courts cannot exempt a court before which the direct effect of Article 86 is pleaded from giving judgment.

21. Nevertheless, if the Commission initiaties a procedure in application of Article 3 of Regulation No 17 such a court may, if it considers it necessary for reasons of legal certainty, stay the proceedings before it while awaiting the outcome of the Commission's action.

22. On the other hand, the national court should generally allow proceedings before it to continue when it decides either that the behaviour in dispute is clearly not capable of having any appreciable effect on competition or on trade between Member States, or that there is no doubt of the incompatibility of that behaviour with Article 86.

23. The competence of such a court to refer a request for a preliminary ruling to the Court of Justice cannot be fettered by Article 9 of Regulation No 17.

(2) Lauder Case

Marty v. Lauder. Case 37/79, Preliminary Ruling of 10 July 1980; (1980) ECR 2481; (1981) 2 CMLR 143; CCH para. 8713; Competition Law CM/M/III/87.

*Facts:* Anne Marty S.A., the plaintiff in the main action, operates a retail outlet in Paris in which it sells perfumes.

Estée Lauder S.A., the defendant in the main action, was formed on 30 May 1967 and is the French subsidiary of the Canadian company Estée

Lauder Cosmetics Limited. Its objects include, in particular, the distribution, sale, import and export of cosmetics, toiletries, sanitary products and perfumery.

By writ of 20 April 1978, Anne Marty formally requested Estée Lauder to open for it an accountant and a depôt for Estée Lauder products and consequently to enter up and fill its first order, details of which were set out in that writ, and to deliver that order, specifying that Anne Marty would pay the amount of that order upon receipt of the invoice.

When Estée Lauder refused to deliver, Anne Marty brought proceedings against it on 5 May 1978 before the Tribunal de Commerce, Paris, claiming that it be ordered, in particular, to deliver the goods and to pay Anne Marty a sum of FF 100 000 as compensation for the damage caused.

In its submission of 4 October 1978 Estée Lauder asked the Tribunal de Commerce, in particular to dismiss Anne Marty's claims and, in the alternative, to 'rule that since Community law is applicable to the contractual relationship between Estée Lauder S.A. and its approved distributors and since the Community rules have made valid the distribution networks which are the outcome of a sales organisation based not only on qualitative but also on quantitative criteria of selection, the refusal given by Estée Lauder S.A., which markets luxury products whose brand image is important, was lawful and well founded'.

Before the national court Anne Marty claimed that Estée Lauder's refusal to sell was contrary to the provisions of public policy laid down in the Regulation of 30 June 1945 and the Order of 24 June 1958 on the refusal to sell. That unlawful practice was said to confer territorial protection on Estée Lauder distributors to the disadvantage of other sellers by eliminating competition in the sector and was contrary to improvement in the service given to customers. According to Anne Marty, Article 85 of the Treaty of Rome also laid down the principle of the prohibition on exclusive distribution contracts, except in the case of the derogation provided for in Article 85(3). Estée Lauder could not in any case rely on Article 85(3). Finally, Anne Marty emphasised that it runs a prestige shop with an excellent reputation and qualifications.

In answer to those arguments Estée Lauder contended that the agreements through which its distribution system is organised are in accordance with the competition rules contained in the law of the European Economic Community, which prevail over internal law. The contracts between Estée Lauder and its authorised distributors in France were notified to the Commission in order to benefit from the exemption under Article 85(3). Estée Lauder also claimed that those agreements had been recognised as valid under the Community rules and that they should consequently be regarded as valid in internal law. In addition, Estée Lauder submitted that its contracts with authorised distributors are in accordance with internal French law in the field of competition, that they contain only terms complying with the conditions of the Fontanet Circular of 30 March 1960, since the contracting parties mutually restricted their contractual activity in order to improve the service provided for the consumer, but without imposing resale prices and without acting in the spirit of voluntary restraint on competition. Finally, Estée Lauder pointed out that Anne Marty is not engaged principally in the sale of perfumery, because its shop sells various goods, in particular clothes.

*The court held:*

The third question

12. The third question seeks to ascertain the powers of national courts to apply Article 85(1), regard being had to the provisions of Article 9(3) of Regulation No 17 which is worded as follows:

"As long as the Commission has not initiated any procedure under Articles 2, 3 or 6, the authorities of the Member States shall remain competent to apply Article 85(1) and Article 86 in accordance with Article 88 of the Treaty..."

13. As the Court held in its judgment of 30 January 1974 in Case 127/73, *BRT* v. *SABAM* (1974) ECR 51, since the prohibitions contained in Articles 85(1) and 86 tend by their very nature to produce direct effects in relations between individuals, those articles create direct rights in respect of the individuals concerned which the national courts must safeguard. To deny, by virtue of Article 9 of Regulation No 17, the national courts' jurisdiction to afford that safeguard would mean depriving the individuals of rights which they hold under the Treaty itself. It follows that the initiation by the Commission of a procedure under Articles 2, 3 or 6 of that regulation cannot exempt a national court before which the direct effect of Article 85(1) is pleaded from giving judgment.

14. Nevertheless, in such a case it is open to the national court, if it considers it necessary for reasons of legal certainty, to stay the proceedings before it while awaiting the outcome of the Commission's action. On that matter, however, it should be noted that, as the Court has already held in its judgment of 6 February 1973 in Case 48/72, *Brasserie de Haecht II* (1973) ECR 77, "Article 9, when referring to the initiation of a procedure under Articles 2, 3 or 6, obviously concerns an authoritative act of the Commission, evidencing its intention of taking a decision under the said articles".

15. An administrative letter such as that sent to the defendant in the main action, far from evidencing such an intention, indicates, on the contrary, that the file on the matter has been closed and that the adoption of a decision is not contemplated.

16. Accordingly, the answer to the third question should be that the jurisdiction of national courts before which the direct effect of Article 85(1) is relied upon is not restricted by Article 9(3) of Regulation No 17. In any case an administrative letter informing the undertaking concerned that the file on its case has been closed does not amount to the initiation of a procedure pursuant to Articles 2, 3 or 6 of Regulation No 17.

Literature:

Consult Leading Cases on the Law of the European Communities Fourth Edition 1982, Chapters 2 and 3, and the literature mentioned there.
- Van der Esch: EEC Competition Rules: basic principles and policy aims LIEI 1980/2 p. 75-80.
- Markert: The Dyestuff Case: a contribution to the relationship between the antitrust laws of the EEC and its Member States. The Anti-trust Bulletin No XIV p. 869-899.
- Verstrynge: The Relationship between national and Community Anti-trust Law: an overview after the Perfumes cases. 1981 Nw.J Int'l L and Bus. Vol 3 Number 2, p. 358.

## Chapter Two

## PRINCIPLES COMMON TO ARTICLES 85 AND 86

### I. SCOPE OF APPLICATION OF ARTICLES 85 AND 86

#### A. Ratione Territorii

1. European Communities

The competition rules of the EEC apply in the ten Member States: Belgium, Denmark (excluding the Faroe Islands and in the future Greenland), the Federal Republic of Germany (including West Berlin), France (including the French Overseas Departments), Greece, Ireland, Italy, Luxembourg, The Netherlands (excluding The Netherlands Antilles) and the United Kingdom (the position of the Channel Islands and the Isle of Man is unclear. See Article 227 EEC and Article 26 of the Act of Accession and Protocol No 3 annexed to the Act of Accession on the Channel Islands and the Isle of Man).

2. Alien Undertakings

a. Introduction

In several instances the Commission has applied the EEC competition rules to Alien Undertakings. The Court of Justice has affirmed the Commission's jurisdiction over these undertakings in competition matters.

The fact that the Commission exercises jurisdiction over Alien Undertakings in competition matters does not however mean that the Commission can exercise its investigation powers under Regulation 17, Article 14, on the territory of non-Member States. Also in the situation where the Commission sends requests for information, enforcement of a possible decision on the basis of Regulation No 17, Article 11(5) and (6), is a delicate matter.

b. Cases

(1) Decision on the Dyestuffs cartel

Decision of the Commission of 24 July 1969 on a proceeding under Article 85 of the Treaty, addressed to B.A.S.F., Cassella Farbwerke, Bayer, Hoechst, (all German firms), Francolor (France), A.C.N.A. (Italy), Ciba, Geigy, Sandoz (all Swiss firms) and I.C.I. (United Kingdom); JO No L 195, 7 August 1969, 11; (1969) CMLR D. 23; CCH para. 9314; Competition Law CM/M/I/26.

*Facts:* In this decision the Commission imposed fines on eleven manufacturers of aniline dyestuffs. The Commission accused the companies of participating in a restrictive practice involving uniform and simultaneous price increases throughout the Common Market.
The Commission noted three price increases. A 15% increase, affecting the majority of dyestuffs based on aniline, took place between 7-20 January 1964 in Belgium and Luxembourg, Italy and the Netherlands.

On 1 January 1965 it was extended to Germany; in addition, a 10% rise in the price of dyestuffs and payments, excluded from the first increase, took place in Germany and the other countries. Finally, on 16 October 1967, an increase of 8% in the price of all dyestuffs was imposed by most manufacturers in Belgium and Luxembourg, Germany and The Netherlands; and in France the increase was 12%. These increases did not take place in Italy.

The Commission considered the infringement of competition to be very serious since practically all the enterprises selling dyestuffs within the EEC - accounting for more than 80% of the market - participated in the concerted practice. Moreover, the effects were felt particularly strongly by a large number of industries using dyestuffs.

The Commission commenced its investigation after it had received information and complaints from the trade organisations of various industries making use of dyestuffs. In the meantime, the German Bundeskartellamt had started proceedings against the enterprises concerned for violation of German anti-trust law (Gesetz gegen Wettbewerbsbeschränkungen).

On the point of jurisdiction the Commission ruled:

"This decision is applicable to all undertakings which took part in the concerted practices, whether they are established within or outside the Common Market. Under Article 85(1) of the Treaty instituting the EEC, all agreements between undertakings, all decisions by associations of undertakings and all concerted practices which may affect trade between Member States and the object or effect of which is to prevent, restrict or distort competition within the Common Market shall be prohibited as incompatible with the Common Market. The competition rules of the Treaty are, consequently, applicable to all restrictions of competition which produce within the Common Market effects set out in Article 85(1). There is therefore no need to examine whether the undertakings which are the cause of these restrictions of competition have their seat within or outside the Community.

Under Article 191(2) of the EEC Treaty decisions take effect by notification to the addressee.

Such notification is carried out when the decision enters into the 'internal sphere' of the addressee. The subsidiaries of the undertakings Ciba, Geigy, Sandoz and ICI in the Common Market which are wholly controlled by their parent companies are part of the 'internal sphere' of these four undertakings. Therefore, notification to those undertakings may validly be made at the seat of one of their subsidiaries.

*The Commission decided:*

1. The concerted practices consisting in fixing the rates of price increase and conditions of application of such increases in the colouring matter sector, which resulted in price increases in 1964, 1965 and 1967 and for which the following undertakings were responsible: B.A.S.F., Cassella Farbwerke, Bayer, Hoechst, Francolor, A.C.N.A., Ciba, Geigy, Sandoz and I.C.I., constitute infringements of the provisions of Article 85(1) of the Treaty instituting the EEC.

2. There shall be imposed:

on B.A.S.F., Cassella Farbwerke, Bayer, Hoechst, Francolor, Ciba, Geigy, Sandoz and I.C.I., a fine of 50,000 units of account. On A.C.N.A. a fine of 40,000 units of account.
These sums should be paid to the Commission within three months of notification of the present decision.

3. As regards Article 2 hereof, the present decision is itself authority for execution, in accordance with Article 192 of the Treaty, against the undertakings designated herein.

4. The present decision is addressed to the undertakings mentioned in Article 1 thereof.
As regards the companies S.A. Ciba, J.R. Geigy S.A., Sandoz S.A. and Imperial Chemical Industries Ltd., it may equally well be notified to the office of one of their subsidiaries established within the Common Market.
(Translation CMLR)

*Sequel*

Most undertakings concerned appealed against these decisions to the Court of Justice in Luxembourg. The Court upheld the Commission's decision, but marginally reduced the fine imposed on A.C.N.A. (Cases 48-49/69, 51-57/69, Judgment of 14 July 1973, see page 44 ).

The authorities in the Federal Republic of Germany also took action against the German undertakings involved on the basis of German competition law. The parties involved raised the question of this parallel application of Community law and national competition law before a German court which referred a question to the Court of Justice in Luxembourg.
(Case 14/68, Walt Wilhelm; see pages 6 and 27).

The Commission addressed its decision, applicable to the alien undertakings, to the subsidiaries established in the Common Market. The Court of Justice did not consider this form of notification irregular. (For the general problems involved in the notification of decisions: see below chapter five)

(2) Decision in Re Continental Can

Decision of the Commission of 9 December 1971 on a procedure under Article 86 of the Treaty; JO No L 7, January 1972, 25; (1972) CMLR D 11; CCH para. 9481; Competition Law CM/M/I/44.

For facts see above page 10.

The Commission ruled on the Question of its jurisdiction:

II - Applicability of Article 86 of the Treaty

1. Under Article 86 of the Treaty instituting the EEC, any abuse by one or more undertakings of a dominant position within the Common Market or in a substantial part of it shall be prohibited as incompatible with the Common Market in so far as it may affect trade between Member States.

A. Undertakings in question

2. Continental Can Company Inc., Europemballage Corporation and Schmalbach-Lubeca-Werke A.G., companies acting directly or indirectly within the Common Market, are undertakings within the meaning of Article 86 of the Treaty.

Being the sole shareholder in Europemballage, which itself holds 85% of the share capital of Schmalbach-Lubeca-Werke, Continental Can controls those two undertakings. Their behaviour can therefore be imputed to it. (Translation CMLR)

(3) I.C.I. Case

I.C.I. v. EEC Commission, Case 48/69, Judgment of 14 July 1972; (1972) ECR 619; (1972) CMLR 557; CCH para. 8161; Competition Law CM/M/III/27.

For facts see above: Decision on the Dyestuffs Cartel, page 41.

The Question of the Community's jurisdiction was raised before the Court by the alien undertakings only.
The United Kingdom Government submitted a memorandum to the Commission in which it objected to the extraterritorial application of the EEC Competition rules.

*The jurisdiction of the Commission*

125. The applicant, whose registered office is outside the Community, argues that the Commission is not empowered to impose fines on it by reason merely of the effects produced in the Common Market by actions which it is alleged to have taken outside the Community.

126. Since a concerted practice is involved, it is first necessary to ascertain whether the conduct of the applicant has had effects within the Common Market.

127. It appears from what has already been said that the increases at issue were put into effect within the Common Market and concerned competition between producers operating within it.

128. Therefore the actions for which the fine at issue has been imposed constitute practices carried on directly within the Common Market.

129. It follows from what has been said in considering the submission relating to the existence of concerted practices, that the applicant company decided on increases in the selling prices of its products to users in the Common Market, and that these increases were of a uniform nature in line with increases decided upon by the other producers involved.

130. By making use of its power to control its subsidiaries established in the Community, the applicant was able to ensure that its decision was implemented on that market.

131. The applicant objects that this conduct is to be imputed to its subsidiaries and not to itself.

132. The fact that a subsidiary has separate legal personality is not sufficient to exclude the possibility of imputing its conduct to the parent company.

133. Such may be the case in particular where the subsidiary, although

having separate legal personality, does not decide independently upon its own conduct on the market, but carries out, in all material respects, the instructions given to it by the parent company.

134. Where a subsidiary does not enjoy real autonomy in determining its course of action in the market, the prohibitions set out in Article 85 (1) may be considered inapplicable in the relationship between it and the parent company with which it forms one economic unit.

135. In view of the unity of the group thus formed, the actions of the subsidiaries may in certain circumstances be attributed to the parent company.

136. It is well known that at the time the applicant held all or at any rate the majority of the shares in those subsidiaries.

137. The applicant was able to exercise decisive influence over the policy of the subsidiaries as regards selling prices in the Common Market and in fact used this power upon the occasion of the three price increases in question.

138. In effect the Telex messages relating to the 1964 increase, which the applicant sent to its subsidiaries in the Common Market, gave the addressees orders as to the prices which they were to charge and the other conditions of sale which they were to apply in dealing with their customers.

139. In the absence of evidence to the contrary, it must be assumed that on the occasion of the increases of 1965 and 1967 the applicant acted in a similar fashion in its relations with its subsidiaries established in the Common Market.

140. In the circumstances the formal separation between these companies, resulting from their separate legal personality, cannot outweigh the unity of their conduct on the market for the purposes of applying the rules on competition.

141. It was in fact the applicant undertaking which brought the concerted practice into being within the Common Market.

142. The submission as to lack of jurisdiction raised by the applicant must therefore be declared to be unfounded.

143. The applicant complains that insufficient reasons were given in the decision, in that it does not mention the relationship existing between the parent company and its subsidiaries by way of justification of the Commission's jurisdiction.

144. The fact that no statement is included showing why the Commission has jurisdiction does not stand in the way of a review of the legality of the decision.

145. Furthermore, the Commission is not bound to include in its decisions all the arguments which it might later use in response to submissions of illegality which might be raised against its measures.

146. Therefore this objection is unfounded.

In cases 52-53/69, Geigy and Sandoz v. Commission, (judgment of 14 July 1972, (1972) ECR 836 and (1972) ECR 845; CCH 8164 and 8165; (1972) CMLR 557; Competition Law CM/M/III/30 and CM/M/III/31), the court followed the same reasoning as in the I.C.I. case and added:

50. Furthermore the applicant claims that the Commission did not take into account its special situation as an undertaking having its registered office outside the Community.

It is argued that by reason of differences of opinion as to the applicability of the principle of jurisdiction based on effects, the applicant was entitled to take the view that the Commission had no jurisdiction to commence proceedings against it.

There, it is said, it must be admitted that in any event the applicant committed a pardonable error, and that any infringements of Article 85(1) of the Treaty are not imputable to an offence on its part.

51. It appears from the examination of the submission concerning the jurisdiction of the Commission that the jurisdiction is based not only on the effects arising from a course of conduct pursued outside the Community, but also on an activity pursued within the Common Market and imputable to the applicant.

52. Therefore this submission is unfounded.

(4) Decision in re Commercial Solvents

Decision of the Commission of 14 December 1972 on a proceeding under Article 86 of the Treaty; J.O. No L 299, 31 December 1972, 7; (1973) CMLR D50; CCH para. 9543; Competition Law CM/M/I/62.

For facts see above, page 14.

C. Commercial Solvents Corporation and its subsidiary Istituto Chemioterapico Italiano.

Istituto Chemioterapico Italiano as an Italian limited company (societá per azioni) which carries on activities in the chemical and pharmaceutical sector. In 1970 its turnover amounted to 5,534 million lire.

In 1972, Commercial Solvents Corp., which is a company operating in the main in the same sector, acquired 51 per cent of the share capital in the Istituto Chemioterapico Italiano.

The board of management of Itituto Chemicterapico at present consist of 10 members of whom five are in the service of the Commercial Solvents Corp. where they hold high executive office. The president of the Commercial Solvents Corp. is also chairman of this board of management.

The executive committee of Istituto Chemioterapico consists of six members, of whom three are representatives of the Commercial Solvents Corp.

In its report on activities for 1972, the Commercial Solvents Corp. indicates that Istituto Chemioterapico is one of its subsidiaries ('our subsidiary') and in its report on activities for 1970 it is stated that Istituto Chemioterapico laboratories constitute the base for Commercial Solvents Corp. research in Europe.

Istituto Chemioterapico, apart from its activity as manufacturer of chemical and pharmaceutical products, acts or has acted as distributor of various Commercial Solvents Corp. products to the exclusion of all other undertakings. Among such products appeared, until 1970, nitropropane and aminobutanol.

A. Applicability of Article 86 jointly to the companies Commercial Solvents Corporation and Istituto Chemioterapico Italiano considered as a group.

The Commercial Solvents Corp. holds controlling power over Istituto Chemioterapico since it holds 51 per cent of its share capital, which permits it to exercise permanently a determining action over the formation of the corporate will and thus over the management of Istituto Chemioterapico, given that the general meeting, by the favourable vote of a number of shareholders representing more than the majority of the share capital, has inter alia the power to appoint the directors, to discuss their responsibilities, to approve the balance sheet.

Besides, Article 2359 of the Italian Civil Code gives to the control of one company by another a defination which rests on the same principle

The composition of the management board and the executive committee of Istituto Chemioterapico indicates well that the Commercial Solvents Corp. exercises in fact its control over Istituto Chemioterapico. In fact five out of ten members of the management board of Istituto Chemioterapico are representatives of the Commercial Solvents Corp. where they hold important executive posts. In particular, the President of the Commercial Solvents Corp. is also chairman of this management board. Besides, among the six members of the executive committee, three are representatives of the Commercial Solvents Corp., which reveals the intention of the Commercial Solvents Corp. to follow closely, day by day, the business, even the routine business, of Istituto Chemioterapico.

On the other hand, it is also significant that the Commercial Solvents Corp. indicates in its annual reports that Istituto Chemioterapico is one of its subsidiaries, which constitutes the base for its research in Europe, which could not be said of undertakings in which one had merely invested capital as a form of placing of funds.

In addition, the prohibition imposed in 1970 by the Commercial Solvents Corp. on its distributors of nitropropane and aminobutanol in certain countries against reselling those products for the manufacture of ethambutol, or against exporting them, indicates in the present case the intention to prevent Zoja being able to obtain supplies of raw material, and shows to what point the Commercial Solvents Corp. exercises close surveillance over the activity of Zoja since the failure of the discussions for a merger, which contributes to the unlikelihood that the Commercial Solvents Corp. is and has refrained from in fact exercising its power of control over Istituto Chemioterapico as regards the conduct of the latter company on the market in the products in question. It is in particular unlikely that as delicate an operation as the attempted takeover referred to above should have taken place without the control of the Commercial Solvents Corp., which was irritated by the conduct of Zoja on the world market even more than Istituto Chemioterapico, and particularly without the participation of the representatives of the Commercial Solvents Corp. on the management board and the executive committee. It may then be concluded that the Commercial Solvents Corp. holds the power of control over Istituto Chemioterapico and exercises it in fact, at least as regards its relations with Zoja, such that in that respect there is no ground for distinguishing between the will and the acts of the Commercial Solvents

Corp. and those of Istituto Chemioterapico. Therefore the companies Commercial Solvents Corp. and Istituto Chemioterapico Italiano should be treated as forming, in their relations with Zoja and for the purpose of application of Article 86, only one single and identical undertaking or economic entity, hereinafter called CSC-ICI group.

(5) Commercial Solvents Case

For facts and references see above, page 14.

The Court held on the question of jurisdiction:

(e) CSC and Istituto as an economic unit

The applicants refer to the case law of the Court and in particular to Judgments 48/69, 52/69 and 53/69 of 14 July 1972 (Rec. 1972, p. 619, 787 and 845), and dispute whether CSC effectively exercises a power of control over Istituto and whether these constitute an economic unit. The two companies have always acted independently, so that CSC cannot be deemed responsible for the acts of Istituto, nor Istituto for those of CSC. Therefore even if CSC holds a dominant position within the world market in raw materials for the manufacture of ethambutol, it has not acted within the Community, and therefore the author of the conduct complained of can only be Istituto which, however, does not have a dominant position within the market in question.

In the disputed Decision in Section II-A CSC's holding of share capital and involvement in the administration of Istituto are set out. It is pointed out in that section that the annual reports of CSC show Istituto as one of its subsidiaries. It is inferred from the prohibition issued in 1970 by CSC to its distributors on reselling nitropropane and aminobutanol for the manufacture of ethambutol, that CSC was not abstaining from exercising its power of control over Istituto. It takes note of an attempt on the part of Istituto to take over Zoja by means of a merger in which it unlikely that CSC played no part. The conclusion is reached that 'CSC holds the power of control of Istituto and exercises its control in fact at least with respect to Istituto's relations with Zoja' and it is therefore proper 'to treat the companies of CSC and Istituto as constituting in their relations with Zoja and for the purposes of the application of Article 86 a single undertaking or economic unit'.

It follows from the passage quoted that there is no foundation in the complaint, which must therefore be rejected, that the Commission altered its position during the course of the present proceedings in that after having agreed in its Decision that the two companies constituted an economic unit in every respect, it restricted its position to the argument that in any case they acted as such in their relations with Zoja.

As to the substance of the submission, besides the particulars given in Section II-A, the disputed Decision contains other particulars which are capable of showing that the argument that, in their conduct vis-a-vis Zoja, CSC and Istituto act as one economic unit is well founded. In this respect the coincidence pointed out in Section II-A of the periods when CSC decided to prolong its production to a stage beyond finishing, and Istituto, a former distributor of nitropropane aminobutanol, began its activities as a producer of ethambutol is highly significant. It is difficult not to associate the decision by CSC to no longer sell nitropropane and aminobutanol with the fact it made an exception in favour of Istituto, which was supplied with dextroaminobutanol for the purposes of its own production of ethambutol and specialities based on this product.

The fact, pointed out in Section II-A of the Decision, that Istituto bought quantities of nitropropane which was still available on the market for resale to paint manufacturers who were forbidden to resell for pharmaceutical purposes outside the Common Market is likewise significant.

As regards the market in nitropropane and its derivatives the conduct of CSC and Istituto has thus been charcterised by an obviously united action, which taking account of the power of control of CSC over Istituto, confirms the conclusions in the Decision that as regards their relations with Zoja the two companies must be deemed an economic unit and that they are jointly and severally responsible for the conduct complained of. In these circumstances the argument of CSC that it did not do business within the Community and that therefore the Commission lacked competence to apply Regulation No 17/62 to it must likewise be rejected.

(6) Decision on the Franco-Japanese ball-bearings agreement

Decision of the Commission of 29 November 1974 on a proceeding under Article 85 of the EEC Treaty addressed to a group of French and Japanese ball-bearings manufacturers; OJ No L 343, 21 December 1974, 19; (1975) CMLR D 8; CCH para. 9697; Competition Law CM/M/I/79.

*Facts:* In October 1972 the Commission published an opinion in which it explicitly drew the attention of undertakings to the applicability of Article 85 of the EEC Treaty to measures designed to restrict Japanese imports into the Community or to regulate for example, their prices and/or quality. The Commission considered that such agreements had to be notified for an exemption under Article 85(3).

The agreement under consideration consisted largely of an exchange of letters between trade associations following negotiations, and revealed a consensus on the part of the parties that the price of Japanese ball-bearings imported into France should be increased so as to align such prices with bearings of French production. Since price competition was therefore neutralised the agreement amounted to a serious restriction of competition in the common market. This was particularly the case since the relevant undertakings were the largest ball-bearing producers in their respective countries. The French side was represented by SKF Compagnie d'Applications Méchaniques (more than 80% of the shares being held by the Swedish Group SKF) and SNR Société Nouvelle de Roulements (a wholly-owned Renault subsidiary), and the Japanese side by four firms: Nippon Seiko Kaisha, Koyo Seiko Ltd., Fujikoshi Ltd. and NTN Toyo Bearing Ltd.

The agreement was also liable to affect trade between Member States. The scope of the price increases permitted under the agreement depended on whether they could affect not only direct imports of ball-bearings from Japan into France but also indirect imports via other Member States. This serious restriction of competition covered the whole of the territory of France, so that trade between France and the other Member States was likely to take place in conditions different from those which would have obtained in the absence of the agreement.

Since the agreement had not been notified, the question of exemption under Article 85(3) could not be examined. In any event, the Commission did not feel that the agreement could have the beneficial effects referred to in Article 85(3), in particular by allowing to consumers some share of the benefit.

*The Commission ruled:*

1. Article 85(1) prohibits as incompatible with the common market all agreements between undertakings, decisions by associations of undertakings and concerted practices which may affect trade betweeen Member States and which have as their object or effect the prevention, restriction or distortion of competition within the common market.

In order to determine whether these provisions apply in this case it is necessary to consider the facts explained above in a more general context as measures taken in Japan at either government or private level, with a view to controlling exports of Japanese products to the EEC either by restricting them or by regulating them as regards price, quality or in any other respect.

Four types of measures can be distinguished and should be differently assessed:

(a) measures taken in pursuance of trade agreements between the Community and Japan. These are acts of external commercial policy, which as such are outside the scope of Article 85 of the EEC Treaty.

(b) measures imposed on Japanese undertakings by the Japanese authorities. These measures are also outside the scope of Article 85. However, in both cases, Article 85 could be applicable to any agreement or concerted practices additional to such measures.

(c) measures resulting from agreements or concerted practices between undertakings which are merely authorised by the Japanese authorities under Japanese law.

Such an authorisation, while required for the measure to be lawful in Japan, would not necessarily mean that Article 85 could not apply, since it would in no way alter the fact that the undertakings concerned were free to refrain from entering into an agreement or engaging in concerted practices.

(d) measures resulting solely from agreements, concerted practices, or decisions by associations of undertakings, entered into or engaged in either unilaterally by Japanese undertakings or in concert with the appropriate European undertakings.

These measures of a private nature may also come within the provisions of Article 85. The Commission has expressly drawn the attention of undertakings to this point, by an Opinion published in the Official Journal in October 1972.

The facts set out above do not constitute measures taken in pursuance of trade agreements between the Community and Japan; nor are the measures in question imposed on Japanese undertakings by the Japanese authorities nor even, to the Commission's knowledge, authorised by those authorities; these are bilateral measures of a private nature, which have not been the subject of any government intervention from either the French or the Japanese side.

*The Commission decided:*

Article 1

The agreement concluded in 1972 through their respective trade associations between the French undertakings SKF, Compagnie d'Applications Méchaniques S.A. and SNR, Société Nouvelle de Roulements and the Japanese undertakings Nippon Seiko Kaisha, NTN Toyo Bearing Kaisha, Koyo Seiko Ltd. and Fujikoshi Ltd, for the purpose of increasing the price of ball-bearings of Japanese origin on the French market, and which is, in particular, manifested by the letters dated respectively 10 March 1972 from the Japan Bearing Association and 27 April 1972 from the Chambre nationale syndicale de la méchanique de haute précision, constitutes an infringement of Article 85(1) of the Treaty establishing the European Economic Community.

Article 2

This Decision is addressed to the undertakings and associations of undertakings listed below: SKF S.A., France; SNR, France; Chambre syndicale nationale de la méchanique de haute précision, France; Nippon Seiko Kaisha, Japan; Koyo Seiko Co. Ltd., Japan; Fujikoshi Ltd. Japan; NTN Toyo Bearing Co. Ltd., Japan; The Japan Bearing Industrial Association, Japan.

(7) Communication in re VEB Pentacon and Elbe Kamera GmbH

Commission Communication of 23 October 1978; Press release IP (78/210); E.C. Bulletin 10-1978, October 1978, p. 31; Competition Law CM/M/II/81.

*The Commission stated:*

In response to the opening of a Commission investigation, a number of clauses of doubtful compatibility with the Treaty competition rules have been deleted from a licensing agreement between two firms in the German Democratic Republic and their licensee in the Federal Republic of Germany and other clauses have been suitably amended. The Commission has frequently invoked Article 85 of the Treaty to deal with such clauses, but this is the first time it has tackled an agreement involving firms in a State-trading country.

The two GDR firms, VEB Pentacon Dresden and Elbe-Kamera-Gesellschaft mbH, both based in Dresden, have patents in the Federal Republic of Germany, France and the United Kingdom for a device for transferring exposed film into developing apparatus. Carl Hostert KG, a company manufacturing such apparatus in Dreisbach in the Federal Republic, was interested in the technique and signed a licensing agreement with the two GDR companies in 1975. The agreement gave the licensee the exclusive right to work the patents registered in the common market. The agreement also specified that the licensee must not contest the validity of the patents covered by the agreement. As the Commission's recent practice has established, such clauses may be anti-competitive for the purposes of Article 85(1) of the EEC Treaty since third parties are thereby prevented from acquiring licences, and thus any additional use of the patent is excluded (exclusivity) and an unacceptable barrier is thereby placed in the way of licensees who might wish to make use of technical knowledge which may otherwise be freely available (no-challenge clauses). There is practically no possibility of exemption for no-challenge clauses under Article 85(3) of the Treaty, since it is always in the public interest for wrongly issued patents to be declared invalid.

A dispute having arisen concerning the application of the licensing agreement, the GDR firms resorted to a clause in the agreement which specified that disputes were to be referred to the arbitration court of the GDR Chamber of Foreign Trade. This did not, however, prevent the Commission from examining the applicability of the rules of competition - which are a cornerstone of the Community's public policy - to the effects of the agreement in question within the common market.

When industrial property right licences exist in one or more Member States such effects are indisputable. After the Commission had intervened the dispute was settled out of court by means of a compromise whose terms included converting the exclusive licence into a non-exclusive licence and deleting the no-challenge clause altogether. The GDR firms also agreed to dispense with a minimum royalty clause, replacing it with a loyalty payment calculated on a unit basis.

In view of this decision by the firms concerned to adapt the agreement completely to Treaty rules, the Commission has terminated its proceeding.

Although the reasoning used by the Commission and Court to justify the application of EEC competition rules to alien undertakings has not always been clear and consistent, it can no longer be doubted that such jurisdiction exists.

The practical application of competition rules to alien undertakings is more problematic. The Commission's powers to request information from non-Community firms and/or to undertake investigations on non-Community territory, are restricted by the fact that such activities would constitute an active interference in the jurisdiction of another State.

Similar problems are raised by the transmission of a statement of objections, the notification of a decision, or the execution of a decision or judgment. In the latter instance the firm or firms in question might not possess executable assets within the Community.

3. Agreements concluded by the Communities with non-Member States

a. General

The Community has concluded agreements with non-Member States which contain provisions on competition law.

These include Association agreements between the EEC and Greece and the EEC and Turkey (Greece became the tenth Member State in 1981). The practical importance of these provisions is negligable because, in the case of Greece, the necessary implementing measures were never adopted and, in the case of Turkey, no implementing procedure was provided for.

Trade agreements containing provisions on competition law have been concluded with Austria, Finland, Iceland, Israel, Norway, Portugal, Sweden and Switzerland. The texts of these provisions are identical, in each case joint committees who are responsible for the administration of the agreements were established, but activity in the sphere of competition has been minimal.

In respect of all the trade agreements the Community made unilateral declarations to the effect that it would assess any practices contrary to the competition clauses on the bases of criteria arising from the application of the rules of Article 85, 86 and 90 of the EEC Treaty.

In three cases the Community has applied Articles 85 and 86 to enterprises established in Switzerland and Sweden after the conclusion of the Trade agreements in question, without reference to the relevant Trade agreements.

The legal effects of the agreements have been unclear but after the Polydor Case (Case 270/80) reproduced below on page 54, it appears that the relevant provisions of those treaties have no direct effect.

b. Cases

(1) Commission Decision of 9 June 1976, Hoffmann-La Roche (Vitamins) O.J. No L 223, 16 August 1976; p. 27; (1976) 2 CMLR D 25; CCH para. 9853; Competition Law CM/M/I/103.

HAS ADOPTED THIS DECISION:

Art. 1. The Hoffmann-La Roche company has committed an infringement of Article 86 by concluding agreements which contain an obligation upon purchasers, or by the grant of fidelity rebates offer them an incentive, to buy all or most of their requirements exclusively, or in preference, from Hoffman-La Roche.

Art. 2. Hoffmann-La Roche is hereby enjoined to terminate the above infringement forthwith.

Art. 3. A fine of 300,000 units of account (three hundred thousand) being 1 098 000 Deutsche Mark (one million and ninety-eight thousand) is hereby imposed on Hoffmann-La Roche. This sum shall be paid within three months of the date of notification of this Decision.
This Decision shall be enforceable in accordance with Article 192 of the Treaty Vitamins establishing the European Economic Community.

Art. 4. This Decision is addressed to Hoffmann-La Roche & Company AG Basle (Switzerland).

Note: In appeal the Commission's way of proceeding as far as jurisdiction is concerned in this case was not challenged.

(2) Commission Decision of 8 December 1977, Hugin-Liptons, O.J. No L 22, 25 January 1978, p. 23; (1978) 1 CMLR D 19; CCH para. 10,007; Competition Law CM/M/I/120.

HAS ADOPTED THIS DECISION:

Art. 1. It is hereby declared that Hugin Kassaregister AB und Hugin Cash Registers Ltd have infringed Article 86 of the Treaty establishing the European Economic Community by refusing to supply spare parts for Hugin cash registers to Liptons Cash Registers and Business Equipment Ltd from 1 January 1973, and that Hugin Kassaregister AB has also infringed Article 86 of the said Treaty by prohibiting its subsidiaries and distributors within the common market from selling such spare parts outside its distribution network.

Art. 2. A fine of fifty thousand (50,000) units of account, that is twenty thousand, eight hundred and thirty-three pounds sterling (£20,833) is imposed on Hugin Kassaregister AB and Hugin Cash Registers Ltd, for which sum the said undertakings shall be jointly and severally liable. This sum is to be paid to Lloyds Bank, Overseas Branch, 6 East Cheap, London EC4, to the account of the Commission of the European Communities, account no. 01-08-634, within three months of the date of the notification of this Decision to the undertakings to which it is addressed.

Art. 3. Hugin Kassaregister AB and Hugin Cash Registers Ltd shall bring to an end without delay the infringements referred to in Article 1 hereof, unless they have already done so of their own accord. Hugin Cash Registers Ltd shall submit for the approval of the Commission, within one month of the notification of this Decision, proposals relating to the resumption of supplies of spare parts for Hugin cash registers to Liptons Cash Registers and Business Equipment Ltd.

Art. 4. In respect of the obligation set out in Article 3 hereof, a periodic penalty payment of 1,000 units of account per day shall be payable by Hugin Cash Registers Ltd in respect of each day of delay from the date stated in the second sentence thereof.

Art. 5. This Decision shall be enforceable in accordance with the provisions of Article 192 of the Treaty establishing the European Economic Community.

Art. 6. This Decision is addressed to 'Hugin Kassaregister AB, Hammarby Fabriksväg, 19-21, Box 4180, 1062 Stockholm, Sweden' and to 'Hugin Cash Registers Ltd, Hugin House, 18-30 Clerkenwell Road, UK-London EC1M 5NN'.

Note: Hugin has appealed against the Decision. The Court has annulled the Decision for lack of proof on the effect on trade between Member States (Case 22/78, Judgment 6 June 1979).

(For other aspects of these Trade Agreements see below page 82).

(3) Polydor Case

Polydor Ltd. and RSO Records Ltd. v. Harlequin Record Shops Ltd. and Simons Records Ltd., Case 270/80, Preliminary Ruling of 9 February 1982; (1982) ECR 329; (1982) 1 CMLR 677; CCH para. 8806; Competition Law CM/M/III/100.

*Facts:*

1. The plaintiffs in the main action are Polydor Records Limited and RSO Records Inc. RSO Records Inc. (hereinafter referred to as "RSO") is the proprietor of the copyrights in a number of sound recordings collectively entitled "Spirits Having Flown" featuring the work of artists known as "The Bee Gees".

Polydor Limited (hereinafter referred to as "Polydor") is the exclusive licensee of RSO under the copyrights in the United Kingdom and under its exclusive licence manufactures gramophone records and cassettes reproducing those recordings, which it sells and distributes in the United Kingdom.

In Portugal records and cassettes reproducing the same recordings are manufactured and marketed by Phonogram and Polygram Discos, companies incorporated under Portuguese law, which are licensees of RSO in Portugal. Those two companies belong to the same group of companies as RSO and Polydor.

Harlequin Record Shops Limited (hereinafter referred to as "Harlequin"), the first defendant in the main action, carries on the business of retail sale of records in the United Kingdom.

Simons Records Limited (hereinafter referred to as "Simons"), the second defendant in the main action, carries on, in the United Kingdom, the business of importing records, which it sells and distributes wholesale to retailers in the United Kingdom.

Since May 1979 Simons has imported into the United Kingdom from Portugal copies of records produced in Portugal by Phonogram and Polygram from the sound recording which is the subject of the copyright. A number of those records were sold by Simons to Harlequin, which sold them to customers in a retail shop.

The imports and sales by Simons and the sales by Harlequin were made without the consent of Polydor or RSO.

On 17 July 1979 RSO and Polydor issued a writ in the Chancery Division of the High Court of Justice claiming inter alia an injunction restraining Harlequin from selling and distributing the records and cassettes. On the same day a Notice of Motion was served claiming an interim injunction restraining such acts until the trial of the action. On 20 July 1979 Simons, at its own request, was added as a defendant to the proceedings and served a Notice of Motion seeking an order to stay the proceedings and to refer three questions to the Court of Justice of the European Communities under Article 177 of the EEC Treaty.

Harlequin and Simons claimed that the records imported by Simons were copies of records made in Portugal by a Portuguese-owned pressing plant for Polygram and were sold by Polygram to Simons' supplier.

By a judgment of 21 December 1979 the Chancery Division of the High Court refused to order a reference under Article 177 and granted an injunction until full trial of the action preventing inter alia Simons from importing the records in question from Portugal and preventing Simons and Harlequin from selling and distributing the records in the United Kingdom.

Harlequin and Simons appealed to the Court of Appeal against that order. They claimed that under Community law Polydor was not entitled to enforce the rights conferred upon it by section 16(2) of the Copyright Act 1956.

This defence is based on the Agreement between the European Economic Community and the Portuguese Republic signed in Brussels on 22 July 1972 (hereinafter referred to as the "Agreement"). That Agreement was adopted on behalf of the Community by Regulation (EEC) No 2844/72 of the Council of 19 December 1972 (Official Journal, English Special Edition 1972 (31 December) (L 301), p. 166). The detailed rules for implementing the safeguard measures provided for in the agreement were laid down by Regulation (EEC) No 2845/72 of the Council of the same date (Official Journal, English Special Edition 1972 (31 December) (L 301), p. 370).

The provisions of the Agreement relied upon by Harlequin and Simons are Articles 14(2) and 23. Article 14(2) reads as follows:

"Quantitative restrictions on imports shall be abolished on 1 January 1973 and any measures having an effect equivalent to quantitative restrictions on imports shall be abolished not later than 1 January 1975".

Article 23 provides as follows:

"The Agreement shall not preclude prohibitions or restrictions on imports, exports or goods in transit justified on grounds of public morality, law and order or public security, the protection of life and health of humans, animals or plants, the protection of national treasures of artistic, historic or archaeological value, the protection of industrial and commercial property, or rules relating to gold and silver. Such prohibitions or restrictions must not, however, constitute a means of arbitrary discrimination or a disguised restriction on trade between the Contracting Parties."

Harlequin and Simons claimed in particular that following the judgment of 5 February 1976 (Case 87/75 Conceria Daniele Bresciani v. Amministrazione Italiana delle Finanze (1976) ECR 129) Articles 14 and 23 of the Agreement had direct effect. Furthermore, they submitted that the case law of the Court of Justice, according to which the provisions of the EEC Treaty on the free movement of goods, and in particular Articles 30 and 36, prevent the proprietor of an intellectual or industrial property right from relying on that right to restrain the importation of a product marketed by him or with his consent, should also be applied in relation to the Agreement with Portugal. Articles 14 and 23 of that Agreement are indeed based on the same principles as Articles 30 and 36 of the EEC Treaty.

3. In view of those arguments the Court of Appeal refused to grant the interim measures claimed by Polydor. It asked the Court of Justice under Article 177 of the EEC Treaty to give a preliminary ruling on the following questions:

"1. Is the enforcement by Company A of their United Kingdom copyrights against a gramophone record lawfully made and sold in the State of Portugal by licensees under the equivalent Portuguese copyrights a measure having equivalent effect to quantitative restrictions on imports within the meaning of Article 14(2) of the said Agreement dated 22 July 1972 made between the European Economic Community and the State of Portugal?

2. If the answer to the first question is affirmative:

(a) Is such enforcement by Company A justified within the meaning of Article 23 of the said Agreement dated 22 July 1980 for the protection of the said United Kingdom copyrights?

(b) Does such enforcement by Company A constitute a means of arbitrary discrimination or a disguised restriction on trade between the State of Portugal and the European Economic Community?

3. Is Article 14(2) of the said Agreement dated 22 July 1980 directly enforceable by individuals within the European Economic Community having regard in particular to the said European Economic Community Council Regulation dated 19 December 1972 giving effect to the said Agreement?

4. Can an importer into the United Kingdom of the gramophone records referred to in Question 1 rely on Article 14(2) of the said Agreement dated 22 July 1972 as a defence when sued by Company A for infringement of their said copyrights in the United Kingdom?"

The order for reference dated 15 May 1980 was lodged at the Court Registry on 8 December 1980.

*The court held:*

7. According to the well-established case-law of the Court, the exercise of an industrial and commercial property right by the proprietor thereof, including the commercial exploitation of a copyright, in order to prevent the importation into a Member State of a product from another Member State, in which that product has lawfully been placed on the market by the proprietor or with his consent, constitutes a measure having an effect equivalent to a quantitative restriction for the purposes of Article 30 of the Treaty, which is not justified on the ground of the protection of industrial and commercial property within the meaning of Article 36 of the Treaty.

8. The first two questions, which may be considered together, seek in substance to determine whether the same interpretation must be placed on Articles 14(2) and 23 of the Agreement. In order to reply to those questions it is necessary to analyse the provisions in the light of both the object and purpose of the Agreement and of its wording.

9. By virtue of Article 228 of the Treaty the effect of the Agreement is to bind equally the Community and its Member States. The relevant provisions of the Agreement read as follows:

Article 14(2). "Quantitative restrictions on imports shall be abolished on 1 January 1973 and any measures having an effect equivalent to quantitative restrictions on imports shall be abolished not later than 1 January 1975."

Article 23. "The Agreement shall not preclude prohibitions or restrictions on imports ... justified on grounds of ... the protection of industrial and commercial property ... Such prohibitions and restrictions must not, however, constitute a means of arbitrary discrimination or a disguised restriction on trade between the Contracting Parties."

10. According to its preamble, the purpose of the Agreement is to consolidate and to extend the economic relations existing between the Community and Portugal and to ensure, with due regard for fair conditions of competition, the harmonious development of their commerce for the purpose of contributing to the work of constructing Europe. To that end the Contracting Parties decided to eliminate progressively the obstacles to substantially all their trade, in accordance with the provisions of the General Agreement on Tariffs and Trade (hereinafter referred to as the "General Agreement") concerning the establishment of free-trade areas.

11. Under Article XXIV(8) of the General Agreement a free-trade area is to be understood to mean "a group of two or more customs territories in which the duties and other restrictive regulations of commerce ... are eliminated on substantially all the trade between the constituent territories in products originating in such territories."

12. In pursuance of the above-mentioned objective the Agreement seeks to liberalise trade in goods between the Community and Portugal. According to Article 2 the Agreement is to apply, subject to special arrangements provided for in respect of certain products, to products originating in the Community or in Portugal which fall within Chapters 25 to 99 of the Brussels Nomenclature.

13. In that connection Articles 3 to 7 of the Agreement provide for

the abolition of customs duties and of charges having equivalent effect in trade between the Community and Portugal. The same principle is applied by Article 14 to quantitative restrictions and measures having equivalent effect. Those provisions are supplemented in Article 21 by the prohibition of fiscal measures or practices of a discriminatory nature and in Article 22 by the abolition cf all restrictions on payments relating to trade in goods. Moreover, in Articles 26 and 28 the Agreement contains certain rules on competition, public aid and dumping. By virtue of Article 32 a Joint Ccmmittee is established which is to be responsible for the administration of the Agreement and to ensure its proper implementation.

14. The provisions of the Agreement on the elimination on restrictions on trade between the Community and Portugal are expressed in terms which in several respects are similar to those of the EEC Treaty on the abolition of restrictions on intra-Community trade. Harlequin and Simons pointed out in particular the similarity between the terms of Articles 14(2) and 23 of the Agreement on the one hand and those of Articles 30 and 36 of the EEC Treaty on the other.

15. However, such similarity of terms is nct a sufficient reason for transposing to the provisions of the Agreement the above-mentioned case-law, which determines in the context cf the Community the relationship between the protection of industrial and commercial property rights and the rules on the free movement cf goods.

16. The scope of that case-law must indeed be determined in the light of the Community's objectives and activities as defined by Articles 2 and 3 of the EEC Treaty. As the Court has had occasion to emphasise in various contexts, the Treaty, by establishing a common market and progressively approximating the economic policies of the Member States, seeks to unite national markets into a single market having the characteristics of a domestic market.

17. Having regard to those objectives, the Court, inter alia, in its judgment of 22 June 1976 in Case 119/75 Terrapin (Overseas) Ltd. v. Terranova Industrie C.A. Kapferer & Co. (1976) ECR 1039, interpreted Articles 30 and 36 of the Treaty as meaning that the territorial protection afforded by national laws to industrial and commercial property may not have the effect of legitimising the insulation of national markets and of leading to an artificial partitioning of the markets and that consequently the proprietor of an industrial or commercial property right protected by the law of a Member State cannot rely on that law to prevent the importation of a product which has lawfully been marketed in another Member State by the proprietor himself or with his consent.

18. The considerations which led to that interpretation of Articles 30 and 36 of the Treaty do not apply in the context of the relations between the Community and Portugal as defined by the Agreement. It is apparent from an examination of the Agreement that although it makes provision for the unconditional abolition of certain restrictions on trade between the Community and Portugal, such as quantitative restrictions and measures having equivalent effect, they do not have the same purpose as the EEC Treaty, inasmuch as the latter, as has been stated above, seeks to create a single market reproducing as closely as possible the conditions of a domestic market.

19. It follows that in the context of the Agreement restrictions on trade in goods may be considered to be justified on the ground of the protection of industrial and commercial property in a situation in which their justification would not be possible within the Community.

20. In the present case such a distinction is all the more necessary inasmuch as the instruments which the Community has at its disposal in order to achieve the uniform application of Community law and the progressive abolition of legislative disparities within the Common Market have no equivalent in the context of the relations between the Community and Portugal.

21. It follows from the foregoing that a prohibition on the importation into the Community of a product originating in Portugal based on the protection of copyright is justified in the framework of the free-trade arrangements established by the Agreement by virtue of the first sentence of Article 23. The findings of the national court do not disclose any factor which would permit the conclusion that the enforcement of copyright in a case such as the present constitutes a means of arbitrary discrimination or a disguised restriction on trade within the meaning of the second sentence of that article.

22. For all those reasons the reply which must be given to the first two questions is that the enforcement by the proprietor or by persons entitled under him of copyrights protected by the law of a Member State against the importation and marketing of gramophone records lawfully manufactured and placed on the market in the Portuguese Republic by licensees of the proprietor is justified on the ground of protection of industrial and commercial property within the meaning of Article 23 of the Agreement and therefore does not constitute a restriction on trade between the Community and Portugal such as is prohibited by Article 14(2) of the Agreement. Such enforcement does not constitute a means of arbitrary discrimination or a disguised restriction on trade between the Community and Portugal.

23. In view of the replies given to the first two questions, it is unnecessary to reply to the third and fouth questions.

## B. Ratione Materiae

1. In General.

The EEC Treaty is applicable to all aspects of economic life with exception of the sectors where the ECSC Treaty and the Euratom Treaty apply. The Treaty is however only applicable to "res in commercio". Non-profit making organisations may fall under the Competition rules of the Community if part of their activities are normal business activities. For an example of a decision involving a non-profit making see Commission Decision of 15 July 1982 in re Stichting Sigarettenindustrie (O.J. No L 232, 6 August 1982, p. 1; Competition Law CM/M/I/179).

The rules are applicable both to the production of goods and the provision of services.

In re Fire Insurance, a Commission Decision of 9 December 1981 (O.J. No L 80, 26 March 1982, p. 36; Competition Law CM/M/I/173) it appears that the British undertaking, The Northern Assurance Co Ltd., contended that Article 85 did not apply to insurance companies. The Commission ruled, however, that Article 85 also applied to the insurance sector.

In case 172/80 a request for a preliminary ruling of the Amtsgericht Rosenheim in Germany, in a dispute pending before that court concerning certain bank charges between Mr. Züchner and the Bayerische Vereinsbank (for the facts see below, page 159), the bank submitted that the Treaty provisions on competition did not apply, at least to a great extent, to banking undertakings. It maintained that by reason of the special nature of the services provided by the banks, they must be considered as undertakings "entrusted with the operation of services of general economic interest" within the meaning of Article 90(2), and thus are not subject, pursuant to that provision, to the rules on competition in Articles 85 and 86 of the Treaty.

*The court held on this point:*

.....

(7) 7. Although the transfer of customers' funds from one Member State to another normally performed by banks is an operation which falls within the special task of banks, particularly in connection with international movements of capital, that is not sufficient to make them undertakings within the meaning of Article 90(2) of the Treaty unless it can be established that in performing such transfers the banks are operating a service of general economic interest with which they have been entrusted by a measure adopted by the public authorities.

(8) 8. As to Article 104 et seq. of the Treaty, those provisions in no way have the effect of exempting banks from the competition rules of the Treaty, which concerns 'Balance of payments', and are restricted to stipulating that there must be co-ordination between the Member States on economic policy, and to that end they provide for collaboration between the appropriate national administrative departments and the central banks of the Member States in order to attain the objectives of the Treaty.

2. ECSC

a. Introduction

The Coal and Steel Community has its own Competition rules, Articles 65 and 66. For undertakings falling under the definition of Article 80 of this Treaty only those Competition rules apply. However, in the case of enterprises with activities falling under the definition of Article 80 and other activities falling under the EEC Treaty both systems may apply.

b. Cases

<u>(1) Commission Decision on the FIAT and Klöckner-Humboldt-Deutz Agreement (IVECO)</u>

Decision of the Commission of 7 April 1975 on a proceeding under Article 66 of the ECSC Treaty; O.J. No L 196, 26 July 1975, p. 41; (1975) CMLR D 64; Competition Law CM/M/I/89.

*Facts:* Fiat a steel-producing undertakinf within the meaning of Article 80 ECSC and Klöckner-Humboldt-Deutz, a mechanical engineering undertaking concluded an agreement to transfer a given part of their assets relating to commercial vehicles and buses for on-highway and off-highway use to a holding company formed under Dutch law, named IVECO. 25 per cent of the shares of Klöckner-Humboldt-Deutz are in the hands of the commercial company Klöckner & Co. of Duisburg which, apart from its other activities, is one of the largest steel stockholders in the Community.

*The Commission ruled:*

.....

Initially, 80 per cent of the share capital in IVECO will be subscribed by Fiat and 20 per cent by Klöckner-Humboldt-Deutz. Whenever the capital of IVECO is increased, Fiat and Klöckner-Humboldt-Deutz will both subscribe in such a way as to preserve the four-to-one ratio in favour of Fiat. The parties will be represented on the board of directors in proportion to their shareholding.

As a result of its 80 per cent shareholding in IVECO and of its majority position in the board of directors, Fiat will be in a position to exercise sole control over IVECO's activities. It can therefore be assumed that Fiat will control IVECO within the meaning of Decision 24/54. The transaction will therefore entail a concentration within the meaning of Article 66(1) between Fiat and the firms transferred by Klöckner-Humboldt-Deutz to the IVECO group.

In 1973 Fiat produced 1.550.000 tonnes of finished rolled products. In manufacturing the vehicles involved in the transaction it used approximately 180.000 tonnes of steel, i.e., about 11.6 per cent of its total output. It used nearly 90 per cent of its output of rolled steel products in its own processing plants.

During the same period Klöckner-Humboldt-Deutz's steel output for the manufacture of vehicles was 11.6000 tonnes - approximately 0.7 per cent of Fiat's total output of finished rolled products.

A consequence of the transaction at issue is that it will be possible for Fiat to supply finished rolled products which Klöckner-Humboldt-Deutz has hitherto purchased from other producers. However, any resulting expansion of Fiat's internal outlets is likely to be negligible and would not bring about any significant change in Fiat's market position as a supplier of finished rolled products.

The proposal transaction then, will not give Fiat the power to determine prices, to control or restrict production or distribution or to hinder effective competition in a substantial part of the market for finished rolled steel products, or to evade the rules of competition instituted under the Treaty, in particular by establishing an artificially privileged position involving a substantial advantage in access to supplies or markets.

The transaction consequently satisfies the tests for authorisation under Article 66(2) of the Treaty and may be authorised.

The effects of this concentration on the markets for commercial vehicles, buses and articulator tractors, have been examined in the light of the competition rules of the EEC Treaty.

Any agreement or concerted practice between the parties going beyond the scope of the transaction here at issue will have to be notified to the Commission for appraisal in the light of Article 65 of the ECSC Treaty or Article 85 of the EEC Treaty.

THE COMMISSION, for these reasons,

HAS ADOPTED THIS DECISION:

Article 1

The formation of the holding company IVECO is hereby authorised.

Article 2

This Decision is addressed to Fiat Società per Azioni, Turin and Klöckner-Humboldt-Deutz AG, Cologne.

For an example of the application of Article 85 EEC to a distribution contract in which the contract goods were iron castings see Case 63/75, SA Fonderies Roubaix-Wattrelos v. (1) Société Nouvelle des Fonderies A. Roux and (2) Société des Fonderies J.O.T., particularly the submissions of the Advocate-General.

3. Euratom

The Euratom Treaty does not contain specific rules on competition policy. Consequently, the EEC competition rules apply to this sector. For example see:

(1) Decision in re United Reprocessors GmbH
Decision of the Commission of 23 December 1975 on a proceeding under Article 85 of the EEC Treaty; O.J. No L 51, 26 February 1976, p. 7; CCH para. 9807; Competition Law CM/M/I/101.

(2) Decision in re KEWA
Decision of the Commission of 23 December 1975 on a proceeding under Article 85 of the EEC Treaty, O.J. No L 51, 26 February 1976, p. 15; Competition Law CM/M/I/102.

4. Agriculture

According to Article 42 of the EEC Treaty the rules on competition shall apply to production and trade in agricultural products only to the extent determined by the Council within the framework of Article 43(2) and (3) and in accordance with the rules laid down therein, account being taken of the objectives set out in Article 39.
Subject to certain exceptions Council Regulation 26/62 declared Articles 85-90 applicable to the agricultural sector. (See below Chapter Six, section IV).

5. Transport

The competition rules of the EEC Treaty apply to the transport sector. However, Regulation 141/62 declared Articles 85-86 inapplicable to transport by air and by sea, and also provided that Regulation No 17 and other implementing Regulations should not apply to the transport sector. Instead special implementing Regulations, Council Regulation 1017/69 of 19 July 1968 (O.J. Special Edition 1968 I) p. 302; Competition Law CM/L/II/10 and Commission Regulations 1629/69 and 1630/69 of 8 August 1969 (O.J. Special Edition 1969 III) p. 371 and p. 381; Competition Law CM/L/II/11 and 12 apply to the sector, transport by rail, road and inland waterway. The Commission has submitted to the Council a Draft Regulation for the application of the competition rules to maritime transport on 15 October 1981 (O.J. No

C 282, 5 November 1981, p. 4) and a Draft Regulation applying the competition rules to air transport on 18 November 1982 (O.J. No C 317, 3 December 1982, p. 3; CM/L/II/21 and CM/L/II/22).

6. Public Enterprise

According to Article 90 EEC public enterprises are subject to the EEC rules of competition with the exception of undertakings entrusted with the operation of services of general economic interest or having the character of revenue producing monopolies.
(See below Chapter Six, Section V).

## C. Ratione Temporis

a. Introduction

The EEC and Euratom Treaties were concluded for indefinite periods of time; the ECSC Treaty, in contrast, was concluded for only 50 years from the date of entry into force. The EEC Treaty entered into force on 1 January 1958 in the six original Member States and on 1 January 1973 for the three new Member States, Denmark, Ireland and the United Kingdom and on 1 January 1981 for Greece. The Treaty contained transitional rules to cover the period of time from the entry into force of the Treaty to the adoption of implementing regulations. The Court of Justice discussed this transitional regime in its Judgment in Case 13/61, the Bosch Case, (Judgment of 6 April 1962: (1962) ECR 45; (1962) CMLR 1; CCH para. 8003; Competition Law CM/M/III/1).

> "Until the entry into force of the Regulation envisaged by Article 87 together with Article 85(3) of the Treaty, Article 85(2) is applicable only to those agreements and decisions which the authorities of the Member States, acting under Article 88 of the Treaty, have expressly declared to come within Article 85(1) and to be negligible for exemption under Article 85(3), or to those agreements which the Commission by decision under Article 89(2), has held to be contrary to Article 85".

Neither the authorities of the Member States nor the Commission used their powers under Articles 88 and 89(2) respectively.

Case 40/70, Sirena v. Eda, (judgment of 18 February 1971; (1971) ECR 69; (1971) CMLR 260; CCH para. 8101; Competition Law CM/M/III/26), involved a contract concluded in 1937.

The Court of Justice held that:

> "If the agreements have been concluded before the entry into force of the Treaty it is necessary and sufficient that their effects continue after this date".

Agreements concluded in the four new Member States before Accession and which had effects within the Communities might possibly fall under the prohibitions of Articles 85 and 86. If not notified, such agreements might be liable to fines under Article 15 of Regualtion No 17. In the light of the Community doctrine of the extra-territorial effect of competition law these agreements will not benefit under the trabsitional regime of Article 25 of Regulation No 17.

b. Cases

(1) Decision on the Sirdar-Phildar agreement

Decision of the Commission in a proceeding under Article 85 of the EEC Treaty; O.J. No. L 125, 16 May 1975, p. 27; (1975) CMLR D 93; CCH para. 9741; Competition Law CM/M/I/87.

*Facts:* The British firm Sirdar Ltd. (formerly called Harrap Bros. (Sirdar Wools) Ltd.) whose main business is the manufacture and sale of knitting yarn and carpet wool, uses the trademark 'Sirdar'. This trademark was registered under various classifications in the United Kingdom trademark register; the trademark has also been registered in all the Member States of the EEC. However, its application for registration under classification No 25 was submitted only in 1965.

In 1943, the largest French manufacturer of knitting yarn, les Fils de Louis Mulliez SA, registered the descriptive trademark "Le Fil d'Art" in France and the international register. Some years later this company registered the phonetic abbreviation of this phrase - "Phildar" - under various classifications in France and in the international register.

In 1962, the French company submitted applications for the registration of the trademark "Phildar" in the United Kingdom under classifications in which the British company had already registered its trademark "Sirdar". (It also submitted an application in respect of classification No. 25 (clothing). The British company opposed the classifications.

Les Fils de Louis Mulliez contested the claim that the Phildar and Sirdar trademarks were likely to be confused, but was anxious, because the registration of the Sirdar trademark in France was previous in time to the Phildar registration and thus tock priority over the latter, to come to terms with the British company. Thus, on 15 December 1964 the parties agreed not to use their respective trademarks on each others home markets. They also agreed not to oppose applications for registration or re-registration of their respective trademarks all over the world. As regards each other's home markets the parties agreed to use trademarks that could not be confused with Phildar or Sirdar and which would not include the termination "Dar".

Finally, the parties undertook not to authorise any third party to use or register trademarks resembling their own marks without the written authorisation of the other party.

As Les Fils de Louis Mulliez SA considered the Agreement of 15 September 1964 to have been void since the accession of the United Kingdom to the European Economic Community, on the grounds that it infringed Article 85 and Articles 30 to 36 of the EEC Treaty, this firm made an application in 1973(No. 1.010.736) to have the Phildar trademark registered in Class 23 in the United Kingdom. This was opposed by Sirdar Ltd.

Les Fils de Louis Mulliez began, moreover, in 1974, to sell knitting yarn under Phildar trademark in the United Kingdom. The goods in question bear the words 'made in France, Roubaix, Paris'. In respect of those sales Sirdar Ltd. has brought an action in the Chancery Division of the High Court. The writ of summons specifies three grounds of complaint - infringement of the registered trademarks of Sirdar Ltd., passing off by Mulliez of its goods as Sirdar goods, and breach of the Agreement of 15 September 1964.

The Commission, in a procedure on the basis of Article 15(6) of Regulation No 17, came to the conclusion that the agreement in question fell under the prohibition of Article 85. On the question of the applicability of the competition rules of the Community to this "Pre-Accession" agreement the Commission rules:

Even in 1964 the Agreement restricted competition in the Common Market, for it was intended to prevent Sirdar knitting yarn from being imported into France, either direct from the United Kingdom or via other Member States. Consequently, the Agreement should have been notified to the Commission in 1964 pursuant to Article 4(1) of Regulation No 17.

The Agreement is therefore not covered by Article 25 of Regulation No 17, as amended by Article 29 of the Act concerning the conditions of accession and the adjustments to the Treaties read in conjunction with Annex 1 (Section V. Competition) thereto, since it does not fall within the scope of Article 85 by virtue of accession but was in fact covered by this Article even before accession.

*The Commission decided:*

Article 1

After preliminary examination, the Commission considers that, on the grounds of the following provisions of the Agreement of 15 September 1964 concluded by the undertakings named in Article 2, Article 85(1) of the EEC Treaty applies, and application of Article 85(3) is not justified.

1. The undertaking by Les Fils du Louis Mulliez SA not to sell knitting yarn in the United Kingdom under the Phildar trademark or under any similar trademark (paragraphs 1 and 5), and

2. The undertaking by Sirdar Ltd. not to sell knitting yarn in France under the Sirdar trademark or under any similar trademark (paragraphs 2 and 6).

Article 2

This Decision is addressed to the following undertakings:
1. Sirdar Ltd; 2. Les Fils de Louis Mulliez SA.

*Sequel*

The English High Court, in a judgment of 19 March 1976, refused a motion for an interlocutory injunction to restrain the defendants from selling or dealing in the U.K. in knitting yarns under the name "Phildar" but refrained from deciding upon the validity under Article 85 EEC and Regulation No 17 of the trademark agreement between the plaintiffs and the defendants.

An appeal was made by Sirdar for the annulment of the Decision of the Commission on 28 March 1975 (Case 34/75). Sirdar considered the Commission's decision to be null and void because the plaintiffs had not been given an oral hearing in accordance with the provision of Article 19(1) of Regulation No 17 and Article 7(1) of Regulation 99/63.

This appeal was later withdrawn.

## II. THE CONCEPT OF TRADE BETWEEN MEMBER STATES

### A. Jurisdiction

#### (1) Consten-Grundig Case

Establissements Consten SA and Grundig-Verkaufs GmbH v. EEC Commission, Joined Cases 56 and 58/64, Judgment of 13 July 1966, (1966) ECR 299; (1966) CMLR 418, CCH para. 8046; Competition Law CM/M/III/5.

*Facts:* On 23 September 1964, the Commission took a decision prohibiting the exclusive dealing agreement concluded between the German manufacturer of radio, TV and recording equipment Grundig-Verkaufs GmbH and the French distributing firm Establissements Consten SA. The agreements provided for exclusive distribution with absolute protection of Consten's sales territory (france). The territorial protection arrangement was designed to make Consten sole supplier of Grundig products in France. For this purpose, Grundig had imposed an export ban on all their dealers in other countries, so that French purchasers could buy Grundig products only from Consten. In addition, Grundig and Consten had signed a supplementary agreement on the use of a special trademark (Gint) in France, the purpose of which was also to hinder the importation by firms other than Consten into France.

Consten had sought to protect its exclusive dealing system by taking action on the basis of the French law on unfair competition (which contained a provision for the protection of exclusive dealing systems) and on the basis of infringement of the Gint trademark, against several parallel importers. On of the undertakings concerned was the Paris firm UNEF. Consten won its action at first instance.

UNEF appealed against this decision and, in the meantime, submitted a complaint against Grundig and Consten to the European Commission. When the Commission commenced an action under Regulation No 17, the Court of Appeal in Paris suspended proceedings pending the decision of the Commission. Grundig and Consten appealed to the Court of Justice in Luxembourg against the unfavourable decision of the Commission.

*The Court held:*

.....

The Complaints relating to the concept of 'agreements ... which may affect trade between Member States'.

The applicants and the German government maintain that the Commission has relied on a mistaken interpretation of the concept of an agreement which may affect trade between Member States and has not shown that such trade would have been greater without the agreement in dispute.

The defendant replies that this requirement in Article 85(1) is fulfilled once trade between Member States develops, as a result of the agreement, differently from the way in which it would have done without the restriction resulting from the agreement, and once the influence of the agreement on market conditions reaches a certain degree. Such is the case here, according to the defendant, particularly in view of the impediments resulting within the Common Market from the disputed agreement as regards the exporting and importing of Grundig products to and from France.

The concept of an agreement 'which may affect trade between Member States' is intended to define, in the law governing cartels, the boundary between the areas respectively covered by Community law and national law. It is only to the extent to which the agreement may affect trade between Member States that the deterioration in competition caused by the agreement falls under the prohibition of Community law contained in Article 85; otherwise it escapes the prohibition.

In this connection, what is particularly important is whether the agreement is capable of constituting a threat, either direct or indirect, actual or potential, to freedom of trade between Member States, in a manner which might harm the attainment of the objectives of a single market between States. Thus the fact that an agreement encourages an increase, even a large one, in the volume of trade between States is not sufficient to exclude the possibility that the agreement may 'affect' such trade in the above-mentioned manner. In the present case, the contract between Grundig and Consten, on the one hand by preventing undertakings other than Costen from importing Grundig products into France, and on the other hand by prohibiting Consten from re-exporting those products to other countries of the Common Market, indisputably affects trade between Member States. These limitations on the freedom of trade, as well as those which might ensure for third parties from the registration in France by Consten of the Gint Trademark which Grundig places on all its products, are enough to satisfy the requirement in question.

Consequently, the complaints raised in this respect must be dismissed.

*Sequel:*

The Court annulled the decision of the Commission in so far as in Article 1 of its Decision it declared that the whole of the contract between Consten and Grundig constituted an infringement of the provisions of Article 85; the Court held that most of the provisions of the contract did not infringe Article 85(1), but dismissed the remaining applications of Grundig and Consten.

See also the Commercial Solvents Case above at page 14.

## B. Concept of Trade

The word "trade" encompasses the production and distribution of goods, trade in agricultural produce, and the provision of services (including services supplied by the liberal professions). For an exception see Article 223 EEC.

### (1) Decision in re GVL

Commission Decision of 29 October 1981 relating to a proceeding under Article 86 of the EEC Treaty; O.J. No L 370, 28 December 1981, p. 49; (1982) 1 CMLR 221 ; CCH para. 10345; Competition Law CM/M/I/165.

*Facts:* The Commission decided that the practice of the German collecting society GVL (Gesellschaft zur Verwertung von Leistungsschutzrechten), which consisted in refusing to conclude contracts with foreign artists who were not resident in the Federal Republic of Germany, constituted an abuse of dominant position and was therefore prohibited.

GVL is the only body in Germany which protects the rights of performing artists such as singers and musicians and collects their royalties from German users of musical works, such as broadcasting companies and others communicating works to the public. It refused to supply its services to foreign artists not resident in Germany, thus depriving them of part of the fees to which they are entitled for communication of their work to the German public. During the proceedings GVL changed its conduct to comply with the rules of competition, but claimed that its refusal was legally well-founded.

It was therefore necessary for the Commission to determine by Decision that an undertaking in a dominant position may not practise discrimination on grounds of nationality. The Commission is aware of the difficulties which the differing royalty arrangements in the Community create for artists. However, it stressed in its Decision that differences in Member States' legal systems regarding the protection of the rights of performing artists cannot provide any justification for this kind of discrimination.

This Decision will enable artists in the Community to ensure that GVL enforces their claims for royalties due to them in Germany.

*The Commission held:*

Trade within the meaning of the competition rules consists of all commercial and business activities, including the provision of services (cf. Judgment of the Court of Justice in 155/73, Sacchi). The sole criterion is whether GVL's conduct was likely directly or indirectly, actually or potentially, to restrict freedom of trade in goods or services in a manner which ran counter to the attainment of the objectives of a single market between States (cf. Judgment of the Court of Justice of 13 July 1966, Consten and Grundig v. Commission/1966/ECR 299).

GVL's refusal to assume responsibility for exploitation of the rights in Germany of foreigners not resident in Germany but resident in one of the Member States hindered the creation of a uniform market for services in the Community. Unlike Germans, such foreigners could not avail themselves of GVL's services. The cross-frontier movement of services which would have developed had it not been for GVL's refusal was thus hindered within the Community. This restriction of the movement of services was appreciable, moreover, since a multitude of foreign holders of rights were prevented from exploiting their rights.

It is irrelevant that GVL restricted its activity to the territory of one Member State. As the Commission has stated in several Decisions, an agreement or conduct which relates to only one Member State may lead to a restriction of trade where trading partners in other Member States are excluded from the agreement or from the advantages of the conduct (Decision of 29 December 1970 - Keramische Fliesen (OJ No L 10, 13.1.1971, p. 15) and Decision of 23 July 1974 - Papiers Peints de Belgique (OJ No L 237, 29.8.1974, p. 3)). In the present case, there can be no doubt as to the direct restriction of trade caused by the discrimination against foreign artists resident in another Member State. The discrimination had the effect of erecting artificial barriers to the provision of services between GVL, as provider of the services in Germany, and foreign artists, as recipients of the services in another Member State, i.e. to economic relations between Member States.

The economic discrimination suffered by foreign artists also affect-

ed their cross-frontier competitive position. This discrimination was likely to place foreign artists in a less favourable position than favoured German and domestic artists, with whose performances they were in competition within the Community, and hence to affect trade between Member States.

## C. Effect on trade between Member States

### 1. Agreements between undertakings in more than one Member State

#### (1) LTM v. MBU Case

La Technique Minière v. Maschinenbau Ulm, Case 56/65, Preliminary Ruling of 30 July 1966; (1966) ECR 235; (1966) CMLR 357; CCH para. 8407; Competition Law CM/M/III/4.

*Facts:* The French company La Technique Minière (LTM), which was engaged in the sale of material for public works contracts, purchased from the German company Maschinenbau ULM (MBU) 37 levellers which were to be delivered over a period of two years. The contract provided that MBU granted the LTM "the exclusive sales right" of the leveller "for France".

The parties agreed that "the supply of machines liable to compete with the goods mentioned in the exclusivity clause could only be carried out with the agreement of Maschinenbau Ulm", and Technique Minière undertook "to ensure the good working of a repairs service and to set up a good stock of spare parts".

After delivery by MBU to LTM of six levellers, LTM asked in Court for the nomination of an expert to examine "whether the machines were unsuitable for the use for which they were intended and unsaleable to French customers". The expert found that they complied "with the terms of the order" and were "perfectly saleable on the French market", and the Tribunal de Commerce de la Seine, at the suit of MBU, gave judgment on 8 January 1964 rejecting two objections of inadmissibility brought by LTM, one of which was based on the EEC Treaty, and declaring annulled the contract in question in so far as it was not executed, the latter company to bear the liability.

LTM appealed against that judgment, asking the Cour d'Appel de Paris to declare the contract "absolutely void" as contrary to Article 85 of the EEC Treaty or, in the alternative, to stay proceedings until the European Court had given an interpretation of the said Article and implementing regulations under Article 177.

MBU then pleaded that notification to the EEC Commission was not compulsory for contracts which were not subject to Article 85(1) and that only a sole distribution contract, which partitioned the market completely, could fall under the application of that provision; whereas in this case competition was capable of taking place in France through parallel imports and the rights of LTM to export the levellers in question.

The Paris Court of Appeal decided to stay proceedings and to ask for a preliminary ruling by the Court of Justice. It submitted the following two questions:

'1. What interpretation should be given to Article 85(1) of the EEC Treaty, and to the Community regulations implementing it, with regard to contracts which have not been the subject of any notification, which grant a "sole right of sale", and which

- do not forbid the concessionaire to re-export the goods which he has acquired from the grantor to any other markets of the EEC,
- do not involve an undertaking by the grantor to forbid its concessionaires in the other countries of the Common Market to sell its products within the territory of the concessionaire who is party to the contracts,
- do not hinder the rights of traders and consumers in the country of the concessionaire to obtain supplies through parallel imports from concessionaires or suppliers in other countries of the Common Market,
- subject to the prior authorisation of the grantor the delivery by the concessionaire of machines liable to compete with the subject-matter of the concession?

2. Does the automatic nullity provided for in Article 85(2) of the EEC Treaty affect the whole of the contract containing a clause forbidden by paragraph (1) of that Article, or may it be limited solely to the prohibited clause?

*The Court held:*

The effects on trade between Member States

The agreement must also be one which 'may affect trade between Member States'.

This provision, clarified by the introductory words of Article 85 which refers to agreements in so far as they are 'incompatible with the Common Market', is directed to determining the field of application of the prohibition by laying down the condition that it may be assumed that there is a possibility that the realisation of a single market between Member States might be impeded. It is in fact to the extent that the agreement may affect trade between Member States that the interference with competition caused by that agreement is caught by the prohibitions in Community law found in Article 85, whilst in the converse case it escapes those prohibitions. For this requirement to be fulfilled it must be possible to foresee with a sufficient degree of probability on the basis of a set of objective factors of law or of fact that the agreement in question may have an influence, direct or indirect, actual or potential, on the pattern of trade between Member States. Therefore, in order to determine whether an agreement which contains a clause 'granting an exclusive right of sale' comes within the field of application of Article 85, it is necessary to consider in particular whether it is capable of bringing about a partitioning of the market in certain products between Member States and thus rendering more difficult the interpenetration of trade which the Treaty is intended to create.

*Sequel*

The Paris Court ruled in favour of MBU, basing itself on the preliminary ruling.

(2) I.C.I. Case

For facts and references see above at page 44.

*The effect of the concerted practice on trade between Member States*

120. The applicant argues that the uniform price increases were not capable of affecting trade between Member States because notwithstanding the noticeable differences existing between prices charged in the

different States consumers have always preferred to make their purchases of dyestuffs in their own country.

121. However, it appears from what has already been said that the concerted practices, by seeking to keep the market in a fragmented state, were liable to affect the circumstances in which trade in the products in question takes place between the Member States.

122. The parties who put these practices into effect sought, on the occasion of each price increase, to reduce to a minimum the risks of changing the conditions of competition.

123. The fact that the increases were uniform and simultaneous has in particular served to maintain the *status quo*, ensuring that the undertakings would not lose custom, and has thus helped to keep the traditional national markets in those goods 'cemented' to the detriment of any real freedom of movement of the products in question in the Common Market.

Therefore this submission is unfounded.

2. Agreements between undertakings in one Member State

(1) Decision on the German Ceramic Tiles Discount Agreement

Decision of the Commission of 29 December 1970 on a proceeding under Article 85 of the Treaty addressed to the members of Interessengemeinschaft der Deutschen Keramischen Wand und Bodenfliesenwerke; JO No L 10, 13 January 1971, p. 15; (1971) CMLR D 6; CCH para. 9409; Competition Law CM/M/I/34.

*Facts:* Purchasers who bought ceramic revetment and paving tiles during a reference period of one year from members of the Interessengemeinschaft or from other German manufacturers are granted a cumulative discount on the catalogue prices of each undertaking. The system encouraged buyers to obtain resales at the highest possible rates by concentrating their purchases on the national producers; this, in turn, discouraged the consideration of offers from other suppliers even if these offers were more favourable. The Interessengemeinschaft comprises nearly all the German producers of ceramic tiles. The discount system is restricted to purchasers situated on the German market. The German market in tiles has an oligopolistic structure, the prices and other conditions of sale of the ceramic tiles are practically identical among the German producers regarding the tiles in question.

Imports from third States account for 35 percent of the market in ceramic revetment tiles, 90 percent of which is accounted for by imports from other Member States, mostly from Italy. Import of ceramic pavement tiles account for 43 percent of the consumption. Most imports come from Japan. The market share of imported tiles has been growing over the last 10 years.

The price of the imported product is in general lower than the price of German tiles.

*The Commission ruled:*

.....

1. The decision on discounts taken by the general meeting of the Interessengemeinschaft on 19 December 1958 and amended on 14 December 1961 is a decision of an association of undertakings.

2. The decision on discounts has the object and effect of noticeably restricting and distorting competition within the Common Market for the following reasons:

(a) The freedom of economic action of nearly all the German producers of ceramic tiles who are members of the Interessengemeinschaft and required to comply with the decision on discounts, is already limited by the fact that they can only give their purchasers discounts which have been jointly fixed. The decision thus suppresses the possibility for these producers of granting individual discounts, departing from the collectively fixed discounts. But, above all, the discount rate does not depend upon the turnover which a purchaser has with a given producer, but is related to the total purchases made from all the German producers, whether or not members of the Interessengemeinschaft. Consequently the discount rate is made independent of the economic relations in fact operating between a given producer and a given purchaser.

(b) The decision on discounts thus succeeds in modifying the competitive positions of the purchasers making up the specialised network through which the sales of ceramic tiles is carried out on the German market:

- The situation of the German purchasers is already affected by the the fact that the decision on discounts deprives them of the possibility of obtaining individual discounts from different producers and causing a discount competition among the members of the Interessengemeinschaft. The suppression of this form of competition is all the more serious if one considers the oligopolistic structure of the market in question and the relatively uniform character of part of the supply.

- But the main effect of the decision on the German purchasers follows from the fact that the system of cumulating the discount bases has the effect of concentrating orders upon the German producers. Firstly, the system of cumulative discounts stepped up in linkage with certain amounts of total purchases and the important differences between the various rates of discount encourages one who has already met part of his needs by purchases from German producers to concentrate all his purchases on German producers with a view to obtaining the highest possible discount rate. In fact, in the case of purchases from non-German producers the purchaser must expect a loss on the discount because those purchases are not taken into account when the cumulative discount is calculated and the latter will therefore be at a lower rate. In order to obtain the highest possible discount, which applies not only to the last individual purchase but all purchases from German producers throughout a year, the purchaser is encouraged not to consider offers, even more favourable ones, from non-German producers, but to concentrate his purchases on the German producers. However, the effect of concentration which results does not only apply for those purchasers who are on the borderline between one discount group and a higher one; more, when the first purchases of the year are made, the purchasers take into account the discount rate which they can obtain by concentrating their orders on German producers. Thus this system of discounts is liable to give rise, even at a stage prior to the passing from one discount rate to another, to a concentration of orders to the prejudice of non-German producers. The only purchases which escape the attraction of orders resulting from this system are those occurring above a given rung of the discount ladder where the purchaser knows that he will not reach the next rung during the current period. The concentrating effect is reinforced by the method of applying the discounts, since the purchaser receives even on his first purchases of the year a discount rate from the members of the cartel which is only one rung lower than the rate reached the previous year. If they are not to be required to make repayments, the purchasers therefore have an interest in making at least a minimum amount of purchases necessary to reach that rate and consequently in rejecting offers from foreign producers.

- In this manner, the decision on discounts leads to a different treatment of trading partners for equivalent services. In effect, a German purchaser who makes a purchase of a given amount from a member of the Interessengemeinschaft and then makes a supplementary purchase from another German manufacturer obtains a higher discount than one who buys tiles of the same quantity and quality from the same producer but makes his supplementary purchase from a non-German producer. In determining the rate of discount to be granted to that purchaser his purchase abroad is not taken into account.

(c) It follows from the above that the system of discounts also modifies the competitive position of the non-German producers in the Common Market:

- In effect the concentration of orders upon the German producers restricts the sales possibilities on the German market of foreign producers and especially the producers of the other Member States for a substantial part of the volume of trade which is carried on there. If conditions were equal these producers should grant, when making sales, rebates of an amount which would compensate the purchaser for the loss of discount on the whole of his purchases made or envisaged from German producers during the reference year. The non-German producers consequently have to surmount, when they make sales on the German market, an artificial obstacle introduced collectively.

- The concentration of orders from the German purchasers of tiles to the disadvantage of foreign suppliers noticeably distorts competition within the Common Market, since it is liable to operate during the whole building up of purchases during the year and in all cases concerns purchase quantities which are far from negligible. In fact, for all purchasers who are positioned within a particular discount rate, all the purchase quantities are liable to be diverted from the offers by foreign producers in so far as they contribute to bringing the purchasers into the discount rate which has been definitively granted. In that respect, account should be taken of the fact that a certain concentration by the purchasers appears immediately above the rate boundaries considered, which shows that the larger part of their purchases is subject to the attractive effect of the system (thus, during recent years, an average of 26 per cent and 35 per cent respectively of turnover in revetment and paving tiles attained in the 17% + 2% bonus discount group was so attained by purchasers who were less than 20 per cent over the minimum purchase amount of 195.000 DM).

- Finally, the better to judge the objects and effect of the decision on discounts, account should be taken of the context in which the decision was taken. In particular the provision in the contract whereby only German undertakings may join the Interessengemeinschaft. It is clear that the provisions of a priori rejects foreign producers who might wish to palliate the unfavourable effects of that decision on their sales in Germany by joining the Interessengemeinschaft. That confirms the finding that the decision on discounts has the object and effect of provoking a concentration of orders on the German producers, to the detriment of other producers.

3. The restriction on competition resulting from the decision on discounts is therefore liable to affect trade between Member States. Indeed:

(a) in order that the condition for application of Article 85(1) should be met, it suffices that the decision on discounts be capable of endangering the freedom of trade between Member States in a manner which could be unfavourable to the attainment of the objectives of a single market between States. But the present decision precisely provokes a concentration of orders of purchasers in the specialised trade in tiles on the German market upon the whole of the producers of that Member State, to the disadvantage of the other producers of the EEC who wish to export tiles to Germany and who are thereby placed, all other things being equal, in a disadvantageous competitive position. That collectively introduced artificial obstacle renders their access to the German markets more difficult than it would have been if that decision had not been taken and is therefore liable to affect trade between Member States in the above-mentioned manner.

(b) the fact that the import of ceramic tiles has strongly increased in recent years in Germany, particularly those coming from Italy, does not prove that the trade between Member States has not been affected. It seems in fact that that increase in imports is to be attributed to special and probably temporary circumstances, external to the decision itself, such as expansions of the internal demand, the play of price advantages or consumer preferences, which have partially compensated in the case of certain foreign producers the unfavourable effects of the decision, and that the increase could have been even stronger without it. In any case, the fact that a decision of an association of undertakings would favour an increase, even a considerable increase, in the volume of trade between Member States would not suffice to exclude the possibility that the decision could not affect that trade within the meaning of Article 85(1).

4. Consequently Article 85(1) is applicable to the decision on discounts taken by the Interessengemeinschaft, which falls under the prohibition set out in that provision.

The Commission considered that in this case there was no reason to apply Article 85(3) and decided:

1. The decision of the Interessengemeinschaft der Deutschen Keramischen Wand- und Bodenfliesenwerke, taken on 19 December 1958 and amended on 14 December 1961, and forming the basis for a 'cartel agreement on discount bases', constituting a breach of the provisions of Article 85(1) of the Treaty instituting the European Economic Community.

2. The declaration of inapplicability provided for in Article 85(3) and requested by the Interessengemeinschaft der Deutschen Keramischen

Wand- und Bodenfliesenwerke is rejected.

3. The Interessengemeinschaft der Deutschen Keramischen Wand- und Bodenfliesenwerke and the undertakings listed in Article 4 below are required to put an end to the violation referred to in Article 1 without delay.

4. The present decision is addressed to the Interessengemeinschaft der Deutschen Keramischen Wand- und Bodenfliesenwerke, of Frankfurt am Main, and to the following undertakings(ommitted).

(2) Vereeniging van Cementhandelaren Case (VCH)

Vereeniging van Cementhandelaren v. EEC Commission, Case 8/72, Judgment of 17 October 1972; (1972) ECR 977; (1973) CMLR 7; CCH para. 8179; Competition Law CM/M/III/36.

*Facts:* On 4 April 1928 the Vereeniging van Cementhandelaren (the Association of cement dealers) was founded in Amsterdam. Its objects were in particular to defend the interests of its members on the Dutch cement market both generally and as against the manufacturers.

On 30 October 1962 the Association (VCH) notified to the EEC Commission under Article 5(1) of Regulation No 17 a series of agreements and decisions concerning the sale of cement in Holland. On 17 December 1965 several amendments and additions to the foregoing were also notified to the Commission.

Following various communications sent by the VCH to the Commission, including those of 29 September 1967, 9 September 1968 and 4 February 1969, the latter began examining the conformity with Article 85 EEC of certain texts. This culminated in a communication of plaints by the Commission to the VCH on 26 January 1970, to which the VCH replied by letter of 29 May 1970. The Commission asked some further questions on 22 October 1970 which were answered by a letter from the VCH of 16 December 1970. An oral hearing was held at the Commission on 17 March 1971. Then, after obtaining the opinion of the Consultative Committee on Cartels and Monopolies, the Commission issued a decision on 16 December 1971, holding that certain texts violated Article 85(1) and could not be granted exemption under Article 85(3) and ordering the violation to be terminated.

*The Court held:*

As to the substance

(a) Effect on competition within the Common Market

The applicant submits that after abolition of the 'fixed prices' system - which was applied only to an unimportant part of the transactions - there only remained a system of 'recommended prices'. These 'recommended prices', which in any case were rarely followed in practice, far from constituting a constraint on its adherents, in reality only represented a basis of calculation which hardly affected the freedom for each of the adherents to calculate its prices according to the data of each individual market. In any case, the differences in production price being slight in the branch in question, competition came into play mainly in the other elements of the transaction, such as product quality and customer service.

Article 85(1) of the Treaty expressly declares incompatible with the Common Market agreements which consist in 'directly or indirectly, fixing ... selling prices or any other trading conditions'.

While a system of 'fixed prices' is clearly contrary to that provision, the 'recommended price' system is equally so. It could not be supposed that the clauses of the agreement relating to the determination of 'recommended prices' are devoid of all useful effect. Indeed the fixing of a price even simply recommended affects competition by the fact that it permits all the participants to foresee with a reasonable degree of certainty what the price policy of their competitors will be. That foresight is all the more certain in that to the 'recommended prices' provisions is attached the obligation to make a demonstrable profit in all cases and these provisions must in addition be considered in the context of the whole of the internal regulations of the applicant association which are characterised by a rigorous discipline supported by inspections and sanctions.

Apart from the fixing of prices properly so called, the agreement covered by the decision under appeal contains a further batch of restrictive clauses concerning other contractual conditions. Such is the case inter alia with the clauses which have the object of preventing the sale of cement to traders other than members of the association or re-sellers authorised by it, of preventing the creation of cement stocks in the hands of third parties who are not subject to the discipline of the association, of strictly limiting the commercial advantages which could be conceded to purchasers and preventing any provisions of services to customers which fall outside the bounds of what is considered "normal". Thus an examination of the whole of the regulation contained in the decision under appeal brings them out as forming a coherent and rigorously organised system which has the object of restricting competition between the members of the association.

(b) Influence on trade between Member States.

According to the applicant association, the Community is not entitled to judge the agreement covered by the decision under appeal because it is a purely national agreement, limited to the Dutch territory, which in no way applies to imports or exports and which is therefore without influence on trade between Member States. In support of this it particularly relies on the fact that the overall production of cement in Holland is far from meeting the needs of the Dutch economy, leaving a large need for imports, that furthermore there are, apart from its members, a large number of unaffiliated sellers of cement and that thus intra-Community trade runs no risk of being unfavourably influenced.

According to Article 85(1) all agreements which have the object or effect of preventing, restricting or distorting competition are incompatible with the Treaty if they are liable to affect trade between Member States. An agreement which extends to the whole of the territory of a Member state has, by its very nature, the effect of consolidating a national partitioning, thus hindering the economic interpenetration to which the Treaty is directed and ensuring a protection for the national production. More particularly, the restrictive provisions by which the members of the applicant association are bound as well as the exclusion by the association of all sales to resellers who are not authorised by it make more difficult the activity or the penetration on the Dutch market of producers or sellers from the other Member States. It therefore appears that the objection based on the fact that the trade between Member States is not liable to be affected by the decision of the applicant association should be dismissed.

*Sequel*

The Court rejected the appeal by the Vereeniging van Cementhandelaren.

(3) Decision in re Papier Peints de Belgique,
Decision of the Commission of 23 July 1974 on a proceeding under Article 85 of the EEC Treaty; OJ No L 237, 29 August 1974; (1974) CMLR D 127; CCH para. 9668; Competition Law CM/M/I/76.

*Facts:* The Commission found that the internal rules of procedure governing the Groupement Belge des Fabricants de Papiers Peints and a number of decisions by this association of undertakings constituted infringements of Article 85(1). It accordingly ordered the relevant undertakings to terminate an agreement and the decisions based on it, where their effect was to restrict the free play of competition in the sale of wallpapers in Belgium.

The Groupement had notified the relevant agreement in 1962, but the notification was incomplete. Following investigations carried out in response to complaints against the Groupement received in 1972, it was found that the Groupement was a comprehensive marketing organisation set up to cover the whole industry concerned. It included collective sales price fixing and imposition of retail proces on dealers, and also the standardisation of general selling conditions, rebates, clearance sales etc. Apart from preventing members of the association from fixing prices and terms individually, it prevented them also from seeking competitive advantages through their own advertising or from individually making better services available to their customers. Furthermore, a resale price maintenance rule was designed to eliminate competition between wallpaper dealers.

The agreement and the decisions covered not only wallpapers produced by members of the Groupement but also imported wallpapers sold in Belgium by the members. In line with the approach taken by the Court and the Commission in earlier cases the effect of such an agreement which covered the entire territory of one Member State and also contained arrangements for aggregated rebates on total turnover, was to consolidate divisions between national markets and to hinder imports from other Member States.

The main interest of the case arises from the ban under Article 85 (1) of a decision between enterprises to impose a collective boycott. This amounted to a particularly serious violation of the rules on competition, since its aim was to eliminate a troublesome competitor. In this case the Commission, considering that the collective boycott went beyond the operation described in the notification, imposed heavy fines on the undertakings involved. The collective refusal to supply originated in the desire of the Groupement to enforce its rules, and particularly its imposed prices policy. Following an individual action by one of its members, the Groupement decided on a collective boycott, from October 1971, of a Belgian wallpaper wholesaler who refused to comply with the prices imposed by the Groupement and to ensure that they were applied by his customers. The wholesaler concerned was a supplier of wallpapers to self-service shops which were retailing below the fixed prices.

The Commission refused to grant exemption from the ban on restrictive practices. Its grounds were the preservation of an artificially high price level for wallpaper on the Belgian market aimed at by the collective pricing agreements, and the inhibiting effect on imports of the aggregated rebate system. Not only did users fail to derive any benefit, they actually suffered loss.

E. The effect on trade between Member States

The agreement constituted by the Règlement d'ordre intérieur, and the decision based on it, may also affect trade between Member States, since wallpaper manufactured outside Belgium and sold in Belgium by the members of the Groupement is also included. Apart from this the aggregated rebate scheme hinders the importation of wallpaper into Belgium. The agreement and the decisions based upon it directly affect freedom of trade between Member States in a way which is detrimental to the attainment of a single market. By its very nature, an agreement extending over the whole area of a Member State has the effect of reinforcing the compartmentalisation of markets at national level; it thereby prevents the economic interpenetration which the Treaty is designed to bring about and protects domestic production.

*The Commission decided:*

Article 1
The Règlement d'ordre intérieur of the Groupement des Fabricants de Papiers Peints de Belgique of July 1971, Circulars 619, 620, 617 C and 617 V and the decision not to supply wallpaper to the dealer Pex and the undertaking International Decor constitute infringements of Article 85(1) of the Treaty establishing the European Economic Community.

Article 2
The application under Article 85(3) for a declaration of non-applicability is refused.

Article 3
The Groupement des Fabricants de Papiers Peints de Belgique and its member undertakings, as named in Article 5(1) to (4) hereof, shall forthwith terminate the infringements specified in Article 1.

Article 4
1. The following fines are imposed in respect of the collective boycott:
(a) on SC Usines Peters Lacroix SA, a fine of 135 000 units of account;
(b) on Les Papeteries de Genval SA, a fine of 120 000 units of account;
(c) on Ets. Vanderborght Frères SA, a fine of 36 000 units of account;
(d) on Papiers Peints Brepols SA, a fine of 67 500 units of account.

2. This decision is enforceable against the enterprises concerned in accordance with the provisions of Article 192 of the EEC Treaty.

Article 5
This Decision is addressed to the Groupement des Fabricants de Papiers Peints de Belgique, Av. Louise 138, 1050 Brussels, and to the following undertakings: (ommitted).

*Sequel*

The parties appealed to the Court of Justice for the annulment of the Decision. (Case 73/74, Papiers Peints v. Commission, judgment of 20 November 1975; (1975) ECR 1491; CCH para. 8334; (1976) CMLR 245; Competition Law CM/M/III/52.

During the oral proceedings the members of the Groupement announced that they no longer contested "the decision of the Commission as from the date on which it was delivered and as regards the future in so far as it prohibited the agreements imposing the obligation to change the prices fixed and to display them" and the agreements "prohibiting the desplay of lower prices or of reductions made by reference to the fixed or recommended prices".

The Groupement stated that it continued to contest the legality of the decision as regards the past, not for the purpose of seeking its annulment in toto but in order to demonstrate that the suspension of deliveries to Mr. Pex did not come within the prohibition in Article 85(1) and that, in consequence, the decision of the Commission imposing the fines for such suspension should be annulled.

Alternatively, the members of the Groupement contended that the fines were so excessive that the Court, which has unlimited jurisdiction in the matter, should reduce them.

The Court held that the control of the market exercised by the Groupement characterised by its pricing and rebates policy, and supported by penalties in order to ensure strict compliance with the conditions of sale, was intended to and did restrict or distort competition in Belgium and consequently, within the Common Market.

The Court annulled Article 4 of the Decision. It considered that the Commission had not fulfilled its obligation under Article 190 of the Treaty to give reasons for its decisions.

*The Court held:*

Effect on trade between Member States

The applicants maintain, first, that the agreements and decisions of the Groupement were not liable to affect trade between Member States.

They maintain, secondly, that even if, in fact, the agreements and decisions were liable to affect trade between Member States, the contested decision did not specify how this trade could be affected.

Thirdly, the members of the Groupement state that they believed in all good faith that the agreements and decisions did not affect trade between Member States, and that there is, accordingly, no justification for fines for a decision which merely enforced the agreement.

The fact that a price-fixing agreement of the type in question only covers the marketing of products in a single Member State does not rule out the possibility that trade between Member States may be affected.

In fact, a restrictive agreement extending over the whole of the territory of a Member State is by its very nature liable to have the effect of reinforcing the compartmentalisation of markets on a national basis, thereby holding up the economic interpenetration which the Treaty is designed to bring about and protecting domestic production.

In this connection it is important to identify the means available to the parties to a restrictive agreement to ensure that customers remain loyal, the relative importance of the agreement on the market concerned and the economic context in which it exists.

The decision of the Groupement concerning the barème de la prime de coopération, the level of which depends on the amount of all purchases from all members during a given year could have the effect of concentrating orders with members of the Groupement with the result that the customer who has already covered part of his requirements from members of the Groupement is encouraged to buy his entire requirements from those members, in order to obtain the highest possible rebate.

The decision does not explain how the fact that 10% of Belgian imports, representing 5% of the total Belgian market, sold by the Groupement subject to its prices and conditions is, in the absence of exclusive arrangements between the members of the Groupement and foreign manufacturers, liable to affect trade between Member States.

Under Article 190 of the Treaty, the Commission is required to state the reasons on which its decisions are based, enumerating the facts forming the legal basis of the measure and the considerations which led it to adopt the decision.

Although a decision which fits into a well-established line of decisions may be reasoned in a summary manner, for example by a reference to those decisions, if it goes appreciably further than the previous decisions, the Commission must give an account of its reasoning.

With regard to the finding in the decision of the territorial protection arising from the restrictive practice and the closing off of the national market, the decision does not clearly set forth the grounds on which the Commission found them to exist, the mere reference to an earlier case constituting insufficient explanation.

Without excluding the possibility that a restrictive pricing practice such as that in dispute may in fact affect trade between Member States, the fact remains that, when the defendant adopted a decision which went appreciably further than its earlier decisions, it ought to have supplied a more detailed statement of the grounds on which it was based.

In this respect, the obligation on the Commission, under Article 190 of the EEC Treaty, to give reasons for its decisions is not satisfied by the straightforward assertions appearing under heading E of the contested decisions entitled "The effect on trade between Member States".

In consequence, Article 4 of Decision No 74/431/EEC of the Commission must, in accordance with the applicant's claim, be annulled.

(4) Fedetab Case

Heintz von Landewijck and others v. Commission, Joined Cases 209-215/78 and 218/78, Judgment of 29 October 1980; (1980) ECR 3125; (1981) 3 CMLR 134; CCH para. 8687; Competition Law CM/M/III/84.

*Facts:* The Commission adopted a decision on 20 July 1978 finding that the system for distributing and selling manufactured tobacco products in Belgium used by the Fédération belgo-luxembourgeoise des Industries du Tabac (Fedetab), Brussels and several of its members constitutes an infringement of the ban on restrictive agreements laid down in Article 85 of the EEC Treaty, and requires that the system be discontinued immediately.

The system was designed to impose fixed profit margins, both horizontally on all the manufacturers who were party to the agreement and vertically at all levels of distribution. It also sought to classify Belgian wholesalers and retailers into a number of different categories, allocate a fixed margin to each, limit the number of new businesses approved in certain wholesale categories, forbid wholesalers in certain categories to resell tobacco products to certain wholesalers in other categories, force firms to observe the resale prices laid down by the manufacturers, encourage manufacturers to agree to impose standardised terms of payment, and force certain categories of wholesalers and retailers qualifying for the highest profit margins to stock a minimum range of brands.

After the Commission had sent Fedetab and its members a statement of its objections to the system, Fedetab replaced it with a 'Recommendation for cigarette sales in Belgium', notified to the Commission on

1 December 1975; this prompted a further statement of objections from the Commission.

This Recommendation, which is still in operation, preserved the old system of dividing up Belgian wholesalers and retailers and allocating each category a fixed profit margin, imposing standard terms of payment on manufacturer's customers, and granting wholesalers and retailers an end-of-year rebate.

Fedetab's distribution system, both as it was before 1 December 1975 and as it is now, following the Recommendation, created appreciable restrictions of competition for it virtually destroys competition at the distribution stage as to the terms offered to dealers.

The system was also apt to affect trade between Member States not only beacause the most important Luxembourg cigarette manufacturer is a member of Fedetab but also because a substantial proportion of the cigarettes and cigars imported into Belgium are sold through the manufacturers belonging to Fedetab, who distribute them alongside their own brands.

*Effect upon trade between Member States*

165. It remains to consider whether the above restrictions are also likely to have a significant effect upon trade between Member States. Only if that is so do the said restrictions fall within the prohibition of Article 85(1).

166. The Commission alleges in the contested decision that the measures prior to the recommendation were likely to affect trade between Member States because certain manufacturing members of Fedetab were responsible for a very substantial part of the manufactured tobacco imported into Belgium and distributed it on the same anti-competitive terms as their own products. Moreover, Belgian importers and manufacturers or those of other Member States who had not subscribed to the restrictive rules drawn up by Fedetab and the FNCG with regard to distribution were subject to the application of those rules when they resold their products, including those originating in other Member States, to a wholesaler or retailer who observed the rules laid down by those two associations, which, having regard to the strong position of the two associations on the market, was the general rule.

167. In view of those considerations the Commission found in paragraph 93 of the decision that although the tax arrangements in force created practical difficulties with regard to parallel imports by wholesalers and retailers, the fact remains that the alteration of trading conditions in Belgium was such as to divert the flow of trade from its normal course (that is, the course which it would have followed in the absence of the restrictions of competition found by the Commission), and so to affect trade between Member States.

168. The Commission alleges in paragraph 106 of the Decision that the measures in the recommendation are liable to affect trade between Member States for the same reasons as those put forward as regards the previous measures.

169. The applicants criticise that statement of reasons maintaining essentially that trade between Member States is not affected by the

market position of the manufacturing and importing members of Fedetab since, solely because of the consequences of the differences in taxation of manufactured tobacco in the Member States, the contested measures govern a purely national situation. At the present stage of the harmonisation of duties on the consumption of manufactured tobacco the individual ways of calculating and levying those duties constitute a fundamental impediment to intra-Community trade and prevent the making of parallel import arrangements. Moreover, even assuming that the contested measures are capable of having an indirect affect upon the volume of manufactured tobacco products imported by the manufacturers, it has in no way been shown that such effect is likely to affect free trade between Member States so as adversely to affect achievement of the aims of a single market between the States.

170. In the face of those conflicting arguments it is right to recall in the first place, as the Court observed in its judgment of 30 June 1966 in Case 56/65 *Société Technique Minière v Maschinenbau Ulm GmbH (1966)* ECR 235, that in order that an agreement, decision or concerted practice may affect trade between Member States it must be possible to foresee with a sufficient degree of probability on the basis of a set of objective factors of law or of fact that the agreement, decision or concerted practice in question may have an influence, direct or indirect, actual or potential, on the pattern of trade between Member States. The influence thus foreseeable must give rise to a fear that the realisation of a single market between Member States might be impeded.

171. In that respect it is right to observe that it is common ground, that as was said in paragraphs 8 and 91 of the decision, a substantial part of the manufactured tobacco products sold in Belgium are imported through manufacturing members of Fedetab who market them using the same distribution networks as for the products which they manufacture themselves. By way of example, in 1974 they imported 51% of the cigarettes and 12 to 14% of the cigars arriving in Belgium, that is some 5% of the cigarettes and 10% of the cigars sold there.

172. Moreover, although because of difficulties of a fiscal and technical nature which the Court pointed out in its judgment of 16 November 1977 in Case 13/77 *INNO v ATAB (1977)* ECR 2115, parallel imports into Belgium of manufactured tobacco are largely excluded, it is necessary to observe that the influence on the trade in question in the present cases is, as clearly appears from the statement of the reasons on which the contested decision was based, above all from the large imports made by manufacturing members of Fedetab. In that respect it must be observed that the restrictions on competition pointed out above in relation to trade margins, end-of-year rebate and terms of payment are likely to distort trade patterns in manufactured tobacco from the course which they would otherwise have followed. *A fortiori* the same is true as regards those of the measures prior to the recommendation which aimed at ensuring strict observance at each stage of distribution of the prices laid down by the manufacturers and importers. In taking concerted action on these fundamental aspects of the sale terms to be allowed to intermediaries, the applicants appreciably reduced still further any inducement the intermediaries may have had of encouraging the sale as regards imported products of certain products in relation to others, in exchange for individual financial advantage.

173. The Commission decision therefore rightly finds that the restrictions on competition by the applicants are likely to affect trade between Member States.

(5) Decision in re Vimpoltu

Decision of 13 July 1983 on a proceeding under Article 85 of the EEC Treaty, O.J. No. L 200, 23 July 1983, p. 44.

*Facts:* The Commission ordered the association of importers and wholesalers of agricultural and horticultural machinery in the Netherlands, "Vimpoltu", to put an end to the restrictions on competition contained in the association's decision of 27 May 1980, which had been notified to the Commission.
The Vimpoltu decision was found to violate Article 85 (1) by prohibiting members from granting retailers a discount of more than 25%, including all bonuses, off the gross selling price, by imposing standard delivery and payment terms and rules on sales promotion, and by requiring an exchange of information on recommended resale prices.
Since the Vimpoltu members account for approximately 90% of imports of agricultural tractors into the Netherlands, the Vimpoltu decision resulted in an appreciable restriction of competition, affecting trade between Member States.

*The Commission held:*

43. The said decision, which applies over the whole territory of a Member State to products almost exclusively imported from other Member States, is apt to affect trade between Member States. Its very nature is such that there is a sufficient likelihood that it could affect, directly or indirectly, actually or potentially, trade between Member States in a manner prejudicial to the attainment of a single Community market. The origin and volume of imports of the products make it likely that the restrictions on competition described above will cause the flow of trade to be diverted from the course in would otherwise have followed.

3. Agreements between undertakings established in Member States and undertakings established in non-Member States.

(1) Decision on the Grosfillex-Fillistorf agreement

Decision of the Commission of 11 March 1964; JO No 58, April 1964,p.915; (1964) CMLR 237; CCH para. 2412,37; Competition Law CM/M/I/1.

*The Commission ruled:*

....

The object of the contract concluded between Grosfillex and Fillistorf is the grant, by a manufacturer established in the Common Market, to a firm established outside the Common Market, of the exclusive right to sell the former's products in a territory situated outside the Common Market, that the object of the contract is not therefore to prevent, restrain or distort competition within the Common Market; however, certain provisions of this contract prohibit Fillistorf from selling in the Common Market countries the goods covered by the contract and any other likely to compete with these, whether manufactured within or outside the Common Market, and that there are therefore grounds for enquiring whether in consequence of these provisions the contract does not have the effect of preventing, restraining or distorting competition within the Common Market, within the meaning of Article 85(1);

On this point, the following circumstances should be taken into account:

- the goods purchased by Fillistorf, which are delivered to it in Switzerland by Grosfillex would, when resold in the Common Market, cross a new customs frontier.

They are therefore not likely to compete with the same goods delivered direct to the Common Market territory. If they did, this would be due to abnormal circumstances of which the Commission has not been informed. There are, indeed, no grounds for supposing that Grosfillex prices on the Swiss market are lower than those charged by Grosfillex within the Common Market, and this seems to be confirmed by the fact that Swiss purchasers of the contract products sold by Fillistorf are not forbidden to resell them in the Common Market;

- the market for household and sanitary plastic goods includes a considerable number of manufacturers who are established in the Member States or in other States and who are able to compete with one another in the territory of the Common Market; the same applies at the distributive stage;

- finally there has been no objection from third parties following the announcement published pursuant to Article 19(3) of Regulation No 17 in the Official Journal of the European Communities No 102 of 4 July 1963.

These circumstances show that competition within the Common Market is not prevented, restrained or distorted to any appreciable extent as a result of the contract in question;

Therefore, the information received by the Commission provides no grounds at present for considering that the contract in question has the object or effect of preventing, restraining or distorting competition within the Common Market, within the meaning of Article 85(1); whereas, one of the conditions for Article 85(1) of the Treaty to be applicable is accordingly not nullified; and that consequently the negative clearance sought may be granted;

The Commission adopted the present decision:

Article 1

According to the information it has received, there are no grounds for the Commission to take action under Article 85(1) of the Treaty establishing the European Economic Community with respect to the agreement concluded on 4 September 1959 between Grosfillex and the firm of Fillistorf.

Note: It is submitted that the export bans used in agreements which affect trade between the EEC and the abovementioned States with whom the Community has concluded Trade agreements (see page 52) will in general no longer be justified. The goods in question will no longer have to cross customs frontiers in two occasions since the customs duties for most industrial products have disappeared as a result of the agreements.

This conclusion is supported by the Decision in re SABA. In re Junghans a clear distinction is made between third countries in general and those States with which the EEC has a Free-Trade agreement.

For other aspects of agreements with undertakings in third States see Annex 18, the Commission's opinion concerning the applicability of the Treaty of Rome to the importance of Japanese products into the Community and Chapter 2, Section I.

(2) Decision in re SABA I

Decision of the Commission of 15 December 1975 on a proceeding under Article 85 of the EEC Treaty; OJ No L 28, 3 February 1976, p. 19; (1976) I CMLR D 61, CCH para. 9802; Competition Law CM/M/I/98.

*Facts:* The Commission authorised the EEC sales system of the German firm SABA, which manufactures radios, televisions and sound reproduction and recording equipment for sale in all Community countries through a network of approved dealers.

There are two aspects of the approval process: (1) in general, any dealer wishing to retail SABA equipment must keep a shop or department specialising in the sale of the relevant goods and must meet certain business and technical requirements so that the goods may be sold in a satisfactory manner. (2) of firms meeting these requirements, SABA appoints only those which further undertake to engage in certain sales promotion activities and to meet certain sales targets.

In the Commission's view the SABA distribution system falls under the prohibition of Article 85(1) because a large number of dealers satisfying all the technical requirements for the sale of this type of equipment are excluded from it. The SABA contracts go beyond straightforward specialist trade arrangements, which would be irreproachable from the anti-trust angle; their ultimate effect is qualitative selection of suitable dealers. The Commission granted however an exemption since it considered that the distribution system, which is based on close two-way cooperation between manufacturer and retailer, helps in the end to rationalise production and distribution, with the consumer as well as reaping the ultimate benefit.

The Commission held on this point:

All SABA dealers in the Community at all stages of distribution are subject to the EEC Distribution Agreements imposed by SABA. German SABA wholesalers, SABA sole distributors and SABA specialist retailers are obliged:

(a) to supply goods for resale within the Common Market only to SABA dealers.

(b) before making delivery, to check by personally consulting the EEC Agreement signed by SABA and SABA dealers and by consulting the catalogue of SABA dealers, whether the relevant retailer has actually been appointed a SABA dealer. Such appointments are made by SABA.

(c) to keep full registers giving serial numbers of SABA articles resold, with dates and purchasers; SABA will request to see these registers or to have the necessary information only where it has reason to believe that the dealer or his customer is in breach of his contract. i.e. has supplied a dealer who is not an authorised SABA dealer.

(d)not to export SABA products to countries outside the EEC nor to import the same from outside the EEC.

However SABA has given the Commission an undertaking to lift these prohibitions once the relevant products are no longer subject to customs duties in trade between the Community and EFTA countries, which will be the case from 1 July onwards.(Exemption has been renewed by Commission Decision of 21 December 1983 (OJ No. L 376, 31 December 1983, p. 43))

(3) Decision in re Junghans

Commission Decision of 21 December 1976 relating to a proceeding under Article 85 of the Treaty; OJ No L 30, 2 February 1977, p. 16; (1977) 1 CMLR D 82; CCH para. 9912; Competition Law CM/M/I/108.

*Facts:* The Commission authorised the EEC sales system of the German firm Gebruider Junghans GmbH, a subsidiary of Karl Diehl KG, manufacturing clocks and watches of all types.
Junghans and Diehl have a relatively small share of the Community market in clocks and watches, though in the case of clocks it is appreciably greater in four countries.
Junghans has established a uniform distribution system to promote sales of its products throughout the Common Market. The main features of the distribution system are the use of particular criteria for the appointment of Junghans retailers and the fact that the channels of distribution are determined by Junghans.
In the Commission's view the Junghans distribution system falls under the prohibition of Article 85(1). The Commission granted an exemption on the basis of Article 85(3) after amendment of the distribution system by Junghans.

*The Commission ruled:*

The prohibition preventing Junghans dealers from exporting from the EEC does not at present have any appreciable effect on competition within the meaning of Article 85(1). This prohibition is designed to protect dealers in third countries from their competitors in the Community. It has the object of restricting competition in third countries.

This prohibition has no appreciable effects on competition within the Common Market and trade between Member States. Owing to the double duty borne by goods twice crossing the customs frontiers of the European Communities, there is no incentive for Junghans dealers and consumers in the Community to buy goods exported by a Junghans dealer to a third country.

However, while at present the Commission sees no reason to object to this export prohibition, this will not necessarily be the case after 1 July 1977 as regards those States with which the EEC has a Free-Trade Agreement. After that date there will be no customs duties on trade between the Community and the countries in question.

4. "de minimis rule"

For the "de minimis rule" and minor agreements see below Chapter 3.

5. Article 86

(1) Commercial Solvents Case

See above, page 14.

(2) Decision in re United Brands Co.

Decision of the Commission of 17 December 1975 on a proceeding under

Article 86 of the Treaty, OJ No L 95, 9 March 1976, p. 1; (1976) I CMLR D 28; CCH para. 9800; Competition Law CM/M/I/100.

*Facts:* United Brand Co. (UBC) is a conglomerate, born of the merger between United Fruit Co. and AMK Corp., a major US meat producer, which derives only some 20% of its total turnover from the sale of bananas. As the world's largest seller of bananas, it holds, in the Commission's opinion, a dominant position on the banana market in a substantial part of the Community. Apart from the fact that it handles 40% of the trade in bananas in the EEC, it wields overwhelming economic power, due largely to the vertical integration of its banana business, and holds other advantages resulting from its multinational and conglomerate character. It owns numerous plantations in tropical banana-growing countries and a fleet of refrigerated banana boats. It also controls banana ripening in consumer countries and takes direct charge of the advertising campaigns and sales promotion activities related to its brand of bananas. It is the only firm on the banana market to have all these advantages and is in a position to use them to place major obstacles in the way of effective competition by its present business rivals, while potential competitors find themselves confronted with major barriers to market entry.

Investigation showed that the market shares held by this company in the northern area of the EEC - Germany, Denmark, Ireland and the Benelux countries - backed up by the marketing policy it pursues, give it a dominant position in these countries. Although UBC also has sizeable market shares in the United Kingdom, France and Italy, the Commission did not consider them in its Decision since different marketing and importing arrangements are obtained there.

The Commission took the view that UBC had been abusing its dominant position in the following ways:

- it prohibited its distributors and ripeners from reselling green bananas, which meant there was market fragmentation;

- it charged its customers prices which differed according to the Member State in which they were located, although there were no objective reasons for such discrimination for equivalent transactions.

- it charged unfair prices for sales to its customers in Germany, Denmark and the Benelux countries;

- finally, for no objectively valid reason, it refused, for nearly two years, to supply one of its main Danish customers.

Because of the seriousness of these violations of Article 86, the Commission imposed a fine of one million u.a. It also ordered UBC to put an end to its infringements of the Treaty (except the refusal to supply, which had already ceased). So that the Commission could check on compliance, UBC was ordered to notify the Commission once it had withdrawn the ban on resale o green bananas by its distributors and ripeners in Germany, Denmark, Ireland and the Benelux countries and to keep the Commission informed of the prices actually charged in those countries over the next two years. Penalty payments amounting to one thousand u.a. per day of delay from the dates stipulated in the Decision were imposed.

The importance of the Decision lies in the fact that the Commission investigated a firm's entire marketing policy in the light of Article 86, not so as to attack its commercial dynamism and economic performance, since this is not the purpose of Article 86, but because a dominant firm has an obligation not to indulge in business practices which are at variance with the goals of integrated markets and undistorted competition in the common market.

The Decision is also significant in that it finds abuse within the meaning of Article 86 on two counts: customers were charged different prices for identical transactions, and unfair prices were imported.

In an attempt to justify the considerable differences in the prices which it charged its customers in different Member States, UBC asserted that it had adjusted its prices to the maximum the market would bear. The Commission took the view that for a dominant firm systematically to charge the highest price it could get, entailing substantial price differences, was not an objective justification for discriminatory prices, particularly if the firm used its dominance to keep markets separated.

In reaching the conclusion that the prices imposed by UBC on its customers were unfair, the Commission relied essentially on the following facts:

In the first place, UBC by its own admission was making a profit on the lowest price quoted for bananas, the price at which it sold to its Irish customers.

Also, UBC was selling bananas withoutthe Chiquita trademark 30 to 40% cheaper than those with, although they were only slightly inferior to Chiquita bananas; furthermore, UBC's main competitors, selling their own brand of bananas of comparable quality, generally sell them at prices below those of Chiquita bananas.

These facts brought the Commission to the view that the prices of this brand of bananas were excessive in relation to the economic value of the commodity supplied. As a guide, it suggested that UBC's prices in Germany, Denmark and the Benelux countries would be acceptable if they came down to not less than 15% below the prices currently charged in Germany.

In taking this action, the Commission had no wish to set itself up as a price-control authority or to interfere in internal price setting by examining cost components or the like. On the other hand, it did wish to make it clear that the provisions of Article 86 which prohibit discriminatory and unfair prices must be enforceable.

United Brands appealed against the Decision of the Commission. The Court upheld the Commission's Decision except the joint dealing with unfair prices.

*The Commission ruled:*

.....

These abuses by UBC of its dominant position are capable of affecting trade between Member States to an appreciable extent as follows.

The prohibition on the sale of green bananas impedes trade between distributor/ripeners in different Member States, and deflects the flow of trade from its normal course. It is capable of affecting trade between those Member States and thus of dividing up the market, particularly as the prohibition applies to all the bananas sold by UBC to its customers from this part of the EEC.

The application in respect of sales, of Chiquita bananas of dissimilar prices for equivalent transactions according to the Member State in which the customer operates and the bananas are to be sold, is liable to encourage or discourage the export of those bananas from one Member

State to another according to the different price levels in the various Member States.

The imposition of unfair prices on customers in certain Member States is liable to affect the quantities of Chiquita bananas traded between Member States, in that it encourages exports from Member States where such unfair prices are not imposed and vice versa.

Olesen is one of the main distributors/ripeners of bananas in Denmark and could have been able to expand its business in other Member States. The cutting off of supplies by UBC prevented it from doing so, for example with the green bananas it was buying for Bremerhaven and then importing into Denmark. Trade has also been affected by the fact that, due to the withdrawal of supplies, Olesen was no longer able to import the same quantities of bananas into Denmark.

(3) Decision in re Hugin-Liptons

Decision of the Commission of 8 December 1977, OJ No L 22, 25 January 1978, p. 23; (1978) 1 CMLR D19; CCH para. 10007; Competition Law CM/M/I/120.

*Facts:* Acting on a complaint in case of refusal to sell, the Commission imposed a fine of 50 000 u.a. (UKL 20 833) on Hugin Kassaregister AB, Stockholm, one of the five major manufacturers of cash registers which supply the Common Market.

The Decision finds that Hugin AB prohibited its various subsidiaries and distributors within the common market from selling its spare parts outside the Hugin network and also, together with its United Kingdom subsidiary, Hugin Cash Registers Ltd. London, refused without valid objective reasons to supply such spare parts to the complainant company, Liptons Cash Registers and Business Equipment Ltd., London, a former distributor of Hugin Cash Registers in the United Kingdom.

Hugin AB is wholly owned by the Federation of Swedish retail trade. Although Hugin AB's share of the EEC market for cash registers is only about 12% it enjoys a monopoly for the supply of spare parts for its own cash registers through its total control of their manufacture and supply. These spare parts are manufactured to Hugin's designs with Hugin's tools, and are sold exclusively through Hugin's sales network. They are essential for the maintenance, repair and reconditioning of Hugin cash registers. Hugin AB's policy of refusing to supply even qualified independent operators not only precludes all competition in the business of service and repair but also effectively contains any independent market for leasing Hugin cash registers or for the sale of used machines.

Liptons is a small company specialising in the sale, leasing, servicing, repairing and reconditioning of all makes of cash registers including those manufactured by Hugin AB, for which purpose it requires spare parts. Liptons had been supplied until 1977 with substantial quantities of spare parts by Hugin AB's United Kingdom importer and subsequently by Hugin UK. Liptons had also acted as distributor for Hugin cash registers from 1969 to 1972. Thereafter, from October 1972 Liptons was refused the supply of spare parts by Hugin AB, Hugin UK and every other Hugin subsidiary and distributor within the EEC to which Lipton applied.

The Commission found that there was a separate market for the supply of spare parts where Hugin holds a dominant position. Hugin abused its dominant position by refusing to supply Liptons without valid objective reason.

*The Commission ruled:*

.....

The abuses by Hugin AB of it dominant position appreciably affect trade between Member States. The prohibition on the export of spare parts from all Member States to any firm other than an authorised dealer directly affects trade between Member States. The refusal by Hugin subsidiaries and the Hugin distributors in other Member States to supply Liptons was a result of Hugin AB's Community wide policy and affected trade between the United Kingdom and the Member States involved. Even if the prohibition is removed in the manner proposed by Hugin AB, its policy of refusing to permit supplies of spare parts to independent companies, such as Liptons, still exists and affects trade between Member States. Hugin AB is thereby preventing Liptons from carrying on its business of maintenance, repair, renting out and re-conditioning Hugin cash registers. Liptons has been prevented from continuing to expand its business within a substantial part of the common market and is unable to purchase other spare parts from other Member States. Due to the size of Hugin AB's share of the overall market for cash registers, the distribution system practised by Hugin AB under which only dealers are supplied with spare parts together with the prohibition imposed on such dealers on selling parts outside the Hugin network, prevent the operation of independent servicing companies anywhere in the common market, and has an appreciable effect on the structure of competition within the common market.
(see also above page 53).

(4) Hugin Case

Hugin Kassaregister AB and Hugin Cash Registers Ltd. V. Commission, Case 22/78, Judgment of 31 May 1979, (1979) ECR 1869; (1979) 3 CMLR 345; CCH par. 8524; Competition Law CM/M/III/78.

For facts see above page 53.

*The Court held:*

15. In its Decision the Commission stated that 'Liptons has been prevented from continuing to expand its business within a substantial part of the common market and is unable to purchase spare parts from other Member States'. According to the Commission the distribution system practised by Hugin 'has an appreciable effect on the structure of competition within the common market'.

16. Hugin contests the validity of those statements. According to Hugin Liptons' activities do not extend beyond a single Member State and there does not really exist a market for spare parts extending beyond the territory of each Member State.

17. The interpretation and application of the condition relating to effects on trade between Member States contained in Articles 85 and 86 of the Treaty must be based on the purpose of that condition which is to define, in the context of the law governing competition, the boundary between the areas respectively covered by Community law and the law of the Member States. The Community law covers any agreement or any practice which is capable of constituting a threat to freedom of trade between Member States in a manner which might harm the attainment of the objectives of a single market between the Member States, in particular by partitioning the the national markets or by affecting the structure of competition within the common market. On the other

hand, conduct, the effects of which are confined to the territory of a single Member State, is governed by the national legal order.

18. For the purpose of applying these criteria to the facts in this case it is necessary to examine separately the effects on Liptons' commercial activities, on the one hand, and on trade in spare parts in general, on the other.

19. It is established that the centre of Liptons' activities is the London region and that, in any event, its commercial activities have never extended beyond the United Kingdom. As regards the future, there is no indication that Liptons envisages extending its activities beyond those geographical limits. That limitation is explained, moreover, by the particular nature of the activities in question. The maintenance, repair and renting out of cash registers and the sale of used machines cannot constitute profitable operations beyond a certain area around the commercial base of an undertaking. This characteristic is reflected in the structure of the undertakings concerned. It appears from the file that in the United Kingdom there exist large numbers of small, local undertakings which specialise in the provision of the services in question. There are grounds for believing that the commercial structure of this trade is the same in the other Member States in which Hugin also applies its policy of not supplying spare parts outside its own distribution network.

20. The conclusion to be drawn from these considerations is therefore that trade between Member States is not affected by the obstacles which Hugin's conduct places in the way of the activities of independent undertakings which specialise in the provision of maintenance services.

21. As regards the distribution of Hugin spare parts as a distinct commercial activity it is established that Liptons has tried in vain to obtain such parts from Hugin dustributors in certain other Member States. Moreover, Hugin does not deny that its policy of not supplying spare parts outside its own network, whilst it does not involve a prohibition on exports, necessarily implies that the refusal to supply independent undertakings applies whatever the geographical location of the undertaking.

22. The question is, therefore, whether it may be assumed that trade between Member States in Hugin spare parts would exist if the market conditions were entirely free and not subject to restrictive practices such as those applied by Hugin in this instance.

23. It should be recalled in this respect that the value of the spare parts is in itself relatively insignificant. Accordingly they are not such as to constitute a commodity of commercial interest in trade between Member States, quite apart from the fact that an independent undertaking would derive no economic advantage from buying them from a Hugin subsidiary in another Member State rather than from the parent company. Indeed, it has not been alleged that Hugin applies differentiated prices on the various local markets. It is logical to suppose that an independent undertaking which could not obtain a spare part from the Hugin subsidiary established in its country would turn to the parent company, that is to say, in this instance, to a supplier based in a non-member country, rather than to a subsidiary in another Member State. If the latter course were followed it would constitute an exception rather than a normal commercial transaction.

24. In the present case Liptons turned to Hugin subsidiaries and distributors in certain other Member States precisely because Hugin's restrictive policy prevented it from satisfying its spare parts requirements through normal commercial channels. Its attempts to obtain spare parts in the other Member States can therefore not be regarded as an indication of the existence, whether actual or potential, of a normal pattern of trade between the Member States in spare parts. In other words, if Liptons had been able to obtain spare parts from a Hugin subsidiary in another Member State it would have been because Hugin was willing to sell those parts outside its own distribution network. In such a case, however, it would be customary for Liptons to apply to the Hugin subsidiary in its own country rather than to a subsidiary in another Member State.

25. In those circumstances Hugin's conduct cannot be regarded as having the effect of diverting the movement of goods from its normal channels, taking account of the economic and technical factors peculiar to the sector in question.

26. It must therefore be concluded that Hugin's conduct is not capable of affecting trade between Member States. Consequently the Commission's decision does not satisfy all the conditions laid down by Article 86 of the Treaty. It must therefore be annulled.

(5) Decision in re Michelin-Netherlands

Commission Decision of 7 October 1981 on a proceeding under Article 86 of the Treaty. O.J. No L 353, 9 December 1981, p. 33; (1982) 1 CMLR 643; CCH para. 10340; Competition Law CM/M/I/164.

*Facts:* In keeping with its longstanding opposition to any policy on prices, rebates and discounts used abusively by a dominant undertaking to maintain or consolidate its position on the market, the Commission imposed a fine of 680 000 ECU on Nederlandsche Banden-Industrie Michelin (NBIM), Amsterdam, a subsidiary of Société Michelin, Clermont-Ferrand, for abusing its dominant position on the Dutch market in replacement tyres for heavy vehicles by pursuing an unlawful policy of discounts.

NBIM's dominant position results first and foremost from the fact that it holds the largest share (some 60%) of the Dutch market in replacement heavy tyres, while none of its main competitors holds more than 8% of the market; but its dominance is also indicated by the wide range of tyres it markets and by its intensive marketing among final consumers. Its position is such that dealers run serious commercial risks in not including Michelin tyres in the range of products they sell.

NBIM applied a discount system consisting, mainly, in fixing a sales target such that the share of Michelin tyres in a dealer's total sales either increased or at least remained stable. This policy of collective discounts not only had the effect of tying dealers to NBIM, but also resulted in discrimination between such dealers. The system's harmful effects on the dealers' commercial autonomy were compounded by a number of its operational aspects such as the failure to publish the criteria applied or to communicate or confirm them in writing to dealers in accordance with normal trade practice. By using such methods to consolidate its position on the market and to dissuade dealers from obtaining supplies from competing manufacturers, NBIM made it more difficult for manufacturers in other Member States to enter the Dutch market, thus

creating an artificial barrier to intra-Community trade.
.....

D. Effect on trade between Member States

51. The discount system applied by NBIM may affect trade between Member States, since, by establishing strong links between the dominant supplier and the dealers, it restricts the dealers' scope in making their purchases. NBIM's entire system is aimed at improving the dealers' performance in its own favour and thus at preventing other manufacturers from obtaining orders. Many of these manufacturers (see point 15) are established in the common market and have large plants which produce heavy tyres for sale on the Netherlands market. Their chances of penetrating the Netherlands market are diminished since, on account of the links established between manufacturers and dealers under the NBIM system, NBIM's market share is roughly fixed, and in consequence other manufacturers' penetration of the Netherlands market cannot exceed a small percentage. The conduct on the part of NBIM which is at issue and its consequent maintenance of its market share is accordingly liable to restrict freedom of trade between Member States in a way that may harm the achievement of the objective of establishing a single market between the Member States, in particular by changing the structure of competition within the common market.

The unfavourable effects of the abusive discount system on trade between Member States is appreciable. The evidence shows that even quite small rebates were considered significant by the dealers. The application of NBIM's discount system and its relation to the attainment of a sales target were uncertain. As a result, the dealers were faced with an invidious choice between making sales efforts for the other manufacturers or for Michelin and it was only natural for the dealers to try to increase their Michelin sales - inevitably at the expense of the other manufacturers because the uncertain and individualised bonus could well turn out to be better than the (known) rebate available from other manufacturers. In this way, the task of those other manufacturers, trying to sell into the Netherlands from other Community countries, was made noticeably more difficult by the action of the dominant undertaking.

52. By making the granting of an extra annual bonus for heavy and light tyres dependent on a specific 'target' in sales of light tyres being reached, NBIM made use of its dominant position on the market in new truck and bus tyres to improve its position on the market in car tyres. This practice was potentially disadvantageous to competitors as regards their scope for selling light tyres. The manufacturers of the car tyres sold on the Netherlands market are indeed also established in the common market and the light tyres sold on this market - apart from a relatively small number produced in the Netherlands - are produced by manufacturers established in other Member States. During a certain period the conduct at issue impeded their sales of light tyres in the Netherlands and could have affected trade between Member States.

*Sequel* The undertakings concerned brought an action for annulment before the Court of Justice. The Court's Judgment essentially confirms the Decision in which the Commission declared that the plaintiff's discount policy was an abuse of a dominant position.
(Case 322/81, Judgment of 9 November 1983, not yet published).

## III. THE NOTION OF UNDERTAKINGS

### A. General

a. Introduction

The notion of "undertakings" appears frequently in Community law, particularly in the EEC competition rules; e.g. Article 85 prohibits agreements betweeen undertakings or decisions of associations of undertakings which distort competition in the common market; and Article 86 prohibits the abuse of a dominant position by undertakings.

Neither the Treaty nor Regulation 17, the principal implementing regulation, define the meaning of "undertakings" for the purposes of competition law. The meaning of the term has, therefore, been developed in the jurisprudence of the Court of Justice and in the decisions of the Commission.

It is irrelevant what form the undertaking possesses as long as it enjoys legal capacity. For instance the undertaking may be organised in the form of a limited liability company, a publicly owned enterprise, a cooperative society, a sole trader, or a partnership.

The undertaking must have an economic aim; it can be engaged in either the production or distribution of goods or in the provision of services. It need not be a profit-making enterprise. Thus, a charitable institution constitutes an undertaking if it engages in trading activities.

b. Cases

1. Decision on the AOIP- Beyrard Agreement

Decision of the Commission of 2 December 1975 on a proceeding under Article 85 of the EEC Treaty; O.J. No L 6, 13 January 1976, p. 8; (1976) 1 CMLR 376; CCH para. 9861; Competition Law CM/M/I/97.

*Facts:* The Commission issued its first 'cease and desist' decision relating to a patent licensing agreement. This prohibits, as incompatible with Article 85, a number of clauses frequently found in patent licensing agreements.

The Commission ruled:

The Decision concerns a licensing agreement between the Association des Ouviers en Instruments de Précision (AICP), the licensee, and an inventor - Mr Beyrard - relating to existing and future patents for a number of liquid variable resistor electrical devices used principally in automatic starters for electric motors.

AOIP is an undertaking within the meaning of Article 85, as is also Mr Beyrard, since by licensing his patents he has commercially exploited his invention.

(2) Sugar Cases

Suiker Unie and others v. Commission, Joined Cases 40-48/73, 50/73, 54-56/73, 111/73, 113-114/73, Judgment of 16 December 1975; (1975) ECR 1663; (1976) I CMLR 295; CCH 8334; Competition Law CM/M/III/53.

*Facts:* The Commission was compelled to intervene to order the Community's main sugar producers and distributors to discontinue the concerted practices they had engaged in since 1 July 1968. These consisted, under the principle of respective market sharing, in making deliveries in the EEC importing countries only with the assent of the main producers in these countries, so as to considerably weaken the competitive pressure which untrammeled sugar imports could have engendered. Market fragmentation along national lines is not only a result of the complete separation of the market but also of the protection arrangements designed to ward off any disturbance of the producers' commercial strategies on their respective markets.

For many years EEC sugar was produced within national market organisations established by the authorities in close cooperation with the home industries. The main result of these arrangements made at official level with the business community was to cut off each of the six Community markets from the others almost completely. On 1 July 1968, national market organisations were replaced by a common market organisation designed to allow the common sugar market to operate and develop as provided for in Article 38(4) of the Treaty. The market stabilisation machinery established by Community regulations in order to guarantee a certain level of income to beet and sugar cane producers while avoiding the emergence of tendencies either to overproduction or to a sugar shortage exert, however, no influence on the free movement of sugar between the Member States or on the free formation of prices between the intervention price and the threshold price.

The various measures taken under the concerted practices engaged in by the sugar producers and their sales organisations in the Community were designed to control sugar trade within the Member States so as to ensure the protection of their respective markets. The deficit situation in certain areas in sugar for human consumption, however, necessitated a number of deliveries between Member States. In order to avoid as far as possible the competitive effects of such intra-Community trade:

- sugar deliveries were made, in general, only from producer to producer or under the producers' direct or indirect control, in order to enable them to resell the imported sugar at the same prices and on the same terms as home-produced sugar (in addition, in Italy, the suppliers, on the one hand, and the purchasers - Italian sugar producers on the other hand formed a grouping; imports into this country were subject to a tendering system organised by the Cassa Conguaglio Zucchero);

- deliveries to dealers and customers of the country of destination were refused, or bids were made only at higher prices adapted to those being charged on the market of the destinee country;

- restrictive clauses were written into the contracts concluded with the national dealers and customers, so as to prevent the latter from disturbing the sales policy pursued by the producers concerned;

- the bids made by the producers - especially the French and Belgian producers - submitted for the auctions organised by the Commission with a view to granting export refunds on exports to non-member countries, were concerted so that the quantities of surplus sugar remaining within the Common Market could be controlled and would exert no competitive pressure.

In the decision it adopted, the Commission endeavoured to restore quickly the scope for competition on the European sugar market in favour of the processing industries and of all the consumers in the Common Market. In addition, since sugar is a commodity consumed in large quantities and since the measures taken by those concerned were obviously in conflict with the aim of market integration, the Commission decided to impose on a number of the undertakings fines related to the seriousness and the length of time during which the infringements are committed and to the size of their shares in the market. The highest fine was 1,500,000 u.a. and the other undertakings were fined from 100,000 u.a. to 1,000,000 u.a. The fines totalled 9,000,000 u.a.

No fines were imposed on certain undertakings involved only occasionally or only to a modest extent in the infringements, or which endeavoured to adopt a pattern of behaviour independent of the producers participating in the concerted practices.

The Commission will ensure that its decision actually has the desired impact, and will carefully examine any implications which it may have for the common sugar market organisation.

*The Court held:*

*The complaint of a concerted practice having as its object the protection of the Netherlands market*

74. Subparagraph 2 of Article 1(1) of the contested decision blames SU and CSM, on the one hand, and RT and Pfeifer & Langer, on the other hand, for having 'since the 1968/69 marketing year (Pfeifer & Langen only since the 1970/71 marketing year)' - that is to say from the 1968/69 to the 1971/72 marketing year - 'committed infringements of Article 85(1) by engaging a concerted practice having as its object and effect the control of deliveries of sugar on the Netherlands market from Belgium and the western part of Germany and consequently the protection of that market'.

*Section 1:* Preliminary submission: the 'Cooperative Vereniging Suiker Unie UA' (SU) was not a legal entity during part of the period to which this complaint refers.

75. I. SU submits that it only commenced business on 2 January 1971 so that there is no foundation for the finding in the decision that the applicant committed infringements 'from the 1968/69 marketing year'.

76. Similarly the Commission infringed Regulation No 17, and in particular Article 15(2) thereof, by imposing on the applicant a fine for an infringement which it could not have committed during most of the period under consideration.

77. The Court shows that in 1966 four Netherlands sugar producing cooperatives, the members of which were beet growers, formed an association known as 'Coöperatieve Vereniging Suiker Unie UA', hereinafter called 'the former association', having as its object in particular, the coordination of the operations of the said cooperatives which had to carry out the instructions of the associations, especially for making the best possible use of plant, investments and prices.

78. Prompted by the wish to attain closer cooperation amounting to an actual merger the four cooperatives formed on 16 July 1970 a company also called 'Coöperatieve Vereniging Suiker Unie UA', which brought

together under its wing the members of the said cooperatives as direct participators, commenced business on 1 January 1971 and is the applicant in this case.

79. After the former association had changed its name to 'Coöperatieve Vereniging Suiker Unie UA', it ceased trading when the applicant commenced business and was dissolved with effect from 1 June 1971.

80. The four cooperatives which were members of the former association were dissolved on 31 December 1970 and on 1 January 1971 the applicant assumed all their rights and liabilities.

81. The applicant states that it cannot be held responsible for acts and things done by the former association which is not its predecessor ('rechtsvoorganger') and which had neither any goodwill nor any assets which it could have transferred to the applicant, quite apart from the fact that a transfer of goodwill is not known in Netherlands law.

82. The applicant is only the legal and economic successor of the four cooperatives,the names of which moreover never included the words 'Suiker Unie'.

83. Even if it must be treated as the legal successor of the former association, there is a case for taking account of the fact that this association was not liable for the obligations arising out of the decision, which were the direct liability of SU.

84. II. As the applicant assumed all the rights and liabilities of the four cooperatives of the old association, it must be treated as the economic successor both of the old association and its members, which is indeed what those members intended.

85. The applicant moreover does not deny that the name 'Suiker Unie' always covered the same undertakings, which were run for the most part by the same persons and had their registered offices at the same address.

86. It does not even claim that its conduct on the sugar market differed from that of the former association.

87. In these circumstances, so far as the sugar market is concerned, the main feature of the conduct of the applicant and its predecessor was its obvious continuity, which means that the whole of this behaviour must be attributed to the applicant.

88. Therefore this submission is unfounded.

3. Decision in re Reuter - BASF

Decision of the Commission of 26 July 1976; O.J.No L 254, of 17 September 1976; (1976)2 CMLR D 44; CCH para. 9862; Competition Law CM/M/I/106.

*Facts:* Acting on a complaint from Mr. Gottfried Reuter, a research chemist and entrepreneur, the Commission decided that the contractual restraint on competition imposed on him when he sold the Elastomer Group to BASF infringed Article 85(1) of the EEC Treaty.

The Decision was based on the following facts. Between 1969 and 1971 Mr Reuter, of Lemförde, near Hannover, sold his entire shareholding

in the Swiss limited company Elastomer AG, which he owned, to BASF AG, Ludwigshafen. Elastomer was the holding company of a group of firms with plants in several countries both within and outside the Community. The group manufactures polyurethanes, which are synthetic substances increasingly used in a large number of industries for the production of various finished goods. The Commercial value of the group consisted primarily of the knowhow and goodwill developed by Mr. Reuter.
In the contract of sale dated 25 June 1971 Mr. Reuter undertook that for a period of eight years he would refrain from engaging in any direct or indirect activities in the field covered by the contract, whether in Germany or elsewhere. All activities relating to polyurethanes, research and development, manufacture, industrial application and marketing were included in this restraint. Every form of activity was prohibited, including the holding of shares in other undertakings and the making of association and consultancy agreements.

The Commission found that the restriction on research and development was intended to eliminate Mr. Reuter as a potential competitor from the polyurethane market, and was thereby a clear infringement of Community competition law.

The restriction on commercial activities - manufacture, application of knowhow and sales - which, taken separately might have been acceptable subject to certain conditions, such as being for a reasonable duration, was considered by the Commission to have become unlawful by the time of the Commission Decision, five years after the business had been transferred.

*The Commission ruled*

.....

The agreement of 18 June 1971 containing the non-competition clause is an agreement between undertakings. Dr. Reuter is also to be regarded as an undertaking for the purpose of Article 85, since he engages in economic activity through those firms of the Elastomer group which remain under his control, by exploiting the results of his own research and as commercial advisor to third parties.

4. Decision in re RAI-UNITEL

Decision of the Commission in a proceeding under Article 85 of the EEC Treaty; O.J. No L 157, 15 June 1978, p. 39; (1978) 3 CMLR 306; CCH para. 10064; Competition Law CM/M/I/30.

*Facts:* The Commission adopted a Decision requesting information relating to a proceeding under Article 85 of the EEC Treaty. The Decision was addressed to Unitel- Film und Fernseh-Produktionsgesellschaft mbH & Co., Munich, whose objections had prevented the Mondovision broadcast of 'Don Carlos' to celebrate the 200th anniversary of La Scala, Milan, on 7 December 1977; its objections were based on the exclusive contracts entered into by Unitel and four of La Scala's principal singers, whereby the latter undertook not to appear in cinema or television performances of the opera if not approved by Unitel.

The information requested was necessary to determine whether the exclusive obligations entered into by these artists constitute restrictions of competition prohibited under Article 85(1). At the end of 1977 the Commission had already asked Unitel to provide this information. The company had refused, claiming that artists were not undertakings for the purposes of Article 85(1) and that the exclusive committments between Unitel and its singers were covered by Regulation No 67/67/EEC of 22 March 1967 on exclusive dealing agreements.

*The Commission ruled:*

1. (a) The Commission takes the view, on the information available to it, that artistes are undertakings within the meaning of Article 85(1) when they exploit commercially their artistic performances. Admittedly the question arises as to whether or not an agreement entered into by an artiste has any appreciable effects on competition. In many cases, particularly where little-known artistes are involved, the answer could well be no. However, there manifestly are appreciable effects in the case of highly successful artistes. In the present case, the agreements prevented a world-wide broadcast from La Scala by RAI. The effects could scarcely have been greater.

However, in the last analysis the Commission's request for information does not turn on whether or not the singers constitute undertakings. Unitel is undoubtedly an undertaking within the meaning of Article 85(1). The Commission is entitled to ask for information when investigating the existence of agreements between undertakings. The question whether the artistes concerned constitute undertakings can only be resolved in the light of information on the economic implications of agreements concerning the commercial exploitation of the artistic services provided. The Commission cannot pronounce on the matter until it has ascertained exactly how the agreements in question are worded.

(b) Regulation No 67/67 does not apply to the provision of services, so no exemption may be claimed for the commercial exploitation of artistic performances. Even if it could that would not affect the Commission's power to obtain information on individual cases covered by the Regulation, since it is entitled under Article 6 to investigate agreements exempted by virtue of the Regulation.

(c) By entering into an exclusive contract with Unitel a singer is prevented from further commercialising his artistic performances in any of the Community Member States. Such a contract may therefore affect trade between Member States. Moreover, it is for the Commission to determine whether there has been an infringement of Article 85. An undertaking which is asked to provide information on an agreement is not entitled to refuse on the grounds that in its opinion the said agreement does not affect trade between Member States.

(5) Decision in re SNPE-LEL

Provisional Decision of the Commission on the basis of Article 15(6) of Regualtion No 17, directed to Société Nationale des poudres et explosifs of Paris and Leafields Engineering Limited of Wiltshire; O. J. No L 191, 14 July 1978, p. 41; (1978) 2 CMLR 758; CCH para. 10064; Competition Law CM/M/I/131.

*Facts:* On 12 June after preliminary scrutiny, the Commission took a provisional decision under Article 15(6) of Regulation No 17 in respect of certain provisions of a cooperation agreement concluded between the Société nationale des poudres et explosifs (SNPE) of Paris and Leafields Engineering Limited (LEL) of Wiltshire.

Both parties are specialised in the manufacture of highly technical products. SNPE in auto-propulsion systems and chemical products and LEL in electronic and precision engineering. They had agreed to cooperate extensively in the development, manufacture and sale of a number of products intended in particular for off-shore submarine applications. Apart from provisions covering the manufacture of the products of one partner by the other, under licence or as subcontractor, and the joint development and manufacture of other products, the agreement, which was properly notified to the Commission, includes a clause under which each firm's national territory is reserved to it alone; neither will grant licences, manufacture or sell directly the products covered by the agreement in the territory of the other.

The Commission believes this market-sharing clause is within the prohibition of Article 85(1) of the EEC Treaty and does not qualify for exemption under Article 85(3). Pending a final decision on the agreement as a whole, the firms are free to continue the cooperation they agreed upon. But they will face fines if they give effect to the relevant clause.

*The Commission ruled:*

.....

1. Société nationale des poudres et explosifs (hereinafter referred to as 'SNPE') is a company incorporated in France in which the French State holds 99.82% of the capital. Its activities are divided between Department A, autopropulsion, Department B, powder and explosives, and Department C, chemicals. A fourth department for engineering was transferred to a subsidiary company, SNPE Chimie Expansion, on 1 January 1976.

During the year 1976 SNPE and SNPE Chimie Expansion employed some 6,000 persons and had a turnover of approximately FF 876 million.

On 21 November 1977 SNPE acquired a controlling interest of 70% in Pyromeca Toulon, a company specialising in the development and manufacture of pyrotechnic units.

2. Leafields Engineering Limited (hereinafter referred to as 'LEL') is a company incorporated in the United Kingdom. Its business is to design, develop and manufacture high-quality devices for the armed services and the off-shore oil industry, such as major components for weapons systems, devices to inflate inflateable equipment, pyromechanisms, gas generators and hydraulic pumps.

In 1976 LEL employed some 158 persons and had a turnover of £ 1.2 million.

In 1974 LEL concluded an agreement with Pyromeca Toulon (and its subsidiary in the United Kingdom, Pyromeca (UK) Ltd, of Windsor) under which each party obtained *inter alia* the right to sell in its territory certain products manufactured by the other party. LEL acquired an 11% share in Pyromeca when the latter was taken over by SNPE.

3. (a) Both SNPE and LEL are firmly established in the market for their respective products and both have specialised and partly complementary activities: SNPE in the fields of autopropulsion and chemical products, LEL in the fields of electronic and precision mechanics. Both have common and competitive interests in these fields as a whole and in particular products which incorporate their own respective specialist skills.

(b) A substantial numner of the parties' products which are covered by the notified agreement are currently still under development and are likely to amount to a growing share in each party's total turnover.

## II. Preliminary assessment under Article 85(1) of the EEC Treaty

Article 85(1) of the EEC Treaty prohibits as incompatible with the common market, all agreements between undertakings which may affect trade between Member States and which have as their object or effect the prevention, restriction or distortion of competition within the common market, and in particular those which share markets or sources of supply.

On the facts at present available, the Commission does not make a final ruling on the notified agreement but has reached the following conclusions on preliminary examination.

12. Both Société nationale des poudres et explosifs (SNPE) and Leafields Engineering Limited (LEL) are undertakings and their agreement of 23 February 1977 is an agreement between undertakings, within the meaning of Article 85(1).

B. Parent - Subsidiary Relationship

Intra-enterprise conspiracy

EEC Competition Law does not as yet recognise the doctrine of "intra-enterprise conspiracy". A notable feature of Commission Decisions under Articles 85 and 86 has been the imputation of a subsidiary's anti-competitive behaviour to its parent company. Also as a basis to establish jurisdiction the Court has followed the Commission's opinion. See however Advocate General Trabucchi in Case 15/74 below page 105.

b. Cases

1. Decision in re Christiani and Nielsen

Decision of the Commission of 18 June 1969 on an application for a negative clearance under Article 2 of Regulation No 17: J.O. No 165, 5 July 1969, p. 12; (1969) CMLR D 36; CCH para. 2412,26; Competition Law CM/M/I/20.

*Facts:* The firms concerned are the Danish company Christiani and Nielsen, Copenhagen, and its Netherlands subsidiary Christiani & Nielsen, The Hague, which have concluded an agreement under which the parent company makes available to its subsidiary its experience, know-how, and in certain cases the services of its technical staff.

The provision of the agreement most directly concerning the rules of competition is that preventing Christiani & Nielsen, The Hague, from exercising its activity outside Netherlands territory without the agreement of the parent company. The Commission nevertheless felt that the agreement in question did not restrict competition, since Christiani & Nielsen of The Hague, although a company with a legal personality of its own, was an integral part of the parent company economically and financially. The two companies were not therefore competing with each other. In these circumstances, the restriction preventing the subsidiary from operating outside the country where its registered office was situated ultimately did no more than apportion work within the economic entity constituted by the Christiani & Nielsen international group.

Christiani & Nielsen (The Hague) is a limited liability company governed by Dutch law. It follows a given economic object and to that end disposes of an organisation comprising staff and material and immaterial elements. Further, it bears the risk and the responsibility of the work which it carries out. The relations between the subsidiary and the parent company are governed by the agreement at present under examination, which sets out obligations binding each of the two companies and which cannot be terminated without the assent of both parties.

For Article 85(1) of the Treaty to apply, there should, between the undertakings in question, be competition which is capable of being restricted. This requirement is not necessarily fulfilled, in relations between two undertakings which carry on their activities in the same sector, by the mere fact of the existence of a separate legal personality for each of the undertakings. In that respect, it is imperative to know whether, on the factual level, autonomous activity of the subsidiary with regard to the parent company is possible on the economic plane.

The company Christiani & Nielsen (Copenhagen) created the company Christiani & Nielsen (The Hague) in order to carry out in optimum conditions on Dutch territory the work in which it has specialised. It was considerations of management which led this undertaking, the activity of which is international, to create subsidiaries in different countries rather than establishing there branches or agencies. That is a piece of marketing strategy which cannot have the effect of causing us to consider, in the present case, a wholly owned subsidiary as an economic entity which can enter into competition with its parent company.

In addition, Christiani & Nielsen (Copenhagen) has the right to nominate directors of Christiani & Nielsen (The Hague) and to give directives to its subsidiary, which is obliged to carry them out. Christiani & Nielsen (The Hague) is therefore an integral part of the economic whole making up the Christiani & Nielsen group.

The unity of the economic organisation of the parent company and the subsidiary is emphasised by the exchange of information, inventions, patents, know-how and by the permanent collaboration between the two undertakings.

In view of the foregoing, the division of markets laid down in the agreements is, in the end, only the distribution of tasks within a single economic entity. It could not be expected in this case that one part of this entity, albeit enjoying separate legal personality, should enter into competition with the parent company. Christiani & Nielsen (Copenhagen), even without any contract, would always have the power to determine the behaviour of Christiani & Nielsen (The Hague), of which it holds the whole of the share capital.

It follows from these factors that the agreement in question cannot have the object or effect of preventing, restricting or distorting competition within the Common Market.

In these circumstances, the information available to the Commission does not permit it to conclude that the agreement in the case is covered by Article 85(1) and therefore the negative clearance may be granted.

*The Commission decided:*

1. There is no ground for the Commission, according to the information made available to it, to intervene under the provisions of Article 85 (1) of the Treaty instituting the European Economic Community with regard to the agreement concluded on 25 August 1931 and renewed on 20 March 1959 between Christiani & Nielsen (Copenhagen) and Christiani &

Nielsen (The Hague).

2. The present decision is addressed to the company Christiani & Nielsen of Copenhagen, Denmark, and to the company Christiani & Nielsen of The Hague, Holland.

2. Decision in re Kodak

Commission Decision of 30 June 1970 on an application for a negative clearance under Article 2 of Regulation No 17. J.O. No L 147, 7 July 1970, p. 24; (1970) CMLR D 19; CCH para. 2412,39; Competition Law CM/M/I/39.

*Facts:* The Kodak group adopted new uniform sales conditions for the companies of the group established within the Common Market. Originally, these conditions contained a clause whereby the companies forbade their customers to export or resell the supplied products for export. On the Commission's request these conditions were removed. The sales conditions formed a system of selective distribution since outlets were chosen on the basis of objective qualitative criteria as to sales, service and display. The Commission did not consider the system contrary to Article 85(1).

*The Commission ruled:*

In the present case, we should examine both the identical nature of the conditions of sale used by the Kodak companies within the Common Market and the content of those conditions.

To be sure, the Kodak companies in the Common Market operate conditions of sale which are absolutely identical; but they do so on the instructions of their parent company, with which they are bound to comply.

When it is established, as is so in this case, that the subsidiary companies in question are exclusively and wholly subject to their parent company, and that the latter in fact exercises its power of control by issuing to them precise instructions, it is impossible for them to behave independently inter se in the areas governed by the parent company.

Consequently the identical nature of the conditions of sale of the Kodak companies in the Common Market does not result from an agreement or concerted practice either between the parent company and its subsidiaries or between the subsidiaries inter se.

But the conditions of sale, apart from the fact that they are identical, constitute agreements between undertakings because they are necessarily the subject of a contract between the Kodak companies and each of their purchasers. (Translation CMLR)

3. Centrafarm v. Sterling Drug Case

Centrafarm B.V. and De Peijper v. Sterling Drug Inc., Case 15/74, Preliminary ruling of 31 October 1974; (1974) ECR 1147; (1974) CMLR 480; CCH para. 8246; Competition Law CM/M/III/46.

*Facts:* Sterling Drug Inc., a company incorporated according to the law of the State of New York, is the titular holder of national patents in several countries - including the Netherlands and Great Britain - relating to the mode of preparation of a medicament named acidum nalidixicum, for the treatment of infections of the urinary passages. For this product the trademark 'Negram' is the property, in Great Britain of the company Sterling-Winthrop Group Ltd. and, in the Netherlands of a subsidiary of the latter, Winthrop B.V.

Centrafarm, of which Mr. De Peijper is a director, imported medicinal preparations manufactured according to the patent method, some of which bore the trademark Negram, without the agreement of Sterling Drug, from England and the Federal Republic of Germany, where they had been put onto the market in a regular manner by subsidiaries of Sterling Drug Inc., into the Netherlands where they were offered for sale.

By importing the goods from Great Britain Centrafarm took advantage of a considerable price differential. It appears that in Great Britain the product is sold for half the price at which it sells in the Netherlands.

On 16 June 1971 Sterling Drug submitted to the president of the Arrondissementsrechtbank at Rotterdam, an application for the immediate adoption of measures of conservation against the actions of Centrafarm and of its director, and requiring them to refrain from any further infringement of the patent belonging to Sterling Drug, together with several subsidiary requests. The president of the Court rejected the application on the grounds of an interpretation of the law on patents (Octrooiwet) according to which a product is held to have been put into circulation in a regular manner even if it is put into circulation abroad by the titular holder of a Dutch patent. Sterling Drug thereupon brought an appeal before the Court of Appeal at The Hague, which found in favour of Sterling Drug, with the exception of certain of its subsidiary requests.

Centrafarm and De Peijper brought an appeal on a point of law before the Hoge Raad against the judgment of the Gerechtshof.

Before deciding further, the Hoge Raad stayed the proceedings and requested the Court of Justice, pursuant to Article 177 of the EEC Treaty, to give a preliminary ruling on the following questions:

1. As regards the rules concerning the free movement of goods:
(a) Assuming that: 1. a patentee has parallel patents in several of the countries belonging to the EEC; 2. the products protected by those patents are lawfully marketed in one or more of those countries by undertakings to whom the patentee has granted licences to manufacture and/or sell; 3. those products are subsequently exported by third parties and are marketed and further dealt in one of those other countries; 4. the patent legislation in the last mentioned country gives the patentee rights to take legal action to prevent products thus protected by patents from being there marketed by others, even where these products were previously lawfully marketed in another country by the patentee or the patentee's licensee, do the rules of the EEC Treaty concerning free movement of goods, notwithstanding what is stated in Article 36, prevent the patentee from exercising the right under 4 above?

(b) If the rules concerning the free movement of goods do not under all circumstances prevent the patentee exercising the right mentioned under (a)4 above,

do they however so prevent him if the exercise of that right arises exclusively or partially from an attempt to partition the national markets of the relevant countries from each other for products protected by the patent, or at least has the effect of thus partitioning those markets?

(c) Does it make any difference to the reply to the questions under (a) and (b) above that the patentee and the licensee do or do not belong to the same concern?

(d) Can the patentee successfully rely in justification of the exercise of the above-mentioned right on the fact that the price differences in the relevant countries which make it profitable for third parties to market in one country products originating from another country and give the patentee an interest in taking action against such practices are the consequence of governmental measures whereby in the exporting country the prices of those goods are kept lower than would have been the case in the absence of those measures?

(e) At any rate where the patent relates to pharmaceutical products, can the patentee successfully rely in justification of the exercise of his patent rights on the fact that the state of affairs described under (a) above prevents him from controlling the distribution of his products, such control being considered by him essential so that measures for the protection of the public can be taken in the event of defects appearing?

(f) Is it a consequence of Article 42 of the Treaty of Accession that, if the rules of the EEC Treaty relating to free movement of goods prevent the exercise of a patent right as before mentioned, those rules cannot be invoked in the Netherlands until 1 January 1975 insofar as the relevant goods originate in the United Kingdom?

II As regards Article 85

(a) Does that fact that a patentee owns parallel patents in different countries belonging to the EEC and that he has in those countries granted to different undertakings associated with the patentee, licences to manufacture and sell (assuming that all the agreements entered into with such licensees are exclusively or in part designed to regulate differently for the different countries the conditions on the market in respect of the goods protected by the patent) mean that this is a case of agreements or concerted practices of the type prohibited by Article 85 of the EEC Treaty, and must an action for infringement as referred to under I(a) above - to the extent that this must be regarded as a result of such agreements or concerted practices - for that reason be held impermissible.

(b) Is Article 85 also applicable if, in connection with the agreements or concerted practices referred to above, it is only undertakings belonging to the same concern that are involved?

The Advocate-General, Mr. Trabucchi, concluded:

The question then arises whether these considerations regarding the application of Article 85 also hold good when the aforementioned agreements are concluded exclusively between undertakings forming part of the same group of companies under the control of one parent company. Or, in such circumstances, which include the subsidiaries' lack of independence as regards decisions on marketing policy, should the application of Article 85 be excluded altogether, the only method available to exercise control over the behaviour of the group acting as a body in concert on the market being Article 86, which prohibits abuse of a dominant position?

Declaring that the prohibition in Article 85 did not apply to agreements which regulate the relationships between members of a group, the Commission had from the outset emphasised the fact that, quite apart from any agreement, there can be no competition between undertakings of this kind. It was on the basis of this elementary principle that the Commission justified its line of reasoning, ushered in by the decision of 18 June 1969 giving negative clearance in *Christiani & Nielsen* (O.J. L 165 of 5 July 1969, p. 12). Under this decision, agreements concluded between undertakings in a group effectively subject to the control of a parent company and who confine themselves to playing their allotted roles in the framework of the same economic entity, escape the prohibition under Article 85, precisely because, under such conditions, neither the subject matter nor the effect of these instruments restricts competition; this is because competition does not, by definition, exist within the group.

Against this background, consideration can reasonably be given to the applicability of the prohibition laid down under Article 85 when, instead of being confined to regulating internal relationships, the agreements between the undertakings in a group are designed to raise barriers against third parties, and to block the avenues open to them for trade and competition.

The precedents established by this Court might be the source of some difficulty because, in holding that, in the case of groups of concerns under the control of a parent company, the prohibition of Article 85 did not apply to contracts subsisting between such concerns, the Court stressed instead their lack of economic independence and the unity of a group forming an economic whole (Case 22/71, *Beguelin*, Rec. 1971, p. 958, paragraph 8 of Grounds; Cases 48/69, 52/69 and 53/69, *ICI and Geigy-Sandoz*, Rec. 1972, p. 665, paragraphs 132-140, p. 837, paragraphs 43-45; Joined Cases 6-7/73, *Istituto Chemioterapico Italiano and Commercial Solvents Company*, (1974) ECR 253-254, paragraphs 36-41).

In my view, however, these precedents do not in principle preclude the applicability of Article 85 to agreements or practices in which the component companies of a group alone participate. *Beguelin* was concerned with a grant by a parent company of exclusive sales rights to one of its subsidiaries, which was established in another Member State, in respect of the products of an undertaking in a third State. It did not matter to competitors or consumers in the Community whether the parent company had the exclusive right of sale in the two States or whether, in one of these States, a subsidiary took its place.

Having regard to the subject-matter of the agreement, the Court decided that the prerequisite of a restriction on competition was lacking.

The other cases cited were concerned with establishing whether anti-competitive conduct on the part of a company established in the common market could be laid at the door of the parent company which controlled it and which was established in a third country. One can thus appreciate the peculiar significance, in such a context, of the concept of the economic whole represented by a group. And this enables us to rule out the possibility that these precedents, which were designed to meet clearly defined situations, can militate against application of Article 85 in the case of agreements and practices operating between the members of the same group where such instruments and practices have the object or effect of restraining competition from third parties.

*The Court held:*

(41) Article 85, however, is not concerned with agreements or concerted practices between undertakings belonging to the same concern and

having the status of parent company and subsidiary, if the undertakings form an economic unit within which the subsidiary has no real freedom to determine its course of action on the market, and if the agreements or practices are concerned merely with the internal allocation of tasks as between the undertakings.

Litterature:

Allen: The Development of European Economic antitrustjurisdiction over alien undertakings. LIEI 1974/2.

Barack: The application of the competition rules (antitrust law) of the European Economic Community. Deventer 1981.

Faull: Extraterritorial application of Article 86 EEC. 1980 ELRev 64-68.

Waelbroeck and March Hunnings: On the enforceability of the EEC and EFTA Free Trade agreements in: 1977 ELRev 16, 1978 ELRev 27 and 1981 ELRev 278.

Bennett: Article 86:effect on trade between Member States re-examined. 1979 ELRev 294-298.

Van Rijn: Intra-Enterprise conspiracy and Article 85 of the EEC Treaty. In: Essays on European Law and Integration 123-139.

Mestmäcker: Providing fair conditions of competition under the Free Trade Agreements of the European Economic Community, 1981 Nw.J. Int'l L and Bus. Vol 3, number 2, 296.

## Chapter Three

## ARTICLE EIGHTY-FIVE

### I. ARTICLE 85 PARAGRAPH 1

### A. Agreements.

1. Horizontal - Vertical

(1) LTM - MBU Case

For facts and references see above, page 69.

*The Court held:*

In order to be prohibited as being incompatible with the Common Market under Article 85(1) of the Treaty, an agreement between undertakings must fulfil certain conditions depending less on the legal nature of the agreement than on its effects on 'trade between Member States' and its effects on 'competition'.

The necessity for an agreement 'between undertakings'

In order to fall within this prohibition, an agreement must have been made between undertakings. Article 85(1) makes no distinction as to whether the parties are at the same level in the economy (so-called horizontal agreements), or at different levels (so-called vertical agreements). Therefore an agreement containing a clause 'granting an exclusive right of sale' may fulfill this condition.

(2) Consten - Grundig Case

For facts and references see above, page 66.

*The Court held:*

The complaints concerning the applicability of Article 85(1) to sole distributorship contracts.

The applicants submit that the application in Article 85(1) applies only to so-called horizontal agreements. The Italian Government submits furthermore that sole distributorship contracts do not constitute 'agreements between undertakings' within the meaning of that provision, since the parties are not on a footing of equality. With regard to these contracts, freedom of competition may only be protected by virtue of Article 86 of the Treaty.

Neither the wording of Article 85 nor that of Article 86 gives any ground for holding that distinct areas of application are to be assigned to each of the two Articles according to the level in the economy at which the contracting parties operate. Article 85 refers in a general way to all agreements which distort competition within the Common Market and does not lay down any distinction between those agreements based on whether they are made between competitors operating at the same level in the economic process or between non-competing persons operating at different levels. In principle, no distinction can be made where the Treaty does not make any distinction.

2. General

(1) ACF - Chemiefarma case
Case 41/69, Judgment of 15 July 1970; (1970) ECR 661; CCH para. 8083; Competition Law CM/M/III/16.

*Facts:* From 1958 the undertaking Nederlandse Combinatie voor Chemische Industrie (Nedchem), which manufactures chemical, pharmaceutical and allied products, was a party to a series of agreements with other European manufacturers of those products.

On 30 May and 11 to 13 June 1958, in conjunction with the undertakings N.V. Amsterdamsche Chininefabriek, Amsterdam, N.V. Nederlandse Kininefabriek Maarssen, Bandoengsche Kininefabriek Holland N.V., Amsterdam, N.V. Pharmaceutische Groothandel van de Amsterdamsche Chininefabriek, Amsterdam and N.V. Bureau voor de Kinineverkoop, Buramic, Amsterdam, it concluded an initial agreement relating to the division of national markets (Germany and the Netherlands) as well as fixing the prices and quotas for the export of quinine and quinidine to all other countries with the following undertakings:

(a) Buchler & Co., Braunschweig;
(b) C.F. Boehringer & Söhne, Mannheim, and its subsidiary, Vereinigte Chininfabriken Zimmer & Co., GmbH, Mannheim.

Pursuant to the provisions of Article 85 of the EEC Treaty, the Bundeskartellamt, to which the agreement was notified on 24 January 1959 in accordance with Article 6(1) of the German law against restriction of competition, requested the parties to the agreement for information on its territorial scope. Following this request Boehringer and Nedchem concluded a new agreement on 14 July 1959 excluding supplies to other States of the EEC.

Negotiations entered into in 1959 between Buchler, Boehringer, Nedchem, the group of French quinine producers (Nogentaise, Pointet-Girard, Taillandier and Pharmacie Centrale) together with Carnegies of Welwyn Ltd and Lake & Cruickshank Ltd of the United Kingdom resulted in an agreement between all those undertakings. First of all on 10, 24 and 31 March 1960 Boehringer (acting also in the name of its above-mentioned subsidiary), Buchler and Nedchem (acting also in the name of all the above-mentioned Netherlands undertakings) concluded an agreement providing for:

- the fixing by agreement of prices and rebates applicable to exports of quinine and quinidine;

- the allocation of export quotas and the reservation of certain markets outside the Community;

- the retention of the clause making the agreement inapplicable to exports in the States of the EEC;

- a system of compensatory quantities in the event of export quotas being exceeded or unfulfilled;

- the prohibition of collaboration outside the Common Market with undertakings which were not parties to the agreement with regard to the production or sale of quinine or quinidine.

- application to be made, in case of dispute, at the option of the parties, to arbitration or to the ordinary courts of law.

It was agreed that this export agreement would terminate on 31 March 1965 but that it might be renewed every five years. Rules drawn up to ensure the strict cooperation of the parties in order to facilitate the implementation of the agreement provided in particular that every month each of the parties to the agreement should supply the other with certain information on the basis of which Nedchem would, for the purposes of quantitative compensation, make periodic calculations of the deliveries in excess of or below the quota of each of the undertakings.

Apart from this agreement, which governed the problem of Buchler's adherence to the agreement concluded on 8 and 14 July 1959 between Boehringer, Buchler, Nedchem, the above-mentioned French group and the two British undertakings, Carnegies and Lake and Cruickshank, in order to settle the conditions for the adherence of the French and British undertakings to the abovementioned agreement of 10, 24 and 31 March 1960, in so far as it related to quinine. Parallel with the export agreement two gentlemen's agreements containing substantially identical provisions were concluded on 9 April 1960 an recorded in writing although they were not signed; one was between the French group Boehringer, Buchler, Nedchem and Carnegies and the other was between the French group, Boehringer, Buchler, Nedchem and Lake & Cruickshank. Those two gentlemen's agreements extended the provisions laid down in the export agreement with regard to price quotas and compensation for quantities, for both quinine and quinidine, to all sales on domestic markets and abroad, and in particular to all sales within the Common Market. Furthermore, they laid down the principle of protection of domestic markets for each of the producers. The two British undertakings agreed not to manufacture quinidine without the approval of the German and Netherlands parties and to purchase this product exclusively from the German and Netherlands parties and to maintain the agreed price on resale. The French undertakings entered into the same obligation with regard to synthetic quinidine. Derogations from the gentlemens agreement could take place only with the agreement of the parties and disputes were to be settled exclusively by arbitration. It was further decided that failure to comply with or termination of the gentlemens agreement would automatically be regarded as failure to comply with or termination of the formal export agreements relating to quinine and quinidine, and vice versa. The gentlemens agreements were kept secret.

The said agreements were supplemented during 1961 and 1962 by an association relating to the joint purchase of raw materials which, in accordance with the decision taken during a meeting on 26 January 1961, was drafted in conformity with the arrangements laid down in a draft agreement instituting a pool of stocks purchased ('bark pool') but which was never signed. The association relating to the joint purchase of raw materials terminated on 31 October 1962.

During a meeting on 2 May 1962 a general increase in prices was decided upon. Agreements were also concluded for the purchase of reserves from the American stockpile which the General Service Administration had decided to sell. In this connection, it was decided durir the meeting on 20 and 21 April 1962 that the quantities purchased by

Nedchem would be divided amongst the members in specific ratio and that in return Nedchem would receive a commission of 2%; this commission would be increased to 7% if the other agreements (the export agreement and the gentlemens agreements) were terminated in advance. On 4 September 1964 the American General Service Administration gave a definite refusal to make any further deliveries to Nedchem alleging that military requirements had arisen.

Following each delivery Nedchem divided it among the other members. The commission was always fixed on the basis of the rate of 2%. When on 13 March 1962 the first regulation in implementation of Articles 85 and 86 of the EEC Treaty came into force, the above-mentioned undertakings decided provisionally to continue the export agreement and to continue to implement the gentlemens agreement.

In the course of a meeting on 29 October 1962 difficulties arose between the parties on the question of the 'bark-pool'. As a preliminary condition to concluding an agreement on bark, Nedchem requested the abolition of the prohibition on exporting bark which was in force in the Congo although Pharmakina, Boehringer's Congolese subsidiary, was in favour of this prohibition. As a result of this Lake & Cruickshank and Boehringer requested revision of the quotas. The scope of the decision taken at this meeting with regard to the gentlemen's agreements gave rise to a dispute between the parties to the present proceedings.

On 2 November 1962 Nedchem notified the other members that the export agreement and the gentlemen's agreement should no longer be regarded as binding; it alleged that the proposals made by Boehringer and Lake & Cruickshank with regard to the 'bark-pool' and the fixing of the new sales quotas were contrary to the spirit of the said agreements.

The other members did not accept those reasons and at the meeting on 14 October 1963, at which all the parties to the agreement were present except Carnegies (which ceased producing quinine in the same month and initimated its withdrawal by letter of 28 October 1963), the parties concerned reached a compromise, the purpose and scope of which are disputed by the parties to the present proceedings.

In the course of 1964 the abovementioned undertakings twice made joint decisions to raise the price of quinine, first by 15% at the meeting on 12 March and subsequently by 25% at the meeting on 28 October, whilst the prices of quinidine were raised by 20%. An agreement modifying the length of the validity of the export agreement (which was in the meantime extended for 12 months only instead of the five years initially provided for) was concluded in December 1964 and January 1965 between Boehringer, Buchler, Nedchem, the French group and Lake & Cruickshank. At the beginning of 1967 the Commission's departments obtained more detail information on the activities of the international quinine cartel through inquiries carried out in the United States of America in connection with Nedchem's purchase of large quantities from the stockpile. In particular the Commission became acquainted with the report of the American Senate Anti-trust Subcommittee. In addition to recording the hearings held by the subcommittee, this document has annexed to it a large number of minutes of the meetings of the members of the cartel, the correspondence exchanged by the parties concerned, the agreements drawn up between them and reports from the director of a British company which was a party to the agreements. These documents date from 1960 to 1963. Consideration of those documents led the Commission to take the view that the implementation of the abovementioned agreements (the export agreement and the gentlemen's agreements) had been continued after October 1963.

*The Court held:*

I - The status and duration of the gentlemen's agreement

The applicant complains that the Commission considered that the export agreement relating to trade with third countries and the gentlemen's agreement governing the conduct of its members in the Common Market constituted an indivisible entity as far as Article 85 was concerned.

The applicant states that the gentlemen's agreement, unlike the export agreement, did not constitute an agreement within the meaning of Article 85(1) and in any event it definitively ceased to exist from the end of October 1962.

The conduct of the parties to the export agreement does not in the applicant's view indicate that they continued the restrictions on competition which were originally provided for in the gentlemen's agreement.

The opposite conclusions reached by the contested decision are therefore alleged to be vitiated because they are based on incorrect findings.

The gentlemen's agreement, which the applicant admits existed until the end of October 1962, had as its object the restriction of competition within the Common Market.

The parties to the export agreement mutually declared themselves willing to abide by the gentlemen's agreement and concede that they did so until the end of October 1962.

This document thus amounted to the faithful expression of the joint intention of the parties to the agreement with regard to their conduct in the Common Market.

Furthermore, it contained a provision to the effect that infringement of the gentlemen's agreement would ipso facto constitute an infringement of the export agreement.

In those circumstances account must be taken of this connection in assessing the effects of the gentlemen's agreement with regard to the categories of acts prohibited by Article 85(1).

The defendant bases its view that the gentlemen's agreement was continued until February 1965 on documents and declarations emanating from the parties to the agreement, the tenor of which is indistinct and indeed contradictory, so that it is impossible to conclude whether those undertakings intended to terminate the gentlemen's agreement at their meeting on 29 October 1962.

The conduct of the undertakings in the Common Market after 29 October 1962 must therefore be considered in relation to the following four points: sharing out of domestic markets, fixing of common prices, determination of sales quotas and prohibition against manufacturing synthetic quinidine.

(2) Decision in re WEA-Filipacchi Music SA

Decision of the Commission of 22 December 1972 on a proceeding under Article 85 of the Treaty, WEA-Filipacchi; J.O. No L 303, 31 December 1972, p. 52; (1973) CMLR D 43; CCH para. 9545 A; Competition Law CM/M/I/65.

*Facts:* The WEA-Filipacchi Music SA company in Paris had, in February 1972, forbidden its wholesale and retail customers to export light music records which it distributes in France; 18 resale agents had given their consent. This was a method of preventing exports of records sold in France to Germany, where they are distributed by the WEA-GmbH company in Hamburg, which belongs to the same group. The price differential between the two markets (the same records of the commonest class were distributed on the German market at a price 50% above that of the French market) had proved an incentive to French resale agents to export to Germany, and the WEA-Filipacchi company was anxious to prevent these exports so as to maintain the higher price level in Germany.

In order to restore the competitive effect which the French resale agents could exert by exporting the records to Germany, the Commission ordered the firms concerned to delete the export prohibition clauses and to disregard them in future. In imposing the fine, it bore in mind not only the seriousness and the obvious illegality of the infringement (this had been pointed out to WEA-Filipacchi Music SA by French resale agents) but also the fact that although the infringement did not last long, it had been discontinued not on the intiative of the firm itself but only through the intervention of the Commission.

This decision is significant in other ways. In the first place, it amplifies the Commission's Communication concerning minor agreements not caught by Article 85(1). The argument adduced by the WEA-Filipacchi firm that it held only a small share of the overall record market in France is not pertinent or an assessment of the restraint in question (apart from the fact that the overall turnover of the group to which the firm belongs is well over the threshold of 15 million u.a.), and the Commission found that there is no single market for classical music, light music and 'pop' music. In addition it must be remembered that the records sold by this firm were interpretations by 'hit' performers working solely for this firm; these performances are individual and can in no circumstances be regarded, because of their properties or their use, or their price, as similar, for the consumer, to the performance of other artists.

Another interesting aspect of the decision is that it makes it clear that a firm cannot use carefully worded clauses to avoid the ban on agreements contained in Article 85. In this particular case, the WEA-Filipacchi company had argued that its circular was only the expression of an opinion and that the consent given by the resale agents, which had signed it and stamped it with their house stamp, was no more than an acknowledgement of receipt. The decision restores these documents to their proper status as agreements between undertakings within the meaning of Article 85(1).

II - Applicability of Article 85(1) of the Treaty instituting the EEC

1. The circular of 7 February 1972, and the consent given by the 18 resellers who signed it and affixed the stamp of their firm, constitute agreements between undertakings within the meaning of Article 85 (1) of the EEC Treaty and in particular such signature and stamp do not constitute mere notice of receipt as claimed by the undertaking WEA-Filipacchi Music SA and some of the resellers in question.

(a) The return of a signed copy usually, in trade practice, amounts to an approval of the contents. A mere notice of receipt is sent by registered letter.

(b) Some resellers refused to sign, giving as their reason the fact that such signature would imply a contractual prohibition on exporting, which is prohibited by Community law.

(c) The words of the circular 'we must guarantee that no export will be made by third parties' prove indisputably that such 'third parties' mean resellers residing in France and who according to the wish expressed by WEA-Filipacchi SA may not export. That interpretation is confirmed by the undertaking Société Centrale de Distribution, of Clermond-Ferrand.

(d) Finally, according to the findings of the Commission, the 'contractual obligations, not only towards our contractual partners but also with regard to the Authors' Rights Societies' mentioned in the circular constitute an unjustified pretext for causing the resellers to declare their agreement to a prohibition on export. There has been no intervention by societies for the exploitation of authors' rights, and the licence contract concluded on 1 July 1971 between WEA-Filipacchi Music SA would be required to prevent the export by third parties of records which they distribute in France.

2. These agreements aim at preventing the export of records distributed in France by WEA-Filipacchi Music SA to other Member States, particularly to Germany. Consequently, they have the object of restricting the competition which the French resellers could exercise by exporting these records to Germany.

*The Commission decided:*

1. It is held that the export prohibitions on gramophone records of WEA-Filipacchi Music SA following the circular of 7 February 1972 and the consents given by the 18 resellers listed in Article 4 of the present decision constitute violations of Article 85(1) of the Treaty instituting the European Economic Community.

2. The undertakings listed in Article 4 of the present decision are required to put an end to these violations.

3. (1) A fine of 60,000 units of account, that is to say 333,251 French francs, is imposed on the undertaking WEA-Filipacchi Music SA.

(2) The present decision constitutes authority to execute on WEA-Filipacchi Music SA in accordance with Article 192 of the Treaty instituting the EEC.

4. The present decision is addressed to the undertaking WEA-Filipacchi Music SA, of Paris, and to the resellers listed below (omitted).

(3) Decision in re Frubo

Decision of the Commission of 25 July 1974 on a proceeding under Article 85 of the EEC Treaty; O.J. No L 237, 29 August 1974, p. 6; (1974) 2 CMLR D 89; CCH para. 9673; Competition Law CM/M/I/78.

*Facts:* Restrictive provisions of an agreement which set up a system of auction sales in Rotterdam for certain types of fruit (mainly citrus fruit) imported into the Netherlands are the subject of this Commission decision. The agreement was concluded between an association of the main Dutch fruit importers (Nederlandse Vereniging voor de Fruit en Groentenimporthandel) and an association of virtually all the Dutch fruit wholesalers (Nederlandse Bond van Grossiers in Zuidvruchten en ander geimporteerd fruit FRUBO). In order to be allowed to take part in auctions, through which most (roughly 80%) of the citrus fruit sold in the Netherlands is handled, dealers had to comply with the conditions imposed by the agreement. The main restriction, apart from a set of technical provisions as to the organisation of auction sales, consisted of the obligation for importers and wholesalers to market citrus fruit grown in non-member countries and intended for sale in the Netherlands only through the Rotterdam auction sales.

As the agreement originally stood, the conditions imposed were even more restrictive, since only Dutch importers were allowed to sell at auction sales and even Community-produced citrus fruit was covered by the agreement. Following objections from the Commission and complaints from twenty-two Dutch wholesalers who took part in the Rotterdam auction sales, the associations concerned made their agreement somewhat more flexible, without however deleting the major restrictions on the freedom for Dutch wholesalers to obtain supplies.
They decided to keep these wholesalers subject to the ban on direct imports from non-member countries and to submit purchases of citrus fruits from elsewhere in the Community to a major restraint, namely customs clearance by another party, thereby compulsorily introducing an additional trading stage. Accordingly, the transactions concerned became virtually impossible.

This Decision is not aimed at the auction sales system as such. It is quite possible that advantages may be derived from the resulting concentration of supply and demand although in certain cases such advantages may be practically eliminated by the disadvantages created by the rigidity inherent in such a distribution system. However, in order to attain the advantages which could be gained from the Rotterdam auction sales, it is not essential to prevent wholesalers from having access to possibly cheaper or better supplies, either because prices were lower on other Community import markets or because, price for price, quicker supplies or fresher fruit could be obtained. It would seem that such opportunities do occur, since a number of wholesalers subject to the agreement at times preferred to obtain supplies elsewhere, despite the penalties which they risked incurring. Moreover, even in the absence of the compulsory supply arrangements complained of, the nature and frequency of direct imports by wholesalers had not been such as to cause the disappearance of this marketing system by reducing its advantages.

*The Commission ruled:*

1. The provisions of the Agreement, which was concluded between two associations of undertakings, bind directly and are effectively applied by the undertakings taking part in the Rotterdam auctions. This Agreement must therefore be considered to be an agreement between undertakings within the meaning of Article 85(1) of the Treaty.

(4) Frubo Case
Nederlandse Vereniging voor de Fruit en Groentenimporthandel, Nederlandse Bond van Grossiers in Zuidvruchten en ander geimporteerd Fruit v. EEC Commission, Case 71/74; (1974) ECR 1031; (1975) 2 CMLR 123; CCH. para. 8285; Competition Law CM/M/III/48.

For facts see above the Decision in re Frubo, page 114 above.

*The Court held:*

Second submission as to substance

28. The applicants deny that the agreement made between them is, as it has been described in the disputed Decision, an agreement between undertakings within the meaning of Article 85(1).

29. In their view, an agreement between undertakings is caught by this provision only if it has actually created obligations which are directly enforceable as between the affiliated undertakings, which is not the position in the present case since only the associations themselves can compel their affiliates to discharge the obligations imposed upon them by the agreement.

30. Article 85(1) applies to associations in so far as their own activities or of those of the undertakings belonging to them are calculated to produce the results to which it refers.

31. To place any other interpretation on Article 85(1) would be to remove its substance.

32. As an association of undertakings, the applicants are therefore subject to the provisions of Article 85.

*Sequel*

The Court rejected the appeal of the applicants.

(5) Decision on the Franco-Japanese ballbearings agreement
For facts and references see above, page 49.

*The Commission ruled:*

It is clear, therefore, that these French and Japanese manufacturers had, through the mediation of their respective trade associations, entered into an agreement in principle for the purpose of increasing the prices of Japanese ballbearings imported into France in order to bring these prices into line with the prices of French manufactured bearings.

Contrary to the agreement put forward by the parties in their reply to the statement of objections and at the hearing, for Article 85(1) of the EEC Treaty to apply it is not essential that this agreement should take the form of a contract having all the elements required by civil law; it is sufficient that one of the parties voluntarily undertakes to limit its freedom of action with regard to the other.

This is indeed so in the case in point since, first in the abovementioned letter of 10 March 1972, the Japan Association informed the Chambre syndicale of the committments entered into by the Japanese manufacturers to raise the price of their bearing export to France and, secondly, in the abovementioned letter of 27 April 1972, the Chambre syndicale noted these commitments on behalf of the French manufacturers.

The parties disputed the contention that this exchange of letters was really an agreement to raise prices.

First, the Japan Association and the Japanese manufacturers concerned claims that the increases mentioned in the letter of 19 March resulted from decisions taken unilaterally in order to adjust to the par values of currencies and to the economic situation in Japan, and that they were unrelated to the requests made by their French competitors.

Secondly, the Chambre syndicale emphasises that although the letter of 27 April does mention the Japanese decisions to increase prices, it also expresses disagreement as to the rates, the dates on which they will apply, the stages and the practical arrangements for these increases, so that this letter could not be seen as an acceptance of the Japanese offer.

These explanations are unconvincing since, in the light of the preceeding negotiations, this exchange of letters forms a consistent and explicit whole and its evidence of a common understanding by the parties that the price of Japanese bearings would be increased, even in the absence of a detailed agreement as to how the agreed price increase was to be effected. It is clear that there was at least agreement in principle on an increase.

. The agreement at issue was concluded following negotiations in which the manufacturing undertakings concerned and their respective trade associations took part, and resulted in an exchange of letters between these trade associations acting on behalf of their members; it is therefore, an agreement between undertakings within the meaning of Article 85 of the EEC Treaty.

3. Joint Ventures

Do joint ventures have to be considered as constituting agreements between enterpises or do they have to be considered as constituting concentration of enterprises?

<u>(1) Decision in re SHV and Chevron agreement</u>
Commission Decision of 20 December 1974 on a proceeding under Article 85 of the EEC Treaty; O.J. No L 38, 12 February 1975, p. 14; (1975) CMLR D 68; CCH para. 9709; Competition Law CM/M/I/85.

For facts see the Decision.

*The Commission ruled:*

The Commission of the European Communities, in the light of the Treaty establishing the European Economic Community (especially Articles 85 and 86) and of Council Regulation No 17 of 6 February 1962 (especially Article 2), has received an application for negative clearance and, failing that, a notification made on 21 December 1970 by Steenkolen-Handelsvereeniging NV (SHV) of Utrecht and by Chevron Oil Europe Inc., incorporated under the laws of the State of Delaware (USA), with its head office in New York (USA) and an office in Brussels.

The purpose of the application is to have the Commission declare that it has no grounds for taking action under Article 85(1) EEC in respect of the general Cooperation agreement concluded between those two companies on 22 October 1969, as amended and supplemented on 24 December 1969 and further amended by letter of 21 May 1973, or in respect of the specific national agreements submitted to the Commission, which derive from the general agreement.

The essence of the notification was published under Article 19(3) of Regulation No 17 in (1973) O.J. CIII/11, 18 December 1973. The Advisory Committee on Cartels and Dominant Positions gave its opinion under Article 10 of Regulation No 17 on 25 April 1974.

The main points of the agreements as they appear from the present text of the co-operation agreements deriving therefrom are as follows:

- under the co-operation agreement, Chevron and SHV have set up through a joint holding company incorporated under Dutch law called Calpam NV, jointly and equally owned subsidiaries also called Calpam, to sell the products covered by the agreement in Belgium, Holland, Luxembourg, Germany and Denmark, where Chevron and SHV hitherto had independent distribution networks;

- they have vested in the Calpam subsidiaries for at least 50 years their distribution networks and all assets relating thereto (plant, equipment etc.)

The general cooperation agreement and the specific agreements forming a Calpam subsidiary for each country involve the following products (except in Germany): paraffin oil (kerosene), household fuel, industrial fuel, asphalt and marine fuels and lubricating oils.

In Germany the agreements for the time being only cover marine fuels and lubricating oils.

The Calpam joint subsidiaries are supplied by the various subsidiaries of Chevron under non-exclusive supply contracts.

For the petroleum products listed above which are distributed by the joint subsidiaries, the signatory companies each agree not to compete against the other without the prior consent of the other.

The price of asphalt sold by the Calpam subsidiaries is fixed by Chevron.

Following the publication pursuant to Article 19(3) of Regulation No 17, the Commission has received no observations from third parties which might lead it to change its views.

The agreements described above involve a lasting change in the structures of the companies involved and above all in that of SHV. SHV ceased to do business as an independent wholesale buyer of petroleum products. SHV and Chevron cease to retail the relevant products separately. Most of the other aspects of the agreement suggest that what is really happening is that the distribution side of Chevron's and SHV's business is being integrated into the new trading structure of the Calpam subsidiaries.

The Calpam subsidiaries are formed for a period lasting until 31 December 2019. This suggests that the assets in question are to be transferred permanently to the Calpam subsidiaries. For both Chevron and SHV this brings about a real concentration between each of them and their joint subsidiaries, confined to the distribution of the products by the agreement.

Chevron, with its subsidiaries other than the Calpam subsidiaries, remains a member of an integrated international petroleum group (Standard Oil of California - Socal) whose activities include crude oil production, oil refining and distribution, petrochemicals and manufacture of fertilizers.

SHV, although associated with other companies in exploration, possesses no refineries and does not constitute a petroleum group. SHV does have interests in coal distribution, chain stores and transport.

The co-operation agreement contains no clauses restricting competition between Chevron and SHV in areas other than those covered by the Calpam joint subsidiaries.

As regards distribution of the products covered by the Agreement, Chevron and SHV have each agreed not to compete with the other without the prior consent of the other. This clause provides SHV with the assurance that the assets transferred by it to the joint subsidiaries will not lose value as a result of competition by Chevron with those subsidiaries. In view of the fact that Chevron has no industrial or commercial interest which could imaginably lead it to compete with its own 50 per cent.-owned subsidiaries, and given also that SHV will disappear as an independent wholesaler on the petroleum product market, with no likelihood of ever returning, the clause in question cannot be said to involve an appreciable restriction of competition.

The foregoing analysis is not affected by the fact that SHV, which jointly with other companies holds exploration licences for the North Sea, might come into possession of crude oil, since SHV's freedom to sell its crude oil to any buyer is umlimited.

The parent companies had included a clause whereby they agreed not to compete in respect of petroleum products not distributed by the Calpam subsidiaries, i.e. lubricating oil, diesel fuel and petrol in the Benelux area and Denmark, and this clause was considered by the Commission to be caught by Article 85(1); the parent companies informed the Commission by letter of 21 May 1973 that the clause had been deleted from their cooperation agreement.

The fact that Chevron fixes the price of asphalt sold by the Calpam subsidiaries does not constitute a restriction of competition in violation of Article 85(1) since in fact asphalt was previously only sold by Chevron.

Hence the operation does not constitute an infringement of Article 85(1), so that negative clearance may be granted pursuant to Article 2 of Regulation No 17.

Finally, Chevron's and SHV's shares of the relevant market in the products in question (a substantial part of the Common Market) do not give either of the undertakings a dominant position, so the agreement does not require investigation under Article 86.

THE COMMISSION, for these reasons,

HAS ADOPTED THIS DECISION:

Article 1

The Commission declares that, on the basis of the facts in its possession, it has no grounds for action under Article 85(1) of the Treaty establishing the EEC in respect of the agreement concluded between Steenkolen-Handelsvereeniging NV and Chevron Oil Europe Inc. on 22 October 1969, as amended and supplemented on 24 December 1969 and further amended by letter of 21 May 1973, or of the specific national agreements submitted to the Commission which derive from the general agreement.

Article 2

This decision is addressed to Steenkolen-Handelsvereeniging NV, Rijnkade 1, Utrecht, and to Chevron Oil Europe Inc. Boulevard du Jardin Botanique 44, Brussels.

<u>(2) Decision in re Vacuum Interruptors I</u>

<u>Commission</u> Decision of 20 January 1977 relating to a proceeding under Article 85 of the EEC Treaty, Vacuum Interrupters Ltd. O.J. No L 48, 19 February 1977, p. 32; (1977) 1 CMLR D 67; CCH para. 10296; Competition Law CM/M/I/111.

*Facts:* This case concerns Vacuum Interrupters Ltd. a joint subsidiary established by Associated Electrical Industries Ltd. and Reyrolle Parsons Ltd. to facilitate and accelerate the launching of a new product hitherto manufactured by neither of the two companies. The Commission gave an exemption pursuant to Article 85(3) valid until 1980.

The vauum interrupter is a particular type of circuit breaker for use in switchgear and is currently at an early stage of development. It has the advantages of being more efficient and more durable than

the liquid and air types now in general use.
It is because of these advantages that undertakings in Japan, the USA and later the United Kingdom have become interested in this type of switchgear. The two parties in this case considered that if research was to achieve any long-term success the design and development of the device would entail financial and technical resources on a scale that neither of them could undertake separately. They therefore decided to create a joint venture for the development of this device, each of the two parent companies providing finance and personnel. The object of the new company is to develop and manufacture vacuum interrupters for incorporation into switchgear manufactured by the parent companies or by competing heavy electrical engineering companies.

The Commission found that the agreements as notified restricted competition within the meaning of Article 85(1) of the Treaty since, in order to develop a specific product, two major British switchgear manufacturers had chosen to cooperate within a joint venture rather than to compete with each other. In view of the circumstances of the case, however, the Commission gave an exemption from the date of the accession of the United Kingdom to the EEC until 1980. Conditions have been attached to the exemption, requiring notification of all changes in the capital structure and in the business activities of the joint venture.

The Commission decided that the consumer was allowed a fair share of the benefit resulting from formation of the joint venture. Durable, efficient interrupters will become available at a reasonable price. Although these interrupters are currently available only for low-power applications, they should in future be capable of use with higher voltages.

*The Commission ruled:*

.....

There is no real vacuum interrupter market yet in the Member States of the EEC, because switchgear, incorporating Vacuum Interrupters Ltd type vacuum interrupters, is still in the development stage. The sales which have taken place to customers within the Member States have been apparently for experimental purposes only (seven vacuum interrupters to two separate customers in West Germany). The prospects for future sales are dependent on the successful development of this type of interrupter and, in particular, the increasing of the power capacity which they can handle. All the indications are that the development will be successful, and that exports to other countries within the EEC will expand. There has been a steady expansion in demand for the vacuum interrupter in both the United States and Japan and there is no reason to believe that a similar expansion will not occur when the manufacturers of switchgear within the EEC develop equipment to incorporate the vacuum interrupter.

A. *Prevention, restriction or distortion of competition*

15. Prior to the signing of the agreement of 25 March 1970 neither Associated Electrical Industries Ltd nor Reyrolle Parsons Ltd were manufacturing vacuum interrupters. However, their experience in the field of heavy electrical equipment and their ability to manufacture components therefor, the extent and quality of their research and development work, some of which was concentrated in the field of vacuum interrupters, their skill in producing electrical equipment generally and the natural growth of their activities in the field of manufacture of electrical equipment might well have led them to extend their range

of products to include vacuum interrupters, thereby making them direct competitors in the relevant product market. They must therefore be assumed to be potential competitors and the agreement of 25 March 1970 to have been concluded between potentially competing manufactures.

16. The object and effect of the agreement is to restrict competition within the common market. There is not at present even one manufacturer of components for electrical equipment within the area of the common market which makes and sells vacuum interrupters. When two companies, each of which is a potential manufacturer and which are each within the common market, merge their activity in the fields of research, development, manufacture and sale by establishing a joint venture concerned with this one product on such terms that, they deprive themselves of the possibility of developing and selling that product independently of, and in competition with each other, there is a restriction of competition.

B. *Effect on trade between Member States*

17. Both Associated Electrical Industries Ltd and Reyrolle Parsons Ltd are major manufacturers of switchgear apparatus in the United Kingdom. It is reasonable to assume that if a market were to develop in the other Member States of the EEC for the vacuum interrupter and if both Associated Electrical Industries Ltd and/or their associated companies and Reyrolle Parsons Ltd had developed and manufactured the vacuum type interrupter independently of each other, each should have been able to obtain a market for it in the other Member States, where they would have been in direct competition not only with each other but also with such other undertakings as might manufacture this type of interrupter.

There could have developed an export trade between each of these undertakings in the United Kingdom and customers in other Member States in which each would have been in competition with the other and with local manufacturers. Exports from the UK to other Member States are now likely to start earlier and form a different pattern, thus affecting the flow of trade from the United Kingdom to other Member States. Both Associated Electrical Industries Ltd and Reyrolle Ltd have as customers in the United Kingdom the Central Electricity Generating Board and other area boards and most of the large industrial undertakings which take electricity from high voltage lines. The fact that two companies, each with an important market position in heavy electrical equipment in the United Kingdom, have combined their activity in the field of vacuum interrupters in a joint subsidiary must reduce the possibility that another manufacturer or other manufacturers of electrical equipment from other Member States of the EEC would be able to enter the United Kingdom for the purpose of manufacturing and selling or selling only the vacuum interrupter in competition with Vacuum Interrupters Ltd. It might well have been easier for such manufacturers to build up a market for the vacuum interrupter in the United Kingdom if they were not to be in competition with one economically and technically strong competitor but with two competitors, each separately economically and and technically weaker. The market position of Vacuum Interrupter Ltd, having regard to that of the parent undertakings and of other manufacturers of switchgear equipment in the UK who are also in a position to sell switchgear equipment utilising the interrupters designed and made by Vacuum Interrupters Ltd, would make it more difficult for new entrants to capture a share of the market. The result therefore of the establishment of Vacuum Interrupters Ltd is that the economic penetration of the United Kingdom by manufacturers of electrical apparatus from the other

Member States of the EEC will be rendered more difficult. Thus the effect of the restriction on competition arising from the creation of the joint subsidiary with which this Decision is concerned is that the potential competition between the parent companies to be offered from the United Kingdom to other Member States will be reduced, as will the potential for competition by companies from other Member States within the United Kingdom. Further, because there are no other manufacturers of vacuum interrupters in the common market at present and there are relatively few potential manufacturers therein, a joint venture between two potential manufacturers affects the structure of competition in the common market. Trade between Member States may thus be affected by the agreement of 25 March 1970.

18. The said agreement is, as set forth in paragraph 15 hereof, concluded between manufacturers who are potential competitors, and there is a restriction in competition as stated in paragraph 16 hereof, which, by virtue of the consequences set out in paragraph 17 hereof, may have an effect on trade between Member States. The said agreement, therefore, comes within the provisions of Article 85(1) of the Treaty.

HAS ADOPTED THIS DECISION:

Art. 1. The provisions of Article 85(1) of the Treaty establishing the European Economic Community are, pursuant to Article 85(3), declared inapplicable to the terms of the agreement of 25 March 1970 made between Associated Electrical Industries Ltd, Reyrolle Parsons Ltd and Vacuum Interrupters Ltd.

Art. 2. Vacuum Interrupters Ltd is required to notify the Commission of any changes during the period of exemption in its share capital and/or the ownership of its shares within 28 days of such becoming effective.

Art. 3. Vacuum Interrupters Ltd is required to notify the Commission of any authorisation given by Associated Electrical Industries Ltd and Reyrolle Parsons Ltd during the period of exemption authorising the undertaking to carry on any other business with full particulars of such authorisation within 28 days of such authorisation being given.

Art. 4. This Decision shall have effect from 1 January 1973 and shall apply until 25 March 1980.
This Decision is addressed to:

1. Vacuum Interrupters Ltd, 68 Ballards Lane, Finchley, London, England;
2. Associated Electrical Industries Ltd, 1 Stanhope Gate, London W1, England;
3. Reyrolle Parsons Ltd, Hebburn, County Durham, England.

*Sequel.*

In 1978 the parties to the agreement applied together with British Switchgear Ltd, Leicestershire, England, for a negative clearance, or, in the alternative for exemption under Article 85(3) concerning an agreement whereby British Switchgear acquired a portion of the shareholding in Vacuum Interrupters Ltd.

(3) Decision in re Vacuum Interruptors II
Commission Decision of 11 December 1980. O.J. No L 383, 31 December

1980, p. 1; (1981) 2 CMLR 217; CCH para. 10296; CM/M/I/160.

*The Commission held:*

A. The restriction of competition

25. 1. The agreement of 27 April 1978 made between Brush, RP and AEI, whereby Brush acquired 20% of the shares in VIL, is an agreement between undertakings within the meaning of Article 85(1) of the EEC Treaty. The object and effect of the agreement is to restrict competition which, for the following reasons, brings it within Article 85(1).

26. 2. Brush, RP and AEI are companies engaged in the field of electrical engineering. All three would have the technical and financial resources, either alone or in conjunction with other companies of their groups specialising in the same field, to develop and manufacture interrupters in general and vacuum interrupters in particular. Brush, which doesn't produce interrupters, can be considered a potential competitor of VIL because of its experience in manufacturing switchgear and the technical expertise and facilities available to it.

27. 3. Since Brush, RP and AEI, which produce switchgear, have, pursuant to this agreement of 1978, not only a contractual obligation but the business interest to buy all their vacuum interrupters from VIL, it can be appreciated that the most important English buyers of interrupters have left the market to the sole benefit of VIL. Brush, in particular, is a very important buyer of interrupters for low-voltage switchgear in which vacuum interrupters can be used. All this constitutes a restriction on the potential sales of the relevant product on the United Kingdom market because producers other than VIL must meet, in addition to normal competitive factors, an additional handicap in that these, the main purchasers of the vacuum interrupter in the UK, have an economic interest in VIL. Unless the terms offered by other manufacturers are very highly competitive it is more likely that these three firms will purchase from VIL.

28. 4. This agreement, which regulates the purchase by one company of a significant shareholding in another company already owned by two competitors gives rise to a situation in which competition between those three companies is likely to be restricted within the meaning of Article 85 of the Treaty.

So, in this case, Brush, as already appears, has the technical and financial ability and the business interest to produce its own vacuum interrupter for incorporation into its own switchgear, now has by virtue of the agreement under consideration, an economic interest as a result of which it is likely to align its decisions and activity in this sphere with its partners in VIL as it now holds a share of the capital in that company. This interest will prevent Brush from acting as an independent enterprise in the field of vacuum interrupters.

Further, Brush, AEI and RP who compete with each other in the switchgear sector of the elctrical engineering industry nevertheless restrict competition between themselves by their agreement to purchase an important component for their equipment from VIL.

B. The effect on trade between Member States

29. 1. The effects of the formation of VIL on Community inter-state trade envisaged by the Commission Decision of 20 January 1977 have been

confirmed in practice, and are likely to be intensified following Brush's accession to VIL membership. There have been no significant imports of vacuum interrupters into the UK. There have been some imports of vacuum interrupters from third countries into other EEC Member States and some exports from the UK to one other EEC Member State.

30. 2. Now that Brush has joined VIL, the chance for manufacturers of electrical equipment in other Member States to penetrate the United Kingdom market as manufacturers and sellers or even only as sellers of vacuum interrupters in competition with VIL is diminished because demand for these products is confined to a small number of buyers, particularly firms like Brush, who fabricate switchgear apparatus and are interested in using the new technology. In fact Brush, along with AEI and RP, are amongst the largest switchgear manufacturers in the United Kingdom who are at the same time each interested in the use of the vacuum interrupter in switchgear and who, by undertakings to purchase in effect all the vacuum interrupters they require from VIL, cease to be potential customers for such manufacturers in other countries. Brush's membership of VIL is of particular importance to the possible restraint of competition being specialised in low-voltage switchgear - switchgear that is particularly suited to the use of the vacuum interrupter.

For these considerations this agreement is an agreement between competing companies, restricts competition, affects trade between Member States, and is consequently within the prohibition of Article 85(1) of the EEC Treaty.

(4) Decision in re De Laval-Stork

Commission Decision of 25 July 1977, on a proceeding under Article 85 of the EEC Treaty; De Laval-Stork O.J. No L 215, 23 August 1977, p. 11; (1972) 2 CMLR D 25; CCH para. 9972; Competition Law CM/M/I/113.

*Facts:* In this case the Commission took a favourable Decision, in respect of an agreement between the American company De Laval and the Dutch company Stork. They formed a joint venture at Hengelo, Netherlands, with the object of combining their production and marketing activities for Europe and the Middle East. Their cooperation covers turbines and compressors used in large-scale plants such as oil refineries.

Under the agreement Stork made part of its Hengelo manufacturing plant available to the joint venture and De Laval provided technical know-how. Both De Laval and Stork remain in business as independent manufacturers.

Cooperation between Stork and De Laval restricts competition in the Community turbine and compressor sector since the production and marketing activities of two competitors have been merged into a single joint undertaking, thus reducing European customers choice. The venture is therefore caught by the prohibition in Article 85(1).

It does, however, bring with it appreciable economic advantages such as increased know-how and a wider product range for Stork and easier penetration of the European market for De Laval which justify exemption under Article 85(3). The various agreements between the two companies do not lead to market dominance; there are a number of important suppliers in the market larger than De Laval and Stork, whose own combined market share is between 10 and 15%.

The joint venture was initially formed in 1971 for a period of five years, renewable with the consent of both parties. The period of exemption has been set at nine years in order to ensure that the cooperation does not last longer than is economically justified.

The Decision imposes conditions and obligations which will ensure that the ability of De Laval and Stork to compete with the joint venture is not unnecessarily limited, that the parent companies are able to make unrestricted use of jointly acquired know-how after the joint venture comes to an end and that the cooperation does not lead to any further restriction of competition in the turbine and compressor industry.

*The Commission ruled:*

.....

2. The agreement made by De Laval and Stork to form De Laval-Stork is an agreement between undertakings within the meaning of Article 85(1).
Such an agreement must be assessed not only in its legal context, that is the formation of a new business entity, whether or not it has distinct legal personality, but also in its economic context. The joint venture agreement, in the context in which it was concluded, has the object and effect of bringing all the research, production and marketing activities of the two parents in the common market under joint control, so that the relations between the two companies and their conduct on the market are altered.

3. The first matter for consideration is whether trade between Member States may be affected. The purpose of this provision, as has been stated in the judgment given by the Court of Justice of the European Communities in the Grundig-Consten and Commercial Solvents cases, is to define the field of application of the Community rules on competition in relation to national legislation.
The agreement has been made by competitors which previously operated independently on the various Community and external markets. De Laval International achieved a considerable proportion of its turbine and compressor sales in the common market, where its know-how and size would have helped it to develop even further. Stork was not in business in the Netherlands alone, since much of its sales were in other Community countries and elsewhere.
The formation of a joint venture by these two undertakings means that production and marketing, no longer being handled by distinct enterprises, will proceed in a different manner and from different places than they would have in the absence of the joint venture. De Laval-Stork's business covers the entire Community and a number of non-member countries. Formation of De Laval-Stork has the further consequence that De Laval International and Stork are likely to refrain from selling in competition with their joint subsidiary, or at least considerably to reduce the extent of such competition. On the other hand the joint subsidiary is not allowed to compete with De Laval International in certain non-member countries, which affects its competitive capacity within the common market.
The formation of the joint subsidiary is therefore likely to alter the normal flow of trade having regard to the size of the undertakings in question. Trade between Member States is likely, therefore, to be appreciably affected.

4. Before considering whether competition within the common market is prevented, restricted or distorted, it should first be considered whether the two undertakings were and remain actual or at least potential competitors in the various relevant markets. Apart from the fact that both undertakings previously carried out research and manufactured and sold most of the relevant products throughout the world, it is clear

that each on its own account previously sold the greater part of its production on these and similar products within the common market. KMS had engaged in research, manufacture and marketing of a large number of the relevant products, and was able, without having to invest too heavily, to extend its business to the other products which are covered by the joint venture. De Laval International, which had decided to try to penetrate the European market, had already been exporting to Europe.

In addition, De Laval International, on its own, could have entered the relevant markets in Europe without any real difficulty, to which end De Laval and KMS had in fact already entered into a licensing agreement in respect of the relevant products. The two companies were at that time either actual competitors, or if not, then the American company despite any difficulties it may have found in organising its European operations from the United States, must be regarded as having been a very powerful potential competitor, both because it was in business on the same markets in the United States, which gave it the opportunity to undertake the same business on the common market without having to begin by acquiring the necessary basic experience, and, secondly, because of its substantial financial power which enabled it and still enables it to make the necessary investments. Thus the two parties were actually or at the very least potentially in competition with each other on the relevant markets.

After the entry into force of the JVA, the parties have remained competitors on the relevant markets. Their involvement in the joint venture and the fact that they are still carrying on business in related product markets or in neighbouring geographical markets mean that there are no insurmountable barriers to stop them reverting to separate business activities in the relevant markets. De Laval remains in business on the American market for similar products, and KMS is continuing to operate the Dutch plant for the manufacture of product ranges which are related to the products covered by the agreement, especially those classes of turbine which are not covered by the JVA. It is clear from the licensing agreement that each of the two parties has, subject to certain conditions, retained the right to sell the relevant products within the Community without passing through the joint venture. Even the fact that research is being jointly undertaken will not prevent either company from continuing to use the results separately. Accordingly the two companies remain real or at the very least potential competitors.

5. The circumstances of this case and the provisions made by the parties in question do not lead to the conclusion that the formation of the joint venture constitutes as a merger.

In the first place the agreement leaves the parents subsisting as economically independent undertakings and there is no evidence to suggest that they have become purely holding companies.

Secondly, it is not the case that at least one of the companies has completely and irreversibly abandoned business in the area covered by the joint venture nor that it is certain that the pooling of this area of business will weaken competition in other areas, particularly in related industries, where the firms involved remain formally independent of each other.

To be regarded as having completely and irreversibly abandoned business in the areas covered by the joint venture, the parties would have had to have given up all their existing capacity to compete actually or potentially and to have ceased to do business in the industry. The withdrawal would have had to have been completely irreversible so that they could no longer be regarded as actual or potential competitors.

They cannot be considered to have done so if they pool only part of their existing activities in these areas, whether it be research or production or marketing of the relevant goods. It is clear from the facts of this case that the association between the parties extends only to part but not all of their activities relating to research, production and marketing and the parties remain actual or at least potential competitors. This fact is further confirmed by the limitation, under the agreement, of the joint venture's activities to a specific territory and the inclusion of certain restrictions in the activities of the two parent companies which would have been unnecessary if the parties had ceased to be able to compete with each other.

The reversible nature of the joint venture is confirmed by the provision in the agreement relating to the conditions to be applied on termination and further from the fact that the agreement has been made for a period of only five years. Although the agreement can be renewed and may therefore create a more durable association the two parties retain the right to terminate the agreement and to revert to fully independent status, hence they remain actual or at least potential competitors.

6. The agreement has the object and effect of restricting and distorting competition within the common market.

Each party controls 50% of the assets of the joint venture, and it is clear from this fact, as from the wording of the agreement, that the consent of both parties is required for any major decision concerning the activities of the joint venture. A number of anti-competitive consequences flow from this by reason of the consultations which will inevitably have to take place between the two parties within the joint venture. Even if an increase in competition between the joint venture and other companies in business on the relevant markets results from the agreement, the effect of the agreement is to eliminate competition between the two parties on the same markets, both as regards research and as regards production and marketing. The two companies have therefore deprived themselves of the opportunity for autonomous costing and pricing, which would be available if their activities were separate. By exchanging information connected with their competitive ability they not only destroy the independence of their market conduct but also remove uncertainty as regards their future behaviour towards their competitors. The pooling of a part of their activities alters the supply structure on the relevant markets, as consumers will no longer be able to choose between the two independent suppliers.

7. The agreement contains further restrictions. For the duration of the agreement certain customers will, as a result of the exclusive licensing agreements entered into in connection with the JVA, no longer be able to choose between the two parties. By these licences the business of De Laval-Stork remains confined exclusively to cases where both the customer's place of business and the place of delivery are within a specific territory, which includes all the Member States of the EEC. Such a customer's scope for choice is thus substantially restricted by the fact that the parties are prevented from making individual offers.
The JVA also contains clauses which will have the effect of restricting competition even after its expiry. As the result of Clause 8, the two parties will be able to derive only limited benefit from their association, since the licences granted under the JVA are restricted in various ways. Once the JVA has expired, the two parties will still not be in a position to engage in full competition with one another.

8. The question then arises whether the effects of these restrictions of competition within the common market are appreciable. The size of the two companies, each of which is multinational with an exclusive turnover, and their position on the relevant markets, where, without being the largest firms, they nevertheless have sizeable market shares, indicate that the restrictions of competition within the common market are appreciable. The agreement therefore comes within the prohibition in Article 85(1) of the EEC Treaty.

*The Commission decided:*

.....

Art. 1. It is hereby declared, pursuant to Article 85(3) of the Treaty establishing the European Economic Community, and subject to the conditions set out below, that the provisions of Article 85(1) are, and shall be, until 1 September 1986, inapplicable to the basic agreement and four implementing agreements made on 1 September 1971 by De Laval Turbine International Incorporated and Sork Roterende Werktuigen BV, formerly known as Stork Pompen NV, of the one part and Koninklijke Machinefabriek Stork BV, on the other part, for the formation of the joint venture De Laval-Stork VOF.

1. If for any reason the joint venture cannot meet an order from a customer, the exclusive nature of the patents and know-how licences granted to it by the parent companies shall not prevent such companies from dealing directly with such customer or from granting non-exclusive licences to third parties to deal with that customer.

2. The licences to be granted under Clause 8(4) of the basic agreement shall afford the parties the opportunity:

- to continue to have the benefit, after the expiration of the period of three years following the dissolution of the joint venture, of the patent and know-how rights licensed to the joint venture to the extent that the exercise of those rights is indispensable for the exploitation of patents and know-how jointly acquired through the joint venture.

- to export the products manufactured under those patent and know-how licences to all common market and non-member countries.

The royalties payable under the licences granted by the parties in accordance with this provision shall not exceed the lowest amount of royalty payable under any licence granted by the parties to third parties in respect of the same patents or know-how.

Art. 2. Exemption is granted subject to the following obligations:

1. The undertakings to which this Decision is addressed shall without delay inform the Commission of any amendment or addition to the abovementioned agreements, and of all matters affecting their interpretation or application, including any arising as a result of arbitration.

2. The undertakings referred to shall furnish the Commission every two years with a full report on the activities of the joint venture.

3. Each of these undertakings shall without delay inform the Commission of the existence, in any of the following forms, of any link between them or of any change made or to be made in such a link:

(a) shareholding of 25% or more;
(b) interlocking directorates;
(c) formation of a joint subsidiary or joint acquisition of an existing undertaking;
(d) grant of patent or know-how licences;
between:

(a) the undertakings themselves; or
(b) any company belonging to the De Laval Turbine Incorporated Group or the Verenigde Machinefabriek NV Group and another company belonging to either of these groups or any other company or companies, where any such company is directly or indirectly engaged within the common market in either the turbine or the compressor industry.

4. Each of the undertakings to which this Decision is addressed shall without delay inform the Commission of any new activity in the turbine or compressor industry other than purely occasional business, engaged in by it independently of the others.

5. Each of the said undertakings shall without delay inform the Commission of any agreements or practices entered into or operated for the transfer of patent or know-how licences or for the substitution of parties thereto and for all allocation or assignment of staff of the joint venture in the event of the dissolution of the joint venture.

Art. 3. This Decision is addressed to:

- De Laval Turbine International Incorporated, PO Box 2072, Princeton, New Jersey 08540, USA,

- Koninklijke Machinefabriek Stork BV, Industriestraat 1, Hengelo, Netherlands,

- Stork Roterende Werktuigen BV, Dr A Philipsweg 51, Assen, Netherlands,

- De Laval-Stork VOF, Industriestraat 1, Hengelo, Netherlands.

(5) Decision in re GEC-Weir-Sodium Circulators

Decision of the Commission of 23 November 1977, relating to a proceeding under Article 85 of the EEC Treaty; General Electric Company and the Weir Group; joint venture in Sodium Circulators, O.J. No L 327, 20 December 1977, p. 26; (1978) 1 CMLR D 66; CCH para. 10070; Competition Law CM/M/I/116.

*Facts:* In this case the Commission, by decision, exempted a joint venture entered into by agreement between The General Electric Company Ltd and the Weir Group Ltd which was notified in April 1977. Prior to the grant of exemption and on the initiative of the Commission, the parties had abandoned a number of restrictive provisions which could not have been exempted. The purpose of the joint venture is to develop, manufacture and sell sodium circulators for use in nuclear fast reactors. The Parties are of considerable industrial significance in the United Kingdom and are established also in other Community countries and elsewhere. The exemption was made subject to a number of reporting obligations upon the parties.

The joint venture arrangements were made wholly by agreement and do not depend for their validity or enforceability on the control of a separate company. However, the arrangements provide for the unified, joint and equal control by the parties of all their activities relating to soium circulators, including planning, financing, research, development, construction and sale.

The agreement and the joint venture fall within the scope of Article 85(1) of the EEC Treaty, primarily because, prior to the agreement, both parties were competitors and, following expiry of the agreement, both parties will again become competitors in respect of sodium circulators. Moreover, for the continuance of the agreement, both parties independently retain, not only horizontally competitive but also vertically overlapping activities in related markets, specifically in the power engineering field.

The Commission found that in these circumstances the very creation of the joint venture in which the parties tock joint control amounted to a restriction of competition, regardless even of the specific restrictive provisions of their agreement. These were viewed by the Commission as reinforcing the implicit restrictive effects of the joint venture.

In addition, the existence of the joint venture was seen by the Commission as providing opportunities and inducements to the parties to enlarge their common activities so as to impair free competition between themselves also in areas outside sodium circulators where they retain independent interests.

The Commission was able to grant an exemption in this case for a number of reasons and notably because of the high risks involved in this particular development work, the complementary expertise of the parties and the urgency to achieve safe and satisfactory technical performance of nuclear reactors in this field. As seen by the Commission, the twelve-year duration of the agreement and of the joint venture is relatively short-term, if considered against the projected long-term future of fast reactor programmes. On completion of the development and on termination of the agreement and the joint venture, both parties will be competitors at arm's length in the manufacture and sale of sodium circulators with enhanced technical versatility and competence.

The Commission also took the view that the conditions for exemption would probably not have been satisfied if the parties had been in a position to manufacture and sell sodium circulators jointly for the entire time or for a significantly long time during the term of the agreement. But in this case the current development work is likely to take some eight years before questions of manufacture and sale can in practice arise. This underlines that while the Commission is willing in appropriate cases to view favourably cooperative development projects in fields of high technology, it will closely assess the possible restrictive effects of joint manufacture and, even more particularly, joint sales arrangements.

*The Commission ruled:*

.....

(d) The joint venture arrangements between the parties are made wholly by agreement and do not depend for their validity or enforcement of the joint control or ownership of a distinct incorporated company. However, the contractual dispositions made by the parties have all the most essential characteristics of a joint venture, commonly so-called; in that they provide for the unified joint and equal control by the parties of all their activities relating to sodium circulators, including planning, financing, research, development, construction and sale.

(e) The relevant terms of the agreement are to the following effect:

(i) each party takes a half share in all the assets, profits, property, losses and liabilities of the joint venture.

(ii) The parties make available to the joint venture the pre-existing and future documents, information, designs, property, assets and rights which are or will be in their possession and concern the sodium circulators to be developed for NPC. The parties each license the joint venture non-exclusively to use their applicable pre-existing information and inventions whether patented or not which concern sodium circulators. All resultant expanses are chargeable to the joint venture.

(iii) All necessary financing of the joint venture is to be provided by the parties in equal amounts and on equal terms as to interest, repayment or otherwise. All surplus funds from time to time available to the joint venture are to be paid out equally to the parties and on like terms.

(iv) The joint venture is controlled by a committee on which the parties are equally represented. Decisions must be unanimous. The joint venture is managed by a manager appointed by the committee.

(v) Agreed numbers of each of the parties personnel are seconded to the joint venture, but remain on the original employing party's payroll and under its administrative control.

(vi) The joint venture is to have total responsibility for the design, development and supply of sodium circulators. All rights in any technical information, designs and patents which result from the development or manufacture of sodium circulators pursuant to the agreement are, subject only to any third party rights, to belong to the joint venture. According to the original notified text of the agreement, the necessary engineering and production work, whether as part of the development or of the subsequent manufacture, was allocated directly to be carried out in pre-established distinct parts, by the joint venture itself and under subcontract from the joint venture, by each of the parties. Following amendment as requested by the Commission, the agreement now attributes a field of primary responsibility to each of the parties, but without rigidly pre-determining exclusive areas of work for each party for the duration of the agreement. The amendment leaves more open a possible future division of contributions, to be decided in the light of any changes in circumstances. The tasks which are within the field of primary responsibility of Weir include in general the hydraulic work and components; those within the field of GEC, the mechanical and electrical work and components.

The agreement restricts competition as follows:

(i) Even in the absence of express provisions, the creation of a joint venture generally has a notable effect on the conduct of parent parties who have a significant holding in the joint venture. Within the field of the joint venture and in related fields such parties are likely to coordinate their conduct and be influenced in what would otherwise have been their independent decisions and activities. Where the parent parties are actual or potential competitors, their participation in a joint venture is accordingly likely to impair free competition between them, regardless of the existence of explicit restrictive provisions to that effect. The fact that a joint venture is not, as it is in this case, a distinct incorporated company, but is created solely by contract, is not a difference of substance, but one of legal form only and does not affect the foregoing conclusions.

(ii) Prior to the agreement which created the joint venture in this case both parties were active and had experience relating to the development and manufacture of pumping equipment for fast reactors. (see 4(e) of I above). Weir had supplied pumps other than sodium circulators for operations in fast reactors and had tendered for an earlier design of sodium circulators. GEC had developed and supplied electromagnetic and rotating pumps as sodium circulators built to a previous specification and GEC has been and is an important supplier of other major reactor equipment and of power plant in general. Each party has considerable background experience within the field of the joint venture and technological versatility in related areas. Each has a considerable industrial base and financial resources and is established through subsidiary companies throughout the Community. Prior to the agreement both parties were therefore competitors for the development and production of sodium circulators which are within the field of the joint venture. Accordingly, the cooperation between them in the field of the joint venture reduces competition.

(iii) The notified agreement exemplified and strongly reinforces the given restrictive effects referred to in 2(a)(i) of II above. It confers equal control of the joint venture upon each party so that neither can make independent business decisions on any matter of importance relating to sodium circulators. The effect of the joint venture and of the agreement is to change each party's position of autonomy in this respect to one of joint activity concerning planning, financing, research, development, production and sale and each party abandons its individual freedom of action in relation to these activities.

(b) As a result of the foregoing, two parties who were, prior to the agreement, independently available for the development, manufacture and sale of sodium circulators are for the duration of the agreement replaced by one; namely the joint venture. While the agreement is in force, customers' demand will therefore be met by the designs and prices of the joint venture, rather than the possibility of alternative designs and prices from the parties independently.

(c) Parent parties will not in general compete with the activities of joint ventures in which they hold substantial stakes, even if they are contractually free to do so. In this case in particular, neither party would, within the context outlined in 4 of I above be likely to devote its resources separately to an individual development effort over and above that required by the joint venture. This effect is here made explicit and ensured by an agreed express non-competition clause. Save in the exceptional circumstances referred to in 3(e)(iv) of I above, neither party is free to act independently or to enter into agreements with third parties in relation to any activity which is competitive with the stated purposes of the joint venture. Neither party is available, save in exceptional circumstances, to cooperate independently in the development of sodium circulators with third parties, to disclose technical information to third parties for this purpose or to tender independently to customers for the supply of sodium circulators.

(d) The sharing between the parties of all development results has the effect that while the agreement is in force both parties maintain the same level and character of sodium circulator technology, so that neither party can obtain a technological advantage over the other in relation to sodium circulators or applicable production methods.

(e) In circumstances such as in this case, the existence of a joint venture in one field is likely to provide opportunities and inducements to parent companies, who each have related interests also in other areas, to enlarge their common activities and impair free competition between them in those other areas. Here each of the parties has highly diversified industrial interests. Apart from their joint activity in the field of the joint venture, the parties have other overlapping, related and competitive activities. By way of examples, both are manufacturers of pumps other than sodium circulators, specifically for power engineering and oil-pipeline applications, and, as to foundry products and high-precision steelcastings, Weir is a major producer and supplier and GEC is a major user. The parties have therefore not only horizontally competitive but also vertically related activities in other areas. Senior employees of both parties are seconded to the joint venture, but remain on the original employing party's payroll and under its administrative control. These employees retain interests in their employers' activities outside the field of the joint venture. Through their continuing association with each other within the joint venture, the coincidence of interests of the parties in other areas can be expected to lead to an impairment of competition between them also in these other areas.

(f) The agreement attributes to each party a separate share of responsibility and work to be contributed to the joint venture. The provisions as originally notified gave to each of the parties for the duration of the agreement substantially unqualified rights to perform the work not only in its own defined field, but also in the field of the other party whenever the other was unwilling or unable to perform its part. These original provisions restricted competition through their effect of reinforcing the exclusivity of the cooperation between the parties and of practically ruling out any likelihood of access to the work by any qualified third parties.

(g) All the foregoing restrictive effects are significantly underlined by the considerable importance of the parties on the affected market.

3. The agreement may affect trade between Member States in respect of all the restrictions referred to in 2 of II above and, in particular, as follows:

(a) Sodium circulators are in operation or planned in the United Kingdom, France, the Federal Republic of Germany, Italy and the Netherlands. Companies which specialise in equipment for sodium circuits and in circulating pumps for nuclear reactors exist in all these countries. Each of the parties has a substantial base in the United Kingdom, has trading activities elsewhere in the Community and specifically each party has expertise relating to sodium circulators. There is a known requirement for such expertise also in Member States other than the United Kingdom. (See 4(e) of I above). In the absence of the notified agreement, either party would have been free.

(i) independently to develop, make or sell sodium circulators also for use in other Member States;

(ii) independently to cooperate in the development of sodium circulators with third parties in other Member States.

By virtue of the agreement and the existence of the joint venture, neither party can choose to engage in any such independent development, manufacture or sale or cooperation.

(b) There are within the Community some 25 companies which specialise in equipment for sodium circuits and in circulating pumps for nuclear reactors. (See 4(e) of I above). The cooperation between the two parties who are of considerable importance of the affected market in the United Kingdom will have the effect of making it more difficult for manufacturers of sodium circulators in the other Member States to sell sodium circulators in the United Kingdom and of making it more likely that any sales by the parties in other Member States will be joint rather than independent.

4. The effect of the restrictions on competition is likely to be appreciable because both parties are groups of siginificant industrial importance, both have considerable financial resources, both are established throughout the Community and the products of the joint venture are very costly and of substantial consequence.

5. Article 85(1) therefore applies to the notified agreement.

*The Commission decided:*

.....

Art. 1. Pursuant to Article 85(3) of the Treaty establishing the European Economic Community, the provisions of Article 85(1) are declared inapplicable to the agreement concluded on 21 March 1977 and amended on 30 September 1977 by Weir Pumps Ltd, the Weir Group Ltd, the English Elelctric Company Ltd and the General Electric Company Ltd. The period during which Article 85(1) remains inapplicable shall be deemed to have begun on 14 April 1977 and shall continue for the duration of the agreement in accordance with its present terms, but not beyond 31 December 1989.

Art. 2. The following obligations are attached to this Decision:

The parties, that is to say, the Weir Group Ltd on its behalf and on behalf of its subsidiary companies and the General Electric Company Ltd on its behalf and on behalf of its subsidiary companies, shall inform the Commission promptly of the occurrence of any of the following matters:

(a) The date when the development contract awarded by NPC becomes effective;

(b) The effective date and nature of any contracts placed during the period of the notified agreement with the joint venture of the parties, or any of them, for the development or production of sodium circulators, other than further development contracts placed by NPC or the United Kingdom Atomic Energy Authority;

(c) The admission of any third party, other than NPC or the United Kingdom Atomic Energy Authority, to the development activity of the joint venture, except as suppliers or subcontractors for minor items or as purchasers laying down their own specifications;

(d) Arbitration awards or settlements arising out of arbitration proceedings in relation to the agreement or the joint venture;

(e) The grant of any licences in pursuance of 3(e)(xiii) of I above, together with the terms thereof;

(f) The conclusion between the parties during the period of the notified agreement of any agreements for joint cooperation between them in the development, manufacture or sale of any products of whatever kind within the fields of power engineering and/or liquid metal technology, but not (unless otherwise notifiable) such agreements principally relating to foundry processes. For the purpose of this paragraph, the expression 'parties' shall include also the future subsidiary companies of respectively The Weir Group Ltd and the General Electrical Company Ltd, any corporation which may control either of them and any subsidiary company of such corporation;

(g) The conclusion of any agreement or arrangement which amends, replaces, supercedes or annuls the notified agreement, as amended on 30 September 1977, and any joint activity by the parties relating to sodium circulators outside the terms of the notified agreement.

Art. 3. This Decision is addressed to:

1. The Weir Group Ltd, 149 Newlands Road, Cathcart, Glasgow G44 4EX, Scotland
on its behalf and on behalf of its subsidiary companies.

2. The General Electrical Company Ltd, 1 Stanhope Gate, London W1A 1EH, England
on its behalf and on behalf of its subsidiary companies.

(6) Decision in re ICI-WANO-Blackpowder
Decision of the Commission of 20 October 1978, relating to a proceeding under Article 85 of the EEC Treaty, Imperial Chemical Industries - WANO-Blackpowder; O.J. No L 322, 16 November 1978, p. 26; (1979) 1 CMLR 403; CCH para. 10089; Competition Law CM/M/I/137.

*Facts:* On 20 October the Commission adopted its first decision under Article 85 of the EEC Treaty prohibiting agreements to set up a joint venture. The agreements, which had been notified to the Commission, were entered into by Wasagchemie GmbH and certain associated companies with subsidiary companies of Imperial Chemical Industries Ltd. The joint company was to operate in the Federal Republic of Germany and to be controlled equally by the Wasag and ICI groups for the manufacture and sale of blackpowder.

Pursuant to the agreements and the parties' participation in the joint venture, neither party (each being a natural competitor of the other in blackpowder and safety fuse) could, without the approval of the other, have made independent decisions within the joint venture field and neither party would have competed with the other or with the joint venture in the blackpowder market.

Blackpowder is a low-power explosive. Its main uses are in the manufacture of fireworks, other pyrotechnical devices, safety fuse and for blasting. Small quantities are used for military purposes. In most of its applications other explosives cannot be used. ICI, which does not have its own production facilities for blackpowder, has a 100% or near 100% share of the sales of blackpowder in the United Kingdom. Wasag, through a controlled company, produces blackpowder and has around 50% of the sales in the Federal Republic of Germany. Each of the parties has, outside the sphere of the agreements, its separate interests in explosives other than in blackpowder and in safety fuse.

It would have been the additional effect of the agreements, particularly in the light of ICI's 100% or near 100% share in the UK blackpowder market and in the light also of its control of distribution and transport facilities for explosives in the UK, that the UK blackpowder market would for the foreseeable future have been blocked to other producers - in France and Italy, for instance.

The main reason why the Commission was not able to grant an exemption in this case was because competition for the UK supply of blackpowder would not have been possible if ICI had participated in the joint venture.

Following receipt of the Commission's objections, the parties informed the Commission that they proposed no longer to implement the agreement for the formation of the joint venture. The Commission nevertheless regards it of importance to have adopted this decision, to establish clearly, also for the benefit of other blackpowder producers and customers, that the agreements in question infringed Article 85(1) and could not be exempted under Article 85(3).

The Commission had also warned the parties that implementation on their part of the joint venture agreements could in this case have additionally amounted to an abuse of ICI's dominant position in the UK blackpowder market.

*The Commission ruled:*

.....

Under Article 85(3) of the Treaty, the provisions of Article 85(1) of the Treaty may be declared inapplicable in the case of any agreement which contributes to the improvement of the production or distribution of goods or to the promotion of technical or economic progress, while allowing consumers a fair share of the resulting benefit, and which does not:

(a) impose on the undertakings concerned restrictions which are not indispensable to the attainment of those objectives;

(b) afford such undertakings the possibility of eliminating competition in respect of a substantial part of the products in question.

1. The implementation of the agreements would afford the parties the possibility of eliminating competition in respect of a substantial part of the products in question in that the implementation of the agreements would result in the insulation of the United Kingdom market by precluding sales into the United Kingdom by suppliers other than WANO and by shutting out all possibilities of competition by WANO in respect of sales into the United Kingdom which are independent of ICI.

2. Accordingly, questions of contribution to the improvement of the production or distribution of goods or to the promotion of technical progress do not fail to be considered, although the parties have submitted that Article 85(3) should be applied to the agreements. However, they have not demonstrated that the production of blackpowder would be improved as a result of the agreements. Although the parties initially alleged in their notification that the pooled technology and resources of ICI and WASAG would enable manufacture on a scale sufficient to

justify developing new processes, it was later admitted that no really new processes were likely for the manufacture of blackpowder. The composition and method of manufacture of blackpowder have remained essentially the same for centuries and no radically new process or methods of manufacture can reasonably be expected to occur by reason of the joint venture. Although the supply by WASAG of all or part of the United Kingdom market for blackpowder would enable an increased rate of use of its plant and on the assumption (which has not been demonstrated) that this could result in economies of scale, these could be obtained independently by ICI in the capital of WANO.

3. The parties have also claimed that the implementation of the notified agreements would lead to a greater security of supply for blackpowder and that, in particular, ICI's participation in the joint venture was necessary for it to obtain suitable supplies of blackpowder and to guarantee supplies of suitable qualities to its customers in the United Kingdom and elsewhere. Security of supply in these circumstances, in which there are considerable under-used production capacities, is not a benefit sufficient for the purposes of Article 85(3). The structure of the industry is such as to exclude any probability of long-term shortage.

4. Even on the assumption (which is not fulfilled) that the agreements, if implemented, could contribute to an improvement in the production or distribution of goods or to the promotion of technical or economic progress, a fair share of any such benefits would not become available to consumers. The result of the agreement would be to enable ICI, an existing monopoly distributor of blackpowder in the United Kingdom, also to become jointly with WASAG a monopoly producer of blackpowder for the Federal Republic of Germany. In that position ICI would be subject to negligible competitive pressure to pass on to the consumer any savings made by increased efficiency.

5. The agreements therefore do not satisfy the tests of exemption of Article 85(3).

In the agreements it was provided that they would not come into operation until approved by the Commission, but the parties in one important respect have been acting as if they were already in force. ICI have been buying from WANO and this necessarily affects the position of other suppliers.

Under the circumstances there remains an interest for the Commission to establish clearly, in particular for the beneift of third parties, that the agreements in question came under Article 85(1) and could not benefit from the exemption under Article 85(1) and could not benefit from the exemption under Article 85(3). This Decision is without prejudice to any view that the Commission may take of any other arrangement which the parties may make in the future.

*The Commisison decided:*

.....

The shareholder's agreement dated 14 October 1975 and the related agreements notified on 28 October 1975 and entered into by Bohlen Industrie AG, Wasagchemie GmbH and other companies controlled by them on the one hand and by Imperial Chemical Industries Ltd and other companies controlled by it on the other hand concerning their joint participation in a joint venture company for the manufacture and sale of blackpowder infringe Article 85(1) of the Treaty establishing the European Economic Community, and may not be implemented.

Article 2

Article 85(3) of the Treaty is not applicable to the agreements referred to in Article 1 above.

Article 3

This Decision is addressed to:

1. Imperial Chemical Industries Ltd, Millbank, London SW1P 3JF, England and to that company on behalf of its subsidiary comapnies.

2. Bohlen Industries AG, 4300 Essen, Huyssenallee 85 and Wasagchemie GmbH, 4300 Essen, Rolandstrasse 9, Federal Republic of Germany, and to those companies on behalf of theri respective subsidiary companies.

## B. Decisions by Associations of Undertakings

### (1) Decision on the German Ceramic Tiles Discount Agreement

For facts and references see above, page 71.

*The Commisison ruled:*

The decision on discounts taken by the general meeting of the Interessengemeinschaft on 19 December 1958 and amended on 14 December 1961 is a decision of an association of undertakings.

### (2) Decision in re CEMATEX I

Decision of the Commission of 24 December 1971 on a proceeding under Article 85 of the Treaty. J.O. No L 227, 8 October 1971, p. 26; (1973) CMLR D 135; CCH para. 2061; Competition Law CM/M/I/41.

*Facts:* CEMATEX is an association without legal personality. It is an association of seven national federations of manufacturers for the textile industry, grouping together the majority of, and the largest, manufacturers of the Common Market countries, the United Kingdom and Switzerland. CEMATEX organises every four years the "International Textile Machinery Exhibitions" (ITMA). The ITMA exhibitions have become the most important in the world for this type of equipment; in principle they are held in each of the countries represented on CEMATEX in turn, but in fact Europe, at the moment of the decision, has only three large towns with adequate facilities for them to be held under satisfactory conditions: Hanover, Milan and Paris.

Hitherto the exhibition rules prohibited exhibitors from displaying their machines at any other fair or exhibition organised in Western Europe for three years out of four. This prohibition had appreciable effects on competition and was reinforced by a recommendation to the manufacturers not to take part in other events either during the fourth year. These rules brought about an excessive concentration by the large manufacturers and sellers concerned. The rules were modified in consequence of observations by the Commission. CEMATEX reduced the previous three year prohibition to two years.

*The Commission ruled:*

The decision of CEMATEX determining the exhibition regulations for each ITMA and renewed every four years is a decision of an association of enterprises, i.e. the national associations of manufacturers of textile machinery. It therefore comes within the scope of application of Article 85.

*Sequel*

By Commission Decision of 24 May 1983, the Decision of 24 December 1971 has been renewed until 31 December 1995.

(3) Decision in re VCH
Decision of the Commission of 16 December 1971 on a proceeding under Article 85 of the Treaty. J.O. No L 7, 8 January 1972, p. 25; (1973) CMLR D 16; CCH para. 2021; Competition Law CM/M/I/45.

For facts see above, page 75.

The rules described in Chapter I above are based on decisions of the general meeting (Algemene ledenvergadering) of the VCH which, both from their terms and under clause 3(c) of the statutes of the VCH, are obligatory on all members of the VCH. As the VCH is an association which has the aim of defending the economic interests of its members, the 'Algemene Bepalingen en Prijsvoorschriften', the Algemene Koop- en Verkoopvoorwaarden 1955 FGB-RBB', the 'Aanvullende Koop- en Verkoopvoorwaarden van de VCH', and the 'Prijsbladen I-IV' must be regarded as the decision of an association of undertakings within the meaning of Article 85(1).

*The Commission decided:*

1. The Algemene Bepalingen en Prijsvoorschriften der VCH, including the Prijsbladen I-IV, referred to in paragraph III, article 5 of those provisions, as well as the Algemene Koop- en Verkoopvoorwaarden 1955 FGB-RBB referred to in paragraph III, article 10, the latter comprising also the Aanvullende Koop- en Verkoopvoorwaarden van de VCH, violate Article 85(1) of the Treaty instituting the European Economic Community.

2. The request for exemption under Article 85(3) made by the Vereeniging van Cementhandelaren for the regulations mentioned in Article 1 is rejected.

3. The Vereeniging van Cementhandelaren is required to put an immediate stop to the infringement held in Article 1 to exist

4. The present decision is addressed to the Vereeniging van Cementhandelaren, of 11-13 Keizersgracht, Amsterdam.

*Sequel*

The parties appealed to the Court of Justice for annulment of the Decision. The Court rejected the appeal. (For the Court's judgement see page 75 ).

(4) re Cauliflowers
Commission Decision of 2 December 1977, on a proceeding under Article

85 of the EEC Treaty, in re marketing of Breton vegetables, O.J. No L 21, 26 February 1978, p. 23; (1978) 1 CMLR D66 ; CCH para. 10070; Competition Law CM/M/I/118.

*Facts:* In a case concerning the admission of buyers it found that certain arrangements made by groups of vegetable growers and dealers based in Brittany for the marketing of Breton cauliflowers, artichokes and early potatoes were in breach of Article 85(1) of the Treaty. The actual arrangements banned by the Commission imposed restrictions on dealers wishing to buy at the two main vegetable auction centres set up in the departments of Nord-Finistère and Ille-et-Vilaine by two growers cooperatives (SICA of Saint-Pol-de-Léon and SICA-SIPEFEL of Saint-Méloir-des-Ondes).

Admission of dealers to the auction centres was conditional on their making all their purchases there and having a packing station close to the auction centre.

Further, in respect of Saint-Méloir-des-Ondes only, admission to the auctions was subject to formal approval by a majority of the dealers already admitted and a buyer was allowed to purchase and dispatch goods on his account only.

These obligations, about which complaints had been made, appreciably restricted competition among Breton dealers and shippers by hampering, if not blocking, access to the auctions for new buyers and, in the case of Saint-Méloir-des-Ondes, by cinfining dealings in the vegetables to dealers already admitted.

A very large quantity of Breton vegetables are marketed through these two auction centres (70% of the cauliflowers and artichokes and 25% of the early potatoes grown in France). A third of their production is exported to other Community countries, particularly Germany.

Since this case concerned farm produce, for which the Commission has made specific arrangements granting certain powers of organisation to producer groups, and because this was the first time it had to give a decision concerning the behaviour of such groups, the Commission did not impose fines.

*The Commission ruled:*

.....

The agreements and decisions concerning the organisation and operation of vegetable auction sales at Saint-Pol-de-Léon and Saint-Méloir-des-Ondes, which are agreements between undertakings or decisions by associations of undertakings as the case may be for the purpose of Article 85 of the Treaty, impose on the parties thereto obligations and rules, some of which restrict competition.

*The Commission decided:*

.....

Art. 1. (a) The clauses in the agreements between SICA de Saint-Pol-de-Léon and the Union des Expéditeurs de Saint-Pol-de-Léon and between SIPEFEL and the Syndicat des Expéditeurs de Saint-Malo, whereby dealers who obtain supplies at auction sales held at Saint-Pol-de-Léon and Saint-Méloir-des-Ondes are required to accept the obligations:

- to buy exclusively at the auction sales to which they have been admitted, and

- to be in possession of a packing centre.

constituting infringements of Article 85(1) of the EEC Treaty.

(b) The decisions taken by the Syndicat des Expéditeurs de Saint-Malo:

- subjecting admission of new buyers to the Saint-Méloir-des-Ondes auctions to a favourable decision by the management bodies set up by the Statutes of the Syndicat, without any reference to fixed and objective conditions of admission,
and

- obliging members to buy, pack and dispatch vegetables only on their own account,
constitute infringements of Article 85(1) of the EEC Treaty.

Art. 2. SICA de Saint-Pol-de-Léon, the Union des Expéditeurs, SIPEFEL and the Syndicat des Expéditeurs de Saint-Malo shall forthwith bring to an end the infringements referred to in Article 1.

Art. 3. This Decision is addressed to the following associations of undertakings:

- Société d'Investissements et de Coopération Agricoles, of Saint-Pol-de-Léon,

- Union des Expéditeurs et Exportateurs en Fruits et Légumes du Finistère, of Saint-Pol-de-Léon,

- Société Interprofessionelle des Producteurs et Expéditeurs de Fruits, Légumes, Bulbes et Fleurs d'Ille et Vilaine SICA-SIPEFEL, of Saint-Méloir-des-Ondes,

- Syndicat des Expéditeurs et Exportateurs en Légumes et Pommes de terre primeurs de la région Malounine, of Saint-Méloir-des-Ondes.

(5) Decision in re Belgian Tobacco Cartel

Commission Decision of 20 July 1978, relating to a proceeding under Article 85 of the EEC Treaty on Belgian Tobacco Cartel C GB - INNO - BM and others (Fedetab) O.J. No L 224, 15 August 1978, p. 29; (1978) 3 CMLR 524; CCH para. 10070; Competition Law CM/M/I/132.

*Facts:* On 20 July the Commission adopted a decision finding that the system for distributing and selling manufactured tobacco products in Belgium operated by the Federation belgo-luxembourgeoise des Industries du Tabac (Fedetab), Brussels, and several of its members constitutes an infringement on the ban on restrictive agreements laid down in Article 85 of the EEC Treaty, and requiring that the system be discontinued immediately.

Fedetab was set up in 1946 and counts among its members practically all the firms in the manufactured tobacco industry in Belgium and Luxembourg. Fedetab members manufacture or import 95% of the cigarettes and 75 to 80% of the cigars and cigarillos sold in Belgium. Practically all the manufactured tobacco imported into Belgium and Luxembourg comes from other EEC Member States.

The case began when the Commission intiated proceedings in response to complaints lodged in 1974 and again in 1975 by SA GB-INNO-BM (a supermarket operator with headquarters in Brussels). SA Mestdagh Frères et Cie (a wholesaler chain), Gosselies, and SA Eugène Huyghebaert (a food wholesaler), Mechelen.

The system was designed to impose fixed profit margins, both horizontally on all manufacturers who were party to the agreement and vertically at all levels of distribution. It also sought to classify Belgian wholesalers and retailers into a number of different categories, allocate a fixed margin to each, limit the number of new businesses approved in certain wholesale categories, forbid wholesalers in certain categories to resell tobacco products to certain wholesalers in other categories, force firms to observe the resale prices laid down by the manufacturers, encourage manufacturers to agree to impose standardised terms of payment, and force retailers to stock a minimum range of brands. A number of complainants had been victims of a concerted refusal to supply by all the Fedetab manufacturers.

After the Commission had sent Fedetab and its members a statement of objections, Fedetab replaced the system with a 'Recommendation for cigarettes sales in Belgium' notified to the Commission on 1 December 1975. This Recommendation, which is still in operation, preserved the old system of dividing up Belgian wholesalers and retailers and allocating each category a fixed profit margin, imposing standard terms of payments of manufacturers customers, and granting wholesalers and retailers an end-of-year rebate.

Fedetab's distribution system, both as it was before 1 December 1975 and as it is now, following the Recommendation, entails appreciable restrictions of competition which do not qualify for exemption from the ban on restrictive practices. The classification of wholesalers and retailers virtually destroys competition at the distribution stage without producing any benefit for the consumer.

The importance of the decision of 20 July is twofold. First, the Commission confirms its opposition to the anti-competitive practice of imposing mandatory profit margins both horizontally on all the parties to the agreement and vertically at all levels of distribution; secondly, it demonstrates the Commission's resolve to preserve as much competition as possible in an industry where governement control on the consumer price has considerably narrowed the potential for competition among wholesalers and retailers alike.

This decision has, however, no power to affect a number of restrictions on competition in the manufactured tobacco industry which still exists in Belgium. These include the obligation under Article 58 of the Belgian VAT Code to adhere to the price fixed by the manufacturer or importer when selling to the final consumers.

One of the complaints in this case SA GB-Inno-BM, has in fact been taken to court several times by the Belgian Association of Tobacco Retailers for failure to comply with that Article. In the course of these proceedings, the Belgian Court of Cassation asked the Court of Justice for a preliminary ruling on whether such resale price maintenance was compatible with various Articles of the EEC Treaty, and in particular Article 30.

The Court of Justice has replied with a number of guidelines to be followed by the Belgian Courts and by the Commission itself when called upon to consider the compatibility of Article 58 of the Belgian VAT Code with the Treaty. (Judgment of 16 November 1977; Case 13/77 GB-INNO-BM/ATAB; Bull. EC 11-1977, point 2.3.38.)

*The Commission ruled:*

.....

1. Of the various measures taken by Fedetab and its members in relation to distribution before 1 December 1975 (see I(c) above), those concerning the approval and classification of wholesalers and retailers by Fedetab, the allowing of fixed margins to the different categories of wholesalers and retailers, the ban on resale to other wholesalers and the keeping of a minimum range constituted both decision by association of under-

takings and also agreements between undertakings; those concerning the manintenance of retail prices and terms of payment constituted agreements between undertakings; and the limitation by Fedetab of access to certain categories of wholesalers constituted a decision by an association of undertakings.

Fedetab and several of its members must fail when they claim that the FNCG Fedetab agreements of 22 May and 5 October 1967 and the additional agreement of 29 December 1970 did not constitute agreements which individually bound the manufacturers who were members of Fedetab.

Even if they did not actually sign the agreements themselves, leaving it to Fedetab to sign on their behalf, it appears that none of them ever disassociated themselves from Fedetab for doing so, nor gave any reason to believe that they were opposed to the agreements whereas Fedetab's statutes empowered it to undertake obligations on their behalf. Consequently it can be concluded that the parties concerned acquiesced in the agreements, a conclusion strengthened by the fact that they carried them out.

The manufacturers likewise fail in their argument that Fedetab members had no hand in the instructions issued by the FNCG to its members on 26 October 1967, 8 May 1970 and 22 March 1972. On the first two occasions, the instructions were evidently no more than measures for applying agreements previously concluded between the FNCG and Fedetab, whilst the additional agreement of 22 March 1972, which followed on from the agreement of 26 October 1967 and the additional agreement of 29 December 1970, was brought into effect on 30 June 1972 by means of individual agreements between wholesalers and Fedetab itself. Fedetab members did not disassociate themselves from Fedetab's action on either occasion; on the contrary, they carried out its instructions.

2. The agreements and decisions described in I(c) have as their object and effect the restriction of competition within the common market for the following reasons:

(a) The practice of dividing wholesalers and retailers up into several categories and allowing fixed margins to each category, which is what Fedetab and its members were doing under the pre 1 December 1975 system, constituted a restriction of competition for both manufacturers and wholesalers, since the manufacturers no longer had the opportunity of competing against each other on mark-ups, and the wholesalers in the services they render to the manufacturers. What the intermediary earns is his category's standard percentage of the price, irrespective of the competititve quality or extent of the services he himself may render. The various criteria considered in classifying FNCG wholesaler-members and retailers took no account of the other services that intermediaries in each category might be good or bad at providing, such as delivery rate, product display, sales incentive, response to emergency requests for stocks, etc. The limitation of wholesalers' margins, notwithstanding any competitive endeavour on their part, to those prescribed for the category in which Fedetab placed them, deprived them in turn of any possibility of competing with each other on resale prices to retailers.

(b) Fedetab's decisions, the agreements it concluded with the FNCG and the additional agreements, the individual arrangements it pressed on wholesalers concerning the behaviour of firms at the various levels of distribution and aiming to ensure compliance with and enforcement of resale prices to be charged by wholesalers to retailers and by retailers to consumers from 13 March 1962 to 1 January 1971 and by wholesalers to retailers from 1 January 1971 to 1 December 1975 all had the object and the effect of preventing wholesalers and retailers from competing on prices in respect of individual brands, since these prices were fixed by the manufacturers operating within the Fedetab association. It should be recalled, in fact, that the individual agreements which Fedetab put to wholesalers and approved retailers had the object of obliging them to maintain the fixed prices and not to give reductions or discount, even for bulk purchases, at the risk of losing the special conditions allocated to the categories in which these wholesalers and retailers were unilaterally and irrevocably placed by Fedetab, which also fixed the margins for each of these categories, Fedetab, with the help of the substantial market power in Belgium, effectively prevented the dealers in question from exercising any freedom of action in this area.

The fact that Belgium, through the new Article 58 of the VAT Code (which came into force on 1 January 1971) and other exercise provisions, compelled the ultimate retailer to sell his merchandise at the price indicated on the tax band does not prevent the system imposed by Fedetab and its members on Belgian wholesalers and retailers from being caught by Article 85. In fact, apart from the fact that Article 58 of the VAT Code does not contain any clause governing wholesalers selling prices, it should be noted that Article 85(1) of the EEC Treaty prohibits significant restrictions of competition within the common market which may affect trade between Member States, even where such restrictions are encouraged by national legislation.

(c) The restriction placed on the number of wholesalers eligible for approval in certain categories between 1 January 1971 and 1 December 1975 constituted a barrier to market entry for those who were not approved.

Under this system there is no incentive for intermediaries to make greater competitive efforts with a view to obtaining improved benefits from manufacturers, or to take their custom exclusively to one manufacturer with a view to being rewarded with a larger rebate, since in both cases the system prevents intermediaries from improving rebates rates. This standard rebate system also imposes on any manufacturer wishing to enter the market a financial burden that will be all the heavier if he receives only a small part of the intermediary's aggregate business, which makes market entry more difficult.

(99) By signing the recommendation, manufacturers undertook to furnish Fedetab, or a body appointed for the purpose, with a list of the wholesalers they supplied; intermediaries were likewise obliged to supply Fedetab with details of all the purchases they had made in the course of the previous year, so as to facilitate the calculation of their end-of-year rebates. In view of the fact that trade discount rates, end-of-year rebates and terms of payment are all standardised, these practices have the effect of preventing all competition in these three areas between the signatory firms, which are not only fully aware of their competitors sales policy but are also safe in the knowledge that it is identical to their own.

(100) (C) The joint, uniform determination of credit periods has the effect, as in the system before 1 December 1975, of preventing competition in this area.

(101) It has also been argued by Fedetab and some of its members that a certain amount of competition over periods of credit continued to exist in spite of the recommendation, but the Commission's information is that all the manufacturers are tending to shorten their credit periods,

settling down at a fortnight or less. This argument must therefore be rejected.

(102) (d) The same applies to the argument that the recommendation does not impose a standardised form of conduct on all manufacturers and that there are in practice several instances of departures from the table of margins allowed by the Ministry of Economic Affairs, and to the argument that the recommendation does not refer to standardised discounts but maximum discounts. The Commission's research has revealed that all the various manufacturers, none of whom, incidentally, has disclaimed the recommendation or indicated its intention to ignore it, have adopted identical operating methods which are in line with the recommendation.

(103) It is difficult to understand why Fedetab and its members should have drafted and notified a recommendation which they did not intend to be complied with. Moreover, its provisions simply extend agreements and decisions which were current before 1975, for which the present signatories of the recommendation have already several times shown wholehearted support, notably by boycotting GB and Delhaize in 1967 and 1972.

(104) Irrespective of whether or not there is truth in Fedetab's assertion that this action was a justified response to the large stores' demands for credit facilities and permission to stock a smaller number of brands, it is nevertheless clear the effect of the action, being that the large stores withdrew their demands in both cases, could not have been achieved without joint action from the members of Fedetab. Moreover, when Fedetab and its members expressly state that an individual manufacturer is unable to stand up on his own pressure from wholesalers, as regards profit margins or credit facilities, they are recognising the very real impact on wholesalers and retailers of the solidarity which they themselves demonstrated.

(105) 3. For the reasons already set out in II(A)(3) above it cannot be accepted that the restrictions on competition flowing from the recommendation were not appreciable by reason of State intervention in the tobacco industry.

(106) 4. Trade between Member States is liable to be affected by the recommendation for the same reasons as apply to the decisions and agreements described in I(c), whose effects on inter-State trade were considered in II(A)(4).

The recommendation is further likely to influence inter-State trade since its provisions for end-of-year rebates mean that if Belgian and other Community importers and manufacturers who did not sign the recommendation want to sell their products, including products coming from other Member States in Belgium, they find that, in entering the market, they face an additional obstacle in the artificial conditions of competition created by the collective measures of Fedetab and its members - who, it should be recalled, account for more than 90% of the total sales of tobacco products in Belgium. Such manufacturers and importers, in order to obtain the collaboration of Belgian wholesalers - and retailers, in the introduction and sale of their products on the Belgian market, must offer them terms of trade at least as generous as those given by Fedetab, and in particular must give them an end-of-year rebate at least equal to that given under the recommendation, without receiving any benefit in return.

(107) The continuing existence of differences between Member States laws

on tax structure and tax collection (in the latter case, at least until 31 December 1977) and of revenue-producing monopolies in two Community countries other than Belgium do not entitle the private sector to bring in its own methods of curtailing the existing opportunities for trading between Member States (e.g. by large distribution undertakings which are capable of creating channels for parallel imports). Nor is there any evidence to indicate that the measures taken by Fedetab and its members are likely to redress the differences between the different national systems.

(108) The foregoing details show that the decisions and agreements considered in II (A) and (B) above fall under the prohibition contained in Article 85 (1) of the Treaty; the question of exemption under Article 85 (3) must consequently be considered.

*Sequel:*

The parties to whom the Decision was addressed brought an action for annulment before the Court of Justice of the European Communities in Luxembourg, see below page 147. (For technical reasons this case has been reproduced after number (5), the ANSEAU-NAVEWA case).

(6) ANSEAU-NAVEWA cases

IAZ International and others v. Commission, joined cases 96-102, 104, 105, 108 and 110/82, Judgement of 8 November 1983 (not yet published).

*Facts:*

The Commission adopted a Decision (17 December 1981) finding that the system of vetting washing-machines and dishwashers for compliance with Belgian pollution control standards constituted, in its present form, an infringement of Article 85(1). The system was based on an agreement concluded in December 1978 between the majority of washing-machine and dishwasher manufacturers and sole importers in Belgium and Association nationale des Services d'eau - Nationale Vereniging der Waterleidingbedrijven (ANSEAU-NAVEWA), a non-profitmaking body representing the local authority water supply companies.

Under this agreement compliance with the pollution control standards was attested by attaching labels to the machines which could only be obtained throught manufacturers or sole importers. Where other importers were refised labels they had to have an individual inspection carried out, the cost of which was prohibitive in comparison with the selling price of the machines. This made parallel imports into Belgium very difficult, if not impossible.

*The Court held:*

....

18. ANSEAU (Case 108/82) and Miele (Case 110/82) contend, moreover, that the Agreement does not exhibit the characteristics constituting an infringement of Article 85(1) of the Treaty.

19. In the first place, ANSEAU observes that there can be no question of an "agreement between undertakings" within the meaning of the above-mentioned provision. ANSEAU is an association of undertakings which does not itself carry on any economic activity. Article 85(1) of the Treaty is therefore applicable to it only in so far as its members are legally bound by the Agreement. In fact they are not since, under both the Agreement and the statutes of ANSEAU, the latter is empowered only to make recommendations.

20. As the Court has already held, in its judgements of 15 May 1975 in Case 71/74 (Frubo (1975) ECR 563) and of 29 October 1980 in Joined Cases 209 to 215 and 218/78 van Landewuck (1980) ECR 3125, Article 85(1) of the Treaty applies also to associations of undertakings in so far as their own activities or those of the undertakings affiliated to them are calculated to produce the results which it aims to suppress. It is clear particularly from the latter judgement that a recommendation, even if it has no binding effect, cannot escape Article 85(1) where compliance with the recommendation by the undertakings to which it is addressed has a profound influence on competition in the market in question.

21. In the light of that case-law, it must be emphasized, as the Commission has pertinently stated, that the recommendations made by ANSEAU under the Agreement to the effect that its member undertakings were to take account of the terms and of the purpose of the agreement and were to inform consumers thereof, in fact produced a situation in which the water-supply undertakings in the built-up areas of Brussels, Antwerp and Ghent carried out checks on consumers' premises to determine whether machines connected to the water-supply system were provided with a conformity label. Those recommendations therefore determined the conduct of a large number of ANSEAU's members and consequently exerted an appreciable influence on competition.

....

27. It is clear from the foregoing considerations that the Agreement is of such a kind as to make parallel imports of washingmachines and dishwashers more difficult, if not impossible, and that it is therefore capable of affecting trade between Member States. In view of the fact that, according to the observations submitted in these proceedings, signatory undertakings' share of the market is approximately 90% and is therefore very considerable, the conclusion must be drawn that the Agreement had a restrictive effect on competition.

....

(7) Fedetab Cases

Heintz van Landewyck and others v. Commission. Joined Cases 209-215/78 and 218/78, Judgment of 29 October 1980; ECR 3125; (1981) 3 CMLR 134; CCH para. 8687; Competition Law CM/M/I/89.

For the facts see above, page 141.

*The Court held:*

V. Substantive submissions on Article 85(1) of the Treaty

*A. Wrong assessment of the nature and scope of the recommendation*

(85) 85. *Jubilé* and *Vander Elst* maintain that the Commission infringed Articles 85 and 190 of the Treaty by wrongly regarding the recommendation as having constituted an agreement between undertakings or a decision of an association of undertakings or as having imposed obligations on the applicants. To constitute such an agreement the recommendation would have had to involve features making it a binding contract under national law. In the present case it is not such a contract since the binding element is lacking.

(86) 86. That argument cannot be accepted. In the present case the applicant members of Fedetab informed the Commission that they wished to be

party to the notification of the recommendation and during the proceedings before the Court they admitted that they had complied with it since 1 December 1975. It follows that the recommendation is a faithful expression of the applicants' intention to conduct themselves on the Belgian cigarette market in conformity with the terms of the recommendation. The necessary conditions for the application of Article 85(1) are therefore satisfied.

(87) 87. Certain applicants including the intervener Agrotab complain further that the Commission wrongly treated the recommendation as a decision of an association of undertakings within the meaning of Article 85(1). The recommendation is said to have been made by Fedetab, a non-profit-making association which as such does not trade.

(88) 88. That argument cannot be accepted either. It is apparent from Article 8 of the statutes of Fedetab that the decisions taken by it are binding on its members. Further, Article 85(1) also applies to associations in so far as their own activities or those of the undertakings belonging to them are calculated to produce the results which it aims to suppress. Since several manufacturers have expressly stated that they are complying with the provisions of the recommendaiton, it cannot escape Article 85 of the Treaty simply because it has been made by a non-profit-making association.

(89) 89. Nor is it possible to accept the argument to the effect that the recommendation has no binding effect and that the decision is wrong in referring in paragraph 61 to a genuine mandatory rule of conduct for all firms in the industry. Apart from the fact that pursuant to Article 8 of the statutes of Fedetab the provisions of the recommendation are binding on its members, it is necessary also to point out that compliance with the recommendation by seven undertakings, the applicants in the present cases, who control a substantial part of the total cigarette sales in Belgium, has a profound influence on competition in the market in question.

*B. Wrong assessment alleged by the applicant HVL*

(90) 90. The applicant HVL, a Luxembourg cigarette manufacturer, complains of infringement of Articles 85 and 190 of the Treaty with regard to it, inasmuch as the Commission wrongly considered that HVL took concerted action with the other parties in respect of the measures prior to 1 December 1975. In that respect the applicant observes that as regards the period prior to 1 December it did not sign any of the agreements referred to in the decision except the letter of 23 December 1971 laying down the maximum periods allowed for payment. It follows that only the measures referred to in that letter can be held against it. Because of pressure from the Belgian market it fell into line with the conduct of the other Belgian manufacturers and importers, but that did not mean that there could be assumed to be an agreement or concerted practice.

(91) 91. That argument cannot be accepted. The applicant has been a member of Fedetab since 1947 and pursuant to Article 8 of the statutes of Fedetab the applicant had to comply with all the decisions taken pursuant to the said statutes. Further, as has already been observed in relation to the previous measures, Fedetab acted in the name of its members, who took part in the adoption and observance of the said measures through the intermediary of their trade association.

## C. Concerted Practices

### (1) ICI Case

For facts and references see above, pages 44 and 70.

*The Court held:*

51. The applicant complains that the Commission has not proved the existence of concerted practices within the meanong of Article 85(1) of the EEC Treaty in relation to any of the three increases mentioned in the contested decision.

52. That decision states that *prima facie* evidence that the increase of 1964, 1965 and 1967 took place as the result of concerted action is to be found in the facts that the rates introduced for each increase by the different producers in each country were the same, that with very rare exceptions the same dyestuffs were involved, and that the increases were put into effect over only a very short period, if not actually on the same date.

53. It is contended that these increases cannot be explained simply by the oligopolistic character of the structure of the market.

54. It is said to be unrealistic to suppose that without previous concertation the principal producers supplying the Common Market could have increased their prices on several occasions by identical percentages at practically the same moment for one and the same important range of products including speciality products for which there are few, if any, substitutes, and that they should have done so in a number of countries where conditions on the dyestuffs market are different.

55. The Commission has argued before the Court that the interested parties need not necessarily have drawn up a common plan with a view to adopting a certain course of behaviour for it to be said that there has been concertation.

56. It is argued that it is enough that they should have previously informed each other of the attitude which they intended to adopt so that each could regulate his conduct safe in the knowledge that his competitors would act in the same way.

57. The applicant argues that the contested decision is based on an inadequate analysis of the market in the products in question and on an erroneous understanding of the concept of a concerted practice, which is wrongly identified by the decision with the conscious parallelism of members of an oligopoly, whereas such conduct is due to independent decisions adopted by each undertaking, determined by objective business needs, and in particular by the need to increase the unsatisfactorily low rate of profit on the production of dyestuffs.

58. It is argued that in fact the prices of the products in question displayed a constant tendency to fall because of lively competition between producers which is typical of the market in those products, not only as regards the quality of the products and technical assistance to customers, but also as regards prices, particularly the large reductions granted individually to the principal purchasers.

59. The fact that the rates of increase were identical was the result, it is said, of the existence of the 'price-leadership' of one undertaking.

60. It is also argued that the large number of dyestuffs produced by each undertaking makes it impossible in practice to raise prices product by product.

61. A further argument is that different price increases for interchangeable products either could not produce economically significant results because of the limited level of stocks and of the time necessary for adapting plant to appreciably increased demand, or would lead to a ruinous price war.

62. Finally, it is said that dyestuffs for which there are no substitutes form only a small part of the producers' turnover.

63. Taking these market characteristics into account and in view of the widespread and continuous erosion of prices, each member of the oligopoly who decided to increase his prices could, it is argued, reasonably expect to be followed by his competitors, who had the same problems regarding profits.

The concept of a concerted practice

64. Article 85 draws a distinction between the concept of 'concerted practices' and that of 'agreements between undertakings' or of 'decisions by associations of undertakings'; the object is to bring within the prohibition of that article a form of coordination between undertakings which, without having reached the stage where an agreement properly so-called has been concluded, knowingly substitutes practical cooperation between them for the risks of competition.

65. By its very nature, then, a concerted practice does not have all the elements of a contract but may *inter alia* arise out of coordination which becomes apparent from the behaviour of the participants.

66. Although parallel behaviour may not by itself be identified with a concerted practice, it may however amount to strong evidence of such a practice if it leads to conditions of competition which do not correspond to the normal conditions of the market, having regard to the nature of the products, the size and number of the undertakings, and the volume of the said market.

67. This is especially the case if the parallel conduct is such as to enable those concerned to attempt to stabilise prices at a level different from that to which competition would have led, and to consolidate established positions to the detriment of effective freedom of movement of the products in the Common Market and of the freedom of consumers to choose their suppliers.

68. Therefore the question whether there was a concerted action in this case can only be correctly determined if the evidence upon which the contested decision is based is considered, not in isolation, but as a whole, account being taken of the specific features of the market in the products in question.

The characteristic features of the market in dyestuffs

69. The market in dyestuffs is characterised by the fact that 80% of the market is supplied by about ten producers, very large ones in the main, which often manufacture these products together with other chemical products or pharmaceutical specialities.

70. The production patterns and therefore the cost structures of these manufacturers are very different, and this makes it difficult to ascertain competing manufacturers' costs.

71. The total number of dyestuffs is very high, each undertaking producing more than a thousand.

72. The average extent to which these products can be replaced by others is considered relatively good for standard dyes, but it can be very low or even non-existent for speciality dyes.

73. As regards speciality products, the market tends in certain cases towards an oligopolistic situation.

74. Since the price of dyestuffs forms a relatively small part of the price of the final product of the user undertaking, there is little elasticity of demand for dyestuffs on the market as a whole and this encourages price increases in the short term.

75. Another factor is that the total demand for dyestuffs is constantly increasing, and this tends to induce producers to adopt a policy enabling them to take advantage of this increase.

76. In the territory of the Community, the market in dyestuffs in fact consists of five separate national markets with different price levels which cannot be explained by differences in costs and charges affecting producers in these countries.

77. Thus the establishment of the Common Market would not appear to have had any effect on this situation, since the differences between national price levels have scarcely decreased.

78. On the contrary, it is clear that each of the national markets has the characteristics of an oligopoly and that in most of them price levels are established under the influence of a 'priceleader', who in some cases is the largest producer in the country concerned, and in other cases is a producer in another Member State or a third State, acting through a subsidiary.

79. According to the experts this dividing-up of the market is due to the need to supply local technical assistance to users and to ensure immediate delivery, generally in small quantities, since, apart from exceptional cases, producers supply their subsidiaries established in the different Member States and maintain a network of agents and depots to ensure that user undertakings receive specific assistance and supplies.

80. It appears from the data produced during the course of the proceedongs that even in cases where a producer establishes direct contact with an important user in another Member State, prices are usually fixed in relation to the place where the user is established and tend to follow the level of prices on the national market.

81. Although the foremost reason why producers have acted in this way is in order to adapt themselves to the special features of the market in dyestuffs and to the needs of their customers, the fact remains that the dividing-up of the market which results tends, by fragmenting the effects of competition, to isolate users in their national market, and to prevent a general confrontation between producers throughout the Common Market.

82. It is in this context, which is peculiar to the way in which the dyestuffs market works, that the facts of the case should be considered.

The increases of 1964, 1965 and 1967

83. The increases of 1964, 1965 and 1967 covered by the contested decision are interconnected.

84. The increase of 15% in the prices of most aniline dyes in Germany on 1 January 1965 was in reality nothing more than the extension to another national market of the increase applied in January 1964 in Italy, the Netherlands, Belgium and Luxembourg.

85. The increase in the prices of certain dyes and pigments introduced on 1 January 1965 in all the Member States, except France, applied to all the products which had been excluded from the first increase.

86. The reason why the price increase of 8% introduced in the autumn of 1967 was raised to 12% for France was that there was a wish to make up for the increases of 1964 and 1965 in which that market had not taken part because of the price control system.

87. Therefore the three increases cannot be isolated one from another, even though they did not take place under identical conditions.

88. In 1964 all the undertakings in question announced their increases and immediately put them into effect, the intiative coming from Ciba-Italy which, on 7 January 1964, following instructions from Ciba-Switzerland, announced and immediately introduced an increase of 15%. This initiative was followed by the other producers on the Italian market within two or three days.

89. On 9 January ICI Holland took the intiative in introducing the same increase in the Netherlands, whilst on the same day Bayer took the same intiative on the Belgo-Luxembourg market.

90. With minor differences, particularly between the price increases by the German undertakings on the one hand and the Swiss and the United Kingdom undertakings on the other, these increases concerned the same range of products for the various producers and markets, namely, most aniline dyes other than pigments, food colourings and cosmetics.

91. As regards the increase of 1965 certain undertakings announced in advance price increases amounting, for the German market, to an increase of 15% for products whose prices had already been similarly increased on the other markets, and to 10% for products whose prices had not yet been increased. These announcements were spread over the period between 14 October and 28 December 1964.

92. The first announcement was made by BASF, on 14 October 1964, followed

by an announcement by Bayer on 30 October and by Casella on 5 November.

93. These increases were simultaneously applied on 1 January 1965 on all the markets except for the French market because of the price freeze in that State, and the Italian market where, as a result of the refusal by the principal Italian producer, ACNA, to increase its prices on the said market, the other producers also decided not to increase theirs.

94. ACNA also refrained from putting its prices up by 10% on the German market.

95. Otherwise the increase was general, was simultaneously introduced by all the producers mentioned in the contested decision, and was applied without any differences concerning the range of products.

96. As regards the increase of 1967, during a meeting held at Basel on 19 August 1967, which was attended by all the producers mentioned in the contested decision except ACNA, the Geigy undertaking announced its intention to increase its selling prices by 8% with effect from 16 October 1967.

97. On that same occasion the representatives of Bayer and Francolor stated that their undertakings were also considering an increase.

98. From mid-September all the undertakings mentioned in the contested decision announced a price increase of 8%, raised to 12% for France, to take effect on 16 October in all the countries except Italy, where ACNA again refused to increase its prices, although it was willing to follow the movement in prices on two other markets, albeit on dates other than 16 October.

99. Viewed as a whole, the three consecutive increases reveal progressive cooperation between the undertakings concerned.

100. In fact, after the experience of 1964, when the announcement of the increases and their application coincided, although with minor differences as regards the range of products affected, the increases of 1965 and 1967 indicate a different mode of operation. Here, the undertakings taking the initiative, BASF and Geigy respectively, announced their intentions of making an increase some time in advance, which allowed the undertakings to observe each other's reactions on the different markets, and to adapt themselves accordingly.

101. By means of these advance announcements the various undertakings eliminated all uncertainty between them as to their future conduct and, in doing so, also eliminated a large part of the risk usually inherent in any independent change of conduct of one or several markets.

102. This was all the more the case since these announcements, which led to the fixing of general and equal increases in prices for the markets in dyestuffs, rendered the market transparent as regards the percentage rates of increase.

103. Therefore, by the way in which they acted, the undertakings in question temporarily eliminated with respect to prices some of the preconditions for competition on the market which stood in the way of the achievement of parallel uniformity of conduct.

104. The fact that this conduct was not spontaneous is corroborated by an examination of other aspects of the market.

105. In fact, from the number of producers concerned it is not possible to say that the European market in dyestuffs is, in the strict sense, an oligopoly in which price competition could no longer play a substantial role.

106. These producers are sufficiently powerful and numerous to create a considerable risk that in times of rising prices some of them might not follow the general movement but might instead try to increase their share of the market by behaving in an individual way.

107. Furthermore, the dividing-up of the Common Market into five national markets with different price levels and structures makes it improbable that a spontaneous and equal price increase would occur on all the national markets.

108. Although a general, spontaneous increase on each of the national markets is just conceivable, these increases might be expected to differ according to the particular characteristics of the different national markets.

109. Therefore, although parallel conduct in respect of prices may well have been an attractive and risk-free objective for the undertakings concerned, it is hardly conceivable that the same action could be taken spontaneously at the same time, on the same national markets and for the same range of products.

110. Nor is it any more plausible that the increases of January 1964, introduced on the Italian market and copied on the Netherlands and Belgo-Luxembourg markets, which have little in commmon with each other either as regards the level of prices or the pattern of competition, could have been brought into effect within a period of two or three days without prior concertation.

111. As regards the increases of 1965 and 1967 concertation took place openly, since all the announcements of the intention to increase prices with effect from a certain date and for a certain range of products made it possible for producers to decide on their conduct regarding the special cases of France and Italy.

112. In proceeding in this way, the undertakings mutually eliminated in advance any uncertainties concerning their reciprocal behaviour on the different markets and thereby also eliminated a large part of the risk inherent in any independent change of conduct on those markets.

113. The general and uniform increase on those different markets can only be explained by a common intention on the part of those undertakings, first, to adjust the level of prices and the situation resulting from competition in the form of discounts, and secondly, to avoid the risk, which is inherent in any price increase, of changing the conditions of competition.

114. The fact that the price increases announced were not introduced in Italy and that ACNA only partially adopted the 1967 increase in other markets, far from undermining this conclusion, tends to confirm it.

115. The function of price competition is to keep prices down to the lowest possible level and to encourage the movement of goods between the Member States, thereby permitting the most efficient possible distribution of activities in the matter of productivity and the capacity of undertakings to adapt themselves to change.

116. Differences in rates encourage the pursuit of one of the basic objectives of the Treaty, namely the interpenetration of national markets and, as a result, direct access by consumers to the sources of production of the whole Community.

117. By reason of the limited elasticity of the market in dyestuffs, resulting from factors such as lack of transparency with regard to prices, the interdependence of the different dyestuffs of each producer for the purpose of building up the range of products used by each consumer, the relatively low proportion of the cost of the final product of the user undertaking represented by the prices of these products, the fact that it is useful for users to have a local supplier and the influence of transport costs, the need to avoid any action which might artificially reduce the opportunities for interpenetration of the various national markets at the consumer level becomes particularly important on the market in the products in question.

118. Although every producer is free to change his prices, taking into account in so doing the present or foreseeable conduct of his competitors, nevertheless it is contrary to the rules on competition contained in the Treaty for a producer to cooperate with his competitors, in any way whatsoever, in order to determine a coordinated course of action relating to a price increase and to ensure its success by prior elimination of all uncertainty as to each other's conduct regarding the essential elements of that action, such as the amount, subject-matter, date and place of the increases.

119. In these circumstances and taking into account the nature of the market in the products in question, the conduct of the applicant, in conjunction with other undertakings against which proceedings have been taken, was designed to replace the risks of competition and the hazards of competitors' spontaneous reactions by cooperation constituting a concerted practice prohibited by Article 85(1) of the Treaty.

(2) Decision in re European Sugar Industry

For facts see page 94, for references page 222.

*The Commission ruled:*

B. 1. The undertakings Suiker Unie and Centrale Suiker Mij, on the one hand, and Raffinerie Tirlemontoise and Pfeifer & Langen, on the other hand, have engaged in a concerted practice regarding deliveries of sugar to the Dutch market.

This concerted practice consists in the fact that the Dutch producers have been buying sugar direct from the Belgian and German producers and reselling it at the same prices and on the same conditions of sale as sugar from their national output. The operation of this concerted practice by the parties concerned is seen with regard to deliveries of Belgian sugar, in the correspondence which shows clearly that Raffinerie Tirlemontoise must not make any delivery to Holland without the consent of the Dutch producers, and in the way in which Raffinerie

Tirlemontoise has compelled its exporters not to deliver to Holland without the consent of the Dutch producers or solely for particular uses not only its own sugar but also that of the other Belgian producers. All other deliveries of Belgian sugar to Holland have been made, by agreement between the producers solely to specific buyers (the Dutch dairy industry). With regard to German sugar the concerted practice results from the fact that Pfeifer & Langen has made deliveries to Dutch producers systematically and in increasing quantities, without there being any other deliveries in appreciable quantities apart from them.

The basic principle of the concerted practice between Raffinerie Tirlemontoise and the two Dutch producers, Suiker Unie and Centrale Suiker Mij, whereby Raffinerie Tirlemontoise, did not, apart from the deliveries intended for its competitors, want to make sugar available for export to Holland during the 1968-69 and 1969-70 seasons, has been confirmed on several occasions and appears in particular in a letter from Raffinerie Tirlemontoise to Exportation de Sucre SA, which states: 'With regard to Holland, the basic principle is that we do not want to do anything that could go against Suiker Unie or Centrale Suiker Mij, just as they do not want to do anything that would disturb us'.

The object or effect of this concerted practice is to prevent, restrict or distort competition within the common market.

In fact all competition in the Dutch market has been eliminated between the above-mentioned Belgian and German suppliers and the Dutch producers. In these sales between producers, the Belgian and German undertakings in question, which are better placed geographically, would sell their sugar individually on the Dutch market, fixing the prices and conditions of sale themselves and using their own marks. Thus in respect of the quantities sold to their competitors, the producers sacrifice an independent commercial activity in the Dutch market.

Moreover, these sales between producers enable Dutch producers to obtain larger quantities of sugar and then to resell them (sugar is largely a homogeneous product) at the same prices and on the same conditions as their own sugar.

Furthermore, with regard, more particularly, to deliveries of Belgian sugar, the parties concerned have claimed that some of the deliveries from Raffinerie Tirlemontoise to Centrale Suiker Mij are made in execution of a contract whereby Raffinerie Tirlemontoise produces lump-sugar that dissolves rapidly for Centrale Suiker Mij which does not have the installations necessary for this production and that other sales made by Raffinerie Tirlemontoise serve to complement the range of qualities of sugar sold by Centrale Suiker Mij. Nevertheless, Raffinerie Tirlemontoise abstains from selling these same sugars in Holland. Consequently, the Dutch users no longer have any opportunity for choice in respect of these sugars, since they are deprived of a direct supply of these sugars from Raffinerie Tirlemontoise. Apart from these deliveries of sugar of special qualities, Raffinerie Tirlemontoise also delivers appreciable quantities of white sugar to the Centrale Suiker Mij which resells it on the same conditions as the sugar that it produces itself.

With regard to the deliveries of sugar from Raffinerie Tirlemontoise to Suiker Unie, the parties concerned have claimed that some of these deliveries relate to sugar intended for denaturation. However, even if the use of the sugar thus sold is limited to the partial market of animal foodstuffs, the users of sugar for this market see the number of offers that are made to them restricted and therefore have a more limited, if not non-existent, choice. Only a minimal part of the sales made by Raffinerie Tirlemontoise to Suiker Unie relates to sugar intended for denaturation. Nevertheless, most of the sugar sold by Raffinerie

Tirlemontoise to Suiker Unie is white sugar delivered in bags which are supplied beforehand by Suiker Unie to Raffinerie Tirlemontoise.

Normally a producer has no incentive to sell products in large quantities to one or more of his competitors. He can obtain a bigger profit by delivering direct to the wholesalers and users concerned. The deliveries are therefore explained by the fact that they have constituted an effective method for restricting competition between the parties concerned and preventing Dutch users from getting the sugar that they want freely from foreign suppliers. The restrictions on competition resulting from the deliveries between producers are particularly serious because they relate to a substantial proportion of the quantities of sugar exchanged between the countries concerned.

Moreover, competition in the Dutch market has been restricted by the fact that Raffinerie Tirlemontoise does not make deliveries of sugar without the consent of its competitors, Suiker Unie and Centrale Suiker Mij. The Dutch producers have mainly given their consent solely for deliveries to the dairy industry since most of the sugar supplied to this industry is used in products derived from milk and does not have any competitive effect on the sale of the Dutch producers' output.

The concerted practice in question has been pursued during the 1970-71 and 1971-72 seasons, by compelling the Belgian and Dutch wholesalers to participate in these concerted deliveries. This follows from the contracts concluded with these wholesalers and the way in which they have been performed. From the 1970-71 season onwards the possible sources of supply for these wholesalers have therefore been restricted by the fact that Raffinerie Tirlemontoise has prevented the Belgian wholesalers from supplying Holland with the sugar from the output of other Belgian producers.

This concerted practice intended to prevent Belgian and German sugar from being delivered freely to the Dutch market in competition with the sugar from the Dutch producers constitutes a restriction of competition capable of affecting trade between the Member States.

Consequently it is covered by the prohibition contained in Article 85(1) of the Treaty. This concerted practice cannot be the subject of a declaration of exemption under Article 85(3) quite simply because it has not been notified to the Commission in accordance with Article 4(1) of Regulation No 17.

*The Commission decided:*

.....

Article 1

(1) It is held that the following breaches of Article 85(1) of the Treaty instituting the European Economic Community have been committed:

Eridania. Societá Generale di Zuccherifici, Cavarzere-Produzioni Industriali, Societá per l'Industria degli Zuccheri Romana Zucchero, Zuccherificio del Volano, Agricola Industriale Emiliana (AIE), SADAM, Zuccherificio di Sermide, on the one hand, and Sucres & Denrées, Béghin, Sucre-Union, Say, Générale Sucrière, Lebaudy-SUC, Raffinerie Tirlemontoise and Süddeutsche Zucker AG, on the other hand, have, since the end of the 1968-69 season, committed breaches of Article 85(1) by engaging in a concerted practice with the object and effect of controlling the deliveries of sugar to the Italian market and consequently protecting that market; Suiker Unie and Centrale Suiker Maatschappij, on the one hand, and Raffinerie Tirlemontoise and Pfeifer & Langen, on the other hand, have since the 1968-69 season (Pfeifer & Langen only from the

1970-71 season onwards), committed breaches of Article 85(1) by engaging in a concerted practice with the object and effect of controlling the deliveries of sugar to the Dutch market from Belgium and the western part of Germany and consequently protecting this market; Pfeifer & Langen, on the one hand, and Raffinerie Tirlemontoise, on the other hand, have, from the 1969-70 season onwards, committed breaches of Article 85(1) by engaging in a concerted practice with the object and effect of controlling the deliveries of Belgian sugar to the market of the western part of Germany and consequently protecting that market; Süddeutsche Zucker AG and Franken, on the one hand, and Béghin and Sucre-Union, on the other hand, have, from the 1970-71 season onwards, committed breaches of Article 85(1) by engaging in a concerted practice with the object and effect of controlling the deliveries of French sugar to the market of the southern part Germany and consequently protecting that market.

It is held that the following measures, which have been found to exist in the context of the concerted practices described above, constitute in themselves breaches of Article 86 or Article 85(1) of the Treaty;

1. Raffinerie Tirlemontoise has, from the 1968-69 season onwards, committed a breach of Article 86 by bringing economic pressure to bear on the Belgian exporters to compel them to restrict their exports;

2. Suiker Unie and Centrale Suiker Maatschappij have during the 1969-70 season, committed breaches of Article 86 by bringing economic pressure to bear on the Dutch importing and exporting within the Community.

3. Südzucker Verkaufs-GmbH has, from the 1968-69 season onwards, committed breaches of Article 86 by preventing its intermediaries from reselling sugar from other sources and by trying its customers by means of loyalty discounts;

4. Westdeutsche Zuckervertriebsgesellschaft and Pfeifer & Langen have, from 1968-69 season onwards, committed breaches of Article 85(1) by concluding agreements with their intermediaries restricting their possibilities of importing and exporting within the Community.

It has been established that Raffinerie Tirlemontoise, Say, Béghin, Générale Sucrière, Lebaudy-SUC, Sucre-Union and Sucres & Denrées committed breaches of Article 85(1) in 1970 by concerting, at the time of the allocations for subsidies on exports to non-member countries, with regard to the amount of subsidies requested and the quantities offered.

Article 2

The above-mentioned undertakings are required to discontinue the said breaches immediately.

Article 3

1. The following fines are imposed:

(a) with regard to Raffinerie Tirlemontoise, a fine of 1,500,000 units of account;

(b) with regard to Sucres & Denrées, a fine of 1,000,000 units of account;

(c) with regard to Société des Raffineries et Sucreries Say, a fine of 500,000 units of account;

(d) with regard to F. Béghin SA, a fine of 700,000 units of account;

(e) with regard to La Générale Sucrière SA, a fine of 400,000 units of account;

(f) with regard to Eridania Zuccherifici Nazionali SpA, a fine of 1,000, 000 units of account;

(g) with regard to Società Italiana per l'Industria degli Zuccheri SpA, a fine of 300,000 units of account;

(h) with regard to Cavarzere-Produzioni Industrali, a fine of 200,000 units of account;

(i) with regard to Agricola Industriale Emiliana (AIE) SpA, a fine of 100,000 units of account;

(j) with regard to Zuccherificio del Volano SpA, a fine of 100,000 units of account;

(k) with regard to SADAM SpA, a fine of 100,000 units of account;

(l) with regard to Cooperatieve Vereniging Suiker Unie UA, a fine of 800,000 units of account;

(m) with regard to Centrale Suiker Maatschappij NV, a fine of 600,000 units of account;

(n) with regard to Pfeifer & Langen, a fine of 800,000 units of account;

(o) with regard to Süddeutsche Zucker AG, a fine of 700,000 units of account;

(p) with regard to Südzucker Verkaufs-GmbH, a fine of 200,000 units of account.

2. This decision is enforceable in accordance with Article 192 of the EEC Treaty with regard to the undertakings on which a fine has been imposed.

Article 4
The present decision is addressed to the following undertakings: (ommitted).

*Sequel*

Sixteen firms appealed to the Court of Justice. The Court gave judgment on 16 December 1975, joining the cases for purposes of the judgment (Cases 40 to 48, 50, 54, 56, 111, 113 and 114/73).

Essentially, the judgment upheld by the Commission's findings as regards the firms' infringement of the rules of competition, notably through market sharing. An exception was made for the Italian market. Disagreeing with the Commission, the Court concluded that the measures taken by the Italian governement to control sugar imports - formation of the Cassa conguaglio zucchero, the imposition of a levy (sovraprezzo) and the tendering procedure for imports - places business under such a tight rein that there was no longer any scope for independent action. The Court therefore decided that concerted action by the Italian, French,

Belgian and German firms, in question could not be regarded as infringing Article 85(1). It should be noted here, incidentally, that in 1975 the Commission initiated proceedings against the Italian Government under Article 169 for these measures.

As regards a number of other alleged infringements, the Court concluded that the Commission had not provided its case. Nevertheless, the judgment as a whole confirmed the Commission's findings and conclusions.

However, the Court made a sharp cut in the fines imposed by the Commission, bringing them down to 1,590,000 u.a. in all. It did this because, in assessing the gravity of the infringements, the Commission had not paid sufficient attention to the fact that competition between firms was already restricted by the common organisation of the sugar market, under which national production quotas are fixed.

In this judgment, the Court had occasion to rule on a number of questions of principle which are of definite importance to the development of Community competition law.

It began by considering the elements of a concerted practice, elaborating upon its definition of the concept in the judgments it delivered on 14 July 1973 in the Dyestuffs cases. The Court defines 'concerted practice' as a form of coordination between firms whereby, without going so far as to conclude a formal agreement, they knowingly eliminate the risk of competition by cooperating to ensure that normal market conditions (given the nature of the goods, the size and number of firms concerned and the size and nature of the relevant market) no longer obtain. Cooperation of this type constitutes a concerted practice, particularly when it enables the firms concerned to crystalise positions they have secured to the detriment of free movement of goods in the common market and freedom of consumers to choose their suppliers.

Here, the Court expressly dismissed the notion that concerted action requires some kind of plan to be prepared: criteria for cooperation set out in the judgment are to be understood in the light of the requirement - inherent in the EEC Treaty rules on competition - that each trader must independently decide the policy he proposes to follow on the common market. Above all, although this requirement does not deny traders the right to adapt intelligently to the way their competitors are behaving or can be expected to behave, it does absolutely rule out any direct or indirect contact between traders where the object or effect is either to influence the market conduct of an existing or potential competitor or to reveal to him market policy decisions or intentions.

Finally, it was held that for the identification of a concerted practice the factors mentioned by the Commission must not be taken in isolation but must be considered together, with due regard for the nature of the relevant market. The Court thus approved the legal approach adopted by the Commission in seeking to establish the existence of a concerted practice, relying on a series of indicators such as deliveries from manufacturer to manufacturer and pressures exerted on dealers or refusal to supply. It stated, for instance, that 'if an economic operator accepts the complaints made to him by another operator in connection with the competition to which the products manufactured by the former operator expose the latter, the conduct of the operator concerned amounts to a concerted practice'.

In this connection the Court considered the evidential value of documents submitted by the Commission for the purpose of proving the existence of the offending concerted practice.

(3) Züchner Case

Züchner v. Bayerische Vereinsbank, Case 172/80, preliminary ruling of 14 July 1981; (1981) ECR 2021; (1982) 1 CMLR 313; CCH para. 8706; Competition Law CM/M/I/96.

*Facts:* Mr. Züchner, the plaintiff in the main action, has an account with the Bayerische Vereinsbank AG, the defendant in the main action, at Rosenheim in the Federal Republic of Germany. On 17 July 1979 he drew a cheque on the defendant bank in the amount of DM 10 000 in favour of a payee resident in Italy. For this a 'service charge' of DM 15, representing 0.15% of the sum transferred, was debited to his account by the defendant.

Mr. Züchner sued the Bayerische Vereinsbank AG before the Amtsgericht Rosenheim for repayment of the charge. He maintains, *inter alia,* that the imposition of the 'service charge' is incompatible with Article 67 of the EEC Treaty because it introduces discrimination between transfers of capital within the country and transfers abroad, and with the competition rules in the Treaty because it is a practice followed by all the banks, or most of them, both in Germany and in the other Community countries and is liable to affect trade between Member States.

The Amtsgericht considered that Article 67 of the EEC Treaty was not relevant to a decision in this case, being a provision which binds only the Member States and has no direct effect as regards citizens of the European Economic Community. It allowed that that was not so, however, in the case of Articles 85 and 86 of the EEC Treaty because they are also binding on citizens of the Common Market. By an order dated 14 July 1980, therefore, it stayed the proceedings and requested a ruling from the Court of Justice on the following question:

'In transfers of capital and other payments between banks within the Common Market, is the debiting of a general service charge at the rate of 0.15% of the sum transferred a concerted practice which may affect trade, and therefore contrary to Articles 85 and 86 of the EEC Treaty?'

*The Court held:*

12. As the Court has stated, in particular in its judgment of 14 July 1972 (Case 48/69 *Imperial Chemical Industries Ltd.* v. *Commission* (1972) ECR 619) a concerted practice within the meaning of Article 85(1) of the Treaty is a form of coordination between undertakings which, without having reached the stage where an agreement properly so-called has been concluded, knowingly substitutes practical cooperation between them for the risks of competition.

13. The Court also stated, in its judgment of 16 December 1975 (Joined Cases 40 to 48, 50, 54 to 56, 111, 113 and 114/73, *Suiker Unie* v. *Commission* (1975) ECR 1663, at p. 1942) that the criteria of coordination and cooperation necessary for the existence of a concerted practice in no way require the working out of an actual 'plan' but must be understood in the light of the concept inherent in the provisions of the Treaty relating to competition, according to which each trader must determine independently the policy which he intends to adopt on the Common Market and the conditions which he intends to offer to his customers.

14. Although it is correct to say that this requirement of independence does not deprive traders of the right to adapt themselves intelligently to the existing or anticipated conduct of their competitors, it does

however strictly preclude any direct or indirect contact between such traders, the object or effect of which is to create conditions of competition which do not correspond to the normal conditions of the market in question, regard being had to the nature of the products or services offered, the size and number of the undertakings and the volume of the said market.

15. The applicant in the main proceedings is of the opinion that in this case there is a concerted practice consisting in the debiting by all or most banks within the Common Market or at least in the Federal Republic of Germany, of a uniform service charge for transfers of sums of a similar amount to other Member States.

16. The defendant in the main proceedings has not denied that, for transfers of funds of this nature a charge at the same rate is imposed by other banks, both in the Federal Republic of Germany and in other Member States. It has however pointed out that this similarity of conduct is not the result of an agreement or concerted practice between those banks, the object or effect of which is to produce results prohibited by Article 85 of the Treaty. It has explained that the justification for imposing the charge lies in the costs involved in such transfers owing in particular to the complex nature of the exchange transactions involved, and it has observed, in addition, that the charge uniformly levied in respect of every transfer above a certain amount represents only a partial contribution towards the total cost of the transfers usually effected.

17. The fact that the charge in question is justified by the costs involved in all transfers abroad normally effected by banks on behalf of their customers, and that it therefore represents partial reimbursement of such costs, debited uniformly to all those who make use of such service, does not exclude the possibility that parallel conduct in that sphere may, regardless of the motive, result in coordination between banks which amounts to a concerted practice within the meaning of Article 85 of the Treaty.

18. Such a practice is capable, precisely because of the fact that it covers international transactions, of affecting 'trade between Member States' within the meaning of the above-mentioned article, the concept of 'trade' used in that article having a wide scope which includes monetary transactions.

19. Moreover, it would fall within the prohibition in Article 85(1) of the Treaty if it were established that its object or effect was to affect significantly conditions of competition in the market in monetary transfers by banks from one Member State to another.

20. That would be the case, in particular, if a concerted practice enabled the banks participating in it to congeal conditions in their present state thus depriving their customers of any genuine opportunity to take advantages of services on more favourable terms which would be offered to them under normal conditions of competition.

21. That is a question of fact which only the court adjudicating on the substance of the case has jurisdiction to decide. In doing so, it must consider whether between the banks conducting themselves in like manner there are contacts or, at least, exchanges of information on the subject of, *inter alia*, the rate of the charges actually imposed for comparable

transfers which have been carried out or are planned for the future and whether, regard being had to the conditions of the market in question, the rate of charge uniformly imposed is no different from that which would have resulted from the free play of competition. Consideration must also be given to the number and importance in the market in monetary transactions between Member States of the banks participating in such a practice, and the volume of transfers on which the charge in question is imposed as compared with the total volume of transfers made by the banks from one Member Country to another.

22. On all those grounds, the reply to the question which has been referred to the Court must be that parallel conduct in the debiting of a uniform bank charge on funds amounts to a concerted practice prohibited by Article 85(1) of the Treaty if it is established by the national court that such parallel conduct exhibits the features of coordination and cooperation characteristic of such a practice and if that practice is capable of significantly affecting conditions of competition in the market for the services connected with such transfers.

## D. Object or Effect

### (1) LTM v. MBU Case

For facts see above, page 69.

The effects of the agreement on competition

Finally, for the agreement at issue to be caught by the prohibition contained in Article 85(1) it must have as its 'object or effect the prevention, restriction or distortion of competition within the Common Market'.

The fact that these are not cumulative but alternative requirements, indicated by the conjunction 'or', leads first to the need to consider the precise purpose of the agreement, in the economic context in which it is to be applied. This interference with competition referred to in Article 85(1) must result from all or some of the clauses of the agreement itself. Where, however, an analysis of the said clauses does not reveal the effect on competition to be sufficiently deleterious, the consequences of the agreement should then be considered and for it to be caught by the prohibition it is then necessary to find that those factors are present which show that competition has in fact been prevented or restricted or distorted to an appreciable extent.

The competition in question must be understood within the actual context in which it would occur in the absence of the agreement in dispute. In particular it may be doubted whether there is an interference with competition if the said agreement seems really necessary for the penetration of a new area by an undertaking. Therefore, in order to decide whether an agreement containing a clause 'granting an exclusive right of sale' is to be considered as prohibited by reason of its object or of its effect, it is appropriate to take into account in particular the nature and quantity, limited or otherwise, of the products covered by the agreement, the position and importance of the grantor and the concessionaire on the market for the products concerned, the isolated nature of the disputed agreement or, alternatively, its position in a series of agreements, the severity of the clauses intended to protect the exclusive dealership or, alternatively, the opportunities allowed for other commercial competitors in the same products by way of parallel re-exportation and importation.

## (2) Consten - Grundig Case

For facts and references see above, page 66.

*The Court held:*

.....

The applicants and the German Governement maintain that since the Commission restricted its examination solely to Grundig products the decision was based upon a false concept of competition and of the rules on prohibition contained in Article 85(1), since this concept applies particularly to competition between similar products of different makes; the Commission, before declaring Article 85(1) to be applicable, should, by basing itself upon the 'rule of reason', have considered the economic effects of the disputed contrast upon competition between the different makes. There is a presumption that vertical sole distributorship agreements are not harmful to competition and in the present case there is nothing to invalidate that presumption. On the contrary, the contract in question has increased the competition between similar products of different makes.

The principle of freedom of competition concerns the various stages and manifestations of competition. Although competition between producers is generally more noticeable than that between distributors of products of the same make, it does not thereby follow that an agreement tending to restrict the latter kind of competition should escape the prohibition of Article 85(1) merely because it might increase the former.

Besides, for the purpose of applying Article 85(1), there is no need to take account of the concrete effects of an agreement once it appears that it has as its object the prevention, restriction or distortion of competition.

Therefore the absence in the contested decision of any analysis of the effects of the agreement on competition between similar products of different makes does not, of itself, constitute a defect in the decision.

.....

## (3) Decision in re WEA-Filipacchi

For facts and references see above, page 112.

*The Commission ruled:*

.....

2. These agreeements aim at preventing the export of records distributed in France by WEA-Filipacchi Music SA to other Member States, particularly to Germany. Consequently they have the object of restricting the competition which the French re-sellers could exercise by exporting these records to Germany.

3. Contrary to the argument relied on by WEA-Filipacchi Music SA, this is not a mere attempt to infringe Article 85(1) but a completed violation. The violation is already complete when an agreement has the object of restricting competition, even if it has not yet had that effect. The objection that the agreement would not have had any effect, particularly because WEA-Filipacchi Music SA would not have been able to obtain judicial enforcement by the imposition of sanctions on those re-sellers who continued to export, is relevant in this instance only for the determination of the amount of the fines.

.....

## (4) First Brasserie de Haecht Case

Brasserie de Haecht v. Wilkin-Janssen
Preliminary Ruling of 12 December 1967, Case 23/67; (1967) ECR 407; (1968) CMLR 26; CCH para. 8053; Competition Law CM/M/III/8.

*Facts:* In 1963 Brasserie de Haecht, whose registered office is at Boortmeerbeek in Belgium, concluded three loan contracts with Oscar Wilkin and his wife Marie Wilkin (née Janssen), the proprietors of a café in Esneux. Under the terms of these contracts, the borrowers undertook to obtain supplies of beer, liquors and soft drinks exclusively from the De Haecht brewery, both for their personal needs and for the purpose of their business.
The period of exclusive purchase in favour of the brewery was to extend at least for as long as the debt was not wholly paid off, plus an additional period of two years. A minimum period of exclusive purchase was stipulated, whatever the length of time taken to repay the debt.

In 1966 Brasserie de Haecht discovered that Mr and Mrs Wilkin had not complied with the exclusive purchase obligation contained in the contract with the brewery comprising the three agreements mentioned above. It brought an action before the Tribunal de Commerce, Liège, for repayment of the loans, the return of the furniture and the payment of damages. In their defence Mr and Mrs Wilkin did not dispute that they had obtained supplies of liquor from other undertakings but pleaded that the agreements in dispute were void under Article 85 of the EEC Treaty. In its judgment of 8 May 1967, the Tribunal de Commerce, Liège, considered that the Community rules (Regulation 67/67/EEC of 22 March 1967, Official Journal of 25 March 1967, p. 849) on the application of Article 85(3) of the Treaty to certain categories of exclusive dealing agreements were not applicable to the dispute pending before it. However, the Tribunal de Commerce held that the exclusive dealing in question arose from an agreement between undertakings and that 'Article 85 does not refer in so many words to a collection of agreements of the same type among the agreements or practices which are prohibited, but the list which it does contain is not exhaustive, and it is possible that the prohibition of certain agreements might be justified by the simultaneous existence of identical agreements which, considered as a whole, affect trade between the Member States of the Common Market'.

The Tribunal de Commerce therefore considered it desirable for the Court of Justice to give an interpretation of Article 85 within the framework of the procedure provided for by Article 177 of the Treaty. Consequently, it put the following preliminary question:

'In order to judge whether the contracts in question are prohibited by Article 85 (1) of the Treaty of Rome, it is necessary to take into account the economic context and the whole of the market, that is to say, in this case, the simultaneous existence of a large number of contracts of the same type imposed by a small number of Belgian breweries upon a very large proportion of liquor licensees or must consideration be limited to an examination of the effects on the market of the said agreements considered in isolation?'

2. The prohibition in Article 85(1) of the Treaty rests on three factors essential for a reply to the question referred. After stating the limits within which the prohibition is to apply, Article 85(1) mentions agreements, decisions and practices. By referring in the same sentence to agreements between undertakings, decisions by associations of undertakings and concerted practices, which may involve many parties, Article

85(1) implies that the constituent elements of those agreements, decisions and practices may be considered together as a whole.

3. Furthermore, by basing its application to agreements, decisions or practices, not only on their subject matter but also on their effects in relation to competition, Article 85(1) implies that regard must be had to such effects in the context in which they occur, that is to say, in the economic and legal context of such agreements, decisions or practices and where they might combine with others to have a cumulative effect on competition. In fact, it would be pointless to consider an agreement, decision or practice by reason of its effects if those effects were to be taken distinct from the market in which they are seen to operate and could only be examined apart from the body of effects, whether convergent or not, surrounding their implementation. Thus in order to examine whether it is caught by Article 85(1) an agreement cannot be examined in isolation from the above context, that is from the factual or legal circumstances causing it to prevent, restrict or distort competition. The existence of similar contracts may be taken into consideration for this objective to the extent to which the general body of contracts of this type is capable of restricting the freedom of trade.

4. Lastly, it is only to the extent to which agreements, decisions or practices are capable of affecting trade between Member States that the alteration of competition comes under Community prohibitions. In order to satisfy this condition, it must be possible for the agreement, decision or practice, when viewed in the light of a combination of the objective, factual or legal circumstances, to appear to be capable of having some influence, direct or indirect, on trade between Member States, of being conducive to a partitioning of the market and of hampering the economic interpretation sought by the Treaty. When this point is considered the agreement, decision or practice cannot therefore be isolated from all the others of which it is one.

The existence of similar contracts is a circumstance which, together with others, is capable of being a factor in the economic and legal context within which the contract must be judged. Accordingly, whilst such a situation must be taken into account it should not be considered as decisive by itself, but merely as one among others in judging whether trade between Member States is capable of being affected through any alteration in competition.

*The Court decided:*

.....

Agreements whereby an undertaking agrees to obtain its supplies from one undertaking to the exclusion of all others do not by their very nature necessarily include all the elements constituting incompatibility with the Common Market as referred to in Article 85(1) of the Treaty. Such agreements may, however, exhibit such elements where, taken either in isolation or together with others, and in the economic and legal context in which they are made on the basis of a set of objective factors of law or of fact, they may affect trade between Member States and where they have either as their object or effect the prevention, restriction or distortion of competition;

.....

*Sequel:*

In 1971 the Commercial Court of Liège asked for a second preliminary ruling. The Court of Justice answered the questions of the Liège court in its ruling of the second Brasserie de Haecht Case,(Case 48/72).

## E. Prevention, Restriction or Distortion of Competition

### A. General

It is submitted that in the practical application of Article 85 there is no substantial difference between the use of the concepts prevention, restriction or distortion of competition. No specific significance can be given to the use of any of the three concepts by the Commission of the Court of Justice.

### B. Cases

#### (1) Decision in re Consten-Grundig

Decision of the Commission of 23 December 1964 on a proceeding under Article 85 of the Treaty; J.O. No 161, 20 October 1964, p. 2545; (1964) CMLR 489; CCH para. 2021,51; Competition Law CM/M/I/4.

For facts see above, page 66.

*The Commission decided:*

.....

The objection has been raised that competition plays such an important part at the production stage that a distortion of competition cannot possibly result from the appointment of a sole distributor.

When products are channelled through several stages of distribution it is sufficient, in order to establish restriction of competition within the meaning of Article 85(1), for competition to be prevented or restricted at one of these stages only. The fact that Article 85(1) juxtaposes the term "prevent" and "restrict" shows, as does the wording of Article 85(3) (b) that it is not necessary, for Article 85(1) to apply, that all forms of competition at all the stages of distribution be prevented.

#### (2) The Consten-Grundig Case

For facts and references see above, page 66.

*The Court held:*

.....

It thus remains to consider whether the contested decision was right in founding the prohibition of the disputed agreement under Article 85 (1) on the restriction on competition created by the agreement in the sphere of the distribution of Grundig products alone. The infringement which was found to exist by the contested decision results from the absolute territorial protection created the said contract in favour of Consten on the basis of French law. The applicants thus wished to eliminate any possibility of competition at the wholesale level in Grundig products in the territory specified in the contract essentially by two methods.

First, Grundig undertook not to deliver even indirectly to third parties products intended for the area covered by the contract. The restrictive nature of that undertaking is obvious if it is considered in the light of the prohibition on exporting which was imposed not only on Consten but also on all the other sole concessionaires of Grundig, as well as the German wholesalers. Secondly, the registration in France by Consten of the GINT trademark, which Grundig affixes to all its products, is intended to increase the protection inherent in the disputed agreement, against the risk of parallel imports into France of Grundig products, by adding the protection deriving from the law on industrial property rights. Thus no third party could import Grundig products from other Member States of the Community for resale in France without running serious risks.

The defendent properly took into account the whole distribution system thus set up by Grundig. In order to arrive at a true representation of the contractual position the contract must be placed in the economic and legal context in the light of which it was concluded by the parties. Such a procedure is not to be regarded as an unwarrentable interference in legal transactions or circumstances which were not the subject of the proceedings before the Commission.

The situation as ascertained above results in the isolation of the French market and makes it impossible to charge for the products in question prices which are sheltered from all effective competition. In addition, the more producers succeed in their efforts to render their own makes of product individually distinct in the eyes of the consumer, the more the effectiveness of competition between producers tends to diminish. Because of the considerable impact of distribution costs on the aggregate cost price, it seems important that competition between dealers should also be stimulated. The efforts of the dealer are stimulated by competition between distributors of products of the same make. Since the agreement thus aims at isolating the French market for Grundig products and maintaining artificially, for products of a very well-known brand, separate national markets within the Community it is therefore such as to distort competition in the Common Market.

It was therefore proper for the contested decision to hold that the agreement constitutes an infringement of Article 85(1). No further considerations, whether of economic data (price differences between France and Germany, representative character of the type of appliance considered, level of overheads borne by Consten) or of the corrections of the criteria upon which the Commission relied in its comparisons between the situations of the French and German markets, and no possible favourable effects of the agreement in other respects, can in any way lead, in the face of the above-mentioned restrictions to a different solution under Article 85(1).

## F. Relevant Market

### (1) Decision on the DRU-Blondel agreement

Decision of the Commission of 17 July 1965, cn a proceeding under Article 85 of the Treaty. O.J. No 131, 17 July 1965, p. 2194; (1965) CMLR 242; CCH para. 9049; Competition Law CM/M/I/6.

*Facts:* The Decision concerns an agreement under which the firm of Diepenbrock and Reigers NV (DRU) of Ulft, Netherlands, who make among other things enamelled household utensils, has granted Etablissements Blondel SA of Paris sole selling rights for these products in France. Neither Blondel nor other purchasers are forbidden to export DRU's products. Rival imports to France are neither excluded by the agreement with Blondel nor by agreements between the producers and dealers in other Member States.

The Commission did find that the agreement has the purpose of restraining competition within the meaning of Article 85(1). In addition, it holds that the agreement is also likely to affect trade between the Member States, since it lays down conditions governing the imports of the products concerned into France from the Netherlands. Nevertheless the Commission is of the opinion that exclusive dealing improves the distribution of goods. It also considers that consumers have a fair share of the benefits resulting from such improvement, for French consumers can obtain the products manufactured in the Netherlands more quickly and easily through the firm that has sole selling rights, and the fact that it is still possible to obtain imports (i.e. rival imports) without going through the latter firms means that there cannot be any significant difference between the price of DRU goods in the Netherlands and in France.

*The Commission ruled:*

Whereas the agreement referred to has been made between enterprises and whereas as a result of it DRU has undertaken to supply only Blondel in the territory covered by the contract, thus preventing any French enterprose other than Blondel from buying DRU's products directly from DRU.

Whereas goods comparable to those produced by DRU can enter the market in question and circulate in it and whereas therefore competition at the production stage is not prevented; whereas, however, for the goods in question, the products of the various manufacturers are individualised by their characteristics; whereas such individualisation, which is emphasised by a brand, enables users to show a preference; whereas for that reason competition at the distribution stage for goods of the same brand is of special importance; whereas under those circumstances the fact that only Blondel can obtain supplies directly from DRU, besides restricting the freedom of the parties to the contract, has the effect of substantially altering the position of third parties, in particular of traders other than the sole distributor who might wish to import the products covered by the contract;

(2) Decision in re Consten-Grundig

For facts and references see above, page 66.

Furthermore, in the case of proprietory goods, such as those in question here, the products of the various manufacturers present external, and to some extent technical, features which are distinguishable one from another. Purchasers of such products, therefore, cannot generally rely upon a comparison of the offers and, particularly, the prices of their suppliers except in the case of the same make.

When, for example, Grundig products are offered to the consumer at a price higher than that of comparable products it is hardly possible for the consumer to ascertain whether the discrepancy is due to differences in production costs caused, perhaps, by a difference in quality, or to the fact that the Grundig sales organisation is more costly to run than that of the other manufacturers. When on the other hand Grundig products distributed by the "official" sales network, in this case that of Consten, are more expensive, for whatever reason, than the same products distributed by an independentsales network, the situation is immediately intelligible to the consumer and he may exercise a real freedom of choice.

For this reason competition at the distribution stage, particularly between wholesalers distributing articles of the same make, assumes special importance. This conclusion is all the more valid in that distribution costs account for a considerable share of the total cost prices.

(3) Consten-Grundig Case

See above, page 164.

(4) Decision in re WEA-Filipacchi

For facts and references see above, page 112.

4. Contrary to the arguments of WEA-Filipacchi Music SA, the restriction on competition is not covered by the Commission's notice of 27 May 1970 on minor agreements, decisions and concerted practices, for the turnover of the group to which WEA-Filipacchi Music SA belongs far exceeds the 15 million units of account (see title II. point 3, of that notice).

5. The share of the global market in records held by WEA-Filipacchi Music SA is of no great importance in assessing the restriction on competition in question since there is no single market for classical music, light music and 'pop' music.

6. Account must be taken also of the fact that the records covered by the agreement contain performances by artists attached exclusively to WEA-Filipacchi Music SA or other undertakings of the same group. The performance of artists in fashion are individual and could not be considered because of their properties as being similar to the interpretations of other artists.

7. Consequently, the restriction on competition is noticeable.

(5) Kali und Saltz - Kali Chemi Case

Kali und Saltz AG and Kali Chemie AG v. EEC Commission
Judgment of 14 May 1975, Cases 19-20/74: (1975) ECR 499; (1975) CMLR 154; CCH para. 8284; Competition Law CM/M/III/48.

*Facts:* The only two German producers of potasch are the companies Kali und Saltz AG (K & S), and Kali-Chemie AG (KC).

K & S, joint subsidiaries of the companies Salzetfurth AG, Wintershall AG and Burbach AG, which make up the BASF group, had a production of 2,2650,000 metric tons in 1973 and was responsible for 88.9% of the German production.

KC, the principal shareholder in which is the company Deutsche Solvay Werke, of the Belgian group Solvay et Cie, was responsible in 1973, with 282,500 metric tons, for 11.1% of the German production.

On 6 July 1970 K & S entered into an agreement the terms of which are as follows:

(i) "KC shall sell to K & S ....its production of potash in so far as this is not marketed independently by KC nor required for its own production of compound fertilisers.

(ii) K & S undertakes to buy annually from KC 280,000 metric tons of K20, less such quantities as KC itself requires under Article 1 thereof....

(iii) ...The parties hereto shall agree in advance as from 1 January 1971, and on each occasion for a period of two years, a provisional programme of allocation having regard to Article 2. They shall agree on the conditions relating to the variety and delivery periods.

(iv) The prices to be paid for the quantities delivered to K & S by KC shall be fixed annually. KC shall receive instalments on account of the prices payable for quantities sold.

(v) This article relates to the marketing of Kieserite produced by KC.

(vi) This agreement .... shall continue in force until 31 December 1980. The parties hereto shall enter into negotiations during the 1979/80 marketing year at the latest with a view to renewing this agreement".

This agreement replaced the sales organisation, Verkaufsgemeinschaft Deutscher Kaliwerke (VDK), which before the merger of the BASF interests in K & S was responsible for the sale of straight potash fertilisers by all the German producers of potash from 1958 until its dissolution in 1970.

Like nitrogen and phosphate, potash is one of the main nutritive substances necessary to obtain the best harvests in agriculture. The crude salts obtained from underground mines and subjected to different refinement processes and treatments for the purpose of obtaining either powdered, non-powdered or crushed varieties.

The potash is supplied as fertiliser either directly to farmers for the purpose of its use as straight potash or as straight potash fertiliser or to manufacturers of compound fertilisers for the purpose of processing.

Figures provided by ISMA of London show that in all European countries straight potash fertilisers are being given up and replaced by compound potash fertilisers. This phenomenon is explained on the one hand by the fact that compound fertilisers, which require only one spreading save labour, and on the other hand by the considerable reduction in available Thomas-Kali from the metallurgic slag which is generally used to complement straight potash fertiliser.

K & S is in a position to offer a complete range, including granulated kinds. KC mainly produces powdered varieties (100% of the production of its factory at Friederichsball and 50% of that at Ronnenberg), whereas manufacturers of compound fertilisers increasingly use only "non-powdered" and highly concentrated varieties of potash. Further, an ever increasing proportion of KC's potash is used in the manufacture of the compound fertiliser RHE-KA-PHOS (nowadays distributed independently after having formerly been distributed by VDK), the surplus, which has been diminishing for several years, being sold as straight fertiliser to K & S.

Whereas German imports of potash are practically insignificant, exports of potash fertilisers are roughly at the same level as domestic consumption. The countries to which exports are made are, in the Community, Denmark, the United Kingdom, Belgium, Luxembourg and the Netherlands and, as regards certain kinds, France, and certain third countries, KC's production accounting in 1971 for only approximately 125,000 metric tons (approximately 90,000 metric tons in 1973) of the total quantity exported.

In France there is a legal monopoly for the sale of potash fertilisers enjoyed by SCPA, whose production is considerable in excess of the national consumption. But the monopoly of imports as regards intra-Community trade must be abolished as a result of the recommendation of the Commission of 25 November 1969.

The United Kingdom, a large importer, will rapidly become an exporter thanks to the operating of installations with a capacity of 600,000 to 900,000 tons per annum.

As for imports into the Community from third countries, they are quantitatively less than imports from France and the Federal Republic of Germany.

The agreement of 6 July was submitted to the Commission at its request on 5 November 1971. It was not formally notified until after the Commission began proceedings on its own initiative on 8 May 1973.

After hearing the oral observations of the companies in question the Commission by Decision dated 21 December 1973:

(a) held that "the agreement of 6 July 1970, concluded between K & S and KC concerning the distribution by K & S of the straight potash fertiliser of KC" constituted "an infringement of Article 85(1) of the Treaty establishing the EEC";

(b) refused "the application for an exemption under Article 85(3)";

(c) ordered the said undertakings to bring the said infringements to an end.

*The Court held:*

1. By application filed at the court on 11 and 12 March 1974, the companies Kali-und-Saltz and Kali-Chemie brought an action for annulment of the Decision of the Commission of 21 December 1973 (O.J. No L 19/22 of 23 January 1974) holding that an agreement of 6 July 1970, concluded between the applicants on the marketing by K & S of part of KC's production of potash, constituted an infringement of Article 85(1) of the EEC Treaty and ordering them to bring the infringement to an end.

2. Since the two applications seek the same relief, it is fitting to join them for the purpose of the judgment.

3. The applicants are the only two producers of potash in the Federal Republic of Germany, K & S having produced more than 2,250,000 metric tons in 1973 while KC produced some 280,000 tons. Potash is delivered as fertiliser, either directly with a view to its use as straight potash or to the producers of compound fertilisers for the purpose of processing. Under the terms of the agreement in question KC supplies K & S with that part of KC's production which KC does not market itself or which is not required for the manufacture of its compound fertiliser RHE-KA-PHOS, while K & S for its part undertakes to purchase the surplus, the parties agreeing moreover to draw up, on each occasion for a period of two years, a provisional programme of allocation of this production.

4. According to the Decision challenged, this agreement has the effect of concentrating practically the whole supply of straight potash fertiliser in the Federal Republic of Germany and thus restricting competition in the market of this product and affecting trade between Member States.

5. In order to find a restriction on competition the Decision challenged states "that the relevant market to take as the basis for the decision in these proceedings is that of straight potash fertiliser". The applicants allege on the other hand that the market in potash products constitutes an entity and cannot be divided into two separate markets,

namely straight potash and compound potash fertilisers, since these two products compete with one another and are to a large extent interchangeable.

6. The arguments on which the Commission has, in the last recitals of its Decision, based its case, show that there is competition between the two products which is effected by their prices and their intrinsic advantages for the consumer. The figures mentioned in the Decision show a considerable increase in consumption of compound potash fertilisers which however has not eliminated straight potash. The Decision challenged states, it is true, that such considerations as the state of the soil, the availability of labour and the weather, point in certain cases to the desirability of using straight potash, but it is not shown that two types of fertilisers constitute different markets. The Decision itself makes a point of the fact that a small number of farmers may in some years buy straight fertiliser and in other compound fertiliser.

7. In these circumstances the conclusion of the Decision that "the declaration of inapplicability of Article 85(1) must in any case be refused because the agreement affords the undertakings the possibility of eliminating competition in respect of a substantial part of the products in question" is not valid.

8. The applicants contest moreover the findings in the Decision challenged that the agreement infringes Article 85(1) in that, although it does not expressly require KC to deliver the whole of its production of potash to K & S, its spirit and the practices followed by the two companies achieve the same result. According to the applicants KC remains free to supply K & S with whatever quantities KC itself decides. This is moreover amply shown by the fact that the part of KC's production supplied to K & S is diminishing and has gone down from 173,500 metric tons in 1971 to 129,400 metric tons in 1973, whereas that used in the processing of its compound fertiliser RHE-KHA-PHOS has increased from 119,700 metric tons in 1971 to 150,800 metric tons in 1973.

9. The fact that KC delivers its surplus production of straight potash to K & S is due to KC not possessing any sales organisation making it possible to market it. Before 1970 it sold this production via the sales agency which then operated between all the German producers of potash for the supply of straight potash fertilisers. The agreement in question is intended to allow KC to concentrate its efforts on the manufacture and sale of the compound product RHE-KHA-PHOS and leaves KC to decide what part of its total production should be sold in this form and consequently the amount of the surplus available for sale to K & S.

10. According to the Decision challenged, the agreement covers the entire production of a Member State and by its very nature affects trade between Member States.

11. The applicants allege that the defendant has not given reasons for its Decision on this point, as is required by Article 190 of the EEC Treaty. In this respect (they claim) neither during the administrative stage nor during the course of the proceedings has it sufficiently taken into account KC's actual position on the market.

12. First, the quantities of straight potash sold by KC to K & S are constantly diminishing. According to the Decision challenged, KC was in a position to set up an independent sales organisation. The appli-

cants have claimed that the cost of such an organisation would be prohibitive for KC having regard to its turnover in straight potash. The examples which the defendant quotes of a possible joint marketing of straight potash and compound fertiliser cannot be related to the position of KC, whose surplus production of straight potash is constantly diminishing.

13. It has therefore not been shown that straight potash can be distributed by an organisation which markets the compound product RHE-KHA-PHOS which competes with it.

14. It follows from the combinations of the circumstances that the continual reduction in the quantities of straight potash which KC has available after manufacturing RHE-KHA-PHOS, and further the concomitant decline in the requirement of straight potash fertiliser in favour of compound fertilisers could prevent KC from setting up an onerous marketing apparatus for the sale simply of its surplus production which decreases every year. This position could lead to allowing exceptional measures to be taken for the sale of this surplus production within the context of an agreement which, if analysed, amounts for KC not to an obligation but to an option to sell to K & S.

15. Accordingly, insufficient reasons appear to have been given for the Decision challenged, at least as regards the rejection of the application for exemption.

(6) Decision in re BMW

See below, page 438.

## G. The "de minimis rule"

(perceptibility test)

### (1) Völk-Vervaecke Case

Franz Völk v. Etablissements J. Vervaecke, Case 5/69, Preliminary Ruling of 9 July 1969; (1969) ECR 295; (1969) CMLR 273; CCH para. 8674; Competition Law CM/M/III/11.

*Facts:* Völk, trading under the name of Josef Erd & Co, manufactures washing machines under the trademark "Konstant". Vervaecke is an undertaking distributing household electrical appliances.

On 15 September 1963 the two undertakings concluded an agreement in which Völk granted Vervaecke the exclusive right to sell its products in Belgium and Luxembourg. Vervaecke undertook to place a monthly order for about 80 appliances with Völk. Völk undertook to protect Vervaecke's sales territory against parallel imports. The agreement was supplemented several times during 1964.

After some time the parties disagreed about the execution of the contract and Völk started proceedings before a German court against Vervaecke. The German court of first instance, the Landesgericht, Kempten, found for Völk. Vervaecke appealed against this judgment to the Oberlandesgericht Munich. Vervaecke submitted in both instances that the agreement was in violation of Article 85 since it contained clauses granting absolute territorial protection. Völk on the other hand, considered that those provisions were valid because the proportion of the market which he had acquired in Belgium and in Luxembourg and that which he had in fact endeavoured to acquire was extremely small.

On 5 December 1968 the Oberlandesgericht, Munich, decided to ask the Court, under Article 177 of the EEC Treaty, to give a ruling on the following question:

'In determining whether the disputed contract of 15 December 1963, as amended on 1 January 1964 and 11 March 1964, falls within the prohibition set out in Article 85(1) of the EEC Treaty, must regard be had to the proportion of the market which the plaintiff in fact acquired or ultimately endeavoured to acquire in the Member States of the European Economic Community, in particular in Belgium and in Luxembourg, the sales sector for which the defendant enjoys "absolute territorial protection"?

*The Court held:*

.....

1. By an order of 5 December 1968, which was received at the Court Registry on 28 January 1969, the Oberlandesgericht, Munich, under Article 177, of the Treaty establishing the EEC, referred to the Court of Justice the question whether in order to decide whether the disputed contract falls within the prohibition set out in Article 85(1) of the EEC Treaty regard must be had to the proportion of the market which the plaintiff has actually acquired or which he has endeavoured to acquire in the Member States of the EEC, in particular in Belgium and in Luxembourg, the sales zone within which the defendant enjoys absolute protection.

2/4. Although the Court is not entitled within the framework of subparagraph (a) of the first paragraph of Article 177 to apply the Treaty to a particular case, it may nevertheless derive from the wording of the decision referring the matter questions which relate exclusively to the interpretation of the Treaty. The question raised relates to agreements which are characterised by the fact that a producer who has granted a distributor the exclusive right of sale of his products for certain countries in the Common Market has undertaken to protect the distributor against deliveries which might be made in those countries by third parties and has obtained from the distributor an undertaking not to sell competing products. The question is thus reduced to whether, in deciding whether such agreements fall within the prohibition set out in Article 85(1) of the Treaty, regard must be had to the proportion of the market which the grantor controls or endeavours to obtain in the territory ceded.

5/7. If an agreement is to be capable of affecting trade between Member States it must be possible to foresee with a sufficient degree of probability on the basis of a set of objectives, factors of law or of fact that the agreement in question may have an influence direct or indirect, actual or potential, on the pattern of trade between Member States in such a way that it might hinder the attainment of the objectives of a single market between States. Moreover the prohibition in Article 85(1) is applicable only if the agreement in question also has as its object or effect the prevention, restriction or distortion of competition within the Common Market. Those conditions must be understood by reference to the actual circumstances of the agreement. Consequently an agreement falls outside the prohibition in Article 85 when it has only an insignificant effect on the markets, taking into account the weak position which the persons concerned have on the market of the product in question. Thus an exclusive dealing agreement, even with absolute territorial protection, may, having regard to the weak position of the persons concerned on the market in the products in question in the area covered by the absolute protection, escape the prohibition laid down in Article 85(1).

*Sequel:*

The Oberlandesgericht, Munich, in a judgment of 19 November 1969, ruled in favour of Völk. The Court considered the agreement to be valid.

For the Commission's point of view on the "de minimis rule", consult the Commission notice of 19 December 1977 (Annex XVI), concerning agreements, decisions and concerted practices of minor importance which do not fall under Article 85(1) of the EEC Treaty.

See, however, the Commission's refusal to apply this notice in re Advocaat Zwarte Kip.

(2) Re Advocaat Zwarte Kip

Decision of the Commission of 24 July 1974 on a proceeding under Article 85 of the Treaty, O.J. No 237, 29 August 1974, p. 12; (1974) 2 CMLR p. 79; CCH para. 9669; Competition Law CM/M/I/77.

*Facts:* By an agreement concluded in 1938, the Dutch firm Van Olffen (currently a wholly-owned subsidiary of Heineken NV) had assigned its rights over a trademark relating to advocaat Zwarte Kip for egg liqueurs in Belgium and Luxembourg to a firm whose rights were ultimately vested in SA Cinoco in which the Stella Artois brewing group holds more than 25% of the shares. From the terms of the initial contract and from subsequent events the agreement was found to have the effect of segregating the Benelux markets and, although this occurred before the EEC Treaty came into force, the same effect continued thereafter. This was borne out by an exchange of letters between the parties by which the assignee was assured that he would have absolute territorial protection and by an action for infringement of the trademark right brought by Cinoco against a Belgian wine trader who had imported from the Netherlands a quantity of advocaat manufactured and marketed under the relevant trademark by Van Olffen.

This Commission Decision will not prevent the Belgian assignee from using his trademark rights as a means of preventing the import and sale of products which infringe his trademark. However products manufactured by the original Dutch trademark holder and imported into Belgium and Luxembourg were not to be considered as infringing products and the existence of the trademark right was therefore not directly attacked.

Moreover, the erection of barriers between Member States on the basis of trademark law was not justified by reason of quality differences between the relevant products. Consumers would not be misled as to quality or origin of products sold under the same trademark in a single market, unless a supplier failed to indicate the origin of the product or its composition. But information for consumers on those points can be provided by means which would not amount to barriers to the free movement of goods.

This decision was made pursuant to a complaint from a parallel importer after a national court had stayed appeal proceedings in respect of infringements. This decision shows the use of the application of Article 85 in relation to trademarks, even though the exercise of trademark rights in a way which is unlawful in relation to the Treaty objectives is in itself contrary to the rules on the free movement of goods.

*The Commission ruled:*

It should be noted that as regards the significance of the restriction, Cinoco has requested the Commission to apply the Communication of 1970 concerning agreements of minor importance. It must, however, be pointed out that this Communication is for guidance purposes only and that the terms of this agreement do not in any case fulfil the essential conditions in favour of small and medium sized undertakings laid down in the Communication.

Van Olffen benefits from the financial and commercial support of NV Heineken, which holds an important position amongst the manufacturers of alcoholic beverages in the Benelux countries and by which it is in fact fully owned. A similar though less pronounced relationship exists between Cinoco and Stella Artois. Further, the position on the Benelux market for advocaat of the parties to the agreement is far from negligible. It should nevertheless be examined whether or not the restriction of competition is significant. Despite the fact that the quantities of advocaat imported by Soenen were very small, the creation of obstacles to trade between Member States based on trademark rights can prevent the importation of extremely large quantities; therefore the potential restriction of competition that can result from such obstacles is very considerable. Consequently, the agreement has the effect of restricting trade within the Common Market to a significant extent.

In re SABA, where Article 85(1) applied, the share of the market of the undertakings concerned ranged in the Federal Republic of Germany for the various types of equipment from 1.8 percent to 11.9 percent, and the share of the market in other Member States was less than 1 percent.

(3) Béguelin Case

Béguelin Import Co. v. Import Export SA, Case 22/71, Preliminary Ruling of 25 November 1971; (1971) ECR 949; (1972) CMLR 81; CCH para. 8149; Competition Law CM/M/III/26.

*Facts:* The Béguelin Company is an import/export company.

On 1 March 1967 it entered into a contract with the Japanese firm Oshawa under which it was appointed exclusive representative in France and Belgium for the sale of gas cigarette lighters manufactured by the Japanese firm under the trademark 'WIN'.

A few days later, the Béguelin/Belgium company set up in France a subsidiary, Béguelin/France, which was wholly owned under its control and Oshawa's exclusive dealership for France was then transferred by contract of 25 March 1967 to the Béguelin/France company.

Shortly afterwards, the exclusive dealership for the Federal Republic of Germany in the WIN trademark was granted by the Oshawa company to the Marbach company, a German firm.

In 1969, a French import/export company G.L. Import Export, Nice, purchased from the Marbach firm a consignment of 18,000 WIN lighters, which were the property of Marbach but which the latter firm had left in bond at the customs in Hamburg: after having taken delivery of them in France, the G.L. Import Export company began to distribute the lighters on the French market.

The Béguelin/Belgium and Béguelin/France companies heard of this and thereupon commenced proceedings before the Tribunal de Commerce, Nice, against the G.L. Import Export company, Nice, and the German firm of Marbach in which they sought:

- first, an injunction against the sale, on pain of penalty, on French territory of lighters acquired by G.L. Import and bearing the WIN trade-mark and

- secondly, an order that the French firm and the German firm should pay the two Béguelin companies compensation for unlawful and unfair competition.

The Béguelin companies based their application in essence on the exclusive dealing contracts granted them by Oshawa.

But the defendant firms in the main action pleaded before the Tribunal de Commerce that the agreements referred to were absolutely void under Article 85 of the EEC Treaty.

*The Court held:*

.....

C. Finally, in order to come within the prohibition imposed by Article 85, the agreement must affect trade between Member States and the free play of competition to an appreciable extent.

(4) re Kawasaki

Commission Decision of 12 December 1978, relating to a proceeding under Article 85 of the EEC Treaty; Kawasaki Motors (UK) Ltd and Kawasaki Motoren GmbH; O.J. No L 16, 23 January 1979, p. 9; (1979) 1 CMLR 448; CCH para. 10097; Competition Law CM/M/I/146.

*Facts:* The Commission has imposed on 12 December a fine of 100,000 u.a. (approximately UKL 67,000) on Kawasaki Motors (UK), a wholly owned subsidiary of Kawasaki Heavy Industries, for preventing the export of Kawasaki motor cycles from the United Kingdom. Kawasaki is the fourth most important supplier of motorcycles in the Community.

The case was brought to the Commission's attention in March 1977 by a private consumer, resident in Belgium, who had sought to buy a Kawasaki motorcycle in the UK because prices there were over 30% lower than in Belgium. The Commission's investigations revealed that Kawasaki Motors (UK) had imposed an export ban on dealers since May 1975. It had been lifted following the Commission's statement of objections under Article 15(6) of Regulation No 17 as an interim measure.

The very considerable price differences referred to by the private consumer were confirmed by the Commission's investigations; in some cases recommended retail prices in other Member States were 50% higher than those in the UK. In particular it was found that the wholesale price charged to dealers in Germany by Kawasaki Motoren GmbH, also a wholly-owned subsidiary of Kawasaki Heavy Industries, was on average, 25% higher than the Kawasaki Motors (UK) recommended retail price to private consumers in the UK.

The export prohibition was imposed in order to protect the high price levels in other Member States, especially the Federal Republic of Germany, from competition from dealers in the UK, thus preventing them from meeting demand from other Community countries. This conduct enabled Kawasaki Motoren GmbH in particular to charge higher prices than would otherwise have been possible. A profit was thereby made from a restriction of competition prohibited by Article 85, and in the Commission's view, a fine was justified.

The Commission welcomes the initiative shown by the private consumer in this case, and will continue to defend the right of consumers and others to buy wherever they wish in the Community.

*The Commission ruled:*

.....

36. The legal advice relied upon by Kawasaki Motors (UK) was that the export prohibition potentially affected trade between the United Kingdom and other Member States, but that Article 85(1) did not apply because the agreement fell within the turnover limits of the Commission's Notice on agreements of minor importance. The latter part of this advice, as was subsequently admitted by Kawasaki Motors (UK), was mistaken since it did not take into account the need to consolidate the turnover of parent and subsidiary undertakings when assessing the importance of an agreement.

37. The above argument does not reduce the gravity of the infringement since both Kawasaki Motors (UK) and Kawasaki Motoren GmbH knew they were restricting competition. The legal advice relied on did not question that competition was being restricted, but made false assumptions as to the importance of the restriction. Moreover, the mistake made in the legal advice was clear and could have reasonably been seen from reading the Commission's Notice. The latter part of the Notice, which was overlooked in the advice, makes it clear that the turnover of parent and subsidiary companies is to be taken into account when assessing whether the agreement falls within the terms of the Notice.

38. In addition, the sales of Kawasaki Motors (UK) in 1975, when advice was given, were approaching the 5% market share threshold of the Notice. For large capacity machines of 750cc and over, which Kawasaki itself regarded as being a separate class of motorcycle, the market share was no less than 29%. In 1976 Kawasaki machines accounted for 5.9% of all motorcycle registrations in the United Kingdom. Kawasaki Motors (UK) cannot have been unaware of these facts.

(5) Distillers Case

Distillers Company v. Commission, Case 30/78, Judgment of 10 July 1980; (1980) 3 CMLR 121; CCH para. 8613; Competition Law CM/M/III/85; (1980) ECR 2229.

*Facts:*

*1. The Distillers Company Ltd. (DCL) and its products*

DCL was established in 1877 through the amalgamation of six Scotch whisky distillers, and now has 38 subsidiaries producing spirits in the United Kingdom: 32 of them produce Scotch whisky, four produce gin, one produces vodka and one Pimm's.

DCL's total turnover for the financial year 1976-1977 in respect of Scotch whisky, gin, vodka and other spirits may be broken down as follows: sales in Europe amounted to 55.7% of turnover, of which 14.7% was obtained in EEC countries other than the United Kingdom and Ireland, sales in North and South America amounted to 27.2% and sales in Africa, Asia and Australia to 17.1%.

DCL is the world's largest distiller and seller of Scotch whisky. In the EEC countries other than the United Kingdom the DCL market share for whisky was, in 1975, 54% in Belgium and Luxembourg, 47% in Denmark,

35% in France, 33% in Italy and Germany, 32% in Ireland and 29% in the Netherlands. For the United Kingdom its market share was between 50% and 30% for the years 1973 to 1977. DCL markets over 50 brands of Scotch whisky, the most familiar being Johnnie Walker, Haig, Black and White, Vat 69, White Horse and Dewar's.

As regards gin, DCL's share of United Kingdom production was approximately 55% during the years 1973, 1974 and 1975. During this same period DCL's sales amounted to approximately 70% of the total gin sales in the United Kingdom. DCL exports large quantities of gin: its market share is 20% in France, 27% in Germany, 30% in the Netherlands, 44% in Belgium and Luxembourg, 20% in Italy, 44% in Denmark and 10% in Ireland. Among DCL gin brands are High & Dry, Gordon's Special Dry London Gin and Booth's Finest Dry Gin.

The DCL group accounts for about one quarter of the vodka sales in the United Kingdom. Its 'Cossack Vodka' brand has the second highest sales in the market.

As for Pimm's, DCL is the only one to sell this; it consists of an aromatised spirit to which is added (except in France) lemonade. To this mixture is added borage, cucumber or mint.

*2. Distribution of DCL spirits*

Each of the 38 British subsidiaries of the DCL group is responsible for the distribution and marketing of its spirits, which bear its own brand names.

In the United Kingdom only a few subsidiaries have their own distributors, whilst most of them sell their brands directly to the wholesale trade, which counts in this case approximately one thousand wholesalers. The wholesale trade itself can be divided into two sectors: the 'tied trade' and the 'free trade'. The tied trade consists essentially of brewery groups which own licensed retail outlets through which the products are sold either by the bottle or by the measure. Most of those breweries also act as wholesalers in the free trade sectors. Purchases by those breweries represent about half the total sales of spirits of DCL's subsidiary companies in the United Kingdom. The free trade consists of a wide range of retailers, including individual licensed shops, chains of nonbrewery retail outlets (such as some of the supermarket chains) and 'multiples' (that is to say, wholesale business which also have their own retail outlets, but which are not controlled by the breweries). They also sell generally by the bottle. In addition, licensed hotel chains may sell by the measure on their premises.

In other Common Market countries most of the DCL subsidiary companies each have their own sole distributors. The spirits supplied to the sole distributors are usually resold to wholesalers who sell them in turn to retailers. There are about 200 sole distributors of DCL spirits in the Common Market. Many other alcoholic drinks, notably brandy, sherry and wine, are also sold by those sole distributors.

For the purpose of duty-free consumption only, the DCL subsidiaries sell spirits directly to ships' chandlers. They number about 1000 in the Common Market.

*3. DCL's conditions of sale and price terms*

On 30 June 1973 DCL notified the Commission of the 'Sellers' Conditions of Sale' applied by each of its subsidiaries for sales of spirits to United Kingdom trade customers only. DCL was seeking an exemption under Article 85(3). The sellers' conditions of sale consisted mainly of:

- provisions relating to terms of delivery and payment;

- a clause (6) prohibiting resale in bond.

On 8 July 1975, in reply to a request of the Commission dated 2 June 1975, DCL submitted a new text of the previously notified Seller's Conditions of Sale, revising Clause 5b (limiting the export prohibition now to territories outside the Community) and removing Clause 6.

On 11 July 1975, DCL submitted to the Commission the text of the circular letter of 24 June 1975 addressed to customers of its subsidiaries established in the United Kingdom and of two appendices, entitled 'Home Trade Conditions of Sale and Price Terms'.

The first section of the latter, entitled 'Conditions of Sale', states that:
'...Following the referendum, we are now amending the Conditions of Sale to permit export by home trade customers to other Common Market countries ...export outside the Common Market is still prohibited'.
Appendix I to the DCL circular letter contains the new version of the Seller's Conditions of Sale.

The second section of the letter, headed 'Price Terms', states:

(a) '... the various allowances, rebates and discounts are designed to meet the particular requirements of the home trade and customers are only entitled to them when the goods are in fact consumed within the UK.'

(b) 'Accordingly, if you wish to buy for export to other Common Market countries you must indicate this on your order and purchase must be made at the gross price'.

(c)'... If ... a customer obtains or claims any home trade allowances, rebates or discounts in respect of goods which he has bought and any of those goods turn up in any country outside the UK, the right is reserved for all companies in the DCL group to sell thereafter to such customer only at the gross price'.

Appendix II to DCL's circular letter, entitled 'Certain Contractual Provisions (relating to price) additional to Conditions of Sale' states that:

The provisions of that Appendix are to form part of every contract made by a purchaser and a subsidiary company of the DCL group for the purchase of any brands of spirits and are additional to seller's conditions of sale (Appendix I);

All allowances, discounts and rebates whatsoever (hereinafter collectively referred to as 'price allowances') are designed to meet the particular market circumstances of the United Kingdom;

Any DCL subsidiary company is entitled to charge the gross price without reduction of such price by any price allowances:

When a DCL subsidiary company has a reasonable belief that any quantity of goods bought by the purchaser from any DCL subsidiary has been or will be consumed outside the United Kingdom;

even when the exports are made by a subsequent purchaser;

regardless of the quantity ordered, until and to the extent that the purchaser produces evidence satisfactory to the selling DCL subsidiary company that the goods will be consumed in the United Kingdom.

On 23 February 1977, DCL addressed a letter to their United Kingdom trade customers informing them that the 'gross price without any reduction of such price by price allowances' is now expressed as 'the gross

EEC export price', which is the price charged to sole distributors in other EEC countries before deduction of any allowances granted to them (the new provisions of Appendix II are hereinafter referred to as 'price terms').

*4. DCL's prices and price allowances*

All prices of spirits supplied to the United Kingdom home market are controlled by the Price Commission which was set up under the Counter-Inflation Act of 1973. The prices may be increased only at minimum intervals of three months, when a producer presents proof that the price increase covers an increase in costs. The export prices applied by DCL to UK trade customers and to sole distributors are not subject to the control of the Price Commission. Spirits intended for export may be circulated under bond.

The various allowances, rebates and discounts (price allowances) granted by DCL's subsidiaries to their trade customers for sales of spirits destined for consumption in the United Kingdom are as follows:

The 'wholesome allowance' is granted to trade customers who purchase a minimum quantity;

The 'aggregate quantity rebate' is granted on the basis of the quantity of spirits purchased annually;

The 'deferred special allowance', which is a loyalty rebate, is applicable only in respect of purchases of a minimum of 1,000 cases of Scotch whisky per annum when the amounts purchased from DCL's subsidiaries represent at least 60% of the total purchases of Scotch whisky by that purchaser;

The 'performance bonus rebate' is applicable only in respect of purchases of Scotch whisky made between March 1977 and March 1978 and is a target bonus granted when purchases of DCL brands in the course of a given year amount to at least 95% of those attained in the previous year;

The 'cash discount' is granted on duty-paid spirits for which United Kingdom customers forward cash with order;

Promotional allowances are granted from time to time by individual DCL subsidiary companies by way of contributions to special promotions for their brands.

The price mechanism can be illustrated by the example of the prices applicable for Johnnie Walker Red Label Whisky. The gross price is a notional resale price at which wholesalers supposedly sell to their retail customers. The gross price of a case of twelve bottles of Johnnie Walker Red Label (without VAT and customs duties) was £ 10.65 on 24 June 1975 and £ 13.51 on 1 March 1977. For whisky bought and consumed in the United Kingdom the maximum allowances were £ 5.30 and £ 6.45 respectively, with an average of £ 5.41. Thus after deduction of the allowances the minimum net prices paid by the trade customers were £ 5.35 and £ 7.06 respectively, with an average of £ 8.20. In contrast, purchasers of the equivalent amount of Johnnie Walker Red Label destined for consumption in a Member State of the EEC other than the United Kingdom had to pay the gross price. As for the price applied in the case of sole distributors in Member countries other than the United Kingdom, this was £ 5.73 and £ 8.35 respectively (after deduction of the cash discount and the distributors' allowances).

*5. Development of parallel exports*

The decision of the Commission states that 'According to information supplied by DCL, parallel exports of DCL Scotch whisky from the United Kingdom to other EEC countries amounted approximately to 100 000 cases in 1974, to 400 000 cases in 1974 and to 550 000 cases in 1975 ... From the date of the circular letter, 24 June 1975, up to 12 July 1976, only one customer had indicated to DCL subsidiary companies that it wished to buy for export to other EEC countries and purchased 1 400 cases at the gross price. The aggregate quantity of Scotch whisky forming part of orders in respect of which DCL subsidiary companies obtained evidence that whisky purchased by United Kingdom trade customers was resold to other EEC countries and required further payment, amounted to over 6 000 cases'. DCL has put the number of cases purchased at the gross export price between 1 January and 31 December 1977 at 340 000.

*6. Complaints*

On 18 May 1976 the undertakings A. Bulloch & Co., A. Bulloch (Agencies) Ltd., John Grant Blenders Ltd., Inland Fisheries Ltd. and Classic Wines Ltd. presented a request to the Commission, pursuant to Article 3 of Regulation No 17, seeking the initiation of the procedure to terminate infringements of Articles 85 and 86 of the EEC Treaty resulting from the DCL price terms contained in the circular letter of 24 June 1975.

These undertakings are related companies all established in the Glasgow area. They purchase large quantities of DCL whisky for resale. Some of the whisky which the complainants had bought in bond at the home trade price and sold to another whisky dealer in the United Kingdom was later found by DCL representatives in supermarkets in France and Belgium. Subsequently DCL asked the complainants for further payment and refused to sell them any in-bond whisky except at the gross price. On 7 March 1977 another request was presented by Madison Benson and Carter Ltd. of London, also raising the difficulties of obtaining DCL Scotch whisky for export.

*The Court held:*

27. Regarding Pimm's; as stated above, the applicant maintains that the price terms do not fall within the prohibition of Article 85(1) of the Treaty solely because its sales in the Member countries other than the United Kingdom are minimal in relation to the sales of other spirits.

28. The applicant's case cannot be accepted. Although an agreement may escape the prohibition in Article 85(1) when it affects the market only to an insignificant extent, having regard to the weak position which those concerned have in the market in the products in question, the same considerations do not apply in the case of a product of a large undertaking responsible for the entire production. In those circumstances there is no reason for the purposes of the action to distinguish between Pimm's and the other drinks produced by the applicant.

## II. ARTICLE 85 PARAGRAPH 2

### A. Automatic Nullity

#### (1) Second Brasserie de Haecht Case

Brasserie de Haecht v. Wilkin-Janssen, Case 48/73, Preliminary Ruling of 6 February 1973; (1973) ECR 77; (1973) CMLR 287; CCH para. 8710; Competition Law CM/M/III/37.

*Facts:* The Commercial Court of Liège, in the proceedings brought before it by the brewery company de Haecht, against the café proprietors Wilkin and Janssen, has asked a second time for a preliminary ruling under Article 177 of the EEC Treaty. The Court would now like to have answers to the following questions:

1. 'Must a procedure under Articles 2, 3 and 6 of Regulation No 17 be considered to be initiated by the Commission from the moment when it acknowledges receipt of a request for a negative clearance or of notification for the purposes of obtaining exemption under Article 85(3) of the EEC Treaty'?

2. 'Can notification of a standard contract referring to legal arrangements made in 1968 be considered as notification of a similar contract entered into during 1963'?

3. 'Is the nullity of contracts exempted from notification to be deemed to take effect from the date when one of the contracting parties duly brings an action for it or merely from the date of the judgment or the decision of the Commission which establishes it?' See also first Brasserie de Haecht Case at page 162.

*The Court held:*

.....

On the third question

24. This question is concerned with whether nullity by virtue of Article 85(2) of agreements exempted from notification is deemed to take effect from the date when one of the contracting parties duly claimed it merely from the date of the judgment or the decision of the Commission establishing it.

25. It follows from the general considerations above that Article 85(2) renders agreements and decisions prohibited pursuant to that Article automatically void.

26. Such nullity is therefore capable of having a bearing on all the effects, either past or future, of the agreement or decision.

27. Consequently, the nullity provided for in Article 85(2) is of retroactive effect.

In case 319/82, Ciments et Betons v. Kerpen & Kerpen GmbH, judgement of 14 December 1983 (not yet published), the Court noted that on the one hand, the nullity pursuant to Article 85(2) is absolute, so agreements falling within its scope do not affect the legal relationships between the contracting parties, while on the other, it applies only to the contractual provisions caught by Article 85(1). The effects of this nullity on the other parts of the agreement must therefor be assessed under national law, not Community law. This also applies to any orders placed or deliveries carried out under such agreements and to the ensuing payment obligations.

## B. Provisional Validity

### (1) Second Brasserie de Haecht Case

For facts and references see above, pages 165 and 183.

General considerations with regard to the questions.

2. By Article 85(2), the Treaty has from its entry into force, rendered any agreements or decisions prohibited pursuant to this Article automatically void.

3. Although the prohibition set out in Article 85(1) is modified by the power of granting exemptions provided for in Article 85(3), the Treaty does not however, contain any transitional provision as to the effects of Article 85(2) on agreements and decisions existing at the date of the entry into force of either the Treaty or of Regulation No 17.

4. This ommission leads to a situation all the more ambiguous from the fact that, apart from the possible intervention by the Commission by virtue of the Regulations and directives referred to in Article 87, the judiciary, by virtue of the direct effect of Article 85(2) is competent to rule against prohibited agreements and decisions by declaring them automatically void.

5. While the first course offers the necessary flexibility to take the peculiarities of each case into account, Article 85(2), the intentions of which are to attach severe sanctions to a serious prohibition, does not of its very nature allow the Court the power to intervene with the same flexibility.

6. Whilst, in defining the powers of the Commission, Regulation No 17, and in particular Article 7 thereof, enabled the Commission to take into account the general principle of legal certainty, it did not modify - as indeed it could not - the effects of Article 85(2), but, on the contrary by Article 1 thereof, it confirmed that, without prejudice, to Articles 6, 7 and 23 thereof, agreements, decisions and concerted practices of the kind described in Article 85(1) shall be prohibited, no prior decision to that effect being required.

7. Thus it was left entirely to the judgment of the courts to determine the lines on which the legal application of Article 85(2) should be reconciled with respect for the said general principle of legal certainty.

8. There is, therefore, room for distinction, in applying Article 85(2), between agreements and decisions existing before the implementation of Article 85 by Regulation No 17, hereinafter called old agreements, and agreements and decisions entered into after that date, hereinafter called new agreements.

9. In the case of old agreements, the general principle of contractual certainty requires, particularly when the agreement has been notified in accordance with the provisions of Regulation No 17, that the Court may only declare it to be automatically void after the Commission has taken a decision by virtue of that Regulation.

10. In the case of new agreements, as the Regulation assumes that so long as the Commission has not taken a decision the agreement can only

implemented at the parties' own risk, it follows that notifications in accordance with Article 4(1) of Regulation No 17 do not have suspensive effect.

11. Whilst the principle of legal certainty requires that, in applying the prohibitions of Article 85, the sometimes considerable delays by the Commission in exercising its powers should be taken into account, this cannot, however, absolve the court from the obligation of deciding on the claims of interested parties who invoke the automatic nullity.

12. In such a case it devolves on the court to judge, subject to the possible application of Article 177, whether there is cause to suspend proceedings in order to allow the parties to obtain the Commission's standpoint, unless it establishes either that the agreement does not have any perceptible effect on competition or trade between Member States or that there is no doubt that the agreement is incompatible with Article 85.

13. Whilst these considerations refer particularly to agreements which must be notified in accordance with Article 4 of the Ragulation, they apply equally to agreements exempted from notification, such exemption merely constituting an inconclusive indication that the agreements referred to are generally less harmful to the smooth functioning of the Common Market.

(2) De Bloos v. Bouyer Case

Etablissements A de Bloos v. Bouyer S.p.r.l. request for a preliminary ruling by the Cour d'Appel of Mons in Belgium. Judgment of 14 December 1977, case 59/77, (1977) ECR p. 2359; (1977) 1 CMLR 60; CCH para. 8444; Competition Law CM/M/III/69.

*Facts:* On 24 October 1959 Etablissements Bouyer SA (hereinafter referred to as 'Bouyer') concluded a contract with Etablissements De Bloos S.p. r.l. (hereinafter referred to as De Bloos) granting De Bloos the exclusive rights to sell products bearing the 'Bouyer' mark for Belgium, the Grand Duchy of Luxembourg and the Belgian Congo (now the Republic of Zaire). The contract was concluded for a term of three years and renewed by tacit agreement until 1973. On 30 January 1963 it was notified to the Commission, pursuant to Articles 4 and 5 of Regulation No 17. On 29 April 1969 the Commission stated in a letter addressed to De Bloos that, in application of Regulation No 67/67 of the Commission of 22 March 1967 (Official Journal, English Special Edition 1967, p. 10), providing for the exemption of certain categories of exclusive dealing agreements, the Commission had decided on 17 July 1968 to take no action (décidé ... de classer) regarding the notification of exclusive dealing agreements which did not, to its knowledge, provide for absolute territorial protection, and that it emerged for the initial examination of the notification of the agreement between Bouyer and De Bloos that it fulfilled that condition.

An action between De Bloos and Bouyer alleging Bouyer's breach of its contractual obligations as defined by the Belgian law of 27 July 1961 on the unilateral revocation of contracts granting exclusive sales concessions of indefinite duration was brought before the Tribunal de Commerce, Tournai, in September 1973, and then before the Cour d'Appel, Mons. Before the Cour d'Appel, Bouyer submitted primarily that under the Brussels Convention on Jurisdiction and the Enforcement of Judgments in Civil and Commercial matters of 27 September 1968 the Belgian courts did not have jurisdiction to hear the case, and in the alternative that, contrary to the Commission's opinion, the agreement at issue, which was concluded in 1959, did provide for absolute territorial protection, so that it could not be exempted from the prohibition in Article 85(1) and must be declared null and void. Pursuant to Article 177 of the EEC Treaty, the Cour d'Appel, Mons, by a judgment of 9 December 1975, referred to the Court of Justice a request for an interpretation of certain provisions of the Brussels Convention.

Following the judgment of the Court of Justice of 6 October 1976 (Case 14/76, De Bloos (1976) ECR 1497) the Cour d'Appel found that the Belgian courts did have jurisdiction *ratione loci*, and held that it should examine the validity of the 1959 agreement in relation to Article 85(1) of the EEC Treaty. Taking into account the Commission's decision to take no action regarding the notification made in January 1963, the Cour 'Appel held that it was necessary to refer the following questions on interpretation and validity to the Court of Justice of the European Communities:

'I. Where a party to proceedings is out of time pursuant to Article 173 of the Treaty establishing the EEC for the purposes of instituting proceedings before the Court of Justice of the European Communities contesting the validity of an act of an institution of the EEC, can a national court submit a preliminary question in that connection?

II. On the assumption that a preliminary question may be referred to the Court of Justice in connection with the validity of an act of an institution of the EEC, notwithstanding the fact that the party contesting the validity of that act is out of time, is the decision adopted by the Commission on 29 April 1969 to take no action with regard to the exclusive agreement in accordance with the Treaty establishing the EEC and the Regulations adopted in implementation thereof?

III. Can an exclusive agreement which fulfils the conditions of Regulation No 67/67/EEC of the Commission of 22 March 1967 continue to benefit after 31 December 1972 from the declaration of inapplicability of Article 85(1) of the Treaty of the EEC?

IV. Is it in all events possible to recognise as provisionally valid, so long as the Commission has not adopted a decision with regard to it, an exclusive agreement which, as the present case, was concluded before 22 March 1967 but which was notified before 1 February 1963?

*The Court held:*

*fourth question*

8. The Court has already ruled, in particular to its judgment of 6 February 1973 (Case 48/72, Brasserie de Haecht (1973) ECR at p. 86) that in the case of old agreements, that is to say - according to the distinction drawn in Articles 4 and 5 of Regulation No 17 - agreements existing before 13 March 1962, 'the general principle of contractual certainty requires, particularly when the agreement has been notified in accordance with the provisions of Regulation No 17, that the court may only declare it to be automatically void after the Commission has taken a decision by virtue of that Regulation'.

9. Similarly it had already been held in the judgment of 9 July 1969 (Case 10/69, Portelange (1969) ECR at p. 316) that: 'In view of the

absence of any legal means enabling the persons concerned to accelerate the adoption of a decision under Article 85(3) - the consequences of which are all the more serious the longer such a decision is delayed - it would be contrary to the general principle of legal certainty to conclude that because agreements notified are not finally valid so long as the Commission has made no decision on them under Article 85(3) of the Treaty, they are not completely efficacious'.

10. Although the fact that such agreements are fully valid may possibly give rise to practical disadvantages, the difficulties that might arise from uncertainty in legal relationships based on the agreements notified or exempted from notification would be still more harmful.

11. The legal consequences stated above result from the indivisability of the prohibition laid down in Article 85(1) and the possibility of exemption provided for in Article 85(3) as implemented by Regulation No 17.

12. These considerations are confirmed by the effects attributed to notification and to exemption from notification of old agreements under Article 6(2) and 7 of the said regulation.

13. Not only may such agreements benefit from an exemption extending retroactively even to the period before their notification, but such of their provisions as are incompatible with Article 85(1) and not capable of benefiting from Article 85(3) may also be regularised retroactively on condition that they are amended with respect to the future at the request of the Commission.

14. Such system is inconsistent with jurisdiction on the part of the courts to make a finding of nullity during the period between notification and the date on which the Commission takes a decision.

15. It follows that, during that period, courts before which proceedings are brought relating to an old agreement the legal effects attributed thereto under the law applicable to the contract, and those effects cannot be called in question by any objection which may be raised concerning its compatibility with Article 85(1).

16. The fourth question should be answered accordingly.

*The Court decided:*

In answer to the questions referred to it by the Cour d'Appel, Mons, by a judgment of 3 May 1977, hereby rules:

During the period between notification and the date on which the Commission takes a decision, courts before which proceedings are brought relating to an old agreement duly notified or exempted from notification must give such an agreement the legal effects attributed thereto under the law applicable to the contract, and those effects cannot be called in question by any objection which may be raised concerning its compatibility with Article 85(1).

<u>(3) Lancome Case</u>

Lancome and Cosparfrance v. Etos and Albert Heijn,
Preliminary Ruling of 10 July 1980, Case 99/79, (1980) ECR 2511; (1981) 2 CMLR; CCH para. 8714; Competition Law CM/M/III/88.

*Facts:*

1. SA Lancôme in Paris manufactures and markets under the Lancôme trademark perfumery, beauty products and toiletries. Cosparfrance Nederland BV is a subsidiary of Lancôme which markets Lancôme products in the Netherlands.

2. In order to market its products. Lancôme has set up a selective sales organisation which covers the whole of the EEC and is based in particular on exclusive distributorship agreements concluded between it and the general agents which it has appointed in the various Member States of the EEC and on sales agreements concluded between Lancôme and retailers established in France. Lancôme notified the Commission on 30 January 1963 of a standard exclusive dealing agreement concluded with its general for Germany, Italy, the Netherlands, Belgium and Luxembourg. Subsequently, Lancôme also notified the Commission of the agreements which its general agents or subsidiaries were applying to their respective authorised retailers.

3. After initiating the procedure on 22 April 1972, the Commission sent a notice of complaints to Lancôme on 24 July 1972. As a result of that notice of complaints, Lancôme amended its contracts so as to enable trade between Lancômes authorised retailers established in the various Member States and to prevent Lancôme products thus exported or imported from being made subject to the system of imposed prices applied in certain Member States. The Director General for Competition therefore sent Lancôme on 16 December 1974 a letter worded as follows:

'Re: Case No IV/19 552 - Lancome sales organisation

Dear Sirs,

Lancôme SA has organised in France and in other countries of the EEC a selective distribution network the main characteristic of which is a limited number of authorised retailers.

This sales organisation is based on a standard exclusive distributorship agreement concluded by Lancôme with its general agents in the various countries of the EEC and on the uniform distributorship agreements concluded by the latter and by Lancôme with their authorised retailers in their respective territories.

The standard exclusive distributorship agreement and the uniform distributorship agreements contained provisions considered by the Commission to be incompatible with Article 85 of the Treaty of Rome. They involved in particular provisions aimed to prevent authorised retailers from reselling Lancôme products to or buying them from general agents or authorised retailers in the other countries of the EEC as well as the obligation to abide by the imposed prices, even in the case of Lancôme products which they were re-importing or re-exporting in the Common Market. For this reason your company was notified of complaints on 24 July 1972 pursuant to Article 19(1) of Regulation No 17. As a result of that notice your company amended the agreements which are the outcome of its sales organisation in the EEC in such a way that authorised retailers are henceforth free to resell Lancôme products or to buy them from any general agent or authorised retailer established in the EEC and to fix their selling prices where the products are reimported from or reexported to other countries of the Common Market.

I have the honour to inform you that in these circumstances, in view of the small share in the market in perfumery, beauty products and toiletries held by your company in each of the countries of the Common Market and in view of the fairly large number of competing undertakings of comparable size on that market and because the financial links between your company and the Oréal group do not seem in this case likely to influence the volume of your turnover for the products in question, the Comission considers that there is no longer any need, on the basis of the facts known to it, for it to take action in respect of the above-mentioned agreements under the provisions of Article 85(1) of the Treaty of Rome. The file on this case may therefore be closed.

I would however draw your attention to the fact that the Commission will keep a close watch to ensure that qualified retailers are not admitted to or excluded from your selective distribution network arbitrarily and that such admittance or exclusion does not constitute an indirect means of hindering freedom of trade between authorised distributors.

Yours faithfully,

W. Schlieder.'

4. The Ahold NV group to which Etos BV and Albert Heijn Supermarkt BV, the defendants in the main action, belong, controls a large chain of retail shops in the Netherlands, principally in the sector of foodstuffs and large-scale consumer goods. At present Etos runs 59 chemist shops in the Netherlands based on the discount sales formula and through this means sells a range of products including drugs, pharmaceutical products, beauty products and perfumes.

Before being taken over by Albert Heijn group (which has since become Ahold), Etos had concluded with Cosparfrance agreements whereby several shops run by Etos were authorised as stockists of Lancôme articles. These agreements came to an end on 20 October 1975.

The defendants in the main action asked Cosparfrance to supply Lancôme products to all their Etos chemist shops and discount drugstores but Cosparfrance refused on the ground that the discount drugstores did not fulfil its qualitative criteria and that moreover it would be contrary to its selective distribution system to supply all the shops in question.

The defendants in the main action however proceeded to sell Lancôme products at prices lower than those which the Netherlands stockists must apply.

5. Lancôme and Cosparfrance, the plaintiffs in the main action, brought proceedings against Albert Heijn Supermarkt and Etos before the Arrondissementsrechtbank, Haarlem, asking that court to prohibit the defendants from selling Lancôme products in their shops which are not authorised as stockists of Lancôme products and in addition to order them to pay compensation for the damage suffered on account of those sales.

In support of those requests, Lancôme claimed that the defendants are guilty of a wrongful act vis-à-vis them by undermining and destroying their sales organisation, in particular by provoking breaches of contract by authorised stockists.

6. The defendants claimed in their defence that the plaintiffs' sales organisation is partially void because it is incompatible with Article 85(1) of the EEC Treaty. They also maintained that the above-mentioned letter of 16 December 1974 constituted merely the opinion of a head of department which is not binding on the Commission.

7. In view of the controversy which has arisen between the parties as to the applicability of Article 85(1) to this case, the court making the reference submitted to the Court of Justice by order of 19 June 1979 a reference for a preliminary ruling.

*The Court held:*

*Provisional validity*

12. As the Court ruled most recently in its judgment of 14 December 1977 in Case 59/77 *De Bloos* v *Bouyer* (1977) ECR 2359, during the period between notification and the date on which the Commission takes a decision, 'courts before which proceedings are brought relating to an old agreement duly notified or exempted from notification must give such an agreement the legal effects attributed thereto under the law applicable to the contract, and those effects cannot be called in question by any objections which may be raised concerning its compatibility with Article 85(1)'.

13. The Court making the reference asks whether a letter such as that of 16 December 1974 sent to Lancôme by the relevant departments of the Commission has the result of putting to an end the provisional protection which, by virtue of the case-law of the Court, is enjoyed, as from the date of notification, by old agreements which were notified within the time-limit provided for by Article 5(1) of Regulation No 17 or which are exempted from notification.

14. With a view to answering that question the considerations which form the basis of the case-law of the Court on 'provisional validity' should be recalled.

15. As the Court has observed in particular in its judgment of 9 July 1969 in Case 10/69 *Portelange* v *Smith Corona Marchant International* (1969) ECR 309, Article 85 of the Treaty is arranged in the form of a rule imposing a prohibition (paragraph (1)) with a statement of its effects (paragraph (2)) mitigated by the exercise of a power to grant exceptions to that rule (paragraph (3)). To treat a given agreement, or certain of its clauses, as automatically void presupposes that the agreement falls within the prohibition of paragraph (1) of the said article and that it may not benefit from the provisions of paragraph (3).

16. The exclusive power to apply Article 85(3) which is conferred on the Commission by Article 9(1) of Regulation No 17, considered in conjunction with the provisions laid down in favour of old agreements by Article 6(2) and 7 of that regulation, has led the Court to conclude that, in the case of those old agreements, the principle of legal certainty in contractual matters requires that, where the agreement has been notified in accordance with the provisions of Regulation No 17, a court may only declare it to be automatically void after the Commission has taken a decision by virtue of that regulation.

17. In the light of those considerations, it appears that the maintenance of the provisional protection from which notified old agreements benefit is no longer justified from the date on which the Commission informs the parties concerned that it has decided to close the file on the case concerning them. After the adoption of such an attitude, which indicates that the Commission does not contemplate taking an individual decision on the notified agreements in question, it is unlikely that the Commission would subsequently exercise in favour of those agreements its power to apply Article 85(3) with, where appropriate, retroactive effect for the period prior to their notification, as permitted by Article 6(2) of Regulation No 17. There is, therefore, no longer any reason to release

national courts, before which the direct effect of the prohibition in Article 85(1) is relied upon, from the duty of giving judgment.

18. The answer to the first question should therefore be that an administrative letter informing the person concerned that the Commission is of the opinion that there are no grounds for it to take action with regard to agreements which have been notified pursuant to the provisions of Article 85(1) has the effect of terminating the period of provisional validity accorded from the date of notification to agreements made prior to 13 March 1962 notified within the period laid down in Article 5(1) of Regulation No 17 or exempted from notification. The opinions expressed in such a letter are not binding on the national courts but constitute a factor which the latter may take into account in examining whether the agreements are in accordance with the provisions of Article 85.

*Sequel:*

For other aspects of the so-called perfumes cases see above at page 29 and page 38 , and below at page 441.

## C. Severability of Offending Clauses

### (1) LTM v. MBU Case

For facts and references see above, page 69.

*The Court held:*

The second question relating to the interpretation of Article 85(2)

Article 85(2) provides that 'Any agreements or decisions prohibited pursuant to this Article shall be automatically void'.
This provision, which is intended to ensure compliance with the Treaty, can only be interpreted with reference to its purpose in Community law, and it must be limited to this context. The automatic nullity in question only applies to those parts of the agreement affected by the prohibition, or to the agreement as a whole if it appears that those parts are not severable from the agreement itself. Consequently any other contractual provisions which are not affected by the prohibition, and which therefore do not involve the application of the Treaty, fall outside Community law.

### (2) Consten-Grundig Case

For facts and references see above, page 66.

*The Court held:*

The Complaints relating to the extent of the prohibtion

The applicant Grundig and the German Governement complain that the Commission did not exclude from the prohibition, in the operative part of the contested decision, those clauses of the contract in respect of which there was found no effect capable of restricting competition, and that it thereby failed to define the infringement.

It is apparent from the statement of reasons for the contested decision, as well as from Article 3 thereof, that the infringement declared to exist by Article 1 of the operative part is not to be found in the undertaking by Grundig not to make direct deliveries in France except in Consten. That infringement arises from the clauses which, added to this grant of exclusive rights, are intended to impede, relying upon national law, parallel imports of Grundig products into France by establishing absolute territorial protection in favour of the sole concessionaire.

The provision in Article 85(2) that agreements prohibited pursuant to Article 85 shall be automatically void applies only to those parts of the agreement which are subject to the prohibition, or to the agreement as a whole if those parts do not appear to be severable from the agreement itself, The Commission should, therefore, either have confined itself in the operative part of the contested decision to declaring that an infringement lay in those parts only of the agreement which came within the prohibition, or else it should have set out in the preamble to the decision the reasons why those parts did not appear to it to be severable from the whole agreement.

It follows, however, from Article 1 of the decision that the infringement was found to lie in the agreement as a whole, although the Commission did not adequately state the reasons why it was necessary to render the whole of the agreement void when it is not established that all the clauses infringed the provisions of Article 85(1). The state of affairs found to be incompatible with Article 85(1) stems from certain specific clauses of the contract of 1 April 1957 concerning absolute territorial protection and from the additional agreement on the GINT trademark rather than from the combined operation of all the clauses of the agreement, that is to say, from the aggregate of its effects.

Article 1 of the contested decision must therefore be annulled in so far as it renders void, without any valid reason, all the clauses of the agreement by virtue of Article 85(2).

## III ARTICLE 85 PARAGRAPH 3

### A. Individual Exemption

Consult Regulation 17 Articles 6, 8 and 9.

#### (1) Consten-Grundig Case

For facts and references see above, page 66.

The complaints concerning the application of Article 85(3).

The conditions of application

The applicants, supported on several points by the German Governement, allege inter alia that all the conditions for application of the exemption, the existence of which is denied in the contested decision, are met in the present case. The defendant starts from the premise that it is for the undertakings concerned to prove that the conditions required for exemption are satisfied.

The undertakings are entitled to an appropriate examination by the Commission of their requests for Article 85(3) to be applied. For this purpose the Commission may not confine itself to requiring from undertakings proof of the fulfilment of the requirements for the grant of the exemption but must, as a matter of good administration, play its part, using the means available to it, in ascertaining the relevant facts and circumstances.

Furthermore, the exercise of the Commission's powers necessarily implies complex evaluations on economic matters. A judicial review of these evaluations must take account of their nature by confining itself to an examination of the relevance of the facts and of the legal consequences which the Commission deduces therefrom. This review must in the first place be carried out in respect of the reasons given for the decisions which must set out the facts and considerations on which the said evaluations are based.

The contested decision states that the principle reason for the refusal of exemption lies in the fact that the requirement contained in Article 85(3) is not satisfied.

The German Government complains that the said decision does not answer the question whether certain factors, especially the advance orders and the guarantees and after-sales services, the favourable effects of which were recognised by the Commission, could be maintained intact in the absolute territorial protection.

The contested decision admits only by way of assumption that the sole distributorship contract in question contributes to an improvement in production and distribution. Then the contested decision examines the question 'whether an improvement in the distribution of goods by virtue of the sole distribution agreement could no longer be achieved if parallel imports were admitted'. After examining the arguments concerning advance orders, the observation of the market and the guarantee and after-sales services, the decision concluded that 'no other reasons which militates in favour of the necessity for absolute territorial protection has been put forward or hinted at'.

The question whether there is an improvement in the production or distribution of the goods in question, which is required for the grant of exemption, is to be answered in accordance with the spirit of Article 85. First, this improvement cannot be identified with all the advantages which the parties to the agreement obtain from it in their production or distribution activities. These advantages are generally indisputable and show the agreement as in all respects indispensable to an improvement as understood in this sense. This subjective method, which makes the content of the concept of 'improvement' depend upon the special features of the contractual relationships in question, is not consistent with the aim of Article 85. Furthermore, the very fact that the Treaty provides that the restriction of competition must be 'indispensable' to the improvement in question clearly indicates the importance which the latter must have. This improvement must in particular show appreciable objective advantages of such a character as to compensate for the disadvantages which they cause in the field of competition.

The argument of the German Government, based on the premise that all those features of the agreement which favour the improvement as conceived by the parties to the agreement must be maintained intact, presupposes that the question whether all these features are not only favourable but also indispensable to the improvement of the production or distribution of the goods in question has already been settled affirmatively. Because of this the argument not only tends to weaken the requirement of indispensability but also among other consequences to confuse solicitude for the specific interests of the parties with the objective improvements contemplated by the Treaty.

In its evaluation if the relative importance of the various factors submitted for its consideration, the Commission on the other hand had to judge their effectiveness by reference to an objectively ascertainable improvement in the production and distribution of the goods, and to decide whether the resulting benefit would suffice to support the conclusion that the consequent restrictions upon competition were indispensable. The argument on the necessity to maintain intact all arrangements of the parties in so far as they are capable of contributing to the improvement sought cannot be reconciled with the view propounded in the last sentence. Therefore, the complaint of the Federal Government, based on faulty premises, is not such as can invalidate the Commission's assessment.

The applicants maintain that the admission of parallel imports would mean that the sole representative would no longer be in a position to engage in advance planning.

A certain degree of uncertainty is inherent in all forecasts of future sales possibilities. Such forecasting must in fact be based on a series of variable and uncertain factors. The admission of parallel imports may indeed involve increased risks for the concessionaire who gives firm orders in advance for the quantities of goods which he considers he will be able to sell. However, such a risk is inherent in all commercial activity and thus cannot justify special protection on this point.

The applicants complain that the Commission did not consider on the basis of concrete facts whether it is possible to provide guarantee and after-sales services without absolute territorial protection. They emphasise in particular the importance for the reputation of the Grundig name of the proper provision for all these services for all the Grundig machines put on the market. The freeing of parallel imports would compel Consten to refuse these sevices for machines imported by its competitors who did not themselves carry out these services satisfactorily. Such a refusal would also be contrary to the interests of consumers.

As regards the free guarantee service, the decision states that a purchaser can normally enforce his right to such a guarantee only against his supplier and subject to conditions agreed with him. The applicant parties do not seriously dispute that statement.

The fears concerning the damage which might result for the reputation of Grundig products from an inadequate service do not, in the circumstances, appear unjustified.

In fact, UNEF, the main competitor of Consten, although it began selling Grundig products in France later than Consten and while having had to bear not inconsiderable risks, nevertheless supplies a free guarantee and after-sales services against remuneration upon considerations which, taken as a whole, do not seemed to have harmed the reputation of the Grundig name. Moreover, nothing prevents the applicants from informing consumers, through adequate publicity, of the nature of the services and any other advantages which may be offered by the official distribution network for Grundig products. It is thus not correct that the publicity carried out by Consten must benefit parallel importers to the same extent.

Consequently, the complaints raised by the applicants are unfounded.

(2) First Decision on the Transocean Marine Paint Association

Decision of 27 June 1967 on a proceeding under Article 85 of the Treaty; J.O. No 163, 20 July 1967, p. 10; (1967) CMLR D 9; CCH para. 2061,85; Competition Law CM/M/I/9.

*Facts:* On 27 June 1967 the Commission of the European Economic Community took its first decision on a co-operation agreement between small and medium-sized enterprises. This decision, which relates to the prohibition of cartels under Article 85 of the EEC Treaty, concerns the Transocean Marine Paint Association, whose membership comprises eighteen medium-sized marine paint manufacturers each established in a different country, five being Member States of the EEC. The members of this association, which has its headquarters in the Netherlands, agreed to pool their technical knowledge to develop certain marine paints, to manufacture them under the same quality standard and to market them under the same trademark. Each member is required, in the country in which it operates, to see that regular supplies of these paints are available by maintaining adequate stocks and ensuring an after-sales service so that purchasers may be able to obtain paints of identical quality, as they require them, in a great number of different countries. This is particularly important as regards the special toxic paints for protecting the parts of a ship's hull below the waterline. The purpose of tis cooperative venture is to tap a world-wide market and to step up competition with the large international marine paint combines.

For this purpose, the agreement originally provided for measures of territorial protection which had the effect of excluding competition between the members almost entirely, to the detriment of buyers. Territorial protection concerned not only the products sold under the common trademark but also marine paints which the members continued to manufacture and sell individually and which still account for the greater part of their turnover. The EEC Commission had opposed these measures because they were not indispensable to the attainment of the objects of the agreement, deemed in themselves reasonable. As a result, the members of the association decided to delete the restrictions on competition objected to, and amended the agreement in consequence.

True, the present version of the agreement does in fact still contain provisions that appreciably restrict competition within the Common Market and are liable to impair trade between States because they give the members of the association, in their own countries, competitive advantage over other members. However, the Commission noted that the agreement tends to improve the distribution of marine paints in the interest of users, and that the restrictions maintained are necessary for the attainment of this objective. Taking the view that during the period when the product is being launched, every member of the association must be able to act vigorously in the market where its chief place of business is located, the Commission allowed that members must be required, in countries in which other members are established to refrain from manufacturing marine paints, either on their own or in cooperation with non-member firms, and to supply there only within the framework of the system of mutual commission.
Here, the Commission allowed for the fact that this system of commission payments does not actually rule out exports, and provide a corrective for any artificial differences between members' prices. The Commission also attributed great importance to the members' relatively weak position on the market for the product in question and to the great competition they face from the other marine paint manufacturers. On these grounds it decided that the cartel prohibition under the EEC Treaty would in this case be inapplicable for a period of five years.
The Commission, nevertheless, laid down certain conditions which will enable it to ascertain whether the members' future activities remain within the bounds of the declaration of exemption.

The Transocean affair is a typical case for a number of decisions the Commission is preparing in the field of co-operation between small and medium-sized enterprises. In its report last year on industrial combination in the Common Market, it urged that small and medium-sized enterprises be encouraged to conclude agreements on joint research, specialisation and reorganisation, so that they may better fulfil their specific role in competition with the large enterprises. In the present decision the Commission stresses its approval of certain forms of co-operation, but points out at the same time that the finding that co-operation is likely to promote competition with larger enterprises does not absolve it from verifying, in accordance with Article 85, whether the competition-restricting methods employed to attain this end (especially measures of territorial protection) do not go beyond what may be regarded as essential in view of the actual market conditions. The Commision thus emphasises its disapproval of market-sharing when it prevents or hampers the economic merging of the national markets into a single common market, which is one of the aims of the EEC Treaty. Under the terms of Article 85 (3) the Commission may declare the provisions of section (1) of that Article inapplicable to any agreement, any decision and any concerted practice which contributes to improving the the production or distribution of goods or to promoting technical or economic progress, whilst allowing consumers a fair share of the resulting benefit, and which does not:

(a) impose on the undertakings concerned restrictions which are not indispensable to the achievement of the above objectives;

(b) afford such undertakings the possibility of eliminating competition in respect of a substantial part of the products in question.

The facts of which the Commission has knowledge allow it to conclude that the notified agreement, in the form in which it has been in force since 15 June 1966, meets the four above-mentioned conditions for a decision, applying Article 85 (3), in the present state of the market.

1. The agreement contributes to improving the distribution of the products. In fact, it allows the members to rationalize and intensify the sale of the marine paints manufactured by them to a common standard and presented under a common trademark. The institution of granted territories in each of which the members there established is primarily responsible for the sale of these paints guarantees, through a judicious geographical distribution of the members and the goods knowledge of the market, that the Transocean paints are offered and stored in a regular manner and in sufficient quantities in a large number of countries and ports and that each member is in a position without difficulty to make deliveries outside its own granted territory, either by itself exporting or through the other intermediary of other members. The members of the association are, therefore, in a position also to give a service to purchasers who wish to be able to obtain the marine paints which they use of an identical quality at any time and in any place at which they may have need of them. Were it not for this agreement, the members would be obliged to create their own distribution networks in a large number of countries, which would involve investments and risks which are excessive for undertakings of a medium size (the need to establish branches or to set up agencies, to maintain depots and after-sales service). Thanks to the association and the coordination of the various individual sale networks of its members, the latter are able, although being medium undertakings, to enter more actively into competition with the big marine paint manufacturers already represented in all the major countries, which results in an increase in the supply of the products

and an improvement in the sales structure in the marine paint sector. The agreement thus involves perceptible objective advantages for the distribution of the products, as compared with the situation which would obtain if it had not been concluded.

2. The consumers obtain a fair share of the resultant benefit, i.e. the advantages which flow from the agreement and which have been set out above. The agreement leads to an increase and an enlargement of the supply of marine paints. The consumer may, as in the past, purchase the products manufactured individually by the members of the association without being obliged to apply to the members of the association established in their country, since no absolute territorial protection has been agreed. Those consumers which decide to use Transocean paints thenceforth avoid the necessity to carry on the ship itself the paint required for its maintenance; they may obtain without difficulty or delay paint of an identical quality in the numerous depots maintained by the members of the association, while avoiding the loss of useful space in their ships. The purchasers of Transocean paint have the possibility of applying to the local member of the association, for example, when they wish to obtain technical advice and have the work of painting supervised. They may, however, apply to members established in other countries when their conditions (price, delivery, date etc.) seem to them more favourable. The ability to purchase from other members usefully corrects the artificial differences which may exist between the prices asked by the members and, when joined to the price competition to which the members are exposed from their competitors, contributes to guaranteeing to the consumers a fair share in the benefits of the agreement.

3. In the present form, the agreement contains no restriction which is not indispensable for obtaining the above-mentioned objectives.

(a) As regards the special Transocean paints, the measures laid down for the concentration of production and sales efforts on the various granted territories are necessary to create as wide and as complete a distribution network as possible, a network which, itself, is a pre-condition for the successful launching of the Transocean products and for an active promotion of the new Transocean marks. Given their relatively modest positions on the market, such a launching requires particularly intensive efforts from the members. In the Common Market, the most important members manufacture only about ... per cent of the production of their countries in marine paints, and all are exposed to a lively competition from producers which are often much bigger. The members must, therefore, during the launching period, make particular efforts to draw the attention of purchasers to the new Transocean paints, of an identical quality and available in all the granted territories and, being producers which hitherto were unknown outside a limited area, to create a reputation as against their competitors which already have available a world sales network. Although the association was created in 1959, that launching period must be regarded as not yet ended. This is explained by the frequent changes which have especially occurred in the composition of the association and appears in practice in the fact that the proportion of Transocean paints sold by the members still represent at the present moment only ... per cent of their total paint production.

In these particular circumstances, the best means of leading the members to promote intensively the sale of Transocean paints in their granted territory consists in imposing upon them the obligation to concentrate their main efforts on that territory so as to ensure that there is available a sufficient and regular supply for their customers, while being able to count on other members not carrying on in that territory such a large activity that it puts in question their own interest in promoting the sales.

At present, intensive action by all the members on their respective territories could not be obtained if they were free to manufacture or have manufactured Transocean paints on the granted territory of other members. This intensive action could further be compromised for lack of a clause relating to commissions, which encourages each member which has received an order which is to be executed in the territory granted to another member to transit it to the latter, and thereby contributes to giving to the members, for the territory for which they are responsible, a privileged position which is necessary if they are to have an interest in exerting an intensive sales effort there. This clause does not, however, exclude the possibility of Transocean paints being imported into the granted territory of each member on payment of a relatively small compensation, which does not have a prohibitive effect, and this encourages the member responsible for that territory to intensify its sales efforts there.

This possibility of trade between Member States in Transocean paints, organised in this way by the clause relating to commission, is not affected by the situation created by the agreement with regard to the right to the trademarks. The present case is characterised by the fact that one and the same mark is used simultaneously in different States by several producers to designate identical products, and this is done by virtue of an agreement which, in order to guarantee unreservedly the interchangeability of the products and to avoid the consumer being led into error, ensures that the products in question are qualitatively identical. In these circumstances, the members established in the Common Market cannot enforce the rights flowing from the marks registered in their favour on their granted territory in order to hinder the imports from other Member States of the Transocean products manufactured by other members. In fact, as the Court of Justice of the European Communities has indicated in Consten-Grundig v. EEC Commission, the fundamental principle of the Community system of competition is opposed to the abusive exercise of the national trademark rights to frustrate the effectiveness of the Community Law on restrictive agreements.

In the light of these various circumstances, it can justly be admitted that the restrictions on competition in Transocean paints do not go beyond what is necessary to attain the objectives of the agreement.

(b) As regards the sale of marine paints other than Transocean paints, the restrictions laid down in the agreement are necessary to encourage the members to use the Transocean marks intensively and thus to promote the sale of Transocean paints.

In fact, the cooperation between the members in the perfecting, the production and the sale of the Transocean paints could not function satisfactorily during the launching period and would not allow an intensification of competition between those products and those of the competitors to be anticipated, if the members were able freely to manufacture or have manufactured, on the granted territory of other members, marine paints other than Transocean paints.

During the launching period, the objectives of the agreement could not be attained without imposing upon the members the obligation to export their own brands to the granted territory of other members only after prior agreement of the latter and on payment of a relatively small compensation. The ability to refuse such authorisation where the envisaged export would clash with the interests of the association gives to the members the guarantee that none of them should, during the period of launching the Transocean paints, be able to pour exclusively or principally its products under its own trademarks on the granted territory of other members to the prejudice of the extension of the sales of the Transocean paints and, consequently, to the prejudice of the common interests of all the members. Furthermore, as a result of this restriction on the liberty to export, those members which receive orders to be executed on the territory granted to another member are encouraged to transmit them to that member, which leads them in practice to offer in preference to their customers Transocean paints, also available at the same quality in the country where the delivery is to take place, and thus to contribute to the promotion of the sales of these paints.

There is no factor indicating that the above-mentioned provisions lead, by the manner in which they are applied, to a restriction of the economic liberty of the members which goes beyond what is indispensable for attaining the objectives of the agreement.

(c) The other restrictions on competition laid down in the agreement should also be held to be indispensable to the intensification of the efforts of each of the members. If manufacture as a sub-contractor for undertakings not belonging to the association were permitted without any limitation, there would be reason to fear that a member would thereby be giving support to those very competitors of the association or competitors of certain of its members against whom the association was intended to encourage a more effective competition. Nor could one exclude the risk that a member should, in the course of its cooperation with undertakings not belonging to the association, a cooperation which would necessarily extend to technical details relating to the manufacturing process, reveal business secrets relating to the perfecting of the Transocean paints and members acquire through the operation of the exchange of information clause secrets which, in the interests of a trusting collaboration, they have undertaken not to divulge.
Finally, the preferential right of members in the grant of licences may in this instance be considered as necessary to prevent the members from making their common technical know-how accessible to third parties by granting them, to the detriment of the other members' interests, licences relating to patents which they could acquire by profiting from the common know-how.

4. The agreement does not give to those concerned any possibility of eliminating competition in a substantial part of the products in question. According to the data available to the Commission, the share in the market of the Common Market members of the association is only about ... per cent, and those members are subject to a lively competition within the Common Market from other manufacturers of marine paints and in particular from the big international groups offering these paints in the Common Market, groups which are in no way hindered from access to that market by the agreement. Thus the last conditions for the application of Article 85(3) is met.

The date of coming into effect of the decision applying Article 85 (3), under Article 6(1) of Regulation No 17, should be fixed at the day on which the notified agreement was amended so as to permit that decision, namely, in this case 15 June 1966. The decision applying Article 85(3) should, under Article 8(1) of Regulation No 17, be granted for a fixed period, namely in the present case for the period ending on 31 December 1972, a period which is necessary to enable an examination of the effects of the agreement and its influence on the market conditions.

For the period preceding the date of coming into effect of the decision applying Article 85(3), i.e. the period from the date of entry into force of Regulation No 17 (13 March 1962) to 15 June 1966, it is necessary, at the request of the parties and in accordance with Article 7(1) of Regulation No 17 to decide whether and to what extent the prohibition laid down in Article 85(1) applies for that period. The conditions of application of that provision are met. There is an agreement existing at the date of entry into force of Regulation No 17 and notified in proper time to the Commission in accordance with Article 5(1) of Regulation No 17, i.e. before 1 November 1962. In its notified version, the agreement contained provisions which could not be regarded as indispenable to the realisation of its objectives and which therefore were an obstacle to a decision applying Article 85(3). Following the communication of the Commission's objections to these provisions made on 30 July 1965 under Article 19(1) of Regulation No 17, the agreement was amended in such a way that, as indicated above, it now meets the conditions laid down in Article 85(3). There is therefore no reason in this case to refuse application of Regulation No 17.

It seems right to subject the decision on conditions in accordance with Article 8(1) of Regulation No 17. These conditions should permit the Commission more easily to determine whether there are or not grounds for it to revoke, under Article 8(3), or alter the present decision or to prohibit those concerned from taking certain courses of action. To that end there should be imposed upon the members of the association the obligation to notify all alterations which may take place in the composition of the association and all amendments and additions to the agreement, as well as all decisions of the board of management and all arbitral awards delivered under Article 23 of the agreement, in so far as they relate to the application or the interpretation of the provisions of the agreement taken into account in the present decision

The fact that this is a cooperation between medium sized undertakings with a view to organising on a world-wide scale a rational system of distribution for the Transocean paints constitutes an essential element in the decision to apply Article 85(3) and it appears, therefore, necessary to impose on the members the obligation to submit annually to the Commission a report on the activity of the association and of its members for the time being and, where appropriate, of its new members, making separate mention of the production and sales of the Transocean marine paints and of the other marine paints manufactured by the members. In order that it should be possible to supervise the effects of the system of commissions on the evolution of the trade in marine paints in the Common Market, there should further be imposed on the members of the association established in the Common Market the obligation to indicate the volume of deliveries for which they are reciprocally required to pay commissions and the amount and rate of the commission relating thereto. In this connection, it is sufficient that these indications should, as has already been the case during the pleading in this case, be sent to the Commission by the general secretary of the association, by agreement with its members, and on the basis of the quarterly reports which they must make under point 11 of the annex to the agreement.

THE COMMISSION, for these reasons,

DECIDES:

1. The provisions of Article 85(1) of the Treaty instituting the European Economic Community are declared inapplicable, under section (3) of that Article, to the agreement concluded on 1 January 1959 and amended on 15

June 1966, creating the Transocean Marine Paint Asssociation.

2. The provision of Article 1 of this Decision takes effect from 15 June 1966. It is applicable until 31 December 1972.

3. By virtue of Article 7(1) of Regulation No 17, the prohibition laid down in Article 85(1) does not apply for the period from 13 March 1962 to 15 June 1966.

4. The present Decision is subject to the following conditions:

(1) The following should be notified without delay to the Commission:

(a) all alterations which may take place in the composition of the association;

(b) all amendments and additions to the agreement;

(c) all the decisions of the board of management and all arbitral awards relating to the application or interpretation of the provisions of the agreement taken into consideration in the present Decision.

(2) The Commission should be supplied once annually, and on the first occasion for the year 1967, with a report on the activity or the association, on the volume of production and on the volume and amount of the sales of each of the members in the marine paint sector, making a distinction between the Transocean paints and the other marine paints which they manufacture, on the volume of deliveries of marine paints for which the members of the association established in the Common Market are reciprocally required to pay commissions and on the amount and rates of the relevant commission.

5. The present Decision is addressed to the members of the association, represented by the latter's general secretary, Mr. F.Ph. Regnault.

*Sequel:*

The General Secretary of the Transocean Marine Paint Association applied on 27 October 1972 for the extension of the exemption under Article 85(3). The exemption was granted by decision of 27 June 1967 and expired on 31 December 1972. A further exemption was granted on 21 December 1973. The Association brought an action for annulment against that Commission Decision on procedural grounds, see page 324. After the Judgment of the Court, the Commission took a new Decision taking into consideration the Court's Judgment. By Decision of 12 December 1979 the Decision was extended again until 31 December 1980.

(3) Decision in re VBVB/VBBB

Decision of 25 November 1981 on a proceeding under Article 85 of the EEC Treaty, O.J. No L54, 25 February 1982, p. 36: (1982) 2 CMLR 344; CCH para. 10351; Competition Law CM/M/I/168.

*Facts:*

1. This proceeding concerns an agreement between the Vereeniging ter Bevordering van de Belangen des Boekhandels (Association for the Promotion of the Interests of the Book Trade - VBBB) and the Vereeniging ter Bevordering van het Vlaamsche Boekwezen (Association for the Promotion

of Flemish Books - VBVB) governing trade in books between the Netherlands and Flanders, which was signed by the associations on 21 January 1949 and amended on 2 July 1958. The agreement was notified to the Commission, pursuant to Regulation No 17, by the VBBB on 30 October 1962 and by the VBVB on 3 November 1962. The proceeding does not concern the systems of collective resale price maintenance operated in the Netherlands and Flanders.

*The Commission ruled:*

APPLICABILITY OF ARTICLE 85(3)

47. Pursuant to Article 85(3), the provisions of Article 85(1) of the EEC Treaty may be declared inapplicable in the case of any agreement between undertakings which contributes to improving the production or distribution of goods or to promoting technical or economic progress, while allowing consumers a fair share of the resulting benefit, and which does not:

(a) impose on the undertakings concerned restrictions which are not indispensable to the attaintment of these objectives.

(b) afford such undertakings the possibility of eliminating competition in respect of a substantial part of the products in question.

48. In regard to the collective exclusive dealing system, it should be pointed out that the parties advanced no arguments for the exemption of this part of the agreement in question in their written observations or in their oral elucidations. Moreover, the parties stated that this clause would not appear in a new agreement. In this connection the Commission considers that the collective exclusive dealing system makes no contribution to the improvement of the production or distribution of the products concerned, namely books, in view of the fact that that clause has the object and effect of establishing a system of market protection for the benefit of the publishers and traders connected with the associations in question, whereby undertakings in the book trade in the one country who are not recognised or registered are restricted in their scope for purchases and sales in the other country, and the free development of other distribution channels and sales methods is limited or hindered.

In regard to the collective resale price maintenance system in trade in Dutch language books between the Netherlands and Belgium, the Commission believes that it would be useful to look more closely at the parties' arguments in relation to all the conditions of Article 85(3), although it is, in principle, unnecessary to consider whether an agreement satisfies all the conditions of Article 85(3) when it has already been found to fail one of those conditions. The Commission's counter-arguments reflect its position on this part of the agreement which is the subject of this Decision.

The Commission also wishes to point out that this Decision discusses certain aspects of collective resale price maintenance in general, since the assessment of the agreement for the fixing of prices of books in inter-State trade cannot be separated from the subject.

## A. CONTRIBUTION TO IMPROVING THE PRODUCTION OR DISTRIBUTION OF GOODS

49. The system of collective resale price maintenance which the agreement establishes for trade in books between Belgium and the Netherlands does not contribute to improving the production of the goods concerned, namely Dutch-language books, or to improving the distribution of such books.

50. The parties have claimed that the collective resale price maintenance scheme established by the agreement contributes to improving the production and distribution of the goods concerned, since the fixed price for Dutch-language books, even beyond national borders, allows subsidisation of less popular books by fast-selling books and thus enables publishers to place a wide range of titles on the market. According to the parties, the fixed price represents a certain security for publishers when they decide to publish a book and such security is necessary if a wide range of titles is to be maintained. With a fixed price, the publisher is sure that the organised book trade will be prepared to stock and promote the sale of less-popular books. The fixed price also makes it possible for smaller publishers, who are often engaged in the publishing of commercially not very attractive books, to hold their own. On the distribution side, the fixed price means that the bookseller can stock a large and varied range of titles in his shop by subsidising the costs on slow-moving titles from the profit on fast-moving ones. This profit enables him to offer ancillary services to the public and to place orders for individual customers.

51. The parties' argument is based on the existence of a link between the principle of cross-subsidisation as practised both by the producer, i.e. publisher, and the distributor, i.e. bookseller, and the system of collective resale price maintenance. The Commission cannot accept this argument, because cross-subsidisation, assuming it is a valid economic or commercial consideration in this case, is not necessarily dependent on a system of collective resale price maintenance. A publisher's decision to offset to some extent the costs of titles that are not very attractive commercially against the profits made on those printed in large number is, in general, an individual, independent decision by each publisher when he sets his selling prices to the trade. For the publisher to be able to pursue his chosen policy there is no need for a system under which the resale price of every book is set by the publisher right down to the final stage of distribution, i.e. sale to the customer, and has to be applied by all recognised, registered or affiliated distributors in the other country. It should be sufficient for publishers to bring out a number of popular books of which they can sell the whole printing so that the relatively high earnings which result enable them to publish less-commercial titles. It cannot be accepted that this necessarily involves resale price maintenance, especially as in practice the publishers of general-interest books generally do not engage in publishing short-run books such as specialised books or the less popular literary works. Nor can the Commission subscribe to the parties' argument in this connection with regard to booksellers. In spite of the resale price maintenance scheme there has clearly already been a sharp drop in the number of general booksellers in the Netherlands, partly due to the rise of self-service shops selling almost exclusively popular books and magazines and the fairly substantial growth in the turnover of book clubs, which generally offer a fairly limited range of books.

52. In determining whether particular restrictions of competition may be exempted from the ban on restrictive practices under Article 85(3),

all that matters is whether the restrictions objectively achieve improvements over the situation which would exist without them. That the cross-border system of collective resale price maintenance may have advantages for certain market operators is not therefore a decisive aspect. It would have to be shown that individual decisions to allow commercially unattractive titles to depend on the publication and sale of books that sell well were not possible or could not reasonably be expected in the prevailing industrial and commercial context. It would also have to be demonstrated convincingly that the continued existence of smaller specialised publishers would be in serious danger under a system of free trade and free price determination. No evidence of this has yet been supplied.

53. In any event the Commission considers that any objective advantages which might derive from the agreement are outweighed by its disadvantages from the viewpoint of competition. The Commission would maintain that the agreement to which this Decision relates has an adverse rather than a favourable effect on the distribution of books, because the system of collective resale price maintenance eliminates any price competition in the distribution of a given title. This is particularly damaging since, in the absence of significant competition between different titles, competition on the price of individual titles within the distributive trade is an important means of rationalizing and improving the distribution system.

B. FAIR SHARE OF BENEFIT FOR CONSUMERS

54. The parties have claimed that the consumer receives a fair share of the benefits for the production and distribution of books resulting from the system of resale price maintenance in the trade in Dutch-language books between Belgium and the Netherlands. As far as the production or publishing of books is concerned, they have maintained that a broader range of titles is available than would be the case without resale price maintenance. In view, among other things, of the fact that may publishers do not publish both general-interest and less-popular books, but restrict themselves to the one or other type, this condition is not considered to be satisfied. Nor can the argument go unchallenged that booksellers would be unable or unwilling to provide ancillary services such as providing full information to customers and passing on individual orders unless there is a system of resale price maintenance. As long as they are able to earn a fair return for the services they provide there is no reason why booksellers should not be able to carry on a normal business without resale price maintenance. Moreover, this system denies the consumer the opportunity of deciding for himself whether to buy books at a price that includes a service charge or to take his custom to a bookseller who does not provide any services and from whom he can buy books more cheaply. The consumer pays the same price for a Dutch-language book published in the other country regardless of his preferences as to additional services; and he is obliged to pay the service charge even if he does not wish to use the service, as is apparently often the case.

55. Secondly, it must be pointed out that even if a wide range of titles and the availability of services are to be regarded as benefiting the consumer, the consumer generally cannot benefit from the advantages of any rationalization that takes place in the book trade. Booksellers are not allowed to grant discounts to good customers. Since the price of the product is, for many customers, an important element in their decision to purchase - and this applies to books as much as to other

products - the Commission considers that the consumer is not receiving a fair share of any benefits resulting from the agreement to which this Decision relates.

56. A further result of the system of collective resale price maintenance for Dutch-language books is that the main group of consumers, which tends to favour the more popular books, is forced to contribute to the cost of publishing short-run titles, which are generally intended for a smaller part of the population. In assessing the relative advantages and disadvantages of any agreement such as that concerned in this case, it cannot be accepted that the advantages it involves for a small minority of the population outweigh the disadvantages for the majority of consumers.

C. INDISPENSABLE NATURE OF THE RESTRICTIONS IMPOSED BY THE AGREEMENT

57. As regards the third condition of Article 85(3), the parties have alleged that resale price maintenance in trade in Dutch-language books between the Netherlands and Belgium is indispensable if the production and distribution of books are to be improved. In the absence of the system, specialist booksellers would lose the major part of their sales of best-sellers to cash-and-carry stores, and as a result would no longer be able to defray the cost of stocking slower-selling titles and of providing ancillary services to the consumer out of profits from best-sellers. They would therefore have to make drastic cuts in the number of slow-selling titles they stocked. Publishers would thus no longer have the assurance that they could sell these titles through booksellers. They would be less-prepared to publish limited-interest works. This would lead to the disappearance of the smaller specialised publishers.

58. The Commission believes that in order to achieve an improvement in the production and distribution of Dutch-language books by specialist booksellers a collective resale price maintenance scheme entailing the imposition of restrictions on competition in trade between Belgium and the Netherlands such as are contained in the agreement that is the subject of this Decision, is not indispensable. If there has been a deterioration in the production or distribution of Dutch-language books in recent years, this phenomenon does not necessarily have anything to do with the question of whether or not a system of cross-frontier resale price maintenance was in operation, but may just as well be attributable to the general worsening of the economic climate. The Commission believes that the parties could use less restrictive means to improve the publication and distribution of Dutch-language books.

59. Again, the Commission recognises the important role which books play as a cultural medium, among others such as the theatre, music, the cinema and painting. It agrees with the parties that a situation must not be allowed to develop in which works of cultural value can no longer be published, but resale price maintenance for all categories of books in trade between Member States is not necessary for this purpose. It must be possible to find other ways of achieving this which do not affect the position of books as a cultural medium but which are more in line with the competition rules of the EEC Treaty.

60. In an attempt to show why it is essential that the resale price maintenance scheme operated by Dutch publishers should also extend to Flanders, even though the improvements in distribution, which the VBBB's rules are alleged to achieve, affect only the territory of the Nether-

lands, and that the converse situation should apply in the Netherlands as regards the VBVB's rules, the parties have advanced the further argument that because of their cultural unity the Netherlands and Flanders form a single market for Dutch-language books. In order to maintain the unity of the market and to make possible the development of Dutch-language culture, prices fixed by the publisher must be respected not only in each of the two territories but also in trade between them. Without such a system the cultural unity of the Dutch-language area would be endangered. In the Commission's view, however, the termination of resale price maintenance in trade betweeen Belgium and the Netherlands will not endanger the cultural unity of the Dutch-language area. Apart from the fact that Dutch-language books form only one element in this cultural unity, the agreement which is the subject of this Decision is only one of the ways in which cultural unity with regard to Dutch-language books manifests itself. The emphasis should rather be placed on forms of co-operation which, while safeguarding the freedom of expression of authors, would act to the advantage of all categories of readers, and which would leave the greatest possible measure of freedom to firms involved in the organisation of the distribution of books.

The Commission also takes the view that it is not for undertakings or associations of undertakings to conclude agreements on cultural questions, which are principally a matter for government (although the Commission recognises that undertakings can also play a valuable part in the dissemination of culture. The Commission is sure that the Member States concerned would not hesitate to take action to protect certain cultural interests should this be necessary. It would refer in this connection to the Treaty on the Dutch-language Union concluded between the Kingdom of Belgium and the Kingdom of the Netherlands, which seeks to bring about integration in the field of the Dutch language and literature in the widest sense and also makes provision for measures in the field of the publishing and dissemination of books.

### D. ELIMINATION OF COMPETITION IN RESPECT OF A SUBSTANTIAL PART OF THE PRODUCTS IN QUESTION

61. Lastly, the parties have claimed that collective resale price maintenance in trade in Dutch-language books between Belgium and the Netherlands does not eliminate competition in respect of a substantial part of the products in question. There is a group of non-recognised publishers who do not take part in the collective system. Recognised publishers compete with one another within individual categories of books. And booksellers compete with one another in the areas of stocking, specialisation, service offered and ordering facilities.

62. Even if booksellers can indeed compete on the prices of books published by non-recognised publishers, the fact is that these publishers' share of total sales of books is small in comparison with that of recognised publishers. By far the largest proportion of books published in one country and sold in the other is governed by the system of collective resale price maintenance. Booksellers cannot compete on prices for any of these titles. The other forms of competition - stocking, specialisation, service offered and ordering facilities - must be regarded as secondary to price competition, certainly from the point of view of the consumer who is often not particularly interested in highly specialised books. Among booksellers, then, competition is eliminated in respect to a substantial part of the products in question.

This conclusion is in no way affected by the fact that a degree of price competition does exist between publishers. Competition of this kind is in any case limited to a small number of titles or series. As a rule most books are completely original works, written by an author following his inspiration at the time of writing. They cannot be compared with one another. In a number of cases, certainly, it is not the author's subjective creativity which is the principle feature, but rather the objective information which the book is intended to convey. Books covering the same ground can therefore to some extent be regarded as substitutes, and may thus constitute a single market. But these works account only for a limited share of the total number of books on the market.

(4) VBVB-VBBB Case
(Dutch Belgian Book Cartel Case)

Vereniging ter Bevordering van het Vlaamsche Boekwezen (VBVB) and Vereniging ter Bevordering van de Belangen des Boekhandels (VBBB) v. Commission, Joined Cases 43 and 63/82, Judgment of 17 January 1984. (Not yet published).

*Facts:* The two associations brought an action for annulment against the Commission Decision. They also applied for suspension of the operation of the Decision in pursuance of Articles 185 and 186 of the EEC Treaty and Article 83 of the Rules of Procedure of the Court as an interim measure until the main proceedings were determined.

*The President of the Court ruled:*

.....

4. It appears both from the file and from the explanations given in the course of the interlocutory proceedings, that in the Dutch-language book market in the Netherlands and in Belgium, relations between publishers, distributors and retailers, so far as they are members of the applicant associations, are governed on the one hand by the agreement in dispute and, on the other, by two systems of rules governing the national book markets, applicable one in the Netherlands and the other in Belgium and including inter alia sale price maintenance agreements.

5. In the contested decision, the Commission expressly stated that its decision did not concern those two national systems.

6. Although, at the present stage of the proceedings, it is not possible to gain a precise conception of the relations between the two national systems and the agreement in dispute, it none the less appears and is admitted by the parties to the main proceedings that such reactions exist, inasmuch as it is the agreement in dispute which, even when the restrictions which result or might result from the national judicial decisions referred to by the contested decision have been taken into account, ensures the integrity of the combination of the national systems. The contested decision is therefore liable to influence the operation of those systems, although the Commission deliberately refrained from calling them in question by that decision.

7. In addition, the applicants have drawn attention to the obligations imposed upon them by Article 4 of the contested decision, which provides:

"The associations of undertakings referred to in Article 5 shall inform their members and affiliates and other parties recognised by or registered with them, in writing, of this decision and of the fact that the restrictions on competition laid down in the agreement referred to in Article 1 have been brought to an end, stating the practical effects that this will have on the terms under which trade in books is carried on between Belgium and the Netherlands. They shall submit a proposal for a notice to this effect to the Commission within four months of receipt of this decision."

8. The applicants contend that the immediate operation of those obligations would make it impossible to reconstruct the relationships between the different parties to the agreement in dispute, in the event of their applications for a declaration that the decision is void being successful.

9. Those two facts justify the need for the suspension, at least in part, of the operation of the contested decision, in order to avoid immediate and, to all appearances, irreversible damage to the applicants.

In its Judgment of 17 January 1984 the Court rejected the application of the associations and upheld the Commission's Decision in full.

*The Court held on exemptions:*

1. The Refusal by the Commission to take alternative proposals into consideration put forward by the applicants

As has been indicated above, the applicants had made certain alternative proposals to the Commission which are mentioned in the considerations of the Decision (points 24 to 31). They complain that these proposals, which could have mitigated the effects of the fixing of prices, were not accepted by the Commission and that the Commission in turn had failed to put forward concrete proposals which could have led to an exemption.

In this connection, it should first of all be noted that the administrative procedure has as its aim the preparation of the Commission Decision with regard to the infringement of the competition rules, but that this procedure also affords the undertakings involved the opportunity to adapt the practices in question to the rules of the Treaty. In the event that an exemption under article 85 sub 3 is sought, it is in the first place the task of the interested undertakings to convince the Commission with evidence that the exemption is economically justifiable, and in the event that the Commission submits objections, to put forward alternatives. The Commisison can indeed in turn give the undertakings indications with regard to possible alternative solutions, but it is not legally obliged to do so, let alone obliged to accept proposals which it considers incompatible with the conditions of Article 85 sub 3.

(Own unofficial translation)

## B. Group Exemptions

Consult Regulation 19/65 (Annex VI), Regulation 1983/83 (Annex VII), Regulation 1983/84 (Annex VIII), Regulation 2821/71 (Annex IX), Regulation 3604/82 (Annex X), the Draft Group Exemption for Patent Licensing Agreements (Annex XI) also based on Regulation 19/65; the Draft Group Exemption for Research and Development Agreement based on Regulation 2821/71 (Annex XIII) and the Draft Group Exemption for Certain Categories of Motor Vehicle Distribution and Servicing Agreements based on Regulation 19/65 (Annex XII).

The competency of the Council and the Commission to enact group exemptions was challenged by the Italian Government. The Court upheld however the competency of the institutions.

(1) Group Exemption Regulation Case

Government of Italy v. EEC Council and EEC Commission, Case 32/65, Judgment of 13 July 1966; (1966) ECR 389; (1969) CMLR 39; CCH para. 8048; Competition Law CM/M/III/6.

*Facts:* By Regulation No 17/62 of 6 February 1962, the Council provided that where parties to an agreement wish to avail themselves of the exemption from prohibition under Article 85(3) that agreement must be notified to the Commission. However, Article 4(2) thereof provides that certain types of agreements therein described shall be exempt from this formality.

By Regulation No 153/62 of 21 December 1962 the Commission introduced a simplified notification procedure for certain so-called exclusive dealing agreements.

Finally by Regulation 19/65 of 2 March 1965 the Council conferred upon the Commission the power to declare by regulation that the exemptions in Article 85(3) shall apply to whole categories of agreements. On 31 May 1965 the Government of the Italian Republic lodged with the Court an application against the Council and, in so far as necessary, against the Commission of the EEC requesting a declaration annulling Regulation No 19/65 of the Council, and a declaration under Article 184 of the Treaty, that Articles 4 and 5 of Regulation No 17/62 of the Council and Regulation No 153/62 of the Commission are inapplicable.

*The Court held:*

The Italian Governement has brought an application against the Council of the EEC and, in so far as necessary, against the Commission. The application is mainly for the annulment of Regulation No 19/65 of the Council, dated 2 March 1965, relating to the application of Article 85 (3) of the Treaty establishing the EEC to categories of agreements and concerted practices.

The application also asks, in reliance on Article 184 of the said Treaty, for a declaration that the following measures are inapplicable: subparagrapgh 2(a) and (b) of Article 4(2) and Article 5(2) of Regulation No 17/62 of the Council, dated 6 February 1962, providing for the notification of agreements in favour of which interested parties wish to claim the benefit of Article 85(3).

Finally, and again relying on Article 184 of the EEC Treaty, the application asks for a declaration that Regulation No 153/62 of the Commission dated 21 December 1962, introducing simplified methods for notifying certain agreements known as exclusive dealing agreements, is inapplicable.

The main relief asked for, that Regulation No 19/65 of the Council be annulled.

Under Regulation 19/65, adopted by virtue of Article 87 of the Treaty, the Council conferred upon the Commission the power to grant by means of regulations and subject to certain conditions, the benefit of the exemption contained in Article 85(3) to certain categories of agreements to which only two undertakings are parties.

The application for the annulment of the said Regulation, which is made in due form, claims that the Regulation was adopted in breach of Articles 2, 3(f), 85, 86, 87 and 222 of the Treaty, and that it amounts to a misuse of powers.

The first submission, that Article 87 has been infringed

The first argument used against Regulation 19/65 is that it lays down provisions concerning the exemption in Article 85(3) without having first defined the scope of the prohibition imposed by Article 85(1) and that in defining the exception before having explicitly stated the rule to which the exception is made, the said Regulation has disregarded Article 87 and infringed the principle according to which everything is permitted which has not been forbidden and replaced it by the converse principle under which everything is forbidden which has not been authorised.

By Article 87 of the Treaty the Council 'shall ... adopt any appropriate regulations or directives to give effect to the principle set out in Articles 85 and 86'.

It is for the Council to decide whether a particular regulation is 'appropriate' and it may come to such a decision on a given point without having to deal exhaustively with the whole of Articles 85 and 86; it may therefore apply the exemption set out in Article 85(3) by means of a regulation which it thinks fit. It does not follow from this that everything which has not been exempted is to be presumed to be forbidden.

Furthermore Article 85(3) of the Treaty provides that the exemption in question may be granted to categories of agreements. The need of undertakings to know their legal position with certainty could justify giving priority to the use of this power, which does not require the Council to adopt rules simultaneously for applying the other provisions of the said Article. Thus, without disregarding Article 86, the Council was entitled to rely on Article 85(3) as its authority for adopting a regulation covering the exemption of categories of agreements. It was in a position to do this without bringing about any alteration in the principles set out in Article 85(1) and without foregoing its right to make any further regulation applying any other provision of the said Article 85 to agreements not provided for by the regulation at issue.

The second submission, that there has been both an infringement of Article 85 and a misuse of powers

It is argued against Regulation No 19/65 first that it infringes Article 85(1) and (3) and at the same time Articles 2 and 3(f) of the Treaty; secondly, that the Regulation constitutes a misuse of powers in assuming that all agreements coming within the exempted category properly fall within the absolute prohibition in Article 85(1), and thus regarding the description set out in Article 85(1) as properly met only by the categories exempted by the said Regulation, but also by all agreements of the kind mentioned in the said categories made between more than two undertakings, or betweeen two undertakings but without fitting one of the descriptions laid down in Article 1 of the said Regulation.

Article 85 lays down the rules on competition applicable to undertakings in Part Three of the Treaty covers the 'policy of the Community'. It aims at bringing about the 'activities of the Community' mentioned in Article 3 and in particular 'the institution of a system ensuring that competition in the Common Market is not distorted', and this is in order to arrive at 'establishing a Common Market' which one of the fundamental objectives set out in Article 2.

Article 85 as a whole should be read in the context of the provisions of the preamble to the Treaty which clarify it and reference should particularly be made to those relating to 'the elimination of barriers' and 'fair competition' both of which are necessary for bringing about a single market.

Article 85 is arranged in the form of a rule imposing a prohibition (paragraph (1) with a statement of its effects (paragraph (2) mitigated by the declaration of the power to grant exceptions to this rule, with provisions for exempting the categories of agreements (paragraph (3) ).

Whether an agreement is caught by Article 85(1) and whether it benefits from the exemption in Article 85(3) are questions which do not depend on the same conditions or have the same consequences. It is therefore of interest to undertakings to see limits set to the scope of each of these two provisions by such regulations as may be made.

Whilst it is true that to grant the benefit of Article 85(3) to a given agreement presupposes that this agreement falls within the prohibition imposed by Article 85(1) the authorisation in Article 85(3) to grant this same benefit to categories of agreements does not imply that because a particular agreement comes within these categories it necessarily fits the descriptions set out in Article 85(1).

In empowering the Council to authorise exemptions to categories of agreements, Article 85(3) only requires it to exercise this power as regards categories of agreements which fit descriptions in Article 85 (1). A Council regulation would indeed have no purpose if the agreements in the categories defined by it could not fit the said descriptions. However, to define a category is only to make a classification and it does not mean that the agreements which come within it fall within the prohibition. Nor does it mean that an agreement within the exempted category, but not exhibiting all the features of the said definition, must necessarily fall within the prohibition. Therefore to grant exemptions by categories cannot amount, even by implication, to passing any pre-conceived judgment on any agreement considered individually.

Regulation No 19/65 does not contravene these principles. Article 1(1) of the said Regulation provides that the Commission may 'by regulation declare that Article 85(1) shall not apply to categories of agreements to which only two undertakings are party' and which contain certain provisions found in exclusive dealing agreements. By paragraph (2) of the same Article, the Regulation which the Commission is to adopt 'shall define the categories of agreements to which it applies and shall specify in particular:

(a) the restrictions or clauses which must be contained in the agreements;

(b) the clause which must be contained in the agreements, or the other conditions which must be satisfied'.

Thus the said regulation limits itself to outlining the action which the Commission is to take, while leaving it to the latter to make clear what conditions an agreement must fulfil in order to benefit from an exemption given to a category of agreements.

The Regulation is made under Article 85(3) and not Article 85(1) as appears from the heading and the recitals in the preamble. Therefore it does not create any presumption of law concerning the interpretation to be given to Article 85(1). Since the intention of the said regulation is to exempt from prohibition categories of agreements and concerted practices, it cannot have the effect, even by implication, of bringing under the prohibition in Article 85(1) categories for which it proposes favoured treatment or of assuming to the detriment of any particular agreement that the terms of the said Article are properly applicable. Thus the regulation in dispute could not alter the requirements to be satisfied before there can be a finding in each case, considered separately, that the characteristics leading to the prohibition in Article 85(1) are present. Thus the doubts, expressed by the applicant, which might arise from the drafting of Regulation No 19/65 are not such as to establish that the system set up by Article 85 has been wrongly applied.

Regulation No 19/65 limits itself to authorising the Commission to lift the prohibition from the agreements described therein in advance and by categories. It does so only in so far as the said agreements may possibly fall within the prohibition contained in Article 85(1), and in doing so it neither infringes Article 85(2) nor Article 3(f) of the Treaty, nor does it give rise to a misuse of powers.

Litterature

Meal: Government compulsion as a defense under United States and European Community antitrust law,
1 Colum.J.Transnat'l (1982) 51-132.

Forrester and Norall: The Laicization of Community law: self-help and the rule of reason: How competition law is and could be applied,
(1984) CMLRev 11-51.

Korah: The rise and fall of provisional validity - the need for a rule of reason in EEC Antitrust,
1981 Nw.J.INT'l & Bus. Vol. 3, number 2, 320.

Schechter: The rule of reason in European Comptition Law,
LIEI 1982/2, 1.

De Jong: The Economics of concerted practices in European Competition policy,
Leiden 1975.

Ritter and Overburg: An attempt at a practical approach to joint ventures under the EEC rules on competition,
(1977) CMLRev

Mok: The jointly owned subsidiary (joint venture) and Article 85 of the EEC Treaty,
in European Competition Policy, Leiden 1975.

Wertheimer: The Haecht II Judgement and its repercussions,
(1973) CMLRev.

Gijlstra and Murphy: EEC Competition Law after the Haecht II and SABAM cases,
LIEI 1979/2.

Kon: Article 85 para. 3: a case for application by national courts,
(1982) CMLRev. 541-563.

Steindorff: Article 85 para. 3: No case for application by national courts,
(1983) CMLRev. 125-130.

E. Picanol: Remedies in national law for breach of Articles 85 and 86 of the EEC Treaty: a review,
LEI 1983/2, 1.

Chapter Four

# ARTICLE EIGHTY-SIX

## A. General

See Chapter II above.

## B. One or more undertakings

(1) Decision in re BP-ABG
Decision of 19 April 1977 relating to a proceeding under Article 86 of the EEC Treaty, O.J. No. L 117, 9 May 1977, p. 1; (1977) 2 CMLR D 1; CCH para 9944; Competition Law CM/M/I/112.

For the facts, see the Decision and the report on the behaviour of the oil companies below.

Firms hold a dominant position where they are able to act fully independently - in other words where they may conduct their business without regard for the reactions of competitors and customers. This can happen when general economic circumstances and particular market conditions combine so that the firms with an established market position, access to raw materials and adequate industrial capacity and capital resources find themselves in a position to control production and distribution on the market.

.....

Economic restrictions such as existed in the Netherlands during the oil crisis can substantially alter existing commercial relations between suppliers who have a substantial share of the market and quantities available and their customers. For reasons completely outside the control of the normal suppliers, their customers can become completely dependent on them for the supply of scarce products. Thus while the situation continues, the suppliers are placed in a dominant position in respect of their normal customers.

.....

(2) Report by the Commission on the behaviour of the oil companies during the period from October 1973 to March 1974.
Commission document Com/75/675 of 10 December 1975.

"Investigation by the Commission in the oil sector

In the present circumstances of the oil products market, the Commission is disturbed about the supply position of oil products distributing firms independent of the integrated groups which have their own refining facilities. These independent firms often encounter grave supply difficulties in connection with the common market refineries and some are in an alarming situation.

The Commission considers that arrangements should be made to ensure that the present circumstances do not give rise to the elimination of independent trading or its absorption by the big companies.

Refusal by the big companies to supply the independent distributors in an equitable manner may give rise to an application of the competition rules of the Treaty and in particular Article 86 thereof.

The same holds good for practices which consist in the big companies applying to their trading partners different conditions for the provisions of equivalent services or subjecting the signature of contracts to the acceptance by their partners of extra services.

The Commission has decided to make the requisite investigations with the firms".

The circumstances to which the Commission referred were those which resulted from the events following the war between Israel and Arab countries of 6 to 16 October 1973, and which completely disrupted the international oil market.

This report contains the result of the enquiry taken by the Commission and provides at the same time information requested by the European Parliament.

(1) The dominant position of the oil companies

The whole of the report shows that the structure of supply was not fundamentally different during the oil crisis from what it had been previously but - bearing in mind the relative scarcity of oil products - in so far as certain oil companies had at their disposal the bulk of the crude oil produced, and transported and refined it, the position of the independents and even of some of the less powerful integrated companies was undermined. Nevertheless, at the same time, refiners in general saw their position strengthened to such an extent that, collectively, they acquired a dominant position on the oil market.

In view of the scarcity of oil products and since sellers and consumers were, as a result, unable to rely on other suppliers even in their own countries, each of the companies with refining capacities in a given country thus became the sole and imposed supplier of all dealers and consumers who were its traditional customers. In the context of their collective dominant position, each of the refining companies was, therefore, in a monopolistic position towards its customers.

A dominant position was created for the supplier in respect of these traditional customers, due to the collective dominant position of all refiners on the entire national market. Such a situation existed in all Member States except Germany.

The definition of what constituted a company's traditional customers gives rise, of course, to some difficulty. In the context of actual problems raised by the crisis, the Commission has taken the view that a company should have considered as a traditional customer, any buyer who, in the twelve months prior to the crisis, had in some way or another been its customer. It is on this basis that the Commission made its assessment of the companies' behaviour in this field.

(2) The supply of oil products

The information gathered on the overall supply of crude oil to all refineries in the common market shows that the contraction in supplies was the result of production cuts ordered by the producing countries and of their embargo directed at the Netherlands and Denmark.

The Commission's investigations did not reveal the existence of any practice forbidden under Articles 85 and 86 in the arrangements for supplying the Community with crude oil. All the oil companies experienced difficulties in their own supply systems in the oil-producing countries. Some of them, with a lesser proportion of concession oil at their disposal, experienced greater difficulties than others in supplying their refineries.

The integrated companies which had no crude oil resources of their own or whose resources were so inadequate that they had concluded supply contracts for crude oil with the large international companies, continued to be supplied on the basis of contracts.

By the same token, the Commission was unable to establish that there had been any agreement between oil companies in Europe, within the meaning of Article 85, to restrict deliveries of refined products. This does not contradict the fact that, locally, dealers or users had to face major supply problems during the most acute phase of the crisis - problems which were caused mainly by a steep rise in demand on the part of anxious customers and by interruptions in the rhythm of deliveries by the refineries and wholesalers. The national authorities did all they could to remedy this.

(3) Prices

The transfer prices charged by the large oil companies, whether for crude oil or refined products, relate to transactions between firms in the same group, that is to say, they are internal prices determined for tax, financial and economic considerations peculiar to the enterprise itself. Where such transactions are purely internal in their effect they are not caught by the rules on competition.

(4) Independent dealers and users

During the crisis the independent companies experienced such difficulties that, in some cases, their very existence was threatened. This was particularly true where the level of maximum prices prevented the independents from buying freely and squeezed their margins to excess.

Many small and medium-sized firms, engaged solely in distribution, have tried either to cover themselves against a recurrence of the same difficulties or to sell out.

The second alternative led to the buying up of a certain number of medium-sized businesses by the big companies. Other firms concluded long-term supply contracts with the refiners which gave them a large degree of security but deprived them at the same time of genuinely free access to the market.

Nevertheless the total of such transactions was small in relation to the total of dealers in oil products in the common market, estimated at around 60,000 wholesalers and retailers.

The crisis thus brought about structural changes in the oil business which are reflected, not in a noticeable reduction in the number of firms, but in the existence of new relationships betweeen the oil companies and a certain number of wholesalers. Nevertheless the Commission discovered nothing in this development indicating abuse by the oil companies of their collective dominant position.

On the other hand, the Commission has examined cases of presumed abuse of an individual dominant position by certain companies in respect of independent dealers who are their customers.

The Commission takes the view that, during the crisis, all the large oil companies were in an individual dominant position, at least in respect of their traditional customers, who had no access to suppliers other than those with whom they had done business. A refusal to sell to such customers can constitute an abuse forbidden by Article 86 since it may affect trade between Member States, which is certainly the case when a sizeable purchaser/dealer is in danger of being squeezed out of the market, a development which would mean appreciable change in the pattern of supply for oil products in a substantial part of the common market.

The question might even be asked whether, in a crisis in which state intervention, in particular, produces a degree of fragmentation of the market, companies in a collective dominant position should not be obliged, according to their share of the market concerned to supply in reasonable quantities and at reasonable prices to buyers who, before this fragmentation of the market, obtained their supplies from other sources. Such an obligation would have the effect of maintaining the competitive marketing structure which existed before the crisis.

3. Züchner Case

For facts and references see above, pages 60 and 161.

*The Court held:*

10. The question of interpretation was raised by the national court with reference to the debiting of a uniform service charge of 0.15% on the relevant transactions. The question arose with regard to both Article 85 and Article 86 of the Treaty. In view of the fact that the order submitting the reference considers only the existence of a concerted practice as a possible infringement of Community rules on competition and having regard to the fact that Article 86 deals with the abuse of a dominant position and does not cover the existence of concerted practices, to which solely the provisions of Article 85 apply, examination of the question which has been referred to the Court must be restricted to the latter article.

## II. DOMINANT POSITION

(1) Deutsche Grammophon Case

For facts and references see above, page 2.

*The Court held:*

.....

The second question

The second question is whether the exercise by the manufacturer of recordings of the exclusive right to distribute the protected articles can be regarded as abusive if the tied selling price in the domestic market is higher than the price of the original product re-imported from another Member State and at the same time the artistes in question are bound by exclusive contracts to the manufacturer of the recordings. With the expression "abusive" the question alludes to the abusive exploitation of a dominant position within the meaning of Article 86 of the Treaty.

This provision prohibits "one or more undertakings exploiting in an improper manner a dominant position in the common market or in a substantial part of it, in so far as trade between Member States is liable to be affected by it".

The criterion for the operation of this prohibition accordingly presupposes a dominant position in the Common Market or in a substantial part of it. A manufacturer of recordings who has a protection right analogous to copyright does not, however, have a dominant position within the meaning of Article 86 of the Treaty merely because he exer-

his exclusive right to market the protected articles.

Since according to this Article the dominant position must at least extend to a "substantial part" of the Common Market it is necessary in addition that the manufacturer, alone or together with other undertakings belonging to the same group is in a position to prevent effective competition in a considerable part of the market in question; in this respect, the possible existence, in particular, of manufacturers who market products of the same kind and the position in the market of these manufacturers must be taken into account.

If the artists in the recordings are bound to the manufacturer by exclusive contracts, inter alia their popularity with the public, the duration and the extent of the obligations undertaken by them and the opportunities for other manufacturers of recordings to obtain artists for comparable performances, must be taken into consideration.

The conditions of Article 86 further presuppose that the dominant position is abusively exploited. A difference between the tied price and the price of the product re-imported from another Member State does not justify without qualification a finding of such an abuse, although it may be conclusive evidence of such an abuse if it is large and cannot be explained on any objective grounds.

## (2) Decision in the Continental Can

For facts see above page 10, for references page 43.

*The Commision ruled:*

.....

B. Dominant position

Undertakings are in a dominant position when they have the power to behave independently, which puts them in a position to act without taking into account their competitors, purchasers or suppliers. That is the position when, because of their share of the market, or of their share of the market combined with the availability of technical knowledge, raw materials or capital, they have the power to determine prices or to control production or distribution for a significant part of the products in question. This power does not necessarily have to derive from an absolute domination permitting the undertakings which hold it to eliminate all will on the part of their economic partners, but it is enough that they be strong enough as a whole to ensure those undertakings an overall independence of behaviour, even if there are differences in intensity in their influence on the different partial markets.

Continental Can has a dominant position in Germany on the market in light containers for preserved meats and fish and in metal caps for glass jars. This dominant position derives from the shares which its subsidiary Schmalbach-Lubeca-Werke holds on the different partial markets in the light container sector and from the economic, financial and technical importance of the group.

Indeed, its share in the German consumption of 'open top' tins made of tin or aluminium for meat and charcuterie lies between 70 and 80 per cent. Metal tins constitute practically the only type of rigid container for preserves of these products: there is in this field only a very weak substitution competition between the various types of container, since only sausages are capable of being packaged in glass jars, when they are intended to be consumed fairly rapidly in places not far distant from the place of manufacture. This exception is not such as to modify noticeably the dominant position of Schmalbach-Lubeca-Werke on this part market.

Likewise, Schmalbach-Lubeca-Werke has a dominant position in Germany on the market in light containers for preserved fish products.

Its share in the German consumption of 'open top' tin or aluminium tins for fish and shellfish lies between 80 and 90 per cent. Metal tins constitute the main type of rigid container for preserves of these products, since the proportion of glass jars (which are in any case heavy containers) - which has been steady for some years - and of plastic jars - which is slightly on the increase - do not together exceed about 30 per cent of the total market. Schmalbach-Lubeca-Werke thus has in any case a dominant position on this part market.

Schmalbach-Lubeca-Werke also has a dominant position in Germany on the market in metal caps, other than crown corks, intended for the preserves industry.

It is the sole licensee in Germany of the 'White Cap' process which is most used of the processes for manufacture of wide aperture metal covers for glass containers, and its share of the market in these covers lies between 50 and 55 per cent.

To judge more precisely the dominant position of Schmalbach-Lubeca-Werke on the German market in the three products aforementioned as well as its general position on that market, we should take into account the following factors:

(a) Schmalbach-Lubeca-Werke has a strong position in Germany in the field of metal containers for drinks. Its share of the German consumption of open tins for beer and other drinks lies between ... and ... per cent. However, given that glass containers are the most used type of container for liquid food products, it cannot be said that Schmalbach-Lubeca-Werke has a dominant position on the market in all containers for drinks, although in that field metal containers represent a special outlet (mainly for beer) which is currently expanding.

(b) Competition in plastic containers is being felt, in a small part of the market, regarding certain preserved fish (e.g. sliced salmon), but it must be noted that Schmalbach-Lubeca-Werke also manufactures plastic containers for various uses in which it registers a turnover of the same size as in the field of metal tins for preserved meat.

(c) Schmalbach-Lubeca-Werke also has important shares in the German market in other types of light metal containers, namely:

- airosol tins made of tin (... per cent);

- 'general line' containers (... per cent);

- open tins for fruit and vegetables (... per cent);

- crown corks (... per cent).

(d) Schmalbach-Lubeca-Werke also manufactures containers of paper-cardboard.

Furthermore, Continental Can has the advantage over most of its competitors of itself manufacturing the machines necessary for the production and use of the metal containers. It has important outlets for these machines in the shape of the big manufacturers of metal containers licensed by Continental Can and the customers of those latter. In this field the size of Continental Can, its technical experience, the breadth of the market secured for its products permit it to maintain an important technological lead.

Continental Can holds patents and especially technical know-how which assure it an important position in the field of manufacture and use of metal containers.

The big manufacturers of metal containers, of a size comparable with Schmalbach-Lubeca-Werke, established in the countries bordering on Germany - Thomassen & Drijver-Verblifa in Holland, Carnaud in France and, outside the EEC, Metal Box in Great Britain, Platmanufaktur-Haustrups in Sweden-Denmark, Sauter in Switzerland and Schmalbach-Lubeca-Werke itself in Austria - are licensed by Continental Can. The exchange of technical information which these make contribute to reinforcing the technological lead of Continental Can and of its licensees over their competitors.

Schmalbach-Lubeca-Werke, which manufactures about 5,000 different products, is in a position to offer to users, thanks to the spread of its 15 factories and of its five sales depots in the principal regions of Germany, a large range of container articles intended for very varying uses, not only in metal but also in plastic and in mixed material (paper-cardboard, etc). This wide assortment gains a freedom of action which the smaller suppliers do not have.

The advantage described in sections 8 to 11 above and the power of independent action which follows for Continental Can are accentuated by the economic importance of the group.

The parent company, Continental Can, is the world's biggest producer of metal containers. In 1969 it registered a net turnover of 1,780 million units of account and a net profit of 90 million units of account. It has assets of an overall value of 1,199.5 million units of account and employs 62,000 persons.

Continental Can's German subsidiary, Schmalbach-Lubeca-Werke is the biggest producer of light metal containers in continental Europe. In Germany itself it made in 1969 a gross turnover, excluding VAT, of 185 million units of account and a net profit of 6.5 million units of account. Its assets represent 100 million units of account (45 million is fixed assets, 55 million in working capital) and it employs 13,000 persons.

As a comparison, the Continental Can group's biggest competitor in Germany Züchner AG of Seesen, registered in 1969 a turnover of about ... million units of account and employs 1,600 persons.

One of the advantages which Continental Can can get from its size is the power to resort to the international capital market. Continental Can thus financed through loans in Eurodollars and Deutschmarks the acquisition in 1969 of a supplementary 60 per cent shareholding in Schmalbach-Lubeca-Werke. Such possibilities of obtaining finance are more difficult to obtain for competitors which do not have an economic and financial power comparable to that of Continental Can.

Continental Can's important shares in the market, its production programme covering all the part markets and some substitution products, its supply of machines for manufacturing and using its products, its technical lead and its economic and financial power based on a very large size, ensure for that undertaking possibilities of independent action which give it a very strong position on the German market in light containers and particularly a dominant position on the German market in light containers for meat and fish preserves as well as in metal covers.

This conclusion is not invalidated by a general reference to the substitution competition as it was at the time of the merger or as it can be expected to be for the immediate future, to which Continental Can is open from the producers of substitute products and from large consumers capable of becoming self-producers of light metal containers.

In this respect other containers are interchangeable with the light metal containers only within narrow limits, especially because of the difference in characteristics and machines attached to each type of container:

(a) Metal containers are rigid, unbreakable, impermeable to gases; they protect the contents against the light and may be hermetically sealed. After the tin is sealed the contents can be sterilised or pasteurised more rapidly than in the case of glass containers. For these reasons certain products are processed basically in metal containers: preserved fruit and vegetables; condensed milk; olive oil (because of the opacity of metal tins); fruit juice (for long distance transportation); techno-chemical products in the particular fields of meat and fish preserves this type of container preponderates.

(b) The different machines necessary to process (fill, close, seal, stop etc.) the various sorts of product in each particular type of container make it difficult for the customer to substitute and interchange those containers in that changes in containers are made by customers only after a deep study of the market and are generally long lasting in character.

Then, even where interchangeability is technically possible, effective transfer to another type of container is strongly impeded by the new investments that such a change implies, particularly for customers of small or medium size. Also, the presence of Continental Can in certain substitution sectors permits it in certain cases to offer the substitution product required.

As regards the potential competition of large buyers capable of becoming self-producers, the amount of investment necessary for an integrated manufacture is such that even the biggest undertakings hesitate to cross that obstacle. Furthermore, the technological lead of the Continental Can group is well known and so many potential self-producers have but little interest in giving up the advantages of such a situation.

On the other hand, it is not to be expected that the competition of the main manufacturers situated in the countries bordering Germany on the German market in 'open top' tins and metal covers, a competition which has been very weak for many years, could develop very strongly in the near future. The factories of some of these manufacturers, like Carnaud and Metal Box, which are the nearest to Germany, are too far from most of the German users of tins for meat and fish, and metal covers for these latter, to decide to entrust them permanently with their supply.

In sum, it may be concluded from the above that Continental Can has, at least for the products mentioned in sections 5, 6 and 7 above, a dominant position within the Common Market.

This dominant position of Continental Can is held by its subsidiary Schmalbach-Lubeca-Werke on the German market, which represents a substantial part of the Common Market. Continental Can thus has for the above-mentioned products a dominant position on a substantial part of the Common Market.

(3) Decision in re European Sugar Industry

For facts see above page 94 and for references page 222.

*The Commission ruled:*

.....

1. The behaviour of the RT towards the two Belgian dealers, Export and Hottlet, who traditionally and because of their size and knowledge of the market deal with the export of Belgian sugar must be judged in the light of Article 86 of the Treaty.

The RT has a dominant position on the Belgian and Luxembourg sugar markets which make up an important part of the Common Market. It controls the greater part of sugar production in Belgium and Luxembourg and has a large amount of surplus sugar at its disposal there. It holds at least 50% of the capital of the NV Suikerfabrieken van Vlaanderen at Moerbeke-Waes and of the SA Raffinerie Notre-Dame at Oreye, which gives it the opportunity to control those undertakings. Although these undertakings are not directly integrated in the marketing organisation of the RT they only seldomly diverge from the price policy fixed by it. They have always applied the same conditions, in their offers or sales contracts, to Belgian dealers.

This dominating position is a result of the size of the share of the market held by RT on the Belgian and Luxembourg markets (85%), as well as of the scope which it enjoys for independent action which allows it to act without taking much account of the activities of its competitors. Thanks to its strong position on the Belgian and Luxembourg markets the RT also exerts influence over certain other Belgian producers (Naveau, Couplet, Donstiennes) so that they also follow on principle the sales policy of the RT towards the Belgian dealers. Furthermore this dominant position is increased still further by the fact that RT also exerts some influence on the sugar markets of other Member States, in particular France, because of its financial participation in the undertakings Say and Raffinerie d'Erstein and its financial links with certain large European sugar producers, and because of its advanced technical knowledge and achievements.

The RT has abused its dominant position by exercising economic pressure on the undertakings Export and Hottlet so as to oblige them only to re-sell the sugar which it supplied to certain clients and for certain uses, and to impose these limitations on their customers. This economic pressure consisted of refusing to sell sugar to the two dealers, especially for exporting to third countries, an activity which represents an important part of the turnover of these dealers, if the sugar was sold for purposes other than those permitted by RT. For lack of other large sources of supply, the two dealers had to give into these pressures from the RT.

The object of these abuses was to limit the prinipal sources of supply of these dealers, who might have wished to buy sugar for other uses than those fixed by the RT, as well as the sources of supply of the dealers' clients.

This abusive exploitation of the RT's dominant position on the Belgian and Luxembourg markets may affect trade between the Member States in the way that might adversely affect the achievement of a single intra-states market, by restricting and in certain cases preventing the sale of sugar in other Member States of the Community. This behaviour of RT is therefore forbidden by Article 86 of the Treaty.

The behaviour of the SU and the CSM towards the three Dutch dealers, Internatio, Jacobson and Dudok de Wit, should be judged according to the provisions of Article 86 of the Treaty.

The two Dutch sugar producers SU and CSM have a dominant position on the Dutch market which constitutes a substantial part of the Common Market. These two producers compete closely in almost all their activities, that is to say the joint purchase of raw materials, rationing of production, collaboration in the use of intermediate products, pooling of research, cooperation on market research, advertising and sales promotions and the harmonisation of ex-factory prices and conditions of sale. Towards other undertakings and particularly towards the three dealers mentioned above, these two producers have acted in a uniform manner and always appear as a single entity.

The dominant position of these two producers is due to the fact that they produce all Dutch sugar and their sales represent more than 85% of the Dutch market, and that they are able to behave independently which permits them to act without taking any particular account of their competitors. This dominant position is strengthened further by the fact that they control by various direct or indirect means almost all sugar imported into the Netherlands. The SU and CSM have exploited this dominant position on the Dutch market in an improper way by obliging the dealers mentioned above to conclude an agreement in which the dealers bound themselves:

- not to sell the large quantities of sugar imported from France in 1969 and 1970 at prices considerably lower than those of the Dutch producers,

- to re-sell to Dutch producers the last amounts to be imported in 50kg sacks or 1kg bags so that those producers could then sell them on the Dutch market, under their trademarks and at their prices,

- not to undertake any further such importation of sugar into the Netherlands without the consent of the Dutch producers.

This argument was maintained by means of economic pressure exerted by the two Dutch producers which consisted of threatening the dealers referred to above with hindering their traditional importing under the temporary admission procedure for the Dutch milk products industry, an activity which represents an important part of their turnovers. The Dutch dealers gave into these threats. From the marketing year 1970/71 onwards, the two Dutch producers integrated these dealers into their import system agreed with RT. These abuses were aimed at limiting the sources of supply of the Dutch dealers who wanted to import sugar freely into the Netherlands, and, in this way, the sources of supply of their clients. This exploitation of the dominant position of SU and CSM on the Dutch market is likely to affect trade between Member States, because it limits and in certain cases prevents the sale in the Netherlands of sugar coming from other Member States of the Community. This behaviour of SU and CSM is therefore forbidden by Article 86 of the Treaty.

3. The behaviour of the SZV towards its buyers must be judged according to Article 86. The SZV has a dominant position in the southern part of Germany which forms a substantial part of the Common Market. It sells by far the greatest proportion of the production of its members. It decides the prices and sales policy itself. When SZV members sell individually they use the same agents. Deliveries by 'outsiders' to dealers and processing factories established in their sales area only play a small part. This area is clearly divided from the WZV and NZV sales areas and from the adjoining French market. Deliveries from the areas of Germany coming from factories not belonging to the SZV are exceptions. Nor are deliveries from neighbouring French areas to dealers or processing plants in South Germany any more numerous or intensive. French producers to deliver in the Saar territory, but in the SZV sales area usually only to the manufacturers themselves (SZ AG and Franken). SZV's share of the market must be estimated at least at 90-95%. This position gives it scope for independent action, which permits it to act without

taking any particular account of its competitors. The SZV has, in the first place, exploited improperly this dominant position by obliging its agents not to sell sugar from other sources without its consent. In this way it has practically excluded the possibility for foreign suppliers of selling sugar through the dealers supplied by the SZV. Consent has only been given for the importation of special kinds of sugar for processing. The parties concerned have emphasised that in the Southern German area there are other dealers who have been able to import freely, and that a series of processing plants have been supplied from abroad too. This in no way alters the fact that the opportunities for foreign suppliers to sell on the southern German market, on which the price level is quite high and close to the target price thus making exports of interest, are considerably restricted by the fact that the dealers who are supplied by SZV, and are consequently bound to it, cannot be clients. The obligation imposed upon the agents not to sell foreign sugar without authorisation constitutes, when imposed by an undertaking in a dominant position, an improper practice and a violation of Article 86.

The SZV has, in the second place, improperly exploited its dominant position by granting fidelity rebates.

The granting of a rebate which does not depend on the amount bought, but only on whether the annual requirements are covered exclusively by the SZV, is an unjustifiable discrimination against buyers who also buy sugar from sources other than SZV. Since the buyers depend for at least part of their supplies on SZV as they have insufficient storage facilities and need regular supplies, the disadvantage of losing the rebate is usually greater than the advantage of buying sugar from outsiders even if they offer it at more favourable prices.

The parties concerned have stated that the fidelity rebate, which was already given before the Community sugar market rules came into force, was very small and only amounted to 0.3% of the selling price; that the offers by French exporters were so advantageous that they would have more than compensated for the loss of the annual rebate; that, furthermore, this rebate was sometimes given in cases where purchases had been made from foreign dealers; and that very often the rebate was immediately deduced from the bill, particularly in two-thirds of the cases in the western part of the SZV sales territory.

The rebate given, although it seems very low, could in fact bring about the effects described above. The loss of this fidelity rebate is quite noticeable even for an undertaking with average annual requirements. With a yearly requirement of 30,000 metric tons, which is not rare, the rebate represents DM 90 000 and for a requirement of 50,000 metric tons, DM 150 000. If the client wishes to buy 3,000 to 5,000 metric tons abroad, the foreign supplier's price must compensate for the loss of the annual rebate. Such favourable offers are, however, practically ruled out. Moreover one must consider that the fidelity rebate is also at stake for future purchases by the client from national producers. It is not possible for the client to use only foreign suppliers for he is usually obliged to buy part of his requirements from nearby national factories and thereby has to submit to the conditions of SZV as the supplier dominating the market.

The facts which have come to the knowledge of the Commission show that in some cases at least the fidelity rebate has been abolished or its continuation made dependent on cessation of imports and that in these cases this has put an end to imports, although the foreign prices quoted were DM 10 to DM 20 per metric ton lower than those of SZV. An important effect of the rebate system is the possibility of controlling the customer's purchases from foreign producers, which can easily be done on the basis of a knowledge of the average amounts bought annually, which do not vary very much.

The fact that the rebate has also been granted in some cases even if purchases have been made from foreign producers and that this control has therefore not been exercised strictly does not alter the fact that the mere warning or risk of the rebate being abolished prevents clients from making further large and regular imports. The small amounts imported other than deliveries from producer to producer are not to be explained by the occasional deliveries temporarily tolerated by SZV.

It does not make much difference that in certain cases the fidelity rebate was granted immediately, that is to say it was deducted directly from the amount on the bill, because the determining factor in this case of purchases from foreign producers is that clients must expect that the rebate will not be granted in future, not only in respect of the next delivery but also for later purchases, which is economically more serious than the loss of the yearly rebate already due to them.

If a fidelity rebate of this kind is granted by an undertaking which holds a dominant position in order to limit opportunities for imports still further and to strengthen that dominant pósition, it constitutes an abuse, which is likely to affect trade between Member States. The granting of the fidelity rebate by SZV is therefore a violation of Article 86.

(4) Commercial Solvents Case

For facts and references see above, page 14.

*The Court ruled:*

.....

(a) Dominant position

9. The applicants dispute the findings in the Decision in question according to which the CSC - Istituto group 'has a dominant position in the Common Market for the raw material necessary for the manufacture of ethambutol', on the basis that it has 'a world monopoly in the production and sale of nitropropane and aminobutanol'.

10. For this purpose they rely on documents which, they claim establish that aminobutanol is produced by at least one other Italian company from butanone, that a third Italian company manufactures ethambutol from other raw material, that a French company produced nitropropane independently and that another undertaking has brought thiophenol on to the market, a product which is said to be used in Eastern Europe to produce ethambutol.

11. Finally CSC produced a statement by an expert according to which there is at least one practical method of producing nitropropane other than the method used by CSC and at least three other processes for producing aminobutanol without using nitropropane.

12. During the course of the administrative proceedings the applicants adduced some of these particulars in support of a request that before taking a decision the Commission should obtain an expert's report to verify the alleged monopoly of CSC as regards the production of raw material for the manufacture of ethambutol. The Commission rejected this request, since it considered that the particulars relied on, even if they were established, would not affect the substance of its Notice of Objections. In the present proceedings the applicants renewed their

request for an expert's report on the point at issue.

13. The Commission replied, without being seriously challenged, that the production of nitropropane by the French company is at present only in an experimental stage and that the researches of this company have been developed only subsequently to the events in dispute. The information as to the possibility of manufacturing ethambutol by using thiophenol is too vague and uncertain to be seriously considered. The statement of the expert produced by CSC takes account only of well-known processes which have not proved themselves capable of adaptation to use on an industrial scale and at prices enabling them to be marketed. The production by the two Italian companies mentioned is on a modest scale and intended for their own needs, so that the processes used do not lend themselves to substantial and competitive marketing.

14. The Commission has produced an expert's opinion from Zoja according to which the production of aminobutanol based on butanone on a substantial industrial scale would be possible only at considerable expense and at some risk, which is disputed by the applicants who rely on two experts, according to whom such production would not present any difficulties or cause excessive costs.

15. This dispute is of no great practical importance since it relates mainly to processes of an experimental nature, which have not been tested on an industrial scale and which have resulted in only a modest production. The question is not whether Zoja, by adapting its installations and its manufacturing processes, would have been able to continue its production of ethambutol based on other raw materials, but whether CSC had a dominant position in the market in raw material for the manufacture of ethambutol. It is only the presence on the market of a raw material which could be substituted without difficulty for nitropropane or aminobutanol for the manufacture of ethambutol which could invalidate the argument that CSC has a dominant position within the meaning of Article 86. On the other hand reference to possible alternative processes of an experimental nature or which are practised on a small scale is not sufficient to refute the grounds of the Decision in dispute.

16. It is not disputed that the large manufacturers of ethambutol on the world market, that is to say CSC itself, Istituto, American Cyanamid and Zoja use raw material manufactured by CSC. Compared with the manufacture and sale of ethambutol by these undertakings, those of the few other manufacturers are of minor importance. The Commission was therefore entitled to conclude 'that in the present conditions of economic competition it is not possible to have recourse on an industrial scale to methods of manufacture of ethambutol based on the use of different raw materials'.

It was justified therefore in refusing the request for an expert's report.

17. For the same reasons the request made during the course of the present proceedings must be rejected, since the fact that CSC had a dominant position on the world market in the production and sale of the raw material in question has been sufficiently established in law.

<u>(5) General Motors Case</u>

<u>General Motors Continental</u> v. <u>Commission of the EEC</u>, Case 26/75, Judgment of 13 November 1975; (1975) ECR 1367; (1976) CMLR 95; CCH para.

8320; Competition Law CM/M/III/50.

*Facts:* In order to be used on the public highway in Belgium, vehicles registered in that country must satisfy the requirements of the Royal Decree of 15 March 1968 which embodies a general regulation concerning the technical standards to be met by motor vehicles and their trailers (Moniteur Belge of 28 March 1968, p. 3266, as subsequently amended on several occasions).

Each type of chassis or unit-construction vehicle manufactured or assembled in Belgium or imported for use in that country must be approved by the Minister for Transport or his representative and be the subject of an approval.

Where a type of vehicle has thus obtained an approval the manufacturer or, where he is established abroad, his sole authorised agent in Belgium shall issue, in respect of each new vehicle of the same type which is in use on the road, a certificate "of conformity" which attests that the vehicle entirely satisfies the requirements contained in the certificate of approval.

The manufacturer of his sole authorised agent subsequently affixes to each vehicle the compulsory type-shield.

Following instructions from the Belgian Minister for Transport, since 15 March 1973 the State testing-stations, which until that date carried out the inspections of used vehicles, have no longer issued certificates of conformity and type-shields for vehicles which have been registered abroad for less than six months; since this date, therefore, the conformity inspections of such vehicles has been carried out by the manufacturer's authorised agent in Belgium.

For the purpose of the Royal Decree of 15 March 1968, a limited company incorporated under Belgian law having its registered office at Antwerp, is the sole authorised agent of Adam Opel AG, Rüsselheim/Main, a manufacturer of private motor cars, and of other manufacturers belonging to the General Motors group.

GMC is responsible for obtaining a certificate of approval for all types of General Motors vehicles included in its Belgian sales programme. It applies for "general" approval for Opel and Vauxhall models; for the American models produced by General Motors, it applies for "low-volume" type approvals, valid for up to 10 units per year. GMC subsequently issues the certificates of conformity and the type-shields for each vehicle sold through its approved dealers.

Private customers and dealers importing vehicles manufactured within the General Motors group into Belgium otherwise than through GMC's standard distribution system - parallel imports - are also obliged to resort to GMC, in its capacity as sole authorised agent for the approval procedures for both new vehicles and, since 15 March 1973, for vehicles registered abroad for less than six months.

Between 15 March and 31 July 1973, GMC charged the same rates for the issue of certificates of conformity and type-shields in five cases of parallel imports as it has charged previously for inspecting certain American models (5,000 BF plus 900 BF VAT).

With effect from 1 August 1973 it implemented its new scale of charges, which distinguishes between GMC vehicles of American manufacture and those of European manufacture: the costs charges for a private motor car manufactured in Europe by an undertaking within the General Motors group and already type-approved in Belgium were 1,250 BF whereas, as regards private motor cars manufactured in the USA by General Motors the costs were 5,300, 7,000 or 30,000 BF, as the case might be.

On 3 August 1973, GMC took action to reimburse part of the amounts charged in the five cases mentioned above. In two cases 4,900 BF and in three cases 4,425 BF was returned.

The Commission of the European Communities considered that by requiring parallel importers of Opel vehicles to pay an excessive price for the technical inspections and administrative costs involved in the issue of certificates of conformity and type-shields GMC had abused a dominant position within a substantial part of the Common Market within the meaning of Article 86 of the Treaty. On 26 July 1974, therefore, acting on its own initiative, it set in motion against GMC the procedure provided for by Regulation No 17/62 of the Council of 6 February 1962, the first regulation implementing Articles 85 and 86 of the Treaty (Official Journal, p. 204).

In pursuance of Article 19(1) of Regulation No 17/62 and of Article 2(1) of Regulation No 99/63 of the Commission of 25 July 1963 on the hearings provided for in Article 19(1) and (2) of Council Regulation No 17 (Official Journal, p. 2268), the Commission informed GMC by letter on 31 July 1974 of the statement of objections which it intended to raise against it.

On 6 September 1974 GMC informed the Commission in writing of its views on these objections.

On 19 December 1974, the Commission adopted Decision No IV/28.851-General Motors Continental, relating to a proceeding under Article 86 of the EEC Treaty.

In Article 1 of this Decision the Commission finds that:

"between 15 March and 31 July 1973, General Motors Continental NV intentionally infringed Article 86 by charging a price that was abusive for the issue of certificates and shields which it was required to issue under Belgian law after inspecting Opel vehicles to check their conformity with the generally approved type and after determining identification of the vehicles".

By reason of this infringement Article 2 of the Decision imposes on GMC a fine of 100,000 units of account, that is, 5,000,000 BF, the decision being enforceable against General Motors NV in accordance with the provisions of Article 192 of the EEC Treaty.

*The Court held:*

.....

The dominant position

4. The applicant maintains, first, that contrary to the statement made in the decision in question, the activity involved in application for vehicle approval and the issue of certificates of conformity could not constitute a dominant position within the neaning of Article 86.

5. Far from constituting a market in itself, this activity is merely ancillary to the market in motor cars, the open and highly competitive nature of which is undeniable.

6. Therefore, the provisions of Article 86 could not be applied to charges the imposition of which was penalized by the decision of the Commission, as the incidence of such charges can only be assessed in relation to the market in motor cars as a whole, in which the applicant does not hold a dominant position.

7. The approval procedure in the context of which the impositions in question were made is, by nature, a duty governed by public law which is so delegated by the Belgian State that, for each make of motor car

the performance of this duty is reserved exclusively to the manufacturer or its sole authorized agent, appointed by the public authority.

8. However, although it entrusted this task of inspection to private undertakings the State took no measures to fix or limit the charge imposed for the service rendered.

9. This legal monopoly, combined with the freedom of the manufacturer or sole authorized agent to fix the price for its service, leads to the creation of a dominant position within the meaning of Article 86 as, for any given make, the approval procedure can only be carried out in Belgium by the manufacturer or officially appointed authorized agent under conditions fixed unilaterally by that party.

10. It thus emerges that the submission which the applicant bases on the fact that it held no dominant position must be rejected.

(6) Decision in re United Brands Co.

Decision of the Commission of 17 December 1975 on a proceeding under Article 86 of the Treaty; OJ No. L 95. 9 March 1976. p.1; (1976) I CMLR D 28; Competition Law CM/M/I/100.

*Facts:* United Brand Co. (UBC) is a conglomerate, born of the merger between United Fruit Co. and AMK Corp., a major US meat producer, which derives only some 20% of its total turnover from the sale of bananas. As the world's largest seller of bananas, it holds, in the Commission's opinion, a dominant position on the banana market in a substantial part of the Community. Apart from the fact that it handles 40% of the trade in bananas in the EEC, it wields overwhelming economic power, due largely to the vertical integration of its banana business, and holds other advantages resulting from its multinational and conglomerate character. It owns numerous plantations in tropical banana-growing countries and a fleet of refrigerated banana boats. It also controls banana ripening in consumer countries and takes direct charge of the advertising campaigns and sales promotion activities related to its brand of bananas. It is the only firm on the banana market to have all these advantages and is in a position to use them to place major obstacles in the way of effective competition by its present business rivals, while potential competitors find themselves confronted with major barriers to market entry.

Investigation showed that the the market shares held by this company in the northern area of the EEC - Germany, Denmark, Ireland and the Benelux countries - backed up by the marketing policy it pursues, give it a dominant position in these countries. Although UBC also has sizeable market shares in the United Kingdom, France and Italy, the Commision did not consider them in its Decision since different marketing and importing arrangements obtain there.

The Commission took the view that UBC had been abusing its dominant position in the following ways:

-it prohibits its distributors and ripeners from reselling green bananas, which meant there was market fragmentation;

-it charged its customers prices which differed according to the Member States in which they were located, although there was no objective reasons for such discrimination; for equivalent transactions, prices were found to have differed between the ports of Bremerhaven and Rotterdam in some cases by as much as, or more than 100%.

-it charged unfair prices for sales to its customers in Germany, Denmark and the Benelux countries;

- finally, for no objectively valid reason, it refused, for nearly two years, to supply one of its main Danish customers.

Because of the seriousness of these violations of Article 86, the Commission imposed a fine of one million u.a. It also ordered UBC to put an end to its infringements of the Treaty (except the refusal to supply, which had already ceased). So that the Commission could check on compliance, UBC was ordered to notify the Commission once it had withdrawn the ban on resale of green bananas by its distributors and ripeners in Germany, Denmark, Ireland and the Benelux countries and to keep the Commission informed of the prices actually charged in those countries over the next two years. Penalty payments amounting to one thousand u.a. per day of delay from the dates stipulated in the Decision were imposed.

The importance of the Decision lies in the fact that the Commission investigated a firm's entire marketing policy in the light of Article 86, not so as to attack its commercial dynamism and economic performance, since this is not the purpose of Article 86, but because a dominant firm has an obligation not to indulge in business practices which are at variance with the goals of integrated markets and undistorted competition in the Common Market.

The Decision is also significant in that it finds abuse within the meaning of Article 86 on two counts: customers were charged different prices for identical transactions, and unfair prices were imposed.

In an attempt to justify the considerable differences in the prices which it charged its customers in different Member States, UBC asserted that it had adjusted its prices to the maximum the market would bear. The Commission took the view that for a dominant firm systematically to charge the highest price it could get, entailing substantial price differences, was not an objective justification for discriminatory prices, particularly if the firm used its dominance to keep markets separated.

In reaching the conclusion that the prices imposed by UBC on its customers were unfair, the Commission relied essentially on the following facts:

In the first place, UBC by its own admission was making a profit on the lowest price quoted for bananas, the price at which it sold to its Irish customers.

Also, UBC was selling bananas without the Chiquita trademark 30 to 40% cheaper than those with, although they were only slightly inferior to Chiquita bananas; furthermore, UBC's main competitors, selling their own brand of bananas of comparable quality, generally sell them at prices below those of Chiquita bananas.

These facts brought the Commission to the view that the prices of this brand of bananas were excessive in relation to the economic value of the commodity supplied. As a guide, it suggested that UBC's prices in Germany, Denmark and the Benelux countries would be acceptable if they came down to not less than 15% below the prices currently charged in Germany.

In taking this action, the Commission had no wish to set itself up as a price-control authority or to interfere in internal price setting by examining cost somponents or the like. On the other hand, it did wish to make it clear that the provisions of Article 86 which prohibit discriminatory and unfair prices must be enforceable.

*The Commission ruled:*

.....

2. Undertakings are in a dominant position when they have the power to

behave independently without taking into account to any substantial extent, their competitors, purchasers and suppliers. Such is the case where an undertaking's market share, either in itself or when combined with its know-how, access to raw materials, capital or other major advantage such as trademark ownership, enables it to determine the prices or to control the production or distribution of a significant part of the relevant goods. It is not necessary for the undertaking to have total dominance such as would deprive all other market participants of their commercial freedom, as long as it is strong enough in general terms to devise its own strategy as it wishes, even if there are differences in the extent to which it dominates individual sub-markets.

*The Commission decided:*

.....

Under Article 16(1) of Regulation No 17/62, the Commission may, by decision, impose on undertakings periodic penalty payments of from 50 to 1,000 units of account per day, calculated from the date appointed by the decision, in order to compel them to put an end to an infringement of Article 86 of the EEC Treaty in accordance with a decision taken pursuant to Article 3 of the Regulation. UBC has infringed Article 86 in several respects. If UBC is to put an end to these infringements, the Commission must be provided with the necessary means to ensure that its requirements in this respect are properly carried out. UBC should accordingly be required to satisfy the obligations set out in Article 3(b) of this Decision. Furthermore, if these obligations are not satisfied, periodic penalty payments should be imposed.

Accordingly, each of the obligations imposed on UBC by Article 3(b) of this Decision should be made subject to a periodic penalty payment of 1,000 units of account in respect of each day of delay.

This Decision is to be enforceable in accordance with Article 192 of the EEC Treaty.

As UBC has appointed United Brands Continental BV, Rotterdam, as its representative in this proceeding, notice of this Decision should be given to that company.

HAS ADOPTED THIS DECISION:

Article 1

It is hereby declared that the United Brands Company has infringed Article 86 of the Treaty establishing the European Economic Community:

(a) by requiring its distributors/ripeners in the Belgo-Luxembourg Economic Union, Denmark, Germany, Ireland and the Netherlands to refrain from re-selling its bananas while still green;

(b) by, in respect of its sales of Chiquita bananas, charging other trading parties, namely distributors/ripeners other than the Scipio Group in the Member States referred to above, dissimilar prices for equivalent transactions;

(c) by imposing unfair prices for the sale of Chiquita bananas on its customers in the Belgo-Luxembourg Economic Union, Denmark, the Netherlands and Germany (other than the Scipio Group);

(d) by refusing from 10 October 1973 to 11 February 1975 to supply Chiquita bananas to Th. Olesen A/S, Valby, Copenhagen, Denmark.

Article 2

A fine of one million units of account is imposed on United Brands Company in respect of the infringements of Article 86 of the Treaty referred to in Article 1 hereof.

Article 3

(a) United Brands Company shall bring to an end without delay the infringements referred to in Article 1 hereof, unless it has already done so of its own accord.

(b) United Brands Company shall:

(i) inform all its distributors/ripeners in the Belgo-Luxembourg Economic Union, Denmark, Germany, Ireland and the Netherlands that it has ceased to apply the prohibition on the resale of green bananas and inform the Commission that it has done so by not later than 1 February 1976;

(ii) inform the Commission by 20 April 1976 and thereafter twice yearly not later than 20 January and 20 July for a period of two years of the prices charged during the previous six months to customers in the Belgo-Luxembourg Economic Union, Denmark, Germany, Ireland and the Netherlands.

Article 4

In respect of each obligation set out in Article 3(b) hereof a periodic penalty payment of 1,000 units of account per day shall be payable in respect of each day of delay from the dates stated therein.

Article 5

This Decision shall be enforceable in accordance with the provisions of Article 192 of the Treaty establishing the European Economic Community.

Article 6

This Decision is addressed to United Brands Company, New York, United States of America, and to its representative United Brands Continental BV, Van Vollenhovenstraat 3002, the Netherlands, which shall be notified thereof.

*Sequel:*

United Brands appealed against the Commission's Decision in a judgment of 14 February 1978. The Court (case 27/76) upheld the Commission decision for the most part. The Court was however of the opinion that the Commission had not adduced adequate legal proof of the lack and evaluations which formed the foundations of its findings that United Brands had infringed Article 86 of the Treaty by directly and indirectly imposing unfair selling prices for bananas. The Court annulled Article 1(c) of the Commission Decision and reduced the fine imposed on United Brands to 850,000 units of account.

## (7) Decision in re Hoffmann-La Roche (Vitamins)

Decision of the Commission of 9 June 1976 relating to a proceeding under Article 86 of the EEC Treaty against the Hoffmann La Roche group, O.J. No L 223, 16 August 1976, p. 27; Competition Law CM/M/I/103.

*Facts:* The Commission issued its decision under Article 86 of the EEC Treaty against Hoffmann-La Roche (Roche), a multinational group with its headquarters in Switzerland and the world's leading vitamin manufacturer.

Roche had entered into exclusive or preferential supply contracts with a number of major bulk vitamin users who incorporated the vitamins into their own medicines, foods and feeding stuffs.

Whether to compensate for the exclusive or to encourage a preferential link, the contracts provided for fidelity rebates based not on differences in costs related to the quantities supplied by Roche but on the proportion of the customer's requirements covered. Furthermore, the rebates were not calculated separately for each group of vitamins but were aggregated across all purchases from Roche, so that Roche was able to benefit from the fidelity arrangement even in respect of those vitamins for which it does not hold a dominant position on the market.

The clause giving Roche the opportunity to align its prices on lower prices charged by competitors could have made the system built upon the contracts somewhat less restrictive, but in fact, as only prices offered by 'reputable' manufacturers in the customer's own country could be considered, the upshot was that Roche was in a position to decide whether or not to bring down its prices and thereby keep the sale.

After finding that each group of vitamins constitutes a separate market, since they are hardly if at all interchangeable, the Commission concluded that Roche dominated the Common Market for the seven relevant groups - Vitamins A, B2, B6, C, E, biotin (H) and pantothenic acid (B3). The principal reasons for the finding of dominance were: the importance of Roche's market shares for individual vitamins (between 47 and 95%), the fact that Roche manufactures a far broader range of vitamins than any of its competitors; the volume of its sales; its technical and commercial advantages over the competition; and the barriers to entry for new competitors on the vitamins market raised by the scale of investment required and by the need for long-term capacity programming.

The Commission considered that Roche was abusing its dominant position by concluding exclusive or preferential contracts since the effect of the contracts was to tie the most important buyers of bulk vitamins to it and to prevent its chief competitors from supplying them. The decision imposed a fine of 300,000 u.a. - or DM 1,098,000, as Roche has an important subsidiary in the Federal Republic of Germany.

*The Commission ruled:*

.....

The relevant market

20. Each group of vitamins constitutes a distinct market because each group is particularly suited to satisfy stable requirements and is not, or at least not to any significant extent, interchangeable with any other group or with any other products.

The relevant product markets for the purposes of this Decision are the following groups of vitamins: A, B2, B6, C, E, Biotin (H), and pantothenic acid (B3).

The relevant geographical market for the purposes of this Decision is the whole of the Common Market.

The dominant position

21. Roche enjoys such a complete freedom of action in the relevant markets enabling it to impede effective competition within the Common Market that it has a dominant position in such markets.

The dominant position results from the following:

- the market share held by Roche for each of the above-mentioned vitamins is very considerable since it ranges from 95% for vitamins B6 and H to 47% (the second producer having about only half this share) for vitamin A.

- Roche produces a far wider range of vitamins than its competitors. Since the requirements of many users extend to several groups of vitamins, Roche is able to employ a sales and pricing strategy which is far less dependent than that of other manufacturers on the conditions of competition in each market.

In assessing the dominant position of Roche account should be taken of the following: Roche is the world's largest producer of all vitamins; itw turnover exceeds that of all other producers and it has technological and commercial advantages not possessed by its competitors. Furthermore, since any entry into the vitamins market requires large and specialised investment and the programming of capacities over long periods in order to be profitable, it is unlikely that the possibility of entry by new competitors to the market would at present have any appreciable effect on the position of Roche.

The abuse

22. The conduct of Roche described above (paragraphs 10 to 18) constitutes an abuse of a dominant position, because by its nature it hampers the freedom of choice and equality of treatment of purchasers and restricts competition between bulk vitamins manufacturers in the common market and furthermore it is likely to affect trade between Member States.

The abusive nature of this conduct appears from the following:

(a) The fact that customers are bound by an exclusive or preferential purchasing commitment in favour of Roche for all or for a very large proportion of their requirements either as a result of an express obligation or exclusivity, or fidelity rebates, or other means.

(b) The fact that the price advantages granted are based not on the differences in costs borne by Roche in relation to the quantities supplied, but on the supply of all or a very large proportion of a customer's requirements.

(c)The fact that in certain cases the rebate is based on all purchases, so that purchases of vitamins of one group are aggregated with purchases of vitamins of other groups ('across-the-board' rebates).

(d) The fact that the agreements generally contain a provision known as the 'English clause', the significance of which is as follows: purchasers are obliged to inform Roche of offers from other manufacturers more favourable than those of Roche; should Roche not match such offers purchasers are free to purchase from such manufacturers without losing the rebate in respect of purchases made from Roche. In some agreements Roche stipulate that the offers should emanate from reputable manufacturers (thereby excluding dealers and brokers).

23. The agreements in question are not identical in so far as the obligations of the purchaser are concerned. Nevertheless, all the agreements are of a type suitable to achieve the desired object, namely that the customer should confine the purchase of all or a large proportion of his requirements of vitamins to Roche. Some agreements contain an express obligation by the purchaser to buy all or almost all of his requirements

from Roche. Other agreements provide for fidelity rebates. In yet other agreements it is evident from their context that price advantages are offered in return for an obligation of exclusivity undertaken by the purchaser. The latter element is present even in those cases where the rebate is described as being in return for a del credere guarantee, since such a guarantee is not given here in favour of independent third parties but for associated or subsidiary companies within well-known multinational groups with a sound financial base and whose commercial transactions call for no guarantee.

24. The exclusivity agreed by Roche with its customers in these agreements amounts to an abuse within the meaning of Article 86 because of its incompatibility with the objective of Article 3(f) of the Treaty, that competition in the Common Market is not distorted, and more particularly because of its incompatibility with paragraph (c) of Article 86.

The fact of agreeing with purchasers that they will buy all or a very large proportion of their requirements from only one source by its very nature removes all the freedom of choice from purchasers in their selection of sources of supply, and ties them to one supplier. The special price offered by Roche is the consideration for the abandonment by its purchasers of their opportunities to obtain substantial proportions of their requirements from competitors. Should a purchaser not observe his obligation of exclusivity - by purchasing some of his requirements from another vitamin manufacturer - the fidelity rebate is forfeited not only in respect of the amount of such purchase, but in respect of all his purchases from Roche. This restrictive effect is aggravated by the fact that the rebate - and hence the exclusivity - is calculated on the basis of all purchases from Roche so that purchases of vitamins of one group are aggregated with purchases of vitamins of other groups (across-the-board rebates).

The agreements in question have further effect of interfering with competition between vitamin manufacturers. The exclusivity established by Roche with its customers denies any access to the customers by other vitamin manufacturers. For quantities of any importance the rate of the rebate given by Roche is such that it is made practically impossible or at the least very onerous for other producers to sell to the customers of Roche.

25. The provision known as the 'English clause' is but a very limited relaxation of the system applied by Roche. The argument that this provision in fact leaves the customer free to purchase from the competitors of Roche is belied by the function of the clause. This provision, whilst enabling Roche to learn of the prices offered by its competitors, leaves to Roche the decision whether the customer in question is free to purchase from the competitor offering vitamins at lower prices; the customer is free to purchase from the competitor only where Roche decides not to match the price offered. This opportunity is further restricted by the requirement that the offer be from a reputable manufacturer in the customer's territory - thereby excluding offers from other territories or other Member States. It is clear that should the sale in question be of interest to Roche, by reason either of the quantity or the type of vitamin involved or the fact that the offer is from a reputable manufacturer, then Roche with its strength in the vitamins market is put in a position to adjust its price and so preserve exclusivity of supply to the customer in question. It is therefore the decision of Roche in each case, depending on the circumstances, whether to admit partially, or to deny access to, a competitor to the market which Roche has reserved for itself.

26. Moreover, in so far as the agreements in question provide for fidelity rebates in return for the reservation by the purchaser of exclusivity towards Roche, the conditions for the application of Article 86(c) are met. The rebates in question lead to discrimination and to the disadvantage both of those customers of Roche who do not benefit thereby and of those who do not benefit to the same extent. The system operated by Roche leads to the fixing of quite different prices for two customers who have bought the same quantities from Roche where one of them has made additional purchases from another manufacturer.

By this means dissimilar conditions are applied to equivalent transactions with other trading parties, thereby placing them at a competitive disadvantage.

27. The conduct in question is likely to affect trade between Member States in that it restricts the trading opportunities of users and suppliers of bulk vitamins in different Member States and this has a direct influence on the patterns of trade between Member States so as to impede the attainment of the objectives of a single market. Furthermore, an examination of the statistics for the import of bulk vitamins in the various Member States indicates that nearly half the turnover in bulk vitamins in the Community is taken up by imports within the Community which is impeded by the agreements in question.

The fine

28. Pursuant to Article 15(2) of Regulation No 17 the Commission may impose fines on undertakings where either intentionally of or negligently they infringe Article 86. In fixing the amount of the fine, regard shall be had both to the gravity and to the duration of the infringement.

It is necessary to impose a fine upon Roche.

Roche has intentionally, or at least negligently, committed the infringement described above. The Roche circulars referred to above provide evidence that the object desired and the effect expected by Roche were the substantial restriction of competition. Roche could not have been unaware that behaviour restricting competition to such an extent was incompatible with Article 86.

In assessing the gravity of the infringement account should be taken of the fact that the conduct in question is of a type which forms a major obstacle to competition, that it is evidenced by a large number of agreements relating to large quantities of vitamins and that these agreements were concluded with major purchasers established in several Member States and whose operations extend to most if not all of the Common Market.

With respect to the duration of the infringement, it may be concluded that the conduct in question began in 1964, that it was evident in an increasing number of agreements, that only at the end of 1974, following intervention by the Commission, were some of the agreements terminated, and that the infringements cannot yet be considered to be at an end since some agreements are still in force.

For the purposes of determining the amount of the fine, however, the Commission only takes into account the period of about five years between 1970, by which date there can be no doubt that Roche was formulating and applying its systematic policy of fidelity agreements, and the end of 1974 when the first terminations of the agreements took place.

29. Although Roche has its registered office outside the common market, it has numerous subsidiaries within the common market, particularly in the Federal Republic of Germany.

In these circumstances, for the payment of the fine, the amount shall be converted from units of account into Deutsche Mark.

*Sequel:*

Hoffmann-La Roche appealed against the Decision. The Court in a judgment of 13 February 1979, Case 85/76, upheld the Decision for the most part but reduced the fine to 200,000 units of account or 732,000 DM. It considered that the Commission had not given enough proof of Roche's dominant position on the market for vitamin B.3. It also considered that the infringement had taken place during a shorter period than the Commission had alleged. Finally Roche had from the initiation of the procedure indicated that it was willing to change the challenged contracts and in the meantime had done so.

(8) Decision in re Hugin-Liptons

For facts and references see above, pages 53 and 89.

*The Commission held:*

Hugin UK and the other Hugin companies established within the common market are wholly controlled subsidiaries of Hugin AB. Hugin AB and Hugin UK, together with all other Hugin companies, are an economic unit and therefore constitute an undertaking within the meaning of Article 86.

The majority of parts for Hugin cash registers are made to Hugin design and with tools belonging to Hugin AB and are exclusive to Hugin AB. These parts are not interchangeable with the parts of other makes of cash registers and cannot otherwise be economically reproduced. Hugin cash registers cannot therefore be properly maintained, repaired or rebuilt without the use of Hugin spare parts. Hugin AB controls the supply of all Hugin spare parts throughout the world.

Hugin AB accordingly enjoys a monopoly in Hugin spare parts throughout the world and thus, with its subsidiaries established in the common market, it holds a dominant position in the common market for the supply of such spare parts. Hugin therefore has a dominant position for the maintenance and repair of Hugin cash registers in relation to companies which need a supply of such parts. It follows therefore, that Hugin AB and Hugin UK hold a dominant position for these products and services in that substantial part of the market consisting of England, Scotland and Wales. Such dominant position extends to the business, such as Liptons carried on, of reconditioning and repairing used in cash registers which also depends upon a supply of Hugin spare parts. As the business of renting out Hugin cash registers depends upon a supply of spare parts in order that the owner may carry out his own maintenance and repair, Hugin AB also has a dominant position in relation to such owners.

In cases in which an undertaking holding a dominant position within the common market or in a substantial part of it for the supply of certain products, and in particular where the dominant position is a monopoly:

(a) refused without objective justification to supply those products to existing substantial customers for and users of the products, and the refusal to supply seriously injures the latter in their business by interfering with and ultimately preventing them from continuing to offer a service or to carry on a line of business, thereby ultimately eliminating all competitors independently of the dominant undertaking from the market for that service or that line of business; and

(b) prohibits its subsidiaries and dealers from supplying those products outside its own distribution network and in particular to buyers in other Member States, thereby making the refusal to supply more effective by denying those products to the customers and users in question,

such conduct amounts to an abuse of a dominant position, where it causes competition to be substantially restricted and trade between Member States to be affected appreciably.

Hugin AB, both directly and through its subsidiaries, has abused its dominant position in the common market in each of the ways described above in a manner likely to strengthen and consolidate its dominant position.

10(a) The stated policy of Hugin AB is that spare parts for Hugin cash registers are only delivered to its own subsidiaries and its own authorised dealers for their own use and are not for resale. From the moment, therefore, that a cash register user purchases a Hugin cash register, the result of Hugin's refusal to supply is to make the user in question totally dependent on Hugin AB for the supply of spare parts and, in effect, for the maintenance and repair of that machine. Purchasers and users are thereby prevented from purchasing such spare parts from any other source and are in addition thereby also deprived of their freedom to choose where they will obtain the maintenance and repair of their machines.

Liptons allege, and Hugin AB does not dispute this, that the maintenance and repair of Hugin cash registers is within the competence of anyone having the skill to maintain and repair competitive cash registers and provided that they have experience and training in the repair of such machines. No other justification has been offered for the refusal to supply spare parts. There is therefore no valid objective reason for depriving companies such as Liptons, which have the requisite skills and training, from competing with Hugin AB, its subsidiaries and authorised dealers in the maintenance and repair of Hugin cash registers nor for depriving the owners and users of such machines from having access to such independent sources of maintenance and repair. Such refusal throughout the common market therefore constitutes an abuse of Hugin AB's dominant position in that it restricts effective competition. The refusal to supply also restricts trade in reconditioned Hugin cash registers which compete with new Hugin cash registers.

(b) With regard to Liptons the conduct of Hugin AB and Hugin UK is an abuse in that Liptons was in 1972 a principal customer for spare parts and had been a customer for spare parts for over 12 years and that the refusal to supply amounted to a withdrawal of supplies which had the result of removing a major competitor in the matter of service, maintenance, repair and the supply of reconditioned machines from a substantial part of the common market. Not only had Liptons been the main distributor for Hugin GB in England, Scotland and Wales, but it had started a substantial business in its own right of the renting out of Hugin cash registers in which it had invested a considerable sum of money. Liptons was also qualified to service, maintain and repair such machines, and this business as it relates to new machines has ceased as a result of Hugin's refusal to supply spare parts. Liptons is now no longer in a position to buy the necessary spare parts for the maintenance and repair of Hugin cash registers for customers requiring that service, not to undertake that service in respect of new machines it might wish to rent to its customers. In addition Liptons is severly restrained in the business it had carried on for over 12 years in reconditioning Hugin cash registers for resale.

Liptons has accordingly been forced gradually to withdraw from these businesses in which it had invested time and money and had established a strong basis for profitable expansion. Without a supply of spare parts Liptons will eventually be eliminated as a competitor in all these lines of business. The fact that Liptons has ceased to be a distributor of Hugin cash registers does not in the circumstances amount to a valid objective reason for refusing to supply spare parts as the business created by the 'main agency' agreement is separate from the other business of servicing, maintaining, repairing, renting out and reconditioning Hugin cash registers which Liptons undertook in its own right both before, during and, to some extent, at least until supplies of spare parts ceased, after the agreement was in force.

12(c) As a result of its policy of not supplying spare parts outside its own network, Hugin AB also abused its dominant position by prohibiting its subsidiaries in France, Belgium, Germany and the UK, and its independent distributors in Ireland, Italy and the Netherlands from supplying spare parts outside the Hugin distribution network. The letters from these companies clearly establish that such a prohibition was in force at the time Liptons endeavoured to obtain spare parts from Hugin AB itself and from the subsidiaries and distributors referred to above. Such conduct shelters Hugin AB from all effective competition in the matter of service, maintenance and repair of Hugin cash registers throughout the common market.

The reasons given by Hugin for its refusal to supply Liptons are not objectively sufficient to justify such refusal. Even if it were correct that a Hugin cash register was a product of such complexity as to require special training beyond that required for any other mechanical, electromechanical or electronic product of a similar kind which, in view of the evidence available, the Commission does not accept, it would still not justify Hugin from withdrawing supplies of spare parts from Liptons at a time when it clearly was in possession of the necessary skills. Hugin cannot, therefore, rely on the fact that because of the lapse of time since the refusal to supply Liptons may have lost those skills if such loss is the result of the deliberate act of Hugin AB. Neither can the argument that there is no market for spare parts be accepted since Liptons was supplied with such spare parts for a period in excess of 12 years at the time when the supply of spare parts was withdrawn by Hugin. Liptons has spent more than five years seeking to obtain such spare parts from Hugin UK, Hugin AB and the other Hugin companies and distributors throughout the common market.

Furthermore, the fact that the system of distribution of Hugin cash registers might be regarded as a system of selected distribution is not itself a valid and objective reason for refusing to supply spare parts to other companies. The criteria for the selection of distributors of a product such as cash registers are not necessarily the criteria appropriate for selecting competent and qualified enterprises who wish to service the product and who need spare parts in order to do so. Also in so far as an enterprise in the position of Liptons has rights under Community law to continued supply of spare parts, it cannot be deprived of these rights by contracts made between the manufacturers and third parties.

The abuses by Hugin AB of its dominant position appreciably affect trade between Member States. The prohibition on export of spare parts from all Member States to any firm other than an authorised dealer directly affects trade between Member States. The refusal by Hugin subsidiaries and the Hugin distributors in other Member States to supply

Liptons was a result of Hugin AB's Community-wide policy and affected trade between the UK and the Member States involved. Even if the prohibition is removed in the manner proposed by Hugin AB, its policy of refusing to permit supplies of spare parts to independent companies, such as Liptons, still exists and effects trade between Member States. Hugin AB is thereby preventing Liptons from carrying on its business of maintenance, repair, renting out and reconditioning Hugin cash registers. Liptons has been prevented from continuing to expand its business within a substantial part of the common market and is unable to purchase spare parts from other Member States. Due to the size of Hugin AB's share of the overall market for cash registers, the distribution system practised by Hugin AB under which only dealers are supplied with spare parts together with the prohibition imposed on such dealers on selling spare parts outside the Hugin network, prevent the operation of independent servicing companies anywhere in the common market, and has an appreciable effect on the structure of competition within the common market.

(9) Hugin case

Hugin Kassaregister and Hugin Cash Registers v. Commision, Judgment of 31 May 1979, case 22/78; (1979) ECR 1869; (1979) 3 CMLR 345; CCH para. 8524; Competition Law CM/M/111/78.

For facts see above pages 53 and 89.

*The Court held:*

Hugin's position on the market.

3. As regards the question whether Hugin occupies a dominant position on the market the Commission takes the view that the facts of the case have shown that while Hugin has only a relatively small share of the cash register market - which is very competitive - it has a monopoly in spare parts for machines made by it and that consequently it occupies a dominant position for the maintenance and repair of Hugin cash registers in relation to independent companies which need a supply of Hugin spare parts. As regards the reconditioning of used machines and the renting out of such machines the Commission also takes the view that Hugin occupies a dominant position as regards cash registers of its own manufacture, since undertakings engaged in such activities depend on supplies of Hugin spare parts.

4. Hugin contests the validity of the Commission's findings on these various points. In its principal argument it states that the supply of spare parts and of maintenance service is certainly not a separate market but is an essential parameter of competition in the market for cash registers as a whole. It states that on that market after-sales service and the quality of repair and maintenance services, including the supply of spare parts, constitute such a significant competitive factor that Hugin runs those services at a loss.

5. To resolve the dispute it is necessary, first, to determine the relevant market. In this respect account must be taken of the fact that the conduct alleged against Hugin consists in the refusal to supply spare parts to Liptons and, generally, to any independent undertaking outside its distribution network. The question is, therefore, whether the supply of spare parts constitutes a specific market or whether it forms part

of a wider market. To answer that question it is necessary to determine the category of clients who require such parts.

6. In this respect it is established, on the one hand, that cash registers are of such a technical nature that the user cannot fit the spare parts into the machine but requires the services of a specialised technician and, on the other, that the value of the spare parts is of little significance in relation to the cost of maintenance and repairs. That being the case, users of cash registers do not operate on the market as purchasers of spare parts, however they have their machines maintained and repaired. Whether they avail themselves of Hugin's after-sales service or whether they rely on independent undertakings engaged in maintenance and repair work, their spare part requirements are not manifested directly and independently on the market. While there certainly exists amongst users a market for maintenance and repairs which is distinct from the market in new cash registers, it is essentially a market for the provision of services and not for the sale of a product such as spare parts, the refusal to supply which forms the subject-matter of the Commission's decision.

7. On the other hand, there exists a separate market for Hugin spare parts at another level, namely that of independent undertakings which specialise in the maintenance and repair of cash registers, in the reconditioning of used machines and in the sale of used machines and the renting out of machines. The rôle of those undertakings on the market is that of businesses which require spare parts for their various activities. They need such parts in order to provide services for cash register users in the form of maintenance and repairs and for the reconditioning of used machines intended for re-sale or renting out. Finally, they require spare parts for the maintenance and repair of new or used machines belonging to them which are rented out to their clients. It is, moreover, established that there is a specific demand for Hugin spare parts, since those parts are not interchangeable with spare parts for cash registers of other makes.

8. Consequently the market thus constituted by Hugin spare parts required by independent undertakings must be regarded as the relevant market for the purposes of the application of Article 86 to the facts of the case. It is in fact the market on which the alleged abuse was committed.

9. It is necessary to examine next whether Hugin occupies a dominant position on that market. In this respect Hugin admits that it has a monopoly in new spare parts. For commercial reasons any competing production of spare parts which could be used in Hugin cash registers is not conceivable in practice. Hugin argues nevertheless that another source of supply does exist, namely the purchase and dismantling of used machines. The value of that source of supply is disputed by the parties. Although the file appears to show that the practice of dismantling used machines is current in the cash register sector it cannot be regarded as constituting a sufficient alternative source of supply. Indeed the figures relating to Lipton's turnover during the years when Hugin refused to sell spare parts to it show that Lipton's business in the selling, renting out and repairing of Hugin machines diminished considerably, not only when expressed in absolute terms but even more so in real terms, taking inflation into account.

10. On the market for its own spare parts, therefore, Hugin is in a

position which enables it to determine its conduct without taking account of competing sources of supply. There is therefore nothing to invalidate the conclusion that it occupies, on that market, a dominant position within the meaning of Article 86.

## III. RELEVANT MARKET

### A. Product Market

#### (1) Decision in re Continental Can

See above, page 43.

#### (2) Continental Can Case

For facts and references see above, page 10.

*The Court ruled:*

.....

D - On the facts set forth in the statement of reasons in the decision

28. The Commission based its decision, inter alia, on the thesis that the acquisition of the majority holding in a competing company by an undertaking or a group of undertakings holding a dominant position may, in certain circumstances, amount to an abuse of this position. This is the case, according to the Commission, if an undertaking in a dominant position strengthens such a position through a merger in such a way that real or potential competition in the goods concerned is in practice eliminated in a substantial part of the Common Market.

29. If it can, irrespective of any fault, be regarded as an abuse if an undertaking holds a position so dominant that the objectives of the Treaty are circumvented by an alteration to the supply structure which seriously endangers the consumer's freedom of action in the market, such a case necessarily exists, if practically all competition is eliminated. Such a narrow precondition as the elimination of all competition need not exist in all cases. But the Commission, basing its decision on such elimination of competition, had to state legally sufficient reasons or, at least, had to prove that competition was so essentially affected that the remaining competitors could no longer provide a sufficient counterweight.

30. In order to justify its thesis the Commission viewed the consequences of the disputed merger from various angles. In this respect a distinction has to be made in the statement of reasons for its decision between four essential elements:

(a) the present market share of the combined undertakings in the products concerned,

(b) the relative proportions of the new unit created by the merger compared to the size of potential competitors in this market,

(c) the economic power of the purchasers vis-a-vis that of the new unit, and

(d) the potential competition of either the manufacturers of the same products, who are situated in geographically distant markets, or of other products made by manufacturers situated in the Common Market.

In examining these various factors the decision on the one hand is based on the very high market share already held by SLW in metal containers, on the weak competitive position of the competitors remaining in the market, on the economic weakness of most of the consumers in relation to that of the new unit and on the numerous legal and factual links between Continental and potential competitors; and on the other hand, on the financial and technical difficulties involved in entering a market characterised by a strong concentration.

31. The applicant contests the exactitude of the data on which the Commission bases its decision. It cannot be concluded from SLW's market share, amounting to 70 to 80% in meat cans, 80 to 90% in cans for fish and crustacea and 50 to 55% in metal closures with the exception of crown corks - percentages which are moreover too high and could not be proved by the defendent -, that this undertaking dominates the market for light metal containers. The decision, moreover, excluded the possibility of competition arising from substitute products (glass and plastic containers) relying on reasons which do not stand up to examination. The statements about possibilities of real and potential competition as well as about the allegedly weak position of the consumers are therefore, in the applicant's view, irrelevant.

32. For the appraisal of SLW's dominant position and the consequences of the disputed merger, the definition of the relevant market is of essential significance, for the possibilities of competition can only be judged in relation to those characteristics of the products in question by virtue of which those products are particularly apt to satisfy an inelastic need and are only to a limited extent interchangeable with other products.

33. In this context recitals Nos 5 to 7 of the second part of the decision deal in turn with a 'market for light containers for canned meat products', a 'market for light containers for canned seafood', and a 'market for metal closures for the food packing industry, other than crown corks', allegedly all dominated by SLW and in which the disputed merger threatens to eliminate competition. The decision does not, however, give any details of how these three markets differ from each other, and must therefore be considered separately. Similarly, nothing is said about how these three markets differ from the general market for light metal containers, namely the market for metal containers for fruit and vegetables, condensed milk, olive oil, fruit juices and chemico-technical products. In order to be regarded as constituting a distinct market, the products in question must be individualized, not only by the mere fact that they are used for packing certain products, but particular characteristics of production which make them specifically suitable for this purpose. Consequently, a dominant position on the market for light metal containers for meat and fish cannot be decisive as long as it has not been proved that competitors from other sectors of the market for light metal containers are not in a position to enter this market, by a simple adaptation, with sufficient strength to create a serious counterweight.

34. Besides, there are in the decision itself indications which make one doubt whether the three markets are to be considered separately

from other markets for light metal containers, indications which rather lead one to conclude that they are parts of a larger market. In the first part of the statement of reasons, where, under letter J, it deals with the main competitors of SLW in Germany and TDV in Benelux, the decision mentions a German undertaking which holds a higher share of production of light metal containers for fruit and vegetables than SLW, and another one which supplies 38 to 40% of the German demand for crown corks: this seems to confirm that the production of metal cans for meat and fish cannot be considered separately from the production of metal cans for other purposes and that, when considering the production of metal closures, crown corks must not be left out. Furthermore, the decision, when examining the possibilities of competition by substitutes, does not - in No. 16 of its second part - confine itself to the three relevant 'markets', but deals with the market for light metal containers for other purposes as well; in this connection it states that these containers could be replaced by containers made of other material to a limited extent only. The fact that the Commission could not maintain this allegation in view of the facts put forward by the applicants in the course of the proceedings, proves in itself how necessary it is sufficiently to define the market concerned in order that the relative strength of the undertakings in such a market might be considered.

35. Since there are in the decision no data on the particular characteristics of metal containers for meat and fish and metal closures (other than crown corks) designed for the food packing industry, whereby these goods constitute separate markets which could be dominated by the manufacturer holding the highest share of this market, it is for this reason characterized by an uncertainty which has an effect on the other statements from which the decision infers the absence of real or potential competition in the market in question. As regards in particular competition by other manufacturers of metal containers, the Commission argued in the course of the proceedings in Court that Contintal licenses 'agreed upon restrictions of competition within the framework of the so-called market information system described... under D 4', but it claims, on the other hand, that TDV and SLW have had 'the possibility of entering into competition with each other'. The argument put forward in no. 19 of the statement of reasons that the plants of certain manufacturers in the country bordering on Germany were located too far away from most German consumers to enable the latter to decide to use them as a permanent source of supply, has not been substantiated. Moreover, this argument is difficult to reconcile with the allegation in No. 25 (a) that the break-even distance for the transport of empty containers are 150-300 kilometers for the relatively large containers, and 500-1000 kilometers for smaller ones. In addition, it is uncontested that transport costs are of no essential significance in the case of metal closures.

36. Besides, as far as potential competition from large consumers capable of manufacturing their own cans is concerned, the decision alleges in No. 18 that such competition is out of the question due to the heavy capital investments involved and the technical lead of the Continental group in this field, whereas in the last paragraph in J No. 3 it is stated that in the Belgian market the Marie Thumas cannery through its subsidiary Eurocan makes metal containers for its own use and for sale to other consumers. This contradiction is a further indication of the Commission's uncertainty with regard to the definition of the market or markets concerned. In letter (e) of No. 30 of the statement of reasons in the decision, it is stated that "except

for Marie Thumas/Eurocan, manufacturers of their own cans do not make more than they themselves need and are not suppliers of empty metal containers", while, on the contrary, under K No. 2, second paragraph, it says that certain German firms who manufacture their own had begun to market their surplus output of metal containers. It can be concluded from all this that some undertakings which have begun to manufacture their own containers were able to overcome the technological difficulties, yet the decision does not contain any criteria for evaluating the power of competition of these undertakings. These considerations show further contradictions which, likewise, affect the validity of the decision contested.

37. All this leads to the conclusion that the decision has not, as a matter of law, sufficiently shown the facts and the assessments on which it is based. It must therefore be annulled.

.....

(3) Commercial Solvents Case

For facts and references see above, page 14.

*The court ruled:*

.....

(b) The market considered

19. The applicants rely on the sixth recital of Section II-C of the Decision in dispute for the conclusion that the Commission considers the relevant market for determining the dominant position to be that of ethambutol. Such a market does not exist since ethambutol is only a part of a larger market in anti-tubercolosis drugs, where it is in competition with other drugs which are to a large extent interchangeable. Since a market in ethambutol does not exist, it is impossible to establish a separate market in the raw material for the manufacture of this product.

20. The Commission replies that it has taken into account the dominant position in the Common Market in the raw material necessary for the production of ethambutol.

21. Both in Section II-B and in the part of Section II-C of the Decision which precedes the finding that the conduct of the applicants "therefore constitutes an abuse of the dominant position within the meaning of Article 86" (II-C, fourth recital), it is a question only of the market in raw materials for the manufacture of ethambutol. In taking the view that "the conduct in question limits the market in raw material as well as the production of ethambutol and thus constitutes the abuse expressly prohibited by the said Article", the Decision in dispute considers the market in ethambutol only for the purpose of determining the effects of the alleged infringement to be better appreciated, it is nevertheless irrelevant as regards the determination of the relevant market to be considered for the purpose of a finding that a dominant position exists.

22. Contrary to the arguments of the applicants it is in fact possible to distinguish the market in raw material necessary for the manufacture of a product from the market on which the product is sold. An abuse of a dominant position on the market in raw materials may thus have effects restricting competition in the market on which the derivatives of the

raw material are sold and these effects must be taken into account in considering the effects of an infringement, even if the market for the derivative does not constitute a self-contained market. The arguments of the applicants in this respect and in consequence their request that an expert's report on this subject be ordered are irrelevant and must be rejected.

.....

(4) Decision in re General Motors Continental

Decision of the Commission of 19 December 1974, on a proceeding under Article 86 of the EEC Treaty; O.J. No L 29, 3 February 1975, p. 14; (1975) I CMLR D 20; CCH para. 9705; Competition Law CM/M/I/83.

For facts see above, page 227.

*The Court held:*

.....

The first paragraph of Article 86 of the EEC Treaty prohibits, as incompatible with the Common Market, any abuse by one or more undertakings of a dominant position within the Common Market or any substantial part of it in so far as it may affect trade between Member States.

7. By virtue of Belgian law and of the authorisation granted to it by Opel. GMC has a dominant position with regard to applications for general type approval and the issue of certificates of conformity and type-shields in Belgium, both for new Opel vehicles and those registered abroad for no longer than six months in a substantial part of the Common Market. Purchasers of such Opel vehicles are obliged to avail themselves to GMC's services before using the vehicles on the public highways in Belgium if:

- the relevant model has not yet received type approval, or

- no certificate of conformity or typeshield has been issued for the relevant vehicle.

Thus whenever a consumer or dealer in Belgium decides to purchase an Opel vehicle outside Belgium, he becomes completely dependent on GMC.

(5) Decision in re Hoffmann La Roche (Vitamins)

See above pages 53 and 233.

(6) Decision in re Hugin-Liptons

See above, pages 53 and 89.

(7) United Brands Case

United Brands v. Commission, Case 22/76, Judgment of 14 February 1978; (1978) ECR 207; (1978) I CMLR 429; CCH para. 8429; Competition Law CM/M/III/71.

For facts see above, page 86.

*The Court held:*

.....

Chapter 1 - The existence of a dominant position

Section 1 - The relevant market

10. In order to determine whether UBC has a dominant position on the banana market it is necessary to define this market both from the standpoint of the product and from the geographic point of view.

11. The opportunities for competition under Article 86 of the Treaty must be considered having regard to the particular features of the product in question and with reference to a clearly defined geographic area in which it is marketed and where the conditions of competition are sufficiently homogeneous for the effect of the economic power of the undertaking concerned to be able to be evaluated.

Paragraph 1. The product market

12. As far as the product market is concerned it is first of all necessary to ascertain whether, as the applicant maintains, bananas are an integral part of the fresh fruit market, because they are reasonably interchangeable by consumers with other kinds of fresh fruit such as apples, oranges, grapes, peaches, strawberries, etc. or whether the relevant market consists solely of the banana market which includes both branded bananas and unlabelled bananas and is a market sufficiently homogeneous and distinct from the market of other fresh fruit.

13. The applicant submits in support of its argument that bananas compete with other fresh fruit in the same shops, on the same shelves, at prices which can be compared, satisfying the same needs: consumption as a dessert or between meals.

14. The statistics produced show that consumer expenditure on the purchase of bananas is at its lowest between June and December when there is a plentiful supply of domestic fresh fruit on the market.

15. Studies carried out by the Food and Agriculture Organisation (FAO) (especially in 1975) confirm that banana prices are relatively weak during the summer months and that the price of apples for example has a statistically appreciable impact on the consumption of bananas in the Federal Republic of Germany.

16. Again according to these studies some easing of prices is noticeable at the end of the year during the 'orange season'.

17. The seasonal peak periods when there is a plentiful supply of other fresh fruits exert an influence not only on the prices but also on the volume of sales of bananas and consequently on the volume of imports thereof.

18. The applicant concludes from these findings that bananas and other fruit form only one market and that UBC's operations should have been examined in this context for the purpose of any application of Article 86 of the Treaty.

19. The Commission maintains that there is a demand for bananas which is distinct from the demand for other fresh fruit especially as the banana is a very important part of the diet of certain sections of the Community.

20. The specific qualities of the banana influence customer preference and induce him not to readily accept other fruits as a substitute.

21. The Commission draws the conclusion from the studies quoted by the applicant that the influence of the prices and availabilities of other types of fruit on the prices and availabilities of bananas on the relevant market is very ineffective and that these effects are too brief and too spasmodic for such other fruit to be regarded as forming part of the same market as bananas or as a substitute therefor.

22. For the banana to be regarded as forming a market which is sufficiently differentiated from other fruit markets it must be possible for it to be singled out by such special features distinguishing it from other fruits that it is only to a limited extent interchangeable with them and is only exposed to their competition in a way that is hardly perceptible.

23. The ripening of bananas takes place the whole year round without any season having to be taken into account.

24. Throughout the year production exceeds demand and can satisfy it at any time.

25. Owing to this particular feature the banana is a privileged fruit and its production and marketing can be adopted to the seasonal fluctuations of other fresh fruit which are known and can be computed.

26. There is no unavoidable seasonal substitution since the consumer can obtain this fruit all the year round.

27. Since the banana is a fruit which is always available in sufficient quantities the question whether it can be replaced by other fruits must be determined over the whole of the year for the purpose of ascertaining the degree of competition between it and other fresh fruit.

28. The studies of the banana market on the Court's file show that on the latter market there is no significant long-term cross-elasticity any more than - as has been mentioned - there is any seasonal substitutability in general between the banana and all the seasonal fruits, as this only exists between the banana and two fruits (peaches and table grapes) in one of the countries (West Germany) of the relevant geographic market.

29. As far as concerns the two fruits available throughout the year (oranges and apples) the first are not interchangeable and in the case of the second there is only a relative degree of substitutability.

30. This small degree of substitutability is accounted for by the specific features of the banana and all the factors which influence consumer choice.

31. The banana has certain characteristics, appearance, taste, softness, seedlessness, easy handling, a constant level of production which enable it to satisfy the constant needs of an important section of the population consisting of the very young, the old and the sick.

32. As far as prices are concerned two FAO studies show that the banana is only affected by the prices - falling prices - of other fruits (and

only of peaches and table grapes) during the summer months and mainly in July and then by an amount not exceeding 20%.

33. Although it cannot be denied that during these months and some weeks at the end of the year this product is exposed to competition from other fruits, the flexible way in which the volume of imports and their marketing on the relevant geographic market is adjusted, means that the conditions of competition are extremely limited and that its price adapts without any serious difficulties to this situation where supplies of fruit are plentiful.

34. It follows from all these considerations that a very large number of consumers having a constant need for bananas are not noticeably or even appreciably enticed away from the consumption of this product by the arrival of other fresh fruit on the market and that even the personal peak periods only affect it for a limited period of time and to a very limited extent from the point of view of substitutability.

35. Consequently the banana market is a market which is sufficiently distinct from the other fresh fruit markets.

Paragraph 2. The geographic market
36. The Commission has taken the Federal Republic of Germany, Denmark, Ireland, the Netherlands and the BLEU as the geographic market and it is in respect of this market that it is necessary to consider whether UBC has the power to hinder effective competition.

37. It takes the view that the economic conditions in this part of the Community allow importer/distributors of bananas to market their products there in the ordinary course without there being any significant economic barriers for UBC to overcome compared with other importer/distributors.

38. The other Member States of the Community (France, Italy, the United Kingdom) must however be excluded from this geographic definition of the market notwithstanding the significant presence of UBC in these States, because of the special circumstances relating to import arrangements and trading conditions and the fact that the bananas of various types and origin are sold there.

39. The applicant points out that the geographic market where an undertaking's economic and commercial power is taken into consideration should only comprise areas where the conditions of competition are homogeneous.

40. Although the Commission had good reason to exclude France, Italy and the United Kingdom from the said market it failed to take account of the differences in the conditions of competition in the other Member States which should have led it to the same conclusions with regard to the latter as it came to in the case of the three countries referred to above.

41. In fact three substantially different systems of customs duty apply in the Member States concerned: a zero tariff in Germany covering a banana quota which meets most of this country's requirements, a transitional tariff in Ireland and Denmark and the Common Customs Tariff of 20% for imports into the Benelux.

42. The Commission has not either taken account of the consumer habits of the Member States concerned (the annual consumption of fresh fruits *per capita* in Germany is equal to 2.5 times that of Ireland and twice that of Denmark), differing commercial patterns, concentrations and monetary points of view.

43. The applicant draws the conclusion from all these findings that the geographic market taken by the Commission includes areas in which the conditions of competition are so different that they cannot be considered as constituting a single market.

44. The conditions for the application of Article 86 to an undertaking in a dominant position presuppose the clear elimination of the substantial part of the Common Market, in which it may be able to engage in abuses which hinder effective competition and this is an area where the objective conditions of competition applying to the products in question must be the same for all traders.

45. The Community has not established a common organisation of the agricultural market in bananas.

46. Consequently, import arrangements vary considerably from one Member State to another and reflect a specific commercial policy peculiar to the States concerned.

47. This explains why for example the French market owing to its national organisation is restricted upstream by a particular import arrangement and obstructed downstream by a retail price monitored by the Administration.

48. This market, in addition to adopting certain measures relating to a 'target price' ("prix objectif") fixed each year and to packaging and grading standards and the minimum qualities required, reserves about two thirds of the market for the production of the overseas departments and one third to that of certain countries enjoying preferential relations with France (Ivory Coast, Madagascar, Cameroon) the bananas whereof are imported duty-free and it includes a system the running of which is entrusted to the "Comité interprofessionnel bananier" ("C.I.B.").

49. The United Kingdom market enjoys "Commonwealth preferences", a system of which the main feature is the maintenance of a level of production favouring the developing countries of the Commonwealth and of a price paid to the associations of producers directly linked to the selling price of the green banana charged in the United Kingdom.

50. On the Italian market, since the abolition in 1965 of the State Monopoly responsible for marketing bananas, a national system of quota restrictions has been introduced, the Ministry for Shipping and the Exchange Control Office supervising the imports and the charterparties relating to the foreign ships which carry the bananas.

51. The effect of the national organisation of these three markets is that the applicant's bananas do not compete on equal terms with the other bananas sold in these States which benefit from a preferential system and the Commission was right to exclude these three national markets from the geographic market under consideration.

52. On the other hand the six other States are markets which are com-

pletely free, although the applicable tariff provisions and transport costs are of necessity different but not dicriminatory, and in which the conditions of competition are the same for all.

53. From the standpoint of being able to engage in free competition these six States form an area which is sufficiently homogeneous to be considered in its entirety.

54. UBC has arranged for its subsidiary in Rotterdam - UBCBV - to market its products. UBCBV is for this purpose a single centre for the whole of this part of the Community.

55. Transport costs do not in fact stand in the way of the distribution policy chosen by UBC which consists in selling f.o.r. Rotterdam and Bremerhaven, the two ports where the bananas are unloaded.

56. These are factors which go to make a relevant market a single market.

57. It follows from all these considerations that the geographic market as determined by the Commission which constitutes a substantial part of the Common Market must be regarded as the relevant market for the purpose of determining whether the applicant may be in a dominant position.

## B. Geographical Market

### (1) Sugar Cases

For facts and references see above, page 94.

*The Court held:*

.....

I - The question whether the 'southern part of Germany' is a substantial part of the Common Market

44. 1. It is clear from the statement of the reasons upon which the decision is based (p. 20 to 21, paragraph 9, p.28 under paragraph 16) that when the Commission refers to 'the southern part of Germany' it means the area which it regards as SZV's sales territory as opposed, on the one hand, to the sales territories which it considers belong to NZV and WZV, two companies, of which the sugar producers of the southern and western regions of the Federal Republic of Germany are members and, on the other hand, to the Länder of Berlain and the Saar, which it states are for the most part supplied by sugar coming respectively from the Federal Republic of Germany and the French Republic.

44. 2. The Commission produced for the Court's file a map (Annex II 10 to the statements of defence in Cases 54 to 56/73) 'based on' the maps annexed to the contracts of WZV's commission agents, which marks the boundaries of the latter's sales territory and bears the letters 'NZV' (in the north) and 'SZV' (in the south), but does not however indicate with any accuracy the boundary between the respective sales territories of these two marketing organisations.

44. 3. If this map is examined in the light of the parties' statements, to the extent to which they agree, it shows clearly that the territory within which the SZV carries on business, that is the 'southern part of

Germany', within the meaning this expression is given in the decision, includes the whole of Bavaria and Baden-Württemberg, part of the Land Hessen bordering on these two Länder, which takes in more than half of Hessen as well as certain parts adjoining the Rhine-Palatine, the Saar, North Rhine-Westphalia and Lower Saxony which are regions of insignificant size compared with the other sectors of SZV's sales territory.

44. 4. In order to ascertain the criteria which determine whether a specific territory is 'a substantial part of the Common Market' reference must be made to Chapter 5.

44. 5. The aggregate annual production of the companies which were members of SZV was at that time on average about 800,000 metric tons, a figure which must be evaluated bearing in mind that, on the one hand, SZAG, the principal member of SZV having its place of business in Baden-Württemberg itself supplied about 70% of this production and, on the other hand, that Franken, having its place of business in Bavaria, is after SZAG the largest producer member of SZV (cf. decision p. 20, paragraph 9).

44. 6. According to the Commission's statistics (cf. Annex I to the rejoinder in Case 55/73, table V, column 29) consumption 'in SZAG's sales territory less the Saar' increased during each of the four marketing years under consideration to 790,000, 792,000, 872,000 and 826,000 metric tons respectively, and these figures could even increase to the extent to which it would have to be conceded that SZV's sales territory exceeds that of SZAG.

44. 7. According to the available statistics the average number of consumers in the region in question for the years which have to be taken into account can be estimated at 22 million at least.

44. 8. If these figures are compared with the corresponding figures relating to the whole of the Community set out in Chapter 5, the 'southern part of Germany' within the meaning which this expression is given in the decision, is found to be sufficiently large, so far as sugar is concerned, to be considered having regard to the other criteria mentioned in Chapter 5 as a substantial part of the Common Market in this product.

44. 9. SZV submits that for the purpose of determining whether the area in question is a substantial part of the Common Market the statistical data relating to this area should not only be compared with the corresponding data relating to the Common Market as it was when the facts giving rise to these proceedings existed but also with the data relating to the Community of 'Nine' in its present form.

45. 0. Article 86 of the EEC Treaty clearly refers in each case to the position occupied by the undertakings concerned on the Common Market at the time when the latter acted in a way which is alleged to amount to an abuse.

45. 1. For this reason alone SZV's argument cannot be upheld.

II - The question whether SZV occupies a dominant position on the sugar market of the southern part of Germany

45. 2. SZV does not deny that in the two principle regions of the area

in question, namely the Länder of Bavaria and of Baden-Württemberg, its share of the market is approximately the 90% to 95% share mentioned in the contested decision (p. 39, paragraph No 3) for the whole of its sales territory.

45. 3. Similarly it concedes that in the Land Hessen its share of the market exceeds 50% and, having regard to the fact that part of this land does not form part of the applicant's sales territory, this statement raises the presumption that, to the extent to which the Land Hessen is co-extensive with this territory, SZV's share of the market is appreciably higher than 50%.

45. 4. These figures are confirmed by the Commission's statistics (Annex I to the rejoinder in Case 55/73, table V, columns 28 to 30) according to which imports, other than deliveries from producer to producer, effected during the four marketing years in question in the sales territory of SZAG, the largest member of SZV, only amounted to 0.19%; 0.73%; 1.62% and 2.93% respectively of the total consumption in SZAG's sales territory.

45. 5. With regard to the deliveries effected in the sales territory of SZV or its members by NZV and WZV or by the members of these marketing organisations there is no evidence at all on the Court's file that the volume of these deliveries was very large.

45. 6. Therefore SZV solely or jointly with its member had the opportunity of preventing effective competition on the market in question.

45. 7. Consequently it had during the period to be taken into consideration a dominant position on this market.

(2) Decision in re Hoffmann-La Roche (Vitamins)

See above pages 53 and 233.

(3) Decision in re Hugin-Liptons

See above page 53, 89, 238 and 241.

(4) United Brands Case

See above page 247.

## IV. ABUSE OF A DOMINANT POSITION

(1) Deutsche Grammophon Case

See above, page 2.

(2) Communication in re Eurofima

The following is the text of a press release issued by the EEC Commission No IP (73) 67 of 16 April 1973, relating to proceedings under Article 86 EEC which were terminated without going to a formal decision.

Acting upon complaints from the industrial sector affected, the Commission has instituted proceedings pursuant to Article 86 of the EEC Treaty, in respect of abuse of a dominant position on the demand side. These proceedings were wound up without any formal decision being taken after the abusive conduct had been terminated.

The complaint was directed against an important undertaking in the service industry. This undertaking had invited tenders for the development for manufacture of certain rolling-stock, which was gradually to replace the conventional type of rolling stock hitherto used in the Member States. Under the terms of the tender, the contractors were obliged, inter alia, to concede to the mandant unlimited rights of use of the patent rights resulting from the development, without any additional compensation.

With regard to the points of the complaint laid before it, the Commission took the view that the undertaking which was inviting tenders occupied a dominant position within the Common Market in so far as it was the most important buyer of the type of rolling-stock concerned. The demand for the granting of unlimited right of use unilaterally taken into consideration the interests of the mandant. The narrow technical co-operation between the mandant and contractor during the development certainly warrants a user right for the mandant for his own needs (maintenance and further construction). The claim to give licences for the future patent rights and for third parties without consulting or giving additional compensation to the contractor is materially improper. This condition of tender represents abuse within the meaning of Article 86.

On the basis of this information on the points of the complaint, the undertaking drew up a contract with the group of companies to which the contract for the execution of the order was awarded. In this contract, the condition objected to has been amended and the user's right to be granted to the mandant has been limited to his own materially justifiable requirements. In order to promote the standardisation of the type of rolling-stock concerned, it may grant licences to third parties, but only with the agreement of the contractor and in exchange for adequate compensation to be fixed as each case arises.

This is the first case where the Commission has taken action against abuse of power on the demand side of the market.

<u>(3) Commercial Solvents Case</u>

See above, page 14.

<u>(4) S.A.B.A.M. Case</u>

Second Judgment of 27 March 1974. (1974) ECR 313;(1974) 2 CMLR 238; CCH para 8269; Competition Law CM/M/III/39.

For facts and further references see above, page 35.

*The Court held:*

.....

3. By the first question it is asked whether an undertaking which enjoys a de facto monopoly in a Member State for the management of copyrights abuses its dominant position by demanding the global assignment of all copyrights without drawing any distinction between specific categories of such rights.

4. By the second question it is asked whether an abuse of a dominant position can consist in the fact that an undertaking stipulates that an author shall assign his present and future rights, and that, without

having to give an account of its action, the undertaking continues to exercise the rights assigned for five years following the withdrawal of a member.

5. It is apparent from the order for reference that the national court, having found that the undertaking in question in fact exercised a quasi-monopoly within Belgian territory and consequently occupied a dominant position in a substantial part of the Common Market, considered it necessary to ascertain whether that undertaking was abusing its dominant position through its statutes and contracts with members.

6. According to the terms of Article 86(a) an abuse must be regarded as consisting in particular, in directly or indirectly imposing unfair trading conditions.

7. It is therefore necessary to investigate whether the copyright association, through its statutes or contracts concluded with its members, is imposing, directly or indirectly, unfair conditions on members of third parties in the exploitation of works, the protection of which has been entrusted to it.

8. For this appraisal account must be taken of all the relevant interests, for the purpose of ensuring a balance between the requirement of maximum freedom for authors, composers, and publishers to dispose of their works and that of the effective management of their rights by an undertaking which in practice they avoid joining.

9. To determine whether, in these circumstances, the practice mentioned in the referring judgment constitute an abuse within the meaning of Article 86 of the Treaty, account must however be taken of the fact that an undertaking of the type envisaged is an association whose object is to protect the rights and interests of its individual members against, in particular, major exploiters and distributors of musical material, such as radio broadcasting bodies and record manufacturers.

10. For an association effectively to protect its rights and interests it must enjoy a position based on the assignement in its favour, by the associated authors, of their rights to the extent required for the association to carry out its activity on the necessary scale.

11. Consequently, it is desirable to examine whether the practices in dispute exceed the limit absolutely necessary for the attainment of this object, with due regard also to the interest which the individual author may have that his freedom to dispose of his work is not limited more than need be. For this purpose, a compulsory assignment of all copyrights, both present and future, no distinction being drawn between the different generally accepted types of exploitation, may appear an unfair condition, especially if such assignment is required for an extended period after the member's withdrawal.

12. The inequitable nature of such provisions must be determined by the relevant court, bearing in mind both the intrinsic individual effect of those clauses and their effect when combined.

13. If abusive practices are exposed, it is also for the Court to decide whether and to what extent they affect the interests of authors or third parties concerned, with a view to deciding the consequence with regard to the validity and effect of the contracts in dispute or certain of

their provisions.

14. It must be concluded that the fact that an undertaking entrusted with the exploitation of copyrights and occupying a dominant position within the meaning of Article 86 imposes on its members obligations which are not absolutely necessary for the attainment of its object and which thus encroach unfairly upon a member's freedom to exercise his copyright can constitute an abuse.

(5) General Motors Continental Case

For facts and references see above, page 227.

*The Court ruled:*

.....

The abuse

11. It is possible that the holder of the exclusive position referred to above may abuse the market by fixing a price - for a service which it is alone in a position to provide - which is to the detriment of any person acquiring a motor vehicle imported from another Member State and subjected to the approval procedure.

12. Such an abuse might lie, inter alia, in the imposition of a price which is excessive in relation to the economic value of the service provided, and which has the effect of curbing parallel imports by neutralising the possibly more favourable level of prices applying in other sales areas in the Community, or by leading to unfair trade in the sense of Article 86 (2) (a).

13. However, the applicant maintains on this point that conduct complained of did not constitute an "abuse" within the meaning of Article 86.

14. In order to demonstrate this point the applicant puts forward a number of arguments based on the actual circumstances in which the charge in question was imposed and, subsequently, largely refunded in the five cases referred to by the Commission.

15. The question whether the applicant abused its dominant position must be considered in the light of all the factors which gave rise to the decision of the Commission.

16. It is not disputed that in the five cases to which the Commission refers, and which arose between 15 March and 31 July 1973, the applicant imposed a charge which was excessive in relation to the economic value of the service provided by way of the approval procedure.

17. However, the applicant maintains on this point that the inspections which it carried out during this period represented an unusual activity on its part, in that it had only been made to assume responsibility for them as from 15 March 1973 when the State testing-stations were discharged from undertaking these same inspections.

18. As these inspections only constituted an occasional activity on the part of the applicant and one of minute importance in relation to the inspections which it normally carries out on the vehicles which it puts directly on the market and which are, therefore, manufactured in accordance with the standards imposed by Belgian legislation, the departments responsible applied the charge which was until then normal for the

inspection of the vehicle which it imported.

19. The applicant again draws attention to the fact that following the complaints made by the parties concerned it very quickly reduced the charge for the inspection of imported vehicles of European manufacture to a level which was more in line with the real cost of the operation and refunded the excess to the parties concerned, and that this took place before the Commission began its investigations.

20. This conduct on the part of the applicant, the truth of which is not contested by the Commission, cannot be regarded as an "abuse" within the meaning of Article 86.

21. The applicant has given an adequate explanation of the circumstances in which, in order to meet a new responsibility transferred from the State testing-stations to the manufacturers or authorised agents of the different makes of motor car in Belgium, it applied, for an initial period, to European cars a rate which was normally applied to vehicles imported from America.

22. The absence of any abuse is also shown by the fact that very soon afterwards the applicant brought its rates into line with the real economic cost of the operation, that it bore the consequences of doing so by reimbursing those persons who had made complaints to it and that it did so before any intervention on the part of the Commission.

23. Although the decision in question may be explained by the Commission's wish to react energetically against any tendency to abuse what is clearly a dominant position, its intervention was unjustified in the actual, temporal and factual circumstances in which it took place.

24. In these circumstances the contested decision must be annulled but the parties must bear their own costs.

.....

<u>(6) Decision in re United Brands</u>

See above, page 86 and 230 and below, page 348.

<u>(7) Decision in re Hoffmann-La Roche (Vitamins)</u>

See above, pages 53 and 233.

<u>(8) Decision in re Hugin-Liptons</u>

See above, page 53, 89, 238 and 241.

<u>(9) Decision in re Michelin-Netherlands</u>

For facts and references see above page 92.

37. NBIM's commercial conduct constitutes an abuse of a dominant position. It restricts dealers' freedom of choice and results in inequality of treatment as between tyre dealers. The access of other tyre producers to the market is also restricted.

Its conduct has the following characteristics:

(a) the application of a discount system that is based on bonuses established individually and selectively for each dealer and linked to the attainment of the individual sales 'targets' established by NBIM and agreed with dealer at the start of each year;

(b) the fact that until 1980 the 'targets' and bonus percentages applicable for each dealer were communicated and confirmed not in writing, but only orally;

(c) in 1977, the bonuses on heavy tyres were linked to purchases of light tyres.

*(a) The discount system*

38. The discount system is clearly aimed at tying the dealers closely to NBIM and thus making it difficult for other producers to gain a foothold in the market. The various bonuses are related to a sales 'target' which is established at the beginning of each annual sales campaign for each dealer, i.e. on an individual and selective basis. Even in periods when the economic situation is poor, the 'targets' are usually set at a level which is higher than the purchases made in the previous year. As a result, great pressure is put on the dealers to outdo themselves each year in their sales of Michelin tyres. The pressure on the dealer to buy Michelin tyres increases during the year and especially towards the end as he will try to achieve his sales 'target' and obtain the highest possible bonus.

This pressure is increased still further through the regular visits made by NBIM representatives, whose job it is to carry out systematic and direct checks on the spot that the 'targets' have been reached and to establish NBIM's resulting position in relation to its competitors (the so-called 'température Michelin'). NBIM defends itself by arguing that, due to a lack of official statistics in the Netherlands concerning sales of the various makes of tyre, it is obliged to estimate such sales through its customers, but this argument cannot be upheld. The information gathered by the Commission shows that these so-called 'estimates' are based on what amounts to a survey, that is to say on questions put directly and individually to the dealers by NBIM representatives.

The fact that use of the term 'température Michelin' was discontinued in 1977 is not relevant, since the practice (which is indeed mandatory for the representatives) of expressing as a percentage the share of Michelin tyres in the relevant dealer's total sales is still observed today, and has the same effect.

39. The resultant organisational links binding the independent trade to NBIM are further strengthened by the structure of the discount system. The table given in point 22 and the related explanatory note show that, up to 1979, NBIM's client dealers, in contrast to those of suppliers of other tyres, could collect only a limited proportion of the total discount accorded to them directly in the form of an invoice discount. The advance bonus, (the remainder of) the annual bonus, the automatic monthly bonus and the four-monthly bonus would certainly follow in due course, assuming that business relations continued on a normal footing, but meanwhile were regularly used by NBIM as a means of pressure (see point 24). Admittedly, the table suggests that in 1978 and 1979 there was a progressive simplification of the system, with NBIM's freedom of action becoming more limited. However, this is true only in respect of the monthly advance bonus, which of course lost its *raison d'être* with the increase in the direct invoice discount.

As far as the other bonuses are concerned, the changes made in 1978 and 1979 were basically concerned only with form. As pointed out in point 22, the range of bonuses applied by NBIM in its discount system was far more limited than the percentages given in fact suggest. Moreover, the discount system was strengthened in 1979 by the introduction of a four-monthly bonus linked to attainment of a sales 'target'.

40. This system applied by an undertaking in a dominant position, a system which has the effect of tying, with respect to organisational and commercial matters, independent dealers closely to the undertaking, constitutes an abuse within the meaning of Article 86, since it is incompatible with the objective of Article 3(f) of the Treaty, namely that competition in the common market should not be distorted.

41. Furthermore, NBIM's policy of granting selective bonuses results in discrimination within the terms of Article 86(c). The Commission has found that different bonuses are granted to dealers whose positions are comparable. The discounts received by the retailers do not in any way correspond to services that, from an economic point of view, are objectively provided and ascertainable. The criteria applied are clearly subjective and essentially based on the loyalty which has been showed to NBIM. Through its policy of individually determined discounts, NBIM applies dissimilar conditions to equivalent transactions with other trading parties, thereby placing them at an unjustified competitive disadvantage or advantage. In any event, this policy gives NBIM the opportunity of practising discrimination.

42. In its reply to the Commission's statement of objections, NBIM denied that the discount system constitutes an abuse within the meaning of Article 86, arguing primarily that the discounts and the 'targets' are a variant of quantity discounts.

NBIM's discounts are indeed linked to the attainment of a sales target clearly defined in numbers and/or guilders. To that extent, the discount system comprises elements which appear to be quantitative in nature. However, the Commission has established that comparable amounts purchased almost never result in the same or comparable discounts being granted to the dealers. The bonuses are quantity discounts only within the strictly individual context of each purchaser. The bonus rates are not established on the basis of objective criteria applicable to all purchasers. They are NBIM's expression of its individual assessment of a given dealer's performance and of its expectations regarding his future performance. These bonuses are set and calculated in such a way that in advance NBIM gains a hold upon the dealer in the efforts he makes to promote Michelin tyres, clearly detrimental to the efforts he puts in for other makes. The opportunity of discriminating between dealers which NBIM gains discourages them from obtaining supplies from other manufacturers at the expense of their purchases from NBIM. Accordingly, the discounts are not comparable to the normal quantity discounts which are customary in the trade and which constitute a reward calculated subsequently according to the objective criteria fixed in advance and known to all.

43. NBIM also point out that, in the period 1975 to 1978, the difference of discount between a small dealer and a large dealer amounted to no more than 2,55%. This difference is described as being marginal and as having a negligible effect on competition. Without going into a detailed analysis of this percentage, the Commission wishes to state that it does not share this view. In the first place, it is well known in the tyre trade that each percentage point more or less can play a crucial role for the dealer's profitability, particularly where the tyres involved are subject to such competition among dealers as Michelin tyres are. It is therefore difficult to see why NBIM should surround its

discount policy with so much secrecy if the margin of manoeuvre held no significance for its sales policy - unless it must be assumed that the lack of transparency is intended to mislead the trade into thinking that the margin is much greater. Furthermore, the Commission has found that, before various rounds of visits, NBIM representatives were instructed to make it clear to the dealers how much it would cost them if they did not place a final order before the end of the year, half-year or quarter. Such instructions would be pointless if the dealers were indifferent to the amount involved, even though it is on occasion barely involved. Lastly, in explaining the 0,5% extra annual bonus referred to above in point 27, NBIM stated that its intention was to give the dealers the opportunity of making up for the loss in income resulting from the temporary shortage of truck tyres. NBIM itself thus confirms the fact that fractions of one per cent are commercially very relevant, and 2,55% all the more so. Furthermore, this fact not only relates to the 'penalty for not reaching the target set', but also to the discrimination as between dealers as a result of the granting of dissimilar bonuses for comparable transactions.

44. NBIM's argument that the discount system is permissible because it allows better planning of the supplier's activities is equally unacceptable. The importance of such planning, even for a firm in a dominant position, cannot override natural market uncertainty.

But the outcome of the system applied by NBIM is that to a great extent tyre dealers are deterred from taking advantage of offers made by competitors during the course of the year. In this respect, the bonuses must be regarded as a variant of loyalty rebates. Though they are not linked to an exclusive purchasing requirement involving all or a very substantial part of the purchaser's requirements. NBIM is able through the discount system to ensure that it obtains a maximum percentage (varying from customer to customer and carefully checked by NBIM) of the purchases made by dealers.

45. NBIM also argues that, in establishing bonuses, it takes account of the extent of the efforts made by the dealer in marketing the relevant products. It claims that it is not guilty of discrimination within the meaning of Article 86(c) of the EEC Treaty, since account is taken only of the individual position of each dealer. As stated above, it is of course permissible, in the light of the competition rules laid down in the EEC Treaty, for an undertaking granting discounts, bonuses etc. to take account of the services which the retailer performs for the undertaking in selling its products. A particular example might be the customer services which the retailer may provide for final consumers and which the manufacturer himself would otherwise have to provide. So as to avoid arbitrariness and to allow checks to be carried out, the conditions which must be met to qualify for the bonus must be defined objectively and made known to the purchasers. The NBIM system must be checked against such criteria if it is to be established that it is not discriminatory. Since the key element in NBIM's discount system is not so much the services which the dealer objectively performs for the undertaking in selling Michelin tyres, but rather NBIM's subjective assessment of the dealer's efforts in marketing Michelin tyres, the above criteria cannot be applied. As a result of this approach, dealers who are objectively in similar circumstances are inevitably treated in dissimilar ways. In view of the essentially oral procedure followed in establishing the bonuses, their complicated nature, the fact that the trade is not informed of the methods used by NBIM and the resulting lack of any means of carrying out checks, it is illusory to

to suppose that discriminatory situations could be avoided.

46. The anti-competitive and discriminatory effects of the discount system are further reinforced by the absence of written notification and confirmation (usually given in writing) of the different targets and bonuses applicable for each dealer.

47. Until 1980, NBIM representatives gave purely oral notification of the 'targets' and associated rebates or 'bonuses' to each dealer personally at the beginning of each year. Written confirmation of this important information was provided by NBIM only in very exceptional circumstances and never as a matter of course. This practice accordingly meant that difficulties regularly arose and that the dealers were heavily dependent on NBIM's unilateral interpretation. The uncertainty resulting from the lack of written confirmation naturally operates to the sole benefit of NBIM given its market position and the relative economic weakness of the individual dealers.

The Commission does not of course have any objections of principle to the purely oral notification of terms of sale. However, if this method is applied by an undertaking in a dominant position and if the terms which it applies are particularly complex in nature and - as demonstrated herein - lend themselves easily to misunderstandings, this combination of factors amounts to abusive conduct. In view of the complexity of the discount system, the failure to provide written confirmation of bonuses and 'targets' made it especially difficult for dealers to make a precise comparison between the net purchase price offered by the major producer and the price offered by other producers. As an element in the commercial policy of an undertaking in a dominant position, this lack of written confirmation increases the undertaking's freedom of action with regard to its direct customers and reduces any inclination on the part of dealers to obtain their supplies from competing producers. The result is to increase the anti-competitive effects of the discount system.

*(c) Combined effect of (a) and (b)*

48. The aim of NBIM's policy is clearly to bind tyre dealers to NBIM as closely as possible. The basis for achieving this is the discount system. Dealers are also aware that the frequent contacts between the representatives and tyre users give NBIM the possibility of influencing the consumer's choice of dealer. This means that the dealers in general will be all the more inclined to take account of NBIM's wishes.

This discount system is of such a nature that it can only be practised by an enterprise in a dominant position. Dealers would never accept this system being imposed by other manufacturers. Michelin's competitors do not therefore use a similar system and are in no position to engage in such practices.

49. Tying purchases to a supplier occupying a dominant position, as is the intention of NBIM's commercial policy, constitutes an abuse within the meaning of Article 86. NBIM's conduct 'is such as to influence the structure of a market where, as a result of the very presence of the undertaking (in a dominant position), the degree of competition is weakened' and, 'through recourse to methods different from those which condition normal competition in products or services on the basis of the transactions of commercial operators, has the effect of hindering the maintenance of the degree of competition still existing in the market or the growth of that competition'.

The behaviour at issue distorts competition between tyre producers. Its aim is to restrict the inclination of dealers to obtain their supplies from competing manufacturers. Access to the Netherlands market for NBIM's competitors is therefore impeded to an extent which would not be possible under normal market conditions.

.....

*Sequel:* The undertaking brought an action for annulment (case 322/81 Michelin NL v. Commission). The Court in its judgment of 9 November 1983 (not yet published) endorsed the Commission's Decision on the definition of the relevant markets and found that during the period taken into consideration Michelin had held a dominant position on those markets. However, the Court held that the Commission's further charge of discrimination between trading partners was not sufficiently proved.

## V. CONCENTRATION

(1) Decision in re Continental Can

For facts and references see above, page 43.

22. The purchase of a majority shareholding in a competing undertaking by an undertaking or a group of undertakings which have a dominant position may, in certain circumstances, constitute an abuse of that position.

23. For an undertaking in a dominant position to reinforce that position by means of merger with another undertaking with the consequence that the competition which would have existed actually or potentially in spite of the existence of the initial dominant position is in practice eliminated for the products in question in a substantial part of the Common Market constitutes behaviour which is incompatible with Article 86 of the Treaty.

24. The acquisition by Continental Can of the competing undertaking Thomassen & Drijver-Verblifa, which itself holds a strong position on a market bordering the German market, constitutes an industrial operation which involves an irreversible alteration in the supply structure in a substantial part of the Common Market.

25. For the major part of the metal containers produced by them, Continental Can in Germany (Schmalbach-Lubeca-Werke) and Thomassen & Drijver-Verblifa had, in effect, the power to compete with each other. This power derives especially from the following data:

(a) The national area of activity of most of the factories of SLW and TDV covers a part of the neighbouring territory, Benelux and Germany respectively, since the economic profit thresholds for the transport of empty containers (by lorry or by train) and their delivery to the customers lies betwen 150 and 300 km for relatively bulky containers (tins containing 1 kg or more) and between 500 and 1,000 km for the smaller containers.

(b) TDV, the premier producer of metal containers in Benelux, which registers an annual turnover of about 60% of the turnover of SLW, is an undertaking which, because of its extended production programme which is comparable to that of SLW, would have been in a position to compete with the latter.

.ch undertaking is already indirectly present on the other's , through SLW's holding in J. Schuybroek of Antwerp and TDV's , in Tedeco Verpackung GmbH of Hamburg, it may be supposed that . two subsidiairy undertakings could have become sales depots or .ıcessionaries in their countries for the products of their respective shareholders.

(d) Finally, the patent licensing, know-how and technical assistance agreements concluded by Continental Can with SLW and TDV may not prohibit these latter exporting the licensed products (metal containers and caps) outside their respective territories.

26. The fact that the sales of SLW in Benelux and of TDV in Germany were relatively weak does not mean that SLW and TDV were not potential competing undertakings, given that situation derived particularly from the agreements and concerted practices which have been described above.

27. It should consequently be considered that SLW and TDV, before being merged into Europemballage, were potentially competing undertakings over a large zone of common action situated on one side or the other of the frontiers of Germany and Benelux. In view of the localisation of the factories of these respective undertakings and of the economic profitability threshold of the transport costs, it may be accepted that that common zone comprised approximately nearly the whole of the territory consisting of Holland, Belgium and Luxembourg, on the one hand, and the North and centre of the Federal Republic of Germany, on the other.

28. This territory represents a substantial part of the Common Market.

29. The acquisition by Continental Can of a major holding in TDV has the effect of suppressing the competition between TDV and SLW in that zone of common action for the types of container described in section 5, 6 and 7:

(a) Thomassen & Drijver-Verblifa, because of its competitive capacity the product which it supplies and the geographic location of its factories, would have been an important competitor to Continental Can on the German market. The German users, whose powers of choice are restricted by the dominant position of Continental Can, would still have had a larger choice of suppliers if TDV had supplied on the geographical market in Germany referred to.

(b) As regards the competition and position of users in Benelux, the appearance of SLW there would also have involved effects promoting competition and an improvement in the situation of the users, all the more since TDV was practically the sole supplier in the containers in question and since supplies by competitors there would have been of an even greater importance for the users than for the German users.

30. Such a favourable development to competition and to the users was made conclusively impossible by the merger between Continental Can and TDV.

(a) The new group has an even stronger position on the German and Benelux market than that previously held by SLW and TDV on their own markets.

(b) The economic and financial power of Continental Can already considerable before the merger, is increased by the turnover, the profits and the production potential of TDV (106.22 million units of account, 3.4 million units of account and 6.900 persons respectively in 1969).

(c) The user's possibilities of having recourse to substitute products exists only to a limited degree, as indicated above.

(d) Competition from foreign manufacturers is not capable of making itself felt significantly on the substantial part of the Common Market in question.

(e) The users have, to be sure, the possibility in certain circumstances to produce themselves the containers which are necessary to them when the SLW-TDV group exceeds certain limits in relation to them with regard to prices and conditions of sale, but that does not establish a competition on the market in container products available to all the users which do not have the power to manufacture them themselves. Apart from Marie Thumas/Eurocan, the self-producers do not manufacture more than they use and do not supply empty metal containers to the market.

31. In so far as before their merger the competition between SLW and TDV was already restricted by the agreements and concerted practices described under 4(b) above, these agreements, while being at the origin of an artificially modified supply structure, did not make that structure irreversible.

On the other hand, return to a competitive situation between Continental Can and TDV in certain regions of Germany and Benelux has been made impossible by the merger of the two groups, the merger crystallising the market structure definitively.

<u>(2) Continental Can Case</u>
See above, page 10.

<u>(3) Eighth Competition Report</u>

Scrutiny of mergers for compatibility with Article 86 EEC

In the absence of more suitable merger control arrangements for EEC industries, the Commission continues to exercise Community surveillance of mergers after they have taken place to ensure that they are not contrary to the prohibition on abuse of dominant positions in Article 86 of the EEC Treaty.

In legal terms the Court of Justice has so far ruled only on a case where a dominant position already held before a merger was strengthened by means of the merger. But the basic considerations set forth in Continental Can refer only in general terms to the need for preserving a borderline beyond which any weakening in competitive forces would jeopardise attainment of the objectives of the common market.

In the period covered by this report, several complaints were filed with the Commission by firms who felt that their interests were harmed by mergers involving other firms. But in none of the cases it considered did the Commission conclude that the circumstances were right for a cease and desist action.

(4) Communication in re Michelin $ Cie.S.A. and Michelin-NL/Actor (April 1979)

The first of these complaints brought into question a transaction involving vertical integration, namely the acquisition by Compagnie Générale des établissements Michelin of a majority holding in the undertaking called Actor NV (Netherlands), a holding company, inter alia, a Dutch company engaged in the retreading of tyres as well as a tyre distribution network in the Netherlands.

The Commission has stated that in the Dutch market for heavyweight replacement tyres of which Michelin is the principle supplier, the latter will only be able to conduct a small part of its total sales through the distribution network which it is acquiring. Accordingly, the concentration as such will not allow it to penetrate the distribution market to the point of putting at risk the continued activity of several other independent distributors who are able to sell tyres on a sufficiently large scale. It follows that there is no reason to fear competing producers who will find their access to the market rendered more difficult nor that users will therefore find their freedom of choice seriously compromised.

On the basis of these facts, there were no grounds under Article 86 of the EEC Treaty for action on the part of the Commission in respect of the concentration concerned.

(5) Communication in re AVEBE/KSH (April 1979)

In view of the degree of structural reorganisation in the Dutch potato starch industry and of the number of complaints filed by suppliers of a firm that had been taken over, the Commission had to consider whether Article 86 of the EEC Treaty applied to the takeover of the potato starch division of Koninklijke Scholten Honing NV (KSH) by the Cooperatieve Verkoop- en Productievereniging van Aardappelmeel en Derivaten 'AVEBE' GA.

As regards supply of the relevant products, the proposed takeover raised no problems since the relevant market is the general starch products market. On this general market the production of maize starch is roughly three times greater than the production of potato starch and is in the hands of major multinationals. The market shares held by AVEBE and KSH, although quite large as regards sales of potato starch and its derivatives, were consequently not large enough to ground a finding that AVEBE dominated the market and was strengthening its dominance to the point of bringing the merger within the prohibition of Article 86.

As regards demand for industrial potatoes, on the other hand, there was the possibility that AVEBE might enjoy a dominant position, strengthened by the merger, in relation to growers in the parts of northern Netherlands and north-western Germany where potatoes are traditionally grown in large quantities.

It was felt however that the strengthening of this dominant position was unlikely to have the effect of leaving on the market only undertakings - in this case growers and suppliers of industrial potatoes - that would depend for their business conduct on the dominant firm.

The common organisation of the market in cereals and rice provides not only for a production refund on potato starch but also for a minimum price to be paid by starch makers to growers from whom they buy industrial potatoes.

The difference in the power relations between the firms in business on the two sides of this market will thus have only a limited effect on price formation, which means that there is no risk that the dominant position will be abused by the charging of unfair prices.

(6) Communication in re PSA Peugeot-Citroën/Chrysler Corp. (April 1979)

The proposal by PSA Peugeot-Citroën to take over the Chrysler corporation's European automobile interests, including Chrysler UK, was likewise scrutinised for compatibility with Article 86 in the light of, among other things, a complaint filed by a British trade union. Since there are other major car makers on the highly competitice European market, the change in the structure of the market resulting from this takeover could not be regarded as abuse of a dominant position.

The Commission was also unable to accept the allegations made by the complainant as to the harmful effect of the takeover in trade in motor vehicles and components between the United Kingdom and France. The Commission took into consideration the principles of the agreement between PSA Peugeot-Citroën and the British Government and the statement of intention made by Peugeot-Citroën concerning (a) the long term future of Chrysler UK as a production unit and (b) the possibilities for component suppliers in the UK to compete with other suppliers for business with Chrysler UK and indeed with the whole of the PSA group.

.....

Draft Regulation Concentration

Concsult also the draft Regulation (EEC) of the Council, first submitted by the Commission to the Council in 1973 (OJ.No.C92, 31 October 1973, p. 1) amended by a Commission proposal submitted to the Council in 1982 (OJ.NO.C36, 12 February 1982,p.3) and again amended in 1984 (OJ C51, 23 February 1984,p.8).

This draft Regulation is not included in this book since its adoption is highly undertain.

Litterature.


- Bishop: Price discrimination under Article 86: political economy in the European Court, 1981 MLR 282-295.
- Baden-Fuller: Article 86 EEC: Economic analysis of the Existence of a dominant position, 1979 ELRev. (423-441).
- Bennett: Hoffman-La Roche: Abuse of dominance on the vitamins market confirmed, 1979 ALRev. 210-221.
- Korah: Concept of a dominant position within the meaning of Article 86, (1980) CMLRev. 295-414.
- Siragussa: The Application of Article 86 to the pricing policy of dominant companies: Discriminatory and unfair prices, (1979) CMLRev. 177-194.
- Temple Laing: Monopolization and the definition of abuse of a dominant position under Article 86 EEC Treaty, (1979) CMLRev. 245-364.
- Zanon: Price Discrimination and Hoffman-La Roche, 1981 JWTL 305-322.

## Chapter Five

## PROCEDURAL ASPECTS

### I. LEGISLATIVE POWERS AND ROLE OF THE NATIONAL AUTHORITIES

### A. Legislative powers

#### (1) Group Exemption Regulation Case

For facts and references see above page 210.

*The Court held:*

The first submission that Article 87 has been infringed.

The first argument used against Regulation No 19/65 is that it lays down provisions concerning the exemptions in Article 85(3) without having first defined the scope of the prohibition imposed by Article 85(1) and that in defining the exception before having explicitly stated the rule to which the exception is made, the said regulation has disregarded Article 87 and infringed the principle according to which everything is permitted which has not been forbidden, and replaced it by the converse principle under which everything is forbidden which has not been authorised.

By Article 87 of the Treaty the Council 'shall ..... adopt any appropriate regulations or directives to give effect to the principles set out in Articles 85 and 86'.

It is for the Council to decide whether a particular regulation is appropriate and it may come to such a decision on a given point without having to deal exhaustively with the whole of Articles 85 and 86; it may therefore apply the exemption set out in Article 85(3) by means of a regulation if it thinks fit. It does not follow from this that everything which has not been exempted is to be presumed to be forbidden.

Furthermore Article 85(3) of the Treaty provides that the exemption in question may be granted to categories of agreements. The need of undertakings to know their legal position with certainty could justify giving priority to the use of this power, which does not require the Council to adopt rules simultaneously for applying the other provisions of the said article. Thus, without disregarding Article 87, the Council was entitled to rely on Article 85(3) as its authority for adopting a regulation covering the exemption of categories of agreements. It was in a position to do this without bringing about any alteration in the principles set out in Article 85(1) and without foregoing its right to make any further regulation applying any other provision of the said Article

85 to agreements not provided for by the regulation at issue.

## B. Regulation 17 Article 9

(Competence of the authorities of the Member States)

See also Chapter I, p. 27 ff.

### (1) Second Brasserie de Haecht Case

For facts and references see above page 183.

*The Court held:*

.....

On the first question

14. The first question asks whether the procedure under Articles 2, 3 and 6 of Regulation No 17 must be considered to be initiated by the Commission from the moment it acknowledges receipt of a request for a negative clearance or a notification for the purpose of obtaining exemption as provided for by Article 85(3) of the Treaty.

The question obviously concerns the provisions of Article 9(3) of the Regulation, under the terms of which "as long as the Commission has not initiated any procedure under Articles 2, 3 or 6, the authorities of the Member States shall remain competent to apply Article 85(1) in accordance with Article 88 of the Treaty".

Without the necessity of re-examining the question whether by the words "authorities of Member States" Article 9 also refers to the national courts acting pursuant to Article 85(2) of the Treaty, it is sufficient in this case to establish that Article 9, when referring to the initiation of a procedure under Articles 2, 3 or 6, obviously concerns an authoritative act of the Commission, evidencing its intention of taking a decision under the said Articles.

A simple acknowledgement of receipt, far from being evidence of intention, merely constitutes an administrative action and cannot be considered as such an authoritative act.

Consequently the simple acknowledgement of receipt of a request for a negative clearance or of a notification for the purposes of obtaining exemption under Article 85(3) of the Treaty cannot be considered as initiating a procedure under Articles 2, 3 or 6 of Regulation No 17.

.....

### (2) S.A.B.A.M. Case (first judgment)

See above page 35.

### (3) First IBM Case

IBM v. Commission, Judgment of 11 November 1981, Case 60/81; (1981) ECR; (1981) 3 CMLR 633; CCH para. 8708; Competition Law CM/M/III/98.

1. For a number of years the Commission, which had received complaints from some of the applicant's competitors, has been conducting an investigation of the marketing practices of the applicant and its subsidiaries in order to determine whether or not those practices amount to an abuse of a dominant position on the market within the meaning of Article 86 of the EEC Treaty.

The applicant was informed by letter of 19 December 1980 signed by the Director General for Competition that the Commission had initiated in its regard a procedure pursuant to Article 3 of Regulation No 17 of the Council of 6 February 1962, the first regulation implementing Articles 85 and 86 of the Treaty (Official Journal, English Special Edition 1959-1962, p. 87) and that it intended to make a decision regarding infringements of Article 86 of the EEC Treaty. A statement of objections as provided for in Article 19 of Regulation No 17 was sent with the letter. At the same time the applicant was invited to submit its reply in writing and was informed that it would subsequently be given an opportunity to state its views orally at a hearing.

.....

2. By letter of 28 January 1981 the applicant requested the Commission to supply it with details concerning the acts of the Commission authorising the initiation of the procedure and communication of the statement of objections, and to send copies of the relevant documents recording those acts.

In a letter of 3 February 1981 signed by the Director of Directorate IV B the Commission refused to supply the said details, stating that the decisions were internal ones which would not be notified outside the Commission.

The applicant informed the Commission by letter of 20 February 1981 that in its opinion the administrative procedure was defective in a number of respects. It therefore asked the Commission to withdraw the statement of objections and terminate the procedure or, alternatively, to answer a number of questions, both general and specific, set out in the letter in order to clarify the Commission's position and to persuade the Commission not to make use of the right which it had reserved itself to put forward further objections at a later stage.

The response to that letter, communicated in a letter of 13 April 1981 after the present application was lodged, was a refusal by the Commission to accede to the applicant's requests, but giving IBM certain information; in addition, it extended on several occasions the period allowed for submitting a written reply to the statement of objections, finally until 31 August 1981.

.....

*The Court held:*

18. Other effects relied on by IBM do not adversely affect the interests of the undertaking concerned. One such is the fact that initiation of a procedure under Article 9(3) Regulation No 17 puts an end to the jurisdiction of the authorities in the Member States - a result which did not in fact occur in this instance as there were no national proceedings, and which essentially results in protecting the undertakings concerned from parallel proceddings brought by the authorities of the Member States.

.....

### C. Liason with National Authorities

Consult Regulation No 17 Articles 10, 13 and 14.

(1) Decision in the Re Deutsche Freiformschmeiden

See below page 299.

### D. Advisory Committee on Restrictive Practices and Monopolies

Consult Regulation No 17 Article 10.

(1) First Boehringer Case

Boehringer Mannheim v. Commission of the EEC,
Judgment of 15 July 1970, Case 45/69; (1970) ECR 769; CCH para. 8085; Competition Law CM/M/III/18.

For facts see above at the ACF-Chemiefarma Case, page 109.

*The Court held:*

.....

IV. The complaints concerning the procedure before the Advisory Committee.

The applicant complains that the Commission did not indicate to the Advisory Committee the amount of the fine envisaged and it has persisted, in its statement in reply, in putting forward this submission despite the defendent's allegation to the contrary.

The Members of the Advisory Committee were informed, by letter of 30 May 1969 from the Commission accompanying the preliminary draft decision in question, of the approximate proportion of the fines intended for the various undertakings. The Director who signed that letter added that at the meeting on 23 June 1969 he would specify "orally the amount of the fines now envisaged". It appears from extracts of the minutes of that meeting that the members of the Committee received these details and were able to give their opinion thereon.

(2) Distillers Case

Distillers Company Ltd v. Commission, Judgment of 10 July 1980, Case 30/78; (1980) ECR 2229 ; (1980) 3 CMLR 121; CCH. para. 8613;

*Facts:*

*1. The Distillers Company Ltd (DCL) and its products*

DCL was established in 1877 through the amalgamation of six Scotch whisky distillers, and now has 38 subsidiaries producing spirits in the United Kingdom: 32 of them produce Scotch whisky, four produce gin, one produces vodka and one Pimm's.

.....

DCL is the world's largest distiller and seller of Scotch whisky.
.....

DCL markets over 50 brands of Scotch whisky, the most familiar being Johnnie Walker, Haig, Black and White, VAT 69, White Horse and Dewar's.

As regards gin, DCL's share of United Kingdom production was approximately 55% during the years 1973, 1974 and 1975. During this same period DCL's sales amounted to approcimately 70% of the total gin sales in the United Kingdom. DCL exports large quantities of gin. Among DCL gin brands are High & Dry, Gordon's Special Dry London Gin and Booth's Finest Dry Gin.

The DCL group accounts for about one quarter of the vodka sales in the United Kingdom. Its "cossack Vodka" brand has the second highest sales in the market.

As for Pimm's, DCL is the only one to sell this; it consists of an aromatised spirit to which is added (except in France) lemonade. To this mixture is added borage, cucumber or mint.

*2. Distribution of DCL spirits*

Each of the 38 British subsidiaries of the DCL group is responsible for the distribution and marketing of its spirits, which bears its own brand names.

In the United Kingdom only a few subsidiaries have their own distributors, whilst most of them sell their brands directly to the wholesale trade, which counts in this case approximately one thousand wholesalers. The wholesale trade itself can be divided into two sectors: the "tied trade" and the "free trade". The tied trade consists essentially of brewery groups which own licensed retail outlets through which the products are sold either by the bottle or by the measure. Most of those breweries also act as wholesalers in the free trade sectors. Purchases by those breweries represent about half the total sales of spirits of DCL's subsidiary companies in the United Kingdom. The free trade consists of a wide range of retailers, including individual licensed shops, chains of non-brewery retail outlets (such as some of the supermarket chains) and "multiples" (that is to say, wholesale businesses which also have their own retail outlets, but which are not controlled by the breweries). They all sell generally by the bottle. In addition, licensed hotel chains may sell by the measure on their premises.

In other Common Market countries most of the DCL subsidiary companies each have their own sole distributors. The spirits supplied to the sole distributors are usually resold to wholesalers who sell them in turn to retailers. There are about 200 sole distributors of DCL spirits in the Common Market. Many other alcoholic drinks, notably brandy, sherry and wine, are also sold by these sole distributors.

For the purpose of duty free consumption only, the DCL subsidiaries sell spirits directly to ships' chandlers. They number about 1,000 in the Common Market.

*3. DCL's conditions of sale and price terms*

On 30 June 1973 DCL notified the Commission of the "Seller's conditions of sale" applied by each of its subsidiaries for sales of spirits to United Kingdom trade customers only. DCL was seeking an exemption under Article 85(3). The seller's conditions of sale consisted mainly of:

- provisions relating to terms of delivery and payment;

- a clause (5b) which imposed an export prohibition on those trade customers and their subsequent purchasers;

- a clause (6) prohibiting resale in bond.

On 8 July 1975, in reply to a request of the Commission dated 2 June 1975, DCL submitted a new text of the previously notified "Seller's conditions of sale", revising clause 5b (limiting the export prohibition now to territories outside the Community) and removing clause 6.

On 11 July 1975 DCL submitted to the Commission the text of the circular letter of 24 June 1975 addressed to customers of its subsidiaries, established in the United Kingdom and of two appendices, entitled "Home trade conditions of sale and price terms".

The first section of the latter entitled "Conditions of sale", states that: "...Following the referendum, we are now amending the Conditions of Sale to permit export by home trade customers to other Common Market countries...export outside the Common Market is still prohibited". Appendix I to the DCL circular letter contains the new version of the Seller's Conditions of Sale.

The second section of the letter, headed "Price terms", states:

(a) "...the various allowances, rebates and discounts are designed to meet the particular requirements of the home trade and customers are only entitled to them when the goods are in fact consumed within the UK".

(b) "Accordingly, if you wish to buy for export to other Common Market countries you must indicate this on your order and purchase must be made at the gross price".

(c) "...If...a customer obtains or claims any home trade allowances, rebates or discounts in respect of goods which he has bought and any of those goods turn up in any country outside the UK, the right is reserved for all companies in the DCL group to sell thereafter to such customer only at the gross price".

Appendix II to DCL's circular letter, entitled "Certain Contractual Provisions (relating to price) additional to Conditions of Sale" states that:

- The provisions of that Appendix are to form part of every contract made by a purchaser and a subsidiary company of the DCL group for the purchase of any brands of spirits and are additional to seller's conditions of sale (the subject of Appendix I);

- all allowances, discounts and rebates whatsoever (hereinafter collectively referred to as "price allowances") are designed to meet the particular market circumstances of the United Kingdom;

- Any DCL subsidiary company is entitled to charge the gross price without reduction of such price by any price allowances:

  - When a DCL subsidiary has a reasonable belief that any quantity of goods bought by the purchaser from any DCL subsidiary has been or will be consumed outside the United Kingdom;

  - even when the exports are made by a subsequent purchaser;

  - regardless of the quantity ordered, until and to the extent that the purchaser produces evidence satisfactory to the selling DCL subsidiary company that the goods will be consumed in the United Kingdom.

On 23 February 1977, DCL addressed a letter to their United Kingdom trade customers informing them that the "gross price without any reduction of such price by price allowances" is now expressed as the gross EEC export price which is the price charged to sole distributors in other EEC countries before deduction of any allowances granted to them (the new provisions of Appendix II are hereinafter referred to as "price terms").
.....

The decision of the Commission states that "According to information supplied by DCL, parallel imports of DCL Scotch whisky from the United Kingdom to other EEC countries amounted approximately to 100 000 cases in 1973, to 400 000 cases in 1974 and to 550 000 cases in 1975... From the date of the circular letter, 24 June 1975, up to 12 July 1976, only one customer had indicated to DCL subsidiary companies that it wished to buy for export to other EEC countries and purchased 1 400 cases at the gross price. The aggregate quantity of Scotch whisky forming part of orders in respect of which DCL subsidiary companies obtained evidence that whisky purchased by United Kingdom trade customers was resold to other EEC countries and required further payment, amounted to over 6 000 cases". DCL has put the number of cases purchased at the gross export price between 1 January and 31 December 1977 at 340 000.

On 18 May 1976 the undertakings A. Bulloch & Co, A. Bulloch (Agencies) Ltd, John Grant Blenders Ltd, Inland Fisheries Ltd and Classic Wines Ltd presented a request to the Commission, pursuant to Article 3 of Regulation No 17, seeking the initiation of the procedure to terminate infringements of Articles 85 and 86 of the EEC Treaty resulting from the DCL price terms contained in the circular letter of 24 June 1975.

These undertakings are related companies all established in the Glasgow area. They purchase large quantities of DCL whisky for resale. Some of the whisky which the complainants had bought in bond at the home trade price and sold to another whisky dealer in the United Kingdom was later found by DCL representatives in supermarkets in France and Belgium. Subsequently DCL asked the complainants for further payment and refused to sell them any in-bond whisky except at the gross price. On 7 March 1977 another request was presented by Madison Benson and Carter Ltd of London also raising the difficulties of obtaining DCL Scotch whisky for export.
.....

*The Court held:*

Procedural irregularities alleged by the applicant

The procedural irregularities alleged by the applicant are in particular the following:

(1) The consultation with the Advisory COmmittee referred to in Article 10 of Regulation No 17 took place on 21 October 1977 whereas the minutes of the hearing before the Commission on 22 June 1977 were not drawn up even as an unrevised draft until 25 October 1977 so that the Committee was not in a position to appreciate the arguments put forward by the applicant at the hearing.

(2) Several supplements to the applicant's answer to the Commission's statement of objections, supplements which the applicant considers were important in judging its case, were not forwarded to the Advisory Committee;

(3) The Commission supplied the applicant with a copy of the intervener's complaint, a large part of which had been excised, and refused to supply the part excised (in so far as that part did not involve business secrets) maintaining that that part of the complaint was irrelevant; on the other hand the whole complaint was forwarded to the Advisory Committee as being one of the most important documents.

In view of what is said above it is unnecessary to consider the procedural irregularities alleged by the applicant. The position would be different only if in the absence of those irregularities the administrative proceedings could have led to a different result. Subject to what the applicant says with regard to the product Pimm's the action is in effect confined to challenging the legality of the Commission's refusal to grant exemption to the price terms under Article 85(3) from the prohibition in Article 85(1). The applicant does not deny that the price terms infringe Article 85(1). Since however it ommitted to notify the said terms to the Commission the applicant has deprived itself by its own act of any possibility of obtaining in the proceedings to which the present application relates a decision granting exemption under Article 85(3). Even in the absence of the procedural irregularities alleged by the applicant the Commission Decision based on the absence of notification could therefore not have been different.
.....

Advocate General Warner considered however in this case:

I turn to the first of the procedural irregularities alleged by DCL, viz. that a number of important documents were not adequately considered, or were not considered at all, by the Advisory Committee.

In the *'Quinine'* cases Mr. Advocate General Gand said, with the Advisory Committee specifically in mind, that 'if a procedural requirement to consult a body is laid down by a provision prior to taking a decision, the ommission or the improper completion of that formality may in certain cases constitute an infringement of an essential procedural requirement invalidating the decision' (see (1970) 2 ECR at p. 710). I would add that I, for my part, view the Advisory Committee procedure with some unease, because of the secrecy that surrounds it. The undertakings concerned are left in the dark as to what the Committee is told or not told by the Commission and as to the content of the Committee's report. They have no opportunity of addressing the

Committee. The question whether such a procedure is compatible with the fundamental principles of Community law, of which this Court is under a duty to ensure the observance, has not been raised or argued in this case. Assuming however that the provisions of Article 10 of Regulation No 17 prescribing that procedure are valid, the risks of injustice that it entails make it, in my opinion, imperative that the procedure should be carried out with scrupulous care.

I would not however hold it against the Commission that it failed to include Lady Hall's report among 'the most important documents'. It does not seem to me that that report added substantially to DCL's Written Comments and I think that the decision to exclude it fell well within the scope of the Commission's discretion under paragraph 5 of Article 10.

As to the Fourth and Fifth Supplements to DCL's Written Comments I feel more doubt. They were manifestly regarded by DCL as important, and I think they were. The Fourth Supplement, Your Lordships remember, contained the results of DCL's investigation of the costs of its sole distributors of Scotch whisky, whilst the Fifth contained DCL's considered answers to two points made by Commission officials at the oral hearing, firstly the point that a solution to DCL's problem might lie in its increasing its prices to United Kingdom wholesalers and reducing its prices to Continental sole distributors, and secondly the point that DCL ought perhaps to charge different prices to sole distributors in different countries in the light of their different costs. The Commission admits of course that the Advisory Committee did not have the 14 days notice of the existence of those documents required by Article 10 (5). Nor does the Commission say that it did not regard the documents as important. Its defence is that the Committee was told of their contents at its meeting and decided not to adjourn to study them further. 'This', says the Commission, 'was a decision which lay entirely within the Committee's discretion and it was not a matter with which the Commission had any right or duty to interfere: by informing the Committee of the existence of the documents, the Commission had fully discharged its obligations. The subsequent action of the Advisory Committee provides no ground for annulling the Commission's Decision.' (Defence para. 174). But to my mind, disregard of procedural requirements by the Committee is just as capable of vitiating the Commission's Decision as disregard of them by the Commission itself.

DCL suggested that the Court, if it should entertain any doubt on the point, should order the Commission to make available to it 'the minutes of the meeting of the Advisory Committee'. In the event the Court asked to be supplied with a copy of the report made under Article 10(6) of Regulation No 17. The Commission complied with the request but asked to be heard further on the question of the confidentiality of that report if the Court envisaged disclosing it to DCL. The Commission no doubt had in mind the procedure adopted in Case 110/75 *Mills* v. *EIB/ 1976/*2 ECR 1613 (see in particular at pp. 1634-1635). If I had thought the present point capable of being decisive of this case, I would have urged Your Lordships to hear the parties on that question. But, since I did not and do not, I leave the point there.

As to the Sixth Supplement, containing the results of DCL's investigation of the costs of its sole distributors of gin, the Commission's defence was, in effect if not in so many words, that it was not one of 'the most important documents'. That was not disputed by DCL.

So I turn to the question of the minutes of the oral hearing.

DCL's complaint here was that the minutes were not only missing from the list of the most important documents sent by the Commission to the Advisory Committee but did not exist even in draft on 21 October 1977 when the meeting of the Committee took place. Your Lordships will have it in mind that Article 9(4) of Commission Regulation No 99/63/EEC required such minutes to be drawn up and to be approved by the persons participating in the hearing. One may wonder why, nearly four months after the hearing, no step had been taken to comply with that requirement.

It was contended on behalf of DCL that the Advisory Committee cannot deliberate validly unless the minutes of the oral hearing are available to it. The Commission pointed out that there is no express requirement in any of the relevant Regulations that the minutes should be available to the Committee.

In the *Buchler* case the point was taken that both the Advisory Committee and the Commission had acted on the basis of a draft of the minutes which did not take into account amendments suggested by the applicant. The Court held that the validity of the decision there in question would only have been affected if that version of the minutes had been misleading in some material respect. This was not so, since the suggested amendments all reltaed to inessential matters. The draft was, therefore, 'able to provide the Advisory Committee and the Commission with complete information on the essential content of the statements made at the hearing' (see paragraphs 16 and 17 of the judgment). A similar objection in Case 48/69 *ICI* v. *Commission/1972/*ECR 619 met with a similar answer (see paragraphs 27 to 33 of the judgment). Those cases are authority for the proposition that there may be an infringement of an essential procedural requirement if the Advisory Committee is presented with draft minutes that are so incomplete or inaccurate as to be liable to mislead it. They do not touch a situation where there are no draft minutes at all.

It seems to me implicit, however, in Regulation No 99/63 read as a whole, and in the light of Article 10 of Regulation No 17, that the minutes must be available for the Advisory Committee. I have in mind in particular Article 1 of Regulation No 99/63 which requires the Commission to hold the hearing before consulting the Advisory Committee. It can hardly have been envisaged that Members of the Committee could then be compelled to ascertain what had been said at the hearing by means other than the minutes prescribed by Article 9(4) of the same Regulation. Nor do I see how the Commission could properly draw up the documents required by Article 10(5) of Regulation No 17, namely the summary of the case, the list of the most important documents and its preliminary draft decision without having a draft of those minutes, at least to hand.

I would therefore hold that the absence of the minutes was prima facie a breach of an essential procedural requirement. I say 'prima facie' because the Commission submitted that, even if that were so, DCL suffered no prejudice in that 'at the hearing DCL's witnesses and advisers merely repeated matters which were essentially contained in earlier documents'. I do not think that what they said amounted to mere repetition. On the other hand I am inclined that it was not so novel or different from what had been said in DCL's Written Comments and in the

Second and Third Supplements thereto that it could have altered the outcome of the case. The new material recorded in the minutes consisted mainly of a powerful submission on behalf of Bulloch. Here again, however, it is not in my opinion possible to form a concluded view without taking into account the contents of the Advisory Committee's report, which has been withheld from DCL. So again, if I had thought the point likely to be decisive of the case, I would have urged Your Lordships to hear argument on the question whether that report was privileged from disclosure in these proceedings.

.....

## II. NOTIFICATION AND APPLICATION FOR NEGATIVE CLEARANCE

### A. General
(How to notify and when)

(1) Decision on the Sirdar-Phildar Agreement

See above page 64.

(2) Second Brasserie de Haecht Case

See above page 183,185.

(3) De Bloos v. Bouyer Case

See above page 186.

(4) VBBB-Eldi Case

VBBB v. Eldi Records, Preliminary Ruling of 20 March 1980, case 106/79; (1980) 3 CMLR 719; CCH. para. 8646; Competition Law CM/M/III/83.

*Facts:*

2. The first plaintiff in the main action is a Netherlands association to promote the interests of the book trade (hereinafter referred to as "the Association"). The other plaintiffs in the main action are publishers and distributors of *inter alia* strip-cartoon books.

The Association drew up a set of rules entitled "Reglement voor het Handelsverkeer in de Nederlandse Uitgeverij en Boekhandel" (Rules for the trade in books in the Netherlands), (hereinafter referred to as "the Rules"). The Rules were sent to the Commission on 30 October 1962, attached to a notification form. The Rules, as they then stood, provided for an exclusive sale and purchase system with certain prices imposed vertically between recognised publishers, bookshops, importers or wholesalers. The recognised booksellers are bound to observe the provisions of the Rules and the agreements made by the Association. If persons seeking recognised status are not members of the Association, they must sign a declaration by which they bind themselves to observe the Association Rules. Publishers are required to fix a single retail price for like copies of each of their books, and the price of books published abroad is generally fixed by converting the retail price determined by the publisher at the prevailing exchange rate. Neither national nor foreign editions may be sold at a price lower than the retail price imposed. Discounts on the retail price may be given only to recognised bookshops and wholesalers and also, as regards publications up to a certain retail price limit, to specially listed businesses and institutions provided, *inter alia,* that they bind themselves to comply with the Association Rules. Discounts may also be obtained by lending library administrators and by "specialised firms", that is to say, for example, that travel agents may obtain discounts on books on guides, and photographers discounts on books on photography, provided that they maintain the retail price of those publications.

3. The Rules have been repeatedly amended. While retaining the main provisions the new versions which were sent to the Commission provide *inter alia* for different relationships between recognised and non-recognised booksellers, the right to reduce or to abolish the retail price in certain cases and to determine special lower prices parallel to the retail price; they also increase the number of cases in which discounts may be given.

4. The parties are in disagreement over the extent to which strip-cartoon books have been covered by the Rules as successively amended.

5. The version of the Rules sent to the Commission on 30 October 1962 was attached to Form B as annexed to Regulation No 27. Under the heading "Information regarding contents of agreement, decision or concerted practice", the form was completed thus: "Zie bijgaand (see attached): Reglement voor het Handelsverkeer in de Nederlandse Uitgeverij en Boekhandel. Artt. 29 b en 30 a". These provisions concerned foreign books. A copy of the Rules, as they stood at 30 October 1962, was attached to the form.

By letter of 18 March 1975 the Commission, in pursuance of Article 11 of Regulation No 17, sent a request for information to the Association "in order to put the Commission in a position to rule, with all the facts of the matter before it, upon the compatibility of the above-mentioned rules and agreements with the competition law of the European Economic Community". The letter is headed *inter alia* "Subject: ... Notifications (a) of the Rules of your Association, (b) ...".

6. The defendent in the main action (hereinafter referred to as "Eldi") is a company which is not a member of the Association and whose business consists *inter alia* of selling strip-cartoon books at reduced prices. The plaintiffs in the main action have sought a temporary injunction against Eldi before the President of the Arrondissementsrechtbank, Amsterdam, asking the court to forbid Eldi to sell or offer for sale to the public the books of recognised publishers at a price other than that fixed or to be fixed by the recognised publishers, and to award a penalty payment to the plaintiffs in the main action amounting to 50 000 guilders for each breach of the injunction which they seek.

One of the most far-reaching claims put forward by Eldi in its defence is that the Rules were contrary to Article 85(1) of the Treaty and that they were null and void because they had not been exempted under Article 85(3). It further contended that the Rules were not even provisionally valid since they had not been notified or had been insufficiently and incorrectly notified for the purposes of Article 5(1) of Regulation No 17.

The plaintiffs in the main action have contested these arguments.

7. By judgment of 3 May 1979 the Vice-President of the Arrondissements-

rechtbank, Amsterdam, stayed the proceedings and in accordance with Article 177 of the EEC Treaty asked the Court of Justice to give a preliminary ruling upon the following question:

"1. Is the Reglement voor het Handelsverkeer in Nederland in its entirety, consequently both in so far as it relates to foreign books and books in Dutch to be regarded as provisionally valid, in the sense that, until the date on which the European Commission takes a decision, the Court in a legal action must accept that the whole Reglement gives rise to the legal consequences which the law applicable to the agreement attributes to it, without those legal consequences being affected by a dispute relating to its compatability with Article 85(1) of the EEC Treaty in view of the fact that, as appears from Form B used for notification pursuant to Article 5(1) of Regulation No 17 of the Council, Rules 29(b) and 30(a) of the said Reglement were notified in good time and the Reglement was also submitted as one of the annexes to the form?

2. Is it relevant in this connexion that it was expressly stated on behalf of the Commission by letter of 18 March 1975 that the whole Reglement would be examined as to its compatability with the Competition rules of the EEC?

3. If Question (1) is answered in the negative, are the rules relating to foreign books to be regarded as provisionally valid in the sense described above or does the whole Reglement lose its provisional validity in that case?

4. If Question (1) is answered in the affirmative, is that question to be answered differently with regard to strip-cartoon books as it has appeared from the evidence submitted that strip-cartoon books up to a certain price limit, which fall within the scope of the Reglement as submitted to the European Commission as an annex to the aforesaid Form B, were excepted from the scope of the Reglement for a certain time and were again included in the definition in Rule 4(a) only from 1 August 1978?"

.....

*The Court held:*

By means of notification the Commission must be supplied with the information necessary to enable it to take the decisions provided for in Regulation No 17. If the agreement has been reduced to writing and if a copy of its entire text is attached to the form, the information given on that form is intended solely to facilitate verification. If that information is correct, and above all if it relates fairly to the provisions which at the time were considered the most important, the objectives of the notification seem to be attained. In that case the agreement must be regarded as properly notified in its entirety, unless the intention to notify only a part of the agreement emerges clearly from the information supplied.

It is therefore necessary to reply to the first question that an agreement may be regarded as properly notified in its entirety and may therefore benefit from the effects of an agreement which has been notified, where its entire text has been attached to the notification form, even though only some of the clauses of the agreement are quoted on the form, provided that the description given there constitutes a fair and accurate record of the provisions which at the time were considered most important.

By the second question the judge making the reference asks whether a letter from the Commission requesting further information, whilst stating that the agreement notified would be examined in its entirety, is relevant as regards the extent of the effects of the notification.

As the letter referred to merely constitutes a request for information under Article 11 of Regulation No 17, and as such a letter cannot in any event - whatever wording is used - alter the effects of the notification, it is necessary to reply to that question that a letter from the Commission requesting, under Article 11 of Regulation No 17 further information about an agreement which has been notified does not in any way alter the effects of the notification.

As the reply to the first question is in the affirmative, the third question, which is asked solely in the event of the reply to the first question being negative, has become irrelevant.

By the fourth question, the judge making the reference, assuming that a particular category of goods fell within the scope of an agreement at the time of its notification, asks whether the fact that the goods were subsequently excluded from the scope of that agreement for a certain period can erase the effects of the notification as regards the category in question.

The effects of the notification extend to the scope of the agreement at the time of its notification. To restrict those effects in the case envisaged by the question would be tantamount to penalising the parties to an agreement for having voluntarily limited its scope, which would be contrary to the spirit of competition law. It is therefore necessary to reply to the fourth question that the re-introduction of a category of goods which fell within the scope of an agreement at the time of its notification, but which was subsequently excluded voluntarily by the parties for a certain period, is covered by the effects of the original notification.

(5) Distillers Case

For facts and references see above, page 179.

.....

*Failure to notify the price terms*

19. It is well to consider in the first place the legal effect of failure to notify the price terms in accordance with the provisions of Regulation No 17 of the Council and the implementing regulation of the Commission.

20. Article 4(1) of Regulation No 17 provides:

'Agreements, decisions and concerted practices of the kind described in Article 85(1) of the Treaty ... and in respect of which the parties seek application of Article 85(3) must be notified to the Commission. Until they have been notified, no decision in application of Article 85(3) may be taken'.

21. Article 6(1) of the same regulations states in this respect that:

'Whenever the Commission takes a decision pursuant to Article 85(3) of the Treaty, it shall specify therein the date from which the decision shall take effect. Such date shall not be earlier than the date of notification'.

22. Article 24 of the same regulation authorises the Commission to adopt implementing provisions concerning *inter alia* the form, content and other details of notifications pursuant to Article 4. Under the powers conferred by that provision the Commission adopted Regulation (EEC) No 1133/68 of 26 July 1968 (Official Journal English Special Edition 1968 (II), p. 400) which provides that notifications under Article 4 of Regulation No 17 shall be submitted on form A/B as shown in the annex to Regulation (EEC) 1133/68 which requires the parties to answer a number of specific questions, the answers to which are necessary to put the Commission in a position to take a decision.

23. It is agreed that the applicant never notified the price terms in accordance with the aforesaid provisions. Even when the Commission asserted in the statement of objections that the applicant had never notified the price terms in accordance with the provisions of Regulation No 17 and Regulation No 1133/68 with the result that they could not be exempted under Article 85(3), the applicant did not proceed to give notification but confined itself to maintaining that refusal to grant exemption under Article 85(3) for that sole reason would be too formal an application of the provisions in question. It adds that the Commission had not insisted on formal notification, for it had used, and had asked the applicant to use, the same reference number for the price terms and the conditions of sale notified in 1973 with a view to exemption, and that that could have led the applicant to believe that the price terms would be considered together with the conditions of sale for the purpose of any exemption.

24. As the Commission rightly maintains, in the absence of notification in accordance with the requirements of the regulation the price terms may not have exemption under Article 85(3). The simple fact that for administrative reasons the same reference number may have been used for the correspondence in relation to the conditions of sale which were duly notified and the correspondence relating to the price terms which were not is irrelevant.

.....

## B. Standard Contracts

### (1) Second Brasserie de Haecht Case

For facts and references see above, page 183.

*The Court held:*

.....

On the second question

This question is concerned with whether notification in 1969 of a standard contract can be considered as notification of a similar contract entered into 1963.

It follows from Regulation No 27/62 of the Commission of 3 May 1962

(OJ 1962, p. 1118) and the forms annexed thereto that the Commission considered that, while it lightens the administrative load, notification of a standard contract is sufficient to allow efficient surveillance of contracts capable of contravening Article 85.

By the mere notification of a standard contract, therefore, the purposes of notification are achieved in respect of contracts in identical terms entered into by the same undertaking.

However, it is evident from these general considerarions that notification given in 1969, and therefore outside the time limits laid down by Articles 5(1) and 7(2) of Regulation No 17, is not such as to make notified standard contracts, even if they existed before the entry into force of that Regulation, old agreements.

It follows from the foregoing that due notification of one standard contract is to be considered as due notification of all contracts in the same terms, including prior ones, entered into by the same undertaking.

## C. Regulation 17 Article 4 (2)

### (1) Fonderies Case

SA Fonderies Roubaix-Wattrelos v. Société Nouvelle des Fonderies A. Roux and Société des Fonderies J.O.T.;
Preliminary Ruling of 3 February 1976; (1976) 1 CMLR 538; CCH para. 8341; (1976) ECR 119; Competition Law CM/M/III/53.

*Facts:* By an agreement concluded on 29 June 1963 the German company Gontermann-Peipers (Gopag) granted the French company Les Fonderies de Roubaix-Wattrelos (Roubaix) the exclusive right to sell Gopag iron castings over the northern half of France. In 1964 a verbal agreement extended this concession to the whole of the French territory. For its part, Roubaix agreed not to manufacture products similar to those which formed the subject-matter of the agreement or to work either directly or indirectly for any undertaking which was a competitor of Gopag. These agreements were recorded in a contract dated 16 March 1966, notified to the Commission on 8 September 1966.

By an agreement concluded on 6 October 1964 Roubaix in its turn granted the Fonderies A. Roux (Roux) the exclusive right to resell Gopag products in 24 Departments in the South of France. Inter alia this agreement specified that: "As the rights of the Fonderies de Roubaix-Wattrelos arise under an agreement concluded with (Gopag), the validity of the present agreement is bound to the existence of the former agreement". Roux also undertook not to manufacture products similar to those which formed the subject-matter of that agreement and not to work either directly or indirectly for any undertaking which was a competitor of Gopag.

A purchase by Roux in March 1972 of castings of Swiss origin formed the basis of the dispute between Roubaix and Roux as a result of which Roubaix brought an action against Roux before the Tribunal de Commerce, Paris, for the payment of damages for breach of contract.

In its defence Roux maintained that the Roubaix-Gopag agreement was void on the ground that it was incompatible with Article 85 and that, as a result, its own agreement with Roubaix was also void. The Tribunal de Commerce accepted this view.

On an appeal from Roubaix, the Cour d'Appel, Paris, reversed this decision by judgment of 5 July 1975 and declared that "in accordance with the case-law of this Court" the notification of the agreement to the Commission conferred upon it a provisional validity until the Commission had given a decision thereon.

As regards the agreement between Roubaix and Roux the Cour d'Appel observes that, as this is an agreement between undertakings within one Member State for the resale of products within that State, under Article 1(2) of Regulation No 67/67 of the Commission of 22 March 1967, it falls outside the scope of Article 1(1) which contains a general statement of the inapplicability of Article 85(1) to certain categories of agreements. As a result, the Cour d'Appel concluded that in order to determine whether, in the absence of notification, this agreement was valid under Article 85 of the Treaty, it was necessary to interpret Article 4(2) of Regulation No 17 of the Council of 6 February 1962, so as to decide whether or not the agreement related "either to imports or to exports between Member States" within the meaning of that provision.

As it therefore considered it necessary to have recourse to Article 177 of the Treaty the Cour d'Appel requested the Court of Justice to give a preliminary ruling: "on the interpretation of the provisions of Article 4(2) (1) of Regulation No 17 ... and to state whether or not a contract which is concluded between two undertakings from one Member State for the purpose of 'selling at least expense' a product which is imported from another Member State by one of the parties using the warehouse and distribution network of the other party must be considered to 'relate to' imports and for this reason be subject to the notification provided for in Article 4(1) of the above-mentioned regulation".

*The Court held:*

.....

Article 4(1) of Regulation No 17 provides that agreements of the kind described in Article 85(1) of the Treaty which come into existence after 12 March 1962 - the date of entry into force of Regulation No 17 - must have been notified to the Commission in order to benefit from the provisions of Article 85(3); however, under the terms of subparagraph (2)(1) of the same article, this notification is not necessary as regards agreements where the only parties thereto are undertakings from one Member State and these agreements do not relate to imports or to exports between Member States.

This second condition must be interpreted with reference to the structure of Article 4 and its aim of simplifying administrative procedure, which it pursues by not requiring undertakings to notify agreements which, whilst they may be covered by Article 85(1), appear in general, by reason of their peculiar characteristics, to be less harmful from the point of view of the objectives of this provision and which are therefore very likely to be entitled to the benefit of Article 85(3).

In the majority of cases, agreements between undertakings from one Member State will be so entitled if they grant exclusive sales concessions in relation to the marketing of goods, where the marketing envisaged by the agreement takes place solely within the territory of the Member State to whose law the undertakings are subject, even if the goods in question have at a former stage been imported from another Member State.

Therefore, the fact that the products involved in such agreements have previously been imported from another Member State does not by itself mean that these agreements must be regarded as relating to imports within the meaning of Article 4(2) of Regulation No 17.

In order that an adequate reply may be given to the national court it is necessary to determine who is responsible for establishing whether or not the agreement exempted from notification are covered by the provisions of Article 85(1) and, if so, whether they benefit from the exemption contained in Article 85(3).

It is for the national court before which an action relating to the validity of such agreements is brought to assess, subject to the possible application of Article 177, whether such agreements may significantly affect trade between Member States.

Assuming this to be the case, these courts also have jurisdiction to find that in spite of the absence of notification, contracts of the type referred to by the question benefit from the exemption relating to categories of agreements provided for in Regulation No 67/67 of the Commission in pursuance of Article 85(3).

In fact, under Article 1(1) of that regulation and subject to the terms of Article 3 thereof, agreements to which only two undertakings from different Member States are party and whereby:

"(a) one party agrees with the other to supply only to that other certain goods for resale within a defined area of the Common Market; or

(b) one party agrees with the other to purchase only from that other certain goods for resale; or

(c) the two undertakings have entered into obligations, as in (a) and (b) above, with each other in respect of exclusive supply and purchase for resale"

benefit by virtue of a general provision from the exemption set out in Article 85(3) and are therefore by reason of this fact alone also exempt from the duty of notification.

There is no reason based on the objectives of Regulation No 67/67 for failing to allow agreements of an identical nature concluded between two undertakings belonging to the same Member State to benefit from this general exemption.

On the contrary, the reasons militating in favour of an exemption by categories in the case of agreements between two undertakings from different Member States are also valid in the case of similar agreements concluded between two undertakings in a single Member State.

It must not be forgotten that Article 1(2) of Regulation No 67/67 provides that: "Paragraph (1) shall not apply to agreements to which undertakings from one Member State only are party and which concern the resale of goods within that Member State".

However, the effect of this provision cannot be to exclude agreements concluded between two undertakings from one Member State.

In fact, the fourth recital in the preamble to Regulation No 67/67 shows that the Commission considers that: "Since it is only in exceptional cases that exclusive dealings agreements concluded within a Member State affect trade between Member States, there is no need to include them in this regulation".

The effect of paragraph (2) is thus to exclude from the scope of Article 85(1) and, therefore, from Regulation No 67/67, exclusive dealing agreements which are purely domestic in nature and are not capable of significantly affecting trade between Member States.

On the other hand, its purpose is not to exclude from the benefit of the exemption by categories those agreements which, although concluded between two undertakings from one Member State, may nevertheless by way of exception significantly affect trade between Member States but which, in addition, satisfy all the conditions laid down in Article 1 of Regulation No 67/67.

*The Court decided:*

.....

1. To the extent to which it exempts from notification agreements which do not relate either to imports or to exports, Article 4(2)(1) of Regulation No 17 of the Council must be interpreted as extending to agreements granting exclusive sales concessions in relation to the marketing of goods, where the marketing envisaged by the agreement takes place solely within the territory of the Member State to whose law the undertakings are subject, even if the goods in question have at a former stage been imported from another Member State.

2. Article 1(2) of Regulation No 67/67 of the Commission, whose effect is to exclude from the scope of Article 85(1) and, therefore, from Regulation No 67/67, exclusive dealing agreements which are purely domestic in nature and are not capable of significantly affecting trade between Member States, is not intended to exclude from the benefit of exemption by categories those agreements which, although concluded between two undertakings from one Member State, may nevertheless by way of exception significantly affect trade between Member States but which, in addition satisfy all the conditions laid down in Article 1 of Regulation No 67/67.

## III. COMPLAINTS

(See Regulation No 17 Article 3)

### (1) GEMA Case

GEMA v. Commission, Case 125/78, Judgment of 18 October 1979; (1979) ECR 3173; (1980) 2 CMLR 177; CCH para. 8568; Competition Law CM/M/III/80.

*Facts:*

By letter of 23 July 1971 the applicant, a German performing right association, submitted a complaint to the Commission in pursuance of

Article 3(2)(b) of Regulation No 17 against:

1. Compagnie Luxembourgeoise de Télédiffusion SA (hereinafter referred to as Radio Luxembourg), whose registered office is in Luxembourg;

2. Radio Music International S.à.r.l. (hereinafter referred to as 'RMI'), whose registered office is in Luxembourg;

3. Radio Télé-Music GmbH (hereinafter referred to as 'RTM'), whose registered office is at Berlin-Wilmersdorf,

for infringements of Articles 85 and 86 of the EEC Treaty. That complaint, which was registered by Directorate General IV of the Commission under No IV/26.932, concerning principally Radio Luxembourg's practices of:

Using its subsidiary, RMI, in order to conclude with music publishers established in Germany and carrying on their business there joint publishing contracts by which the publishers grant to RMI one half of the royalties payable in respect of their performing rights over the musical work published jointly in return for broadcasts in German at favourable listening times,

and

Through the medium of the Secretary General of Radio Luxembourg in association with Edition Intro Gebrüder Meisel KG, managing a music-publishing company, Radio Télé-Music GmbH, in which each of the two partners holds one half of the capital, and whose purpose is to conclude, with other publishers, composers and authors, publishing contracts relating to musical works frequently broadcast by Radio Luxembourg in its German-language programmes at favourable listening times.

The applicant maintained that the effect of the practice followed by Radio Luxembourg and its subsidiaries of jointly publishing pieces of light music which are broadcast frequently by Radio Luxembourg is to obtain for Radio Luxembourg as a member of the applicant association, increased royalties in respect of performing rights. Since the applicant - which is the only performing right association in Germany - has to apportion all the royalties it receives on the basis of a fixed scale of distribution, the result of the said practice is to put the other publishers of light music in an unfavourable position.

By letter of 23 January 1974 the Commission sent to the aforementioned three companies in accordance with Article 19(1) of Regulation No 17 a statement of the objections raised against them which concluded that there was an infringement of Article 86 of the Treaty. A copy of that letter was sent to the applicant. Radio Luxembourg and RMI replied to the statement of objections in a memorandum dated 9 April 1974. On 23 April 1974 the Commission conducted hearings of the parties.

By letter of 31 January 1978 the applicant called upon the Commission 'to adopt a formal decision in the inquiry into Proceedings IV/26/932 - Radio Luxembourg ... within two months of the receipt of this letter' failing which the applicant would institute against the Commission the proceedings for failure to act for provision is made in the second and third paragraphs of Article 175 of the Treaty.

In a letter dated 22 March 1978 the Commission informed the applicant in particular that:

'The Commission considers that the most recent information in its possession does not entitle it to grant your application in pursuance of Article 3(2) of Regulation No 17 for a decision recording an abuse of a dominant position by Radio Luxembourg and the other aforementioned undertakings. In the light of recent developments the Commission considers it doubtful whether it is possible to demonstrate convincingly to the Commission and the Court of Justice of the European Communities that Radio Luxembourg:

Occupies a dominant position in a substantial part of the Common Market; and

Abuses such a position'.

After setting out in detail the reasons on which its opinion was based the Commission concluded as follows:

'For those reasons the Commission considers that a decision under Article 86 would not be justified in the present circumstances. In accordance with Article 6 of Regulation No 99/63/EEC the Commission allows you the opportunity of submitting in writing any comments which you may have on the foregoing within two months of receipt of this notification'.

In that letter the Commission also expressed its opinion that performing right associations are able in other ways to take precautions against the practice of certain broadcasting companies of giving preference in broadcasting to their own pieces of light music. The Commission suggested that the applicant should have discussions on that subject with two of its officials. Those discussions took place in Brussels on 14 April 1978. The applicant was represented by Professor Mestmäcker and Mr Arendt. According to the applicant the discussion covered all the points raised by the Commission in its letter of 22 March 1978.

By a telex message of 28 April 1978 the applicant informed the Commission that it considered its proposals, which involved in particular amending the articles of association of GEMA in order to frustrate Radio Luxembourg's practice of concluding joint publishing contracts, to be impracticable.

On 30 May 1978 the applicant lodged this application for failure to act against the Commission, relating to its failure to comply with the application made by the applicant on 23 July 1971 in pursuance of Article 3(2) of Regulation No 17.
.....

*The Court held:*

A. The application for failure to act.

15. Article 3 of Regulation No 17 provides in particular as follows:

(1) Where the Commission, upon application or upon its own initiative, finds that there is infringement of Article 85 or Article 86 of the Treaty, it may by decision require the undertakings or associations of undertakings concerned to bring such infringement to an end.

(2) Those entitled to make application are:

(a) Member States;

(b) natural or legal persons who claim a legitimate interest'.

16. Article 6 of Regulation No 99/63 provides that:

'Where the Commission, having received an application pursuant to Article 3(2) of Regulation No 17, considers that on the basis of the information in its possession there are insufficient grounds for granting the application, it shall inform the applicants of its reasons and fix a time-limit for them to submit any further comments in writing'.

17. As is shown by the phrase '...shall inform the applicants of its reasons', it follows that the communication referred to in Article 6 of Regulation No 99/63 only seeks to ensure that an applicant within the meaning of Article 3(2)(b) of Regulation No 17 be informed of the reasons which have led the Commission to conclude that on the basis of the information obtained in the course of the inquiry there are insufficient grounds for granting the application. Such a communication implies the discontinuance of the proceedings without, however, preventing the Commission from re-opening the file if it considers it advisable, in particular where, within the period allowed by the Commission for that purpose in accordance with the provisions of Article 6, the applicant puts forward fresh elements of law or of fact. The applicant's argument that an applicant under Article 3(2) of Regulation No 17 is entitled to obtain from the Commission a decision within the meaning of Article 189 of the Treaty on the existence of the alleged infringement cannot, therefore, be accepted.

18. Moreover, even assuming that such a communication is in the nature of a decision within the meaning of Article 189 of the Treaty and that it is therefore capable of being contested by way of Article 173 of the Treaty, that in no way implies that the applicant within the meaning of Article 3(2) of Regulation No 17 is entitled to require from the Commission a final decision as regards the existence or non-existence of the alleged infringement. In fact the Commission cannot be obliged to continue the proceedings whatever the circumstances up to the stage of a final decision. The interpretation put forward by the applicant would remove all meaning from Article 3 of Regulation No 17 which in certain circumstances allows the Commission the opportunity of not adopting a decision to compel the undertakings concerned to put an end to the infringement established. It therefore follows from the nature of the procedure to establish an infringement laid down by Article 3 of the regulation that it cannot be accepted that a natural or legal person who, in pursuance of Article 3(2)(b) of the regulation, has requested the Commission to establish the said infringement, is entitled to demand a final decision on the proceedings instituted by the Commission following his complaint.

19. As regards the letter of 22 March 1978 it must be noted that the Commission informed the applicant of its view that a decision by way of Article 86 of the Treaty would not be justified and set out the facts and reasons on which that opinion was based. In addition, in accordance with Article 6 of the aforementioned Regulation No 99/63 it fixed a time-limit of two months for the submission by the applicant of any further comments in writing.

20. It follows that the Commission acted in accordance with the aforementioned provisions of Article 6 of Regulation No 99/63 by informing the applicant of the outcome of the proceedings and of the reasons for the discontinuance of the inquiry into its complaint. It must be added that it emerges from the terms of the letter, which is in two separate sections, that the Commission's suggestion for discussions with the applicant in order to examine other suitable methods of dealing with the consequences of the practices called in question by it falls outside the scope of the procedure to establish an infringement of the rules on competition instituted by the Commission following the submission of the original complaint. Contrary to the argument put forward by the applicant that suggestion cannot therefore confer on the letter an interlocutory character.

21. It results from the foregoing considerations that by replying by means of the letter of 22 March 1978, which was in accordance with the requirements of Article 6 of Regulation No 99/63, to the applicant's letter of 31 January 1978 calling upon it to act, the Commission addressed to the applicant an act which constitutes a definition of its position within the meaning of the second paragraph of Article 175 of the Treaty.

22. It follows that in this instance the Commission has not failed to act on the applicant's application to it and that the circumstances contemplated by Article 175 are not present.

23. The application on the grounds of failure to act must therefore be dismissed as inadmissable.

.....

(2) Demo-Studio Schmidt Case

Demo-Studio Schmidt v. Commission, Case 210/81, Judgment of 11 October 1983 (not yet published).

*Facts:* Natural or legal persons who claim a legitimate interest are entitled, under Article 3(2) of Regulation No 17, to apply to the Commission to have it require undertakings bring to an end infringements of Articles 85 and 86. The Commission examines such applications. Where it arrives at the conclusion that the complaint cannot be taken up, it informs the applicant by letter of its reasons and fixes a time limit for submission of any further comments in writing in accordance with Article 6 of Regulation No 99/63/EEC. The Commission considers that this communication is not a Decision within the meaning of Article 189 of the EEC Treaty and cannot be challenged before the Court of Justice.

On several occasions, after having received a letter of rejection pursuant to Article 6 of Regulation No 99/63/EEC, complainants have applied for a formal Decision on the object of their complaint. In the case of Demo-Studio Schmidt the Commission did adopt a Decision in the form of a letter expressing a final opinion, rejecting the complainant's request for supply of Revox products.

Although the Commission thus acknowledged that a formal decision can be adopted on the rejection of a complaint, it did not concede the applicant's entitlement thereto. In certain cases formal rejection of a complaint may be of general interest, notably when required to throw

Light on a new point of law. However, this does not imply that an individual is entitled to oblige the Commission to take action in cases involving restrictions of competition.

*The Court held:*

1. By application lodged at the Court Registry on 13 July 1981, Oswald Schmidt, trading as Demo-Studio Schmidt, Wiesbaden, Federal Republic of Germany, brought an action under the second paragraph of Article 173 of the EEC Treaty for a declaration of the nullity of the measure dated 11 May 1981 concerning a proceeding for the application of Articles 85(1) and 86 of the EEC Treaty, in which the Commission, expressing its "final decision", notified the applicant that it considered that there were no grounds for upholding his complaint seeking a declaration that Willi Studer Revox GmbH (hereinafter referred to as "Revox) had infringed the competition rules laid down in Articles 85 and 86 of the EEC Treaty by refusing to approve him as a specialist reseller or to supply him with its products.
...

11. Although the formal complaint lodged by the applicant on 7 June 1980 sought an order that Revox should supply him immediately, it must be interpreted - as indeed it was interpreted by the Commission during the phase prior to these proceedings and as is apparent from an analysis of the pleadings submitted to the Court - as a request for the Commission to establish an infringement of the provisions of Articles 85 and 86 of the Treaty, in accordance with Article 3(1) and (2) (b) of Regulation No. 17 and, by decision, to require Revox to bring the infringement to an end.

12. The Commission does not dispute the fact that its decision on the applicant's compleint does constitute a measure which the Court may be upon to declare void, since a "notice" or "communication" of that kind is definitive.

13. However, the Commission states that it leaves it to the Court to assess to what extent the applicant really has an interest in taking legal proceedings, regard being had in particular to the fact that, in the Commission's opinion, the powers vested in it by Article 85 do not include the power to compel a company to approve a dealer as a specialized distributor or to supply him with products.

14. As the Court held in its judgment of 25 October 1977 in Case 26/76 Metro v. Commission (1977) ECR 1875) "It is in the interests of the satisfactory administration of justice and of the proper application of Articles 85 and 86 that natural or legal persons who are entitled, pursuant to Article 3 (2) (b) of Regulation No. 17, to request the Commission to find an infringement of Articles 85 and 86 should be able, if their request is not complied with either wholly or in part, to institute proceedings in order to protect their legitimate interests".

15. The Court considers that the refusal to grant Mr Schmidt a dealership for Revox products, which was regarded by him as constituting an infringement of Articles 85 and 86 of the Treaty, was capable of affecting his legitimate interests. Moreover, as the Court held in its judgment of 6 March 1974 (joined cases 6 and 7/73 Istituto Chemioterapico Italiano SpA (1974) ECR 223) and in its order of 17 January 1980 (Case 792/79R Camera Care Limited v Commission (1980) ECR 119), where the Commission has found an attitude on the part of a producer which

constitutes an infringement of Articles 85 and 86, it has the power to order the undertaking in question to take any measures necessary to bring the infringement to an end.

## IV. ADMINISTRATIVE PROCEDURE

### A. Requests for information

(See Regulation No 17 Article 11)

(1) Decision in re Theal/Watts
Commission Decision of 21 December 1976, in a proceeding relating to Article 85 of the Treaty; Theal/Watts, O.J. No. L 30, 10 February 1977; (1977) 1 CMLR D44; CCH para. 9913; Competition Law CM/M/I/109.

*Facts:* In this case, the Commission fined a British firm and a Dutch firm for using trademark rights and export bans to protect an exclusive dealing agreement. The firms are Cecil E. Watts Ltd, Sunbury-on-Thames, which manufactures devices for cleaning and maintaining records, and its Dutch sole distributor Theal BV (now known as Tepa BV), Amsterdam.

In 1972 Dutch wholeslaers decided to take advantage of the fact that prices in the United Kingdom were lower than Dutch prices by effecting parallel imports of Watts products into the Netherlands although Watts had prohibited its British wholesalers from exporting.

Between 1972 and 1975 Theal brought court proceedings against four Dutch retailers, one of whom - Mr. J.D. Wilkes - made an application to the Commission in 1974.

On Theal's application the court issued orders enjoining each retailer from selling goods manufactured by Watts which were not obtained from Theal. The injunctions were based on the fact that the sales infringed Theal's rights in respect of the trademark borne by Watts goods.

The goods were genuine Watts products and the trademarks were lawfully affixed in the country of origin. Theal also threatened other retailers with proceedings on the same grounds.

Apart from the fine of 10,000 u.a. imposed on each of the firms for its infringement of clearly established rules of competition, the Commission also fined Theal 5,000 u.a. for providing incorrect information. When notifying the exclusive dealing agreement Theal had ommitted to mention its right to use Watts trademarks.

*The Commission decided:*

.....

Art. 1. 1. The oral exclusive distribution agreement made between Theal N.V. and Mr. Cecil E. Watts, now between Tepa B.V. and Cecil E. Watts Ltd, including the grant of the exclusive right to use trademarks in the Netherlands, constitutes an infringement of Article 85(1) of the Treaty establishing the European Economic Community.

2. The supplying of incorrect and misleading information in the notification dated 24 January 1963 made by Theal N.V., now Tepa B.V., infringed Article 15(1) of Regulation No 17 of 6 February 1962.

Art. 2. The application for a declaration under Article 85(3) that Article 85(1) is inapplicable is refused in respect of the agreement referred to in Article 1 hereof.

Art. 3. The undertakings to which this Decision is addressed shall bring the infringement referred to in Article 1(1) to an end without delay. In particular these undertakings shall refrain from all further action of any kind calculated to prevent the importation into or resale in the Netherlands of any Watts products.

Art. 4. 1. The following fines are imposed for infringement of Article 85(1):

(a) On Tepa B.V. a fine of 10,000 units of account, that is 36,200 Dutch guilders;

(b) On Cecil E. Watts Limited, a fine of 10,000 units of account, that is 4,166 pounds sterling.

2. In addition a fine of 5,000 units of account, that is 18,100 Dutch guilders, is imposed on Tepa B.V. for supplying incorrect and misleading information in a notification made under Article 5 of the aforesaid Regulation No 17.

Art. 5. This Decision shall be enforceable in accordance with the provisions of Article 192 of the Treaty establishing the European Economic Community.

Art. 6. This decision is addressed to Tepa B.V. of Amsterdam, Postbus 396, Netherlands, and Cecil E. Watts Limited of Darby House, Sunbury-on-Thames, Middlesex, England.

*Sequel:* In Appeal the Court upheld the Decision of the European Commission.

(2) Decision in re CSV I

Decision of the Commission of 25 June 1976 relating to a proceeding under Article 85 of the EEC Treaty, O.J. No L 192, 16 July 1976, p. 27; CCH para. 9854; Competition Law CM/M/I/104.

*Facts:* On 13 March 1967 a proceeding was brought by the Commission on its own initiative under Article 85 of the Treaty against the Dutch joint selling agency for simple nitrate fertilisers, Centraal Stikstof Verkoopkantoor (CSV), of the Hague, and against the manufacturers who hold shares therein. The first statement of objections was sent on 29 May 1968. On 27 June 1969 CSV and its members applied for negative clearance and amended CSV's rules and regulations and its terms of sale in such a way that CSV would thereafter only deal with sales in the Netherlands and outside the EEC. These changes were accepted by the Commission subject to a subsequent review of their results.

In a second statement of objections dates 23 December 1974 the Commission took the view that CSV should cease operating as a joint selling agency, even though it was then only concerned with sales in the Netherlands and outside the Community, because of the effects on the individual exports to other EEC countries of the CSV shareholder companies. On 27 March 1975 these companies, namely, Unie van Kunstmestfabrieken NV and Nederlandse Stikstof Maatschappij NV together with CSV itself, notified to the Commission all the agreements referred to in the statement of objections dated 23 December 1974.

On 29 August 1975 the lawyers acting for the notifying companies proposed to the Commission to make certain changes to the agreements and practices which in their opinion would meet the objection raised by the Commission.

In his reply dated 17 October 1975, the Director-General for Competition, after reviewing the proposed changes, states 'As has already been observed in the statement of objections, it is difficult for the restrictions imposed by the agreement to escape liability under Article 85(1) or to qualify for exemption under Article 85(3)'. Nevertheless his staff 'would carefully consider the possible effects resulting from the adoption of the measures proposed on 29 August 1975'.

On 22 December 1975 the Commission requested CSV to supply the information set out in Article 1 of this decision in preparation for a meeting between Commission officials and CSV representatives. CSV had until 19 January 1976 to supply this information.

On 14 January 1976 CSV and its lawyers orally informed the Commission that part of the information requested concerned CSV's exports outside the EEC under an agreement bringing all European manufacturers of nitrate fertilisers together in Nitrex AG, Zurich, Switzerland, which was responsible for the operation of the agreement. The notifying firms considered that if the information supplied to the Commission included documents relating to the activities of Nitrex, those members of their staff who were also on the Nitrex Board of Directors could be regarded by the Swiss authorities as committing an offence under the Swiss criminal code.

Notwithstanding the fact that the Commission again wrote on 16 January 1976 stating that if necessary it would issue a decision requiring the information to be supplied, on 19 February 1976 CSV refused to supply the information. The ground for the refusal was that CSV's legal advisers in Switzerland had stated that the production of the documents called for by the Commission could expose those producing them to the risk of imprisonment or fines under Article 273 of the Swiss Criminal Code and that it would therefore be preferable, if prosecutions were brought, to be able to plead compulsion (état de contrainte) under Article 34 of that Code. The information would therefore not be supplied except in response to a legally enforceable decision. CSV therefore stated that it was obliged not only to refuse to supply the documents called for but also to inform the Commission it would appeal against the decision requiring the production of such documents.

*The Commission ruled:*

As the Commission stated in its letter of 16 January 1976, the Commission requires this information, because without it the effects of CSV's conduct on competition within the Community cannot properly be assessed. The reason given by CSV for refusing to comply with the request is unacceptable. This information requested concerns the business activity of the Dutch firms belonging to CSV and of CSV itself. The information is available within the Community and the Commission is entitled to call for it. The Commission's staff may not disclose any information aquired if it is covered by the obligation of professional secrecy.

Part of the information has also been supplied to an international combine established in Switzerland. However, the fact that information has been supplied to a body governed by Swiss law does not mean that it can no longer be supplied to the Commission. Nor are the Commission and its staff released from their obligation of professional secrecy simply because the information has been supplied to the combine based in Switzerland.

Even if Swiss law could be interpreted to mean that the supply of information to the Commission amounted to unlawful disclosure, this would still not warrant delaying the performance of obligations imposed by the Commission in order to enforce the rules of competition.

Under Articles 15(1)(b) and 16(1)(c) of Regulation No 17 the Commission may, by decision, impose on undertakings or associations of undertakings:

(a) fines of from 100 to 5,000 units of account where, intentionally or negligently, they supply incorrect information in response to a request made pursuant to Article 11(3) or (5) or do not supply information within the time limit fixed by a decision taken under Article 11(5);

(b) periodic penalty payments of from 50 to 1,000 units of account per day, calculated from the date appointed by the decision, in order to compel them to supply complete and correct information which it has requested by decision taken pursuant to Article 11(5).

Having regard therefore to the facts stated above, measures should be taken to limit as far as possible the duration of CSV's refusal to comply with the request for information. Periodic penalty payments should therefore be imposed pursuant to Article 16 of Regulation No 17 for each day beyond a time limit which, having regard to the circumstances of the case, may reasonably be set at 80 days from the notification of this Decision. In view of the size of the firms concerned and of the grounds for their refusal to supply information, the amount of the penalty payments may reasonably be fixed at the equivalent in Dutch guilders of 1,000 units of account per day of delay. The calculation of the sum due, taking into account the date on which the liability to pay commences, shall be reserved for a later decision of endorsement.

HAS ADOPTED THIS DECISION:

Art. 1. Centraal Stikstof Verkoopkantoor BV (CSV) shall forward to the Commission:

(a) in respect of 1974/75 and 1975/76:

- the monthly returns sent to it by Unie van Kunstmestfabrieken NV and Nederlandse Stikstof Maatschappij NV containing statements and forecasts of production and individual sales of simple nitrate fertilisers, the documents which CSV sent in reply and the correct and final versions of these statements and forecasts resulting from the discussions between CSV and those companies;

- the annual equalisation accounts;

- reports of the Planningscommissie;

- forecasts for future years, together with their covering notes;

(b) in respect of the two months immediately preceding its reply:

- all documents relating to production and sales of simple nitrate fertilisers exchanged between CSV on the one side and Unie van Kunstmestfabrieken NV and Nederlandse Stikstof Maatschappij NV on the other.

Art. 2. The information called for in Article 1 shall be supplied within 80 days from the day on which the addressee receives this Decision.

Art. 3. In conjunction with the obligation to supply the information specified in Article 1 there shall be imposed a periodic penalty payment of the equivalent in Dutch florins of 1,000 units of account per day of delay beginning on the 81st day following that of the notification of this Decision.

Art. 4. This Decision is addressed to Centraal Stikstof Verkoopkantoor BV, Thorbeckelaan 360, 2025 The Hague, Netherlands.

Application may be made to the Court of Justice of the European Communities, Luxembourg, for review of this Decision as provided in the Treaty establishing the European Economic Community, and in particular in Articles 173 and 185 thereof.

(3) Decision in re RAI/Unitel

Decision of the Commission of 26 May 1978, in a proceeding relating to Article 85 of the Treaty, O.J. No L 157, 15 June 1978; (1978) 3 CMLR 306; CCH para. 10054; Competition Law CM/M/I/130.

*Facts:* The Commission adopted a Decision requesting information relating to a proceeding under Article 85 of the EEC Treaty. The Decision was addressed to Unitel Film- und Fernseh-Produktiongesellschaft mbH & Co, Munich, whose objections had prevented the Mondovision broadcast of 'Don Carlos' to celebrate the 200th anniversary of La Scala, Milan, on 7 December 1977; its objections were based on the exclusive contracts entered into by Unitel and four of La Scala's principal singers, whereby the latter undertook not to appear in cinema or television performances of the opera if not approved by Unitel.

The information requested was necessary to determine whether the exclusive obligations entered into by artists constitute restrictions of competition prohibited under Article 85(1). At the end of 1977 the Commission had already asked Unitel to provide this information. The company had refused, claiming that artists were not undertakings for the purposes of Article 85(1) and that the exclusive commitments between Unitel and its singers were covered by Regulation No 67/67/EEC of 22 March 1967 on exclusive dealing agreements.

The Commission did not agree with Unitel's view, pointing out:

(i) firstly, that artists are undertakings within the meaning of Article 85(1) when they commercialise their artistic performance; that the question does arise as to whether or not an agreement entered into by an artist has any appreciable repurcussions on competition, although in many cases, particularly when little-known artists are involved, the answer is clearly no; that the Commission cannot pronounce on the matter until it has copies of the complete texts of the contracts in question;

(ii) secondly, that Regulation No 67/67/EEC does not apply to the provision of services, so no exemption may be claimed for the commercialisation of artistic performances.

The Commission further considered that the impact of Unitel's activities on trade depended among other things on the identity and influence of its shareholders.

Unitel responded to the Decision by providing the information, so that the Commission is now in a position to consider the substance of the case.

*The Commission ruled:*

.....

Art. 1. Unitel Film- und Fernseh-Produktionsgesellschaft mbH & Co, is hereby required to supply the following information within one month of notification of this Decision.

1. the complete texts of the agreements entered into between Unitel and the singers whose performances of 'Don Carlos' in La Scala, Milan, on 7 December 1977 was prevented from being televised by RAI on account of their appearance in the Salzburg production of the same opera;

2. details of the legal structure of Unitel with copies of the documents embodying the company's constitution and rules;

3, the names of all Unitel shareholders and exact details of their holdings.

Art. 2. The attached Annex forms an integral part of this Decision.

Art. 3. This Decision is addressed to Unitel Film- und Fernseh-Produktionsgesellschaft mbH & Co., Amiraplatz 1/IV, D 8000 Munich 2.

Proceedings against this Decision may be instituted in the Court of Justice of the European Communities in Luxembourg in accordance with the provisions of the EEC Treaty, and in particular Articles 173 and 185 thereof.

(Annex referring to Regulation 17, Articles 15 and 16 ommitted).

(4) Decision in re Telos

Commission Decision of 25 November 1981 in re request for information to Telos, O.J. No L 58, 2 March 1982, p. 19; (1982) 1 CMLR 267; CCH para. 10356; Competition Law CM/M/I/170.

*The Commission held:*

16. Under Article 15(1)(b) of Regulation No 17, the Commission may by decision impose on undertakings fines of between 100 and 5000 units of account where, intentionally or negligently, they supply incorrect information in response to a request made pursuant to Article 11.

17. Where incorrect information has been supplied, it is, contrary to Telos' submission, immaterial as regards application of Article 15(1)(b) whether this was in response to a 'simple' request for information under Article 11(1) or to a decision under Article 11(5) requiring information to be supplied.

18. Telos gave the Commission an incorrect answer to the second part of the question ('who has prohibited you') by its reply to the effect that there was no contractual agreement under which it was prohibited from exporting and that it made no distinction between French and foreign clients. In its answers Telos falsely claims that Victor Hasselblad and/or Hasselblad (GB) had not taken any action to prevent it from exporting equipment to the United Kingdom and that it had sold equipment to, and had decided not to do business with, Camera Care of its own free will.

19. The instructions issued by Victor Hasselblad in 1974 to the effect that its sole distributors' markets should be protected against imports continued to apply to Telos and is to be regarded as being tantamount to an export prohibition. Telos also complied with this prohibition by stipulating that any equipment sold by it to Camera Care was not to be sold on the territory allotted to Hasselblad (GB) (that is the United Kingdom). In its reply to the Commission, Telos should have replied that Victor Hasselblad had instructed it in June 1974 to protect sole distributors' allotted territories, by neither exporting itself, nor permitting exports by retailers supplied by itself, to these territories.

20 However, the statement is also incorrect in that it makes no mention of the other steps taken by Hasselblad (GB) and by Victor Hasselblad to hinder exports to the United Kingdom, which are also tantamount to export prohibitions.

21. Any statement is incorrect which gives a distorted picture of the true facts asked for, and which departs significantly from reality on major points. Where a statement is thus false or so incomplete that the reply taken in its entirety is likely to mislead the Commission about the true facts, it constitutes incorrect information within the meaning of Article 15(1)(b).

22. In reality, the telephone conversation of 5 July 1978, the letter from Hasselblad (GB) and above all the action taken by Victor Hasselblad in mid-November 1978 renewed the prohibition which had existed since 1974 of exports of Hasselblad products to the territories allotted to another sole distributor and made it clear to Telos that both firms regarded parallel exports in general to the United Kingdom as posing a serious problem and as being harmful to business. This was even true of exports by completely independent retailers.

23. Hasselblad (GB) acted on the mistaken assumption that the equipment in question had been exported by a French retailer who had been supplied by Telos. It was for this reason that Telos was asked 'to look into the matter'. This made it clear to Telos that the wish on the part of Hasselblad (GB) to stamp out exports to the United Kingdom by - independent - retailers was directed in the first place against sole distributors, particularly since Telos was aware of Victor Hasselblad's instruction that national markets be protected and had promised to keep a watch on this type of transaction.

24. When it intervened in 1978, Victor Hasselblad sought, therefore, Telos' cooperation in refraining in future from engaging in exports to the contractual territories of a sole distributor.

25. The purpose and effect of the action taken by Victor Hasselblad (GB) was, therefore, to prohibit exports to the United Kingdom. Telos also understood the purpose of this action correctly and, referring to the letter from Hasselblad (GB) and to its contractual relationship with Victor Hasselblad, discontinued its exports to Camera Care.

26. Telos, however, did not reveal to the Commission these prohibitions by Victor Hasselblad and Hasselblad (GB), giving the impression that it had not been subjected to any pressure as regards exports to the United Kingdom and that it had severed relations with Camera Care of its own free will. By stating immediately thereafter that it did not distinguish between French and foreign customers, Telos also tried to strengthen this impression. Moreover, this statement is also false, because Telos did indeed distinguish between clients in its own and clients in another sole distributor's territory.

27. The incorrect information supplied had significant repurcussions on the course of the proceedings since it gave the Commission the mistaken impression that no pressure had been exerted on Telos. It was only in June 1980, when investigations were carried out on the premises of Telos and Hasselblad (GB), that the Commission became aware of the true facts and was for the first time in a position to institute proceedings under Article 85(1) of the Treaty against Victor Hasselblad and its sole distributors on the ground that they had engaged in concerted practices.

28. Telos also supplied the incorrect information intentionally. Telos did clearly regard the measures taken by Hasselblad (GB) and Victor Hasselblad as constituting an export prohibition and an obligation to supervise exports of other dealers. Telos also realised that the Commission's request for information was concerned generally with export prohibitions and in particular the boycott on supplies to Camera Care.

29. In this case a serious infringement of the fundamental principles of the common market was concealed. Precisely by framing its answer in the manner it did, Telos sought to divert attention away from the existence of a serious infringement, viz. a concerted practice aimed at prohibiting exports. The incorrect reply delayed the proceedings considerably and, if no investigations had been carried out on the premises of the undertakings concerned, it is highly likely that the conduct of Victor Hasselblad and Hasselblad (GB) towards Telos would not have come to light. In view of the above considerations, a fine of 5000 ECU appears appropriate.

## B. Investigatory Powers of the Commission

(See Regulation 17 Article 14)

### (1) Decision in re Deutsche Freiformschmeiden

Commission Decision of 8 December 1977, concerning an investigation to be made at the Vereinigung deutscher Freiformschmeiden (V.d.F.), Dusseldorf, pursuant to Article 14(3) of Council Regulation No 17.

O.J. No L 10, 13 January 1978, p. 32; (1978) 1 CMLR D 63; CCH para. 10004; Competition Law CM/M/I/119.

*The Commission decided:*

Having regard to the Treaty establishing the EEC and in particular Article 85 thereof,

Having regard to Council Regulation No 17 of 6 February 1962, and in particular Article 14(3) thereof,

Having consulted the Federal Cartel Office, Berlin, being the competent authority for the purpose of Article 14(4) of Regulation No 17,

WHEREAS:

There are sufficient grounds for suspecting that agreements for the maintenance of local prices and for restricting interpenetration are being applied on the common market for heavy forgings weighing over four tons. Such agreements and restrictions are contrary to Article 85 of the Treaty, as is the contract sharing which is also suspected.

In order to ascertain the facts the Director-General for Competition gave orders on 14 January 1977 that investigation should be made at several undertakings and associations of undertakings pursuant to Article 14 of Regulation No 17.

The checks which were due to be carried out on 18 January 1977 at the V.d.F., in the presence of a representative of the competent German authorities, could not be carried out because the V.d.F. refused to submit to the investigation unless they were authorised by a Decision of the Commission of the European Communities.

A Decision must therefore be adopted requiring the V.d.F. to submit to the investigation and in particular to allow the requisite business records to be examined.

Articles 15(1)(c) and 16(1)(d) of Regulation No 17, the full texts of which are annexed to this Decision, empower the Commission by decision to take actions against undertakings by:

(a) imposing fines where undertakings intentionally or negligently produce the rquired books or other business records in incomplete form during investigations under Article 14, or refuse to submit to an investigation ordered by decision pursuant to Article 14(3);

(b) imposing periodic penalty payments calculated daily from the day appointed by the Decision, in order to compel them to submit to an investigation which it has ordered by decision pursuant to Article 14(3).

HAS ADOPTED THIS DECISION:

Art. 1. (1) The V.d.F. is hereby required to allow an investigation to be made in its business premises in Düsseldorf. In particular it is required to allow the Commission's officials authorised for the purpose of this investigation to enter its premises during normal office hours and to produce the requisite business records for examination by those officials.

2. In particular it shall produce all records of the V.d.F.:

(a) concerning its relations with other associations of undertakings in the Community;

(b) of meetings with member companies and meetings of working groups and sales management personnel;

(c) concerning the joint office in Zurich, including details of any payments made to that office.

Art. 2. The investigation shall be carried out in the business premises of the V.d.F. in Düsseldorf and shall begin on 13 December 1977.

Art. 3. This Decision is addressed to the V.d.F., Düsseldorf. It shall be notified by being handed over personally to a representative of the V.d.F. by the Commission's officials authorised for the purpose of the investigation immediately before the investigation is to begin.

Art. 4. Proceedings against this Decision may be instituted in the Court of Justice of the European Communities in Luxembourg in accordance with Article 173 of the EEC Treaty. Pursuant to Article 185 of the EEC Treaty, such proceedings shall not have suspensory effect.

(2) National Panasonic Case

National Panasonic (UK Ltd) v. Commission, Judgment of 26 June 1980, Case 136/79; (1980) ECR 2033; (1980) 3 CMLR 169; CCH para. 8682; Competition Law CM/M/III/84.

*Facts:*

National Panasonic (UK) Limited (hereinafter referred to as 'Panasonic') a company formed under English law with its registered office in Slough, Berkshire (United Kingdom), is a 100% subsidiary of the Matsushita Electric Trading Company Limited, a company formed under Japanese law which in turn belongs to the Japanese industrial Matsushita Group.

Panasonic's company object is the distribution in various countries (the United KIngdom, including the Channel Islands, Ireland and Iceland) of electrical and electronic goods produced by other undertakings of the Matsushita Group.

On 27 June 1979 at approximately 10 a.m. two officials of the Commission, duly authorised agents, arrived without prior notice at Panasonic's sales offices in Slough and notified the directors of the undertaking of a Commission decision of 22 June 1979 authorising an on-the-spot investigation of all the company's documents. The assistant to Panasonic's managing director asked those officials to await the arrival of the undertaking's solicitor who had to travel from Norwich and they replied that they had full authority to commence the investigation immediately. The inspection therefore began at 10.45 a.m. in the absence of Panasonic's solicitor who only arrived three hours later and the inspection lasted approximately seven hours. At about 5.30 p.m. the Commission's agents left Panasonic's offices with copies of several documents and notes which they had made.

By application of 23 August 1979, which was received at the Court Registry on 24 August 1979, Panasonic appealed against the decision authorising the investigation. After hearing the report of the Judge Rapporteur and the views of the Advocate General, the Court decided to open the oral procedure without any preparatory inquiry.

*The Court held:*

.....

*(a) The infringement of Article 14 of Regulation No 17*

8. The applicant maintains first of all that the contested decision is unlawful because it does not comply with the spirit and letter of the provisions of Article 14(3) of the Regulation No 17 of the Council. To this end it maintains that on a proper construction those provisions provide for a two-stage procedure which permits the Commission to adopt a decision requiring an undertaking to submit to an investigation only after attempting to carry out that investigation on the basis of a written authorisation to its own officials. This interprestation is confirmed, according to the applicant, by Article 11 of the same regulation which is similar in structure and provides for a two-stage procedure and by Article 13(1) which makes a distinction between an investigation carried out by the Commission informally and that ordered by decision.

9. These arguments do not appear to be well-founded. In order to enable the Commission to accomplish its task of ensuring that the rules of competition in the common market are complied with, the eigth recital of the preamble to Regulation No 17 provides that it 'must ... be empowered, throughout the common market, to require such information to be supplied and to undertake such investigations as are necessary to bring to light any agreement, decision or concerted practice prohibited by Article 85(1) or any abuse of a dominant position prohibited by Article 86'. For this purpose, that regulation provides for separate procedures, which shows that the exercise of powers given to the Commission with regard to information and investigations is not subject to the same conditions.

10. Article 11(2), (3) and (5), which concerns the Commission's power to request the information it considers necessary, provides as follows:

'2. When sending a request for information to an undertaking or association of undertakings, the Commission shall at the same time forward a copy of the request to the competent authority of the Member State in whose territory the seat of the undertaking or association of undertakings is situated.

3. In its request the Commission shall state the legal basis and the purpose of the request and also the penalties provided for in Article 15 (1)(b) for supplying incorrect information.

.....

5. Where an undertaking or association of undertakings does not supply the information requested within the time-limit fixed by the Commission, or supplies incomplete information, the Commission shall by decision require the information to be supplied. The decision shall specify what information is required, fix an appropriate time-limit within which it is to be supplied and indicate the penalties provided for in Article 15(1)(b) and Article 16(1)(c) and the right to have the decision reviewed

by the Court of Justice'.

It follows from those provisions that the article in question in fact stipulates, for the exercise of that power, a two-stage procedure, the second stage of which, involving the adoption by the Commission of a decision which specifies what information is required, may only be initiated of the first stage, in which a request for information is sent to the undertakings or associations of undertakings, has been carried out without success.

11. On the other hand, Article 14 of the same regulation on the 'investigating' powers of the Commission is different in structure. Article 14 (2) and (3), which defines the conditions for the exercise of those powers, provides as follows:

'2. The officials of the Commission authorised for the purpose of these investigations shall exercise their powers upon production of an authorisation in writing specifying the subject-matter and purpose of the investigation and the penalties provided for in Article 15(1)(c) in cases where production of the required books or other business records is incomplete. In good time before the investigation, the Commission shall inform the competent authority of the Member State in whose territory the same is to be made of the investigation and of the identity of the authorised officials.

3. Undertakings and associations of undertakings shall submit to investigations ordered by a decision of the Commission. A decision shall specify the subject-matter and purpose of the investigation, appoint the date on which it is to begin and indicate the penalties provided for in Article 15(1)(c) and Article 16(1)(d) and the right to have the decision reviewed by the Court of Justice.'

This provision does not of course prevent the Commission from carrying out an investigation solely pursuant to a written authorisation given to its officials without adopting a decision, but in other respects it contains nothing to indicate that it may only adopt a decision within the meaning of Article 14(3) if it has previously attempted to carry out an investigation by mere authorisation. Whereas Article 11(5) expressly makes the adoption of a Commission decision subject to the condition that the latter has previously asked for the necessary information by means of a request addressed to those concerned and specifies in Article 11(3) the essentials which such a request must contain, Article 14 makes the investigating procedure by means of a decision subject to no preliminary of this kind.

12. The applicant wrongly relies in support of its argument on the wording of Article 13(1) of the same regulation which provides that, at the request of the Commission, the national authorities must undertake the investigations which the Commission considers to be necessary under Article 14(1) or which it has ordered by decision pursuant to Article 14(3). By making a distinction between the two investigatory procedures, that provision clearly shows by the use of the word 'or' that those two procedures do not necessarily overlap but constitute two alternative checks, the choice of which depends upon the special features of each case.

13. The difference in the rules on this subject contained in Articles 11 and 14 is explained, moreover, by the diversity of the needs met by

those two provisions. Whereas the information which the Commission considers necessary to know may not as a general rule be collected without the cooperation of the undertakings and associations of undertakings possessing this information, investigations, on the other hand, are not necessarily subject to the same condition. In general they aim at checking, by measures such as those listed in the second subparagraph of Article 14(1) of Regulation No 17, the actual existence and scope of information which the Commission already had and do not therefore necessarily presuppose previous cooperation by undertakings or associations of undertakings in possession of the information necessary for the check.

14. The applicant maintains in another connection that if it were necessary to interpret Article 14 differently from Article 11, that is as meaning that it permits the Commission to adopt an investigating decision without previously carrying out an investigation such as that provided for in Article 14(2) the Commission might, by having recourse to the procedure laid down in the same article for requests for information, escape the conditions laid down in Article 11 and thus evade the guarantees given by the latter to the undertakings and associations of undertakings concerned.

15. Such arguments however do not take into account the distinction made by the regulation itself between the 'information' referred to in Article 11 and the 'investigation' referred to in Article 14. The fact that the officials authorised by the Commission, in carrying out an investigation, have the power to request during that investigation information on specific questions arising from the books and business records which they examine is not sufficient to conclude that an investigation is identical to a procedure intended only to cbtain information within the meaning of Article 11 of the regulation.

16. For all these reasons, it is necessary to dismiss the first submission as unfounded.

*(b) The infringement of fundamental rights*

17. The applicant then claims that by failing previously to communicate to it beforehand the decision ordering an investigation in question, the Commission has in this instance infringed fundamental rights of the applicant, in particular the right to receive advance notification of the intention to apply a decision regarding it, the right to be heard before a decision adversely affecting it is taken and the right to use the opportunity given to it under Article 185 of the Treaty to request a stay of execution of such a decision. The applicant relies in particular on Article 8 of the European Convention for the Protection of Human Rights and Fundamental Freedoms of 4 November 1950 whereby 'everyone has the right to respect for his private and family life, his home and his correspondence'. It considers that those guarantees must be provided *mutatis mutandis* also to legal persons.

18. As the Court stated in its Judgement of 14 May 1974 in Case 4/73, *J. Nold, Kohlen- und Baustoffgrosshandlung v. Commission of the European Communities* (1974) ECR 491 at 507, fundamental rights form an integral part of the general principles of law, the observance of which the Court of Justice ensures, in accordance with constitutional traditions common to the Member States and with international treaties on which the Member States have collaborated or of which they are signatories.

19. In this respect it is necessary to point out that Article 8(2) of the European Convention, in so far as it applies to legal persons, whilst stating the principle that public authorities should not interfere with the exercise of the rights referred to in Article 8(1), acknowledges that such interference is permissable to the extent to which 'it is in accordance with the law and is necessary in a democratic society in the interests of national security, public safety or the economic well-being of the country, for the prevention of disorder of crime, for the protection of health or morals, or for the protection of the rights and freedom of others'.

20. In this instance, as follows from the seventh and eighth recitals of the preamble to Regulation No 17, the aim of the powers given to the Commission by Article 14 of that regulation is to enable it to carry out its duty under the EEC Treaty of ensuring that the rules on competition are applied in the common market. The function of these rules is, as follows from the fourth recital of the preamble to the Treaty, Article 3(f) and Articles 85 and 86, to prevent competition from being distorted to the detriment of the public interest, individual undertakings and consumers. The exercise of the powers given to the Commission by Regulation No 17 contributes to the maintenance of the system of competition intended by the Treaty which undertakings are absolutely bound to comply with. In these circumstances, it does not therefore appear that Regulation No 17, by giving the Commission the powers to carry out investigations without previous notification, infringes the right invoked by the applicant.

21. Moreover, as regards more particularly the argument that the applicant was in this instance denied the right to be heard before a decision was taken regarding it, it is necessary to state that the exercise of such a right of defence is chiefly incoporated in legal or administrative procedures for the termination of an infringement or for a declaration that an agreement, decision or concerted practice is incompatible with Article 85, such as the procedures referred to by Regulation No 99/63/EEC of the Commission of 25 July 1963 (Official Journal, English Special Edition 1963 to 1964, p. 47). On the other hand, the investigation procedure referred to in Article 14 of Regulation No 17 does not aim at terminating an infringement or declaring that an agreement, decision or concerted practice is incompatible with Article 85; its sole objective is to enable the Commission to gather the necessary information to check the actual existence and scope of a given factual and legal situation. Only if the Commission considers that the data for the appraisal thereof collected in this way justify the initiation of a procedure under Regulation No 99/63/EEC must the undertaking or association of undertakings concerned be heard before such a decision is taken, pursuant to Article 19(1) of Regulation No 17 and to the provisions of Regulation No 99/63/EEC. Precisely this substantive difference between the decisions taken at the end of such a procedure and decisions ordering an investigation explains the wording of Article 19(1) which, in listing the decisions which the Commission cannot take before giving those concerned the opportunity of exercising their right of defence, does not mention that laid down in Article 14(3) of the same regulation.

22. Finally, the argument that the absence of previous information deprived the applicant of the opportunity of exercising its right under Article 185 of the Treaty to request the Court for a stay of execution of the decision in question is contradicted by the very provisions of Article 185. That article presupposes in fact that a decision has been

adopted and that it is effective whereas the previous notification, which the applicant complains that the Commission did not send it, should have preceded the adoption of the contested decision and could not have been binding.

23. In view of these considerations, the second submission is not well founded.

*(c) Absence of a statement of the reasons upon which the decision was based*

24. The applicant also maintains that the contested decision is irregular in that it failed to state or to state properly the reasons on which it was based, in particular because it in no way indicates the reasons why the Commission applied Article 14(3) of Regulation No 17 in this instance without attempting first of all to carry out an informal investigation.

25. Article 14(3) of Regulation No 17 itself lays down the essential constituents of the statement of the reasons upon which a decision ordering an investigation is based by providing that it 'shall specify the subject-matter and the purpose of the investigation, appoint the date on which it is to begin and indicate the penalties provided for in Article 15(1)(c) and Article 16(1)(d) and the right to have the decision reviewed by the Court of Justice'.

26. It is an established fact that the preamble to the contested decision states the purpose, which is to check facts which might show the existence of an export ban contrary to the Treaty, and indicates the penalties laid down in Article 15(1)(c) and 16(1)(d) of Regulation No 17. It also established that Articles 1 and 2 of that decision state the subject-matter of the investigation decided upon and the place where and date on which that investigation will be carried out. Finally, the second paragraph of Article 3 of the decision indicates the possibilities of instituting proceedings before the Court of Justice against such a decision in accordance with Article 173 of the Treaty.

27. In view of these factors, it follows that the contested decision fulfils the requirements laid down in Regulation No 17 as regards the statement of the reasons upon which it is based and that it is necessary to dismiss this submission as unfounded.

*(d) The violation of the principle of proportionality*

28. The applicant points out in addition that the principle of proportionality, as established by the case-law of the Court of Justice, implies that a decision ordering an investigation adopted without the preliminary procedure may only be justified if the situation is very grave and where there is the greatest urgency and the need for complete secrecy before the investigation is carried out. It points out, finally, that the contested decision violates such a principle by not indicating in the statement of the reasons upon which it is based that any of those facts exists.

29. The Commission's choice between an investigation by straightforward authorisation and an investigation ordered by a decision does not depend on the facts relied upon by the applicant but on the need for an appropriate enquiry, having regard to the special features of the case.

30. Considering that the contested decision aimed solely at enabling the Commission to collect the necessary information to appraise whether there was any infringement of the Treaty, it does not therefore appear that the Commission's action in this instance was disproportionate to the objective pursued and therefore violated the principle of proportionality.

31. For all these reasons, since this last submission cannot be accepted either, it is necessary to dismiss the application as unfounded.
.....

(3) Decision in re Federation de la Chaussure

Commission Decision of 27 October 1982 in re inspection visit at Fédération nationale de l'Industrie de la Chaussure de France, O.J. No L 319, 16 November 1982, p. 12;(1983)ICMLR 575 ; CCH para. 10435; Competition Law CM/M/I/181.

*The Commission held:*

1. On 4 March 1982, the Director-General for Competition gave written authorisation for two officials of the inspection directorate to carry out an investigation at the Fédération nationale de l'industrie de la chaussure de France (hereinafter referred to as 'the FNICF') in Paris, pursuant to Article 14 of Council Regulation No 17.

The investigation was carried out on 9 and 19 March 1982 at the FNICF's head office in the presence of several members of its management, in particular the secretary-general and one of his advisers, and a representative of the competent French authority.

The main purpose of the investigation was to obtain information on the application of French measures to improve the situation of the footwear and leather industry, in order to assess whether and to what extent the FNICF had, on behalf of its members, entered into undertakings to limit imports or to impose other restrictions within the meaning of Article 85 of the EEC Treaty.

2. Having produced his authorisation, the inspector drew the attention of the FNICF's management to the provisions of Articles 14 and 15 of Regulation No 17 concerning the Commission's powers of investigation, and in particular to the provisions of Article 15(1), as set out in the authorisation and under which the Commission may by decision impose fines on undertakings and associations of undertakings where they submit to an investigation but, intentionally or negligently, produce the required books or other business records in incomplete form.

When they were duly called upon, the FNICF's representatives expressed willingness to submit to the investigation and to comply with all obligations which might arise therefrom.

3. On 9 March 1982, the Commission's official requested FNICF to supply, for the purpose of an examination within the meaning of Article 14(1)(a) of Regulation No 17:

(1) correspondence, internal memoranda and minutes of meetings with other associations representing the footwear industry in France or in

certain other Community countries;

(2) records or minutes of meetings of the FNICF's management bodies: firstly, the Federal Council, comprising representatives of the regional unions, specialist member groupings of the FNICF and individual member manufacturers, and, secondly, the Bureau of the Federal Council, presided over by a board of three persons.

The documents requested were those covering the period from 1 January 1981 to the date of the investigation.

In response to this request, the representatives of the FNICF produced various files of correspondence and records of meetings with other organisations representing the footwear industry, but failed to produce any of the records or minutes of meetings of the FNICF's Federal Council and of the Bureau of the Federal Council since 1 January 1981.

The Secretary-General of the FNICF has stated that the last three meetings of the Federal Council took place in October 1981, in December 1981 and on 24 February 1982 and that minutes of these meetings were drawn up; he has also confirmed that these documents existed at the very time of the investigation at the FNICF's head office.

4. In a written statement, recorded in the minutes on 10 March 1982, the Secretary-General of the FNICF confirmed that 'the FNICF's management bodies had been given a verbal account of the gentlemen's agreement (accord de bon volonté) reached on 25 November'.

This 'gentlemen's agreement' of 25 November 1981, specifically mentioned by the Secretary-General of the FNICF, was one of the very vehicles for preparing and implementing the French measures to improve the situation in the footwear and leather industry which were mentioned in the investigation authorisation.

The principal aim of the investigation was thus to collect all the information relating to this agreement, in so far as it was likely to contain specific provisions for increasing sales of French footwear on the domestic market and hence to limit imports of such products into France.

The inspector also drew the FNICF's attention to a document which had come to the Commission's notice during a previous investigation carried out at another French trade association and which, according to the management representatives of that association, had actually been discussed at the meeting on 25 November 1981 mentioned by the Secretary-General of the FNICF.

This document, which is unsigned and has no title or heading, comprises three sections ( A, B and C) relating to the agreement to be signed by the wholesale and retail trade associations, the FNICF and the public authorities with a view to limiting imports according to percentage increases of sales on the domestic market varying from 10 to 25%.

One of the main objectives of the investigation was to determine precisely the conditions under which this document was submitted to the FNICF's Federal Council and the board of the Federal Council for discussion, any preparatory work done during previous meetings of those same bodies, any decisions adopted in this connection and any instructions given to the various members of the FNICF.

5. On 10 March 1982, the inspectors repeated their request, which was recorded in the minutes, for the following documents to be produced:

(1) correspondence, internal memoranda and records of meetings with various other trade organisations since 1 January 1981;

(2) minutes or records of meetings held by the FNICF's Federal Council and by the Bureau of the Federal Council since 1 January 1981.

The written reply from the Secretary-General of the FNICF, recorded in the same minutes, states that the documents referred to in (1) 'were given to the inspector', but that 'the documents referred to at (2) are confidential documents dealing with all the problems of the FNICF, and therefore go far beyond the investigators' terms of reference, so that the agreement of the FNICF's bureau must be obtained before they can be produced'.

The inspectors immediately recorded a statement in the minutes that 'the FNICF had produced documents which were incomplete within the meaning of Article 15(1)(c) of Regulation No 17'.
.....

7. Under Article 14 of Regulation No 17, the Commission, in carrying out the duties assigned to it by Article 89 of the EEC Treaty, may undertake all necessary investigations into undertakings. To this end, the officials authorised by the Commission are vested with the powers described in Article 14(1) of the said Regulation *inter alia* to examine the books and other business records, to take copies of or extracts from the books and business records, and to enter any premises of undertakings.

Under Article 14(2) of the said Regulation, the officials authorised by the Commission for the purpose of these investigations shall exercise their powers upon production of an authorisation in writing specifying the subject matter and purpose of the investigation and the penalties provided for in Article 15(1)(c) of the Regulation in cases where production of the required books or other business records is incomplete.

Under Article 15(1) of Regulation No 17, the Commission may, by decision, impose on undertakings fines of from 100 to 5 000 units of account where, intentionally or negligently, they produce the required books or other business records in incomplete form during investigations under Article 14.

The FNICF does not dispute the fact that the inspector drew its attention at the beginning of the interview to the provisions of Articles 14 and 15 of Regulation No 17 and that it thereupon agreed to submit to the investigation and to all the obligations arising therefrom under those provisions.

Consequently, the argument that the FNICF was not informed until the end of the interview of its right to refuse to submit to an investigation which the Commission had not ordered by decision taken pursuant to Article 14(3) is at variance with the fact that the FNICF's representatives acknowledged that their attention had been drawn in good time to all the provisions of Articles 14 and 15 of that Regulation, and these representatives admit, in their letter dated 14 May 1982, that there was no reason to refuse such an investigation.

8. The request for the FNICF to produce the minutes of its Federal Council and its other management bodies was in conformity with the aim of the investigation authorisation issued to the inspectors.

These documents constitute business records within the meaning of Article 14(1)(a) of Regulation No 17; it has not been contested that these documents were at the FNICF's head office at the time of the investigation.

Undertakings or associations of undertakings which are the subject of an investigation are not entitled to assess whether a request for documents to be produced is justified or whether the period in respect of which they are required is appropriate. Furthermore, undertakings or associations of undertakings may invoke the confidentiality of such documents only within the framework of Article 20 of Regulation No 17.

It is not for representatives of undertakings or associations of undertakings to choose between documents which they consider to be relevant to the subject of an investigation and those which they consider not to be relevant. According to the case law of the Court of Justice of the European Communities (see the judgment of 18 May 1982 in Case 155/79, AM & S Ltd v. Commission of the European Communities), officials authorised by the Commission are empowered to request those books and other business records necessary for them to carry out their tasks and to decide which of them should be copied as being relevant to their investigation.

9. In producing documentation which was clearly incomplete to Commission inspectors carrying out an investigation under Article 14 of Regulation No 17, the FNICF intentionally infringed Article 15(1)(c) of Regulation No 17. Furthermore, it must have been aware of the extent of the Commission's investigatory powers.

The conditions for the application of Article 15(1) are thus fulfilled.

10. The infringement committed by the FNICF is clearly serious because the failure to produce the documents requested made the Commission's task of ensuring compliance with the Treaty rules on competition more difficult. Furthermore, the FNICF indicated in its letter dated 14 May 1982 that its bureau had, after the investigation, maintained an identical position thereby accentuating the intentional nature of the infringement.

A fine must therefore be imposed in proportion to the gravity of the infringement committed by the FNICF.

.....

## C. Enquiries into sectors of the economy

(Regulation 17 Article 17)

On 9 October 1969 the Commission decided to start an enquiry into the beer industry on the basis of Article 12 of Regulation No 17. The main purpose of this inquiry is to determine the extent to which the exclusive supply contracts customarily applied in the brewery sector involve, either individually or in conjunction with others, in the economic or legal context in which they are concluded, elements to which the provisions of Article 85, paragraph 1, of the EEC Treaty are likely to apply.

The Commission has addressed requests for information, in the form of a decision, to a Belgian brewery and to two French breweries in application of Article 11(5) of Council Regulation No 17/62. This phase of the procedure means that these undertakings are henceforth obliged to provide the Commission with all the information it requests and, if they fail to do so, are likely to have fines or penalty payments imposed on them for each day's delay in complying with such requests.

This procedure is fairly rare, since in the majority of cases undertakings answer requests for information from the Commission within the required time-limit. So as to carry out this general investigation into the beer industry - which will enable the Commission to collect all necessary information for an assessment of 'brewery contracts' from the point of view of the rules of competition - requests for information have been addressed since May 1970, to numerous large breweries in the Common Market, which supplied their replies within the given time-limit. These replies are now being studied.

Decisions of 18 June 1971, J.O. No L 161, 19 July 1971, p. 72; CCH para. 9444; Competition Law CM/M/I/39 A-C.

For a more recent example see the Report by the Commission on the behaviour of the oil companies in the Community during the period from October 1973 to March 1974, Brussels, 14 December 1975, Studies Competition, Approximation of legislation Series No. 26 and Fifth Report on Competition Policy, April 1976 page 15.

See also Eighth Report on Competition Policy, April 1979, page 38, on the inquiry into the behaviour of the oil companies on the jet fuel markets.

## D. Legal Privilege

### (1) AM & S Case

AM & S Europe Ltd v. Commission, Case 155/79, Judgment of 18 May 1982; (1982) ECR 1575 ; (1982) 2 CMLR 264 ; CCH para. 8757; Competition Law CM/M/III/102.

*Facts:*

AM & S Europe Limited is a company incorporated in England. It has a subsidiary which owns and operates a zinc smelter at Avonmouth.

On 10 February 1978 the Member of the Commission responsible for competition policy directed investigations to be made of various undertakings, including the applicant, pursuant to Article 14 of Regulation No 17 of the Council.

On 20 and 21 February 1979 three officials of the Commission carried out an investigation at the applicant's premises in Bristol the purpose of which, as stated in the mandates which the officials produced, was to investigate '...competitive conditions concerning the production and distribution of zinc metals and its alloys and zinc concentrates in order to verify that there is no infringement of Articles 85 and 86 of the EEC Treaty'.

At the conclusion of that investigation those officials left the premises of AM & S taking with them copies of a certain number of documents and leaving with AM & S a written request for further specified documents.

By letter of 26 March 1979 AM & S sent to the Commission photocopies of certain documents but at the same time refused to make available others which its legal advisers considered were covered by legal privilege, that is to say, the principle of legal professional privilege or confidentiality as understood in common law jurisdictions. The applicant further suggested that contact might be made with its solicitors should the Commission need further confirmation regarding the documents for which privilege was claimed.

The Commission did not accept that invitation. Instead, by decision of 6 July 1979 taken under Article 14(3) of Regulation No 17, it required AM & S to submit to a fresh investigation at its premises at Bristol and Avonmouth and to produce certain business records which were divided into three groups (Article 1(a) (b) and (c) of the decision). Article 1(b) concerns 'all documents for which legal privilege is claimed, as listed in the appendix to AM & S Europe Limited's letter of 26 March 1979 to the Commission'.

On 25, 26 and 27 July 1979 two officials of the Commission proceeded to carry out a further investigation at AM & S's premises in Bristol pursuant to the decision of 6 July 1979.

On that occasion AM & S made it clear that it was unwilling to show to the inspectors the entirety of the documents for which privilege was claimed but that, without prejudice to any argument that it might wish to raise disputing the rights of the Commission to look at any part of the documents which the applicant regarded as covered by privilege. AM & S was prepared to permit part of the documents to be seen so that the inspectors might reasonably satisfy themselves that the documents were indeed privileged. The solicitors for AM &S offered, moreover, to come to Brussels in order to put their arguments to the appropriate departments of the Commission.

The Commission's inspectors thereupon stated that they would stop the investigation as far as it concerned the documents for which privilege was claimed but that the Commission reserved all rights relating to those documents. As for the meeting sought by the solicitors for AM & S, they stated that for various reasons a meeting could not be held until after 7 September 1979.

On 23 August 1979 the solicitors for AM & S wrote to the Director of the Directorate A of Directorate General IV (Competition) to ask him to fix a date for a meeting at which the question of the privileged documents might be discussed.

Following upon that letter a meeting was arranged which took place in Brussels on 18 September 1979 and at which were present counsel for AM & S and its solicitors and, for the Commission, Mr Riboux, Head of Division, in the absence of the Director of Directorate A, along with other officials.

At that meeting AM &S expressed its desire to reach agreement on a procedure whereby two conflicting interests might be reconciled, namely, (i) the Commission's desire to be satisfied that a document was indeed privileged and (ii) the need to maintain the secrecy of communications passing between legal advisers and clients for the purpose of obtaining legal advice. The procedure suggested was, in essence, that of allowing to be seen certain parts of the document in question which, according to AM & S, would enable its character to be clearly identified.

The Commission representatives refused to accept the proposal made by AM & S. They stated that they were bound by the decision of 6 July 1979, which they interpreted as meaning that an inspector must have the right, if he chose to exercise it, to read the whole of the document.

.....

*The Court held:*

(a) The interpretation of Article 14 of Regulation No 17

15. The purpose of Regulation No 27 of the Council which was adopted pursuant to the first subparagraph of Article 87(1) of the Treaty, is, according to paragraph (2) (a) and (b) of that article, 'to ensure compliance with the prohibitions laid down in Article 85(1) and Article 86' of the Treaty and 'to lay down detailed rules for the application of Article 85(3)'. The Regulation is thus intended to ensure that the aim stated in Article 3(f) of the Treaty is achieved. To that end it confers on the Commission wide powers of investigation and of obtaining information by providing in the eighth recital in its preamble that the Commission must be empowered, throughout the Common Market, to require such information to be supplied and to undertake such investigations 'as are necessary' to bring to light infringements of Articles 85 and 86 of the Treaty.

16. In Articles 11 and 14 of the regulation, therefore, it is provided that the Commission may obtain 'information' and undertake the 'necessary' investigations, for the purpose of proceedings in respect of infringements of the rules governing competition. Article 14(1) in particular empowers the Commission to require production of business records, that is to say, documents concerning the market activities of the undertaking, in particular as regards compliance with those rules. Written communications between lawyer and client fall, in so far as they have bearing on such activities, within the category of documents referred to in Articles 11 and 14.

17. Furthermore, since the documents which the Commission may demand are, as Article 14(1) confirms, those whose disclosure it considers 'necessary' in order that it may bring to light an infringement of the Treaty rules on competition, it is in principle for the Commission itself, and not the undertaking concerned or a third party, whether an expert or an arbitrator, to decide whether or not a document must be produced to it.

(b) Applicability of the protection of confidentiality in Community law

18. However, the above rules do not exclude the possibility of recognising, subject to certain conditions, that certain business records are of a confidential nature. Community law, which derives from not only the economic but also the legal interpenetration of the Member States, must take into account the principles and concepts common to the laws

of those States concerning the observance of confidentiality, in particular, as regards certain communications between lawyer and client. That confidentiality serves the requirement, the importance of which is recognised in all of the Member States, that any person must be able, without constraint, to consult a lawyer whose profession entails the giving of independent legal advice to all those in need of it.

19. As far as the protection of written communications between lawyer and client is concerned, it is apparent from the legal systems of the Member States that, although the principle of such protection is generally recognised, its scope and the criteria for applying it vary, as has, indeed, been conceded both by the applicant and by the parties who have intervened in support of its conclusions.

20. Whilst in some of the Member States the protection against disclosure afforded to written communications between lawyer and client is based principally on a recognition of the very nature of the legal profession, inasmuch as it contributes towards the maintenance of the rule of law, in other Member States the same protection is justified by the more specific requirement (which, moreover, is also recognised in the first-mentioned States) that the rights of the defence must be respected.

21. Apart from these differences, however, there are to be found in the national laws of the Member States common criteria inasmuch as those laws protect, in similar circumstances, the confidentiality of written communications between lawyer and client provided that, on the one hand, such communications are made for the purposes and in the interests of the client's rights of defence and, on the other hand, they emanate from independent lawyers, that is to say, lawyers who are not bound to the client by a relationship of employment.

22. Viewed in that context Regulation No 17 must be interpreted as protecting, in its turn, the confidentiality of written communications between lawyer and client subject to those two conditions, and thus incorporating such elements of that protection as are common to the laws of the Member States.

23. As far as the first of those two conditions is concerned, in Regulation No 17 itself, in particular in the eleventh recital in its preamble and in the provisions contained in Article 19, care is taken to ensure that the rights of the defence may be exercised to the full, and the protection of the confidentiality of written communications between lawyer and client is an essential corollary to those rights. In those circumstances, such protection must, if it is to be effective, be recognised as covering all written communications exchanged after the initiation of the administrative procedure of Regulation No 17 which may lead to a decision on the application of Articles 85 and 86 of the Treaty or to a decision imposing a pecuniary sanction on the undertaking. It must also be possible to extend it to earlier written communications which have a relationship to the subject-matter of that procedure.

24. As regards the second condition, it should be stated that the requirement as to the position and status as an independent lawyer, which must be fulfilled by the legal adviser from whom the written communications which may be protected emanate, is based on a conception of the lawyer's role as collaborating in the administration of justice by the courts and as being required to provide, in full independence, and in the overriding interests of that cause, such legal assistances as the client

needs. The counterpart of that protection lies in the rules of the professional ethics and discipline which are laid down and enforced in the general interest by institutions endowed with the requisite powers for that purpose. Such a conception reflects the legal traditions common to the Member States and is also to be found in legal order of the Community, as is demonstrated by Article 17 of the Protocols on the Statutes of the Court of Justice of the EEC and the EAEC, and also by Article 20 of the Protocol on the Statute of the Court of Justice of the ECSC.

25. Having regard to the principles of the Treaty concerning freedom of establishment and the freedom to provide services the protection thus afforded by Community law, in particular in the context of Regulation No 17, to written communications between lawyer and client must apply without distinction to any lawyer entitled to practise his profession in one of the Member States, regardless of the Member State in which the client lives.

26. Such protection may not be extended beyond those limits, which are determined by the scope of the common rules on the exercise of the legal profession as laid down in Council Directive No 77/249/EEC of 22 March 1977 (Official Journal No L 78, p. 17), which is based in its turn on the mutual recognition by all the Member States of the national legal concepts of each of them on this subject.

27. In view of all these factors it must therefore be concluded that although Regulation No 17, and in particular Article 14 thereof, interpreted in the light of its wording, structure and aims, and having regard to the laws of the Member States, empowers the Commission to require, in the course of an investigation within the meaning of that article, production of the business documents the disclosure of which it considers necessary, including written communications between lawyer and client, for proceedings in respect of any infringements of Articles 85 and 86 of the Treaty, that power is, however, subject to a restriction imposed by the need to protect confidentiality, on the conditions defined above, and provided that the communications in question are exchanged between an independent lawyer and his client.

28. Finally, it should be remarked that the principle of confidentiality does not prevent a lawyer's client from disclosing the written communications between them if he considers that it is in his interests to do so.

(c) The procedures relating to the application of the principle of confidentiality

29. If an undertaking which is the subject of an investigation under Article 14 of Regulation No 17 refuses, on the ground that it is entitled to protection of the confidentiality of information, to produce, among the business records demanded by the Commission, written communications between itself and its lawyer, it must nevertheless provide the Commission's authorised agents with relevant material of such a nature as to demonstrate that the communications fulfil the conditions for being granted legal protection as defined above, although it is not bound to reveal the contents of the communications in question.

30. Where the Commission is not satisfied that such evidence has been supplied, the appraisal of those conditions is not a matter which may

be left to an arbitrator or to a national authority. Since this is a matter involving an appraisal and a decision which affect the conditions under which the Commission may act in a field as vital to the functioning of the Common Market as that of compliance with the rules on competition, the solution of disputes as to the application of the protection of the confidentiality of written communications between lawyer and client may be sought only at Community level.

31. In that case it is for the Commission to order, pursuant to Article 14(3) of Regulation No 17, production of the communications in question and, if necessary, to impose in the undertakings fines or periodic penalty payments under that regulation as a penalty for the undertaking's refusal either to supply such additional evidence as the Commission considers necessary or to produce the communications in question whose confidentiality, in the Commission's view, is not protected in law.

32. The fact that by virtue of Article 185 of the EEC Treaty any action brought by the undertaking concerned against such decisions does not have suspensory effect provides an answer to the Commission's concern as to the effect of the time taken by the procedure before the Court on the efficacy of the supervision which the Commission is called upon to exercise in regard to compliance with the Treaty rules on competition, whils on the other hand the interests of the undertaking concerned are safeguarded by the possibility which exists under Articles 185 and 186 of the Treaty, as well as under Article 83 cf the Rules of Procedure of the Court, of obtaining an order suspending the application of the decision which has been taken, or any other interim measure.
.....

## E. Statement of objections

(Regulation No 17 Article 19. 1)

### (1) ACF Chemiefarma Case

For facts and references see above, page 109.

*The Court held:*
.....
C - Submissions relating to procedure and form

I - Submissions relating to the notice of complaints

The applicant complains that in the notice of complaints communicated to it on 30 May 1968 the Commission failed to give sufficient information on the objections made against it and the evidence on which they were based.

By this ommission the Commission is said to have hampered review by the Court of the legality of the contested decision.

Article 19(1) of Regulation No 17 obliges the Commission, before taking a decision in connection with fines, to give the persons concerned the opportunity of putting forward their point of view with regard to the complaints made against them.

Article 4 of Regulation No 99/63 of the Commission provides that the

Commission shall in its decision deal only with those objections raised against undertakings and associations of undertakings in respect of which they have been afforded the opportunity of making known their views.

The notice of complaints fulfils this requirement since it sets forth clearly, albeit succinctly, the essential facts on which the Commission relies.

The requirement imposed on the Commission by Article 19 is met when in the course of the administrative procedure it supplies the details necessary to the defence.

In the present case the Commission has clearly set out the essential factors on which it based the complaints listed, referring expressly to statements contained in the minutes of certain meetings of the undertakings concerned and to correspondence relating to the protection of domestic markets which was exchanged between those undertakings in October and November 1963.

Furthermore, maintaining on the basis of its investigations that the undertakings concerned had continued to exchange information on their sales with a view to possible quantitative compensation and that up to the end of 1964 they had maintained a policy of uniform prices, the Commission thereby deduced that after 1962 they had continued to apply the gentlemen's agreement on production and sale in the Common Market.

Consequently the objections raised with regard to the notice of complaints are unfounded.

<u>(2) Bayer Case</u>

Bayer v. Commission, Case 51/69, Judgment of 14 July 1972, (1972) ECR 745.
For facts see above, page 109.

*The Court held:*
....
(b) The divergence of the 'statement of complaint' from the order instituting the administrative proceedings

The applicant contends that the statement of complaint refers to the possibility of the imposition of fines, while the initiating decision only refers to the proceedings for establishing an infringement. The Commission had thereby infringed Article 19 of Regulation 17 as well as Articles 2 and 4 of Regulation 99/63, in conjunction with Article 162 (2) of the EEC Treaty, and Article 27 of the Standing Orders of the Commission.

However, the Commission substantiates its attitude vis-a-vis the companies against which it is instituting proceedings for the infringements of the rules of competition, not from the decision instituting these proceedings, but solely from the statement of complaint. Moreover, although the order instituting the hearing particularly ('notamment') quoted Articles 3 and 9(2) and (3) of Regulation No 17, in fact it referred to the Regulation as a whole, and thus to Article 15, which governs the imposition of fines.

The objection is therefore without foundation.
.....

(3) Geigy Case

Geigy v. Commission, Case 52/69, Judgment of 14 July 1972, (1972) ECR 787.
For facts see above, page 109.

*The Court held:*
....

(d) The continuation of investigations after the service of the statement of complaint.

The applicant contends that, even after service of the notification of the complaint, the Commission undertook investigations, thus misconstructing the legal nature of this notification, which - according to Regulations No 17 and No 99 - was intended to conclude the process of investigation. Moreover, the contested decision relied on contentions which did not appear in the notification of the complaint, for instance, that the telegrams had been dispatched simultaneously.

The Commission is justified and in certain circumstances even obliged to initiate new investigations during the administrative proceedings if additional investigations are considered necessary. Such investigations would only necessitate an amendment of the statement of complaint if the Commission, as the result of these investigations, had cause to make new allegations against the companies, or establish its allegations of infringement on substantially different grounds. Such was not the case here. The matters with which the applicant was charged were clearly apparent from the text of the notification of the complaint. It contained all the necessary particulars for the establishment of the complaint alleged against the applicant and described the methods by which the price increases of 1964, 1965 and 1967 had been enforced and effected. Furthermore, the right to a hearing was not curtailed by the fact that the exact description of these events relating to the decision appealed from had been changed on the basis of facts which those concerned had been able to notify to the Commission during the administrative proceedings.
The applicant's contention is therefore without foundation.

(4) Continental Can Case

For facts and references see above, page 10.

*The Court held:*
.....

(b) The applicant also argues that the statement of objections of 15 March 1971 was not accompanied by a sufficient statement of reasons, for the Commission had simply cited its objections without mentioning the supporting reasons. The statement of reasons in the decision was also sufficient since it merely repeated the statement of objections of 15 March 1971 without taking into condsideration the reply given by the affected parties on 9 August 1971, and also because it made no mention of supporting reasons for the objections made.

As far as the first plea is concerned, Article 4 of Regulation No 99/63 states that the Commission should only take into consideration in its decisions those objections on which the addressee has had the opportunity to express an opinion. The statement of objections fulfils this requirement as it indicates the essential facts on which the Commission bases its case in an admittedly concise, but nevertheless clear form. In its communications of 15 March 1971 the Commission clearly presented and stated the essential facts on which it based its objections and indicated the extent of the dominant position held by Continental and how it had been abused. The criticisms made of the statement of objections are therefore unfounded.

As far as the second plea is concerned, the Commission is admittedly obliged to provide the reasons for its decision, but it does not need to refute all the arguments adduced during the administrative proceedings.

(c) The applicants go on to discern a formal error in the contested decision, since the administrative proceedings are headed 'Continental Can Company' in the Official Journal of the European Communities of 8 January 1972, whereas the French version, which alone is authentic, is entitled 'Europemballage Corporation'.

This circumstance, however, on account of the economic and legal links between Continental and Europemballage, cannot effect the validity of the contested measure.

(5) Sugar Cases

For facts and references see above, page 94.

*The Court held:*

.....

II - Submissions based on defects in the notification of objections

1. SZV takes the view that the notification of objections which was sent in identical wording to forty-eight undertakings, although each of the latter were only affected by some of the facts alleged, did not set out with sufficient accuracy the complaints specifically made against the applicant or the evidence used against it.

None of the documents mentioned in the notification of objections to justify the complaint that it engaged in a general concerted action based on the principle 'chacun chez soi' ('each in his own home') which was also made against the applicant, emanated from SZV or was sent to it.

Since it consequently feared that the replies given by the other undertakings would be construed against it, SZV requested the Commission to send it copies of them, which the Commission refused to do on the ground that it was under a duty to respect the principle of professional secrecy.

This complaint, which is the only one made against the applicant by the contested decision, is not that SZV engaged in a concerted practice but that it abused a dominant position.

This complaint has been clearly and accurately formulated on pages 91 to 93, 107 to 108 and 121 to 123 of the notification of objections and supported by documents emanating from SZV or which explicitly mentions SZV.

The submission must therefore be rejected.

(6) First IBM Case

For facts and references see above, page 269.

*The Court held:*

.....

18. Other effects relied on by IBM do not adversely affect the interests of the undertakings concerned. One such is the fact that initiation of a procedure under Article 9(3) Regulation No 17 puts an end to the jurisdiction of the authorities in the Member States - a result which did not in fact occur in this instance as there were no national proceedings, and which essentially results in protecting the undertaking concerned from parallel proceedings brought by the authorities of the Member States. Another such effect is the fact that communication of the statement of objections is recognised as crustallising the Commission's position, which means in effect that the Commission is prevented, pursuant to Article 4 of Regulation No 99/63, from relying in its decision, in the absence of a frech statement of objections, on the existence of any objections other than those on which the undertaking has been given an opportunity to make known its views, though it does not prevent the Commission from withdrawing its objections and thereby altering its standpoint in favour of the undertaking.

19. A statement of objections does not compel the undertaking concerned to alter or reconsider its marketing practices and it does not have the effect of depriving it of the protection hitherto available to it against the application of a fine, as is the case when the Commission informs an undertaking, pursuant to Article 15(6) of Regulation No 17, of the results of the preliminary examination of an agreement which has been notified by the undertaking. Whilst a statement of objections may have the effect of showing the undertaking in question that it is incurring a real risk of being fined by the Commission, that is merely a consequence of fact, and not a legal consequence which the statement of objections is intended to produce.

20. An application for a declaration that the initiation of a procedure and a statement of objections are void might make it necessary for the Court to arrive at a decision on questions which the Commission has not yet had an opportunity to state its position and would as a result anticipate the arguments on the substance of the case, confusing different procedural stages both administrative and judicial. It would thus be incompatible with the system of the division of powers between the Commission and the Court and of the remedies laid down by the Treaty, as well as the requirements of the sound administration of justice and the proper course of the administrative procedure to be followed in the Commission.

21. It follows from the foregoing that neither the initiation of a procedure nor a statement of objections may be considered, on the basis of their nature and the legal effects they produce, as being decisions within the meaning of Article 173 of the EEC Treaty which may be challenged in an action for a declaration that they are void. In the context of the administrative procedure as laid down by Regulations No 17 and No 99/63, they are procedural measures adopted preparatory to the decision which represents their culmination.

22. In support of its submission that the application is admissible

IBM relies further on the special circumstances of the case and on the nature and implications of the submissions which it puts forward on the substance of its case, claiming that a judicial review ought to be made available at an early stage in this case both in accordance with the principles of international law in such matters and pursuant to general principles flowing from the laws of the Member States. The present application is intended to establish that the administrative procedure was wholly unlawful from the beginning under the rules of Community law and international law, particularly those concerning the power to initiate such procedures. Any continuation of that administrative procedure is unlawful, it claims, and the fact that IBM may subsequently have the final decision declared void is not sufficient to give it effective legal protection.

23. It is not necessary for the purpose of this case to decide whether, in exceptional circumstances, where the measures concerned lack even the appearance of legality, a judicial review at an early stage such as that envisaged by IBM may be considered compatible with the system of remedies provided for in the Treaty, because the circumstances referred to by the applicant in this case are in any event not such as would make it possible to regard the action as admissible.

24. Moreover, in this instance adequate legal protection for IBM does not require that the measures in question be subject to immediate review. If, on the conclusion of the administrative procedure and after any observations which IBM may submit in the course of it have been examined, the Commission were to adopt a decision which affects IBM's interests, that decision will, in accordance with Article 173 of the EEC Treaty, be subject to judicial review in the course of which it will be permissible for IBM to advance all the appropriate arguments. It will then be for the Court to decide whether anything unlawful has been done in the course of the administrative procedure and if so whether it is such as to effect the legality of the decision taken by the Commission on the conclusion of the administrative procedure.

25. The application must therefore be dismissed as inadmissible.

.....

## G. Service of statement of objections

(1) Geigy Case

For facts and references see above, page 318.

*The Court held:*

.....

(c) Service of the Statement of Complaint

The applicant objects that the Commission notified the complaint in a manner which did not comply with the law of Switzerland, where this notification had to be served. The Swiss Confederation did not recognise as lawful the service by post of foreign legal proceedings of this kind in its sovereign area. According to general principles of public international law, therefore, the notification of the complaint did not take place in a proper manner and was therefore invalid. This procedural error infringed the applicant's right to a hearing set out in Article

19 of Regulation No. 17 as well as Articles 2 and 4 of Regulation 99.

The notification of the complaint provided in Article 2(1) of Regulation 99 is intended to give the parties an opportunity to explain themselves in the hearing which has been instituted against them by the Commission in the exercise of its authority under Articles 3 and 15 of Regulation No. 17. As there is no applicable agreement between the Community and the Swiss Confederation, service depends on international practice and must be resolved with mutual regard to the spheres of jurisdiction of both the Community and the Swiss Confederation.

(2) Frubo Case

For facts and references see above, page 115.

*The Court held:*

.....

Second submission as to form

The applicants criticise the Commission first for having addressed its first statement of objections of 12 November 1969 only to their members and not to the applicants themselves and, secondly, for having, after the second statement of objections of 19 November 1973, continued the procedure on the basis of the new text of Article 9 of the agreement as it appeared after the amendment of 21 February 1974.

The applicants cannot claim that they were not informed by the undertakings which they organise, because the subject of the statement of objections was, of course, the agreement concluded between the two associations.

Moreover, the nature of the amendment of 21 February 1974 did not require a fresh statement of objections.

## H. Hearings

### a. General

NOTICE ON THE PROCEDURES FOR APPLYING THE COMPETITION RULES OF THE EEC AND THE ECSC TREATIES (ARTICLES 85 AND 86 (EEC) AND 65 AND 66 (ECSC)

1. In its Eleventh Report on Competition policy the Commission announced that it envisaged creating the post of Hearing Officer; it has now taken the decision to do so.

To ensure his independence in the performance of his duties, the Hearing Officer will have the right of direct access to the Member of the Commission with special responsibility for competition policy. Administratively he will belong to the Directorate-General for Competition.

The Hearing Officer's task will be to ensure that the hearing is properly conducted and thus to contribute to the objectivity of the hearing itself and of any decision taken subsequently. He will seek to ensure in particular that in the preparation of draft Commission decisions in competition cases due account is taken of all relevant facts, whether favourable or unfavourable to the parties concerned.

In performing his duties he is to see to it that the rights of the defence are respected, while taking account of the need for effective application of the competition rules in accordance with the regulations in force and the principles laid down by the Court of Justice.

b. Cases

(1) ACF-Chemiefarma Case

For facts and references see above, page 109.

*The Court held:*

.....

III - Complaints relating to the drawing up of the minutes of the hearing

The applicant complains that the Commission failed to observe Article 9(4) of Regulation No 99 by ommitting to submit to the undertakings concerned within a reasonable time the complete and accurate minutes of the hearing, by fixing too short a period of time for it to submit its observations and by failing to ensure, prior to adopting the contested decision, that it concurred with the draft minutes.

In the course of the administrative procedure the applicant, which had been given a period of three weeks within which to submit its observations on the draft minutes which the Commission had submitted to it, nether exercised its right to propose amendments nor requested an extension of the period allowed.

There is thus no foundation in the complaint now made against the Commission that it concurred with the minutes before adopting the contested decision.

The applicant further maintains that by its failure to submit the minutes to it in Dutch, the Commission infringed the principles contained in Articles 217 and 248 of the EEC Treaty together with the provisions of Regulation No. 1 of the Council.

Under the terms of Article 3 of Regulation No. 1 of the Council, documents which an institution of the Community sends to a person subject to the jurisdiction of a Member State shall be drafted in the language of such State.

The failure to communicate a Dutch version of the draft minutes thus constitutes an irregularity in drawing up that document which is capable of affecting its validity.

It is clear, however, from the arguments put forward by the applicant that it was able in due time to acquaint itself with the contents of the minutes.

The applicant has not alleged that this resulted in the minutes containing any substantial inaccuracies or ommissions with regard to it.

It must therefore be concluded that the irregularity which has been found did not in this case have harmful consequences capable of vitiating the administrative procedure.

In these circumstances the abovementioned complaints must be rejected.

(2) Continental Can Case

For facts and references see above, page 10.

*The Court ruled:*

.....

A - On the irregularity of the administrative procedure

(a) The applicants argue that the contested decision was irregular on account of the fact that Continental had been given no opportunity to state its point of view in the administrative procedure in accordance with Article 19 of Regulation No. 17/62 of the Council and Article 7 of Regulation No. 99/63 of the Commission. Therefore, it was argued, the decision offended against the right of being heard.

It is established that the applicants, by letter of 14 May 1970 sent through their representative, requested the Commission, which had previously directed its inquiries as to the acquisition of the TDV shares and debentures to Continental, to apply in future to Europemballage. From the minutes supplied by the applicants of the hearing of the parties on 21 September 1971, it is moreover clear that amongst the people taking part in this hearing was Mr. Charles B. Stauffacher, in his capacity as a member of the Board of Directors of both the applicants. From these circumstances it is clear that Continental has had the opportunity to state its case in the administrative procedure.

(3) Transocean Marine Paint Association Case

Transocean Marine Paint Association v. Commission, Judgment of 23 October 1974, Case 17/74; (1974) ECR 1603; (1974) CMLR 454; CCH para. 8241; Competition Law CM/M/III/44.

*Facts:* see in first instance above, page 193.

On 22 October 1972 the Association applied for the simple renewal, for a period of ten years, of the exemption granted in 1967, but the Commission did not follow this course. It considered, just as in 1967, that the agreement was covered by the provisions of Article 85 paragraph 1 and that exemption on the basis of Article 85 paragraph 3 was justified, but, in view of changes which had occurred since 1967 in the competitive situation, such exemption must be subject to stricter conditions than those imposed by the original Decision.

In this connection, the Commission puts forward the following factors:

(a) the total turnover of the Association and its percentage of the market in marine paints had considerably increased;

(b) the turnover of one group of members, Nippon Paint, had increased substantially and this group accounts for 60% of the turnover in marine paints of the Association;

(c) five members had withdrawn, eight new members had joined;

(d) two members, Astral (France) and Urruzola (Spain), had formed links with two large paint manufacturing groups, AKZO and BASF, which are not members;

(e) a movement towards concentration had occurred both in the marine paint sectors and in the general paint sectors.

These circumstances led the Commission, by its Decision of 21 December 1973 to subject the exemption to new conditions set out in Articles 2 and 3 of that Decision. Under Article 2, it requires the abolition of certain commissions which the members had agreed to pay one another when they executed orders in each other's territory.

The terms of Article 3 are as follows:

"This Decision is subjected to the following obligations:

1. That the Commission shall be informed without delay of the following matters:

(a) Any amendment or addition to the Agreement,

(b) Any decision taken by the Board of Directors or the result of any arbitration held, pursuant to the restrictive provisions of the Agreement, in particular Articles 3 to 9 thereof,

(c) Any change in the composition of membership,

(d) Any links by way of common directors or managers between a member of the Association and any other company or firm in the paints sector or any financial participation by a member of the Association in such outside companies or vice-versa including all changes in such links or participation already in existence.

2. A report is to be submitted by the Association annually to the Commission on the activities of the Association and in particular on improvements in the production and marketing of marine paint products achieved".

The application is directed against Article 3(1)(d) and therefore aims at the annulment of part of the contested decision.

*The Court held:*

.....

By Decision of 21 December 1973 the Commission, pursuant to Article 85 paragraph 3 of the EEC Treaty, renewed, subject to new conditions, the exemption from the prohibition contained in Article 85(1), which had been granted, by Decision of 27 June 1967, to an agreement restricting competition on the market in marine paints, concluded between the undertakings constituting the Transocean Marine Paint Association (hereinafter referred to as the Association).

Inter alia, Article 3 paragraph 1(d) of the Decision requires members of the Association to inform the Commission without delay of "any links by way of common directors or managers between a member of the Association and any other company or firm in the paints sector or any financial participation by a member of the Association in such outside companies or vice versa including all changes in such links or participations already in existence".

This action has been brought for the purpose of annulling that single provision.

The applicants firstly state that the obligation in issue was mentioned neither in the "notice of objections" of 27 July 1973, nor at the time of the hearing on 27 September 1973, and that furthermore it was not mentioned in any letter or memorandum from the Commission, prior to the Decision, so that they were never given the opportunity to make their views known on this subject. Accordingly, as regards the clause in issue, the Commission is said to have infringed rules of procedure laid down by Regulation No. 99/63 of the Commission of 25 July 1963 (OJ No 127 of 20.8.1963), on the hearing provided for in Article 19 of Regulation No 17 of the Council of 6 February 1962 (OJ No. 13 of 21.2.1962) and in particular Articles 2 and 4 of the said Regulation No 99/63.

Secondly, the applicants allege an infringement of Article 85 of the Treaty and of Article 8 paragraph 1 of Regulation No. 17, in that the obligation imposed upon the undertakings is wider in scope that anything which may be imposed upon them under Article 85.

In a communication of 27 July 1973 entitled "notice of objections", drawn up in Dutch, the Commission stated that a simple renewal of the exemption could not be envisaged, since the position of the members of the Association on the marine paints market had changed as a result of the increase in the number of undertakings composing the Association, the increased size of certain of them and the links which two of the members, Astral and Urruzola, had forged with large industrial chemical concerns.

The Commission added that it was nevertheless willing to renew the exemption for a period of five years, but at the same time making it subject to fresh conditions and obligations, one of which was formulated so as to involve, for the members of the Association, apart from the obligations contained in Article 4 of the Decision of 27 June 1967, the further obligation to notify to the Commission without delay "iedere wijziging in de deelnemingsverhoudingen van de leden" (literally: any change in the participating relationship of the members).

The applicants claim that at no time could they infer from this statement that the Commission intended to impose on them a condition such as that contained in the provision in issue, and one to which they would not be able, by reasons of its breadth, to adhere and which, without good reason, would harm their interests. If they had been in a position to realise the Commission's intentions they would not have failed to make known their objections on this matter so as to draw the Commission's attention to the inconvenience which would result from the obligation in issue and to the illegality by which it is vitiated. Since they were not given this opportunity, they allege that the Decision, insofar as the obligation in issue is concerned, must be annulled since it is vitiated by a procedural defect.

The defendant replies, firstly, that the requirement laid down in Article 2 of Regulation No. 99/63, according to which 'the Commission shall inform undertakings and associations of undertakings in writing of the objections raised against them', in the same way as the obligations imposed upon it by Article 4 of the same Regulation, to deal with 'those objections raised against undertakings and associations of undertakings in respect of which they have been afforded the opportunity of making known their views', do not relate to the conditions which the Commission intends to attach to a decision granting exemption.

The Commission adds that the concern which is given expression in the clause in issue was known to the applicants, in particular because of the importance attached to the case of the companies Astral and Urruzola, and this both in the communication of 27 July 1973 and during the course of the hearing.

According to Article 19 of Regulation No. 17 of the Council, the Commission, before taking decisions as provided for in Articles 2, 3, 6, 7, 8, 15 and 16 of that Regulation, shall give the undertakings or associations of undertakings concerned the opportunity of being heard on the matters to which the Commission has taken objection. In reference to Article 6, this provision relates to decisions taken pursuant to a request for the application of Article 85(3).

According to Article 24 of the same Regulation the Commission shall have to adopt implementing provisions in this context, which it did in Regulation No. 99/63.

It is clear both from the title and from the first recital of this Regulation that it is concerned with all the hearings provided for in Article 19 of Regulation No. 17 of the Council and, accordingly, also applies to procedures with regard to Article 85(3). However, the obligations imposed upon the Commission by Articles 2 and 4 of Regulation No. 99/63 to inform an undertaking, in writing or by giving notice in the Official Journal, of the objections raised against it and to deal, in its decisions, only with these objections, is essentially concerned with the statement of the reasons which would lead it to apply paragraph (1) of Article 85, either by ordering that an infringement be terminated or imposing a fine upon the undertakings, or by refusing to give the latter negative clearance or the benefit of paragraph (3) of the same provision.

On the other hand, the Commission cannot be expected to anticipate the conditions and obligations to which it is entitled to subject the exemption laid down in Article 85(3). In fact, the investigation of a request for exemption may bring to light various ways in which the operation of an agreement or the control of that operation may be undertaken, thus prompting the Commission to withdraw the objections which it had raised against the request and justifying the grant, possibly subject to certain conditions, of the benefit of Article 85(3).

It is clear, however, both from the nature and objective of the procedure for hearings, and from Articles 5, 6 and 7 of Regulation No. 99/63, that this Regulation, notwithstanding the cases specifically dealt with in Articles 2 and 4, applies the general rule that a person whose interests are perceptibly affected by a decision taken by a public authority must be given the opportunity to make his point of view known. This rule requires that an undertaking be clearly informed, in good time, of the essence of conditions to which the Commission intends to subject an exemption and it must have the opportunity to submit its observations to the Commission. This is especially so in the case of conditions which, as in this case, impose considerable obligations having far-reaching effects.

Since Article 85(3) constitutes, for the benefit of undertakings, an exception to the general prohibition contained in Article 85(1) the Commission must be in a position at any moment to check whether the conditions justifying the exemption are still present. Accordingly, in relation to the detailed rules to which it may subject the exemption, the Commission enjoys a large measure of discretion, while at the same time having to act within the limits imposed upon its competence by Article 85. On the other hand, the exercise of this discretionary power is linked to a preliminary canvassing of objections which may be raised by the undertaking.

It is clear from the file that this requirement was not fulfilled in respect of the obligation at issue.

The statement contained in the communication of 27 July 1973 could be interpreted in widely differing ways, inter alia, as requiring merely that the information which had already to be supplied under Article 4 of the Decision of 17 June 1967 be supplemented by the notification of any links which might exist between the undertakings which are members of the association. The ambiguity of this statement is highlighted by the fact that during the proceedings before the Court the Commission suggested different versions of it both in English, which is the language chosen by the applicants as the language of the case, and in French, in the translation in the statement of defence and in the correction proposed during the oral procedure.

Although it is clear from the minutes of the hearing that the links between two members of the Association, the companies Astral and Urruzola, and two important industrial chemical concerns were examined in depth - which moreover prompted the Commission to dispense with its requirement that these two members should leave the Association - the said minutes show that at no time was the general condition later contained in the Decision the subject of an exchange of points of view. This fact confirms the applicants' assertion that they were convinced that the obligation as stated in the 'notice of objections' concerned only the mutual relations between members of the Association and not such links as might exist with outside undertakings, including those operating outside the common market and concerned with the manufacture of paints other than marine paints.

Accordingly, the conditions stated in Article 3(1)(d) of the Decision was imposed in breach of procedural requirements and the Commission must be given the opportunity to reach a fresh decision on this point after hearing the observations or suggestions of the members of the Association.

Notwithstanding the importance of the subject matter of this part of the Decision, it is nevertheless capable of being severed, for the time being, from the other provisions, and a partial annulment is therefore possible and is justified by the fact that, taken as a whole, the Decision is favourable to the interests of the undertakings concerned.

The provision in issue should therefore be annulled and the case remitted to the Commission.

Costs

Under Article 69(2) of the Rules of Procedure, the unsuccessful party shall be ordered to pay the costs, if a submission has been made to that effect.

The defendant party has failed in its pleas.

The defendant party should therefore be ordered to pay the costs.

THE COURT hereby:

1. Annuls Article 3(1)(d) of the Decision on 21 December 1973;
2. Refers the case back to the Commission;
3. Orders the Commission to pay the costs.

## I. Notification of Decisions

(1) ICI Case

For facts and references see above, page 44.

*The Court held:*

.....

On the plea relating to notification of the Decision

The applicant contends that the Commission, by providing in Article 4 of the decision challenged that notification thereof may be made at the registered office of the subsidiaries of the applicant established in the Common Market, and by proceeding accordingly, violated the Treaty, or at least essential procedural requirements. The German subsidiary of the applicant, to whom the decision was notified by the Commission, had received no mandate in this respect from the parent company, and under German law it was under no obligation to bring the documents in question to the latter's notice.

Article 191 of the Treaty, second paragraph, provides that "decisions shall be notified to the persons to whom they are addressed and shall take effect upon such notification". Article 4 of the Decision challenged could not in any event alter this rule, and hence could not affect the applicant's rights.

Irregularities in the procedure of notification of a decision are external to the legal act and therefore cannot vitiate it. In certain circumstances these irregularities might prevent the time from bringing an action from starting to run. The final paragraph of Article 173 of the Treaty provides that the time for bringing an action for annulment against individual acts of the Commission starts to run upon the notification of the decision to the applicant, or, failing that, from the date on which the latter had knowledge of it.

In the present case, it is apparent that the applicant had complete knowledge of the text of the decision and made use, within the time limits, of its rights to bring an action. In these circumstances, the question of any irregularities of notification becomes immaterial.

The abovementioned pleas are, therefore, inadmissable on the grounds that they are immaterial.

(2) Continental Can Case

For facts and references see above, page 10.

(d) The applicants go on to argue that the contested decision was irregular because it was not duly notified to Continental. The undertaking had received one or two letters from the Commission by post in December 1971, although the decision should have been notified through diplomatic channels.

A decision is properly notified within the meaning of the Treaty, if it reaches the addressee and puts the latter in a position to take cognisance of it. This was so in the present case, because the contested decision actually reached Continental and the latter cannot make use of its own refusal to take cognisance of the decision in order to render this communication ineffective.

J. Publicity

(1) ACF-Chemifarma Case

For facts and references see above, page 109.

*The Court held:*

.....

VIII - The complaint relating to the publicity given to the decision

The applicant complains that the Commission violated the principles on which Article 21 of Regulation No 17 is based by communicating the contested decision to the press and publishing it in its entirety in the Official Journal of the Communities although it does not appear amongst the decisions publication of which is prescribed by that Article.

The defendant is thus alleged to have influenced public opinion to the detriment of the applicant's reputation and its stock market position.

Article 21 of Regulation No 17 which provides for the publication of certain decisions does not include those adopted under Article 15 of the said Regulation.

Although the Commission was not obliged to publish the contested decision, there is nothing in the letter or the spirit of the abovementioned Article 21 to prevent it from publishing it since this did not amount to divulging the undertakings' business secrets.

The Commission's communication to the press altered neither the meaning nor the content of the decision.

The publicity thus given to the decision may even contribute to ensuring the observance of the rules of the Treaty on competition.

The present complaint is thus unfounded.

(2) Sugar Cases

For facts and references see above, page 94.

*The Court held:*

.....

Section 2 Procedural and formal submissions

I - Submissions concerning the administrative procedure

1. Premature publication, a breach of the principle that everyone has the right to a fair trial.

SU, CSM and Pfeifer & Langen blame the Commission for having infringed the principle that everyone has the right to a fair trial by issuing certain public statements giving the impression that the infringements alleged had been found to exist. What is more, they did so before the undertakings concerned had been able to defend their position on the complaints affecting them.

Thus the Commission deprived itself of the opportunity of determining impartially the facts of the case and the arguments put forward by the applicants.

There is nothing in the Court's file to support the presumption that the contested decision would not have been taken or would have been drawn up in a different way, if the public statements which are the subject-matter of this decision had not been made, whether or not they are open to criticism under another legal head.

Moreover the decision has not upheld all the complaints set out in the notification of objections.

This submission must therefore be dismissed.

K. Reasoning of Commission's Decisions

(1) ACF Chemifarma Case

For facts and references see above, page 109.

VII - Submission of the infringement of an essential procedural requirement through failure to supply a statement of reasons

With regard to the infringement of an essential procedural requirement the applicant puts forward a series of complaints with regard to the reasoning of the contested decision.

It complains first of all that the decision ommitted to refer to important parts of its reply to the notice of complaints, which dealt in particular with the characteristics of the market in pharmaceutical products and the pointlessness of territorial protection.

Those ommissions hamper any review of the Commission's power to intervene under Article 85 of the Treaty on the ground of a potential obstacle to trade between Member States.

Under Article 190 of the Treaty the Commission is required to state the reasons on which its decisions are based, ennumerating the facts forming the legal base of the measure and the considerations which led it to adopt the decision.

Nevertheless the Commission is not required to discuss all the issues of fact and of law which may have been touched on by every interested person in the course of the administrative procedure.

With regard more particularly to decisions imposing a fine, the statement of reasons is to be considered sufficient if it indicates clearly and coherently the considerations of fact and of law on the basis of which the fine has been imposed on the parties concerned, in such a way as to acquaint both the latter and the Court with the essential factors of the Commission's reasoning.

It is clear from the decision that the Commission considered that the position of the market in pharmaceutical products was not decisive in finding an infringement of the rules of the Treaty on competition.

Consequently the Commission has not infringed an essential procedural requirement by ommitting from the reasons for its decision factors which it rightly or wrongly considered irrelevant to the proceedings.

With regard to territorial protection the decision sets forth clearly and coherently the reasons of fact and law for which the Commission alleged that the applicant together with other undertakings had shared out the markets within the Community.

(2) Cement Convention Case

See below page 378.

L. Administrative file

(1) ACF Chemifarma Case

For facts and references see above, page 109.

*The Court held:*

.....

II - The objection relating to the consultation of the administrative file

The applicant maintains that the Commission infringed the rights of the defence by refusing in the course of the administrative procedure to allow it to consult essential documents on which the contested decision was based.

The defendant replies that it had enabled the applicant to consult the documents which were of importance for the appraisal of the complaints.

The notice of complaints alleges that the applicant together with other producers of quinine had until 1966 adopted a policy of common prices, particularly with regard to sales in Italy, Belgium and Luxembourg.

According to this statement this concerted conduct is clear in particular from the uniformity of the prices maintained by the undertakings for their sales in the said countries.

In support of this statement the notice of complaints (last subparagraph of paragraph 11) refers to the outcome of investigations carried out by the Commission's staff in those countries.

In the course of the administrative procedure the applicant requested the Commission to acquaint it with the facts referred to.

The Commission rejected this request on the ground that it must protect the business secrets of undertakings.

Nevertheless the Commission itself alleged that those undertakings regularly exchanged information on the amounts sold in the States in question.

Furthermore in case of doubt the Commission could have requested the opinion of the other undertakings concerned with regard to the applicant's request for the communication of the documents relating to them.

It does not appear that the Commission consulted the said undertakings in this way.

Nevertheless, throughout the administrative procedure the applicant did not dispute that it had carried out a concerted policy with regard to prices until the end of October 1964.

<u>(2) United Brands Case</u>

For facts and references see above, page 247.

*The Court held:*

.....

Section 1: Complaints relating to denial of due process

The applicant complains of the speed with which the administrative procedure took place, of material errors in the Statement of Objections to which it drew the Commission's attention and which have not been rectified - for example the profits it was alleged to have made in Ireland -, of the brevity or ambiguity of the statement of the reasons on which some of the objections such as that relating to unfair prices were based and takes the view that this conduct on the part of the Commission amounts to a breach of the principle of due process.

Article 11 of Regulation No 99/63/EEC of the Commission of 25 July 1963 states that the latter 'shall have regard...to the time required for preparation of comments', 'The time limits shall be not less than two weeks'.

Following a preliminary investigation lasting about one year the administrative procedure was initiated on 19 March 1975.

UBC had two months (from 11 April 1975 to 12 June 1975) within which to submit its observations and it is UBC which asked for the hearing which took place on 24 June 1975 as provided for in Article 19(2) of Regulation No 17 of the Council (First Regulation implementing Articles 85 & 96 of the Treaty) of 6 February 1962.

It is evident from these dates that the procedure was carried out within normal time periods and cannot be criticised on the ground that it was rushed.

As far as the allegation is concerned that the statement of the reasons upon which the objections were based was inadequate Article 4 of the said Regulation No. 99/63 provides that the Commission in its decisions shall deal only with those objections raised against undertakings in respect of which they have been afforded the opportunity of making known their views.

The Statement of Objections satisfies this requirement since it sets out, summarily but clearly, the principal facts upon which the Commission relies.

In its communication of 19 March 1975 the latter clearly stated the principal facts upon which it based the objections made and indicated to what extent UBS is in a dominant position and has abused it.

It does not therefore seem that during the procedure before the Commission there was any breach of the principle of due process.

As far as the other objections are concerned they relate to the substance of the case.

Consequently this submission is unfounded.

(3) Hoffmann-La Roche Case

Hoffmann-La Roche S.A. v. Commission of the European Communities, Case 85/76, Judgment of 13 February 1979; (1979) ECR 461; (1979) 3 CMLR 211; CCH para. 8227;

For facts see above page 53, 233, 247, 254 and 258.

*The Court held:*

.....

*Second submission: Irregularities in the administrative procedure*

7. On this point the applicant in the first place submitted in its application that the procedure initiated by the Commission its own initiative against it pursuant to Articles 3 and 15 of Regulation No. 17 of the Council was irregular having regard to the fact that documents for internal use by its departments came unlawfully into the possession of the Commission.

However during the written and oral procedure before the Court it stated that it withdrew this submission and itself produced for the Court's file with other documents the documents the use of which by the Commission it had previously regarded as being unlawful.

In these circumstances this submission may be rejected without any further examination since the Court is of the opinion that it need not examine it of its own motion.

8. The applicant submits in the second place that in the disputed decision documents, particulars whereof were not given during the administrative procedure, and other evidence which the Commission refused to let it inspect because of the duty to respect professional secrecy were

taken into account.

Thus the applicant first of all refers to the documents mentioned in Recital 12 to the contested decision, namely four internal circulars issued by Roche, which according to the decision were dated September 1970 (actually 8 September 1972), December 1970, May 1971 (actually mid-August 1971) and August 1971 and also to the minutes of the European Bulk Managers meeting on 12 and 13 October 1971 (actually on 12 and 13 October 1972).

It refers in the second place to the evidence which the Commission obtained from other vitamin manufacturers and with the help of which it calculated the market shares which it claims Roche has, and also to the information requested and obtained from the applicant's customers for the purpose of determining whether or not the contracts, the conclusion whereof is regarded by the Commission as an abuse of a dominant position had as their effect the restriction of competition and of trade between Member States.

9. Observance of the right to be heard is in all the proceedings in which sanctions, in particular fines or penalty payments, may be imposed a fundamental principle of Community law which must be respected even if the proceedings in question are administrative proceedings.

Article 19(1) of Council Regulation No. 17 obliges the Commission, before taking a decision in connection with fines, to give the persons concerned the opportunity of putting forward their point of view with regard to the complaints made against them.

Similarly, Article 4 of Regulation No. 99/63 of the Commission of 25 July 1963 (Official Journal, English Special Edition 1963, p. 47) on the hearing provided for Article 19 of Regulation No. 17 provides that the Commission shall in its decisions deal only with those objections raised against undertakings and associations of undertakings in respect of which they have been afforded the opportunity of making known their views.

10. Although the Court in its judgment of 15 July 1970 in Case 45/69 (Boehringer Mannheim GmbH v Commission of the European Communities (1970) 2 ECR 769) held that these requirements are satisfied as far as concerns the notification of complaints - the first stage of the administrative procedure - if the notification sets forth clearly, albeit succinctly, the essential facts upon which the Commission relies, this ruling is subject to the proviso that 'in the course of the administrative procedure it supplies the details necessary of the defence'.

11. Thus it emerges from the provisions quoted above and also from the general principle to which they give effect that in order to respect the principle of the right to be heard the undertakings concerned must have been afforded the opportunity during the administrative procedure to make known their views on the truth and relevance of the facts and circumstances alleged and on the documents used by the Commission to support its claim that there has been an infringement of Article 86 of the Treaty.

12. The Commission does not deny that, since it took the view that it was bound to observe professional secrecy, it refused to pass on the data that it had obtained from competitors or customers of Roche which

formed the basis, together with other data, of its assessment of the market shares and of the view that the disputed contracts restrict competition.

13. Although Article 20(2) of Regulation No. 17 provides that 'Without prejudice to the provisions of Articles 19 and 21, the Commission and the competent authorities of the Member States, their officials and other servants shall not disclose information acquired by them as a result of the application of this regulation and of the kind covered by professional secrecy', this rule must, as the express reference to Article 19 confirms, be reconciled with the right to be heard.

14. The said Article 20 by providing undertakings from whom information has been obtained with a guarantee that their interests which are closely connected with observance of professional secrecy, are not jeopardised, enables the Commission to collect on the widest possible scale the requisite data for the fulfilment of the task conferred upon it by Articles 85 and 86 of the Treaty without the undertakings being able to prevent it from doing so, but it does not nevertheless allow it to use, to the detriment of the undertakings involved in a proceeding referred to in Regulation No. 17, facts, circumstances or documents which it cannot in its view disclose if such a refusal of disclosure adversely affects that undertaking's opportunity to make known effectively its views on the truth or implications of those circumstances, on those documents or again on the conclusions drawn by the Commission from them.

15. However if such irregularities have in fact been put right during the proceedings before the Court they do not necessarily lead to the annulment of the contested decision in so far as remedying them at a later stage has not affected the right to be heard.

16. The documents to which the applicant has referred are, on the one hand, those mentioned in Recital 12 to the contested decision, that is to say the same documents as those in the case of which it had criticised the manner of their coming into the possession of the Commission, although it later produced them for the Court's file so that both parties could and did make their submissions concerning them.

On the other hand as far as concerns the data on the basis of which the Commission has calculated the market shares and its analysis of the effects of the disputed contracts the parties, during the written procedure at the request of the Court produced, following an exchange of information, an agreed document which shows that the Commission in the case of all the vitamins in question had disclosed the bases of its calculation of the market shares according to their value for 1972, 1973 and 1974 with the result that Roche was in a position to estimate it market shares according to the quantities sold on the basis of the sales attributed to certain competitors in the documents produced by the Commission.

17. Thus the parties have been able to agree on an estimate of the market according to quantity and value - although they have remained in disagreement as to which of the two criteria is determinative - as far as concerns vitamins A, B, and H and also vitamins C and E subject in the case of the latter to an examination of the market to be taken into consideration from the standpoint of the interchangeability for certain uses of these two vitamins with other products, only the market

shares of vitamins $B_2$ and $B_6$ remaining unagreed.

18. Finally the Commission also produced during the written procedure at the request of the Court the minutes of the meeting between Unilever and Roche mentioned in Recital 3 to the contested decision as well as the reports of the inquiries carried out by its officials with some of Roche's customers, who entered into the disputed contracts, or, in the case of those undertakings which wished to remain anonymous, a note summarising the said reports.

19. In these circumstances the submission based on the alleged breach of the principle of the right to be heard cannot be upheld.
.....

## V. INTERIM MEASURES BY THE COMMISSION

### (1) Camera Care Case

Camera Care Ltd v. Commission, Case 792/79 R, Order of the Court of 17 January 1980; (1980) ECR 119; (1980) 1 CMLR 334; CCH para. 8645; Competition Law CM/M/III/82.

*Facts:* Camera Care Limited, a company engaged in the repair, hire and sale of professional photographic equipment, whose registered office is in Belfast, asked the Commission by complaint dated 26 June 1979 and received by the Commission on 5 July to open an investigation under Article 3 of Regulation No. 17 to establish whether Victor Hasselblad A/B, an undertaking manufacturing cameras and photographic equipment, whose registered office is in Göteborg, Sweden, Hasselblad (GB) Limited, whose registered office is in Wembley, England, and Safveans A/B, whose registered office is in Göteborg, were in breach of Articles 85 and 86 of the EEC Treaty.

According to Camera Care Limited the infringements by the companies concerned consisted mainly of:

(a) withholding direct supplies of Hasselblad products from the applicant and preventing other persons from making indirect supplies;

(b) withholding and preventing direct and indirect supplies with the object and/or effect of maintaining a fixed price structure and of preventing or determining price competition at the retail level;

(c) maintaining and applying provisions of supply agreements with certain dealers which restrict or prevent export from, in particular, France and Germany to the United Kingdom.

In its application Camera Care Limited als asked the Commission to make an interim decision requiring Hasselblad A/B and Hasselblad (GB) Limited to bring to an end forthwith the practices complained of and to make supplies of Hasselblad products to the order of the applicant at the prices and upon the terms usually applied.

On 27 August 1979 the Commission informed Camera Care Limited that its complaint of 26 June had been receiving its attention and that it had advised Hasselblad (GB) Limited of its essential points in requesting that company to supply certain supplementary information together with

its comments. The Commission also informed Camera Care that it regretted it could not comply with its proposal to take interim measures because under Community law there was no legal basis for this.
.....

*The Court held:*

Faced with the refusal by the Comission to adopt interim measures the applicant brought an action on 5 November 1979 based on both Article 173 and Article 175 of the Treaty seeking either the setting aside of the Communication referred to above or a declaration by the Court that the Commission was in breach of the Treaty for refraining from meeting the request for the adoption of interim measures.

In an application for the adoption of interim measures lodged on the same day under Article 186 of the Treaty, the applicant asked the Court as a matter of urgency to make an injunction against the Commission ordering it to take an appropriate decision with regard to Hasselblad or, alternatively, to take urgent measures itself.

In its written observations on the subject of the application for interim measures, the Commission expressed doubts upon the admissibility of the main action. At the same time, however, it indicated that it thought interim measures might be justified at that stage. Although it believed it possessed the powers needed to do this, in the absence of any clear indication on this point in Regulation No. 17, it did not wish to take measures on its own initiative and consequently requested the Court to settle this question of principle at the outset.

By order of 26 November 1979 the President of the Court referred the application for interim measures to the Court under the first paragraph of Article 85 of the Rules of Procedure.

By an application of 10 December 1979 the Hasselblad companies applied to be allowed to intervene in the main action and with regard to the application for the adoption of interim measures. The Court allowed the interventions by order of 12 December 1979.

The parties presented oral argument on 9 January 1980.

Definition of the action

Because of the doubt about the legal nature of the communication from the officers of the Commission which is at the root of the case, the applicant has based its action upon both Article 173 and Article 175 of the EEC Treaty. Although the action cannot, for the purposes of the final judgment, be defined as resting upon both these articles, there seems to be no need to resolve the question at this stage.

However the action may in fact be defined, if it were to succeed the Commission would in any event be required under Article 176 of the Treaty to 'take necessary measures to comply with the judgment of the Court of Justice'. The two actions have in fact the same object in that the applicant's purpose is that the Commission should adopt the interim measures sought by the applicant.

Power of the Commission to adopt interim measures

The hesitation shown by the Commission stems from the fact that Regulation No. 17 does not expressly confer upon the Commission, after receiving applications under Article 3 of the Regulation or when proceeding on its own initiative under the same provision, the power to adopt interim measures pending the time when it is in a position to adjudicate upon the substance of the case.

It is recalled that Article 3(1) of the Regulation provides that: "Where the Commission, upon application or upon its own initiative, finds that there is infringement of Article 85 or Article 86 of the Treaty, it may by decision require the undertakings...concerned to bring such an infringement to an end". Paragraph (3) of the same article adds that the Commission, before taking a decision under paragraph (1), may "address to the undertakings...concerned recommendations for termination of the infringement".

It is obvious that in certain circumstances there may be a need to adopt interim protective measures when the practice of certain undertakings in competition matters has the effect of injuring the interests of some Member States, causing damage to other undertakings, or of unacceptably jeopardising the Community's competition policy. In such circumstances it is important to ensure that, whilst enquiries are being carried out no irreparable damage is caused such as could not be remedied by any decision which the Commission might take at the conclusion of the administrative procedure.

Although it is true that, from the point of view of both the efficacy of competition law and the protection of the legitimate interests of the Member States or undertakings concerned, the adoption of protective measures may seem to be necessary in certain circumstances, the provisions of Regulation No. 17 must nevertheless be examined to see whether they can accommodate this legal requirement.

It is as well to observe on this point that Article 3 of the Regulation entitles the Commission to take two types of action in order to bring to an end any infringements that it finds: first, the Commission may take "decisions" which, according to Article 189 of the Treaty, are binding upon those to whom they are addressed and which, according to Articles 15 and 16 of Regulation No. 17, may be accompanied by fines and periodic penalty payments; secondly, before taking a binding decision, the Commission is always entitled under Article 3(3) to address to the undertakings concerned "recommendations for termination of the infringement". The object of this last provision is to enable the Commission to inform the undertakings concerned of its assessment of the situation with regard to Community law in order to persuade them to comply with its point of view without immediately resorting to legal enforcement. It cannot, however, be construed as a limitation upon the practical ways in which the power to take a decision, which is the core of Article 3, may be exercised.

As regards the right to take decisions conferred upon the Commission by Article 3(1), it is essential that it should be exercised in the most efficacious manner best suited to the circumstances of each given situation. To this end the possibility cannot be excluded that the exercise of the right to take decisions conferred upon the Commission should comprise successive stages so that a decision finding that there is an infringement may be preceded by any preliminary measures which may appear necessary at any given moment.

From this point of view the Commission must also be able, within the bounds of its supervisory task conferred upon it in competition matters by the Treaty and Regulation No. 17, to take protective measures to the extent to which they might appear indispensable in order to avoid the exercise of the power to make decisions given by Article 3 from becoming ineffectual or even illusory because of the action of certain undertakings. The powers which the Commission holds under Article 3(1) of Regulation No. 17 therefore include the power to take interim measures which are indispenable for the effective exercise of its functions and, in particular, for ensuring the effectiveness of any decisions requiring undertakings to bring to an end infringements which it has found to exist.

However, the Commission could not take such measures without having regard to the legitimate interests of the undertaking concerned by them. For this reason it is essential that interim measures be taken only in cases proved to be urgent in order to avoid a situation likely to cause serious and irreparable damage to the party seeking their adoption, or which is intolerably for the public interest. A further requirement is that these measures be of a temporary and conservatory nature and restricted to what is required in the given situation. When adopting them the Commission is bound to maintain the essential safeguards guaranteed to the parties concerned by Regulation No. 17, in particular by Article 19. Finally, the decisions must be made in such a form that an action may be brought upon them before the Court of Justice by any party who considers he has been injured.

As the President of the Court has indicated, in the context of the ECSC Treaty, in his interlocutory order of 22 October 1975 in Case 109/75R (National Carbonising Company (1975) ECR 1193), it is in accordance with the key principles of the Community that any interim measures which prove to be necessary should be taken by the Community institution which is given the task of receiving complaints by governments or individuals, of making inquiries and of taking decisions in regard to infringements which are found to exist, whilst the role of the Court of Justice consists in undertaking the legal review of the action taken by the Commission in these matters. In this regard, the rights of those concerned are safeguarded by the fact that if interim measures decided upon by the Commission adversely affect the legitimate interests of any party the person concerned may always obtain the revision of the decision made, by the appropriate judicial course, applying if necessary for emergency measures under Article 185 or Article 186 of the EEC Treaty.

It follows from these considerations that the Commission possesses the powers needed to meet the request of the applicant if it thinks this request is justified in the circumstances. The applicant must therefore be referred back to the Commission so that it may, without prejudice to the rights and interests of the party concerned by the complaint, take a decision upon the request for interim measures upon the conditions set out above.

.....

<u>(2) Ford Interim Case</u>

Ford Werke AG and Ford of Europe v. Commission, Joined Cases 228-229/

82R, Order of the President of the Court. (1982) ECR 3091, Judgment of the Court of 28 February 1984 (not yet published).

*Facts:* By circular of 27 April 1982 Ford Werke AG informed its German distributors that after 1 May 1982 it would no longer accept any orders for right-hand drive vehicles placed with it by those distributors and that the "Visit Europe Plan" was to be maintained only for left-hand drive vehicles. The Commission considered that that development prevented it from granting the application for negative clearance, or for an exemption under Article 85(3) of the EEC Treaty, which had been submitted to it in 1976 by Ford Werke AG when the latter notified the Haupthändlervertrag (main dealer agreement) between it and its German distributors. Within the framework of its examination of that application, it adopted an interim decision on 18 August 1982 requiring Ford Werke AG to resume deliveries of the vehicles referred to in the circular. Ford Werke AG and Ford of Europe Incoporated both brought actions for a declaration that that decision was void and applied for the adoption of an interim measure suspending its operation.
.....

*The President held:*

According to Article 185 of the Treaty, actions brought before the Court of Justice do not have suspensory effect. The Court may, however, as follows from that provision read in conjunction with Article 83(2) of the Rules of Procedure of the Court, if it considers that the circumstances so require, direct that the operation of contested measures be suspended. It may also, pursuant to Article 186 of the Treaty, prescribe any necessary interim measures.

It is clear from the consistent case-law of the Court that measures of this nature cannot be considered unless the factual and legal grounds relied on to obtain them establish a prima facie case for granting them, In addition there must be urgency in the sense that it is necessary for the measures to be issued and to take effect before the decision of the Court on the substance of the case in order to avoid serious and irreversible damage to the party seeking them. Finally they must be provisional in the sense that they do not prejudge the decision on the substance of the case.
.....

As the Court stated in its order of 17 January 1980 in Case 729/79 R Camera Care Limited, the Commission must be able, within the bounds of the supervisory task conferred upon it in competition matters by the Treaty and Regulation No. 17, to take protective measures to the extent to which they might appear indispensable in order to prevent its final decision from becoming ineffective. It is nevertheless necessary for those interim measures to be taken only in cases of proven urgency, in order to prevent the occurrence of a situation likely to cause serious and irreparable damage to the party applying for their adoption or intolerable damage to the public interest. The measures must be of a temporary and conservative nature and must be limited to what is necessary in the given situation.

*The Court held:*
....

17. With regard to the parties' arguments, as set out above, it is

appropriate first to examine whether, in adopting the contested interim measure, the Commission kept within the limits of its powers as established by the provisions of Community law and by the interpretation placed on those provisions by the Court in its order of 17 January 1980.

18. In that order the Court did not examine in detail the form and nature of the interim measures which the Commission may adopt. As the order makes clear, the power to adopt such measures is based on Article 3(1) of Regulation No. 17, which the Commission also mentioned in the references in the preamble to the contested decision.

19. That provision states that "Where the Commission, upon application or upon its own initiative, finds that there is infringement of Article 85 or Article 86 of the Treaty, it may by decision require the undertakings ... concerned to bring such infringement to an end." As the Court stated in the aforementioned order the protective measures which the Commission may adopt as interim measures are those which appear indispensable in order to prevent the exercise of the power to make decisions given by Article 3 from bedoming ineffectual or even illusory because of the action of certain undertakings. It follows that the interim measures must come within the framework of the final decision which may be adopted by virtue of Article 3.

20. In this case the main proceedings relate to the dealer agreement. It is solely in relation to that agreement that the Commission is in a position to make a finding that there is an infringement of Article 85 (1) and the final decision which the Commission may adopt under Article 3 (1) is that which requires Ford AG to bring the operation of that agreement to an end.

21. The contested interim decision does not relate to that agreement but solely to Ford AG's refusal to supply right-hand dirve cars to German dealers and that refusal, according to the Commission, does not infringe either Article 85 or Article 86 of the Treaty. The measure ordered by that decision therefore does not come within the framework of a final decision which mat be adopted. In view of its unequivocal wording and in particular of its express order to Ford AG to refrain from taking any measures having the same effect as the circular, the decision ordering interim measures cannot be interpreted in the manner in which the Commission submitted, in the course of the proceedings before the Court, that it should be interpreted, namely as allowing the company to maintain its refusal to supply on condition that it ceases to operate the dealer agreement.

22. Even on the assumption that the Commission, when adopting in pursuance of Articles 6 and 8 of Regulation No. 17 a decision in application of Article 85 (3) of the Treaty, may regard the refusal to supply as a circumstance which prevents an exemption from being granted in respect of the dealer agreement or may subject the grant or continuation of such an exemption to the requirement that supplies be resumed, it would still have no authority to convert that requirement, by means of a decision ordering interim measures, into a separate, enforceable order which leaves no choice to the undertaking concerned.
....

## VI. DECISIONS OF THE COMMISSION

### A. Negative Clearance

(Consult Regulation No. 17 Article 2)

(1) Decision in the Prym-Beka Agreement

Commission Decision of 8 October 1973 on a proceeding under Article 85 of the Treaty. O.J. No. L 296, 24 October 1973, p. 24; (1973) CMLR p. 250; CCH para. 9609; Competition Law CM/M/I/72.

*Facts:* After examining the contractual relations agreed upon between William Prym-Werke KG and SA Manufacture Belge d'Aiguilles Beka, concerning needles for household sewing machines, the Commission gave an exemption to agreements on a long-term exclusive supply agreement which was part of an undertaking by one of the parties to cease manufacture and transfer it to the other party. Since the undertaking relating to the specialisation was binding on only one of the parties, the agreement did not qualify under the block exemption regulation, although in relation to production it was likely to have certain specialisation effects.

It has previously been pointed out that the instances of incompatibility with Article 85 derive not only from decisions prohibiting agreements but also from cases of negative clearance or authorisation which reveal constraints of competition discontinued or altered at the Commission's initiative to enable Article 85(3) to be applied. In this connection, it should be noted that in this case the parties to the agreement had to abandon the commitment to share customers within the Common Market, as originally envisaged by the agreement. In earlier decisions on specialisation agreements (concerning the rationalisation groups in the German Steel Industry and the agreement among French producers of light-weight paper) the Commission had previously insisted upon the abandonment of provisions intended to organise among the parties the allocation of production quotas, the distribution of profits through an equalisation scheme or the coordination of commercial policies within the Common Market.

The agreement under consideration resulted from the following situation. At the time it was concluded both the undertakings concerned manufactured and sold needles for household sewing machines. Prym needed its own manufacturing facilities to supplement the large range of haberdashery articles of all kinds which it sold. Considering it necessary to rationalise production in view of the world market situation but believing that automated plant would only be fully used if a minimum turnover could be achieved, the two undertakings decided that manufacturing operations should be concentrated in a single factory. Stolberg should stop. The plant and equipment involved would be transferred to Eupen.

To consolidate their collaboration, Prym acquired a 25% interest in Beka and the two parties concluded an agreement for supplies to Prym on a long-term basis and to confirm that each should retain its traditional clientele. In its statement of the matters to which it had taken objection, the Commission informed the parties that it could not grant an exemption while the customers-sharing arrangement remained in force in respect of Community trade. Finally Prym and Beka agreed that this clause should not apply in respect of the EEC market.

The positions of the undertakings concerned and the conditions on the market in question may be described as follows:

Prym manufactures, in addition to semi-finished brass products, chains and the like a whole range of haberdashery goods intended mainly for clothing, such as fastenings of all kinds, buckles and needles. It has several factories, employing about 4,500 persons.

Beka manufactures solely needles for both household and industrial sewing machines. It has one factory, at Eupen, which employs 350 persons. At present 25% of its capital is held by Prym and 75% by the Belgian Bekaert company. which is one of the world's major producers of wire and wire products.

Annual world production of needles is estimated at 1,400 million, valued at approximately 50 million units of account. There are between 25 and 30 manufacturers, mainly in Western Europe, North America and the Far East.

Prior to the agreement's implementation, Beka produced 90 million needles per annum (about 6% of world production) and Prym 40 million (about 3% of world production).

Prym and Beka together account for about 10% of the EEC market. Their main rivals in Europe are the German Schmetz company, which is three times larger than Prym and Beka combined, the needle factories of the American Singer and Torrington Groups and the Dutch Muslof company, but the Japanese and Hong Kong manufacturers have also been exerting very great pressure on the market.

The Commission found that both the committments entered into by Prym (the ban on the manufacture of needles and the exclusive supply obligation) as well as those entered into by Beka (the obligation to meet all Prym's requirements and to grant preferential selling prices) had as their object and effect an appreciable restriction of competition within the Common Market and that they could adversely affect the free flow of trade between Member States so as to prejudice the attainment of a single market.

However, the Commission also took the view that the agreement could be exempted from the ban in Article 85(1) since the rationalisation of production arising from the concentration of manufacturing activity at the Beka factory would result in an improvement in the quality of the needles and a fall in their cost price, to the benefit of consumers. These advantages could not be achieved and maintained unless Prym undertook, as was the case, not only to stop its own production but also and above that to obtain supplies solely from Beka over an extended period. Moreover, in view of the strong competitive pressure from other manufacturers both in the Community and in non-member countries, the agreement did not afford the partners scope for eliminating competition in respect of a substantial part of the products in question. The consent to the parties contained in the Commission decision, is valid until 31 December 1984, but can be extended. It takes account of the fact that the favourable effects of the agreement are associated with a continuing long-term cooperation between the parties.

*The Commission ruled:*

.....

Under Article 2 of Regulation No. 17 the Commission may grant negative clearance if it finds, on the basis of the facts in its possession, that there are no grounds under Article 85(1) of the EEC Treaty for action on its part in respect of the agreement in question.

Even in its amended version of 10 October 1972 the agreement concluded between Prym and Beka has as its object and effect a considerable restriction of competition within the common market in as much as it provides, for an indefinite period, as follows:

1. Prym is forbidden to manufacture needles for domestic sewing machines or cause them to be manufactured on its behalf by third parties;

2. Prym is obliged to buy its total requirements of needles for domestic sewing machines exclusively from Beka;

3. Beka is obliged to deliver to Prym all the quantities of such needles it requires and at preferential (selling) prices.

The agreement may affect trade between Member States because it gives to a Belgian undertaking the exclusive right to supply Prym which is liable to jeopardise freedom of trade between Member States in a manner prejudicial to the attainment of the objectives of a single market.

The circumstances therefore exist in which the prohibition contained in Article 85(1) of the Treaty becomes applicable; and there are thus no grounds for the Commission to grant the negative clearance applied for, even in respect of the amended version of the agreement of 10 October 1972.

*The Commission decided:*

.....

Article 1
The application for negative clearance in respect of their supply agreement of 11 August 1968, which was submitted on 9 April 1970 by the undertakings William Prym-Werke KG of Stolberg and SA manufacture Belge d'Aiguilles Beka of Eupen, is rejected.

Article 2
Pursuant to Article 85(3), Article 85(1) of the Treaty establishing the European Economic Community is declared inapplicable to the agreement referred to in Article 1 in its version modified on 10 October 1972.

Article 3
The declaration in Article 2 takes effect from 10 October 1972; it shall apply until 31 December 1984.

Article 4
This Decision is addressed to the undertakings William Prym-Werke KG, Zweifallestrasse 5/7, Stolberg/Rhineland (germany), and SA manufacture Belge d'Aiguilles Beka, Hütte 77, Eupen (Belgium).

.....

## B. Termination of Infringement

### (1) Consten-Grundig Case

For facts and references see above, page 66.

*The Court held:*

.....The complaint concerning the inclusion in the operative part of the decision of the finding of infringement.

The German Government supports the submission that there was an infringement of an essential procedural requirement on the ground that the finding that an infringement of Article 85 of the EEC Treaty had been committed should have been included solely in the preamble to and not in the operative part of the decision.

That finding constitutes the basis of the obligations of the parties to terminate the infringement. Its effect on the legal situation of the undertakings concerned does not depend on its position in the decision.

This complaint therefore does not disclose any legal interest requiring protection and must consequently be rejected.
.....

(2) Decision in re Continental Can

See above, pages 43, 219, 243 and 263.

(3) Decision in re WEA-Fillipacchi

For facts and references see above, pages 112, 164, 170,

*The Commission held:*

IV Applicability of Article 3(1) of Regulation No. 17

Article 3(1) provides that if the Commission finds that Article 85 of the Treaty is being infringed it can, by means of a decision, oblige the undertakings concerned to put an end to the said infringement.

Insofaras the 18 resellers listed in Article 4 of the present decision have undertaken not to export the records distributed in France by WEA-Fillipacchi Music SA, it suffices for the re-establishment of free competition that they should abolish the export prohibitions and no longer abide them in future.

(4) Decision in re Commercial Solvents

See above, page 46.

(5) Decision in re European Sugar Industry

See above, pages 115 and 222.

(6) Commercial Solvents Case

For facts and references see above, page 14.

*The Court held:*

.....

II The measures ordered and the sanctions imposed by the disputed Decision

The disputed Decision ordered CSC and Istituto under penalty of a fine to supply Zoja within a period of 30 days with 60,000 kg. of nitropropane or 30,000 kg. of aminobutanol and to submit to the Commission within two months proposals for the subsequent supply of Zoja, and imposed on them jointly and severally a fine of 200,000 units of account, i.e. 125,000,000 lire.

In the first place the applicants disagree that the provision of Regulation No. 17/62(3) whereby the Commission, where it finds that there is such an infringement, may require the undertakings concerned to bring such an infringement to an end, enables the Commission to order specific supplies.

In the second place they complain that the Commission has misused the powers intended to prevent competition from being distorted within the Common Market and applied the provisions of Article 86 beyond the territory of the Community by ordering supplies disproportionate to the needs of Zoja for the supply of its customers within the Community and which correspond rather to its activities in the world market.

As to the first submission, according to the wording of Article 3 of Regulation No. 17, where the Commission finds that there is an infringement of Article 86, "it may by decision require the undertakings... concerned to bring such an infringement to an end". This provision must be applied in relation to the infringement which has been established and may include an order to do certain acts or provide certain advantages which have been wrongfully withheld as well as prohibiting the continuation of certain action, practices or situations which are contrary to the Treaty. For this purpose the Commission may if necessary, require the undertakings concerned to submit to it proposals with a view to bringing the situation into conformity with the requirements of the Treaty.

In the present case, having established a refusal to sell incompatible with Article 86, the Commission was entitled to order certain quantities of raw material to be supplied to make good the refusal of supplies as well as to order that proposals to prevent a repetition of the conduct complained of be put forward. In order to ensure that its decision was effective the Commission was entitled to determine the minimum requirements to ensure that the infringement was made good and that Zoja was protected from the consequences of it. In choosing as a guide to the needs of Zoja the quantity of previous supplies the Commission has not exceeded its discretionary power.

Therefore the first submission is unfounded.

As to the second submission, it has been established above that it cannot be inferred from the expression "in so far as it may affect trade between Member States" that only the effects of a possible infringement on trade within the Community must be taken into account when it is a question of defining the infringement and its consequences. Moreover the rather limited measure that the applicants suggested would have resulted in the production and sales outlets of Zoja being controlled by CSC-Istituto in Zoja being in a position where its cost price would have been affected to such an extent that its production of ethambutol would have been in danger of being unmarketable. In these circumstances the Commission could well consider that the maintenance of an effective competitive structure necessitated the measures in question.

Although the disputed Decision and during the course of the present proceedings the Commission has constantly avoided meeting the complaint in the way that the applicants argued it, it has on the other hand ever since the Notice of Objections maintained that since the conduct complained of aimed at eliminating one of the principal competitors within the Common Market, it was above all necessary to prevent such an infringement of Community competition by adequate measures. Both in the disputed Decision and in the written procedure the measures taken were justified by the necessity of preventing the conduct of CSC and Istituto having the effect referred to and eliminating Zoja as one of the principal manufacturers of ethambutol in the Community. This reasoning is at the root of the litigation and cannot therefore be considered as insufficient.

This submission, therefore, also fails.

III The penalty imposed

The disputed Decision imposed jointly and severally on the companies CSC and Istituto a fine of 200,000 units of account, that is to say 125,000,000 lire. Although the seriousness of the infringement justifies a heavy fine, the duration of the infringement should also be taken into account, which in the Decision was calculated as two years or more, but it might have been shorter if the Commission, which had been put on inquiry by the complaint of Zoja on 8 April 1971, that is six months after the first refusal by CSC-Istituto, had intervened more quickly. Moreover the ill effects of the conduct complained of have been limited by reason of the fact that CSC-Istituto have provided the supplies ordered by the Decision.

Having regard in particular to these circumstances it is proper to reduce the fine to 100,000 units of account, namely 62,500,000 lire.

(7) Decision in re Advocaat Zwarte Kip

See above, page 176.

(8) Decision in re United Brands Co

See above, pages 86, 230, 258.

(9) Decision in re Hugin Liptons

For facts and references see above, page 53.

*The Commission decided:*

.....

Art. 1. It is hereby declared that Hugin Kassaregister AB and Hugin Cash Registers Ltd have infringed Article 86 of the Treaty establishing the European Economic Community by refusing to supply spare parts for Hugin cash registers to Liptons Cash Registers and Business Equipment

Ltd from 1 January 1973 and that Hugin Kassaregister AB has also infringed Article 86 of the said Treaty by prohibiting its subsidiaries and distributors within the Common Market from selling such spare parts outside its distribution network.

Art. 2. A fine of fifty thousand (50,000) units of account, that is twenty thousand eight hundred and thirty-three pounds (£ 20,833), is imposed on Hugin Kassaregister AB and Hugin Cash Registers Ltd for which sum the said undertakings shall be jointly and severally liable. This sum is to be paid to 'Lloyds Bank, Overseas Branch, 6 East Cheap, London EC4' to the account of the Commission of the European Communities, account No 01-08-634, within three months of the date of the notification of this Decision to the undertakings to which it is addressed.

Art. 3. Hugin Kassaregister AB and Hugin Cash Registers Ltd. shall bring to an end without delay the infringements referred to in Article 1 hereof, unless they have already done so of their own accord. Hugin Cash Registers Limited shall submit for the approval of the Commission, within one month of the notification of this Decision, proposals relating to the resumption of supplies of spare parts for Hugin cash registers to Liptons Cash Registers and Business Equipment Ltd.

Art. 4. In respect of the obligation set out in Article 3 hereof, a periodic penalty payment of 1,000 units of account per day shall be payable by Hugin Cash Registers Ltd in respect of each day from the date stated in the second sentence thereof.

Art. 5. This Decision shall be enforceable in accordance with the provisions of Article 192 of the Treaty establishing the European Economic Community.

Art. 6. This Decision is addressed to 'Hugin Kassaregister AB, Hammarby Fabriksväg, 19-21, Box 4180, 1062 Stockholm, Sweden, and to 'Hugin Cash Registers Ltd, Hugin House, 18-30 Clerkenwell Road, UK - London EC1M 5NN'.

(10) Decision in re Distillers

Decision of the Commission of 20 December 1977, in a proceeding relating to Article 85 of the Treaty, Distillers Company Limited; O.J. No. L50 of 22 February 1978; Competition Law CM/M/I/122.

*Facts:* The Commission took a decision requiring the group companies of the Distillers Company Ltd to put an end to the price differentiation which hindered its cutomers in the United Kingdom from exporting Scotch whisky, gin, vodka and Pimm's. DCL's price terms, which had been the subject of complaints by United Kingdom dealers in spirits, and the bans on exports to other EEC countries previously contained in DCL's Conditions of Sale, amount to infringements of Article 85 of the EEC Treaty.

The DCL Group is the most important producer and distributor of spirits in the United Kingdom and of Scotch whisky in the Community. During the last four years, its share in the production and sale of Scotch whisky in the United Kingdom has been between 40 and 50% and its share in sales of gin in the region of 70%.

The DCL group has thirty-eight main subsidiary companies which deal in spirits (chiefly Scotch whisky, gin, vodka and Pimm's). They organise distribution through about a thousand wholesalers in the UK and through sole distrbutors, usually handling only one brand, in the other Community countries.

On behalf of these subsidiaries DCL notified the Commission of its Conditions of Sale to British customers. Bans on exports to other EEC countries which had been contained in these Conditions of Sale were withdrawn by DCL in June 1975 after the Commission intervened.

But DCL simultaneously put into effect price terms according to which allowances and rebates usually granted to United Kingdom customers were not to be extended to them if they exported the spirits to other EEC countries. Accordingly, a United Kingdom dealer wishing to export Scotch whisky has to pay a price which is approximately double that which applies to his purchases for resale in the United Kingdom.

These practices of differential pricing amount to an indirect export ban which is as detrimental to the establishment of a common market as the direct prohibitions previously contained in the Conditions of Sale and certainly as effective in restricting parallel exports. This was evidenced by complaints which were officially submitted to the Commission by a number of United Kingdom dealers.

On the other hand, practices of this nature also preclude price levels which are favourable to British customers by virtue of brisk competitive conditions in the United Kingdom, from affecting market conditions in other EEC countries and thus from benefiting consumers in those countries also.

The Commission did not accept the reasoning that, because of the higher distribution costs borne by DCL's sole distributors in other common market countries, the United Kingdom market had to be isolated in this way to protect such sole distributors from competition from other dealers.

*The Commission decided:*

.....

Art. 1. The prohibition to export from the United Kingdom to other EEC countries and the prohibition to resell in bond contained in the seller's conditions of sale, which have been notified to the Commission on 30 June 1973, and which are part of the contracts for the sale of spirits entered into by 38 subsidiary companies of the Distillers Company Limited with their trade customers established in the United Kingdom, constituted an infringement of Article 85(1) of the Treaty establishing the European Economic Community, from 1 January 1973 to or to about 24 June 1975.

Art. 2. The application for a declaration under Article 85(3) that Article 85(1) is inapplicable is refused in respect of the provisions and the period referred to in Article 1 hereof.

Art. 3. The price terms, which are part of the contracts referred to in Article 1 hereof and which are set out in Appendix II of The Distillers Company Limited circular letters of 24 June 1975 and 23 February 1977, constitute an infringement of Article 85(1) of the Treaty establishing the European Economic Community and an application of Article 85(3) is not justified.

Art. 4. The Distillers Company Limited to which this Decision is addressed shall ensure that the infringement referred to in Article 3 hereof is brought to an end without delay. In particular The Distillers Company Limited and its subsidiary companies shall refrain from all further action by means of their price terms calculated to restrict the exportation from the United Kingdom into other EEC countries of their spirits bought by trade customers established in the United Kingdom.

Art. 5. This Decision is addressed to the Distillers Company Limited, 21 St James' Square, London, United Kingdom, which shall notify it to its subsidiary companies listed in Annex 1 hereto (Annex ommitted).

C. Exemptions

(Consult Chapter Three Part III on Article 85(3))

VII. SANCTIONS AND PENALTIES

A. Fines

(1) B.A.S.F. Case

B.A.S.F. v. Commission, case 49/69, judgment of 14 July 1972, (1972) ECR 713; Competition Law CM/M/3/28. For facts see page 53.

*The Court held:*

.....

On the fine

The applicant additionally contends that the objective pursued by the Commission could have been achieved under Article 3 of Regulation No. 17 without the imposition of fines. The fines provided in this Regulation were not intended as a punishment or to expiate activities in the past, but to prevent a repetition thereof. Moreover, the judgment in dispute did not adequately substantiate the computation of the fine and in particular did not adequately investigate the actual gravity of the actions complained against.

However, Article 15 of Regulation No. 17 does not limit the imposition of fines to cases concerning the repetition of infringements which have aready been established and declared prohibited by the Commission under Article 3. The interpretation of Article 15 in such a limited sense would considerably reduce the deterrent value of the fines. This cannot, therefore, be accepted as a correct interpretation. In view of the number and the magnitude of the activities in respect of which the claimant participated in the unlawful conduct, as well as in respect of the consequences on the realisation of the common market in dyes, the amount of the fine is commensurate with the gravity of the offence against the Community's rules of competition.

Therefore the applicant/s contention is without foundation.

.....

(2) Bayer Case

For facts and references see above, page 317.

*The Court held:*

.....

On the fine

The applicant objects that the decision appealed against did not take into account the fine imposed upon it by the Bundeskartellamt (German Federal Cartel Office) by its decision of 28 November 1967.

As the Bundeskartellamt's decision has been cancelled, the issue concerning legal protection on which this objection is based does not apply, therefore, the justification of the objection need not be further investigated.

In view of the number and the magnitude of the activities in which the claimant participated in the unlawful conduct, as well as in respect of the consequences on the realisation of the common market in dyes, the amount of the fine is commensurate with the gravity of the offence against the Community's rules of competition.

(3) Decision in re WEA-Filipacchi

For facts and references see above, page 112.

*The Commission held:*

.....

V - Applicability of Article 15(2) of Regulation No. 17

Article 15(2)(a) of Regulation No. 17 provides that the Commission may by means of a decision impose on undertakings fines of from 1,000 to 1,000,000 units of account, it being possible to raise the latter figure to ten percent of the turnover of the preceeding business year of each of the undertakings having taken part in the infringement, where such undertakings, wilfully or through negligence, have infringed the provisions of Article 85(1) of the Treaty instituting the EEC. In determining the amount of the fine, the gravity and the duration of the infringement shall be taken into account.

1. It was deliberately that WEA-Filipacchi Music SA infringed Article 85 (1). According to the findings of the Commission, at least three French resellers drew the attention of that undertaking to the fact that the export prohibition constituted a violation of Community law. The undertaking nonetheless in a circular of 24 February 1972 warned all the resellers who had refused to sign the agreement following the first circular of 7 February 1972.

2. The export prohibitions constitute a grave infringement of Article 85 of the Treaty instituting the EEC for they prevent the attainment of a single market. This fact is well-known since the Commission's decision in The Agreement of Grundig Verkaufs-GmbH of 23 September 1964 and since the Judgment of the Court of Justice of 13 July 1966 in the Consten-Grundig case.

3. Imposing the fine, account should be taken of the following factors:

(a) Little time elapsed between the beginning of the violation by the dispatch of the circular of 7 February 1972, and the finding that the violation existed, on 28 June 1972, following an inspection made under Article 14(1) and (2) of Regulation No. 17. The termination of the violation in application of the present decision does not, therefore, follow from the free determination of WEA-Filipacchi Music SA but from the intervention by the Commission.

(b) According to the findings of the Commission WEA-Filipacchi Music SA has inflicted no economic sanction on the undertakings which had refused to sign the circular of 7 February 1972. However, if that undertaking has not imposed such sanctions, that is because the French re-sellers had brought to its attention as from February 1972 that the procedure constituted a violation of Community law and that an economic sanction imposed on one of those traders would very probably have led them to file a complaint against WEA-Filipacchi Music SA under Article 3 of Regulation No. 17.

4. For these reasons, the Commission considers that it should in the present case impose on WEA-Filipacchi Music SA a fine of 60,000 units of account.

(4) Decision in re European Sugar Industry

For facts and references see above, page 222.

*The Commission ruled:*

IV. 1. Where the Commission finds that there is infringement of Article 85 or Article 86 it may, under Article 3(1) of Regulation No. 17, by decision require the undertakings concerned to bring such infringements to an end. Taking into account the above considerations, the Commission is in this case in a position to establish (see Article 1 of this decision) infringements of Article 85 and Article 86, and in accordance with Article 3 of the abovementioned Regulation it requires the undertakings concerned to bring such infringements to an end.

2. According to Article 15(2)(a) of Regulation No. 17 the Commission may by decision impose on undertakings or associations of undertakings fines from 1,000 to 1,000,000 units of account or a sum in excess therof but not exceeding 10% of the turnover in the preceeding business year of each of the business undertakings participating in the infringement where, either intentionally or negligently they infringe Article 85(1) or Article 86 of the Treaty.

The parties concerned have, deliberately or, at least negligently, committed infringements consisting of the concerted practice described above, because they knew, or in any case could have known, the restrictive effects of these practices on competition. The measures which the various parties concerned took as regards their agents, certain buyers, or the tenders for refunds for exports to third countries (cf. II-E+F) should be considered, in order to determine the amount of the fines, in conjunction with the concerted practices in which they engaged (cf. II-A to D).

In fixing the amount of the fines, regard is to be had, in accordance with Article 15(2) both to the granting and to the duration of the infringements.

(a) In judging the gravity of the infringements, the following general observations should be made:

On the one hand, account should be taken of the fact that it is a matter of a product of particular importance to the consumer and that the measures taken by those concerned are obviously contrary to the objective of integration of the markets envisaged in the Treaty. In this connection it should not be forgotten that the various practices are directed towards the same goal although the methods of implementing them vary according to the special features of the market concerned and the sugar supply situation. The effect of every such practice is to reduce to the minimum the possibilities of importing sugar freely without the control of the national producers.

On the other hand, it must be borne in mind that the production of, and trade in, sugar were regulated up to 30 June 1968 by national market organisations, which even provided for sales territories for marketing sugar. This explains a tendency for old practices to become a habit and a slowness to adapt and take advantage of the opportunities that the Community organisation of the sugar market has opened up for free intra-Community trade. However, the special characteristics of the Community sugar market, the organisation of which includes certain restrictions, though without thereby eliminating opportunities for competition, must be taken into consideration.

As regards the duration of the infringements, it must be stated that in general they covered a period of several years.

(b) In assessing the amount of fines to be imposed on the various undertakings, account must be taken of the nature and duration of the infringements in which they participated, the extent of their participation, their situation on the market and this position in relation to their clients.

RT participated both in the concerted practice relating to exports to Italy and on the concentration on sales policy with regard to the SU, CSM and Pfeifer & Langen, as well as in the tendering procedure for export refunds. It was able to exert influence on the Belgium and Luxembourg markets over its principal clients who were the first in line for possible exports.

Sucre & Denrées took part in the concentration of the tendering procedure for export refunds, as well as in the concerted practice relating to deliveries to Italy, and played a decisive part in organising those deliveries, because it coordinated all the supply and negotiated with Eridania the conditions on which the deliveries were made.

Say played an important part within the framework of the group of French and Belgian producers as regards the exports to Italy and also participated in the concentration on tendering procedures for export refunds, without however having taken part in the agreements concerning the other Community markets.

Béghin is not only the most important producer in the group of French and Belgian producers exporting to Italy and not only participated in the concentration of tendering procedures for export refunds, but has made large scale direct sales to its German competitors (SZ, AG and Franken).

Générale Sucrière took part in the concertation on deliveries to Italy and in the offers within the tendering procedure for export refunds. In 1971/72 it took over control of the Lebaudy-Sommier undertakings which also took part in the group of French and Belgian producers exporting to Italy.

Eridania was the undertaking around which the group of Italian importers organised itself in order to control sales in Italy of sugar produced in the other Member States of the EEC. It was this undertaking which sought and worked out the delivery agreements with suppliers in France and Belgium and South Germany. By the concerted organisation of those deliveries Eridania has been able to maintain, and even strengthen its position on the Italian market.

The Societa Italiana per l'Industria degli Zuccheri, of which the Gruppo Pedano has recently taken control, has always participated in the activity of the group of Italian importers and has often profited from the result obtained in the tendering procedures, thanks to tenders submitted on the basis of the understanding with the suppliers' group.

The Cavarzere-Produzioni Industriala, which together with the Societa Generale di Zuccherifici which recently absorbed le Zucherificio e Raffineria di Pontelongo forms one single group (Gruppo Padano), has also always taken part in the activities of the group of Italian importers and benefited from the results obtained by the group in the tendering procedures for importing sugar into Italy.

The Roman Zucchero and the Zuccherificio del Volano have always been connected, especially as regards marketing policy, and they have recently come under the control of AIE. These undertakings have always been in agreement with the activity of the importers' group, and AIE as well as the Zuccherificio del Volano have also profited from the results obtained in the tendering procedures although to a lesser extent than the abovementioned undertakings (the Roman Zucchero has only occasionally taken part in the tendering procedures and for marginal quantities).

SADAM is in the same position as AIE or the Zuccherificio del Volano as regards its participation in the tendering procedure of the Cassa Conguaglio Zucchero.

SU is the most important Dutch producer, and as such is concerned and takes part to a greater extent in the control of imports to the Netherlands in cooperation with the principal potential suppliers, RT and Pfeifer-Langen.

The same applies essentially to CSM. However, a smaller fine should be imposed on it than on SU, because its share of the market is smaller and it has exerted less influence on the national market.

Pfeifer and Langen, by its production and its influence within the SZV, is the most important undertaking in the Western area of Germany. It has played a decisive part in ensuring that a substantial part of the sugar imports into its sales territory since the marketing year 1968/69 would be placed under its control, thanks to the cooperation with the RT, either by buying from its foreign competitors a large share of its unsatisfied requirements, or by concertation with RT whereby RT refrains from making any competing offers in its sales territory apart from the deliveries from producer to producer. Furthermore, Pfeifer and

Langen has taken part during the last two marketing years in the concerted practice between producers relating to direct deliveries of sugar to Dutch producers.

SZ AG is one of the most important producers in the Community and exerts a dominant influence in the SVZ. It only participated in the suppliers group exporting to Italy during one marketing year (1969/70), but it subsequently continued in agreement with the Italian producers to export sugar to Italy, principally by means of deliveries from producer to producer. On the other hand, it has bought increasing quantities of sugar from Sucre-Union and Béghin, and in this way has considerably weakened the competition which might have resulted from the free sale of these quantities of sugar in southern Germany.

The activity of SZV must also be judged in the context described above. It has been made responsibke for marketing sugar of the SZ AG and of its other members in the southern part of Germany.

There is no need to determine a fine for Sucre-Union. Although this undertaking did participate in the Belgian and French suppliers' group exporting to Italy, in the agreement on direct deliveries to German funds for exports to third countries, it has nevertheless been the only one always to play the part of an outsider as far as this was possible, and also to make, in addition to direct sales to foreign competitors, quite large sales to dealers and processing undertakings in the market of destination. The same applies to the undertaking Lebaudy-SUC, which has only played a limited part because of its modest position on the market and its economic dependence on the Générale Sucrière, and has carried out to a fairly large extent intra-Community deliveries. The participation of the Italian undertakings Romana Zucchero, Société Générale de Sucreries (ex-Pontelongo) and Zuccherificio di Sermide in the practices of the group of importers and suppliers on the Italian market has been only occasional and quantitatively very limited, and there is consequently no reason to impose fines on them.

The imposition of a fine on Franken does not seem justified either, since the role of this undertaking in the southern German sales area was not important and it only followed the example of SZ as regards direct sales to foreign competitors. Likewise there is no need to impose a fine on WZV. It appears sufficient to require the said undertakings to bring the infringements to an end without imposing other sanctions.

Taking into account all the factors mentioned above the Commission considers it appropriate to fix the fines provided for in Article 3 of this Decision.

3. This Decision is enforceable, in accordance with Article 192 of the EEC Treaty.

(5) Sucrière Case

S.A. Générale Sucrière and others v. Commission of the European Communities

Joined Cases 41, 43 and 44/73 - interpretation, Judgment of 9 March 1977; (1977) ECR 445; Competition Law CM/M/III/64.

For facts see judgment below.

*The Court held:*

.....

1. Decision of 2 January 1974 (OJ No L 140, p. 17 et seq.) the Commission

- found that the plaintiff and defendant undertakings had infringed Articles 85 and 86 of the EEC Treaty;

- imposed fines on all these undertakings and in particular:

- on Société anonyme Générale Sucrière a fine of 400,000 u.a....that is FF 2,221,676;

- on Société des Raffineries et Sucreries Say 'a fine of 500,000 u.a. ...that is FF 2,777,095;

- on Société F. Béghin 'a fine of 700,000 u.a....that is FF 3,887,933.

The Say and Béghin companies later merged and are now the Béghin-Say company.

The said undertakings instituted proceedings against the Commission for annulment of this decision (Joined Cases 40 to 48, 50, 54 to 56, 111, 113 and 114/73); in some of these cases the Commission was supported by Unione Nazionale Consumatori which intervened at that time in those cases and is now one of the defendants in the present case. The Court's decision in these proceedings is contained in its judgment of 16 December 1975 (1975) ECR 1663).

Paragraph 3(a) of the operative part of this judgment annuls the fines imposed on the Italian undertakings and Süddeutsche Zucker AG. Paragraph 3(b) thereof:

- 'reduces the fines imposed...on the other applicants:

.....

- in the case of Say (Case 43/73) to 80,000 u.a. (FF 444,335.20);

- in the case of Béghin (Case 44/73) to 100,000 u.a. (FF 555,419);

.....

2. On 6 February 1976 Générale Sucrière paid the Commission Lit 50,000, 000 in respect of the fine imposed upon it. On 13 February 1976 Béghin-Say paid the Commission Lit 50,000,000 and 62,500,000 being the fines imposed on the former companies Say and Béghin respectively.

The Commission informed the said companies that these payments were not accepted in full discharge. It does not object to the undertakings concerned paying their debts in the currency of any of the Member States; however the amount of the debt is determined by the sum in national currency mentioned in the judgment. If therefore the companies wished to pay in lire then they should have paid sums corresponding, at the rate of exchange applicable on the day of payment, to FF 444,335.20 in the case of Générale Sucrière, and FF 999,754.20 (444 335.20 + 555 419) in the case of Béghin-Say, In these circumstances Générale Sucrière and Béghin-Say still owe FF 144 510.20 and FF 153 210.20 respectively or the actual equivalent value of these sums in the currency of another Member State.

The companies have challenged this view. In their opinion the amount of the debt is determined by the sums fixed by the Court in units of account, as the figures in national currency in the judgment were merely intended to be an indication of the amount. The combined effect of Articles 10 and 27 of Financial Regulation of the Council of 25 April 1973 'applicable to the general budget of the European Communities' (OJ L 116, p. 1) is, on the one hand, that the value of a unit of account shall be 0.88867088 grammes of fine gold and, on the other hand, that a unit of account shall be converted into the respective national currencies on the basis of the relationship between the weight of fine gold contained in a unit of account and the weight of fine gold corresponding to parity in respect of each of those currencies as declared to the International Monetary Fund (IMF). One unit of account so calculated is equivalent to Lit 625; the companies have therefore fully discharged their debts.

Since this exchange of views between the companies and the Commission did not culminate in any agreement on the abovementioned issue, on 30 September 1976 Générale Sucrière and Béghin-Say made the present application.

3. Pursuant to Article 102(2) of the Rules of Procedure of the Court all the parties affected by the disputed judgment were given an opportunity to submit their observations in writing. Only Centrale Suiker Maatschappij, Raffinerie Tirlemontoise, Sucres et Denrées, Süddeutsche Zucker AG, Südzucker-Verkauf GmbH, Pfeifer & Langen and the Commission have submitted observations.

On hearing the report of the Judge-Rapporteur and the views of the Advocate-General, the Court decided to open the oral procedure without holding any preparatory enquiry.

Decision

1. The Générale Sucrière and Béghin-Say companies - the latter was formed as a result of the merger of the former companies Say and Béghin - pursuant to Article 40 of the Protocol on the Statute of the Court of Justice of the European Economic Community and Article 102 of the Rules of Procedure have lodged applications for interpretation, in so far as they are affected, of paragraph 3(b) of the operative part of the judgment of the Court of 16 December 1975 given in Joined Cases 40/73 etc. (Suiker Unie and others v. Commission of the European Communities (1975) ECR 1663) to which the Générale Sucrière, Say and Béghin companies were parties.

2. In this judgment the Court annulled or varied in part the Commission Decision of 2 January 1973 (OJ L 140, p. 17 et seq.) which, inter alia, imposed on the said companies and several other undertakings under Article 15 of Regulation No. 17 of the Council fines expressed in units of account and in national currency for infringing Articles 85 and 86 of the EEC Treaty.

3. More particularly the court held that these fines should be fixed in the case of Générale Sucrière at '80.000 u.a. (FF 444 335.20), in

the case of Say at 80.000 u.a. (FF 444 335.20) and in the case of Bẽghin at 100.000 u.a. (FF 55 419).

4. For the purpose of establishing parity between each sum expressed in units of account (hereinafter referred to as 'u.a.') and the corresponding sum in national currency the Court - as the Commission did in its decision - took into account Article 18 of Regulation No. 17 according to which for the purpose of applying Article 15 the u.a. shall be that adopted in drawing up the budget of the Community.

Sucrière v. Commission

5. Thus the Court applied the provisions both of Articles 10(1) and 27 of the Council's Financial Regulation of 25 April 1973 applicable to the general budget of the European Communities (OJ L 116, p. 1) according to which, on the one hand, the value of the u.a. shall be 0.88 867 088 grammes of fine gold and, on the other hand, the financial contributions from Member States shall be expressed in u.a. and shall be converted into the respective national currencies on the basis of the relationship existing between the weight of fine gold corresponding to parity in respect of each of those currencies as declared to the International Monetary Fund.

6. According to the applicants the amount of their debts is to be determined by the sum expressed by the Court in u.a., the sum in national currency only being relevant as an indication of the amount, so that they were entitled to pay in the national currency of any Member State whatsoever, and consequently in Italian lire by applying the beforementioned method for the purpose of converting the u.a. into Italian lire.

7. Although the Commission does not object to the applicants paying their debts in a national currency of the Community other than French francs, it is nevertheless of the opinion that the amount of the debts is determined by the sums fixed by the Court in this currency and that concequently, if the applicants wish to pay in another national currency, the conversion must be carried out at the exchange rate on the free foreign exchange market applicable on the date of payment.

8. The essence of both the applicants' and the Commission's claim is that the Court should interpret its judgment in accordance with the argument put forward by each of them.

9. 1. As provided by Article 15(2) of Regulation No. 17 the Commission may...impose...fines of from 1,000 to 1,000,000 u.a. or a sum in excess thereof but not exceeding 10% of the turnover in the preceding business year of each of the undertakings participating in the infringement...

10. This provision prevents the Commission and, should the occasion arise, the Court, from fixing fines which do not fall within the limits so laid down.

11. To the extent to which this provision, for the purpose of defining these limits takes the u.a. into consideration the Commission and the Court, in order to convert the u.a. into national currency, have to adopt the method found in Article 18 of Regulation No. 17 and in the provisions to which it refers.

12. Nevertheless there is nothing in the wording of Article 15 of the regulation which justifies the conclusion that the Commission and the Court are bound to express the amount of a fine in u.a. with reference to a sum expressed in u.a.

13. A first objection to this conclusion is that for the purpose of fixing the upper limit of fines Article 15 refers not only to a sum expressed in u.a. but also to a sum to be calculated by reference to the turnover of the undertaking concerned, which can only be expressed in a national currency.

14. The said conclusion in the second place fails to appreciate the inference which must be drawn from the fact that, under the provisions of Articles 187 and 192 of the EEC Treaty when read together, the decisions of the Commission and of the Court imposing a pecuniary obligation on persons other than States shall be enforceable, and any enforcement which may be necessary shall be governed by the rules of civil procedure in force in the State in the territory of which it is carried out.

15. Thus, since the u.a. is not a currency in which payment is made, the Commission and the Court are of necessity bound to fix the amount of the fine in national currency.

16. These considerations are not invalidated by the fact that the choice of the appropriate national currency might create difficulties for undertakings whose business and financial operations are spread over several Member States or for undertakings established in third countries.

17. In such circumstances the judgment must be understood as meaning that the amount of the respective debts of the applicants is determined by the sums expressed in French francs, since the sum expressed in u.a. have only been mentioned to make it possible to check whether the prescribed limits within which the fines must fall have in fact been observed.

18. The order in which the judgment has in each case mentioned the two sums and the way in which it has placed them side by side are not conclusive.

19. 2. Consequently the Commission could and can require the applicants to pay their debts in French francs.

20. Nevertheless no legal provision prevents the Commission from accepting payments in another national currency of the Community.

21. As far as the rate to be applied in this case is concerned for the purpose of converting one of these currencies into another the applicants cannot rely on the fact that Article 18 of Regulation No. 17 refers to the provisions applicable to the budget of the Community.

22. Since it is a fact that the parties of the various national currencies adopted by these provisions no longer in most cases reflect the actual position in the market, it cannot be assumed that they apply by analogy to circumstances which, as in this case, are not explicitly covered by any legal provision.

23. Although the Commission is entitled to accept payments in a national currency of the Community other than that in which the debt has been determined, the fact remains that it must see to it that the actual

value of the payments made in another currency corresponds to that of the sum fixed in national currency in the Court's judgment.

24. Therefore the conversion of the two national currencies in question must be effected at the exchange rate on the free foreign exchange market applicable on the day of payment.

25. The applicants object to this solution on the ground that it would lead to discrimination in favour of undertakings established in countries which have so-called soft currencies.

26. This reasoning is based on the supposition, which has just been stated is mistaken, that the Commission and the Court have to fix the fine in u.a.

27. 3. The applicants have only requested that paragraph 3(b) of the operative part of the disputed judgment should be interpreted in so far as it affects them.

28. However as provided for in Article 102(1) of the Rules of Procedure an application for interpretation 'must be made against all the parties to the case in which judgment was given'.

29. This means that an interpreting judgment is binding not only on the applicants but also on any other party, in so far as that party is affected by the passage in the judgment which the Court is asked to interpret or by a passage which is exactly similar thereto.

30. Since paragraph 3(b) of the operative part of the judgment, which has to be interpreted uses, as far as concerns the former applicants Suiker-Unie, Centrale Suiker Maatschappij, Raffinerie Tirlemontoise, Sucres et Denrées, Südzucker-Verkauf GmbH and Pfeifer en Langen, wording similar to that which is the subject-matter of these applications - in that it mentions the amount of the fine first of all in u.a. and then, in brackets, in the national currency of the undertaking in question, accordingly in Netherlands guilders, Belgian francs, French francs or Deutschmarks as the case may be - the Court's interpretation of this specific paragraph of the operative part of the judgment under consideration is also binding on the other undertakings.

Costs

31. Under Article 69(2) of the Rules of Procedure the unsuccessful party shall be ordered to pay the costs and where there are several unsuccessful parties the Court shall decide how the costs are to be shared.

32. In this case the Générale Sucrière and Béghin-Say companies as well as the other companies which have submitted observations in support of the applicants' conclusions - namely Centrale Suiker Maatschappij, Raffinerie Tirlemontoise, Sucres et Denrées, Süddeutsche Sucker AG, Südzucker-Verkauf GmbH and Pfeifer & Langen - have failed in their pleas.

33. It is therefore appropriate to order that each of those companies shall bear its own costs and one-eighth of the Commission's costs.

On those grounds,

THE COURT

hereby rules:

1. Paragraph 3(b) of the operative part of the judgment of the Court of 16 December 1975 given in joined cases 40/73 etc (Suiker Unie and Others v. Commission (1975) ECR 2026) is to be interpreted as meaning that:

a. the amount of the debts arising out of the fines imposed respectively on each of the undertakings concerned under the said paragraph 3(b) is to be determined by the sum expressed in the national currency of each undertaking; therefore in the case of the applicants, this is the sum expressed in French francs.

b. although the Commission is under no obligation to do so, it is nevertheless entitled to accept payment by each of the said undertakings in a national currency of the Community other than the one determined in accordance with subparagraph (a) above and in these circumstances the conversion of one currency into the other must be effected at the exchange rate on the free exchange market, applicable at the date of payment.

2. Each of the Générale Sucrière, Béghin-Say, Centrale Suiker Maatschappij, Raffinerie Tirlemontoise, Sucres et Denrées, Südzucker-Verkauf GmbH and Pfeifer & Langen companies shall bear its own costs and one eighth of the Commission's costs.

<u>(6) Decision in re Miller International Schallplatten</u>

Commission Decision of 1 December 1976 relating to a proceeding under Article 85 of the Treaty, O.J. No. L 357, 29 December 1967, p. 40; Competition Law CM/M/I/107.

*Facts:* Miller, a subsidiary of the American Corporation MCA Records Inc. itself conrolled by MCA Inc. Universal City, manufactures records, tapes and cassettes which it distributes under the Europa and Sonic labels.

The terms of sales for the goods applying to German and other buyers and the exclusive dealing agreement with the French sole distributor contained express export prohibitions in respect of the relevant goods.

Miller was seeking thereby to protect exclusive importers or licencees in other countries, notably in the Community.

*The Commission ruled:*

.....

20. Under Article 15(2)(a) of Regulation No. 17, the Commission may by decision impose on undertakings fines of from 1,000 to 1,000,000 units of account, or a sum in excess thereof but not exceeding 10% of the turnover in the preceding business year of each of the undertakings participating in the infringement where, either intentionally or negligently, they infringe Article 85(1) of the Treaty. In fixing the amount of the fine, regard must be had both to the gravity and to the duration of the infringement.

21. Miller has intentionally infringed Article 85(1). It knew and intended that its prohibition on export would prevent its customers from competing in the goods in question in other Community countries. Miller was also aware that export prohibitions were contrary to Community law, or at least chose to ignore any doubt on this question. So much is evi-

dent from the reference to EEC Regulation in the formulation of the export prohibition, which however never came into force, in the agreement with the Dutch sole distributor and from a statement by the manager of the company, made in the course of the hearing, that he knew that such a prohibition was not permitted. Furthermore, it has been well known since the Decision of the Commission of 23 September 1964 in the Grundig/Consten Case and the judgment of the Court of Justice of 13 July 1966 in Case Nos. 56 and 58/64, Grundig/Consten, that prohibitions on export constitute a serious infringement of Article 85 of the EEC Treaty. Furthermore, in its Decision of 22 December 1972 in the WEA-Filipacchi Music SA case, the Commission found that export prohibitions on records produced by that undertaking were infringements of Article 85(1) of the EEC Treaty, and it fined the undertaking for having imposed the same.

22. In fixing the amount of the fine the gravity and duration of the infringement as well as the position of the undertaking should be taken into account.

a. Export prohibitions constitute a serious infringement of Article 85 of the EEC Treaty, since they prevent the creation of a single market.

The export prohibitions imposed by Miller International Schallplatten GmbH affected large numbers of retailers in the common market, Miller was, however, aware of instances of exports being made to other Member States and did not apply sanctions.

b. Miller imposed the export bans under its terms and conditions of sale in about 1970 and in its exclusive dealing agreements of 11 June 1971 with its French distributor. It enforced them until May 1975. The infringements thus continued over a considerable length of time.

c. Miller is a medium-sized firm which, although belonging to the American MCA group does not itself have a very high turnover.

23. In the light of these considerations the Commission considers that Miller should be fined 70,000 units of account.

(7) Miller International Schallplatten Case
Miller International Schallplatten v. Commission, Case 19/77, Judgment of 1 February 1978, (1978) ECR p. 1629. Competition Law CM/M/III/72.

For facts see above, page 362.

*The Court held:*

.....

17. The applicant had requested in the alternative that the fine of 70,000 units of account should be annulled or reduced.

It has maintained that it did not intentionally commit the infringements of which it is accused and furthermore that those infringements were not serious.

It claims that in adopting the clauses prohibiting exports it did not intentionally infringe the prohibitions contained in Article 85 (1) of the Treaty.

This lack of awareness is said to be demonstrated by the opinion of a legal advisor consulted by the applicant concerning the drafting of its terms and conditions of sale, which opinion, produced as an annex to its reply, does not mention the fact that a clause prohibiting exports might be incompatible with Community law.

18. As is clear from the foregoing as a whole, the clauses in question were adopted or accepted by the applicant and the latter could not have been unaware that they had as their object the restriction of competition between its customers.

Consequently, it is of little relevance to establish whether the applicant knew that it was infringing the prohibition contained in Article 85.

In this connection the opinion of a legal advisor, on which it relies, is not a mitigating factor.

It must thus be held that the acts prohibited by the Treaty were undertaken intentionally and in disregard of the provisions of the Treaty.

19. With regard to the gravity of the infringement, the clauses prohibiting exports constitute a form of restriction on competition which by its very nature jeopardises trade between Member States.

Consequently, the Commission was entitled to consider that the infringements which it found were of a certain gravity and to take this into account with regard to the provisions of Article 15 of Regulation No. 17.

20. The applicant has further maintained that the amount of the fine is extremely burdensome for an undertaking of its nature.

21. Nevertheless by its refusal to produce its accounts, which the Court requested, it has prevented verification of this statement.

22. It follows that the application in respect of Article 2 of the contested decision is not well founded and accordingly must also be dismissed.

(8) Pioneer Cases

Pioneer Electronic (Europe) N.V. and Others v. Commission, Joined Cases 100-103/80, Judgment of 7 June 1983, not yet published.

*Facts:* After receiving a complaint from IFFLI SA, Metz, a French parallel importer of hi-fi equipment, the Commission imposed fines on Pioneer Electronic Europe N.V., Antwerp, Musique Diffusion Francaise, Pioneer's French sole distributor, C. Melchers & Co., its German sole distributor, and Pioneer High Fidelity (GB) Ltd (formerly Shriro UK Ltd), the British sole distributor. At the instigation of Musique Diffusion Francaise these firms had engaged in two concerted practices preventing parallel imports into France of Pioneer equipment from the Federal Republic of Germany and the United Kingdom, where it was much cheaper. In 1975, for example, Pioneer's best-selling amplifier was sold to the retail trade 27% cheaper in the Federal Republic of Germany than in France, and 38% cheaper in the United Kingdom.

Pioneer Electronic Europe, the subsidiary of a Japanese multinational ranking among the world's leading suppliers of hi-fi equipment, is responsible for distributing Pioneer equipment throughout Europe.

Commission investigations revealed that Pioneer Electronic Europe had organised a meeting with its sole distributors, at which the question of parallel imports was discussed. Following this meeting as well as Pioneer Electronic Europe's intervention, the German sole distributor refused to meet a substantial order from a German dealer in the absence of an assurance that the products would not be exported. At the same time the British sole distributor entered into arrangements with Musique Diffusion Francaise and took measures affecting its main customers in order to prevent Pioneer Equipment being re-exported from the UK to other Member States. These concerted practices had the object and effect of isolating the French market for Pioneer hi-fi equipment.

.....

In this case the fines imposed on the firms involved, taking account of the behaviour of each firm and the duration of the infringements, were as follows: Pioneer Electronic Europe, 4 350 000 EUA (BFR 175 476 825); Musique Diffusion Francaise 850 000 EUA (FF 4 942 597); C. Melchers & Co. 1 450 000 EUA (DM 3 596 667); and Pioneer High Fidelity (GB) Ltd (formerly Shriro (UK) Ltd) 300 000 EUA (UKL 194 925).

.....

*The Court held:*

D - Submissions relating to the size of the fines

(a) The general level of the fines

101. The applicants maintain that, in fixing the amounts of the fines, the Commission failed to observe the last subparagraph of Article 15(2) of Regulation No. 17, which provides that regard shall be had both to the gravity and to the duration of the infringement. According to the applicants, the Commission did not base itself on the gravity of their conduct nor on its duration. They say that it took advantage of these cases in order to introduce a new policy intended to increase the general level of fines for certain infringements of Community law although such a change in policy was justified neither by the nature of the infringements in question nor by the particular circumstances of the case. The imposition of such large fines in the present cases is solely due to the fact that the cases came before the Commission at a time when it was changing its policy, which is not only contrary to the provisions of the regulations but in fact leads to arbitrariness.

102. Moreover, the method thus described is manifestly discriminatory. The facts of the present cases arose at the same time as those of other cases in which the Commission adopted a decision before the decision in the present case, imposing significantly lower fines.

103. The Commission admits that the present cases are the first in which it has imposed a level of fines considerably higher than in the past. Before the adoption of the contested decision it had not imposed fines exceeding 2% of the total turnover of the undertaking, even for serious infringements. In these cases the fines range from 2 to 4% of turnover.

104. According to the Commission, however, such a level is fully justified

by the nature of the infringements. After 20 years of Community competition policy an appreciable increase in the level of fines is necessary, in its view, at least for types of infringement which have long been well-defined and are known to those concerned, such as prohibitions on exports and imports. In fact those constitute the most serious infringements since they deprive consumers of all the benefits resulting from the elimination of customs duties and quantitative restrictions; they hinder the integration of the economies of the Member States and leave distributors and retailers in a position of subordination towards procedures. Heavier fines are particularly necessary where, as in the present case, the principal aim of the infringement is to maintain a higher level of prices for consumers. The Commission states that many undertakings carry on conduct which they know to be contrary to Community law because the profit which they derive from their unlawful conduct exceeds the fines imposed hitherto. Conduct of that kind can only be deterred by fines which are heavier than in the past.

105. In that connection it must be remembered that the Commission's power to impose fines on undertakings which, intentionally or negligently, commit an infringement of the provisions of Articles 85(1) or 86 of the Treaty is one of the means conferred on the Commission in order to enable it to carry out the task of supervision conferred on it by Community law. That task certainly includes the duty to investigate and punish individual infringements, but it also encompasses the duty to pursue a general policy designed to apply, in competition matters, the principles laid down by the Treaty and to guide the conduct of undertakings in the light of those principles.

106. It follows that, in assessing the gravity of an infringement for the purpose of fixing the amount of the fine, the Commission must take into consideration not only the particular circumstances of the case but also the context in which the infringement occurs and must ensure that its action has the necessary deterrent effect, especially as regards those types of infringement which are particularly harmful to the attainment of the objectives of the Community.

107. From that point of view, the Commission was right to classify as very serious infringements prohibitions on exports and imports seeking artificially to maintain price differences between the markets of the various Member States. Such prohibitons jeopardise the freedom of intra-Community trade, which is a fundamental principle of the Treaty, and they prevent the attainment of one of its objectives, namely the creation of a single market.

108. It was also open to the Commission to have regard to the fact that practices of this nature, although they were estab-ished as being unlawful at the outset of Community competition policy, are still relatively frequent on account of the profit that certain of the undertakings concerned are able to derive from them and, consequently, it was open to the Commission to consider that it was appropriate to raise the level of fines so as to reinforce their deterrent effect.

109. For the same reasons, the fact that the Commission, in the past, imposed fines of a certain level for certain types of infringement does not mean that it is stopped from raising the level within the limits indicated in Regulation No. 17 if that is necessary to ensure the implementation of Community competition policy. On the contrary, the proper application of the Community competition rules requires that the Com-

mission may at any time adjust the level of fines to the needs of that policy.

110. The submission must therefore be rejected.

(b) The alleged absence of intention on the part of Pioneer

111. Pioneer argues that it did not act intentionally since it could not know that its conduct was unlawful.

112. On the basis of the assessment, carried out above in part B(d), of the evidence adduced as regards Pioneer's conduct, the Court finds that Pioneer must have been fully aware that its conduct was of such a nature as to encourage restrictions on competition. That is sufficient for a finding that that undertaking acted intentionally. This submission must therefore be rejected.

(c) The use of turnover as the basis for calculating the fines

113. Melchers claim that it is unlawful to fix the fines in proportion to the undertaking's turnover, as the Commission has done in the present cases. It argues in fact that turnover gives no indication of the profitability of the undertaking or of its ability to pay a fine.

114. In any event, Melchers, MDF and Pioneer claim that the fine cannot be calculated, as the Commission has done in the present case, on the basis of the total turnover of the undertaking, since the goods in respect of which the infringement was committed represent only a part of that turnover.

115. Pioneer argues that the fine imposed on it must be reduced because the turnover on which the Commission based its calculations also related to sales of hi-fi equipment to countries not affected by the infringement.

116. According to Melchers, the Commission ought to have taken into consideration the fact that only about 10% of its turnover related to hi-fi products, whilst in the case of the other applicants those products accounted for the whole of their turnover. Melchers adds that, in fixing the ceiling for fines at 10% of the turnover, Article 15(2) of Regulation No. 17 refers to the turnover in the sector in which the infringement was committed. Because the Commission did not observe this method of calculation, the amount imposed on Melchers amounts to 18% of its turnover on the hi-fi market, thus exceeding the limit fixed by the aforementioned provision.

117. The Commission replied that only the total turnover of an undertaking can give an indication of the maximum fine which the undertaking is capable of paying. For that reason, the limit laid down in Article 15 (2) of Regulation No. 17 must, in its view, be understood as referring to the total turnover. Likewise in all the other cases in which, in the Commission's view, regard must be had to turnover in order to fix the amount of a fine, it is the total turnover which is relevant and not the turnover resulting from the transactions concerned by the infringement. It stresses however that, owing to the large number of unquantifiable criteria to be taken into consideration in fixing a fine, no mathematical formula of general application is possible.

118. Under the terms of Article 15(2) of Regulation No. 17, the Commission may impose fines of from 1,000 to 1,000,000 Units of Account or a sum in excess thereof but not exceeding 10% of the turnover in the preceding business year of each of the undertakings participating in the infringement. Article 15(2) provides that in fixing the amount of the fine within those limits the gravity and the duration of the infringement are to be taken into consideration.

119. Thus the only express reference to the turnover of the undertaking concerns the upper limit of a fine exceeding 1,000,000 Units of Account. In such a case the limit seeks to prevent fines from being disproportionate in relation to the size of the undertaking and, since only the total turnover can effectively give an approximate indication of that size, the aforementioned percentage must, as the Commission has argued, be understood as referring to the total turnover. It follows that the Commission did not exceed the limit laid down in Article 15 of the regulation.

120. In assessing the gravity of an infringement regard must be had to a large number of factors, the nature and importance of which vary according to the type of infringement in question and the particular circumstances of the case. Those factors may, depending on the circumstances, include the volume and value of the goods in respect of which the infringement was committed and the size and economic power of the undertaking and, consequently, the influence which the undertaking was able to exert on the market.

121. It follows that, on the one hand, it is permissible, for the purpose of fixing the fine, to have regard both to the total turnover of the undertaking, which gives an indication, albeit approximate and imperfect, of the size of the undertaking and of its economic power, and to the proportion of that turnover accounted for by the goods in respect of which the infringement was committed, which gives an indication of the scale of the infringement. On the other hand, it follows that it is important not to confer on one or the other of those figures an importance disproportionate in relation to the other factors and, consequently, that the fixing of an appropriate fine cannot be the result of a simple calculation based on the total turnover. This is particularly the case where the goods concerned account for only a small part of that figure. It is appropriate for the Court to bear in mind those considerations in its assessment, by virtue of its powers of unlimited jurisdiction, of the gravity of the infringements in question.

122. To the extent to which reliance is to be placed on the turnover of undertakings involved in the same infringement for the purpose of determining the proportions between the fines to be imposed, the period to be taken into consideration must be ascertained in such a way that the resulting turonvers are as comparable as possible. The submissions put forward in this respect by MDF and Pioneer are not of such a nature as to influence appreciably the assessment made by the Court. Therefore it is not necessary to examine those submissions in detail.

(d) The duration of the concerted practices

123. According to MDF and Pioneer, the concerted practices could only have commenced on 19 and 20 January 1976 at the time of the Antwerp meeting. Pioneer and Melchers observe that the concerted practice between MDF. Pioneer and Melchers was consummated on 27 January 1976 when the

employees of Melchers told Mr Schreiber that the goods would not be delivered. Lastly, the applicants maintain that there is no evidence that the concerted practice between MDF, Pioneer and Shriro continued for two years. It is argued that, as the duration of the infringement is one of the factors to be taken into account in fixing a fine, it is appropriate to reduce the fines considerably on that ground.

124. As a result of the finding that the infringements committed were confined to the period "late January/early February" and in view of the findings relating to Melcher's refusal to sell, it is no longer necessary to deal with these submissions. The duration of the concerted practices established by the Court will enter into the general assessment to be made by it within the framework of its powers of unlimited jurisdiction.

(e) The imposition of a single fine for two concerted practices

125. According to MDF, there is reason to believe that the Commission considered that the two concerted practices in which MDF participated constitute two distinct infringements. By combining the fines calculated for each of those two infringements into a single fine, the Commission infringed the general principle concerning the overlapping offences.

126. Pioneer, for its part, claims that the Commission infringed its right to a fair hearing by imposing on it a single fine for two infringements. In the absence of a specific fine for each infringement, it is not possible to know how the Commission assessed the gravity of each infringement or whether the criteria applied in considering each infirngement were proper.

127. In that connection, it suffices to observe that the Commission maintains that, in the case of MDF and Pioneer, it treated the infringements as a single offence and therefore imposed a single fine on each undertaking. In fact, there is nothing to indicate that the Commission did not follow that procedure, which is justified in the present case since MDF and Pioneer participated in two concerted practices which were both designed to prevent parallel imports to a particular country of goods produced by the same firm. These submissions must therefore be rejected, without its being necessary to express a view on the possible existence of principles of Community law relating to the overlapping of fines imposed for several separate infringements.
.....

The claim for a reduction of the fines

129. In fixing the amount of the fines regard must be had to the duration of the infringements established and to all the factors capable of affecting the assessment of the gravity of the infringements, such as the conduct of each of the undertakings, the role played by each of them in the establishment of the concerted practices, the profit which they were able to derive from those practices, their size, the value of the goods concerned and the threat that infringements of that type pose to the objectives of the Community.

130. In relation to the criteria used by the Commission in fixing the fines, regard must be had in particular, in the case of all the undertakings, to the shorter duration of the infringements resulting from the partial nullity of the contested decision and to the considerations set out

above in part D(c) concerning the relationship between the total turnover of the undertakings and the other factors to be taken into account for the purpose of determining the gravity of the infringements.

131. On the basis of all those considerations and regard being had to the particular circumstances of each of the undertakings, the fines should be fixed as follows:

132. As regards Pioneer, regard must be had particularly to the central position which that undertaking occupies in the distribution network of the products in question, which enabled it to play the role of intermediary in exerting considerable influence on the conduct of national distributors. In respect of that undertaking the fine should be fixed at 2,000,000 Units of Account, that is to say BFr 80,679,000.

133. In the case of MDF, which was the instigator and essential beneficiary of the two concerted practices, a fine of 600,000 Units of Account, that is to say FF 3,488,892, should be imposed.

134. As a result of the partial nullity of the contested decision there is no difference between the duration of the two concerted practices in which Melchers and Shriro (now Pioneer GB) were involved. To establish the relationship between the fines to be imposed on those two undertakings regard must be had in particular to the fact that Shriro was entirely dependant on Pioneer in the pursuit of its activities, whereas Melchers, as a result of the diversity of its activities, of which the sale of Pioneer products constituted only a small part, could more easily have resisted the pressure exerted upon it. Regard being had also to all the other circumstances of the cases, the fine to be imposed on Melchers should be fixed at 400 000 Units of Account, that is to say DM 992 184, and the fine to be imposed on Pioneer GB should be fixed at 200 000 Units of Account, that is to say £ 129 950.

135. In view of the reduction of the fines decided above and the fact that since the date of the contested decision the undertakings have had the use of the sums in question without having to arrange a guarantee or pay interest, the submissions put forward by MDF and Melchers regarding the difficulties which payment of the fines would entail for them must be rejected. That applies equally to MDF's claim to be allowed to pay the fine in several instalments. It is for the Commission to decide, in an appropriate case and having regard to the current financial situation of the undertakings, whether it is desirable to allow payment to be deferred or effected in instalments.

(9) ANSEAU-NAVEWA case

For facts and references see above, page 146.

*The Court held:*

....

54. Furthermore, Disem-Andries maintains that the Commission made a mistake in its assessment inasmuch as, in calculating the amount of the fine imposed on it, it did not take account of its adverse financial situation.

55. That argument cannot be accepted either. As the Commission has rightly observed, recognition of such an obligation would be tantamount

to conferring an unjustified competitive advantage on undertakings least well adapted to the conditions of the market.

56. For its part, ANSEAU contends that no account was taken in the Decision of the fact that it does not carry on any economic activity of its own, that it did not derive any financial benefit from the implementation of the Agreement and, moreover, that the infringement established was terminated by the date on which the decision was adopted.

57. In that regard it is clear from the statement of reasons contained in the Decision that the fine imposed on ANSEAU, being equal in amount to the highest fines imposed on the undertakings which were parties to the Agreement, was fixed by reference to the fact that on the one hand ANSEAU bore most of the responsibility, but that on the other hand it was necessary to take account of the fact that it was a non-profit-making association.

58. That approach must be regarded as justified, notwithstanding the fact that ANSEAU is a non-profit-making association, particularly in view of the fundamental rôle which it played in the drawing-up and implementation of the Agreement.
....

(10) Hasselblad case

For facts and references see below, page 428.

*The Court held:*
....
57. In that regard, it must be pointed out that the amount of the fine is determined on the basis of a number of considerations, including the gravity of the infringement and its duration. An undertaking's turnover is only one of the factors which may be taken into account. The aim of the concerted practice established by the Commission was to prevent any imports into the United Kongdom of Hasselblad cameras intended for Camera Care and as such the practice consituted a flagrant breach of the rules on competition contained in the Treaty. However, it would appear that the Commission fixed the amount of the fine on the basis of various considerations, one of which was the fact that the applicant's practice in connection with the Silver Service Guarantee was in breach of the rules on competition and the applicant had delayed repairs to cameras which were the subject of parallel imports, matters which the Commission failed to prove in the proceedings before the Court. Furthermore, Article 3 of the decision must be declared by the Court to be void in one respect, and in relation to a specific period. Accordingly, the infringements found by the Commission have been established before the Court only in part. A further consideration is that the applicant is not a large undertaking. In the circumstances, the Court has decided to reduce the fine from ECU 165 000 to ECU 80 000.
....

B. Double jeopardy

(1) Walt Wilhelm Case - see above, pages 6 and 27.

(2) Decision in re Boehringer
Decision of the Commission of 25 December 1971 on a proceeding under Article 85 of the Treaty. J.O. No. L 282, 23 December 1971, p. 46;

(1972) CMLR D 121; CCH para. 9484; Competition Law CM/M/I/43.

*The Commission held:*

....

The Commission, in the light of the Treaty instituting the EEC (especially Article 85) and of Council Regulation No. 17 of February 1962, of the Commission's Decision of 16 July 1969 imposing on the company Boehringer Mannheim GmbH a fine of 190,000 units of account and of the judgment delivered on 15 July 1970 by the Court of Justice in case 45/69 reducing the amount of the fine imposed by the Commission to 180,000 u.a., has received a request, made on 3 September 1969 by Boehringer, that the Commission deduct from the amount of the fine the 80,000 dollar fine imposed by the US District Court, Southern District of New York by a judgment of 3 July 1969. This request was confirmed by Boehringer on 3 November 1970. The applicant undertaking has been heard and the Consultative Committee on Cartels and Monopolies gave its opinion on 13 July 1971.

I. The members of the international quinine cartel were the subject of proceedings in the United States for the violation of the anti-trust provisions of American law. On 25 September 1968 a Grand Jury of the US District Court, Southern District of New York, preferred a bill of indictment, inter alia, against the company Boehringer Mannheim GmbH and one of its subsidiary companies of which it holds all the share capital, namely, Vereinigte Chininfabriken Zimmer & Co GmbH (VCZ).

The indictment contained five counts:

1. The first of these accused the undertakings of having, between the end of 1958 and at least the summer of 1966, restricted in an unjustified manner, by means of a concerted infringement, the internal and external trade of the United States and of having thereby violated section 1 of the Sherman Act. According to the indictment this violation took the form of the uninterrupted application of agreements and concerted practices the object of which was:

(a) to fix, stabilise and increase the price of quinine, quinidine and other products extracted from the quinquina bark;

(b) to divide the markets as regards the sale of quinine and quinidine;

(c) to establish sales quotas;

(d) to reserve the production of synthetic quinidine for Nedchem, Boehringer and Buchler;

(e) to eliminate the other producers of quinine, quinidine and other products extracted from the quinquina bark, especially by systematically making more advantageous offers than those of such producers;

(f) to divide up the supplies of the quinquina bark;

(g) to exert an influence on the sale of the American reserve stock of quinine by temporarily maintaining the prices of that product at a given level and by appointing Nedchem to acquire that stock on behalf of all the undertakings covered by the indictment (cf. point 14 of the latter).

According to the indictment, the effects of the violation were as follows:

(a) the prices of the products extracted from the quinquina bark were increased, fixed and maintained at an artificial level, which was not the result of the free play of competition;

(b) competition between the importers and the American resellers was restricted and hindered;

(c) competition between the producers was restricted and hindered on the American market;

(d) the American purchasers of products with a quinine base (in whatever form) suffered damage;

(e) competition was restricted and hindered on purchase of the American reserve stock;

(f) potential competitors were excluded from purchase of the products forming the reserve stock of the American Government and/or from their resale to the United States (point 16 of the indictment).

2. In the second count the undertakings were accused of having, between the end of 1958 and at least the summer of 1966, also committed the violation, the nature and effects of which were set out in the first count with the aim of monopolising the internal and external trade of the United States and of having thereby violated section 2 of the Sherman Act (see points 20 and 22 of the indictment).

3. In the third count the undertakings were accused of having, between the end of 1958 and at least the summer of 1966, monopolised the internal and external trade of the United States and of having thereby violated section 2 of the Sherman Act, the conduct of the undertakings which allowed such monopolisation to take place or which served for its exploitation and the latter's effect having been set out in the first count.

4. In the fourth count the undertakings were accused of having, at the same time and by that same conduct, violated section 73 of the Wilson Tariff Act.

5. Finally, in the fifth count, they were accused of having at the same time, by the restriction of competition for which they were responsible on purchase of the American reserve stock of quinine, by the division of the quantities of quinine purchases on that occasion by Nedchem and therefore also by the influence which they exerted on the level of prices in the United States and, consequently, on the price at which the American stock of quinine was sold, and finally by the concealment of their agreement from the American authorities committed a fraud against the United States and thus violated section 371 of title 18 of the US Code.

On 3 July 1969 Boehringer stated through its representatives before the US District Court that it admitted guilt on the first two counts ('nolo contendere'). Thereupon a fine of $ 40,000 was imposed on Boehringer on each of the counts, i.e. a total of $ 80,000. During the hearing of the attorney for the Anti-trust Division of the Department of Justice claimed against Boehringer a fine of $ 50,000 on each count, submitting that the violation alleged in the indictment, and in the execution of which Boehringer had played a preponderant part, had consisted in acquiring the American quinine reserves at a low price and then after acquiring them making a general increase in the prices of quinine. For his part, counsel for Boehringer emphasised the fact that on selling its reserves to Nedchem, the United States was perfectly aware that that company belonged to a world cartel. On 3 July 1969 the proceedings brought against Boehringer were dropped, with the consent of the Government, as regards counts 3, 4 and 5 ('dismissal order') as well as the proceedings which had been brought against its subsidiary the company VCZ & Co. GmbH ('nolle prosequi order') (see the extract from the court records concerning criminal case 68 CRIM 870 and the record of the hearing of 3 July 1969). On 11 July 1969 Boehringer paid the fine imposed on it, i.e. $ 80,000.

By its decision of 16 July 1969, the Commission imposed on Boehringer a fine of 190,000 units of account. The Commission, at the time when it took that decision was indeed aware of the fact that anti-trust proceedings had been brought in the United States against Boehringer and that that company had been indicted on 25 September 1968, but it had not yet been made aware that Boehringer had been condemned to a fine by the American Court and had already paid it.

On 3 September 1969 Boehringer asked the Commission to count as part of the fine of 190,000 units of account which it had imposed on it by its decision of 16 July 1969, the fine of $ 80,000 which the US District Court of New York had imposed on it on 3 July 1969 and which it had paid on 11 July 1969. This request was made on the following grounds:

From a comparative examination of the decision of 16 July 1969 and the American indictment which was the base of the judicial proceedings ending in the condemnation of Boehringer it appeared, according to the latter, that it was for the same facts as those upon which the American Court had already condemned it that the Commission had imposed a fine, namely the agreements relating to prices and discounts, to the division of the market by a partitioning system, the establishment of a system of quotas and compensating deliveries and finally the limitation of production of quinidine.

Thereby the same conduct, it was argued, would be penalised twice through application of basically comparable legal rules, which would amount to an inadmissible case of double penalty. According to Boehringer, it was for the Commission, under a general principle of law appearing in the laws of all the Member States (expressing the principle of non bis in idem) and under a general requirement of equity expressed by the Court of Justice in Wilhelm v. Bundeskartellamt, to include in the fines already imposed those to be imposed or at least to take them into account when calculating the latter fines. Comparing the two sets of proceedings, it will be seen that it is practically the same facts which were punished in both cases.

By letter of 17 February 1970 the Commission communicated to Boehringer the reasons why it did not think it could consider a decision reducing the amount of the fine which had been imposed on it. By letter of 12 March 1970 Boehringer adopted a position on the matter and expounded its point of view during the oral hearing which it had claimed and which took place on 24 April 1970. For the establishment of the present decision the Commission refers to the text of Boehringer's letters of

12 March 1970 and to the record of the hearing of 24 April approved by that undertaking.

By a judgment delivered on 15 July 1970, the Court of Justice reduced the amount of the fine imposed on Boehringer to 180,000 units of account. Boehringer has also asked the Court to take the earlier fine into account but when the Commission objected that the request was inadmissible since it was already before the Commission itself, Boehringer left it to the Court to determine whether it could give a decision on the matter even without a prior decision of the Commission. But as the Commission then announced that it would shortly give a decision on the matter and the Advocate-General submitted that the Court ought not 'for various reasons' to give a decision on the request, the Court decided not to take into consideration, in the present case, the penalties imposed by the American authorities on the ground that those penalties came about solely with regard to restrictions on competition which occurred outside the Community.

By its letter of 3 November 1970 Boehringer confirmed that it persisted in its request which it had made to the Commission for the fine to be taken into account.

II. The Commission starts from the fact that the Court, in its judgment of 15 July 1970, refused to take the American fine into account only 'for the present case' and thereby it did not give definitive judgment on Boehringer's request, which itself was not examined in substance during the proceedings.

Boehringer's request of 3 September 1969 should be rejected for the following reasons:

This request aims at having the fine imposed in the United States taken into account in that imposed by the Commission. The Treaty instituting the EEC and its implementing regulations on competition do not provide for such an obligation to take other penalties into account. In the Commission's opinion, nor does an examination of the national laws of the Member States reveal the existence of a general principle of law which would require fines imposed by courts of non-Member States to be taken into account in those imposed under Community law.

The Court of Justice in Wilhelm v. Bundeskartellamt held that the Community and the Member States had an obligation to take account of previous penalties imposed for the same set of facts. This obligation derives, for the Court of Justice, from the existence of a general principle of equity set out in Article 90(2) of the ECSC Treaty. That judgment of the Court concerned only the clash of penalties imposed under Community law and the national law of the Member States. In that connection it should be remembered that the territorial area of application of Community law on competition created by the EEC Treaty and that of the national competition laws of the Member States partially overlap and that the economic circumstances and the legal situations which gave rise to their application can be closely linked. The obligation both on the Community organs and on the Member States to take account of penalties imposed previously contributes to ensuring respect for the general requirements of equity in not penalising the same conduct twice.

The same does not apply in cases of clash between penalties imposed under

Community law and under the laws of the non-Member States. An examination of the laws of the Member States reveals the existence of no general principle of law common to all such legal systems providing that penalties imposed by non-Member States should be taken into account in those imposed by the Community, and in the criminal law of only two Member States is the judge obliged to take account of the size of fines imposed and paid abroad, whereas in other Member States a conviction abroad constitutes only an obstacle to any criminal proceedings. In three Member States (France, Belgium and Luxembourg) a penalty imposed and paid abroad does not then prevent criminal proceedings when the offence has also been committed on their national territory. In those Member States the principle non bis in idem thus is not applied when the criminal judge founds his jurisdiction on the territoriality principle, since he is not required in such a case to take account in his sentence of the penalty imposed abroad.

Furthermore, the principle non bis in idem, whether it appears under the guise of preventing prosecution or of an obligation on the national judge to take account of penalties imposed and paid abroad, may apply only when the offence is the same ('dieselbe Tat'). That condition is not met in the present case. The American judge penalised behaviour of the applicant within the international quinine cartel, behaviour which restricted competition in the United States. The Commission, on the other hand, imposed a fine on the members of that same cartel whose behaviour restricted competition within the Common Market. That unlawful behaviour corresponds, certainly, at least in part, to applying the agreement on exports concluded between the members of the cartel but, to know whether it is the 'same offence', it is not necessary to take account, from the competition law point of view, of the decision or agreement by which the participants in the agreement agreed to adopt behaviour which such an agreement (or decision) provoked and the legally protected interests which it attacked. The behaviour of the members of the quinine cartel which, in execution of the export agreement of April 1962, consisted in selling quinine and quinidine for export at jointly fixed prices should not, for that reason, be considered as constituting the 'same offence'.

Nonetheless it is the 'same offence' since the Commission in its Decision, especially aimed at the restrictions on competition which produced effects within the common market, particularly those which were the objects 'gentleman's agreements' concluded between the participants in the cartel on 7 April 1962. These 'gentleman's agreements' guaranteed in particular to their signatories the protection of their national market and prohibited the French members manufacturing synthetic quinidine. As regards the export agreement, the Commission held as the only thing against it that it laid down identical prices on export to Italy, Belgium and Luxembourg. It appears, on the other hand, on reading the documents relating to the proceedings in the United States that the American court put the emphasis on facts which, as appears from the decision of 16 July 1969, were not proved to the Commission to constitute infringements of Article 85 of the EEC Treaty. The American authorities in particular saw in the agreement on the supply of bark, in the agreement on the acquisition by Nedchem of the American stocks of quinine and in the practice of especially high sales prices until the middle of 1966, particularly serious restrictions on competition, whereas the Commission, for its part, considered the agreement on the supply of bark and the agreement on the conering of the American quinine reserves did not constitute an infringement of Article 85. On the

other hand, the Commission considered that the infringements ended in February 1965, while the American authorities accepted that they continued until the middle of 1966.
Between these two dates very large price increases took place for quinine and quinidine, increases which the American authorities imputed to the international quinine cartel.

In view of all these circumstances we should reject the application made on 3 September 1970 by Boehringer for the fine of $ 80,000 imposed on it in the United States to be taken into account in that of 180,000 units of account which the Court of Justice fixed for the violation which it committed of the competition rules of the EEC Treaty.

THE COMMISSION, for these reasons,

HEREBY DECIDES:

1. The application made by the Company Boehringer Mannheim GmbH for the fine of $ 80,000 imposed on it on 3 July 1969 by the US District Court of the Southern District of New York to be taken into account in the fine which the Commission imposed on it in its decision of 16 July 1969 and which the Court of Justice of the European Community reduced to 180,000 units of account in its judgment of 15 July 1970, is rejected.

2. This Decision is addressed to the company Boehringer Mannheim GmbH of Sandhofer Strasse 112-132, Mannheim.

(3) Second Boehringer Case

Boehringer Mannheim GmbH v. EEC Commission, Judgment of 14 December 1972, Case 7/72; (1972) ECR 1281 ; (1972) CMLR 864; CCH para. 8143; Competition Law CM/M/III/36.

For facts see above, page 370.

*The Court held:*

.....

In a judgment of 16 July 1969 the Commission of the European Communities imposed on the applicant a fine of 190,000 units of account for infringement of Article 85 of the EEC Treaty. This amount was reduced to 180, 000 units of account by a judgment of the Court on 15 July 1970 in Case 45/69. On 3 July 1969 a New York District Court condemned the applicant to pay a fine of $ 80,000, because it had violated the Federal antitrust laws of the United States; the applicant paid this fine on 11 July 1969. By letter of 3 September 1969 it requested the Commission to set off this fine paid in the United States against the fine imposed by the decision of the Commission of 16 July 1969. The Commission rejected this request in a decision of 25 November 1971.

The applicant complains that the Commission thereby violated a general principle of law prohibiting duplication of sanctions for one and the same act.

The Commission is under a duty, in fixing the amount of a fine, to take into account the sanctions already imposed on an undertaking in respect of the same act, in cases of sanctions for infringements of the antitrust law of a Member State which are therefore breaches of laws committed in the territory of the Community. The question as to whether the Commission can also be under a duty to set off a sanction imposed by authorities of a non-Member State, need only be determined if the acts alleged in the case against the applicant by the Commission on the one hand and by the American authorities on the other hand are identical.

Even if the acts attracting both the sanctions arise out of the same body of agreements, they are nonetheless in essence distinct from each other, as regards both their purpose and also their territorial impact.

The fines imposed by the Community were particularly directed against the genetlemen's agreement for the sharing-out of the dominant markets in the Common Market and Great Britain, and against the agreements restricting production of synthetic quinidine in favour of the Nedchem, Boehringer and Buchler companies. The conviction in the United States may well have been based in part on these agreements, but it was concerned with a large body of facts, at the centre of which lay in particular the quinquina bark agreement, the acquisition and the sharing out of the contents of the American stickpile by the cartel, and the maintenance, from then until mid-1966, of abnormally high selling prices in the United States. The parties are in dispute as to which acts are material to the American conviction, since judgment was entered against the applicant on a guilty plea (nolo contendere) so that only the indictment is available, by means of which doubts as to the scope of the conviction could have been settled. However, it still remains for the applicant to prove identity of acts, and this it could not do in the circumstances.

We must in any case reject the view that the mischief lies in the cartel agreement itself and not in the execution of its terms. In this connection we need only refer to the judgment of 15 July 1970 (Case 45/69) in the case between the same parties, when the Court took a contrary view, since, on the basis of its findings that the cartel concluded that the infringements of the Treaty were less far reaching than the Commission had supposed, and it drew the appropriate conclusions with regard to the assessment of the fine. In accordance with Article 85 of the Treaty this judgment only took into account such acts done in execution of the cartel agreements as were likely to affect trade between the Member States and to distort competition within the Common Market. Moreover the applicant has brought forward nothing that could support the view that the conviction in the United States extended to acts done outside that country in execution of the cartel agreements and to its effects in such places. In this respect, also, it has not been shown that the acts alleged were identical.

There is therefore no reason to set off - even partially - the amount of the fine imposed on the applicant in the United States against the fine of 180,000 units of account imposed upon the applicant for infringement of Article 85 of the Treaty.

The application is hereby refused.

Under Article 69(2) of the Rules of Procedure, the unsuccessful party is to be ordered to bear the costs. The applicant has been unsuccessful in its suit.

THE COURT, rejecting all further and contrary submissions,

HEREBY DECIDES:

1. The application is unfounded and is refused.

2. The applicant is ordered to bear the costs in the case.

## C. Regulation 17 Article 15 (6)

### (1) Cement Convention Case

CBR at al. v. EEC Commission, Judgment of 15 March 1967, Cases 8-11/66; (1967) ECR 75; (1967) CMLR 77; CCH para. 8052; Competition Law CM/M/III/17.

*Facts:* On 6 July 1956 74 undertakings (44 German, 28 Belgian and 2 Dutch) entered into an agreement called the 'Noordwijkse Cement Accoord' (hereinafter referred to as 'the NCA').

This agreement divided up the market in respect of the supply of cement and clinker by means of quotas. It also contained clauses concerning the building of new cement works, the collective fixing of prices and conditions of sale, obligations as to exclusive sales and exclusive purchasers, and certain prohibitions on exports.

The last-mentioned aspects of this agreement formed the subject-matter of a later agreement, which is not in issue in the present proceedings, made between the members of the original cartel on the one hand and the trade organisation concerned on the other.

On 31 October the NCA agreement was notified to the EEC on Form B in accordance with the provisions of Regulation No. 17.

On 8 April 1965 the member undertakings of the NCA received, directly or indirectly, a letter signed by Mr von der Groeben, a member of the Commission. This letter stated that it did not constitute a notice under Article 15(6) of Regulation No. 17, and amongst other matters informed the undertakings to which it was addressed that the agreement notified was probably prohibited under Article 85(1) and could not be authorised under Article 85(3). The said letter advised that it was advisable to strike out a certain number of clauses of the agreement and invited the undertakings to state their views.

At the request of the undertakings a number of meetings took place between their representatives and officials of the Commission, followed by an exchange of letters. In particular on 11 June 1965 a meeting took place at which the protagonists seem to have drawn different conclusions about the result which certain proposed amendments to the clauses of the agreement notified might have on the validity of the said agreement.

On 14 December 1965 the Commission decided to pursue the matter in writing and to send to the parties to the agreement notices under Article 15(6) of Regulation No. 17. For this purpose the Commission conferred on the President of the Working Party on Competition, Mr von der Groeben, authority to sign to the Director General for Competition the task of signing and dispatching the said notices.

On 3 January the Director General for Competition sent a registered letter which after describing the agreement in question, ended with the following paragraphs: 'The Commission has subjected the agreement in question to a preliminary examination. It has reached the conclusion that the requirements for applying Article 85(1) of the Treaty are met and that there is no justification for applying Article 85(3) to the agreement in the form in which it has been notified. This preliminary examination is notified to you by the Commission pursuant to Article 15(6) of Regulation No. 17 (First Regulation implementing Articles 85 and 86 of the Treaty, dates 6 February 1962, Official Journal of the European Communities, 1962, No 13, p. 204 et seq.).

The Commission takes this opportunity of informing you that the provisions of Article 15(5) of the aforesaid Regulation No. 17, whereby the application to the agreement notified of the provisions concerning fines set out in Article 15(2)(a) of the said Regulation was provisionally suspended, will cease to apply to the agreement as from the date of receipt of this letter.

I should be obliged if you would let me know within a period of six weeks (from the receipt of this letter) whether you have ceased to apply the agreement in question'.

This notice forms the subject-matter of the applications made to the Court which were joined by an order of the Court of 4 May 1966.

The applicants notified the Commission of the agreement of 6 July 1965 known as the 'Noordwijkse Cement Accoord'and the Commission, in the terms of the minutes of its 343rd meeting, 'took on 14 December 1965 a decision' worded as follows: 'A notice under Article 15(6) of Regulation No. 17 shall be addressed to the undertakings which are parties to the agreement registered with the Commission under No. IV/A-00851; the Chairman of the Working Party on Competition is hereby authorised to have the notices sent by the Director-General for Competition'. On 3 January 1966 the Director General for Competition carried out this instruction by sending the undertakings a registered letter, with a form of acknowledgement of receipt, in which the Commission informed them that, after a preliminary examination 'the provisions of Article 15(5) of...Regulation No. 17, whereby the application to the agreement notified of the provisions concerning fines set out in Article 15(2)(a) of the said Regulation was provisionally suspended, will cease to apply to the agreement as from the date of receipt of this letter'.

Admissibility

The Commission claims that the application for annulment lodged by the said undertakings are inadmissible, on the ground that it has issued a mere opinion and not a decision within the meaning of Article 189 of the Treaty, and that Article 15(6) of Regulation No. 17 does not make provision for any measure in the nature of a decision.

Regulation No. 17, under which the measure of 14 December 1965 was taken, empowers the Commission to impose fines on undertakings which intentionally or negligently infringe Article 85(1) of the Treaty. However, by virtue of Article 15(5) undertakings which have notified their agreements and which keep within the limits of the activity described in the said notification are exempted from this system of fines. Finally, Article 15(6) empowers the Commission to withdraw the benefit of this exemption from fines if, after preliminary examination, it is of the opinion that Article 85(1) of the Treaty applies and that application of Article 85(3) is not justified.

The effect of the measure of 14 December 1965 and 3 January 1966 was that the undertakings ceased to be protected by Article 15(5) which exempted them from fines, and came under the contrary rules of Article 15(2) which thenceforth exposed them to the risk of fines. This measure deprived them of the advantages of a legal situation which Article 15(5) attached to the notification of the agreement, and exposed them to a grave financial risk. Thus the said measure affected the interests of the undertakings by bringing about a distinct change in their legal position. It is unequivocally a measure which produces legal effects touching the interests of the undertakings concerned and which is binding on them. It thus constitutes not a mere opinion but a decision. Any doubt which might be raised by the question whether the notification of the said decision was made in proper form in no way alters the nature of that decision and cannot affect the admissibility of the application.

It is also necessary to consider whether the two requirements under Article 15(6) of Regulation No. 17 concerning Article 85(1) and Article 85(3) of the Treaty consecutively do not necessarily imply that the Commission must proceed by way of a decision.

To exclude an agreement from the benefit of the exemption from a fine under Article 15(5) of Regulation No. 17, the Commission must according to Article 15(6), first be of the opinion that Article 85(1) of the Treaty applies. Therefore it must consider the facts of the case and apply to them the terms of Article 85(1), and issue a finding that the various constituent elements described in this provision are present. The Commission is wrong when it objects that the agreement is prohibited without the necessity for any prior decision. Although under Article 1 of the Regulation agreements 'of the kind described' in Article 85(1) of the Treaty 'shall be prohibited, no prior decision to that effect being required', the Commission must nevertheless find that the agreement submitted to it is indeed of the kind described in Article 85(1) and objectively considered does contain all the constituent elements prescribed in that Article. In particular the questions whether the agreement, notified under Article 5 of the Regulation, may affect trade between Member States, or has as its effect the distortion of competition, are 'met' and with reference to which there is no justification for applying Article 85(3).

Even though such an assessment may be explained by a concise statement of reasons in view of the preliminary nature of the procedure, the reasons must nonetheless appear from the decision itself with sufficient clarity to allow the Court and all parties concerned to ascertain whether the provisions have been applied correctly. It is not disputed that the Commission would be infringing the Treaty if it made use of Article 15(6) of the Regulation in cases where the requirements for applying this provision were not clearly met. Such a risk of violating the Treaty thus presupposes the need for a statement of reasons so that appropriate judicial review may be carried out. Furthermore, the necessity to reach a finding that the infringement of Article 85(1) was obviously of a serious nature, far from reducing this obligation, makes it all the more imperative.

Thus, irrespective of all the other submissions, which now become superfluous, the Decision of 14 December 1965, notice of which was given to the undertakings by letter dated 3 January 1966, must be annulled for having failed to state the reasons on which it was based.

*The Court decided:*

.....

1. Annuls the decision of 14 December 1965, notice of which was given to the applicant undertakings by letter dated 3 January 1966;

2. Orders the Commission to pay the costs.

## VIII. THIRD PARTY RIGHTS

Consult Regulation 17/62 Article 3, Regulation 99/63 Articles 5, 6, 7 and 9.

(1) Metro Case

Metro SB Grossmärkte GmbH & Co KG v. Commission, Case 26/76, Judgment of 25 October 1977; (1977) ECR 1875; Competition Law CM/M/III/67.

For facts see judgment below.

*The Court held:*

.....

The applicant complains that the Court should:

'Declare to be void and annul the Decision of the Commission of the European Communities of 15 December 1975, No K 75 1852, relating to a procedure under Article 85 of the EEC Treaty (IV/847 - SABA) and the dismissal by the defendant on 14 January 1976 of the objections submitted to it in the course of the abovementioned procedure.

Order the defendant to bear the costs of the proceedings.

The defendant contends that the Court should:

Dismiss that part of the application as unfounded which seeks the annulment of the Commission Decision of 15 December 1975.

Dismiss the remainder of the application as inadmissible or alternatively as unfounded.

Order the applicant to bear the costs.

The intervener SABA supports the conclusions of the Commission.

The intervener Verband des SB-Grosshandels e.V. supports the conclusions of the applicant.

Decision

1. The first head of the application lodged by the undertaking Metro-SB-Grossmärkte GmbH & Co. KG (hereinafter referred to as 'Metro'), which

was received at the Court Registry on 11 March 1976, is for the annulment of the Commission Decision of 15 December 1975 (Official Journal No L 28 of 3 February 1976, p. 19) relating to a proceeding under Article 85 of the Treaty with regard to the selective distribution system established by the undertaking Schwarzwälder ApparateBau-Anstalt August Schwer und Söhne GmbH (hereinafter referred to as 'SABA') for distributing its electronic equipment for the leisure market in the Common Market.

The second head of the application is for the annulment of the Commission's refusal, contained in its letter of 14 January 1976, to review its decision of 15 December 1975 in order to take account of the objections repeated by the applicant, albeit it had already taken the opportunity of making them known in the course of the hearing by the Commission of the parties and of third persons in accordance with Article 19 of Regulation No. 17 of (the Council of 6 February 1962 and of Regulation No. 99/63 of) the Commission of 25 July 1963, before the adoption of the contested decision.

In Article 1 of that Decision it is recognised that the Conditions of Sale for the Domestic Market (May 1972 version) laid down by SABA do not fall within the prohibition contained in Article 85(1) of the Treaty, whilst in Article 2 the Commission decides that the other provisions of the relevant distribution system qualify for an exemption under Article 85(3).

2. Although the application is for the annulment of the contested decision in its entirety consideration of the submissions put forward indicates that the lawfulness of Article 2 alone of that decision is thereby called in question.

Admissibility

(a) The letter of 14 January 1976

3. The Commission has contested the admissibility of the application in so far as it is directed against the refusal contained in its letter of 14 January 1976.

4. That refusal is merely a confirmation of the decision of 15 December 1975 and annulment of the refusal would follow from annulment of the decision so that, in so far as this second head is concerned, the application must be considered as devoid of purpose and accordingly inadmissible.

(b) The decision of 15 December 1975

5. SABA, which has intervened in the dispute in support of the conclusions of the Commission, considers that the application is inadmissible since the decision contested by Metro is not of direct and individual concern to the latter.

6. The second paragraph of Article 173 of the Treaty states: Any natural or legal person may...institute proceedings against a decision addressed to that person or against a decision which, although in the form of a regulation or a decision addressed to another person, is of direct and individual concern to the former'.

Since the contested decision was not addressed to Metro it is necessary to consider whether it is of direct and individual concern to it.

7. Metro is a so-called self-service wholesale trading undertaking having some 30 establishments in the Federal Republic of Germany and in certain other Member States.

This form of distribution, which means that Metro competes in particular with specialist wholesalers, consists in obtaining from producers wholesale supplies of a wide range of foodstuffs (food department) and other products (non-food department) in order to resell them, principally to retailers, who will themselves resell the products, but also to commercial or industrial undertakings or small businesses which wish to apply the goods purchased for commercial purposes and, lastly, to private customers termed 'institutional consumers', although it should be noted that this latter practice forms the subject-matter of dispute between the parties.

Metro distributes these products through the so-called 'cash and carry' system whereby purchasers serve themselves in sales areas where the goods are stored in such a way that they may be removed easily by the customers themselves, are displayed simply and are paid for in cash, which results in lower prices and makes it possible to operate satisfactorily on lower profit margins than those of the traditional wholesale trade.

This form of marketing is thus characterised both by special sales methods and by the nature of the customers sought by the wholesaler.

8. When the applicant applied to SABA for recognition as a wholesaler for the distribution of electronic equipment for the leisure market SABA refused because the applicant would not agree to a number of conditions to which SABA subjects the grant of the status of a SABA wholesaler and which, the applicant maintains, are not compatible with the structure of the self-service wholesale trade as Metro engages in it.

Specific instances of this are the prohibition on SABA wholesalers regarding the supply of SABA equipment to trade consumers, that is to say to dealers or small businesses outside the trade in electrical goods but using the equipment for commercial purposes within their business, likewise the prohibition on supplies to institutional consumers and the obligations imposed on wholesalers under the cooperation agreements linking them with SABA.

The intervener SABA, on the one hand, maintains that those conditions are compatible with Metro's business activity and that its refusal to appoint the latter as wholesaler stems instead from Metro's sales policy, which is intended to combine in one unit the roles of wholesaler and retailer and to which SABA cannot agree in view of the structure of its distribution system whereby a clear distinction is maintained between those two operations in accordance, as SABA maintains, with the requirements of Federal German legislation.

9. Since the defendant refused to appoint the applicant, on 7 and 9 November 1973 the latter lodged with the Commission, in accordance with Article 3(2)(b) of Regulation No. 17, a request for a finding that the distribution system established by SABA was contrary to Articles 85 and 86 of the Treaty and that SABA should be required to terminate

that system.

10. For its part, in order to obtain negative clearance within the meaning of Article 2 of Regulation No. 17 and Article 85(3) of the Treaty that Article 85(1) was inapplicable, SABA notified to the Commission in 1962, 1963, 1969 and 1972 its conditions of sale for the domestic market, the sole distributorship agreements concluded with undertakings established in other Member States, the 'distribution agreements' which SABA distributors, wholesalers and retailers in the Federal Republic of Germany are required to sign and the agreements for SABA wholesalers in the EEC and for SABA specialist retailers.

On 22 July 1974, after Metro had submitted its complaint, SABA also notified the model cooperation agreement which it requires its appointed wholesalers to sign.

11. Since the Commission considered that Metro could claim a legitimate interest in a possible finding that an infringement had taken place it investigated the claims of both Metro and SABA.

Although it had earlier informed Metro that it considered that it could not find in favour of Metro's complaint, whilst inviting it in a Telex message of 6 December 1974 in accordance with Article 6 of Regulation No. 99/63 to submit its comments, the Commission partially altered its attitude following the submission of those comments by the applicant and upon hearing the latter and required SABA to discontinue the undertakings whereby it obliged wholesalers inter alia to prohibit sales to trade consumers.

After SABA had agreed to this amendment amongst others the Commission adopted the contested decision, which nevertheless upholds a number of aspects of the distribution system which the applicant had criticised in the course of the administrative procedure.

12. Since Metro considered that the distribution system thereby approved retained features unlawfully preventing its appointment as a SABA wholesaler it lodged this application.

13. The above-mentioned facts establish that the contested decision was adopted in particular as the result of a complaint submitted by Metro and that it relates to the provisions of SABA's distribution system, on which SABA relied and continues to rely as against Metro in order to justify its refusal to sell to the latter or to appoint it as a wholesaler, and which the applicant had for this reason impugned in its complaint.

It is in the interests of a satisfactory administration of justice and of the proper application of Articles 85 and 86 that natural or legal persons who are entitled, pursuant to Article 3(2)(b) of Regulation No. 17, to request the Commission to find an infringement of Articles 85 and 86 should be able, if their request is dismissed either wholly or in part, to institute proceedings in order to protect their legitimate interests.

In those circumstances the applicant must be considered to be directly and individually concerned, within the meaning of the second paragraph of Article 173, by the contested decision and the application is accordingly admissible.

## IX. JUDICIAL REVIEW

### A. Introduction

Article 164 EEC Treaty: The Court of Justice shall ensure that in the interpretation and application of this Treaty the Law is observed.

Article 172 of the EEC Treaty provides that regulations made by the Council pursuant to the provisions of the Treaty may give the Court of Justice unlimited jurisdiction in regard to penalties provided for in such regulations.

Article 17 of Regulation 17/62 provides that the Court of Justice shall have unlimited jurisdiction within the meaning of Article 172 of the Treaty to review decisions whereby the Commission has fixed a fine or periodic penalty payment; it may cancel, reduce or increase the fine or periodic penalty payment imposed.

Article 173 of the EEC Treaty is the basis of the judicial review by the Court of acts of Council and Commission. This provision is the basis for actions for annulment of all Commission Decisions in the field of EEC competition law.

Article 175 of the EEC Treaty gives the possibility for an application of the Commission's failure to act.

Article 185 of the EEC Treaty provides that actions brought before the Court shall not have suspensory effect. The Court of Justice may, however, if it considers that circumstances so require, order that application of the contested act be suspended.

Article 186 of the EEC Treaty provides that the Court may in any cases before it prescribe any necessary interim measures.

A full discussion of legal review is outside the scope of this book. Readers are advised to consult: Kerse: EEC Antitrust procedure, London 1981 with 1982 and 1983 supplement.

For a more complete treatment of Judicial Reveiw readers are advised to consult Brinkhorst and Schermers: Judicial Remedies in the European Communities, 2nd edition; Schermers: Judicial protection in the European Communities, 3rd edition.

### B. Cases

#### (1) Metro case

See above page

#### (2) Camera Care case

See above page

#### (3) Demo-Studio Schmidt case

See above page 290.

(4) Ford Interim case

See above, page 340.

## Litterature

- Kerse: EEC Antitrust procedure, Londone 1981 with a 1982 and 1984 supplement.
- Forrester: Legal professional privilege: Limitations on the Commission's power of inspection following the AM&S judgment, (1983) CMLRev. 75-85.
- Harding: The use of fines as a sanction in EEC competition law (1979) CMLRev. 345-364.
- Joshua: The element of surprise: Competition investigations under Article 14(3) of Regulation 17, (1983) ELRev. 324.
- Korah: Commission has powers to grant interim measures, (1980) ELRev. 135-139.
- Korah: Comfort letters:Reflections on the perfumes cases, (1980) ELRev. 14-39.
- Livingston and Sherliker: Comfort letters and Articles 85 and 86 procedure and jurisdiction, (1981) NLJ 287-290.
- Livingston and Sherliker: Confidentiality in UK and EEC anti-trust procedures, (1982) JBL 31-36.
- Livingston and Sherliker: EEC Law. Requests for information under Regulation 17/82, NLJ 659-661.
- Philip: EEC Competition law and privileges against self-incrimination, LIEI 1981/1, 49-88.
- Temple Laing: The powers of the Commission to order interim measures in competition cases, (1981) CMLRev. 49-61.
- Temple Laing: Community anti-trust law - compliance and enforcement, (1981) CMLRev. 335-362.
- Sherliker: Interim measures and Articles 85 and 86, A stitch in time, (1980) NLJ 931-932.
- Thompson: EEC Commission hearings in competition cases, (1982) JWTL 443-450.

Chapter Six

# SPECIFIC TOPICS IN COMPETITION LAW

## I. MAIN PROHIBITED HORIZONTAL AGREEMENTS

### A. Market sharing agreements and quotas

a. Introduction

Market sharing agreements are particularly restrictive of competition and contrary to the achievement of a single market. Agreements or concerted practices for the purpose of market-sharing are generally based on the principle of mutual respect of the national markets of each Member State for the benefit of producers resident there. The direct object and result of their implementation is to eliminate the exchange of goods between the Member States concerned. The protection of their home market allows producers to pursue a commercial policy - partiuclarly a pricing policy - in that market which is insulated from the competition of other parties to the agreements in other Member States, and which can sometimes only be maintained because they have no fear of competition from that direction. The fixing of delivery quotas in relation to total sales, combined in some cases with a compensation scheme to ensure that the quotas are respected, means that the members of the group give up any possibility of obtaining an advantage over their competitors by applying an individual sales policy. Maintenance of the equilibrium as fixed by the quotas directly endangers intra-Community trade as soon as the sales quotas are applied to one or more markets within the Community.

b. Cases

(1) The Quinine Cartel

See above, page 109 , the ACF-Chemiefarma Case.

(2) Decision in re SNPE-LEL

See above, page 99.

13. The agreement has as its object and effect the restriction of competition within the common market:

(a) The undertakings concerned are actual competitors, particularly in the field of pyromechanisms, and at least potential competitors in other areas. Each party is of significant importance in its respective country as regards civilian and military uses of its respective products.

(b) In respect of the products listed in Annex 1 to the agreement (see paragraph 10), Clause 2.2 of the agreement prohibits all manufacturing or trading activity of SNPE in the United Kingdom and of LEL in France (see paragraph 5). These provisions impose territorial limitations on the activities of the parties and amount to a sharing of the market in their products.

(c) The isolation of national markets is a particularly grave restriction as it runs counter to the principal objective of the Treaty to establish a single market comparable to a home market. Such restrictions of competition are in opposition to principles of free trade in goods and services established by the Treaty. The sharing of markets is explicitly cited in Article 85(1)(c) of the Treaty as a particular example of a restrictive trade practice which is prohibited and has been condemned in a number of Commission Decisions which have been upheld by the Court of Justice.

(d) Certain other provisions of the notified agreement, in particular those referred to under paragraph 6, 7 and 8, will be subject to a separate assessment by the Commission. Some of these appear to bind the parties to cooperate in such a manner that in important areas they no longer make independent decisions in their future business activities. These provisions also appear to prevent the parties *inter alia* from freely granting subcontracts or licences to third-party undertakings in the other party's country.

(e) Although, according to the parties, the products listed in Annex 1 to the agreement represent only a minimal or not significant part of their output (less than 2% for SNPE, 10% for LEL), the restrictions of competition referred to in paragraph 13(b) are appreciable because the products are highly specialised in their particular applications, are offered on the European market only by a very limited number of manufacturers apart from SNPE, LEL and Pyromeca and there is no substantial competition to the parties within the Community from other producers.

14. For these reasons and also because the agreement brings about a territorial sharing of the parties' manufacturing and selling activities, the agreement may appreciable affect trade between Member States.

15. In respect of Clause 2.2 of the agreement (see paragraph 13(b) and (c)), SNPE have stated *inter alia* that this clause 'did not aim at a market sharing with an absolute territorial protection'. The leading idea behind this clause was that the technical complexity of the products concerned and the necessary exchange of information thereon would require that the parties be bound to maintain a close confidentiality, to provide the preconditions for a joint exploitation which could achieve a reliable cooperation between technical teams, thus promoting the communication of know-how between the parties concerned. The two parties, as they each supply their own complementary technological skills for the realisation of a complete product, recognise it as legitimate that they should not offer the same product to third-party users in the other party's country' (SNPE letter of 20 December 1977).

16. LEL have similarly stated that the objective of Clause 2.2 is 'to ensure the technical interchange takes place to allow a natural and positive development of the products of our joint technologies. The agreement does not limit the opportunities for consumers to purchase the products to which the agreement relates from other sources within the EEC. On the contrary, the agreement enables each party to offer customers a full range of products of both companies which otherwise would not be available within the EEC' (LEL letter of 20 December 1977).

17. These arguments refer in substance to the general purpose of the agreement concerning the sharing between the parties of technological information and do not affect the conclusion that Article 85(1) applies. Clause 2.2, whether it is considered in isolation or within the general framework of the agreement, has as its object and effect the creation of a territorial partitioning of SNPE's and LEL's respective activities which relate to the products listed in the agreement.

18. On a preliminary examination, therefore, the agreement in this respect infringes Article 85(1) of the EEC Treaty.

## III. Preliminary assessment under Article 85(3) of the EEC Treaty

Under Article 85(3) of the Treaty, the provisions of Article 85(1) may be declared inapplicable in the case of any agreement between undertakings which contributes to improving the production or distribution of goods or to promoting technical or economic progress, while allowing consumers a fair share of the resulting benefit, and which does not (a) impose on the undertakings concerned restrictions which are not indispensable to the attainment of these objectives, nor (b) afford such undertakings the possibility of eliminating competition in respect of a substantial part of the products in question.

19. At this stage of the proceedings, it can be left open whether or not the restrictions on competition which are referred to in paragraph 13(d) fulfil the requirements for an exemption.

In any event, Clause 2.2. of the notified agreement (paragraphs 5 and 13(b) and (c)) does not meet the requirements for exemption for the following reasons:

(a) Even on the assumption that specialisation of manufacturing activities and joint research and development of new products are in principle likely to contribute to improving production, the obligations of each party not to grant licences, or to produce or to sell directly in the other's country cannot contribute to such a development. The question whether the provisions contained in Clause 2.2 are indispensable to the attainment of such benefits does not therefore arise.

(b) In any event, consumers cannot draw any kind of benefit from the territorial allocation of the manufacturing and marketing activities of the parties. The parties themselves are the sole effective beneficiaries of the agreed partitioning of the market.

(c) Because of the limited number of other manufacturers of the products concerned, SNPE's and LEL's reservation to themselves of their respective home markets affords them the possibility of eliminating competition in respect of a substantial part of the products in question.

20. The relevant arguments of the parties, as outlined in paragraphs 15 and 16, do not displace the Commission's conclusion that the obligations of the parties as contained in Clause 2.2 of the agreement cannot benefit from the exempting provisions of Article 85(3).

21. On a preliminary examination of the notified agreement, the provisions contained in Clause 2.2 do not satisfy the tests of exemption contained in Article 85(3).

## B. Joint Price Fixing

a. Introduction

Joint price fixing of goods sold in the Common Market is also likely to affect adversely trade between Member States and seriously restrict competition.

.....

The prohibition of cartels also covers agreements concluded between enterprises of one and the same Member State for the purpose of fixing prices and resale conditions for imported products or for fixing prices and selling conditions for products or their own manufacture as regards their exports to markets within the EEC. Such agreements eliminate all possibility of price competition between members of the cartel so that - where their share of the market is not negligible - competition within the Common Market is restricted and trade between Member States affected by the resultant bias against imported and exported products.

b. Cases

(1) Decision on the Quinine Cartel

See above, page 109,the ACF-Chemiefarma Case.

(2) Decision on the Dyestuffs Cartel

See above, pages 41, 44, 70 and 149.

## C. Joint sales agencies

a. Introduction

In 1968 and 1969 the Commission gave negative clearance to three joint selling agencies for fertilisers manufactured respectively in Belgium, France and Italy.

The first two clearance decisions, dated 6 November 1968, concerned the Belgian agency (Cobelaz-Usines de Synthèse et Cobelaz-Cokeries) and the French agency (Comptoir Francais de l'Azote - CFA). Negative clearance in the third case was given on 3 June 1969 to the Italian agency SEIFA (Società per lo Sviluppo dei Consumi dei Fertilizzanti).

The agreements notified conferred powers on the agencies covering national territory, other Community countries and non-member countries.

Before granting negative clearance, the Commission had asked the agencies to abandon all responsibilities in respect of intra-Community trade; this was then done. However, when clearing the agencies, the Commission also decided that the fertiliser industry should be monitored closely and that it should check particularly whether the surviving parts of the agreements did not in fact involve market fragmentation by country.

The enquiry carried out under Council Regulation No 17 yielded a certain amount of information on the selling agencies and on the general situation in this industry. The main points are as follows:

The Belgian agency - *Cobelaz*

The Cobelaz-Usines de synthèse agreement was extensively amended on 1 July 1969; since then Cobelaz has had no responsibilities for marketing synthetic nitrogenous fertilisers in Belgium. It deals exclusively with sales outside the Communities. As regards ammonium sulphate from coke ovens, Cobelaz now markets the production of only one company, and it has become, so to speak, the company's sales department.

The French agency - *Comptoir francais de l'azote (CFA)*

On 1 June 1969, the members of this agency withdrew all its responsibilities for marketing in France. The CFA has now no activities within the nine countries, being responsible only for exports outside the Community.

The Italian agency - *Società per lo sviluppo dei consumi (SEIFA)*

SEIFA gave up all sales business on 30 June 1972 and was absorbed by Montecatini-Edison SpA on 3 July of that year, when it ceased to exist as a separate legal entity.

However, although these agencies no longer operate in the Community, there does not seem to have been any substantial corresponding increase in the volume of intra-Community trade.

French producers export only 4 to 6% of their total production to other Community countries, and Italian producers less than 1%. Only Begium exports half of its production, France and Germany taking equal shares. But here marketing policy is selective: Belgian producers steer clear of the Dutch market (which takes only 2% of their sales) for fear of a retaliatory inflow of Dutch products into Belgium.

b. Cases

(1) Decision in re CSV II

Decision of the Commission of 20 July 1978 on a proceeding under Article 85 of the Treaty. O.J. No L 242, 4 September 1978, p. 15; CMLR I (1979) II; CCH para. 10.076; Competition Law CM/M/I/135.

For the facts see the decision below.

1. The proceeding concerns the cooperation in the marketing of straight nitrogenous fertilisers between two Dutch fertiliser manufacturers, Unie van Kunstmestfabrieken BV (UKF) and Nederlandse Stikstof Maatschappij (NSM) operating through the joint sales agency Centraal Stikstof Verkoopkantoor BV (CSV), founded in 1948.
.....

D. Structure of nitrogenous fertiliser supply in the Netherlands

9. Unie van Kunstmestfabrieken BV (UKF) combines the fertiliser interests of NV Nederlandse Staatsmijnen (Dutch State Mines - DSM) following the merger in 1972 of DSM and Verenigde Kunstmestfabrieken (VKF), itself the result of a merger between NV Maatschappij tot exploitatie van Kooksovengassen Mekog and the phosphate fertiliser manufacturer Albatros. UKS is the largest nitrogenous fertiliser manufacturer in the European Economic Community. Its Dutch production facilities are in the Nether-

lands at Geleen, IJmuiden, Pernis and Amsterdam. Through DSM it is entitled to half the output of Ammoniak Unie NV, a joint subsidiary of DSM and BASF at Pernis.

Outside the Netherlands, UKF has production facilities at Ince Marsh in the United Kingdom with UKF Fertilisers UK Ltd (formerly Shellstar). In Ireland UKF sells through CFD Albatros, in France through its subsidiary Lecoester SA, in Belgium through Moreels Guano, in Germany through UKF Deutschland and in the United States through the local DSM subsidiary, Nyrpo Inc., and Columbian Nitrogen Corporation. In 1976 the DSM Group's total sales were Fl 9934 million, of which 1683 million were accounted for by fertilisers.

10. Nederlandse Stikstof Maatschappij (NSM) is a company in which 69% of the shares are held by Montedison and 25% by ICI. It is a very important manufacturer of ammonia, nitric acid, ammonium nitrate and above all urea, of which it may be regarded as the world's largest manufacturer. Its production facilities are at Sluiskil. NSM began producing ammonium nitrate at 33.5% N in 1975, specifically for the French and British markets, and it is planning to enter production of a comparable product based on magnesammon.

NSM manufactures no compound fertilisers, but supplies on the basis of a long-term agreement Zuid-Chemie, a Gesa subsidiary manufacturing compound fertilisers in the Netherlands, with ammonium nitrate solution, an intermediate product used in their manufacture.

In 1976 NSM's sales were Fl 1100 million.

.....

12. In addition to the two manufacturers (UKF and NSM) belonging to CSV, there is also another Dutch straight nitrogenous fertiliser manufacturer, Esso Chemie, an Esso subsidiary. This company entered the market in 1968 as an importer and in 1969 as an ammonia producer. It also produces straight nitrogenous fertilisers which it sells exclusively through a division of Windmill Holland BV, Europoort, which sells them on the Dutch market alongside its own compound fertilisers. It has gained a Dutch market share of between 20 and 25%. It manufactures ammonia, nitric acid, urea and calcium ammonium nitrate at 26%.

## E. Background to the agreements

13. Centraal Stikstof Verkoopkantoor NV (CSV) was formed at the Hague on 27 August 1948 as a limited liability company under Dutch Law with the object of engaging in all business activities relating to the sale of chemical fertilisers.

Its founders were:

- NV Nederlandse Staatmijnen,

- NV Maatschappij tot exploitatie van Kooksovengassen (Mekog), and

- NV Nederlandse Stikstofmaatschappij.

At the time, these three firms accounted for virtually all the straight nitrogenous fertiliser production capacity in the Netherlands, and they formed this company to handle joint sales of their straight nitrogenous fertilisers in the Netherlands and for export. Original shareholdings were 50, 25 and 25% respectively.

14. On 11 April 1963 the CSV shareholders entered into an 'agreement between manufacturers of straight nitrogenous fertilisers' as a sequel to a similar agreement entered into on 4 April 1955, which had expired on 30 June 1962: 'to ensure supplies to agriculture and horticulture on the best economic terms by expanding the consumption of nitrogenous fertilisers as far as possible' the firms agreed to reinforce their future cooperation as regards the marketing of nitrogenous fertilisers manufactured by them.

The agreement was amended and provisionally renewed on 23 June 1969. The preamble to the current version of the agreement, which dates from 1976, defines its object in the following terms: 'the manufacturers wish to strengthen their future cooperation while maintaining the same objectives, by pooling the sale and marketing of their straight nitrogenous fertilisers on the Dutch market and on markets outside the European Economic Community and by engaging in joint advertising on those markets'.

15. By an agreement entered into on the same day by the manufacturers and CSV, entitled 'CSV agreement', CSV's shareholders entrusted CSV with the task of 'marketing all straight nitrogenous fertilisers manufactured by them in the Netherlands and on export markets outside the common market'.

16. Following the merger between NV Nederlandse Staatmijnen and NV Maatschappij tot exploitatie van Kooksovengassen (Mekog) in Unie van Kunstmestfabrieken BV, the parties to the manufacturers' agreement are currently UKF and NSM. Their shareholdings in CSV are now 75 and 25% respectively.

## F. Content of the agreements as they currently apply

18. *The manufacturers' agreement*

(a) Article 1 of the agreement defines the products to which it relates.

'(1) The item "nitrogenous fertilisers" is taken to mean all products manufactured from synthetic ammonia, with the exception of nitric acid, containing more than 1% nitrogen - including those containing other nutrients - provided they are available to a manufacturer on Dutch territory and are intended to be used as fertilisers. It also includes ammonia and aqua ammonia for agricultural use in the Netherlands, and ammonia, nitric acid and ammonium nitrate supplied by two manufacturers to Dutch manufacturers of compound fertilisers.

(2) The item "straight nitrogenous fertilisers" is taken to mean nitrogenous fertilisers, particularly nitric acid and ammonia, containing less than 5% phosphorus ($P_2O_5$) or potassium ($K_2O$) as plant nutrients.'

(b) The manufacturers undertake (Article 2) to make all their sales in the Netherlands and in non-EEC countries jointly through CSV. This does not extend to sales by the manufacturers to CSV, between manufacturers, sales to other manufacturers for processing under contract, sales to persons employed by the firms or sales of waste.

All exports to EEC Member States are to be handled individually by the manufacturers themselves.

CSV's sales on the Dutch market are to be made in accordance with terms of business determined by CSV and approved by the manufacturers. For exports outside the EEC, the manufacturers lay down general guidelines for CSV and in individual cases may give special instructions.

(c) The manufacturers are free (Article 3) to determine their production capacities and to abandon production of existing lines for others. Should they decide to set up new plant they will inform CSV so that it can make the necessary arrangements to increase joint sales potential.

Each of them freely and independently determines the amount of each type of nitrogenous fertiliser it will manufacture. Before the beginning of each year CSV informs the manufacturers of the quantities of each type of straight nitrogenous fertiliser it believes it can sell in each of the next few months both on the Dutch market and on export markets outside the EEC. This information is updated monthly.

(d) Article 4 of the agreement allots to each manufacturer a proportional share of supplies to the Dutch market relating firstly to total CSV Dutch sales and secondly to sales of ammonia for agricultural use in the Netherlands and of nitrogenous fertilisers for processing into compound fertilisers in the Netherlands.

For the first part, the proportions are 75% for UKF and 25% for NSM up to 300 000 tonnes of pure nitrogen, 60% for UKF and 40% for NSM between 300 000 and 450 000 tonnes, and 70% for UKF and 30% for NSM above that. The second part is to be allocated in such a fashion that UKF accounts for 75% of aggregate supplies and NSM for 25%.

(e) The manufacturers undertake to agree before the beginning of each year on their percentage share of supplies of each type of product and on the distribution of their sales outside the EEC. The agreement also contains detailed arrangements (Article 5) for dealing with surpluses and shortfalls in terms both of quantities and of revenue.

In particular, should it be found at the end of the year that the tonnage of nitrogen supplied by one of the manufacturers does not correspond to the quota allotted to it, CSV is to equalise supplies by upward or downward adjustments so that the manufacturer who has remained below his sales quota is authorised to sell to another who has exceeded it, at the average gross price, in the form of a product to be agreed, the quantity of nitrogen to make up the difference between the quota and the quantity actually supplied. But this equalisation will not take place if it is found that the manufacturer who has not made full use of his supplies quota has not supplied CSV in good time with the quantities requested.

It is also provided (Article 6) that in the event of surplus production, the quota for exports outside the EEC will be allotted in such a fashion that the share of each manufacturer in total sales for the relevant year corresponds for each product to that manufacturer's sales in the two preceding years.

(f) Article 7 requires CSV to pay each manufacturer a uniform average price per tonne supplied, calculated separately for each type of fertiliser; this average price varies depending on whether the product was supplied to the home market or exported outside the common market.

(g) It is further provided (Article 11) that the Board (Raad van Commissarissen) of CSV is to consist of four members, three appointed by UKF and one by NSM. A Steering Group (Stuurgroep) consisting of representatives of each manufacturer is set up (Article 12) to handle monthly liaison with CSV and issue instructions to it; these instructions are to be binding provided representatives of both manufacturers agree to them in the presence of CSV's management.

19. *The CSV agreement*

(a) The CSV agreement, which was entered into and renewed at the same time as the manufacturers' agreement, confers on CSV the task of determining, with the agreement of the manufacturers, the terms of business applicable in the Netherlands and for exports outside the common market (Article 2).

It provides that the relevant products are to be sold in CSV's name on behalf of the manufacturers, who retain the right to put their trade marks on packagings (Article 3).

CSV undertakes to pay the amounts accuring to each manufacturer under the manufacturers' agreement, notably under the clauses concerning supply quotas (Articles 5 and 7).

(b) Consultations between CSV's management and the Steering Group on the manner in which CSV is to perform the tasks conferred on it by the manufacturers are as a rule to be held monthly. CSV's management is required to comply with instructions given by the Steering Group. Should it disagree with these instructions it must say so during the course of the same meeting; the final decision is then suspended until the Board of CSV has settled the question (Article 1 (4)). The Steering Group is also to verify annually CSV's budget (Article 8).

Apart from a number of technical provisions, the agreement expresses the general acceptance by CSV of all the arrangements made for the performance of the manufacturers' agreement.

20. *CSV's terms of business*

(a) CSV's Dutch sales of nitrogenous fertilisers, for direct consumption in agriculture and horticulture are made through CSV's Dutch representatives, with whom orders must be placed, namely:

- Cebeco (Nationale Coöperatieve Aan- en Verkoopvereniging voor Land- en Tuinbouw GA Cebeco-Handelsraad), Rotterdam,

- Cocon, Rotterdam, acting for Cehave NV, Veghel, and Coöperatieve Centrale Vereniging 'Landbouwbelang' GA, Roermond,

- ANK (BV Algemene Kunstmesthandelmaatschappij), Rotterdam, hereinafter referred to as 'the representatives'.

Orders for CSV must be placed by one of these three representatives (Article 1).

(b) CSV may refuse to meet all or part of an order, specifying reasons

(Article 2).

Where it is unable to meet demand for one or more specific varieties of product, CSV, after consulting all interested buyers so as to distribute the available quantities as fairly as possible, may supply an equivalent quantity of pure nitrogen in the form of a fertiliser of an available variety (Article 6).

(c) Sales prices are determined at the beginning of each agricultural marketing year; they are uniform within each category of fertiliser regardless of the origin of the product (Article 8).

Buyers may qualify for staggered rebates (staffel-korting) varying according to the month of delivery. The value of the rebate declines monthly from the beginning of the marketing year, i.e. October (Article 11).

(d) Orders which have been sent to CSV by the dates specified in the terms of business and which have been accepted and confirmed by CSV will be delivered in specified instalments per month or per period in accordance with a table given in the terms of business. Deliveries are to be made at the prices laid down in Article 8 minus the staggered rebates provided for in Article 11 (Article 20). These Articles further contain a table which, for the most important products, determines the supply schedules which the wholesaler must comply with in order to qualify for these rebates.

(e) Where CSV lowers its prices in the course of a marketing year, it reimburses the difference between the agreed price and the reduced price (Article 7) to buyers who have fully complied with the terms of business, as regards stocks of products whose price has been reduced and which can still be identified as having been definitely delivered by CSV. To qualify for this arrangement buyers have since 1970 had to keep full accounts and at all times give CSV's inspectors every facility for investigations.

Deliveries are after loading ex-works, either at the warehouse or on board barge (Article 12).

Lastly, for deliveries by barge and rail, CSV has since 1970 given higher rebates to buyers placing orders of a determined quantity or proving that they are grouping their orders. Failure to comply with the delivery schedule renders the buyer liable to an additional carriage charge. Deliveries by rail are made free at all Dutch stations where the quantity is 25 tonnes or more (Article 15).

21. Before the beginning of each marketing year the CSV members prepare and notify to CSV their production and sales forecasts ('produktieraming' and 'afzetraming') for the whole of the coming year. For each product (calcium ammonium nitrate, magnesammon, lime nitrate, urea, nitric acid, urean, ureak) they specify month by month:

(a) how much they plan to produce;

(b) how much they plan to sell themselves by way of straight fertilisers:

- for technical use in the Netherlands,

- for technical use in the EEC (with no distinctions according to Member

State),

- for agricultural use in the EEC and the USA (where their sales are no longer pooled);

(c) stocks in hand and quantities remaining available for sale through CSV.

22. This information is discussed by the Planning Committee. It is collected in a single paper that is passed on to both of them. Each month the manufacturers adjust their figures, send them to CSV and receive in return a paper setting out, product by product and manufacturer by manufacturer, the volumes produced and sold on the various markets in the previous month and the corrected forecasts for the remaining months of the year.

The Planning Committee meets monthly to discuss stocks, production and sales by the two manufacturers in order to verify whether they are in line with the forecasts. CSV informs the manufacturers of any sales problems it meets, or of any scope for expansion, so that this can be taken account of in future production.

23. One of the results of this system is that there is practically no chance of exports within the EEC, which are included in the end-of-year allocation to manufacturers, exceeding the level set for them at the beginning of the year, as additional quantities not allocated by the forecasts to a given market are automatically made available to CSV in order, according to CSV, 'to avert the risk of their being sold twice' and the quantities needed to meet orders from the other Member States during the year cannot be diverted from or added to production programmes, especially when production facilities are operating to capacity as in 1973/74.

With the same object of preventing quantities from being sold twice, the Nitrex Supervisory Committee - whose services are used both by CSV and by other European manufacturers of straight nitrogenous fertilisers for sales in countries with centrally planned economies - can declare CSV's allocation to Nitrex of quantities of fertilisers for markets outside the Community irrevocable.

24. The manifacturers also investigate at home and within Nitrex, the possibility of planned exchanges of products between manufacturers (produktenruil) and purchases from or sales to other manufacturers or importers. As regards deliveries from manufacturer to manufacturer, these take place both between CSV members themselves, notably as regards products which they both manufacture but of which they are in short supply, or in order to economise on transport costs, and between CSV members and manufacturers to whom they are linked through joint subsidiaries (UKF and BASF through Ammoniak Unie) or by interlocking shareholdings (NSM-Montedison/ICI).

25. Every two months the Steering Group meets to discuss all technical and economic questions arising: sales in the Netherlands, carriage, price, rebates, terms of business, comparison between quantities available and sales effected or about to be effected, deliveries to competitors, manufacturers of compound fertilisers such as Zuid Chemie etc., imports, exports within and outside Nitrex, use of liquid fertilisers, safety at production plant, market exploration and so on.

26. From the minutes of these various committee meetings it can be seen that CSV, on the basis of its sales forecasts, from time to time makes recommendations to manufacturers on stocks, production and ranges. At times of shortfall as in 1973/74 it has even been found that CSV does not hesitate to put pressure on manufacturers to give precise figures for their sales in the EEC and either to reduce their sales or to sell at a higher price or to refrain from entering into new EEC export contracts without consulting it and the other manufacturer, or again to replace the products due to be exported by products of another quality. Moreover, at these meetings, when CSV has confronted the manufacturers, with its requirements to meet the sales forecasts, the manufacturers have on occasion acted in concert in reserving a specified quantity of the relevant product for export to EEC countries and have then allocated this quantity between themselves.

27. CSV produces estimated production and sales accounts (poolafrekening) from time to time during the marketing year, and final accounts at the end of the year. Sales in the Netherlands are organised by CSV so that UKF and NSM supply exactly the quotas given to them by the manufacturers' agreement. The application of those quotas is possible principally because, throughout the marketing year, CSV and the manufacturers have periodically brought up to date the details of sales and deliveries already made by both manufacturers and compared them with the quotas, so that each manufacturer's production can be tailored to the fulfilment of its quota.

28. When the accounts are drawn up, an average gross price is also calculated per tonne per product for the home market, for exports to non-Community countries and for intermediate products. This price is paid to each manufacturer according to its product supply quotas for the above markets. Packaging costs (verpakkingskosten), distribution costs (distributiekosten) and carriage costs are shared out between UKF and NSM. Deliveries of nitric acid from Hoogovens (one of UKF's parent companies) are also within the 'poolafrekening' but are calculated separately.

29. Application of the quotas laid down in the accounts is ensured by a sale at the average gross price by any manufacturer which has not achieved its quota to one which has exceeded it of a corresponding quantity of nitrogen in an agreed form of fertiliser (those sales are entered in the accounts under the heading 'switch agreements'), so as to liquidate, over two marketing years if necessary, any positive or negative balance arising from the differences between on the one hand the quantity of straight nitrogenous fertilisers which the manufacturers had on hand at the beginning of the year (i.e. their production, less any corrections arising from the previous year) and on the other the sum of their sales (afzet) - including sales in other EEC Member States - and their year-end stocks (eindvoorraden).

30. These stocks are made up of the quantities of fertiliser which CSV has been unable to dispose of. They are allocated in the final accounts to each manufacturer according to the quantities of each type of fertiliser which he has sold during the year either through CSV or independently.

31. In the case of UKF, the sales taken into consideration (afzet) extend also to sales of compound fertilisers in proportion to their nitrogen content, though CSV itself is not directly involved in these sales.

For both UKF and NSM, deliveries of intermediate products (halffabrikaten) to other firms in the fertiliser industry, such as Zuid Chemie, are taken into account. Although sales of nitrogen for technical uses are theoretically conducted separately - a technical coordination committee called the 'Technische Ureum Commissie', meeting every month, is responsible for market information and the coordination of prices among the manufacturers - they (including, since 1974, export sales outside the EEC) are included in the accounts.

.....

A. Agreements or concerted practices

60. The cooperation between UKF and NSM is based on agreements within the meaning of Article 85(1), namely the manufacturers' agreement (producentenovereenkomst) and the CSV agreement (CSV-overeenkomst), to which effect is given through the uniform terms of business determined by CSV and by concerted practices. CSV merely provides the framework for this cooperation. As shareholders in CSV, UKF and NSM determine CSV's business policy. The shareholders have the right of veto, which effectively prevents CSV from taking any business decisions without the agreement of both of them. If necessary they can issue instructions via the Steering Group to CSV's management. If CSV's management wishes to influence the business policy of one or other of the shareholders on its own account, i.e. if it issues 'instructions' or 'recommendations' or exerts 'pressure', it is merely acting in accordance with the cooperation between UKF and NSM applied via CSV pursuant to the agreements between them, whose practical execution is left to CSV.

B. Restriction of competition within the common market

61. These agreements have as their object and effect an appreciable restriction of competition within the common market. The two manufacturers, UKF and NSM, act in concert in the production and sale of straight nitrogenous fertilisers not only on the Dutch market and the other markets allocated to CSV, but also on markets in the other Member States.

62. In the first place, the agreements have as their object and effect the joint sale of products manufactured by the two undertakings on their home market and outside the EEC. The consequence is that buyers in the relevant markets can no longer approach two independent suppliers, but must deal exclusively with CSV, which charges uniform prices and applies the same terms of business for deliveries of UKF and NSM products. Customers can no longer choose between competing offers. UKF and NSM products are, admittedly, still separately identifiable to some extent and customers may voice a preference for one or the other when placing an order with CSV. But this has no appreciable effect on competition because the same prices and conditions apply to the products of both firms and, moreover, both are guaranteed a fixed share of the Dutch market by means of the exchange system and the quota arrangement.

63. If such cooperation did not exist, UKF and NSM would be capable of doing business on the relevant markets independently, and thus of competing with one another. UKF is the largest manufacturer of nitrogenous fertilisers in the Community, and NSM is not far behind. UKF operates its own production plants through subsidiaries in Belgium, France and the United Kingdom. NSM has ties with ICI and Montedison, the largest

fertiliser manufacturers in the United Kingdom and Italy respectively.

UKF and NSM have a sufficiently broad range of products (NSM has recently extended its range (see point 10)). In the Netherlands they account for 46 and 34% of production respectively, and have a market share of 50 and 17% respectively. In the Community as a whole UKF has a 10% market share (including that of its UK plant) and NSM a 6.4% share. Other domestic and foreign manufacturers, including smaller firms and others, like Esso Chemie, which have a narrower range of products, are capable of marketing their products throughout the Community without assistance, either via their own marketing network or via the normal trade outlets and cooperatives.

64. The cooperation by joint sales between UKF and NSM affects their entire production and distribution policy. The prices that can be charged ary considerably from one market to another; a lower return in non-member countries can generally be balanced by a higher one in the Community (barring a few exceptions of limited duration). Prices subject to government approval within the Community are not fixed prices; they may accordingly be undercut. Improved use of production capacity and imports from other member or non-member countries can be used to boost supplies; there are no technical barriers to trade or excessive transport costs to hinder imports, especially when they come by sea or inland waterway. When the situation arises that supply constantly exceeds demand and local manufacturers' prices are appreciably undercut, then these local manufacturers lose sales and revenue.

65. This being so, UKF's and NSM's objective is to match their supplies as closely as possible to demand. The basic reason behind the cooperation between UKF and NSM is therefore to establish and exchange sales estimates (correct to the nearest kilogram), broken down by type of fertiliser, use, destination and delivery date. CSV's shareholders act on the sales estimates relayed to them by CSV and make arrangements for the appropriate quantities to be produced and placed at CSV's disposal according to the agreed schedule. The two shareholders' total production consists of these quantities, plus the quantities they market independently without CSV's intervention as a sales agent.

The detailed information thus exchanged with regard to UKF's and NSM's production and sales plans is further supplemented by an exchange of production and sales figures and details of stocks. All these figures are constantly updated to give an accurate picture of actual or expected developments on the market, regularly discussed and then corrected again.

66. The quantities placed at CSV's disposal are irrevocable or may be declared so, either by CSV itself or, where non-member countries are concerned, by Nitrex. There is, however, no sales guarantee given to the shareholders. If one of them produces more than it can sell, either independently or via CSV, it must stock up the surplus or cut down its production. If CSV's domestic sales do not come up to expectations the excess quantity is automatically earmarked for export to non-member countries. If they still fail to find a market, the quota arrangement of Article 6 of the manufacturers' agreement comes into effect. The fact that Article 6 has never been applied even during a period of substantial surplus in production capacity suggests that a pupose of the coordination system is to prevent such a situation.

67. In effect, this means that when the manufacturers draw up their first production and sales forecasts for the coming agricultural year they are free to decide at their own discretion on the quantities they will sell independently and the quantities they will offer CSV. These plans are, however, coordinated at or before the time they are exchanged and harmonised with those of CSV. Any corrections in the course of a farm year are equally carefully harmonised. It is not easy for an individual manufacturer - if only for technical reasons, above all when he is working at full capacity as during the 1973/74 crisis - to decide unilaterally to increase production in order to push up his own export figures in the short term.

In addition, the production and sales accounts refer to total production, including sales made independently by UKF and NSM. The quantities produced by both firms and made available to CSV and those remaining unsold are lumped together in the accounts under the heading 'end of year stocks' (eindvoorraden) and made available to CSV in the following year. However, these quantities are not considered as made available to CSV by the producers in proportion to the unsold stock held by each of them, nor in terms of the quantities made available to CSV or sold through its agency during the previous year, but in proportion to their total sales including their individual sales for that year. This puts at a disadvantage a producer who proportionally has made the largest individual sales, particularly to other Member States. Since the amount held in stock may not correspond to the amount supposed to have been made available to CSV, the situation is clarified by completion of 'switch agreements', i.e. delivery agreements between the producers or by including the amounts in question in agreements of this type.

68. The proceeds from sales in the Netherlands and from non-member countries (46% of total sales) are distributed as evenly as storage, transport and packing costs. This pooling of proceeds also covers products - such as intermediate products and urea for industrial uses (5% of total sales) - marketed without recourse to CSV's services as sales agency.

If UKF and NSM calculate to the last kilogram and cent in these matters, and if the total production and sales of both manufacturers are taken into account in their joint planning to the extent described, then they must inevitably refrain from competing with one another on markets not included in their pooling arrangements in order to safeguard the joint sales policy they pursue through CSV. When deciding on their sales policy for markets not covered by CSV they must take their CSV sales policy into account just as much as they take their quantities and pricing policies for their individual exports into account when they decide on their CSV sales policy.

69. It can be seen from the results of their cooperation - particularly in 1973/74 - that UKF's and NSM's sales policy in other Community markets was specifically discussed during their meetings, leading to decisions of a clearly practical nature. CSV caused its shareholders to provide it with precise figures for their sales in the EEC and persuaded them to reduce their sales, to sell at a higher price, to refrain from entering into further similar agreements without first consulting it and the other manufacturer, or to supply the EEC markets with products of a poorer quality. The records of these meetings show CSV's requests as taking the form of 'instructions', 'pressure' or 'recommendations'.

The parties have asserted that 1973/74 was not a typical year, characterised as it was by the shortage induced by the crisis, the danger of supplies draining off to non-member countries (where, for a limited period, they fetched higher prices) and the attendant risk of a shortfall in supply on the domestic market. They maintain that the words 'instructions', 'pressure' and 'recommendations' are not to be taken literally; the manufacturers were still free to determine their own sales policy, even in these difficult years.

70. The events of 1973/74 demonstrate that decisions concerning the quantity or prices of products sold in one Member State can have repercussions not only in that Member State but in others too. Despite the parties' assertions it seems quite predictable that, faced with an unstable market, they should use their information exchange scheme to improve the coordination of their sales policies on other EEC markets. There is, on the other hand, no need for UKF and NSM specifically to coordinate the individual export details when market conditions are normal. It is sufficient to have a coordination system which will allow them to concert the general orientation of their sales policy.

71. The cooperation between UKF and NSM makes the two firms interdependent, gives them influence over each other and leads them to coordinate their sales policy even on markets which they do not supply jointly through CSV.

As the Court of Justice of the European Communities held in its judgment of 16 December 1975, ground of judgment 174, the 'requirement of independence ... does ... strictly preclude any direct or indirect contact ... the object or effect whereof is either to influence the conduct on the market of an actual or potential competitor or to disclose to such a competitor the course of conduct which they themselves have decided to adopt or contemplate adopting on the market'.

72. The joint sale by CSV of straight nitrogenous fertilisers manufactured by UKF and NSM, combined with an information agreement that is inextricably bound to it, thus has the effect of depriving the manufacturers of much of their freedom to determine independently how much to produce and for which markets. Even if the manufacturers did not invariably follow in practice the lines laid down in CSV, this does not alter the fact that UKF and NSM substituted for the inherent risks of competition a form of practical cooperation which created conditions of competition that differed from the normal conditions of the market.

### C. Capacity to affect trade between Member States

73. The cooperation between UKF and NSM effected through CSV is capable of affecting trade between Member States. This is clear from an overall assessment of the various aspects of this cooperation, all of which are inextricably interdependent: joint domestic sales, joint sales to non-member countries (except the USA) and the coordination by UKF and NSM of their entire business policy as regards straight nitrogenous fertilisers, including production, storage and sales.

74. There is no need to decide whether cooperation has an appreciable effect on competition in the common market and on trade between Member States if it consist simply and solely of making specified quantities of products available to a distribution agency for sales in non-member

countries.

In the case at issue, however, the agreements cover more than just sales in non-member countries: that aspect is an integral part of a more extensive form of cooperation involving joint domestic sales and coordination and effectively covering UKF's and NSM's entire straight nitrogenous fertiliser business.

75. The sales policies of the parties cannot be considered on the basis of each market individually. They needed to coordinate their joint domestic sales and joint sales in non-member countries (with the exception of the USA) for the reason that since their proceeds from sales on the domestic market were - except over one specific period - and still are substantially higher than those from sales in non-member countries, UKF and NSM cannot possibly be indifferent about how much of the quantites they make available to CSV is sold domestically and how much is sold in non-member countries. The parties solved this problem by dividing up their domestic sales into fixed quotas; the remainder of the quantities made available to CSV by UKF and NSM were automatically earmarked for export to non-member countries. These non-Community sales have brought in lower proceeds, and consequently do not need to be regulated by a permanent quota system: provision is simply made for such sales to be effected in the event of surplus production, i.e. if one or both of the parties produces, and makes available to CSV, more than CSV can manage to market.

76. The events of 1973/74 show (see point 69) that the sales policy determined within CSV can influence the decisions taken by UKF and NSM with regard to sales on non-CSV markets in the Community. The amounts CSV or one of its shareholders supplies to the Dutch or any other Community market may affect the prices on that market and the other party's income and also have repercussions on other markets. An increase in supply to these markets which are an obvious area for expansion because they fetch higher prices than exports to non-member countries, and in the case of Germany higher even than in the Netherlands, is extremely likely to result in exports to other Member States by those purchasing from CSV and its members.

Cooperation is consequently not confined to just one Member State and non-member countries, it affects the whole production and sales policy followed by UKF and NSM, including trade between Member States. The nature and the accuracy of the year-end production and sales accounts, which include figures for quantities exported to other Member States, along with prior exchange and discussion of all important production and sales factors, demonstrate that UKF and NSM were not free to determine independently their production policy or their policy on exports to other Member States.

77. The parties fail in their submission that inter-State trade is subject to technical barriers and cannot therefore be appreciably influenced by private arrangements. If nitrogenous fertilisers with a higher or lower nitrogen content are used in a given Member State, there is nothing to prevent manufacturers in other Member States from including such fertilisers in their production programmes and exporting them.

78. The parties also fail in their argument that inter-State trade has increased and has not therefore been affected.

The volume of UKF's and NSM's export business within the common market has admittedly increased and has even led those companies to establish production and sales facilities in several countries. But, as the Court of Justice emphasised in its judgment of 13 July 1966, the fact that an agreement encourages an increase, even a large one, in the volume of trade between Member States is not sufficient to exclude the possibility that the agreement may affect such trade by constituting a threat, either direct or indirect, actual or potential, to freedom of trade between Member States in a manner which might harm the attainment of the objectives of a single market between States.

79. The cooperation between UKF and NSM does not merely jeopardise their freedom to determine independently their sales policy on non-CSV markets, but also has a restrictive effect on imports.

The concentration of supplies from two manufacturers of this size and importance on a Community market constitutes an economic unit which discourages foreign manufacturers from pursuing a more active export policy, effectively preventing them from altogether doing so. This danger increases in proportion to the power and solidarity of manufacturers in the country of destination.

Between them, UKF and NSM have something in the region of a 16% share in COmmunity production; their most important competitors - BASF, Ruhrstickstoff AG, Gesa, ICI, Montedison and the Carbochimique Group - each have a substantially smaller share of between 7 and 8%. The two firms have well-sited factories with large production capacities, not all of which is used. With a 67% share of Dutch production, UKF and NSM hold a very strong position on their home market. The concentration of supplies by UKF and NSM and the annual agreements with CSV fixing quantities for the greater part of their purchases effectively reduce the alternatives open to Dutch purchasers when they wish to place subsequent orders in the course of the year.

The Netherlands import less of the relevant products than the other Member States, and such imports as there are have had no appreciable influence on the high prices prevailing there. These high prices have been successfully maintained for years, in spite of lower prices in other Member States and considerably lower prices in non-member countries. The cooperation in question resulted in the continuous coordination of market policies and is a force to be reckoned with for foreign manufacturers proposing to import into the Netherlands larger quantities at appreciably lower prices.

80. The cooperation between UKF and NSM through CSV thus has appreciable effects on the structure of competition in the common market and is capable of affecting trade between Member States. This finding which is based on close and lengthy observation of the market and of the operation of the CSV cooperation arrangements, differs from the conclusions reached by the Commission in its comparable Decisions concerning Cobelaz/Kokerie, Cobelaz/Synthèse, CFA and Seifa, where the Commission made it clear that its sympathetic attitude was strictly a result of the circumstances then pertaining. There is therefore no inconsistency in the finding that inter-State trade is affected in the present case.

## D. Information Agreements

### a. Introduction

Under information agreements firms work together to exchange information, through a central agency, on quantities, prices, discounts and other terms of business, and on their suppliers and customers. A distinction can be drawn between agreements which are for purely statistical purposes and those which identify individual firms - depending on how the central reporting agency collates and passes on the information.

The essential points in the assessment of an information agreement were stated by the Commission as long ago as 1968, in the Cooperation Notice. There is an important distinction between information arrangements which do not affect competition and arrangements in which the exchange of information has to be regarded as being in restraint of competition. The distinction of course can only be drawn case by case, after consideration of all the circumstances. But the following general criteria may be stated.

(1) The type of information exchanged is the first material point. The provision of collated statistical material is not in itself objectionable from the point of view of competition policy. The Commission has no fundamental objection where national trade associations representing the same economic interests in different countries exchange statistics, either direct or through a reporting agency, which set out production and sales figures for the industry in question without identifying individual businesses, as is the practice in official statistics. Nor will the Commission as a rule object to a breakdown of data by product, country or period of time which goes beyond what is required in official statistics. But the Commission does reserve the right to investigate such cases where the breakdown of figures might enable an individual party to an information agreement to identify the competitive behaviour of the other parties.

On the other hand, the organised exchange of individual data from individual firms, such as figures on quantities produced and sold, prices and terms for discounts, higher and lower rates, credit notes and general terms of sale, delivery and payment, will generally be regarded by Commission as practices which have as their object or effect the restriction or distortion of competition within the common market, and which are therefore prohibited.

The area between permissible and prohibited exchange of information is thus defined by the distinction between a purely statistical arrangement with a breakdown of data by product, country and period of time which is not conducive to collusion, and the kind of arrangement which clearly relates to individual firms. One circumstance which in the Commission's view would certainly suggest a prohibited agreement or practice would be the regular communication of invoices or other information on an individual firm to the central reporting agency. This sort of information normally constitutes a trade secret and is not required for the preparation of periodical statistics. The Commission believes that in such cases it is enough to provide the agency with collated figures on quantities supplied and turnover in the period covered.

Parties to an information agreement which lies in the area between what is permissible and what is prohibited must be prepared to have the

Commission investigate their actions particularly closely if the trend on the relevant markets points to covert market sharing or price fixing.

(2) In assessing information agreements the Commission also pays close attention to the structure of the relevant market. The tendency for firms to fall in line with the behaviour of their competitors is particularly strong in oligopolistic markets. The improved knowledge of market conditions aimed at by information agreements strengthens the connection between the undertakings, in that they are able to react very efficiently to one another's actions, and thus lessens the intensity of competition.

(3) Lastly, the Commission also takes into account the fact that this form of cooperation between firms normally improves only the sellers' knowledge of the market. And that debars buyers from exploiting whatever 'concealed competition' subsists between sellers in oligopolistic markets and from thus preventing the price structure from becoming rigid.

The Commission's attitude to information agreements follows the line indicated by the Court of Justice in relation to concerted practices in its judgment against European sugar manufacturers:

'The criteria of coordination and cooperation ... must be understood in the light of the concept inherent in the provisions of the Treaty relating to competition that each economic operator must determine independently the policy which he intends to adopt on the common market ... Although it is correct to say that this requirement of independence does not deprive economic operators of the right to adapt themselves intelligently to the existing and anticipated conduct of their competitors, it does however strictly preclude any direct or indirect contact between such operators, the object or effect whereof is either to influence the conduct on the market of an actual or potential competitor or to disclose to such a competitor the course of conduct which they themselves have decided to adopt or contemplate adopting on the market.'

b. Cases

(1) Decision in re White Lead

Decision of the Commission of 12 December 1978 on a proceeding under Article 85 of the Treaty. O.J. No L 242, 4 September 1978, p. 15; CMLR I (1979) 464; CCH para. 10.111; Competition Law CM/M/I/142.

For the facts see the Decision below.

1. The proceeding concerns cooperation in the white lead industry since 1971 between Associated Lead Manufacturers Ltd (ALM), London, Lindgens & Söhne GmbH & Co (Lindgens), Cologne, and BV Chemische Industrie en Handelsmaatschappij Wed. Hondorff Block & Braet (Hondorff), Schoonhoven, Netherlands.

2. White lead (lead carbonate) is produced by directly dissolving metallic lead or dissolving lead oxide by the addition of acids. It is a white powder used as a white pigment in the manufacture of paints for outdoor use or as a stabilising agent in the plastics industry. It is supplied either as a powder (dry white lead) or as a paste (white lead ground).

11. (f) The agreement of 1 January 1971 and the background to it

In 1970 the Community white lead manufacturers got together to try to reach an accommodation in order to prevent prices falling still further. The objectives of this understanding were protection of home markets, regulation and allotment of export markets by quotas, exchange of information on quantities delivered and observance of prices set by the appropriate price leader in accordance with an agreed scheme. 'There should be established as many monopoly markets as possible in order to avoid a competitive fight specially carried out by the representatives and local dealers being accustomed to take away business one from the other by undercutting prices mutually.'

At the meeting on 16 December 1970, a draft agreement was discussed which provided for quotas of one third each, price leaders and delivery quotas for each export market, including markets in the Community, exchange of delivery figures so that cases where quotas were exceeded or unfulfilled could be regulated, and the establishment of a price scheme.

The minutes stated that the EEC countries, were to be omitted from the agreement: 'For legal reasons from the heading 'EEC is to be taken out of the draft text.' Legal doubts about the inclusion of the EEC countries had already been raised at the meeting of 1 June 1970, but the exchange of delivery figures was regarded as unexceptionable.

12. Accordingly the revised draft agreement of 20 January 1971, which was finally adopted on 15 April 1971 and took effect from 1 January 1971, contained no express reference to the designation of price leaders in the then EEC countries or to quotas for particular Member States. But the obligation to provide details of all exports including exports to EEC countries, was not removed. All that was removed was the explicit reference to the purpose of these figures, namely to establish cases where quotas were exceeded or unfilled.

The most important provisions of the agreement were:

- the fixing of overall export quotas of one third each for Lingdens, Hondorff and the two British parties ALM and Mersey;

- the allocation of subquotas and designation of price leaders for each export market outside the then Member States;

- the establishment of the 'schedule price', based on the price quoted on the London Metal Exchange;

- quota balancing arrangements: a party who had not fulfilled his one third quota was entitled to export corresponding quantities, mainly to 'regulator countries' such as Eastern Block countries, the USA and Brazil; to make this possible the price leader in the relevant export market would himself quote prices £5 higher; where quotas were exceeded or unfilled, balances could be carried over to the following year;

- monthly notification of all export deliveries, broken down by country, the information to be distributed by a central office.

13. From the beginning of 1971 onwards, the parties sent exact details of their exports and in return were notified of total deliveries, stating

who had exceeded or fallen short of his subquota and his overall export quota of one third.

EEC markets (except home markets) could not be omitted from these figures, 'as otherwise a proper calculation would be impossible' (letter from Lingdens dated 8 January 1971).

(b) Restriction of competition within the common market

24. The object and effect of this cooperation was the restriction of competition within the common market in various respects.

25. The parties exchange monthly statements of their deliveries of white lead, broken down by country, including EEC countries, through a central office. In this way they reduce or even remove the risks which would arise if they were not aware of each other's market policy and the amounts they delivered through the absence of reliable statistics and the lack of knowledge of demand in the two different sectors of paints and plastic material. The information provided on deliveries during the previous month is very precise. It makes it possible to recognise another party's intentions in good time, where he plans for instance to begin supplying a market which he has hitherto supplied only occasionally if at all, or to raise the quantities sold, which on a shrinking market would sooner or later lead to price cuts and thus increase the danger of a general collapse in prices, which is exactly what cooperation was intended to prevent.

26. This exchange of information cannot be explained by appealing to the need for more exact statistics or for greater knowledge of market conditions, of which the benefit is in any case reserved to the manufacturers; the supplier is identified, so that the information would normally constitute a trade secret not to be made available to competitors. The parties have explicitly classified similar statistics on production and deliveries of substitute products as trade secrets not to be divulged to competitors. The systematic knowledge of such accurate market data restricts the scope for competition between the parties.

27. This exchange of information in itself restricts competition, but the fact that it is compelemented by a system of delivery quotas produces another anti-competitive effect. To fix delivery quotas in this way is to limit or control markets in the sense of Article 85(1)(b). This is still true even if the quotas are not always meticulously observed, for a quota agreement conflicts with this provision even if it has the limitation or control of markets merely as its object. A quota agreement cannot be judged differently under competition law depending on whether the parties have spread their deliveries in accordance with the quota by constant observation of each other's actions (made possible through the exchange of information) or whether one or other party has attempted to exceed his quota on the assumption that at any rate this will not elicit any immediate reaction from the other, particularly in the form of economic countermeasures (e.g. deliveries to the home market of the party who has exceeded the quota). An agreement does not cease to be anti-competitive simply because it is temporarily or even repeatedly circumvented by one of the parties to it.

28. The quota arrangement was intended to extend to all exports; this is quite clear from the preliminary negotiations and is implicit in the

manner in which the agreement has been applied. The quota arrangement and the exchange of information on deliveries made sense only if they applied to all exports, and not merely to exports outside the Community, which make up about half of total sales. The parties' own national markets were excluded from the quota arrangement, but only because these were reserved for their respective national manufacturers. A manufacturer who finds his sales falling further and further, and therefore feels compelled to cooperate with his competitors on export markets in order to keep prices from falling, is hardly likely to ruin the prices on his own domestic market, which he has dominated for years, by engaging in an ill-advised marketing policy. On condition, therefore, that these markets are respected by the parties to the agreement, they can safely be excluded from the quota system. This consideration does not, however, apply to markets on which several parties are operating at the same time; here there is a need for coordination and the instruments for achieving it were set out in the 1971 agreement. For this reason ALM has allowed certain continental markets to be protected as this would, according to it, entail no alteration to its commercial pólicy. The exchange of information allowed it to control deliveries on these markets.

29. In the present case, however, the quota system agreed by the parties had not only the object but also, to some extent at least, the effect of limiting or controlling markets. Variations from quotas were calculated from the inception of the agreement until the end of 1977 and were carried forward from one year to the next without interruption. Even if a balancing operation is not carried out every year, the fact that the amount by which each party to the agreement has exceeded or fallen short of his quota is calculated each month contains an express or implied invitation to the parties to conduct the balancing operation which is the basis of the quota system. Deliveries do not have to be turned down to reduce the variation. Merely a policy of not looking for orders will reduce the quantities delivered in favour of the other parties. This, however, constitutes a restriction on competition.

### E. Collective Exclusive Reciprocal Dealing

#### a. Introduction

Collective obligation for exclusive purchasing from specific manufacturers or importers, or for exclusive deliveries to certain buyers within a Member State can also give rise to very serious restrictions on competition likely to affect trade between Member States. Where the obligations are reciprocal these collective exclusive dealing agreements can result in the splitting of an otherwise unified market into two separate parts, one made up of manufacturers adhering to the agreements and their recognised clients, and the other of the producers not adhering to the agreement and the clients who have not been selected. This artificial division of the market of a Member State, which is the result of such exclusive reciprocal agreements, means that the market as a whole is never open to producers of the other Member States, and that buyers of the Member States itself can never choose from among all the goods available within the Common Market.

When, as is generally the case, the manufacturers who are parties to such agreements within a Member State hold a strong position in the market and where the selected clients represent a major part of the distribution network of the market concerned, these agreements tend to isolate certain sectors of the economy of the Member States within the Community.

Undertakings of mutual exclusivity between manufacturers and dealers are often the extension at the distributive level of agreements between manufacturers for fixing quotas and prices. By establishing such exclusive trade relations with buyers, the producers party to the agreement tend to shield themselves from competition from other suppliers.

## F. Aggregated Rebate Cartels

a. Introduction

Isolation of an economic sector of a national market within the Community can also occur even where exclusive agreements have not been made between producers of a Member State where such agreements grant to the buyers in that State rebates, the rates of which are fixed jointly in relation to the total purchases made during the period under consideration from all the producers who are parties to the agreement. A cumulative system of rebates encourages buyers to obtain rebates at the highest possible rates by concentrating their purchases on the national producers and, therefore, not taking offers from other suppliers into consideration even if these offers are more favourable. This way of attracting custom restricts sales possibilities of foreign producers on the market concerned and producers from other Member States in particular. An artificial obstacle, collectively imposed makes access to the market of a Member State more difficult and is prejudicial to the establishment of a single market within the Community.

b. Cases

(1) Decision on the German Ceramic Tiles Discount Agreement

See above, page 71 and 138.

## G. Other prohibited practices

a. Introduction

The Commission has prohibited other horizontal agreements which it feels lead to restrictions of competition in the Common Market. Examples include collective boycotts (Papier Peints), restrictions on the freedom to obtain supplies (Frubo), voluntary restraint agreements (Franco-Japanese ballbearings) and reciprocal collective exclusive dealing Papier Peints, Bomée).

b. Cases

(1) Decision in re Papier Peints de Belgique

For facts and references, see above, page 77.

*The Commission ruled:*

.....

D. The boycott of Pex and International Decor

1. The decision to cease supplying Pex and International Decor taken by the Groupment in October 1971 is a decision by an association of undertakings within the meaning of Article 85(1).

2. This decision constitutes a restraint on Pex's and International Decor's competition since that time with other wallpaper dealers.

3. The claim by the Groupment and its members that they were justified in refusing to supply, because Pex would not comply with the General Conditions of Sale and charge the fixed prices, nor ensure that his customers would comply with them, is not a valid defence: the General Conditions of Sale and the collectively fixed prices are in violation of Article 85(1).

The further claims that Pex had debts outstanding with a member of the group, Papiers Peints Brepols SA, does not justify the other members of the group in refusing to supply him. Moreover, Pex's debts with Papiers Peints Brepols SA date from a period when the latter was calling for a boycott of Pex in its circular of 4 October 1971, thus starting the process which led to the Group deciding on the boycott on 29 October 1971 (first unpaid account 29 June 1971, falling due on 30 September 1971; second unpaid account 30 August 1971, falling due on 30 November 1971).

The Groupment's last claim - that GB Enterprises SA, which had been supplied by Pex, does not charge the prices fixed by the group or observe the prohibition on displaying price reductions - is without substance, even if in individual cases GB Enterprises SA has charged the public higher prices than those fixed, since GB Enterprises SA is free to set its prices at will.

(2) Decision in re Frubo

For facts and references see above, page 114.

*The Commission ruled:*

.....

1. The provisions of the agreement, which was concluded between two associations of undertakings, bind directly and are effectively applied by the undertakings taking part in the Rotterdam auctions. This Agreement must therefore be considered to be an agreement between undertakings within the meaning of Article 85(1) of the Treaty.

2. The present version of the Agreement contains certain provisions which have as their object and effect the restriction of competition within the common market. Article 9(1) prohibits importers and wholesalers authorised to take part in the Rotterdam auctions from marketing, otherwise than through these auctions, citrus fruit produced in third countries and apples and pears produced outside Europe with this fruit is intended for consumption in the Netherlands and has not yet either been sold or purchased at another fruit import auction or sold after unloading and clearance through customs from an importer or wholesaler established in another Member State

This prohibition in effect basically restricts the freedom of supply of the wholesalers taking part in the Rotterdam auctions, and hence their ability to compete since it prevents them from becoming importers themselves and thus compels them to obtain at the Rotterdam auctions the bulk of their supplies of fruit from third countries intended for consumption in the Netherlands. Although Article 9(1) does not prevent wholesalers from obtaining supplies at other EEC fruit import auctions, that is to say the Antwerp and Hamburg auctions, only meagre supplies are available at these two other auction centres. Moreover, while Article 9(2) allows Dutch wholesalers to purchase from undertakings established in other EEC Member States, it must be stated that the conditions governing such purchases are so restrictive as to be virtually prohibitive, the practical result of these conditions being that Dutch wholesalers may consign to the Netherlands fruit from third countries purchased by them in some other Member State only if it has been both unloaded and cleared through customs in that other Member State. It is thus prohibited for a Duteh wholesaler to consign to the Netherlands fruit from third countries which he has himself imported into another Member State or which has not first been unloaded and cleared through customs by an importer or wholesaler himself established in another Member State. Removal of the requirement that the fruit must have been unloaded in the other Member State makes no appreciable difference to these restrictive effects, since the ban on the marketing in the Netherlands of fruit from third countries imported by Dutch wholesalers themselves into another Member State remains unaffected thereby. It is therefore clear that Article 9 of the Agreement effectively restricts the freedom of supply of the wholesalers taking part in the Rotterdam auctions and that this restriction is particularly marked since the wholesalers are responsible for a major share of the distribution of citrus fruit intended for consumption in the Netherlands.

The abovementioned prohibition also has the effect of restricting the freedom of sale within the common market of importers established in other Member States of the Community. Thus, although the Agreement does not prohibit these importers from taking part as sellers in the Rotterdam auctions whenever they wish to sell in the Netherlands a quantity of fruit which, say, could have been sold at remunerative prices on their domestic market, such importers may not sell directly, that is without passing through the auctions, to the Dutch wholesalers taking part in these auctions fruit which they themselves have imported but have not yet unloaded or cleared through customs. In other words, the Agreement prevents an importer from another EEC Member State from forwarding to a Dutch wholesaler directly, that is without going through the Rotterdam auctions, part of an order of citrus fruit from a third country when he finds that he will be unable to sell the entire order on his own national market.

3. The obligation on the wholesalers parties to the Agreement to obtain the bulk of their supplies of fruit intended for consumption in the Netherlands only at the public import sales, and the resulting restriction on the freedom of sale of importers from the other Member States are likely to affect trade between Member States. With the exception of citrus fruit imported in the Community (i.e. Italy), fruit purchased at the Antwerp and Hamburg auctions and fruit imported in third countries and purchased in other Member States from undertakings which have already cleared it through customs and unloaded it, wholesalers bound by the Agreement may not import directly, that is without passing through the Rotterdam auctions, fruit intended for consumption in the Netherlands. This prohibition applies not only to fruit purchased by Dutch wholesalers in third countries and imported by them into the Netherlands

but also to fruit from third countries which was either purchased by these Dutch wholesalers in other Member States before being unloaded and cleared through customs or which they themselves have imported into these other Member States. The fact that the Dutch wholesalers taking part in the auctions are prevented from supplying the Dutch market with fruit which they themselves had either previously imported into other Member States or otherwise purchased freely from importers and wholesalers in other Member States of the Community is likely to affect trade between Member States.

Moreover, the overall effect of these restrictions on Dutch wholesalers in their freedom to carry on their business (including the prohibition on importing directly from third countries) is to damage the competitive structure of this sector of the common market by weakening the competitive position of these wholesalers in their dealings with importers and with other wholesalers of the Community. This capable of affecting the flow of trade between Member States in such a manner likely to hinder the establishment of a single market among these States.

(3) Decision on the Franco-Japanese Ballbearings Agreement

See above, pages 49 and 116.

(4) Decision in re Bomée Stichting

Decision of the Commission in a proceeding under Article 85 of the Treaty of 21 November 1975. O.J. No L 329, 23 December 1975; CMLR I (1978) D 14; CCH para. 9792; Competition Law CM/M/I/96.

For the facts see the decision below.

I. The facts

The Bomée-Stichting is a trade association, with legal status under Dutch law, formed in the Hague on 17 November 1937 for an indeterminate period. Its object is to promote the orderly marketing of branded goods of this description in the interests both of manufacturers and importers and of wholesalers, retailers and consumers. The association seeks to attain this objective by all legal means; in particular by facilitating concerted practices by the firms in this sector, by fixing the Bomée conditions, by collaborating in the drafting and enforcement of individual sales conditions and by setting up a special tribunal for the sector (Article 3 of the Bomée Statutes).

Its members are Dutch manufacturers and importers of perfumes, toiletry articles and cosmetics, of which most, about 60, belong to the association. They sell Bomée articles through approximately eight wholesalers whom they appoint. Several thousand retailers controlling approximately 6 500 sales points supply the consumer. The Bomée members are also grouped in three other associations: Mepacos (importers and manufacturers), Vegrocos (wholesalers) and SPD (retailers). Representatives of these associations are on the Bomée Board of Directors. They deal in most of the main brands, Balmain, Dior, Chanel, Rubinstein, Ricci, Nivea, Pond's, Valdélis, 4711, Revlon, Lanvin, Lancôme and Rochas; roughly half of all Bromée articles are imported into the Netherlands from other EEC Member States. In 1974. Bomée's share of the Dutch market was about 70% in cosmetics, about 40% in toiletries and about 90% for perfumes.

The members of the association have adopted uniform conditions for the sale of Bomée articles. The association ensures that they are complied with strictly, both by its members (who also undertake to require their customers to comply) and by wholesalers and retailers who accept them. Acceptance becomes effective when a member has a brand added to the published list Bomée articles. Eight days after publication, compliance with the Bomée conditions for goods bearing that brand become compulsory (Clauses 2 and 3 of the 1972 Bomée conditions).

As a rule, any wholesaler or retailer who buys an article which is subject to the Bomée conditions must thereafter comply with them, in respect of all such articles which he acquires thereafter by whatever means (Clause 3(2)).

As they stood when notified in October 1962, the 1953 Bomée-Stichting conditions had the main aim of enforcing resale price maintenance and ancillary measures, such as those regulating the supply of dealers through recognised distribution channels.

After the Dutch authorities had rejected Bomée-Stichting's application under Dutch law for exemption from the prohibition on resale price maintenance agreements, the association had to delete all RPM clauses from its conditions of sale. Individually, however, several members have RPM clauses in their own conditions of sale.

On 5 May 1972 Bomée-Stichting notified the Commission of the text of the new conditions which became operative on 3 January 1972.

Although the RPM clauses had been deleted, together with the clauses which, in the 1953 edition, banned all members other than manufacturers or importers from importing the relevant articles into the Netherlands without the consent of the appropriate manufacturer or importer, the 1972 conditions (Bomée-voorwaarden 1972) still contained the following clauses:

- wholesalers may supply Bomée articles only to retailers (Clause 10(3));

- retailers may sell Bomée articles only to the consumer (Clause 10(5));

- wholesalers may obtain Bomée articles only from manufacturers or importers who are members of the association (Clause 11(1));

- retailers may obtain Bomée articles only from manufacturers or importers who are members of the association or from wholesalers appointed by such manufacturers or importers (Clause 11(2));

- any dealer other than a manufacturer or importer who imports a Bomée article must inform the association, specifying the country of origin (Clause 11(3));

- wholesalers and retailers may be obliged to return their stocks of Bomée articles to the manufacturer or importer if the latter lodges a request with the association's tribunal (Rechtspraakcommissie) (Clause 19(1)).

In response to a statement of objections addressed to it by the Commission on 22 June 1973 stating that these clauses were incompatible with the rules on competition in the European Community, Bomée-Stichting amended its conditions of sale with effect from 19 December 1974 (Bomée-voorwaarden 1974).

This new version contains the following stipulations:

- members, manufacturers and importers are prohibited from supplying Bomée articles to firms other than wholesalers and retailers who have accepted the Bomée conditions (Clause 10(1));

- wholesalers who have accepted the Bomée conditions are prohibited from supplying Bomée articles to firms other than retailers who have accepted the Bomée conditions (Clause 10(3a));

- retailers who have accepted the Bomée conditions are prohibited from supplying Bomée articles to other firms, being confined to consumer sales (Clause 10(5a)).

However Clause 10(3a) and (5a) is supplemented by paragraphs (3b) and (5b), which provide that these conditions do not apply to deliveries to firms established outside the Netherlands.

The conditions of sale contain the following further stipulations:

- wholesalers who have accepted the Bomée conditions may obtain Bomée articles only from manufacturers or importers who are members of the association (Clause 11(1));

- retailers who have accepted the Bomée conditions may obtain Bomée articles only from manufacturers and importers who are members of the association of from wholesalers appointed by such manufacturers or importers (Clause 11(2)).

However, Clause 11 is supplemented by a new paragraph (3) to the effect that the obligations imposed by paragraph (1) and (2) do not apply where the goods are obtained from firms established outside the Netherlands.

The association's tribunal may order disciplinary measures against any person who does not comply with these mandatory provisions (Clause 20).

On 8 July 1975 Bomée-Stichting wrote to inform the Commission that it was amending Clause 1(2) so that the definition of Bomée articles would extend only to products marketed 'in the Netherlands'. This notification became effective on 25 August 1975.

On 7 July 1975 the firm Maxis BV of Muiden lodged a complaint with the Commission in respect of the Bomée conditions, it had experienced difficulties in obtaining Bomée products.

## II; Applicability of Article 85 (1) of the EEC Treaty

6. Article 85(1) of the EEC Treaty prohibits, as incompatible with the common market, all agreements between undertakings , decisions by associations of undertakings and concerted practices which may affect trade between Member States and which have as their object or effect the prevention, restriction or distortion of competition within the common market.

The conditions of sale jointly framed and applied by all the members of Bomée-Stichting constitute a decision by an association of undertakings within the meaning of Article 85(1).

7. Clause 10(1), (3) and (5) and Clause 11 of this decision of the trade association have as their object and effect the restriction of competition within the common market since they are designed to ensure that all trade passes exclusively through the distribution channels collectively recognised by the parties. The resulting restrictions have noticeable effects on the relevant markets in view of the number and size of the firms involved and of the large range of worldrenowned articles and products on the Bomée list. Furthermore, these are standard conditions to which an unlimited number of firms may become party.

Clause 10(1) of the 1974 Bomée conditions, whereby manufacturers and importers who are members of the association may supply Bomée articles in the Netherlands only to wholesalers and retailers who have accepted the Bomée conditions, means that other dealers are unable to obtain Bomée articles from the manufacturers or importers and that the manufacturers and importers are prevented from supplying dealers who have not accepted the Bomée conditions. The effect of this is to restrict the business freedom of manufacturers, of importers and of dealers who have not accepted the Bomée conditions.

Clause 10(3) of the 1974 Bomée conditions, under which wholesalers, who have accepted the Bomée conditions may supply Bomée articles in the Netherlands only to retailers who have accepted the Bomée conditions, and Clause 10(5), under which these retailers may sell Bomée articles in the Netherlands only to the consumer, prevent wholesalers and retailers from supplying other Dutch dealers at the same stage of distribution as themselves, who would be free to resell the products on terms that might be better for the consumer. Similarly they cannot supply other Bomée wholesalers, and wholesalers cannot supply the consumer.

Clause 11 of the 1974 Bomée conditions, under which wholesalers must obtain Bomée articles only from member manufacturers and importers and under which retailers may only obtain them from manufacturers or importers or their appointed wholesalers, restricts the freedom of wholesalers and retailers to buy from other Dutch suppliers.

The investigation of this case discloses that these restrictions on competition form a coherent and carefully adjusted system which is collectively applied and imposed by the members on wholesalers and retailers, and which clearly has as its object and effect the elimination of competition between the market participants concerned and other dealers and to ensure that as far as possible trade in Bomée articles in the Netherlands is channelled through the manufacturers, importers, wholesalers and retailers participating in the Bomée system. The effect of these restrictions is to consolidate existing distribution structures and the positions of the undertakings concerned on the relevant markets in such a way that new market entrants and firms which refuse to accept the Bomée conditions, such as Maxis BV, find it difficult to penetrate the market. The Bomée system makes it particularly difficult for market positions to be modified by the free play of competition.

The scope of the appraisal is not affected by the consideration that the Bomée conditions have been modified since 19 December 1974 in order to permit the parties to purchase the products concerned in other Member

States for resale. The amendment of the Bomée product description which came into force on 25 August 1975 and which limited the description to those products marketed in the Netherlands, served only to clarify the initial easing of the conditions. Neither modification takes the 1974 Bomée conditions out of the scope of the prohibition contained in Article 85(1). Serious obstacles still exist, particularly with regard to the marketing in the Netherlands of those products which are imported by the members themselves. These products may not be distributed freely by importers, wholesalers and retailers (the traders on the relevant market), but only through the prescribed distribution channels. Importers are not free to deliver to any wholesaler or retailer and neither the member wholesalers nor retailers may sell their merchandise within their respective groups. Therefore the means by which imported products penetrate the Dutch market are not the result of individual decisions by the parties on the different distribution levels, but are influenced by the restrictive agreements which the parties have concluded with their competitors.

The restrictive clauses reffered to above may substantially affect trade between Member States within the meaning of Article 85(1) of the Treaty in that they apply to goods which are mainly imported from other Member States and sold in the Netherlands. Trade flows may therefore be deflected from their natural course and trade between Member States affected.

They further have the effect of consolidating the division of the common market into national markets, which goes against the economic interpenetration aimed at by the Treaty, in that they make it difficult for manufacturers and dealers in other Member States to do business on the Dutch market.

In view of the size and number of the firms which belong to Bomée-Stichting, of the large number of dealers who accept the Bomée conditions, and of the range and reputation of the branded articles to which the conditions apply, the restrictive clauses discussed above have a substantial effect on trade between Member States in a manner detrimental to the creation of a single market.

Although the adverse effect upon trade between Member States is mitigated by the opportunity, first given on 19 December 1974 and later confirmed on 25 August 1975, for the wholesalers and retailers concerned to obtain supplies direct from other Member States, this relaxation of the rules does not compensate for the collective and cumulative effect of the restrictions referred to above, to which the admission of the products imported into the Netherlands by the members themselves remain subject.

Clause 10(1), (3) and (5) and Clause 11 of the 1974 Bomée conditions accordingly fall within the scope of Article 85(1) of the Treaty establishing the EEC.

## II. DISTRIBUTION AGREEMENTS

### A. General

The supplier of goods and services can ensure the distribution of his products in a number of ways. He can carry out distribution himself, either through employees or through branches or subsidiaries. Alternatively, he might wish to entrust the distribution of his goods to other persons; the most common of such relationships are those involving commercial agents and distributors.

The commercial agent represents a supplier of goods and services (known as the principal) and in seeking business for his principal the agent usually has the power to conclude contracts in his own name or in the name of his principal - for the account of the latter.

The ownership of the goods in question and the risk involved in transactions concluded by the agent remain with the principal. The distributor, on the other hand, is completely independent of the supplier and normally bears the risk in all transactions with third parties. The ownership of the goods is vested in the distributor.

In such commercial relationships the parties often undertake reciprocal obligations to protect their respective positions. The most common types of protective clauses are as follows:

(a) Exclusivity clauses.
Where a supplier agrees with a distributor to supply only the latter with certain products or where a distributor agrees to purchase certain products only from the supplier or where both parties agree to supply or purchase the goods in question to or from each other. Such clauses are frequently reinforced by the allocation of specially defined sales areas. In many cases the supplier undertakes not to deal directly or indirectly with any other party in the defined territory. A corresponding restriction requires the distributor not to sell directly or indirectly outside the allocated sales area.

(b) Customer limitation clauses.
Examples of such clauses are:

i. Where either party undertakes not to deal with particular customers;

ii. Where either party undertakes not to deal with certain types of outlets, e.g. supermarkets;

iii. Where either party undertakes not to sell to customers at certain stages in the production cycle, e.g. where a wholesaler undertakes not to sell to other wholesalers or where the manufacturer undertakes not to sell directly to consumers.

(c) Non-competition clauses.
Where, for example, a supplier agrees with a dealer not to distribute the goods in question or a distributor agrees with a manufacturer not to start producing or distributing competing products;

(d) Sales promotion clauses.
Such clauses include the following obligations: to advertise; to maintain a sufficient supply of the goods in question; to comply with the packaging and trade mark requirements of the manufacturers; to establish an adequate sales network; to provide specialised training for staff; to provide after sale service and to honour product guarantees.

(e) Resale price maintenance clauses.
Where a distributor undertakes to sell the products in question under conditions and at prices fixed by the supplier. In many instances the

distributor is required to impose the same obligation on all further purchasers of the product.

Typical distribution agreements feature some or all of the above clauses. Clearly the restraints involved can help to improve the distribution process. But it is also clear that such restrictions limit the freedom of action of the parties to the agreement and in many instances the limitation of the parties' freedom of action will entail consequences for third parties. The question now arises whether restrictive clauses in distribution agreements fall under the prohibitions of EEC competition law. In particular, can vertical agreements be subject to Article 85(1) EEC?

During the early 1960's the issue was disussed at length by various commentators. A small minority of these denied the applicability of Article 85 to such vertical agreements. Their principal argument was that Article 85 is applicable only to restrictive agreements between enterprises at the same levels of production or distribution; no competition can exist between enterprises at different levels of the production cycle. Such agreements might, nonetheless, result in an abuse of a dominant position and thus fall under the prohibition of Article 85 EEC.

In the Bosch case, both the Commission and the Advocate-General argued that Article 85 'referred as much to vertical as to horizontal agreements'. The Court did not comment upon the question in its judgment. The point at issue was raised again in three cases decided by the Court during the course of 1966; LTM v. MBU; Consten-Grundig v. the Commission; and Italy v. the Council and the Commission. The Government of the Republic of Italy, in all three cases, and the applicant, in the Grundig case, contended that Article 85 EEC was not applicable to vertical agreements. The Court emphatically rejected these arguments. In the LTM v. MBU case the Court said:

"To fall under this prohibition an agreement must have been made between undertakings. No distinction is made in the provision as to whether the parties are placed at the same level (so called 'horizontal' agreements) or at different levels (so called 'vertical' agreements) of the economic process. Therefore, a contract containing a clause granting exclusive right of sale may fulfil this condition".

And in the Consten-Grundig case the Court stated:

"In addition, it is pointless to compare on the one hand the situation under Article 85 of a producer bound by a sole agency agreement to the distributor of his products and on the other hand that of a producer who includes within his undertaking the distribution of his products by some means, e.g. by commercial travellers, and who thus escape Article 85".

The Commission and the Court of Justice obviously entertained no doubts as to the relevance of Article 85 to distribution arrangements.

In March 1962 the Council enacted Regulation No 17, the first implementing regulation under Article 87 EEC. This regulation established the negative clearance procedure and the notification for exemption procedure. The regulation also made provision for existing restrictive agreements, defined the powers and competence of the Commission, the Court of Justice and the national authorities, and empowered the Commission to impose fines and periodic penalty payments in order to ensure compliance with the Treaty rules. Although Regulation No 17 does not give much indication of the Commission's policy with regard to distribution agreements, the Commission realised that the majority of agreements notified under the regulation would involve distribution. The Commission tried to forestall the anticipated flood of notifications in a number of ways.

In December 1962 the Commission issued its Announcement on exclusive agency contracts concluded with commercial agents which declared that such agreements do not generally fall under Article 85(1). However, by March 1964 38,000 agreements, including 31,000 distribution agreements, had been notified, despite the fact that a simplified notification procedure was introduced by Regulation 27 of 1962 (as amended). In order to solve this problem the Commission was authorised by Council Regulation 19/65 to grant group exemptions in respect of certain types of agreements including exclusive distribution arrangements. On the basis of this enabling regulation the Commission adopted Regulation 67/67 which granted group exemption for categories of exclusive distributorship contracts. A number of test decisions adopted during the late 1960's further classified the status of exclusive distribution agreements and by 1970 the number of outstanding notifications had been sharply reduced. From 1970 onwards the Commission began to develop its attitude to other distribution agreements including national resale price maintenance and selective distribution.

A number of actions for annulment before the Court (Metro case, Case 26/76, Miller International, Case 19/77, BMW Belgium Cases 32/78 and 36 to 82/78, Distillers Case 30/78) and a number of preliminary rulings (Perfumes cases, Cases 253/78, 1 to 3/79, 37/79 and 99/79 and the L'Oréal case, Case 31/80) clarified important aspects of EEC competition law in the field of distribution.

After a few years study and after the publication of a draft regulation and amendments to the draft regulation, the Commission adopted in June 1983 Regulation No 1983/83 on the application of Article 85(3) of the Treaty to categories of exclusive dealing agreements, replacing from 1 July 1983, Regulation 67/67; (Annex

## B. Commercial Agency Agreements

### a. Introduction

The concept of commercial agency exists in the law of all Member States. A commercial agent is an independent entity who represents a principal and has power to conclude contracts for the account of the latter. Apart from Del Credere guarantees the principal always bears the risk. The commercial agent usually enjoys an exclusive right to represent his principal. Nevertheless, in most of the Member States it is sometimes difficult to distinguish between commercial agents, employees and independent traders. In its judgment in the Sugar Case, the Court noted: 'the laws of the Member States and economic practice have developed a great variety of forms of agreement which distinguish in particular between those where the intermediate trader negotiates with customers or comes to an agreement with them in his own name and for his own account, or in his own name but for the account of the principal, or again in the name of and for the account of the latter. The Court contended that for the purpose of applying Articles 85 and 86 of the Treaty, however, the relationship between an economic operator and his intermediate must only be determined in the light of Community law.

The Commission would have appeared to have taken such difficulties into account when drafting its announcement on exclusive agency contracts made with commercial agents.

The Commission considered that agency contracts do not fall under the prohibition of Article 85(1), but stress the importance of distinguishing between commercial agents and independent traders. It felt that the decisive criterion was the agreement between the parties as to the assumption of the risk involved in the performance of the contract. If the 'agent' does assume the risk, the possible application of Article 85(1) will not apply because the agent merely carries out an auxillary function in the distribution process.

b. Cases

<u>(1) Sugar Cases</u>

For facts and references, see above pages 94, 157, 252 and 319.

On the obligation imposed by Südzucker Verkauf GmbH on its agents not to resell sugar from other sources without its consent.

*The Court held:*

.....

B. The evaluation of the Commission's view

SZV submits that, since the relationship to itself of the intermediaries with whom it entered into the disputed agreements was that of commercial representatives, Article 86 does not apply to these contracts.

(a) 1. With regard to the prohibition of competition stipulated in order to ensure that the goods which it or its members manufacture are distributed, can choose either to use commercial employees - that is to say persons bound to it by contract of employment - or traders with whom it enters into contracts of a different kind.

So far as the legal position of the traders and the terms of these contracts are concerned, the laws of the Member States and economic practice have developed a great variety of forms of agreement which distinguish between those where the intermediate trader in particular negotiates with customers or comes to an agreement with them in his own name and for his own account, or in his own name but for the account of the principal, or again in the name of and for the account of the latter.

If the contracts on the Court's file, which are at issue, are examined they are found to be in law trade representatives contracts, in particular because they expressly confer upon the intermediaries the attributes of trade representative within the meaning of German law and because under their terms the representative is under a duty to negotiate or conclude sales of sugar in the name of and for the account of the principal, to carry out the latter's instructions and to look after his interests and, finally, because they allot them specific territories where they are to act as representatives.

It is agreed that, without prejudice to certain small differences, German law, which governs the contracts in dispute, proceeds on the basis of the principles that such trade representatives are prohibited, even if there is no stipulation in the contract to that effect, from competing with their principal without the latter's consent and that any infringement of this prohibition of competition may even render the representative liable to an action against him for damages.

However for the purposes of applying Articles 85 and 86 of the Treaty the relationship between an economic operator and his intermediaries must only be determined in the light of Community law, so that the fact that a trade representative's contract, which imposes upon the representative a prohibition of competition, complies with the national law governing this contract or that this law even imposes a similar prohibition is not determinative when considering whether such a contract is not caught by Article 86.

However it must be admitted, independently of the content of the applicable laws of Member States, that, in general, the fact that a producer or an association of producers forbids its agents who sell in its name and for its account, to act at the same time for competing producers without consent, corresponds to its nature and spirit of a legal and economic relationship of the kind in question.

In fact, if such an agent works for the benefit of his principal he may in principle be treated as an auxiliary organ forming an integral part of the latter's undertaking, who must carry out his principal's instructions and thus, like a commmercial employee, forms an economic unit with this undertaking.

In these circumstances the abuse is not due to the fact that the principal forbids such an auxiliary organ, without his consent, to trade in products which could compete with his own.

The position is different if the agreement entered into between the principal and his agents, whom the contracting parties call 'trade representatives', confer upon these agents or allow them to perform duties which form an economic point of view are approximately the same as those carried out by an independent dealer, because they provide for the said agents accepting the financial risk of the sales or of the performance of contracts entered into with third parties.

In fact in such a case the agents cannot be regarded as auxiliary organs forming an integral part of the principal's undertaking with the result that, if a clause prohibiting competition is agreed between principal and agent and the principal is an undertaking occupying a dominant position, that clause may constitute an abuse within the meaning of Article 86 as it is likely to consolidate that dominant position.

However the Commission has not alleged and the agreements produced for the Court's file do not disclose that the relations between SZV and its agents included the conditions which have just been mentioned, that is to say stipulations which enable the conclusion to be drawn that the agents have in relation to the applicant a position very similar to that of an independent dealer.

In particular the Commission has not denied that the trade representatives in question were mainly concerned with distribution for the account of the applicant without acting at the same time as independent dealers to any great extent.

2. However even clauses prohibiting competition imposed by an undertaking occupying a dominant position on trade representatives may constitute an abuse, if foreign competitors find that there are no independent operators who can market the product in question on a sufficiently large scale, and are in practice forced to apply to the said undertaking's trade representatives if they wish to sell this product in the latter's sales territory, or if the said undertaking enlarges the scope of the prohibition of competition to such an extent that it no longer corresponds to the nature of the legal and economic relationship in question.

With regard to the first of these exceptions the Commission has not denied that there are two groups of economic operators in south Germany trading in sugar, which, since they are under no obligation to SZV, are not bound by the prohibition of competition imposed by the latter on its trade representatives. They are the 1270 wholesalers referred to above, and, in particular, a not inconsiderable number of dealers, whose business consists mainly or to a great extent of importing and exporting sugar.

It does not appear that this case is concerned with dealers in the second group.

The result of all these considerations is that the clauses prohibiting competition in the disputed contracts are not in themselves an abuse within the meaning of Article 86.

## C. Closed exclusive dealing agreements and export bans

a. Introduction

"Closed" agreements are agreements which contain absolute territorial protection clauses, usually in the form of an export ban. Export bans involve an undertaking on the part of a distributor not to sell directly or indirectly outside his assigned territory. The supplier, in turn, undertakes to ensure that unauthorised sales made by himself or by other distributors and customers will not take place in the protected sales territory. The effect of such an agreement is the partitioning of markets without the corrective possibility of parallel imports.

b. Cases

(1) Consten-Grundig case

See above, page 66 .

(2) Pioneer Cases

See above, page 364 .

(3) Decision in re Hasselblad

Commission Decision of 2 December 1981 in a proceeding under Article

85 of the Treaty. O.J. No L 161, 2 June 1982, p. 18; CMLR 2 (1982) 233; CCH para. 10401; Competition Law CM/M/I/176.

*Facts:* Following a complaint from a UK photographic retailer, Camera Care, it came to the Commission's notice that the Swedish manufacturer and its British distributor had taken steps, together with Hasselblad's sole distributors in Belgium, Denmark, France, Germany and Ireland, to prevent or to impede trade in Hasselblad equipment within the Community. Ancillary measures were introduced to support the partitioning-off of markets, the firms concerned set up a system of reciprocal checks on the serial numbers stamped on Hasselblad equipment and exchanged price lists and terms of sale in order to trace the sources of uncontrolled exports. In addition, Hasselblad (GB) Ltd discriminated in its warranty arrangements and after-sales service against Hasselblad equipment which it had not itself imported. The firm further sealed off the UK market by applying a selective distribution system incompatible with the rules of competition and by requiring exports to be authorised by them.

The Commission considered that these practices were caught by Article 85(1) of the Treaty and also that in view of the practices and measures at issue the exclusive distribution agreements entered into between Victor Hasselblad and its distributors could not qualify for the exemption for certain categories of exclusive dealing agreements provided for in Regulation No 67/67/EEC. Under Article 3(b)(2) of this Regulation, the exemption does not apply where, as in this case, the parties take measures 'to prevent dealers or consumers from obtaining from elsewhere goods to which the contract relates or from selling them in the territory covered by the contract'.

84. These practices constituted a particularly serious infringement since the Swedish and British firms put pressure on the other sole distributors. The Commission took this into account and also the duration of the infringement in imposing fines of 560 000 ECU on Victor Hasselblad and 165 000 ECU on Hasselblad (GB) Ltd. On the other hand, much smaller fines were imposed on the Belgian, French and Irish sole distributors, who took an active part in the market partitioning, but under pressure from Victor Hasselblad and Hasselblad (GB) Ltd. Since the Danish and German sole distributors were found to have only participated in supporting measures (serial number checks and exchange of price lists) which were not directly related to the obstruction of individual export transactions, the Commission decided not to impose any fines on them.

*The Commission ruled:*

42. As stated in the judgment given by the Court of Justice of the European Communities on 16 December 1975 in Joined Cases 40 to 48, 50, 54 to 56, 111, 113 and 114/73 ('Suiker Unie' (1975) ECR 1663), the concept of a 'concerted practice' refers to a form of coordination between undertakings which knowingly substitutes for the risks of competition practical cooperation between them which leads to conditions of competition which do not correspond to the normal conditions of the market. If an undertaking acts on the complaints made to it by another undertaking in connection with the competition from the former's products, this constitutes or is evidence of a concerted practice.

43. Victor Hasselblad took up the complaints made by its sole distributors Prolux and Hasselblad (GB) concerning parallel imports and contacted Têlos, Ilford, and, on the occasion of Camera Care's imports,

also Prolux. It made clear to them and put into practice its general sales policy of protecting its sole distributors from imports. Victor Hasselblad expressly prohibited Ilford from engaging in exports and requested Têlos to keep an eye on the matter. It evidently also contacted Prolux on account of the matter of exports.

44. Ilford subsequently gave Victor Hasselblad an oral and written commitment that it would comply with the ban and Têlos gave an assurance that it would keep an eye on exports and would not itself supply Camera Care any more. Prolux refused to meet orders from the United Kingdom. Têlos gave a similar assurance to Prolux in December 1974 and to Hasselblad (GB) between July and September 1978. Accordingly, Têlos, Ilford and Prolux also acted on and adopted either explicitly (Ilford and Têlos) or tacitly (Prolux) the respective complaints made by the other sole distributors.

45. In addition to Victor Hasselblad, which, in its capacity as manufacturer, played a major role in formulating this policy of market compartmentalisation, Hasselblad (GB) and Prolux knowingly and intentionally prompted the other sole distributors to act as they did. By acting in this way, the sole distributors in question (Hasselblad (GB), Ilford, Têlos, Prolux and Polack) arranged also among themselves not to export to other Member States in the common market. They thus complied with Victor Hasselblad's general sales policy, which had been notified to them, viz. to afford the sole distributors the maximum feasible territorial protection. This coordinated behaviour made normal market conditions, as they would have evolved in the presence of free circulation of goods, unattainable.

46. For the purpose of applying Article 85(1), it need not be decided whether the export ban imposed on Ilford amounts to an agreement. It is sufficiently decisive that Victor Hasselblad and its sole distributors combined to apply a policy of market compartmentalisation.

47. Têlos's and Ilford's submission that they complied with the manufacturer's export ban only in form (Têlos) or only as a result of extreme pressure being exerted on it (Ilford) is irrelevant to the question whether there was a concerted practice. For a concerted practice to exist it is sufficient for an independent undertaking knowingly and of its own accord to adjust its behaviour in line with the wishes of another undertaking. The motive or knowledge that the act is unlawful is irrelevant.

48. Moreover, the provisions in the sole distributorship agreement to the effect that the serial numbers of equipment sold and the name and address of the purchaser should be registered and should be notified to Victor Hassleblad upon request have been used by Victor Hasselblad and by Hasselblad (GB), Ilford, Têlos, Prolux and Polack to trace the source of exports within the Community. Such systematic checks were clearly not isolated measures but part of an overall system of market partitioning. All of the abovementioned sources of exports were detected by serial number checks. The latter is therefore the use for an unlawful purpose of a contractual provision which in itself is lawful.

49. The exchange of price lists and business secrets between Victor Hasselblad, Hasselblad (GB), Ilford, Têlos, Prolux, Nordić and Polack was another ancillary device to ensure the market partitioning. No objections will normally be raised under competition law merely because

a manufacturer asks its sole distributors for their price lists and for information regarding their terms of business (price rebates, bonuses etc.). However, Victor Hasselblad used the information it received to inform its sole distributors of the prices charged by the other sole distributors. As can be seen from Victor Hasselblad's letters of 18 June 1974 and 13 October 1978 to Têlos and to Hasselblad (GB) respectively, this exchange of information was designed precisely to prevent exports ('pirate exports') or to remove the incentive for them.

The exchange of price information between Prolux and Têlos and between Hasselblad (GB) and Têlos clearly served the same purpose. Polack asked for the price information at a time when parallel imports from Denmark to the United Kingdom were expanding. The exchange of information between Têlos and Nordic took place without any reasons being given but included details of pricing and discount arrangements, and this at a time when parallel imports were also taking place.

50. The Court of Justice in its Judgment of 17 October 1972 in the 'Cimenteries' case, (1972) ECR 977, and the Commission in several Decisions: (COBELPA/VNP, 8 September 1977 (O.J. No L 242, 21.9.1977, p. 10), Vegetable parchment 23 December 1977 (O.J. No L 70, 13.3.1978,p. 54), have pointed out that the mutual notification between competitors of prices and of the conditions governing discounts, bonuses, rebates, etc., which rank as business secrets, constitutes an anti-competitive measure within the meaning of Article 85(1). This is all the more so where, as is usually the case, such information is sought or given for an anti-competitive purpose or with anti-competitive effects (Court of Justice, Judgment in 'Suiker Unie' (1975) ECR 1663 and 1965 *et seq.*). It was precisely in order to eliminate competition in the form of parallel imports that the parties concerned exchanged the information in question.

51. The joint submission by the parties concerned that they never increased their prices to match those charged by another sole distributor but, if anything, adjusted their prices downwards in no way affect the above assessment. First, it shows that in this case, the arrangement for exchanging information influenced the market behaviour of the parties concerned. Secondly, if information had not been exchanged in the manner described, the price reductions, where they occurred, would have been larger. The joint submission statement that the price lists were 'generally known' is not true of the secret price rebates and bonuses. Further, the fact that it is possible, although bothersome and time-consuming, to obtain price lists with the help of third parties such as dealers in no way detracts from the assessment that the exchange of price information brings about an artificial change in the conditions of competition (cf. Commission Decision in Vegetable Parchment).

## B. EFFECT OF THESE MEASURES ON THE SOLE DISTRIBUTORSHIP AGREEMENTS

52. Under Article 3(b) of Regulation No 67/67/EEC, sole distributorship agreements do not benefit from block exemption where the parties to them take direct or indirect steps to protect the allotted territories or endeavour otherwise to prevent imports.

53. Under the agreements as written, there was no lawful means by which Victor Hasselblad or its sole distributors could control the resale of Hasselblad equipment to an extent larger than that permitted under the exemption provided for in Regulation No 67/67/EEC or could demand, say,

that resellers supply the equipment only to dealers supplied by Hasselblad sole distributors.

54. In its Judgment of 1 October 1975 (Case 25/75 - Van Vliet/Dalle Crode (1975) ECR 1103), the Court of Justice declared that the effect of a sole distributorship agreement must not be to prevent imports from other Member States being carried out outside the 'official' distribution network, thereby upholding the Commission's constant endeavours to ensure that sole distributorship arrangements do not restrict supplies of the relevant contract goods and do not divide up markets.

55. As implemented, the sole distributorship agreements between Victor Hasselblad and the sole distributors Hasselblad (GB), Ilford, Têlos, Prolux, Polack and Nordic do not, therefore, fall within the block exemption provided for in Article 1(1) of Regulation No 67/67/EEC, with the result that Article 85(1) of the Treaty applies to them because of their exclusivity.

56. An anti-competitive measure can consist in sole distributors giving no, or slower, or lower quality repair service in respect of parallel-import goods. The Commission has repeatedly stated that, compared with a purchaser of goods that have been imported through regular channels, a purchaser of parallel-import goods must not be discriminated against either financially or technically or as regards access to after-sales service (cf. Commission Decision of 23 October 1978: Zanussi (O.J. No L 322, 16.11.1978)). This does not mean that a sole distributor is not allowed to provide any additional guarantee services in respect of goods imported and resold by him. However, parallel-import products must not be placed at a disadvantage in so far as the manufacturer's guarantee and the sole distributor's guarantee are identical. The distributor's guarantee must not assure the user priority in speed of repair. Prompt repair work is an important feature of any guarantee, particularly where, as in the present case, the products in question are, for the most part, used by professionals and where the speed of guarantee and repair services is a fundamental feature of the after-sales service.

57. Hasselblad (GB) practises a more rapid repair service for 'normally' imported cameras, thereby placing purchasers of parallel-import Hasselblad equipment at a disadvantage. This constitutes a measure acting in restraint of competition. This behaviour on the part of Hasselblad (GB) is caught by Article 3(b) of Regulation No 67/67/EEC because it is intended to dissuade dealers or consumers from obtaining the goods from within the common market.

58. It is irrelevant here that it is a unilateral measure since even unilateral action is, as is clear from the ninth recital of Regulation No 67/67/EEC, sufficient for Article 3 of that Regulation to apply. For the same reason, the sole distributorship agreement between Victor Hasselblad and Hasselblad (GB) does not benefit from the block exemption in Article 1(1) of Regulation No 67/67/EEC.

(4) Hasselblad case

For facts and references see above, page

*The Court held:*

....

30. The first distributorship agreement between Victor Hasselblad and

the applicant was concluded in 1958. That agreement contained a clause prohibiting sales by the applicant outside the United Kingdom. In 1975 that agreement was replaced by a new sole distributorship agreement not containing any prohibition on exports. The terms of the agreement were thus such that it could qualify for block exemption under Regulation No. 67/67/EEC of the Commission. The Commission maintains in its decision, however, that the agreement does not qualify for such exemption on the ground that the contracting parties took steps to obstruct the provision of supplies of products referred to in the agreement to dealers elsewhere in the Common Market, which renders the exemption contained in Article 1 inapplicable by virtue of Article 3 of the same regulation.

31. In that connection the Commission relies, in particular, on the conduct of Victor Hasselblad and of the applicant, considered above, as regards furnishing Camera Care with supplies.

32. The Commission also contends that the applicant introduced a guarantee, known as the 'Silver Service Guarantee', covering only Hasselblad cameras imported into the United Kingdom through the applicant. Every Hasselblad camera is guaranteed by the manufacturer for a period of one year. The sole distributor is under an obligation to carry out the necessary repairs. The Silver Service Guarantee extends the one-year period to 24 months for cameras imported through the applicant. The Commission claims that in its advertisements the applicant offered users covered by the Silver Service Guarantee a twenty-four hour repair service and that it accords priority to such repairs.

33. According to the Commission's decision (para. 57), the fact that the applicant advertises or practices a more rapid repair service for 'properly' imported cameras and thus places parallel imports of Hasselblad products at a disadvantage constitutes a measure in restraint of competition.

34. In that regard it must be remembered that in reply to a question put to it by the Court, the Commission was unable to show that cameras which were the subject of parallel imports had to wait longer for repairs with the applicant than did the same cameras in other Member States; it was only able to show that the applicant reserved special advantages for its own customers (a twenty-four hour repair service and two-year guarantee). In the circumstances, such conduct cannot be regarded as restricting the supply of parallel imports of cameras where such cameras are fully covered by the manufacturer's normal guarantee which the distributor is under an obligation to provide.

35. The view must therefore be taken that although the Commission's objection to the Silver Service Guarantee is unfounded, the existence of a concerted practice aimed at restricting parallel imports intended for Camera Care has been established and is sufficient to exclude block exemption under Regulation N. 67/67/EEC.

36. The applicant also submits that the Commission did not provide it with an opportunity to express its views concerning the sole distributorship agreement concluded with Victor Hasselblad and that Article 2 of the decision should therefore be declared void. That argument cannot be accepted. It is clear from the statement of objections that the Commission informed the applicant that the alleged conduct had the effect of excluding the agreement from the exemption provided for in Reg. 67/67/EEC.

## D. Regulation 1983/83

Regulation 67/67 on the application of Article 85(3) of the Treaty to categories of agreements, decisions and concerted practices has been replaced on 1 July 1983 by Commission Regulation 67/67.

Regulation 1983/83 has the same structure as Regulation 67/67 but differs especially as far ad the territorial scope is concerned. Regulation 1983/83 also covers exclusive dealing agreements for the whole of the common market, so individual exemptions are no longer necessary for those type of agreements as was the case with Regulation 67/67 (see Decision on the Durodyne/Europair Agreement op 19 December 1974, O.J. No L 29, 3 February 1975, p. 11).

Regulation 1983/83 also covers exclusive dealing agreements between parties in one Member State as did Regulation 67/67 in the interpretation of the Court of Justice in Case 63/75 Fonderies Roubaix v. Fonderies Roux.
For the text of Regulation 1983/83 see Annex No. VII.

## E. Specific territorial

## Problems

1. Where the supplier is situated inside the EEC and the distributor is situated outside the EEC, or where both the supplier and the distributor are established inside the EEC but the sales territory lies outside the EEC.

Cases:

(1) Decision on the Grosfilex-Fillistorf Agreement

See above, page 83.

(2) Decision in re Junghans

See above, page 86.

(4) Decision on the Rieckermann/AEG-Elotherm Agreement

Decision of the Commission of 6 November 1968 on a proceeding under Article 85 of the Treaty. J.O. No L 276, 14 November 1968, p. 25; (1968) CMLR D 78; CCH para. 9267; Competition Law CM/M/I/17.

*The Commission decided:*

.....

Under this agreement, the export company Johs. Rieckermann KG, Hamburg, has undertaken to market exclusively in Japan the inductive heating equipment manufactured by AEG-Elotherm GmbH, Remscheid-Hasten. Rieckermann is required to purchase equipment of this type for export to Japan exclusively from AEG-Elotherm. AEG-Elotherm is required to market its equipment in Japan through Rieckermann only and to ensure that its other customers do not sell such equipment there.

In the Commission's view, the ban of Article 85(1) of the EEC Treaty does not apply to this agreement as it does not impair competition to an appreciable extent within the Common Market. This agreement has been treated as a test case and the Commission is now able to use a simplified procedure to deal with the bulk of roughly 1,100 notifications and applications filed with it in respect of such exclusive dealing agreements on exports.

Through this Decision, the Commission makes it clear that, in respect of most exclusive dealing agreements to which export companies not equipped for selling within the Common Market are party, there is no need for notification and no point in applying for negative clearance. Exclusive dealing agreements concluded with such firms will, as a rule, not appreciably impair competition within the Common Market, even if the manufacturer grants his exporter absolute territorial protection for the relevant exporter market and if the exporter has undertaken not to sell competing products on this market.
.....

## F. National Resale Price Maintenance and Price Terms in intra-Community trade

a. Introduction

Purely national systems of resale price maintenance do not generally come under the Community law prohibiting cartels. To the extent that they are limited to compelling retailers in a Member State to respect certain prices for the resale within that State of products supplied by a manufacturer established on that market or by a concession holder appointed for that territory, trade between Member States will not, generally, be affected within the meaning of Article 85 of the EEC Treaty. That is why the Commission considers that the question of vertical resale price maintenance is essentially a matter of national competition policy. The Commission ensures, however, that intermediaries and consumers are enabled to obtain supplies of the product concerned at the most favourable prices and wherever they choose within the Community.

With this in view, the Commission pointed out the fact that a system of vertical resale price maintenance was authorised in a Member State in no way constitutes a sufficient reason for not applying the prohibition referred to in Article 85(1) to measures intended to make them watertight, that is to say measures which prevent the sale in the country concerned of products imported at prices below the price level fixed by resale price maintenance. Other clauses which may be covered by the provisions of Article 85(1) are those prohibiting exports, re-exports or re-imports and which are intended to preserve the price system operated within a Member State. The same was also considered to apply with regard to systems of fixed re-export prices under which all foreign customers are obliged to charge for re-exports those prices fixed by resale price maintenance in the country for which the exports were intended.

b. Cases

(1) Decision in re Deutsche Philips GmbH

Decision of the Commisison of 5 October 1973 relating to proceedings under Article 85 of the EEC Treaty; O.J. No L 293, 20 October 1973, p. 40; (1973) CMLR D 241; CCH para. 9606; Competition Law CM/M/I/71.

*Facts:* In 1973 the Commission fined Deutsche Philips GmbH for various restrictive practices including export bans, re-import price fixing and customer limitation clauses, all of which were designed to protect a vertical price maintenance system. In 1967 the Commission had initiated proceedings against Deutsche Philips and other subsidiaires of Philips Gloeilampenfabriek Eindhoven (Holland), for having applied export bans. The parent company decided to lift bans on exports to other Member States, and called upon the subsidiaries concerned to amend their agreements accordingly. Deutsche Philips made the necessary amendments, but not to all its agreements. It did not lift the ban on exports to EEC countries which was contained in its agreement for electric razors until after the Commission had initiated new proceedings for breach of Article 85(1).

*The Commission ruled:*

.....

Since the price-fixing applied without exception to all goods covered by the agreement, which German retailers had purchased from DPG direct or from domestic or foreign suppliers, the German retailers were obliged to observe the fixed prices applying in Germany when reselling goods covered by the agreement and imported from another EEC country into Germany. This re-import price-fixing thus prevented the German retailer from entering into competition with other German retailers as regards prices when reselling re-imported goods in Germany.

This reimport price-fixing cannot be justified by the fact that it serves to protect the price-fixing which is legally permitted in Germany by preventing the sale of imported goods below the prices fixed in Germany and thus makes it possible to maintain the price-fixing. The fact that vertical price-fixing is allowed in a given Member State is not sufficient justification for exempting measures designed to preserve this price-fixing from the scope of Article 85(1). A market-sharing policy conflicting with the objectives of the common market cannot be considered to comply with the competition rules in the EEC Treaty simply because the national legislature has permitted the fixing of consumer prices for certain goods.

*The Commission decided:*

.....

Article 1

It is hereby established that the following obligations imposed by Deutsche Philips GmbH on its German dealers constitutes infringements of Article 85(1) of the EEC Treaty:

- the ban on exports contained in the price-fixing and distribution agreement for Philips electric shavers;
- the reimport price-fixing contained in the price-fixing and distribution agreements for Philips electric shavers, for large domestic appliances, for domestic appliances, for experimental apparatus and for ordinary lamps and discharge lamps;

- the price-fixing, the ban on horizontal supplies by wholesalers, the ban on horizontal supplies and advertising by retailers, the ban on direct supplies and the ban on reverse deliveries, contained in some of the agreements aforesaid or in the agreement for colour television sets in wholesale trade, the extent that they applied to trade between Member States.

Article 2

1. A fine of 60,000 (sixty thousand) units of account, or 219,600 (two hundred and nineteen thousand six hundred) Deutsche Marks is hereby imposed on Deitsche Philips GmbH by reason of the maintenance of its ban on exports contained in its price-fixing and distribution agreement for Philips electric shavers (March 1967 version) until October 1972.

2. This Decision shall constitute an obligation on Deutsche Philips GmbH enforceable under Article 192 of the EEC Treaty.

Article 3

This Decision is addressed to Deutsche Philips GmbH, Hamburg.

(2) Decision in re Gero Fabriek

Decision of the Commission of 22 December 1976 relating to a proceeding under Article 85 of the EEC Treaty; O.J. No L 16, 19 January 1977, p. 1; Competition Law CM/M/I/110.

*Facts:* Gero-Fabriek NV, Zeist, Netherlands (hereinafter referred to as 'GERO'), manufactures silver-plated stainless-steel cutlery, specialising in stainless steel spoons and forks. In 1963 it was the biggest of the 11 Dutch spoon and fork manufacturers and had 1,100 employees on its payroll. In 1969 over 90% of its sales were in the Netherlands and roughly 6% in Belgium. In the Netherlands, GERO sells to two categories of customers: firstly it deals with retailers, with whom it concludes its general terms of retail sale, and secondly, it sells directly to large buyers, such as hotels, hospitals and other institutions which, because of the special range and quantities they require, do not buy through retailers. The general terms for wholesale apply to these large buyers.

In Belgium GERO sells exclusively to retailers through its wholly owned subsidiary, GERO International BV, Brussels. Gero has, however, stated that it is to appoint an exclusive distributor for Belgium.

In the Netherlands GERO's sales accounted for approximately 60% of the market in 1971, though this fell to 50% by 1975. Its current share of the Dutch wholesale market is about 15%. In contrast, in Belgium its sales rose from 10% of the market in 1971 to 19% in 1974, and now stand at about 15%. In other Member States, GERO sells only very small quantities, chiefly in Germany and France, where exclusive distributors are also to be appointed.

By 1963 about 2,400 of the 11,000 or so retailers of forks and spoons in business in the Netherlands accepted GERO's terms of sale. At present Gero has about 1,900 customers in the Netherlands and 425 in Belgium.

In its notification of 8 August 1963, GERO describes its general terms of sale as a standard form of agreement, of the type whereby an individual agreement is signed separately with each buyer. The notification also states that these terms of sale apply exclusively to supplies within the Netherlands. One of the main features was a system of fixed retail sales prices.

Since 1958 GERO has been applying general terms for retail sales to sales to Belgian dealers; these were not notified to the Commission; These terms contain, in respect of Belgium and Luxembourg, exactly the same clauses on resale prices as the terms for the Netherlands which were notified to the Commission.

*The Commission ruled:*

.....

In order to apply its provisions on resale prices in Belgium and the Netherlands, GERO has used two price lists, one in Belgium francs and the other in Dutch guilders. The range of products contained therein is not the same for the two Member States, since the Dutch price list contains a whole series of products which do not appear in the Belgium list.

The current price lists date from September 1974 for Belgium and Luxembourg and from October 1974 for the Netherlands. Since September and October 1974, the official exchange rate has been Bfrs. 14,5026 to the guilder. The rate of VAT included in the price list is 16% in the Netherlands and 18% in Belgium.

Irrespective of the different tax rates, GERO's prices in the Netherlands have regularly differed by a few percentage points from their prices in Belgium. For example, without making any allowance for the higher VAT in Belgium; a set of 12 Zilmeta spoons (model 519 831) costs Bfrs. 520 in Belgium but only Fl 34 05 in the Netherlands (a 5.3% difference without allowing for VAT). In the majority of cases, GERO products were cheaper in the Netherlands than in Belgium.

Likewise, the system of imposed retail prices makes it impossible for dealers to fix their own retail prices by reference to their own costs and commercial policy. The free formation of prices and the ability to pass onto purchasers any possible resulting benefits are hindered or at least substantially reduced. The system is thus clearly contrary to the prohibition in Article 85(1).

These restrictions may substantially affect trade between Member States. Not only do they apply to the distribution of GERO products in the Member States where the bulk of the products are sold, but they also have the object of totally hindering trade between those Member States and the others. Even if the various export prohibitions were lifted, the system of retail prices imposed on dealers would be likely to influence trade between Member States by deflecting trade flows away from the channels which they would naturally have if prices were fixed freely.

The application of imposed retail prices means that import and export patterns are different from what they would be if prices were fixed freely. The number of dealers affected (more than 2,000) and the share of the market in the relevant goods (estimated at about 50% for the Netherlands) are sufficiently large for the adverse effect on trade between Member States to be regarded as appreciable.

(3) Decision in re Distillers

For facts and references see above, page 349 .

*The Commission ruled:*

.....

2. Price Terms

2.1. *Application of Article 85(1) of the EEC Treaty*

The price terms applied to transactions for sales of spirits between DCL subsidiary companies and their United Kingdom trade customers are laid out in the DCL circular on 23 February 1977.

(a) The price terms have as their object the restriction and distortion of competition within the common market.

Under the price terms, DCL United Kingdom trade customers have to inform the selling DCL subsidiary company that they wish to export to other EEC countries. Purchases must then be made at the gross price.

This gross price was until 22 February 1977 the price before deduction of any allowances, rebates or discounts normally granted to United Kingdom trade customers. Since 23 February 1977, it is the price before deduction of any allowances or discounts to sole distributors in the other EEC countries. In both cases, United Kingdom trade customers are charged different prices for identical goods dependent on whether they resell in the United Kingdom or in another common market country.

The price terms tend to restrict competition in EEC countries other than the United Kingdom and amount to an indirect export prohibition.

The price terms, in providing for the application to DCL United Kingdom trade customers of a different price for spirits exported to other EEC countries from that charged when the spirits are resold for consumption in the home market and in reserving price allowances for spirits for resale and consumption in the United Kingdom, restrict the opportunity of such customers reselling in an EEC country other than the United Kingdom. Sales by DCL United Kingdom trade customers and by their subsequent purchasers in EEC countries other than the United Kingdom are indeed rendered, at the very least, more difficult. Competition in such countries on the part of DCL United Kingdom trade customers and traders purchasing from them is thereby restricted.

DCL admitted that their price terms were intended, following the removal of the export prohibition, to protect DCL sole distributors from competition on the part of traders purchasing from DCL trade customers in the United Kingdom and reselling for consumption in the sole distributors' territories.

The non-applicability of price allowances on spirits for export and the application to the same customers of different prices for spirits for export and for spirits for United Kingdom consumption are clearly an attempt to impede parallel imports from the United Kingdom into EEC countries other than the United Kingdom, with the same object as a formal export prohibition and can be regarded as a more efficient way to discourage export.

DCL United Kingdom trade customers are requested by DCL to indicate their intention or that of their subsequent purchasers to export to other EEC countries. Furthermore, the price terms provide for the exaction of penalties for non-observance. A customer who has not observed the price terms, or who is suspected of not observing them, may have to pay the gross price, even on spirits for consumption in the United Kingdom. He may later obtain reimbursement with reasonable interest of the amount equivalent to the price allowances to the extent to which he provides proof of consumption in the United Kingdom. Nevertheless, the application of this provision may strongly affect the commercial position of such a customer and amounts to a sanction and an effective incentive to observe the agreed price terms.

DCL argued that such price terms, restricting the allocation of price allowances to spirits sold for consumption in the United Kingdom, could not have been designed to impede imports into other EEC countries since they have been in existence for a considerable period of time and certainly antedated the commencement of such imports. This argument does not alter the assessment that the price terms have as their object the restriction of competition in EEC countries other than the United Kingdom, but demonstrates that since the existence of such price terms was simply a consequence of the non-exportation clause, the clarification of 24 June 1975 was clearly designed to maintain the effects of this non-exportation clause.

These price terms have as a further object to distort competition by preventing the price advantages attributable to the competitive conditions in the United Kingdom from affecting the competitive structure in the rest of the common market.

As stated in the circular letter of 24 June 1975 and Appendix II, the price allowances 'are designed to meet the particular requirements of the home trade'. DCL explained that these price allowances were intended to fit in with the competitive conditions of the United Kingdom spirits market which was characterised by the power of the purchasers and the strong price competition between the different brands of spirits.

The reservation of price allowances on spirits for United Kingdom consumption prevents the effect of favourable pricing in the United Kingdom from being extended to the DCL spirits market in common market countries other than the United Kingdom. This amounts to an isolation of the United Kingdom market in respect of such price advantages attributable to the competitive conditions which prevail in the United Kingdom with the effect of preventing them from affecting the competitive conditions in other common market countries. Accordingly, consumers in those countries cannot benefit from the better price advantages in the United Kingdom.

(b) As the price terms clearly have as their object the restriction and distortion of competition within the common market, it is not necessary to show their actual repercussions in order to establish the applicability of Article 85(1) of the EEC Treaty. However, it should be noted, as a subsidiary matter, that the effect of price terms is to restrict and distort competition to a considerable extent within the common market.

The prices at 24 June 1975 and 1 March 1977 a case of 12 bottles of Johnnie Walker Red Label are used as an example. The price terms have entailed, for a British purchaser who wishes to export, a buying price 99% and 92.7% (or ... % 'average' price) higher than the price he would pay in the absence of this restriction. An increase of this size considerably distorts competition within the common market.

Moreover, as a result of the price terms, the price paid by a United Kingdom trade customer of DCL wishing to export has at these dates been ... % and ... % higher than that paid for the same product by the sole distributors in the other common market countries. Indeed, sole distributors have higher costs due to their obligations of promoting the spirits. It has been argued that these costs approximate to the difference between the buying price of the parallel importer and that of the sole distributor. However, such differences in the buying price make it distinctly difficult for the DCL United Kingdom trade customers and, even more so, for their subsequent customers to compete with the sole distributors in the other EEC Member States or at the very least, render parallel export unattractive.

DCL has strictly implemented its price terms and effectively pursued those who breached them. DCL either asked for the price difference when spirits bought at the home trade price were later found in EEC countries other than the United Kingdom or charged certain customers the gross price for purchases suspected of being intended for exports. Such customers could then bring proof of actual consumption in the United Kingdom and be entitled to a refund. For a year following the application of the price terms of 24 June 1975, no cases of spirits purchased at the gross price were exported, except on one occasion, namely that of a United Kingdom customer who had purchased some 1400 cases of Scotch whisky at the gross price with the intention of exporting them to other EEC countries.

DCL has stated that from July 1976 to July 1977, United Kingdom trade customers purchased approximately 250 000 cases of Scotch whisky at the gross price. However, this figure still leaves open how many of these cases were exported since the gross price is also charged for certain purchases even when the customer does not necessarily intend to export.

In any event, the said volume of parallel exports remains even lower than before 24 June 1975 (550 000 cases) at a time when a formal non-exportation clause was imposed on DCL customers. It can reasonably be assumed that exports would have reached a significantly higher level in the absence of the restriction resulting from the price terms.

The complaints have stressed the difficulties which, due to the DCL practices, they face in their trading of spirits. They find themselves in practice debarred from exporting to other EEC countries after purchase at the gross price. DCL subsidiaries tend to charge them systematically the gross price with the effect that an extra burden is imposed on their trading activities in the United Kingdom.

Furthermore, these price terms enable DCL to maintain a price to sole distributors which is somewhat higher or at least similar to that charged to United Kingdom trade customers, although sole distributors are at a higher level in the distribution chain and bear promotional expenses which the United Kingdom wholesalers do not bear.

Accordingly, in view of DCL's market position in relation to Scotch whisky, gin, vodka and Pimm's in the United Kingdom, the price terms appreciably restrict and distort competition within the common market.

(c) The price terms are likely to affect trade between Member States; they hinder or, at the very least, make it more difficult for United Kingdom customers to export DCL spirits to the other common market countries, which they would do to a large extent in the absence of these terms. Thus they tend to partition the common market by hindering exchanges between the United Kingdom and other EEC countries for a substantial part of the products in question and are prejudicial to the establishment of a single market among the Member States.

## G. Selective Distribution

### a. Introduction

Enterprises frequently make use of selective criteria when choosing the outlets for their products. The standard thus employed can be either qualitative or quantitative. Selective distribution systems utilising both quantitative and qualitative criteria are not unusual. Qualitative criteria include minimum requirements as to trained personnel, maintenance of sufficient stocks of the goods in question, and the provision of after-sales service. Quantitative criteria serve to limit the number of outlets in any area by making use of population and presumed income estimates. During the years it has become clear that quantitative criteria are not allowed by the Commission and the Court. The Commission and the Court consider that selective distribution agreements might fall under the prohibition of Article 85(1) if the selective criteria are not applied in an objective manner.

### b. Cases

#### (1) Decision in re BMW

Decision of the Commission of 13 December 1974 on a proceeding under Article 85 of the EEC Treaty; O.J. No L 29, 3 February 1975, p. 1; (1975) I CMLR D 44; CCH para. 9701; Competition Law CM/M/I/80.

*Facts:* The Commission granted an exemption to the standard form contracts by which BMW organised the sales of motor cars and motorcycles. BMW's distribution system can be described as a system of the selection of dealers on the basis of several objective criteria as to qualifications and which involve certain minimum requirements imposed on all dealers and sales outlets. Accordingly BMW vehicles or parts were not sold by firms which, although they were willing to sell them, would not undertake to provide the additional services which BMW required them to provide at the dealer stage or to set up the prescribed service infrastructure (selection on qualitative criteria, namely, firm of sufficient business standing, employment of staff trained in cooperation with BMW, after sales services according to BMW requirements, minimum maintenance of stocks, minimum guarantees). In addition, there is quantitative selection of retailers by the manufacturer which amounts to further restriction of competition in BMW products. Firms may occasionally be excluded although they are willing and able to meet the qualitative requirements, should BMW decide not to increase the number of approved dealers as a matter of marketing policy (qualitative selection). There are no predetermined objective criteria as to this additional form of selection.

The Commission found that the standard form contracts included restrictions of competition but held, nevertheless, that Article 85(3) applied to the contracts.

*The Commission decided:*

The Commission has to decide whether the selective distribution system operated by BMW, containing a partial prohibition on dealing in competing products, can be exempted under Article 85(3) from the prohibition contained in Article 85(1) of the Treaty.

In considering the selective distribution system operated by BMW in Germany, the Commission is prepared to accept that such a system may contribute both to improving the production and distribution of goods and to promoting technical progress.

Limiting the number of dealers can be regarded as more beneficial, so far as it is based on the requirements by BMW of minimum standards for selection and continued employment of dealers. By such means the following can in particular be ensured:

- that BMW motor vehicles are received and stored in technically perfect condition and are delivered to customers after a pre-delivery check carried out in accordance with BMW's instructions;

- that both maintenance and preparation and also services carried out under guarantee and extended free service are not only sufficiently available but are also of an adequate quality for the consumer;

- that any modifications to vehicles which become necessary may be carried out;

- that sufficient plant equipment and BMW-trained personnel are available for the provision of the above services;

- that the store of spare parts is adequate in range and quality; and

- that BMW may rapidly and fully inform its appointed dealers of technical problems as they arise.

BMW has in addition reserved the right to make individual appointments from those applicants satisfying the objective requirements for BMW dealers, on the basis of consideration for which there are no universally predictable and objective criteria (see 8 and 13 above). The reservation of such a right is to be accepted in the present case, in so far as it relates to the selection by BMW of its main dealers. The restrictive influence which BMW has over the selection of BMW retail dealers by BMW main dealers facilitates rationalisation, because BMW also cooperates directly with BMW retail dealers with the aim of improving service. The cooperation between BMW and its dealers, which goes beyond the mere marketing of products, provides, in the view of the Commission in this particular case, a major factor justifying the BMW selective distribution system. It can be considered to be a method of rationalising the sale and service of BMW vehicles and parts and thereby provides a better service to the consumer than a system of free marketing to which such cooperation is not attached. Motor vehicles, being products of limited life, high cost and complex technology, require regular maintenance by specially equipped garages or service depots, because their use can be dangerous to life, health and property and can have a harmful effect on the environment. It is therefore of importance that those responsible for the maintenance of vehicles are made aware of the latest technical knowledge which the manufacturer has acquired in the development and construction of the vehicle. Moreover, continual cooperation between BMW and its main dealers and retail dealers may assist BMW in the preparation of its maintenance instructions and training programmes, and may also lead indirectly to improvements in the design of vehicles.

In the present case it can also be accepted that consumers receive a fair share of the benefit resulting from the improvements and progress achieved through the standard forms of agreement used by BMW. The measures which are restrictive of competition not only have direct advantages for the consumer in the form of improved service, but also allow adequate competition at the ditribution level, so that there remains a pressure to pass on to customers the benefits resulting from rationalisation. Such competition is assured by the fact that not only are consumers free to purchase goods and request service wherever they wish within the common market, but also that BMW dealers are free to purchase BMW products not only from the BMW dealer for their territory but also from any other BMW dealer anywhere in the common market. A corresponding freedom is enjoyed by the consumer, who may choose parts of other makes from BMW dealers, unless they are such as are of particular importance for the safety of BMW vehicles and do not satisfy the standards of quality of BMW parts.

The restrictions imposed on parties to the standard agreements are considered to be indispensable to the attainment of the improvements and technical progress mentioned.

The provisions on selective distribution are indispensable, because on economic grounds a continuing cooperation between BMW and dealers would be subject to a limitation if BMW had to cooperate with all dealers prepared to sell BMW goods and provide pre- and after-sales service to customers. The minimum requirements placed by BMW on the provision of services could not be met if BMW were only to issue service instructions to each main dealer or retail dealer on delivery of its products. Moreover, BMW has left untouched the option of every customer to have his vehicle serviced at an independent establishment, the latter being able to purchase all its requirements of BMW parts from any BMW main dealer or retail dealer.

The BMW standard agreements provide the parties with no opportunity to eliminate competition in respect of a substantial part of the goods concerned. In the first instance, they concern BMW vehicles, which compete with a range of other vehicles throughout the common market; in the second, as has already been stated competition between BMW and competing products is maintained at the various levels of distribution within the network of BMW.

For none of its motor cars - even with a narrow definition of the market - does BMW have a share of the German market which would exclude competition in respect of a substantial part of the products concerned. In that respect the Commission had to consider whether the fact that in Germany BMW has a considerable share of the market in motorcycles of 250 cc capacity and above militated against the granting of an exemption. The BMW share of motorcycles of 250 cc capacity and above registered in Germany in 1972 was approximately 32%. In 1973 BMW produced 197.446 motor cars and 20.856 motorcycles and sold 193.378 motor cars and 19.918 motorcycles. Its turnover for motor cars was DM 1.040.000.000 and for motorcycles DM 79.035.000. Bearing in mind that lesser importance of the trade in motorcycles when compared with that in motor cars and the great similarity in sales and service methods for the two products, it would be unreasonable to impose on BMW a different method of distribution for motorcycles; moreover, BMW is subject to effective competition in the motorcycle market in Germany and even more so in the other countries of the common market.

All the conditions laid down in Article 85(3) have therefore been fulfilled.

*Sequel*
This Decision has not been renewed. The Commission is however working on a special group exemption for the automobile industry. A draft has has been published in O.J. No C 165, 24 June 1983,p. 2 (see Annex XII).

(2) L'Oréal Case

L'Oréal v. de Nieuwe AMCK, case 31/80
Preliminary ruling of 4 December 1980; (1980) ECR 3775; CMLR 2 (1981) 235; CCH para. 8715; Competition Law CM/M/III/90.

*Facts:* By an order of 17 January 1980, which reached the Court on 23 January 1980, the Rechtbank van Koophandel (Commercial Court) of the legal district of Antwerp, in pursuance of Article 177 of the EEC Treaty, requested the Court to give a preliminary ruling on questions relating to the interpretation of Articles 85 and 86 of the Treaty.

These questions are referred to the Court in the course of an action brought by the Belgian company L'Oréal NV and the French company L'Oréal S.A. before the President of the Rechtbank van Koophandel, Antwerp, in summary proceedings, against the company De Nieuwe AMCK. The L'Oréal companies have established in Belgium for Kerastase hair-care products a selective distribution network of which the company De Nieuwe AMCK is not a part. The action is primarily for a declaration that the defendant's actions in offering for sale or selling Kerastase products bearing an express statement that they may be sold only by Kerastase hairdressing consultants, and should the occasion arise, in obtaining stocks of those products by being party to a breach of contract, are acts contrary to fair trading practice. The plaintiffs also seek an injunction forbidding the defendant to offer for sale or sell the products referred to above or obtain stocks thereof.

The defendant in the main proceedings contended before the national court that the selective distribution network set up by L'Oréal was illegal as being contrary to the Community rules on competition. In reply, the plaintiffs in the main proceedings referred to a letter dated 22 February 1978 addressed to L'Oréal S.A. by the Commission. By that letter the Commission informed the company that by reason of the small portion of the market for perfumery, beauty and toilet preparations occupied by L'Oréal in the various countries and the large number of competing undertakings of a similar size, the Commission took the view that there was no need for it to intervene under Article 85(1) of the Treaty with regard to L'Oréal's distribution system and that the matter had therefore been allowed to rest.

.....

*The Court held:*

(18) 13. With regard to the first question referred to the Court by the national court concerning the possibility that the distribution system in question may receive an exemption under Article 85(3), it should be recalled that under Article 9(1) of Regulation No 17 cited above the Commission has sole power, subject to review by the Court, to declare the provisions of Article 85(1) of the Treaty inapplicable pursuant to Article 85(3) of the Treaty. The jurisdiction of the national courts is restricted to determining whether the agreement, decision or concerted practice which is the subject of the action before them is in accordance with Article 85(1) and, if appropriate, to declaring the agreement, decision or practice in question void under Article 85(2).

(19) 14. It is therefore in relation to those provisions that the national court will have to examine the validity of L'Oréal's distribution system. It is for the Court of Justice to provide it for this purpose with the points of interpretation of Community law, which will enable it to reach a decision.

(2) 15. As the Court observed in its judgment of 25 October 1977 (Case 26/76, *Metro v Commission* (1977) ECR 1875), selective distribution systems constitute an aspect of competition which accords with Article 85(1) provided that resellers are chosen on the basis of objective criteria of a qualitative nature relating to the technical qualifications of the re-seller and his staff and the suitability of his trading premises and that such conditions are laid down uniformly for all potential resellers and are not applied in a discriminatory fashion.

(21) 16. In order to determine the exact nature of such 'qualitative' criteria for the selection of re-sellers, it is also necessary to consider whether the characteristics of the product in question necessitate a selective distribution system in order to preserve its quality and ensure its proper use, and whether those objectives are not already satisfied by national rules governing admission to the resale trade or the conditions of sale of the product in question. Finally, inquiry should be made as to whether the criteria laid down do not go beyond what is necessary. In that regard it should be recalled that in Case 26/76, *Metro v Commission* cited above, the Court considered that the obligation to participate in the setting up of a distribution system, commitments relating to the achievement of turnovers and obligations relating to minimum supply and to stocks exceeded the requirements of a selective distribution system based on qualitative requirements.

(22) 17. When admission to a selective distribution system is made subject to conditions which go beyond simple objective selection of a qualitative nature and, in particular, when it is based on quantitative criteria, the distribution system falls in principle within the prohibition in Article 85(1), provided that, as the Court observed in its judgment of 30 June 1966 *(Socété Technique Minière v. Maschinebau Ulm GmbH*, Case 56/65, (1966) ECR 235), the agreement fulfils certain conditions depending less on its legal nature than on its effects first on 'trade between Member States' and secondly on 'competition'.

(23) 18. To decide, on the one hand, whether an agreement may affect trade between Member States it is necessary to decide on the basis of a set of objective factors of law or of fact and in particular with regard to the consequences of the agreement in question on the possibilities of parallel importation whether it is possible to foresee with a sufficient degree of probability that the agreement in question may have an influence, direct or indirect, actual or potential, on the pattern of trade between Member States.

(24) 19. On the other hand, in order to decide whether an agreement is to be considered as prohibited by reason of the distortion of competition which is its object or its effect, it is necessary to consider the competition within the actual context in which it would occur in the absence of the agreement in dispute. To that end, it is appropriate to take into account in particular the nature and quantity, limited or otherwise, of the products covered by the agreement, the position and the importance of the parties on the market for the products concerned, and the isolated nature of the disputed agreement or, alternatively, its position in a series of agreements. In that regard the Court stated in its judgment of 12 December 1967 (in Case 23/67 *Brasserie de Haecht* (1967) ECR 407) that, although not necessarily decisive, the existence of similar contracts is a circumstance which, together with others, is capable of constituting an economic and legal context within which the contract must be judged.

(25) 20. It is for the national court to decide, on the basis of all the relevant information, whether the agreement in fact satisfies the requirements necessary for it to fall under the prohibition laid down in Article 85(1).

(26) 21. Consequently, the answer to the first question must be that the agreements laying down a selective distribution system based on criteria for admission, which go beyond a mere objective selection of a qualitative nature, exhibit features making them incompatible with Article 85(1) where such agreements, either individually or together with others, may, in the economic and legal context in which they occur and on the basis of a set of objective factors of law or of fact, affect trade between Member States and have either as their object or effect the prevention, restriction or distortion of competition. It is for the Commission alone, subject to review by the Court, to grant an exemption in respect of such agreements pursuant to Article 85(3).

(3) Decision in re AEG Telefunken

Decision of the Commission of 6 January 1982 in a proceeding under Article 85 of the Treaty in re the selective distribution system of AEG Telefunken; O.J. No L 117, 30 April 1982, p. 15; CMLR 2 (1982) 386; CCH para. 10366; Competition Law CM/M/I/175.

*Facts:*

86. The Commission established that the selective distribution system for Telefunken branded products operated in the Community by Allgemeine Elektrizität-Gesellschaft (AEG-Telefunken), the German company which manufactures in particular electronic leisure equipment, constituted, in the form practised between 1976 and 1980, an infringement of Article 85(1) of the Treaty. The Commission imposed a fine of 1 000 000 ECU on AEG-Telefunken.

In 1973 AEG-Telefunken notified the Commission of a distribution system under which its Telefunken 'five star' range could only be sold within the Community by wholesalers and retailers recognised by the firm on the basis of certain conditions of admission. The firm stated that any dealer who satisfied these conditions would be admitted.

In fact, AEG-Telefunken applied a different system. On account of their pricing policy, admission to the distribution system was refused, rendered difficult or made subject to further conditions in the case of certain distribution organisations and certain dealers whose pricing threatened the company's own pricing policy, even though they satisfied the letter of the conditions laid down. It also directly and indirectly exercised substantial influence on the setting of retail prices by dealers.

As applied, AEG-Telefunken's selective distribution system, which regulated trade between the different Member States, appreciably restricted competition.

87. In setting the amount of the fine the Commission took account of the fact that AEG-Telefunken is a major manufacturer of electronic leisure equipment and that the infringement had had a substantial effect on the market and on trade between Member States. However, as mitigating circumstances, the Commission bore in mind that this was the first case in which it was taking a Decision on the application of a selective distribution system which was incompatible with the rules of competition but which in itself gave no cause for objection and also that the discrimination and influence brought to bear on prices had very often been initiated by approved dealers.

*The Commission held:*

1. Decisions of the Court of Justice concerning selective distribution systems

53. Selective distribution systems may constitute an aspect of competition, which accords with Article 85(1), provided that resellers are chosen on the basis of objective criteria of a qualitative nature relating to the technical qualifications of the reseller and his staff and the suitability of his trading premises, and that such conditions are laid down uniformly for all potential resellers and are not applied in a discriminatory fashion (judgment of the European Court of Justice of 25 October 1977 in Case 26/76, Metro (1977) ECR, page 1875). It follows, as the Court stated in its judgment of 10 July 1980 in Case 99/79, Lancôme (1980) ECR, page 2511, and in its judgment of 16 June 1981 in Case 126/80, newspaper distributors (1981) ECR (not yet published) that agreements laying down a system of selective distribution based on criteria for admission which go beyond a simple objective selection of a qualitative nature are in principle caught by the prohibition in Article 85(1), particularly where they are based on quantitative selection criteria. These judgments further make clear that it is important for the appreciation of selective distribution systems whether these agreements, either individually or together with others, in the economic and legal context in which they are concluded and on the basis of a body of objective features of law and fact, are capable of affecting trade between Member States and have, as either their object or effect, the prevention, restriction or distortion of competition (judgment of the European Court of Justice of 11 December 1980 in Case 31/80, L'Oréal

(1980) ECR, page 3775).

54. The above decisions of the Court show that the distribution system applied by AEG can escape the prohibition provided for in Article 85(1) only if it is clear from the economic and legal context within which the distribution agreement is operated and from all the attendant circumstances:

- that all resellers who meet the technical qualifications necessary for selling the products covered by the distribution agreement have, in principle, access to the goods,

- that dealers are not automatically excluded from the distribution network because they might jeopardise the pricing policy pursued by AEG, and

- that authorised contracted dealers are free to set their resale prices on their own initiative without direct or indirect interference from AEG.

Furthermore, the Commission has already pointed out, in its Decision of 15 December 1975 (IV/847, SABA (O.J. No L 28, 3.2.1976, p. 19) that, in the case of selective distribution systems, competition must be ensured by allowing authorised dealers to determine their selling prices at their own discretion.

2. The overall connection between distribution contract and practical application

55. These conditions, under which a selective distribution system may be deemed not to fall under Article 85(1), are not met by the AEG distribution agreement as actually applied.

56. AEG has in fact applied a distribution system completely different from the wording of the notified standard agreement: for certain sales outlets and certain dealers, access to the distribution system was made impossible, difficult or subject to additional conditions, although these dealers met the required qualitative criteria laid down in the standard contract. In addition, AEG brought considerable influence to bear, both directly and indirectly, on dealers' resale prices.

57. The non-authorisation of certain dealers and the fixing of selling prices occured as the distribution agreement was implemented and were directly and intrinsically connected with it.

Discrimination arose when certain dealers were refused access to the system; under the terms of the distribution agreement these dealers were not allowed to be supplied with AEG products.

58. The influence brought to bear on prices was also included in the actual application of the distribution agreement by AEG-Telefunken. The fact that AEG was entitled under the terms of the standard contract to impose a ban on supplies and to claim compensation in the event of default or damage - and so actually exclude dealers from the distribution network - provided it with the means of persuading dealers to toe the line on prices. This means was also used by AEG. It induced dealers to agree arrangements concerning selling prices. Where, with regard to prices, dealers behaved, or seemed likely to behave in a manner calculated to

'disrupt the market', AEG, in discussions over supplies 'clearly brought to attention how important market pricing was' (point 49 above), explained pricing policy 'in detail' (point 41 above), 'induced' dealers to increase their prices (point 43 above), 'made it clear' that further cut-price advertising 'would lead to a considerable worsening of relations' or sought a 'neat, unusual way of keeping the customer in check' (point 51 above).

59. An appraisal of the economic context and of all the actual circumstances therefore shows that these measures are closely connected with the distribution agreement. Without them, it would have been impossible or difficult for AEG to influence prices. In particular, the relatively close and intended permanent contractual relationship between manufacturer and dealer through the distribution agreement enabled AEG to establish direct contact with its dealers. Furthermore, the distribution agreement frequently led dealers, because of their confidence in regular supplies, to invest financially in the Telefunken brand name. Generally speaking, therefore, exclusion from the distribution network would have entailed considerable disadvantages for dealers. Those dealers bound by the distribution agreement were therefore all the more inclined to comply with AEG's wishes concerning price discipline.

60. The refusal to admit dealers to the system and the influence brought to bear on prices are thus not isolated measures but are directly connected with the distribution agreement.

(4) AEG-Telefunken case
AEG v. Commission, case 107/82, judgment of 25 October 1983 (not yet published). For facts see above page 443.

*The Court held:*

....

33. It is common ground that agreements constituting a selective system necessarily affect competition in the Common Market. However, it has always been recognized in the case-law of the Court that there are legitimate requirements, such as the maintenance of a specialist trade capable of providing specific services as regards high-quality and high-technology products, which may justify a reduction of price competition in favour of competition relating to factors other than price. Systems of selective distribution, in so far as they aim at the attainment of a legitimate goal capable of improving competition in relation to factors other than price, therefore constitute an element of competition which is in conformity with Article 85 (1).

34. The limitations inherent in a selective distribution system are however acceptable only on condition that their aim is in fact an improvement in competition in the sense above mentioned. Otherwise they would have no justification inasmuch as their sole effect would be to reduce price competition.

35. So as to guarantee that selective distribution systems may be based on that aim alone and cannot be set up and used with a view to the attainment of objectives which are not in conformity with Community law, the Court specified in its judgment of 25 October 1977 (Metro v. Commission), (1977) ECR 1875) that such systems are permissible, provided that resellers are chosen on the basis of objective criteria of a qualitative nature relating to the technical qualifications of the reseller and his staff and the suitability of his trading premises

and that such conditions are laid down uniformly for all potential resellers and are not applied in a discriminatory fashion.

36. It follows that the operation of a selective distribution system based on criteria other than those mentioned above constitutes an infringement of Article 85(1). The position is the same where a system which is in priciple in conformity with Community law is applied in practice in a manner incompatible therewith.

37. Such a practice must be considered unlawful where the manufacturer, with a view to maintaining a high level of prices or to excluding certain modern channels of distribution, refuses to approve distributors who satisfy the qualitative criteria of the system.

38. Such an attitude on the part of the manufacturer does not constitute, on the part of the undertaking, unilateral conduct which, as AEG claims, would be exempt from the prohibition contained in Article 85(1) of the Treaty. On the contrary, it forms part of the contractual relations between the undertaking and resellers. Indeed, in the case of the admission of a distributor, approval is based on the acceptance, tacit or express, by the contracting parties of the policy pursued by AEG which requires inter alia the exclusion from the network of all distributors who are qualified for admission but are not prepared to adhere to that policy.

....

*Sequel:*

The Court upheld the Commission decision in full, notwithstanding the fact that the Commission had not succeeded in proving a number of individual cases.

## H. Guarantees and after sales service

a. Introduction

The Commission is scrutinising guarantee arrangements applied by the European manufacturers of domestic electrical appliances with a view to ensuring that the guarantees given are valid in any Member State where they market their products.

b. Cases

(1) Zanussi guarantee

Decision of the Commission of 23 October 1978 in a proceeding under Article 85 of the Treaty in re Zanussi guarantee, O.J. No L 322, 16 November 1978, p. 36; CMLR I (1979) 81; CCH para. 10090; Competition Law CM/M/I/138.

*The Commission ruled:*

The Zanussi Group (Zanussi), which is headed by Industrie A. Zanussi SpA, Pordenone, Italy, is in business chiefly in the domestic electrical appliances industry, manufacturing refrigerators, cookers, dishwashers, washing machines and television sets. In 1976 Zanussi recorded sales totalling aroung 525 million units of account and employed approximately

30.000 personnel on production in this field in Italy. The appliances are sold in Italy through wholesalers and are imported into the other common market countries by the Zanussi Group companies.

Zanussi's output of domestic electrical appliances is about 3.8 million units annually, half being exported; About three quarters of all appliances exported go to common market countries. Zanussi holds sizeable market shares for the relevant appliances in the Community countries, with refrigerator market shares of approximately 25% in Italy, 15% in Belgium and 10% in the Netherlands, a washing machine market share of some 20% in Denmark and a dishwasher market share of about 25% in Italy. With the exception of IAZ UK and IAZ Belgium, which also handle the Irish and Luxembourg markets respectively, the sales subsidiaries import Zanussi appliances only in their own Member State. At the next stage of distribution, Zanussi appliances throughout the Community are marketed by dealers (wholesalers, retailers and department stores), who are all allowed by Zanussi, without exception, to resell wherever they wish within the common market at prices which they themselves set.

Zanussi appliances are distributed in the Community under different trade marks, including Zanussi, Rex, Castor and Zoppas. Their technical characteristics often differ according to the country in which they are to be sold. These differences, which concern matters such as wring, amperage plugs, closing devices and others, flow chiefly from differences in the regulations applied in the Member States to ensure safety in the use of electrical equipment or compliance with other standards for their operation.

Zanussi gives Community users a guarantee according to which, during a limited period, it will carry out certain operations free of charge in the course of the after-sales service scheme which it has set up on the common market. Although they sometimes differ from country to country and from appliance to appliance, guarantee services mainly concern mechanical parts of Zanussi appliances and consist in repairing or replacing defective parts without charges and in supplying the required labour.

Until May 1977 guarantee service from Zanussi in the different Community countries was provided through the dealers, who, when they sold the appliance, were obliged to give the user the relevant guarantee certificate, having filled in their name and the date of sale. Among the conditions on the guarantee certificate were the following:

(a) the user of a Zanussi appliance was entitled to service under guarantee only from the Zanussi subsidiary which imported the appliance;

(b) guarantee service was refused when the appliance had been used in a country other than that into which it was originally imported by the local subsidiary;

(c) guarantee service was also refused when the appliance had been modified, or when alterations had been carried out by persons not approved by the local subsidiary.

When the Commission informed Zanussi that the restrictions contained in the terms of its guarantees in the Member States were incompatible with Article 85 of the Treaty, the company decided to change its guarantee scheme to make it consistent with the rules on competition yet still conform to local technical and safety standards for electrical appliances. In May 1977, therefore, it instructed its subsidiaries to provide guarantee services for all Zanussi appliances regardless of their origin, pending the introduction of a new and more comprehensive guarantee scheme which would no longer be incompatible with Article 85. On 11 October 1977 Zanussi notified to the Commission the new terms on which, from 15 February 1978, it would provide its guarantee service to purchasers in the Community.

These are as follows:

1. in the Community, Industrie A, Zanussi will guarantee all appliances which it has manufactured and which are distributed under any of its trade marks for sale in a Community country;

2. after-sales service under guarantee will be provided by the Zanussi subsidiary in the Community country where the appliance is used on the terms applied locally by that subsidiary;

3. after-sales service under guarantee may be refused:

(a) if the appliance is defective by reason of its having been installed and/or used in a manner inconsistent with technical and safety standards in the country where the guarantee is claimed;

(b) if the appliance has not been used for normal purposes or has not been used in accordance with the manufacturer's requirements and instructions;

4. after-sales service under guarantee may also be refused if any adjustment or adaptation has been made to the appliance other than properly executed adjustments required to make it conform to the technical and safety standards in force in the country where the claim under the guarantee is made;

5. any adjustment to meet technical and safety standards which may be required to ensure that the appliance works properly may be made by the local Zanussi subsidiary or by a qualified person capable of carrying them out properly. The full costs of adjusting the appliance will be charged to the user; if the Zanussi subsidiary carries out the work, such work will be invoiced on the terms applying in the place where the adjustment is requested and made.

These terms, translated into the several Community languages, are printed on the guarantee certificates provided by Zanussi through its dealers, who are required, on delivery of the goods, to hand over either the completed and signed certificate (as in the case of Denmark, Italy and the United Kingdom) or (in the other Member States) a form attesting to the purchase and entitling the customer to apply for a guarantee certificate from Zanussi.

No comments from other interested parties have been received following publication of the notice summarising the notified agreement and stating the Commission's intention to give negative clearance in respect of that agreement.

(a) Restrictive nature of the guarantee scheme in force until May 1977

The effect of the pre-May 1977 guarantee scheme was to restrict or distort competition within the common market, since the user could only seek service under the Zanussi guarantee from the subsidiary which imported the appliance into its own Member State; Zanussi was released from its obligation to provide guarantee service if the appliance was used in a Member State other than that in which the importing subsidiary was established. The result was that Zanussi dealers were placed in an artificially disadvantageous competitive situation vis-à-vis other firms which also distributed Zanussi appliances, or similar appliances of other brands, when in their own country they resold Zanussi appliances bought elsewhere in the Community or when in another Member State they resold a Zanussi appliance bought in their own country, since in these users could not benefit from the Zanussi guarantee.

The clause laying down that the user's right to claim the guarantee and the manufacturer's obligation to provide it ceased to exist if the appliance had been adjusted in any way or had been altered by somebody who had not been authorised to do so by the importing subsidiary also restricted competition within the common market, since it prevented dealers who planned to import or export from making the appliance conform to safety and technical standards in other Member States, when it was essentially to comply with these in order to sell the appliances.

The guarantee scheme was likely to affect trade between Member States since it could reduce or at any rate appreciably distort Community inter-State trade in Zanussi appliances. Free after-sales service for Zanussi appliances is of great importance to the user on account of the position of these appliances in relation to supply and demand within the common market.

Article 85(3) could not be applied to the agreements in the original guarantee scheme. Admittedly, the Zanussi guarantee meant that service could be provided free of charge, so that the appliances could be used in optimum technical conditions to the benefit both of users and of dealers. But the offending clauses caused each dealer to confine his business to his own Member State. By discouraging dealers from expanding their business beyond the confines of the national competitive arena, the agreements prevented the latest design and technical improvements available in certain Member States from becoming available throughout the common market. Even admitting that the agreement did have certain beneficial effects, there was no evidence of the consumer being allowed a fair share of the resulting benefits. The freedom of users to acquire Zanussi appliances where they wished in the light of varying terms of sale, and particularly as regards guarantees, was directly attached. At any rate it could not be accepted that the restrictions imposed by Zanussi were indispensable to the smooth operation of the guarantee scheme, since their effect was to prevent or hinder the performance of guarantee service where inter-State trade was handled by firms that were not Zanussi subsidiaries.

The argument which was put forward as justification of the scheme, and which could not be accepted, was that the differences betweeen technical and safety standards in the various Member States were so great that domestic electrical appliances, including those made by Zanussi, had to be manufactured to such dissimilar specifications that they could not be distributed anyway in a country other than where they conformed to the technical and safety standards and hence there could be no movement in these goods between Member States.

However, even admitting that these differences did constitute an obstacle to free movement, this could not justify the incorporation of the standards in question into the dealers' contracts in such a way (here by the provision for the termination of the guarantee) as to aggravate this obstacle; moreover, for the appliances in question the differences between the effectively binding technical and safety standards in force in the Member States were not so great as to prevent the movement of the goods across national frontiers or, more generally, to eliminate the economic advantages which third parties might gain from exporting or importing once the necessary adjustments had been made.

(b) Non-restrictive nature of the guarantee scheme introduced in May 1977 and consequent inapplicability of Article 85

The guarantee scheme introduced by Zanussi on a temporary basis in May 1977, subsequently confirmed in the certificates issued after 15 February 1978, no longer has the effect of restricting competition within the common market; the agreements between Zanussi and its dealers are therefore no longer caught by the prohibition in Article 85(1) of the Treaty.

The new general terms of guarantee printed on the certificates, which are now the same for the different Member States, entitle users to service under guarantee from Zanussi anywhere inside the Community, regardless of where they first bought their appliance or where it is being used.

The fact that guarantee service will be provided on the terms locally applied by the Zanussi subsidiary inthe State where the appliance is used, and not on the terms pertaining in the country where the appliance is bought, does not constitute a discrimination between Zanussi appliances sold by that subsidiary and appliances retailed by other subsidiaries.

The new terms of guarantee will henceforth allow dealers and users to adapt their appliances, or have them adapted, so that they will conform to the technical and safety standards of the country where they are used, without the Zanussi guarantee thereby being invalidated. These adjustments, moreover, can be done either by Zanussi or by any qualified person who is capable of carrying them out correctly. Thus a Zanussi appliance which has been imported into a Member State and then adapted by the importer himself to conform to the local technical and safety standards will continue to be covered by guarantee.

The current guarantee scheme is no longer such, therefore, as to discourage dealers from importing Zanussi appliances from, or exporting them to, other Member States. Neither does it tend to dissuade the user from buying a Zanussi appliance in some other Community country from that in which the appliance will be in use.

The Commission is therefore able to issue a negative clearance within the meaning of Article 2 of Regulation No 17 for the new guarantee scheme introduced by Zanussi, as this no longer contains anti-competitive clauses which may affect trade between Member States.

## I. Exclusive Purchasing

Exclusive purchasing agreements and requirements clauses are types of exclusivity clauses whereby one of the parties to an agreement for a certain period undertakes to purchase all his supplies of a particular type of goods only from the other party to the agreement. Contracts of this nature are very common in the beer and petroleum retail trades and cover in those sectors usually very long periods. Such contracts can have a restrictive effect on competition because of the reduction in the number of possible outlets for competing suppliers and because retailers bound by such contracts are prevented from seeking supplies elsewhere. The Commission has adopted in June 1983 a Regulation on the application of Article 85(3) of the Treaty to categories of exclusive purchasing agreements including special provisions for beer supply agreements and provisions for service station agreements (see Regulation No 1984/83, Annex

### (1) First Brasserie de Haecht Case

See above, page 165 .

### (2) Decision in re BP Kemi/DDSF

Commission Decision of 5 September 1979 in re proceeding under Article 85 of the EEC Treaty in re BP Kemi/DDSF. O.J. No L 126, 14 November 1979, p. 32; CMLR 3 (1979) 684; CCH para. 10165; Competition Law CM/M/I/146.

*Facts:* Acting on a complaint lodged by a Danish household spirit producer, the Commission took a Decision establishing that the agreements and concerted practices operated by the Danish firms BP Kemi A/S (BP Kemi) and A/S De Danske Spritfabrikker (DDSF), for the supply and distribution of synthetic ethanol in Denmark constitute an infringement of the competition rules.

Synthetic ethanol is used in the production mainly of ethanols, solvents and household spirit.

Accounting for approximately 45% of the synthetic ethanol produced for sale within the EEC, the British firm BP Chemicals Ltd (BPCL) - a wholly-owned subsidiary of the BP group - is the largest synthetic ethanol producer in the Community.

BP Kemi, another wholly-owned subsidiary of the BP group, is a trading company operating only in Denmark where one of the products it sells is ethanol produced by BPCL.

Before Denmark joined the Community, DDSF held the legal monopoly of synthetic ethanol production in Denmark and was also the main distributor; imports of the product were subject to a licensing system. Following the termination of its monopoly as required by the Accession Treaty, DDSF decided to cease its production; after negotiations with the British producing company, BPCL, in 1973, it entered into purchasing and cooperation agreements with BP Kemi, BPCL's sister company and distributor in Denmark.

Under the purchasing agreement DDSF undertook in practice to buy its total requirements from BP Kemi, at least until 1979.

In theory this exclusive purchasing obligation was modified by an alignment clause: but even if DDSF obtained a lower quotation from another supplier, it was permitted to accept it only if BP Kemi refused to align downwards; in addition there were astringent requirements as to quantities and origin.

In return for its purchasing obligation DDSF did not obtain exclusive distribution rights, since BP Kemi wished to take advantage of the opening of the Danish market in order to make direct sales to large customers. DDSF's interests were, however, protected by a cooperation agreement which restricted BP Kemi's freedom of action (in particular, BP Kemi undertook to keep to DDSF's list prices and to pay compensation should its sales exceed a given share of the market) and set up a system whereby information was exchanged between the parties.

BP Kemi and DDSF terminated the cooperation agreement at the end of 1974 but continued to apply identical prices and exchange information until the end of 1976. The purchasing agreement remained in force until 15 July 1979.

The exclusive purchasing obligation appreciably restricted competition. Since Denmark's largest distributor - and the only one with the technical facilities necessary for supplying certain categories of customer - was in practice bound for at least six years to a single producer, this obligation cancelled out the effects of the opening of the Danish market after accession (the BP Group's market share, initially 90%, is still nearly 80%).

This restriction did not qualify for exemption from the Treaty's prohibition of restrictive practices accorded by Commission Regulation No 67/67 to certain categories of exclusive dealing agreements. The Regulation aims to facilitate marketing and rationalise distribution by ensuring that tasks are shared out between producers and distributors: this objective is clearly not attained if, as in this case, the supplier develops his own distribution network in the territory concerned. Furthermore, the exclusive purchasing obligation imposed on DDSF was linked with the restrictions on competition contained in the cooperation agreement and maintained by concerted practices after expiry of the agreement.

.....

*The Commission ruled:*

57. Contrary to the view of the parties the question here is not at whose wish DDSF's obligation to buy its total requirements of synthetic ethanol from BP Kemi was agreed upon, whether the principal motive was DDSF's desire for secure supplies or BP Kemi's desire for secure sales, or whether the purchasing obligation suited both parties' interests. The decisive question is whether the obligation had the restriction of competition as its object or effect.

58. As the Court of Justice has pointed out 'competition may be distorted within the meaning of Article 85(1) not only by agreements which limit it as between the parties, but also by agreements which prevent or restrict competition which might take place between one of them and third parties. For this purpose, it is irrelevant whether the parties to the agreement are or are not on a footing of equality as regards their position and function in the economy. This applies all

the more, since, by such an agreement, the parties might seek, by preventing or limiting the competition of third parties in respect of the products, to create or guarantee for their benefit an unjustified advantage at the expense of the consumer or user, contrary to the general aims of Article 85.

59. When a purchaser undertakes to buy all his requirements for a given product from one manufacturer during a certain period, other manufacturers of the product in question are prevented from supplying the purchaser with the product during the period concerned. Depending *inter alia*, on the length of the period and on the economic context, including the market shares and positions of the purchaser and seller such a purchasing obligation may constitute a restriction on competition within the meaning of Article 85(1).

60. It is true that when any agreement concerning the purchase of a given quantity of a product has been concluded, other producers of the product in question are excluded to that extent (but no further) from covering the needs of the purchaser, but such producers are able to compete for each such contract before it is signed. This is the result of the normal role of competition which gives any interested party the possibility of putting forward his offer and which enables the purchaser to decide freely which of the offers is the most attractive when all factors are taken into account. However, when a purchasing obligation of a longer duration is entered into, the relationship of supply is frozen and the role of offer and demand is eliminated to the disadvantage of *inter alia* new competitors who are thereby prevented from supplying this customer and old competitors who in the meantime may have become more competitive than the actual supplier. If the conditions of the market are thereby influenced to an appreciable extent, it is possible that competition is restricted within the meaning of Article 85(1).

61. In the present case the purchasing obligation means that all foreign suppliers except BPCL are prevented for a period of six years from selling to DDSF which represent not only the largest, but also in a number of respects the only practical sales possibility for them in Denmark. The restrictive character of this obligation on the part of DDSF is not affected by the fact that BP Kemi has no obligation to supply DDSF with more than 25 000 tonnes a year. DDSF is obliged to purchase all its requirements up to 25 000 tonnes from BP Kemi, with a resulting exclusion of other suppliers in respect of such quantities. Furthermore, since the actual consumption of DDSF has not exceeded ... hl, which corresponds to approximately ... tonnes (the specific gravity of pure alcohol is around 0,8), the limit of 25 000 tonnes is of no practical importance. Moreover, even if the limit of 25 000 tonnes were reached, this would not mean that DDSF would be free to buy possible quantities in excess of 25 000 tonnes from other sources of supply since in such a situation DDSF would be obliged first to give BP Kemi the opportunity of supplying such excess quantities.

62. The parties have argued that the English clause in its different versions means a protection of the interests of DDSF since DDSF as a result of the clause can buy at a lower price when the conditions of the clause are fulfilled, and since the clause means that such purchases may possibly be made from another supplier. However, the conditions for the clause coming into play are so severe that its practical importance is limited. The clause, moreover, by its nature confirms the restrictive relationship between the parties and means a protection of

the interests of BP Kemi.

63. The English clause in the Cooperation Agreement, according to its terms, could be invoked only if the quantity offered by the competitor corresponded to DDSF's total annual requirements; thus the purchase of smaller quantities from other suppliers was not possible. However, even if DDSF had found another supplier who could have supplied DDSF with its annual requirement, DDSF might have abstained from invoking the clause since this, according to the clause, would have meant that BP Kemi could withdraw from the contract.

The English clause contained in the addendum relaxes the purchasing obligation only to an insignificant extent. Minimum purchases are still provided for, the quantity being not less than two million litres in shipments of not less than 500 000 litres for delivery over not more than six months. Moreover, the offer has come from a 'serious Western European supplier of alcohol'. This excludes *inter alia* offers of smaller quantities from West European countries, and occasional offers on the spot market, which are frequently used by consumers to supplement existing supplies in order to cover their requirements. Although DDSF could not afford to be completely dependent on such sources, their use as a supplement would have been economically attractive. Furthermore, even if DDSF should receive an offer fulfilling the said conditions, DDSF might not invoke the clause for fear that BP Kemi would use the right this gives it to terminate the agreement.

64. In so far as the conditions for the application of, for instance, the English clause in the addendum could have been fulfilled and DDSF, as a result could decide to apply the clause, the result is that BP Kemi was being informed of details of an offer made by one of its competitors; such information concerning the market behaviour and supply possibilities of a competitor would be of importance to BP Kemi. Consequently the English clause restricted competition between BP Kemi and its competitors because it provided it with information about their prices which it would not otherwise have been likely to get. The application of the English clause also means that it was up to BP Kemi in each case to decide, in view of all circumstances, whether a competitor who was offering ethanol at lower prices and under the conditions stipulated in the clause was to be allowed to supply DDSF. DDSF was not free to purchase from such a competitor if BP Kemi decided to meet the price offered by this competitor; it not being necessary for BP Kemi to underquote the competitor's offer. This is not contradicted by the fact that BP Kemi in the case of the offer concerning ethanol produced by Veba-Chemie actually offered a lower price.

65. In spite of the alleged advantage of the English clause for DDSF, it is even doubtful whether the clause could help in bringing the prices down to the level prevailing in a competitive situation. In a competitive situation it would be expected that a supplier who learns that his price has been underquoted by a competitor would seek to get the order through a further price reduction, but a competitor with knowledge of the English clause might not reduce his price further, if this were possible, because he might think such a reduction was likely to be useless.

66. The purchasing obligation as supplemented by the English clause appreciably limits - and limited - other suppliers than BP Kemi's chances of selling on the Danish market. The overcapacity existing every-

where shows that quantities could be made available by such other sources of supply and the transport costs play only a secondary role as for instance shown by the fact that certain imports from the USA take place. As to prices, the prices on the Danish market were always attractive, even for producers from countries in which relatively high domestic prices apply, such as Germany for example. In practice synthetic ethanol produced by Veba-Chemie had been offered to DDSF at a price lower than that charged by BP Kemi. It is, of course, true that import duties were levied upon imports into Denmark until 30 June 1977 but even in 1973 when they made up 25.2% of the selling price they did not prevent foreign suppliers from making offers or proposals of negotiation to DDSF in order to begin business with DDSF and to enter a new market which shortly would be no longer cut off by customs tariffs. If DDSF had not been bound by the purchsing obligation as supplemented by the English clause, DDSF would also have been free itself to look for offers on the spot market or elsewhere which did not fulfil the conditions of the English clause but which would have been economically attractive for the company. DDSF was thus deprived of the possibility of using other sources, either occasionally or on a permanent basis and with a view to growth, and thus to lessen the degree of its dependence on BP Kemi.

67. The restrictive effects of the purchasing obligation as supplemented by the English clause are particularly clear in the market in question. The undertaking tied to BP Kemi by these clauses, DDSF, is the largest buyer on the Danish market with a market share of 71% in 1973 and 56% in 1976. Considering that BP Kemi itself had a market share in the said years of 21% and 28% respectively, only a minor part of the market was open to other suppliers. Moreover, supply is oligopolistic throughout the Community. Apart from BPCL the only producers to be taken into consideration are SODES in France and Veba-Chemie and Erdölchemie in Germany. However, Erdölchemie is not a really independent competitor; it is a joint undertaking in which Bayer and BP (through a German subsidiary) each holds a 50% stake, and which, since Bayer has no other interests in the ethanol field, is strongly influenced by BP. Apart from these producers, there are only a few suppliers to be considered as competitors of BP Kemi on the Danish market; these trade in ethanol produced inthe Community or in non-member countries and sell only limited quantities.

68. When on such a market, which already displays a weak competitive structure, one of the most important suppliers entering into long-term contracts with one of the most important purchasers, which induce the purchaser to take all his requirements or the major part of his requirements from the same supplier, there exists an appreciable disadvantage for the supplier's competitors and for purchasers, and there is thus a restriction of competition for the purpose of Article 85(1). A six-year agreement certainly goes beyond what is appropriate under EEC rules of competition to the natura of the legal and economic relationship between the parties. Certainly, DDSF's interest in a regular guaranteed supply is to be recognised, as is BPCL's interest in lasting and steady sales of its output. But these interests could be met by concluding purchasing agreements stipulating fixed quantities, without reference to the purchaser's unspecified or not precisely specified requirements and without the restrictions resulting from an English clause; such agreements could be regularly renewed after renegotiating to adapt them to changing interests and the shifting competitive position.

69. DDSF has argued that since DDSF can terminate the purchasing obliga-

tion every time agreement cannot be obtained between the company and BP Kemi in respect of price increases made by BP Kemi, what is under consideration is not a binding six-year agreement but a number of successive agreements made every time price increases have taken place and only entered into after negotiations where each of the parties has been free to defend its interests.

However, the purchasing obligation has been entered into for six years. It is binding for the parties during this period and it is in no way automatically terminated by a price increase.

70. DDSF has furthered referred to the official Danish statistics concerning foreign trade and indicated that, since the import prices (duties excluded) since 1973 have been lower for ethanol imported from the United Kingdom than from any other EEC country, DDSF would in any case only have bought ethanol produced by BPCL.

As regards this argument it should be indicated that when DDSF is buying from BP Kemi it is not paying the import price but a higher price which contains the profit of BP Kemi; a comparison of import prices does not therefore seem to be relevant. Moreover, offers which are not accepted, such as the favourable offer concerning ethanol from Veba-Chemie, which did not result in a sale because of the subsequent price reduction made by BP Kemi, naturally do not appear from the statistics. Also, it should be noted that the import prices from other countries concern relatively small quantities and therefore do not reflect the more favourable prices which DDSF would probably have obtained, if it had been free to buy from sources other than BP.

71. BP Kemi has argued that the purchasing obligation has not restricted competition because of the governmental measures applied in France and Germany; these measures have meant that exports from these countries have only been allowed to the extent that national requirements could be met.

However, the production capacities in France and Germany exceed the actual production in these countries to a significant extent and considerable exports from Germany and in particular from France have taken place. To Denmark, for instance, in 1976 - when the governmental measures in France and in Germany were still in force and when the customs duties in Denmark were insignificant - the exports were around 14 000 hl from France and around 8000 hl from Germany. Furthermore, SOFECIA in January 1973 offered DDSF ethanol 'to cover the consumption in Denmark' and in October 1973 DDSF and SODES decided to maintain the contact, although SODES 'understood that (because of the purchasing obligation) there was no immediate possibility for supplies of spirits from SODES to DDSF'. It also seems that SODES did not foresee any difficulties in continuing its supplies to other customers in Denmark.

Under these circumstances it must be assumed that the governmental measures in France and Germany would not have prevented DDSF from getting at least some of its supplies from manufacturers in these countries if the company had been free to do so.

2. Restriction of competition between BP Kemi and DDSF

(a) General

72. BP Kemi and DDSF have contended that the competition between them is not a type of competition which is protected by Article 85(1). Their argumentation may be summarised as follows:

73. Although formally BP Kemi - and not BPCL - is the party to the agreements, this is merely the result of the internal allocation of tasks within the BP Group. In effect therefore, the agreements should be considered as having been made between a producer, BPCL, which was incapable of supplying the entire Danish market, and a distributor, DDSF, which was wholly dependent on BPCL for its supplies. Thus each party was dependent on the other, and the situation was fundamentally the same as that which exists in a sole distributorship arrangement where the producer has reserved to himself the right of selling the contract product to certain customers in the territory of the sole distributor. Competition between a producer and a sole distributor is not the kind of competition which Article 85 is designed to protect; in fact, it is of the essence of any sole distribution arrangement that the freedom of the producer to sell in the distributor's allotted territory be restricted, and it would be senseless to require a manufacturer in such a situation to compete with his distributor since, in the long run, the result would necessarily be the elimination of the distributor with no resulting benefit for competition in general.

74. The Commission agrees with the parties that since both BP Kemi and BPCL belong to the BP Group BPCL should be included in the assessment of the agreements with DDSF. It is not true to say, however, that there is no competition between BP Kemi and DDSF to which Article 85(1) applies.

75. The competition between the parties in this case is protected by Article 85(1). The Court of Justice has ruled that Article 85(1) makes no distinction between businesses operating in competition with each other at the same level or between businesses not competing with each other and operating at different levels and that it is not possible to make a distinction where the Treaty does not make one. However, Article 85(1) makes no distinction either between businesses operating at different levels and competing with each other. Consequently, an agreement between such competing businesses at different levels may have the object or effect of restricting competition within the meaning of Article 85(1).

76. That there is competition between the parties is shown among other things by what happened in 1977, when BP Kemi began to compete with DDSF on prices, with the result that DDSF's market share was reduced. Moreover, the parties have elsewhere referred to the fact that prices constitute only one dimension of competition, and that the range of offers and customer service also play a role in competition for customers. Lastly, on the price clause in the Cooperation Agreement, DDSF has itself stated that it was 'intended to provide DDSF with the necessary protection against undercutting by its own supplier'.

77. Of course a producer is not obliged to enter the territory of his sole distributor, but if circumstances prompt him to do so, either directly or through a subsidiary or affiliated company, he becomes an operator on the market in the territory like the distributor. Economically he then exercises functions on the market similar to those of the

distributor, and any restriction of his free behaviour on the market becomes a restriction of competition just as a restriction in an agreement between two distributors on the market.

To exclude the relationship between a manufacturer and his distributor in a given territory from the application of the rules of competition would mean that they could freely agree to sell at identical prices or to divide customers between them. The producer and the dealer may have completely different views on sales policy, which will find their expression in different prices, terms and customer service, to the advantage of the customer.

## III. PERMITTED FORMS OF COOPERATION

### A. General

The Commission has endeavoured to define those agreements which do not come under the prohibition and those which do come under such a ban but which are entitled to exemption. The Commission adopted a large number of individual decisions granting negative clearance where it was shown that the agreements which had been submitted did not restrict competition within the Common Market, so that it was not necessary for the Commission to intervene under Article 85.

Thus the intention regarding a certain number of types of agreements has been clarified in the light of the provisions of Article 85 and the individual cases examined. In order to indicate its favourable attitude towards cooperation, particularly between small and medium sized enterprises, and also to dispel the uncertainty that still exists with regard to forms of cooperation which do not come under the ban on agreements, the Commission endeavoured to explain, in more general terms, by means of its Communication concerning Cooperation between Enterprises those forms of cooperation which do not normally involve any restriction on competition.

Most of the individual decisions on negative clearance arising from the examination of the terms of the agreements have shown that they do not entail any restriction of competition within the meaning of Article 85 because the situation of the market and the position of third parties on the market are not appreciably affected.

In its Communication concerning Agreements of Minor Importance, the Commission laiddown quantitative criteria 'for the general definition of cases of this kind'. Agreements between enterprises which are limited by their minor position on the market and by their limited economic and financial position are, in general, incapable of appreciably affecting either the intensity of competition or the freedom of choice of third parties.

In recent years, particular forms of cooperation have been exempted from prohibition through a series of individual exemption decisions where the agreements fulfilled the necessary conditions. Exemption is normally granted for each separate case since it cannot be decided on without the particular characteristics of the agreement and their effects on the market being studied. It is for this reason that the decisions so far published do not allow for the formulation of premature generalisations, since the conditions for exemption can only be defined for each separate case. It is only in certain fields that certain types of agreement to the extent that their characteristics can be placed within a general delimitation can be eligible for block exemptions. Certain general considerations emerge as to the possible authorising of certain categories of agreement concerning standardisation, specialisation, research and development as well as the use of the results obtained, and the Commission has therefore been authorised to draft regulations for block exemption in this area. Several important individual decisions were also handed down in these matters, and the results of these are being examined with a view to defining the conditions under which general solutions can be found and put into operation. In other fields, specific decisions are still necessary so that the situation is clarified by proceeding from case to case.

The Commission widened the scope for cooperation for small and medium sized undertakings by adopting, pursuant to the Council's empowering Regulation 2821/71 of 20 December 1972, a block exemption regulation for certain specialisation agreements, provided the share of the market held by the undertakings participating and their turnovers did not exceed specified ceilings. The adoption of this Regulation is based on the consideration that specialisation agreements generally contribute to improving the production process and that they are particularly suited to strengthening the competitive position of small and medium sized firms.

Only specialisation in the manufacture of products is included within the scope of the Regulation, to the exclusion of specialisation in distribution or in the supply of services, for in this field, the danger of market sharing is difficult to assess and the Commission's experience insufficient. Such types of specialisation must be dealt with by single decisions.

In adopting a block exemption regulation for certain specialisation agreements, the Commission's aim was to encourage the conclusion of certain agreements which satisfied the conditions set out in the Regulation, since the Regulation authorised such agreements without the need for notification. Agreements which do not qualify for exemption under the Regulation because they may not fulfil precisely all the requirements of the Regulation may nevertheless qualify for individual exemption where the Commission finds, following notification, that the conditions for applying Article 85(3) are met.

Incompatibility with Article 85 derives not only from decisions prohibiting agreements but also from cases of negative clearance or authorisation which reveal restraints of competition discontinued or altered at the Commission's initiative to enable Article 85(3) to be applied.

(See Commission Notice concerning agreements, decisions and concerted practices in the field of cooperation between enterprises, Annex    ).

## B. Specialisation Agreements

a Introduction

Favourable results from the point of view of the economy as a whole can be obtained by means of specialisation agreements.

The basis of specialisation agreements is the agreed allocation of production between the parties, accompanied by mutual obligations on each party to supply the other exclusively with the products in which he specialises for sale in the territory of the other party. Such agreements prevent a member producer from recommencing the manufacture of a product given up in favour of another producer or from marketing directly under his own mark in the territory of another producer the product in which he specialises. The consumers, therefore, have no longer the possibility of stimulating competition between the products of manufacturers participating in the agreement.

Such agreements do, however, provide a means of obtaining specialisation which contributes to lower costs by the setting up of long production runs and a better utilisation of available production capacity by the concentration of effort on a limited number of products. The obligation of reciprocal supply gives each party, in spite of the specialisation of their production, the possibility of continuing to offer for sale to their customers a complete range of products, while the fact that each party represents its partners in the group within the territory in which it has a sales network at its disposal, facilitates the marketing of the products concerned. The agreements concerned also generally aim at promoting among the members of the group a more highly developed technical cooperation, thus creating the motive force for standardisation and rationalisation, for example by means of exchange of information and indeed by jointly working out new products. The specialised enterprises are thus able to offer improved and better adapted products at more advantageous prices.

The Commission has not failed to recognise, however, the limitations of this useful trend, limitations which the decisions adopted have already underlined. The essential condition for granting exemption to such agreements is that specialisation shall not compromise the effectiveness of competition in such a way that the parties to the agreements can utilise the savings in costs for their exclusive profit instead of sharing them fairly with their customers. Even if the real advantages obtained for the customers are not immediately apparent when the agreement is examined, there must nevertheless be established with sufficient probability that any such advantages will accure in the future as a result of the progressive development of the specialisation, thus enabling the parties to achieve a reduction in selling price - a result which will be encouraged by the pressures of competition. Although such agreements may enable the parties thereto to strengthen their position on the market, they must remain subject to effective competition from other manufacturers established in the Common Market or distributing goods similar to those covered by the specialisation agreement. Competition at the distribution level must also be ensured by allowing intermediaries to make parallel imports of the specialised products covered by the agreement.

On the other hand, a specialisation agreement cannot be authorised under the terms of Article 85(3) even if the advantages implied by the agreement cannot be obtained by other means, when it reduces the number of suppliers to a figure below the minimum required to maintain effective competition. Article 85(3)(b) excludes any exemption for agreements which give the contracting parties the possibility of eliminating competition for a substantial part of the products concerned.

(Consult Regulation 3604/82/EEC of the Commission on the application of Article 85(3) to categories of specialisation agreements Annex X).

b. Cases

(1) Decision in re agreement of Jaz and Peter I

Decision of the Commission of 22 July 1969, on a proceeding under Article 85 of the EEC Treaty; J.O. No L 195, 7 August 1969, p. 11; (1969) CMLR D 23; CCH para. 9269; Competition Law CM/M/I/25.

*Facts:* The French company Jaz and the German company Peter concluded a specialisation agreement in 1967 under the terms of which Jaz concentrated on producing electric clocks and Peter specialised in the manufacture of mechanical clocks. Jaz ceased producing mechanical clocks and Peter ceased producing electric clocks.

In return for this specialisation each party undertook to supply the other party exclusively with the specialised products. The Commission considered that the agreement fell under Article 85(1). In the first place it prevented the enterprises concerned from resuming manufacture of their abandoned lines and marketing their specialised products directly, under their own trademark, in the other country. In the second place they deprived consumers of the possibility of prompting competition between the goods manufactured by the two firms. However the Commission found that the agreement could be exempted under Article 85(3).

The agreement in question permits the participating undertakings to increase their productivity within the framework of enlarged activity thanks to the specialisation in their principle manufactures and the exchange of technical information with a view to attaining a reduction in the cost price of their products. The obligation to make reciprocal exclusive supply of the specialised articles bearing the marks of the partner charged with their resale, which is an integral part of the specialisation agreement, is intended to guarantee to each of the parties that the henceforth greater quantities of the specialised articles which they manufacture will not only be in fact acquired by the partner but may also be more easily put by it onto its national market thanks to the renown already enjoyed by its trademarks.

The agreement allows each of the parties to concentrate entirely on the manufacture of the product which already hitherto account for the main part of its production and for which it has available bigger and better manufacturing possibilities than its partner, taking into account its technical equipment and its long experience. It thus puts each of the parties in a position to manufacture in much greater quantities the articles for which it is specialised. This concentration of production involves not only a better utilisation of the industrial plant available to each, whence a reduction in the unitary cost of manufacture of the specialised products, but also the elimination of the burdens which result from the maintenance of previous non-profitable manufactures, thus allowing important overall economies. Furthermore, the obligation agreed upon to make reciprocal exclusive supply gives to each of the parties the certainty of being able to depend upon minimum orders from its partner, which facilitates the drawing up of its manufacturing programme. It also gives it, in spite of the specialisation of its manufactures, the possibility to continue to offer for sale a complete range of mechanical end electrical time pieces, in all price ranges, which permits it to satisfy all categories of customer. Consequently, the agreement contributes to improving both production and distribution of the products in question.

By reason of the competition which exists on the Community market in time pieces because of the existence of numerous undertakings operating in the Member States as well as the pressure exerted by imports from non-Member States, it is unthinkable that Jaz and Peter could appropriate to their own profit the cost economies which result from the agreement. It can therefore be expected that they would pass on, even if only in part, to their purchasers the reduction in manufacturing costs which is one of the aims of the agreement. As an indication that the agreement has already given rise to price reductions, one can mention the fact that the prices to the French consumers recommended by Jaz for the alarm clocks manufactured by Peter are 7 per cent lower than those recommended by Jaz before the conclusion of the agreement for similar alarm clocks manufactured by its old French supplier and also that the price of Articles sold by Peter on the German market have remained unchanged since 1967 in spite of the severe increase in certain elements in the cost price, particularly wages. The agreement has already resulted in other real advantages for consumers since, thanks to the exchange of technical information between the parties and the permanent control exercised by them over the manufactures of each other the consumers have been offered improved articles better adapted to the tastes of the country to which they are aimed, and their conditioning and methods of protection during transportation have also been improved following the observations made about the deliveries received by the two parties. It can therefore be concluded that the consumers have a fair share in the profit resulting from the agreement.

The agreement does not compromise any restrictions which are not indispensable to the attainment of the objects sought:

(a) without the giving up by each party of the manufacture of the articles in which its partner specialises, the sought-for increase in productivity would not be possible, since it derives from the specialisation itself.

(b) The obligation to make reciprocal exclusive supply as operated in this case (obligation to supply under the partner's trademark and to take delivery of minimum quantities) gives each of the partners a guarantee that not only will it put onto the market in its partner's country given quantities of the articles which it will then be alone in manufacturing because of the specialisation, but also that it will itself be able to take the whole benefit from the sale in its own country of the specialised articles of its partner; Jaz and Peter could not reasonably be expected, without such guarantee, to take the risk of concentrating each on certain manufactures and making new investments with a view to increasing their production of improved specialised articles.

(c) The increase in productivity by increasing the quantities produced as specialised articles, which is the main object of the agreement, is realised in the present case by the withdrawal by each of the parties in favour of its partner, in the sector in which the latter has specialised, from parts of production and market in which it was previously engaged. This objective can only be attained if each of the parties abstains from purchasing from third parties the articles which it needs to complete its range and which it can obtain from its partner.

(d) The reciprocal concession of the right of priority for the marketing of new articles which the parties aim at manufacturing and distributing should, also, be considered as indispensable to the realisation of the improvement of production and the promotion of technical progress to which the agreement contributes. The development of an ever closer collaboration between the parties, particularly in the field of joint research and exchange of information, would be imperilled if the latter had not agreed from the beginning thereby to have the possibility of participating within certain limits, and within their respective territories, in the benefits which the partner could derive from the perfecting and sale of any new products.

There are in the countries of the Common Market numerous manufacturers of time pieces capable of competing effectively with Jaz and Peter in their respective markets. Considerable imports, particularly from Switzerland, Japan and the Eastern European countries, are regularly made into France and Germany. The middle man has always the power to make parallel imports. Jaz and Peter remain free to export under their own trademarks out of Germany and France and they are at liberty to buy from other manufacturers for resale outside Germany and France. Therefore the agreement, although it puts the parties in a position to increase the share of the market in time pieces which they have within the EEC, a rather large share as regards Jaz, does not nevertheless give them on the whole the possibility of eliminating competition in a substantial part of the products in question. Consequently all the conditions for the decision to apply Article 85 are met.

(2) Decision in re the agreement Jaz and Peter II

Decision of the Commission of 23 December 1977 relating to a proceeding under Article 85 of the Treaty. Jaz-Peter. O.J. No L 161, 3 March 1978, p.17;(1978)2 CMLR 186; CCH para. 10013; Competition Law CM/M/I/127.

*The Commission ruled:*

.....

5. The provisions of Commission Regulation (EEC) No 2779/72 of 21 December 1972 concerning the application of Article 85(3) of the Treaty to certain categories of specialisation agreements, which was made after the Decision of 22 July 1969, are not applicable to the present agreements because the market shares of one of the parties in one Member State exceeds that fixed by Article 3 of the Regulation. It must therefore be examined whether or not a decision tc renew the exemption can be taken.

6. The agreement continues to fulfil the conditions required for the application of Article 85(3) for the following reasons:

(a) The agreement allows each of the parties to concentrate entirely on manufacturing those products for which it has bigger and better manufacturing facilities than its partner, taking into account its technical equipment and its experience. Each can manufacture in much greater quantities the articles in which it specialises. Jaz is now producing four times as many alarm clocks and electrical pendulum clocks as it did 10 years ago before the agreement. Peter's production of large mechanical alarm clocks has increased by 25% over the same period. This concentration and development of production means not only a better use of the industrial plant available to each, and hence a reduction in the unit cost of manufacture of the specialised products, but also the elimination of the burdens which result from maintaining previous non-profitable manufactures. Furthermore, the obligation agreed upon to make reciprocal exclusive supplies gives each party the certainty of being able to depend upon minimum orders from its partner, thereby facilitating the preparation of its manufacturing programme. It also enables them, in spite of their specialised manufactures, to continue to offer for sale a complete range of mechanical and electrical timepieces in all price ranges.

All these advantages both for production and distribution have led to an appreciable increase in the competitiveness of both Jaz and Peter, which in turn has led to a considerable expansion in the two undertakings sales in Community and third country market. In 10 years Jaz's turnover has more than quadrupled. Over 20% of its turnover is now found in non-domestic markets whereas in 1967 this company exported only 10% of value of production. The expansion has been less rapid for Peter but the German company has been able, during the same period, to increase its turnover by 170%.

The combined effects of the technical cooperation and of the investments, which have, through economies of cost, been able to be developed in the field of research, have also enabled the two undertakings to achieve substantial improvements in the quality of their products. The degree of precision in mechanical and particularly electrical mpvements attained by Jaz and Peter has increased considerably over 10 years and includes the use of electronic components and quartz synchronisation devices. In addition numerous technical refinements (repeating alarms, digital numerical displays, movements governed by tuning fork vibrations) have been added to the various products manufactured. It is clear, therefore, that the overall effect of the agreement has not only been an improvement in production and distribution but also the promotion of technical progress.

Peter's obligation to deliver its stopwatches exclusively to Jaz for sale on the French market has also involved an improvement in distribution. It should be emphasised that Peter's stopwatches cannot, by reason of their style of manufacture as well as their price level, be considered as competing with those which Jaz continues to manufacture in much more restricted amounts. The stopwatches manufactured by Jaz, which have a logarithmic movement, are in a price range which is clearly higher than Peter's models, which have a running-type movement. The fact that Jaz has taken over the sale of Peter's stopwatches under its own trademarks has allowed it to offer to French purchasers, though its numerous sales outlets in France, a complete range of timepieces of this type. A substantial increase can be discerned in the sale of Peter's stopwatches on the French market as compared with the period preceeding the agreement.

(b) The competition on the Community market in time pieces, due to the large number of undertakings operating in the Member States and to the pressure from imports from non-Member States, has ensured that Jaz and Peter could not solely appropriate for their own profits the cost economies which result from the agreement. By offering increasingly large quantities of improved articles of high quality at competitive prices, the two undertakings have been able to afford customers a fair share of the resulting benefit. Jaz and Peter's price evolution demonstrates that not only have the prices of some current quality articles been reduced and for the most part have remained unchanged for periods of several years but also that the increases in respect of omproved articles have generally been lower than the general rate of price increases. For these reasons it may be concluded that the agreement will continue to afford the consumer a fair share of the resulting benefit in the future.

(c) The agreement does not contain any restriction which is not indispensable to the attainment of the objectives sought:

- unless each party had given up manufacturing the articles in which its partner specialises, the desired increase in productivity would not have been possible, since it stems from the specialisation itself;

- the obligation to supply under the partner's trademark and to take delivery of minimum quantities gives to each of the parties a guarantee that not only will it put onto the market, in its partner's country, given quantities of the articles which it will then be alone in manufacturing because of the specialisation, but also that it will itself be able to take the whole benefit from the sale in its own country of the specialised articles of its partner. Jaz and Peter could not reasonably be expected, without such guarantee, to take the risk of concentrating each on certain manufactures and making new investments to increase their production of specialised articles and to improve the quality thereof;

- the increase in productivity by increasing the quantities produced as specialised articles, which is the main object of the agreement, is achieved in the present case by the withdrawal by each of the parties in favour of its partner, in the sector in which the latter has specialised, from those areas of production and of the market in which it was previously engaged. This objective can only be attained if each of the parties abstains from purchasing from third parties the articles which it needs to complete its range and which it can obtain from its partner;

- the reciprocal concession of a priority right to market new articles which the parties propose to manufacture and distribute has never been applied since the agreement came into force. However, this must be considered as indispensable to achieve the improvement in production and the promotion of technical progress to which the agreement contributes. The development of an ever-closer collaboration between the parties, particularly in the field of joint research and exchange of information, would be imperilled if they had not agreed from the outset to be able by these means to participate within certain limits, in their respective territories, inthe benefits which the partner could derive, by reason of the specialisation, from the perfecting and sale of any new products.

(d) There are in the countries of the common market numerous manufacturers of timepieces capable of effectively competing with Jaz and Peter in their respective markets. Considerable imports, particularly from Japan, Switzerland and the Eastern European countries, are regularly made into France and Germany. The midlle-man trade is always in a position to make parallel imports. Jaz and Peter remain free to export under their own trademarks out of Germany and France and they are at liberty to buy from other manufacturers for resale outside Germany and

France. Consequently, although the agreement puts the parties in a position to increase their market share within the EEC, a rather large share in the case of Jaz, it does not however afford them on the whole the possibility of eliminating competition in a substantial part of the products in question.

7. Consequently, the Commission Decision of 22 July 1969 can, under Article 8(2) of Regulation No 17, be renewed since all the requirements for the application of Article 85(3) of the Treaty continue to be met.

## C. Agreements on Joint Research and Development and Utilisation of Results

a. Introduction

Efforts made in pure and applied research determine the competitivity of enterprises and the possibilities of development of the economy as well as the pace of technical innovation. That is why the Commission has tried to remove, within the common market, obstacles to the cooperation of enterprises in reasearch and development within the limits of the rules of competition laid down by the EEC Treaty.

To the extent that they do restrict competition, agreements between small and medium sized enterprises concerning joint research and development only, do not generally present any particular danger to competition. It is rather at the stage of utilisation of the results of research that problems with regard to the law on cartels may arise. The Commission will therefore, have to examine, on the basis of individual decisions already adopted as well as decisions to be adopted, the conditions under which certain categories of agreements on research and development of products and processes up to the stage of industrial application as well as utilisation of the results obtained, including provisions regarding the use of industrial property rights and of secret technical know-how, can be exempted from the prohibition. The regulation which the Commission is authorised to adopt should define the limits laid down by Community law on cartels for cooperation in research and development which it considers necessary for the purpose of ensuring the possibilities of technical and economic development and the competitive capability of enterprises in an enlarged market but which must not allow restrictions of competition, such as the sharing or protection of national markets.

In its notice on Cooperation between Enterprises, the Commission made it clear that agreements arrived at for the purpose of undertaking joint research do not generally restrict competition on condition that the enterprises are not restricted as far as their own research activities are concerned, and that the results of the joint research are made available to all participants in proportion to their participation. In principle, third parties must not be excluded from access to the results of joint research, although the constitution of a joint research organisation justifies the obligation not to grant licences to third parties unless there is prior joint agreement on the part of the contracting parties to do so or unless this is reached by a majority vote.

Particular circumstances may, however, arise in the case of some agreements for joint research which distinguish them from the usual cases envisaged by the Commission in its notice on cooperation. This notice concerns, in particular, cooperation agreements between small and medium sized enterprises. In the case where large enterprises take part, something which the Commission considers as a possibility, the notice referred to above should only be taken with certain reservations.

The Commission has published a draft Regulstion on the application of Article 85(3) of the Treaty to categories of research and development cooperation agreements (see Annex XIII).

b. Cases

(1) Decision in re Henkel-Colgate

Decision of the Commisison of 23 December 1971, on a proceeding under Article 85 of the EEC Treaty; J.O. No 114, 18 January 1972, p. 14; CCH 9461; Competition Law CM/M/I/52.

*Facts:* Henkel and Colgate have decided to coordinate their development projects concerning textile detergents. A research company set up in Switzerland and in which they both have equal holdings will synthesize the indivisual research studies so far effected and will continue them to the point where they are exploitable commercially. The results of the joint research (patents or know-how) will be accessible to both partners in the same way and both may exploit them without restriction. Each partner will be entitled to obtain, subject to the payment of a due of 2% maximum, a licence for all countries. The importance of this decision is to be seen in the fact that joint research decided on between two firms of world scale on an oligopolistic market is thus made subject to the prohibition on combinations and agreements laid down in the Community. Competition at research level plays a special role in this market; the improvement of the quality and method of use of the products which must result from individual research is one of the principal means of conquering shares in the market and improving one's position in relation to competing firms.

(2) Decision on the Bayer and Gist-Brocades Agreement

Commission Decision of 15 December 1975 on a proceeding under Article 85 of the Treaty; O.J. No L 30, 5 February 1976, p. 13; CMLR I (1976) D 98; CCH para. 9770; Competition Law CM/M/I/98.

*Facts:* The Commission authorised long-term specialisation agreements relating to penicillin production between two large European drug manufacturers, Bayer in Germany and Gist-Brocades in the Netherlands.

In this industry distinctions must be made between different market levels for the various manufacturing stages; that of raw penicillin, of 6 APA (6 aminopenicillanic acid) an intermediate product (obtained by biological or chemical process), and of processing into ampicillins and other semisynthetic penicillins, and of the finished product (the various branded preparations sold to hospitals and dispensing chemists). Before they entered into the agreement Bayer and Gist-Brocades were large manufacturers operating independently at these various stages of manufacture. Since raw penicillin can be processed into an intermediate product or into branded preparations for direct sale, and since the intermediate product is sold as such to outsiders while semisynthetics are sold in bulk, the various manufacturing stages each constitute a separate market.

In order to increase production, the two firms entered a long-term agreement under which raw penicillin manufacture was undertaken mainly by Gist-Brocades, with its superior experience of fermentation techniques, while Bayer was made responsible for the production of intermediate products, partly by its own biological process and partly by the chemical process developed by Gist-Brocades. Gist's raw penicillin output is largely for processing into an intermediate product by Bayer, the remainder being processed into traditional penicillin preparations by Gist itself. Bayer uses part of its 6 APA production for its own purposes and processes part under sub-contracting agreements with Gist-Brocades.

The firms have thus achieved a measure of specialisation, supported by reciprocal long-term supply contracts and arrangements for joint investment. In view of their size and technical know-how, each could have manufactured both products but in fact have decided provisionally to abandon part of their business. Competition between the parties in research is also restricted. The agreements are therefore within Article 85(1) However, after amendments had been made, the Commission was able to regard this specialisation as deserving exemption.

Where a product specialisation agreement is concluded between two large firms both having good market knowledge and financial power, it cannot automatically be assumed that each is incapable of acting alone, without help from a major competitor, in bearing the costs and economic risks inherent in extending its production capacity so as to rationalise manufacture. In this case, however, the Commission concluded that production could be more economic as a result of the specialisation. Bayer used a low-quality and low-yield penicillin strain, needed the assistance of a firm experienced in fermentation techniques in order to improve its product. For technical reasons it was more rational to contribute to financing the extension of production capacities at Gist-Brocades and to convert its own plants to the manufacture of the intermediate product on a larger scale.

Most important, once amended, the agreements contained no restrictions which were not indispensable to the attainment of their objectives. The two parties retain full freedom to decide how to use and extend their production capacities and, apart from their firm supply commitments, to decide how much to produce. Only should one of the companies wish the other to supply it with quantities exceeding the capacity of the jointly financed plant will the other have to make an appropriate contribution to financing the extension.

Before amendment, the agreements contained no such provision for independent action in the market outside the specialisation agreements. The plants were to be transferred to joint subsidiaries in which the two parties were to own equal shares and appoint an equal number of directors. The inevitable result would have been joint control over production and investment. Such an extensive restriction of competition between the two firms could not have been regarded as necessary to their specialisation.

This is the first case in which two firms have of their own accord abandoned a plan to form joint subsidiaries in response to objections by the Commission. In a market having various levels it was important that, despite the long-term specialisation, the firms remained independent of each other in respect of the quantities to be manufactured and the investments to be made.

In fixing the period of the validity of the exemption at eight years, the Commission took account of both the extensive investment required in order to operate the specialisation scheme and of the oligopolistic structure of the market. Conditions were attached to the Decision so that the Commission would be able to monitor the practical effects of cooperation, particularly the position of other firms on the market, and to verify that competition is not effected by financial connections or interlocking directorates between the two parties or between them and other persons in this market.

## D. Joint Advertising, joint use of quality labels, standardisation and joint purchasing

a. Introduction

As the Commission has stated in its Notice on Cooperation between Enterprises, joint advertising as such does not constitute a restriction on competition if the participating enterprises are not prevented from carrying out their own publicity. As, in the case of joint research it cannot of course be excluded that, contrary to the general case which the Commission had in mind in its Notice, joint advertising by enterprises of a certain size may come under the general ban. Such a situation can arise when a market is characterised by an oligopolistic structure where advertising as a means of competition plays a decisive role.

Joint advertising which aims to draw the attention of buyers to certain classes of products is generally linked with associations for standards which establish a common quality label guaranteeing to customers that the quality of a product bearing such a label is up to established standards. The Commission has also stated that, in general, agreements on the use of a common label do not restrict competition if competitors, whose products satisfy the required quality conditions, may use the labels on the same terms as the members themselves.

Certain problems concerning competition may arise from agreements which are concerned solely with the uniform application of standards and types. Since agreements of this kind need not be notified in accordance with Article 4(2) Section 3 a of Regulation No 17, the Commission was never made aware of them. As the effectiveness of these agreements is linked with the obligation on the part of participating enterprises to manufacture or sell only those products or parts of products which have been the object of jointly fixed standards, types, kinds, dimensions and categories, they may come under the general ban on cartels. In general, such agreements do, however, help to rationalise production by means of better utilisation of production capacities and of the improvement of supply facilities due to uncreased interchangeability of the products concerned to the benefit of the consumer. Such agreements will, however, only provide the possibility of eliminating competition and present real advantages for the consumer to the extent that they do not provide a means of restricting or removing price competition as well as competition relating to conditions and quality among the participants to the agreement. The Commission will obviously take this into account when determining the conditions under which block exemptions can be granted for certain types of agreement in the field of standardisation.

b. Cases

(1) Decision in re SOCEMAS

Decision of the Commission of 17 July 1968 on a proceeding under Article 85 of the Treaty; J.O. No L 201, 12 August 1968, p. 4; (1968) CMLR D 28; CCH para. 9101; Competition Law CM/M/I/12.

*Facts:* SOCEMAS is a société anonyme which was established in 1959 by a large number of chain stores selling food and provisions. At the time of notification for negative clearance the number of chain stores belonging to SOCEMAS was 69, representing about 20,000 shops scattered around France. SOCEMAS is not a profit-making organisation. It is required by the objects of association: to make market studies in France and abroad with a view to reducing the costs and sales prices of the articles sold by its members: to carry out studies of products, their standardisation and their conformity with the regulations on health and deception: to seek out articles manufactured in France and capable of being sold abroad on good terms: to circulate among its members the results of its research and measures.

In accordance with the provisions of its articles of association SOCEMAS carries on, in particular, a search abroad for products, food or otherwise, which are of interest as regards quality of price. On the French market, the food and provisions stores or their central purchasing departments themselves take up directly the same search. However, each food and provisions store or central purchasing department remains free to search abroad and buy there those products which are of particular interest to it.

When it is involved, SOCEMAS clarifies all the factors - namely, the technical characteristics of the products, purchase price, delivery period, conditions of payment, etc. - and on the basis of the results obtained makes proposals to the food and provisions stores. Where the latter consider the offer interesting, they give orders to SOCEMAS which, if the quantity of merchandise to be bought is sufficiently great, conclude a contract with the foreign supplier concerned. But if the order is too small, it asks its members concerned to enter into direct relations with the foreign supplier.

SOCEMAS is not concerned with the actual carrying out of the importation into France of the bought goods, their invoicing, payment and distribution after crossing the frontier among the food and provisions stores concerned; all these operations are entrusted to another specialised undertaking, the National Purchasing, Import and Representation Corporation, which has since 1947 always carried them out on behalf of the food and provisions stores.

The prices of resale on the French market of the products imported from abroad are freely fixed by each food and provisions store.

Hitherto, SOCEMAS has not extended its activity to the export of French products.

There is no need to consider here the other activities provided for in the articles of association of SOCEMAS concerning the study of products, their standardisation and their conformity with the regulations in force on the French market.

It follows from the information obtained:

- that in 1965 imports from EEC countries carried out through SOCEMAS amounted to 0.1% of the overall turnover of the food and provisions stores and that it has not been possible to affirm that such imports exceeded, at their best, for any given product - e.g. tinned fish from Germany - 1% of the annual production of that Member State;

- that the foreign products of any origin actually purchased through SOCEMAS hitherto represents only a minimal part of their total turnover.

- that these purchases have been the object of fairly rapid development, but those carried out in the EEC countries have remained stationary over recent years;

- that those products which according to the statistics of recent years have remained in large part the same - where there is therefore an increase in the volume of purchases from abroad rather than of the variety - come from all the countries in the world and also from the EEC countries other than France;

- that they are in general articles typical of such countries, which are not manufactured in France, or else in certain cases products the price or quality of which make them preferable to similar French produced articles; those which come from EEC countries are, in particular, certain types of biscuit, tinned fish, wines, glass-ware and toys.

*The Commission decided:*

.....

The negative clearance requested may be granted under the provisions of Article 2 of Regulation No 17 if the Commission finds that, according to the information it has received, there are no grounds for it to intervene, under Article 85(1) of the Treaty, with respect to the articles of association and activities of SOCEMAS.

Under Article 85(1) of the Treaty, the following practices shall be prohibited as incompatible with the common market: all agreements between undertakings, all decisions by associations of undertakings and all concerted practices, which may affect trade between Member States and the object of effect of which is to prevent, restrict or distort competition within the Common Market.

The food and provisions chain stores (M.A.S) associated within SOCEMAS are undertakings. The provisions in the articles of association whereby SOCEMAS concludes contracts abroad on behalf of its members which authorise it to do so is an agreement between those undertakings.

Before the formation of SOCEMAS, the food and provisions stores grouped in five central marketing departments and the other food and provisions stores explored the foreign markets and made purchases therein through the central purchasing department or directly. Thereafter, the central purchasing departments have ceased their activity outside France and nearly the whole of the products imported by the food and provisions stores have been so imported following the intervention of SOCEMAS.

The activity of SOCEMAS consists essentially in the transmission to its members of purchase offers from foreign markets on conditions more favourable than those which were possible for them before the creation of that organisation. Nevertheless, the food and provisions stores remain free to accept them or not. Furthermore, they are not bound to obtain their supplies only through SOCEMAS and each food and provisions store or central purchasing department thus retains legally its freedom to make imports independently. Therefore, that agreement does not have the object of preventing, restricting or distorting competition.

In order to appreciate whether the agreement has the effect of preventing, restricting or distorting competition, account must be taken not only of the facts at present known, but also of their evolution so far as it is possible to foresee them with a minimum degree of certainty.

The purchases abroad of products capable of being sold in the shops of the food and provisions stores made by SOCEMAS represent only a very minor part of the different markets in the products in question. As regards the purchase in the EEC countries other than France, they have remained stationary over recent years and no appreciable extension of their amount or range is to be expected, given that for the food and provisions stores they represent a complementary supply relating to certain types of product for which the taste of consumers develops only slowly.

Consequently the creation of SOCEMAS and its activity do not have any noticeable effects on the position of the suppliers on the markets for the products concerned, which permits the affirmation that the agreement under examination does not have the effect of preventing, restricting or distorting competition within the Common Market.

Therefore, the agreement has neither the object nor the effect of preventing, restricting or distorting competition.

Since one of the conditions of application of Article 85(1) has not been met, it is not necessary to examine whether the agreement meets the other conditions, namely, in this case, whether the agreement is capable of affecting trade between Member States.

The agreement therefore does not fall within the field of application of Article 85(1) of the Treaty and the Commission may affirm, in answer to the request of SOCEMAS, that according to the information it has received there are no grounds for it to intervene with regard to the agreement in question under Article 85(1) of the Treaty. The negative clearance may therefore be granted.

(2) Decision on the Trans Marine Ocean Paint Association (First)

For facts and references see below, page 195.

(3) Trans Marine Ocean Paint Association Case

For facts and references see below, pages 202 and 324.

## F. Rationalising Participation in Fairs and Exhibitions

a. Introduction

The regulations on exhibitions often restrict the freedom of exhibitors to take part, either directly or indirectly, for a given period in activities of this kind other than those organised periodically by the association itself. There is a need to rationalise participation in fairs and exhibitions and of the trend, which is often uneconomic, for the proliferation of this type of activity. The limitation on the participation of exhibitors in other similar types of activities is a rationalisation factor in the trend towards a concentration of specialised exhibitions.

This concentration provides the opportunity of a periodic comparison of practically all the products concerned in one and the same place and thus assists the marketing of these items in the interests of consumers.

However, competition between manufacturers or their general agents as well as the activities of the organisers of the fairs and exhibitions should not be restricted to such an extent as to hinder the development of the advantages offered by such concentration.

b. Cases

(1) Decision in re CEMATEX I

See above, page 138.

## G. Subcontracting

See the Commission Notice on Subcontracting, Annex XVIII.

## IV. AGRICULTURE

(1) Decision in re European Sugar Industry

For facts and references see above, page 222.

The concerted practice described above and covered by the prohibition in Article 85(1) of the Treaty cannot benefit from the exceptions laid down in inthe first sentence of Article 2(1) of Regulation No 26.

The first of these exceptions, that established in favour of 'such ... agreements, decisions and practices ... as form an integral part of a national market organisation', cannot be invoked where a common organisation of the market has not left any place for the national market organisations. It follows from the third recital in Regulation No 26 that the second of these exceptions, that made in favour of 'agreements, decisions and practices ... necessary for attainment of the objectives set out in Article 39 of the Treaty' is only intended to apply in so far as the application of Article 85(1) of the Treaty would jeopardise attainment of the objectives of the common agricultural policy in the sugar sector. The necessary means for attaining these objectives were laid down in Regulation No 1009/67/EEC and its implementing Regulations (in particular the minimum price for sugar beet, sugar price support systems, basic and maximum production quotas for each undertaking, measures intended to facilitate the sale of surplus production). The practices in question cannot be included in this context no matter from what point of view one examines them (artificial separation of the Community market in sugar for human consumption from that of surpluses, the sharing of the national markets in sugar for human consumption, descrimination in deliveries, measures to restrict imports, concertation in respect of tendering procedures).

The means of attaining the objectives of the common agricultural policy in the sugar sector should allow the common sugar market to operate and develop as provided for in Article 38(4) of the Treaty i.e. in such a way that there is free movement of the product between the Member States. If Regulation No 1009/67/EEC provides for basic amounts per Member State these amounts are only factors in calculating the quotas to be attributed to each undertaking with the sole aim of limiting the guarantee regarding prices and sales, and they are therefore not a form of sharing out production between Member States.

Among the objectives of the common agricultural policy as defined in Article 39 of the Treaty, the recitals in Regulation No 1009/67/EEC emphasise the importance of the necessary guarantees in respect of employment and standards of living of Community growers of sugar beet and sugar cane. The practices in question are not part of the means provided to this end by Community rules and mentioned above, and were adopted for purposes totally alien to these objectives.

Concentration with regard to the Community tendering procedures determining the export refunds leads to a distortion of competition between the undertakings concerned, whereas competition is the whole point of the system of tenders provided for in Regulation No 1009/67/EEC.

The practices in question cannot be considered in any way necessary for attaining the objectives of Article 39 of the Treaty in the sugar sector. They even conflict with the measures laid down in the Community rules as necessary for attaining the said objectives in this sector.

(2) Decision in re Frubo Case

For facts and references see above, page 115 .

*The Court held:*

.....

First submission as to form

The applicants contend that the defendent has not, pursuant to the procedure provided for under the regulation, ruled on the applicability or otherwise of Regulation No 26 of the Council of 4 April 1962 applying certain rules of competition to production of and trade in agricultural products.

The defendent maintains that if, when a decision is taken applying Article 85 to agricultural products, it follows the procedure of Regulation No 17 and decides that an agreement whose exemption has been applied for does not come under Regulation No 26, this does not affect the rights of the applicants.

Article 2 of Regulation No 26, implementing Article 42 of the EEC Treaty, provides that the production of or trade in agricultural products are subject to the requirements of Article 85.

Nevertheless, Article 2(1) of Regulation No 26 provides as follows:

"Article 85(1) of the Treaty shall not apply to such of the agreements, decisions and practices referred to in in the preceding Article as form an integral part of a national market organisation or are necessary for attainment of the objectives set out in Article 39 of the Treaty".

Article 2(2) reads: "After consulting the Member States and hearing the undertakings or associations of undertakings concerned and any other natural or legal person that it considers appropriate, the Commission shall have sole power, subject to review by the Court of Justice, to determine, by decision which shall be published, while agreements, decisions and practices fulfil the conditions specified in paragraph 1".

Article 2(3) reads: "The Commission shall undertake such determination either on its own initiative or at the request of a competent authority of a Member State or of an interested undertaking or association of undertakings".

To require the Commission to consult the Member States even in cases where it is in no doubt that the exceptions provided for under Regulation No 26 cannot apply would oblige the Commission to fulfil unnecessary formalities and needlessly delay enquiries into the matters concerned.

First submission as to substance

The applicants contend that, because the disputed Decision withheld application of Article 2 of Regulation No 26 to the disputed agreement on the ground that the agreement was not essential for the attainment of the objectives laid down under Article 39, the Decision infringed not only Article 2 but also Article 39, 40 and 85 of the Treaty.

The stabilisation of markets referred to in Article 39 covers not only adjustment of supply to demand in order to develop Community production but also the compatibility of trade in products imported from third countries with paragraphs (c), (d) and (e) of the said Article.

The agreement did, in fact, have the beneficial effects of concentrating the supply of and demand for fruit imported from third countries in the Rotterdam import auctions and thus of ensuring the stability of the market, the availability of supplies and their reaching concumers at reasonable prices.

The exception provided for under Article 2(1) of Regulation No 26 however, applies only to agreements "necessary to the attainment of the objectives set out in Article 39 of the Treaty".

The applicants have not shown in what respect their agreement, which is concerned with products coming from third countries, can be necessary to "increase agricultural productivity" or to "ensure a fair standard of living for an agricultural community", as the first two objectives of the common agricultural policy are expressed.

In consequence the Commission could reasonably regard Article 2 of Regulation No 26 as inapplicable.

(3) Re Cauliflowers

Commission Decision of 2 December 1977 relating to a proceeding under Article 85 of the EEC Treaty; Groupement d'Exportation du Leon (Grex) O.J. No L 21, 26 January 1978, p. 23; (1978) 1 CMLR D66; CCH para. 10005; Competition Law CM/M/I/118.

*Facts:* Vegetable production in Brittany is geographically concentrated on the narrow band of coastal land roughly 150 kilometres long in the North of the French Departments of Finistère, Côte-du-Nord and Ille-et Vilaine. The main crops grown in this area, which enjoys a mild, humid climate, are cauliflowers, artichokes and early potatoes. Some 70% of the French cauliflowers and artichokes and 25% of early potatoes come from this area.

Aggregate cauliflower production in all the Community countries is nearly 1,500,500 tonnes. Most of this is grown in three Community countries, Italy, France and the United Kingdom, which together account for about 90% of all Community cauliflower output. Figures for 1976 show that 570,000 tonnes were produced in Italy, 443,000 tonnes in France and 254,000 tonnes in the UK. France alone accounts for some 30% of Community cauliflower output, chiefly in the vegetable growing area in Northern Brittany. This area produces more than 300,000 tonnes of cauliflowers, representing some 70% of all French production. There are two varieties of cauliflower cultivated in Brittany, winter cauliflowers, harvested from December to the end of May, and Autumn cauliflowers, harvested from October to December. Production of winter cauliflowers varying between 240,000 tonnes and 280,000 tonnes, is concentrated chiefly arounf Saint-Pol-de-Leon in northern Finistère and Paimpol in Côtes-du-Nord, whereas autumn cauliflowers, with production ranging from 35,000 to 50,000 tonnes depending on the season, are grown almost exclusively around Saint-Malo in Ille-et-Vilaine.

Community production of early potatoes is in excess of two million tonnes, the main producer countries being Germany with 800,000 tonnes, France with 500,000 tonnes and the United Kingdom with 450,000 tonnes. Brittany accounts for approximately 25% of French output of early potatoes, most of them coming from the area around Saint-Malo.

In December 1960, about 3,000 farmers agreed to form an organisation on 31 March 1961, they formed an agrocultural cooperative called the 'SICA-Marché de Vente aux Enchères du Nord Finistère (SICA de Saint-Pol-de-Leon) at Saint-Pol-de-Leon. On 22 November 1961 the SICA S-P-de Léon and the Union des Expéditeurs et Exportateurs en Fruits et Légumes du Finistère signed an agreement requiring shippers belonging to the latter association to obtain supplies only from the auction sales held by the SICA S-P-de-Léon. Between 1964 and 1966 agreements were entered into by the SICA with three major agricultural cooperatives - the Société de Commercialisation des Primeuristes (SOCOPRIM), the Syndicat spécialise des Producteurs de l"Armor (SYPA) and the Coopérative des Agriculteurs de Bretagne - which led to the formation of an association of marketing groups where the member producer groups undertook to sell all their produce through the auction sales held by the SICA de Saint-Pol-de-Léon. In the Ille-et-Vilaine a similar process of organisation led to the introduction in 1965 of auction sales at Saint-Méloir-des-Ondes; managed by an agricultural cooperative which included not only the growers that took part in the auction sales but also, unlike the system at the auction sales at Saint-Pol-de-Léon, all the shippers admitted to the auction sales as buyers. This cooperative, called Société Interprofessionelle des Producteurs et Expéditeurs de Fruits, Légumes, Bulbes et Fleurs d'Ille-et-Vilaine - SICA-SIPEFEL (SIPEFEL), has also entered into agreements with two other producers organisations (APPRM and Coopérative des Agriculteurs de Bretagne) for the formation of the Association de Mise en Marché de Saint-Méloir-des-Ondes, whose member producers are required to sell solely through the auction sales.

In March 1967 a third system of auction sales, the SICA du Goëlo Trégor, was set up at Paimpol; following amalgamation with a major cooperative in the Cotes-du-Nord, this became l'Union des coopératives de Paimpol et Tréguier in 1974.

Meanwhile, in 1965 the amalgamation of all the producers organisations in Brittany had led to the formation of the Comité Economique Agricole Régional Fruits et Légumes de la région Bretagne. This Committee (CERAFEL) is an association of producers organisations which, under the French law No 62-933 of 8 August 1962, may extend the rules applied by its members to production and marketing, with the exception of sales contracts themselves, to the whole region.

As a result of this organisation of growers into particularly well structured and coordinated groups, the bargaining strength of growers and buyers on the Brittany cauliflower and artichoke markets is now quite different from what it was in 1960. The marketing of more than 90% of all cauliflowers, artichokes and early potatoes grown in Brittany is handled by three associations of producers organisations, which sell their produce by auction at Saint-Po-de-Léon, Paimpol and Saint-Méloir-des-Ondes.

These associations are:

- Associations des Groupements de Mise en Marché du Nord Finistère, formed by the SICA de Saint-Pol-de-Léon, SOCOPRIM, SYPA and the producers in the Saint-Pol-de-Léon vegetable growing area belonging to the Coopérative des Agriculteurs de Bretagne;

- Union des Coopératives de Paimpol et Tréguier, consisting of the Coopérative de Goëlo Trégor, the Cooperative La Presqu'île and the Côtes-du-Nord producers belonging to the Coopérative des Agriculteurs de Bretagne;

- Association de Mise en Marché de Saint-Méloir-des-Ondes, consisting of the SIPEFEL member producers, the APPRM and the producers in the Saint-Malo vegetable-growing area belonging to the Coopérative des Agriculteurs de Bretagne.

The remainder of the cauliflowers, artichokes and early potatoes grown in Brittany (less than 10%) is marketed by four cooperatives: l'Union des Cooperatives Agricoles du Nord-Finistère la Paimpolaise, la Perrosienne and the GAARM (Groupement des Associations Agricoles pour l'organisation de la Production et de la Commercialisation des Pommes de Terre et Légumes de la Région Malouine). All these producer groupings, including the four independent cooperatives, belong to CERAFEL.

On the distribution side the organisation of dealers and shippers (hereinafter referred to as 'dealers') varies according to where they do their business. The 60 dealers who buy at the Saint-Pol-de-Léon auction sales belong to one or other of the two associations of dealers on that market.

The Union des Expéditeurs et Exportateurs en Fruits et Légumes du Finistère (Union des Expéditeurs), the more powerful of the two, consists of 44 dealers, including the largest in business on that market, the remainder belonging to the GEEP (Groupement des Expéditeurs Primeuristes du Nord-Finistère). At Paimpol only 14 dealers regularly buy at the auctions held by the Union des Coopératives de Paimpol et Tréguier. Unlike the dealers at Saint-Pol-de-Léon and Saint-Méloir-des-Ondes, they belong to no association. Lastly, the 46 dealers who buy at the Saint-Méloir-des-Ondes auctions are members of SIPEFEL and are also affiliated to the Syndicat des Expéditeurs et Exportateurs en Légumes et Pommes de Terre Primeurs de la Région Malouine (Syndicat des Expéditeurs de Saint-Malo).

The auctions at Saint-Pol-de-Léon, Paimpol and Saint-Méloir-des-Ondes are held in a large hall using the system of a display dial against which bids are made as the price indicated falls. Each buyer admitted to the auction has his own button, which he presses when he wishes to make a bid; the needle on the dial then stops at the price indicated. The three dial auction centres at Saint-Pol-de-Léon, Paimpol and Saint-Méloir-des-Ondes can be linked up electronically, so that goods offered for sale at Centre A may also be purchased by buyers at Centres B or C. Such link-ups are used as follows:

- between Saint-Pol-de-Léon and Paimpol for the winter cauliflowers and artichokes sold on those markets;

- between Paimpol and Saint-Méloir-des-Ondes, but only for winter cauliflowers for sale at Paimpol; and

- between all three centres, but only for early potatoes.

Payment for all transactions between growers and dealers is carried out through the agency of the particular organisation holding the relevant auction (SICA de Saint-Pol-de-Léon, SIPEFEL, or Union des Coopératives de Paimpol et Tréguier). Under the current terms of payment to be made within two or three weeks depending on the product, the dealer makes payment for his purchase to the organiser at the price shown on the auction dial for the quantities taken. The organiser then transmits the amount due to each grower in accordance with the quantities sold by him, less three centimes per kilogram of produce or per head of cauliflower to cover the costs of running the auction.

Each year the Council of the European Communities, under the common agricultural policy, sets intervention prices for cauliflowers below which producers organisations may not offer their members produce for sale. For each quantity thus withdrawn from the market producers are paid the intervention price. These operations are entirely financed by the EAGGF, which pays the sums to be repaid to the various regional bodies. In Brittany CERAFEL is resonsible for the receipt, apportionment and payment of these sums on behalf of the local producers organisations. For other vegetables CERAFEL may itself set a withdrawal price, but financing of withdrawal operations is then handled through an equilisation system extending to all the participating growers.

Vegetables offered for sale at the auctions are either packed or in bulk. At Saint-Pol-de-Léon and Paimpol 45% of artichokes, more than 60% of cauliflowers and all early potatoes are already packed before being put up for auction. This is done by packers with specially equipped facilities who are under contract to the SICA. The remainder, sold in bulk, is packed by the dealers in their own facilities. Virtually all vegetables sold at the Saint-Méloir-des-Ondes auctions, except early potatoes, are prepacked.

The main sales outlets for cauliflowers grown in Brittany are the export markets, as 50 to 60% are exported, giving an approximate volume of 100, 000 tonnes. The main export markets are Germany (40 to 50,000 tonnes), the United Kingdom 15 to 30,000 tonnes) and the Benelux (20 to 25,000 tonnes). From external trade statistics for the past ten years it can be seen that the volume of sales to these three markets has remained fairly stable, apart from a slight increase in sales to Germany. Virtually all the other vegetables grown in Brittany are for French domestic consumption, only 10% of the early potatoes and less than 6% of the artichokes being exported.

*The Commission ruled:*

.....

Article 2(1) of Council Regulation No 26 of 4 April 1962 provides that Article 85(1) of the Treaty shall not apply to such of the agreements, decisions and practices referred to in the preceding Article as form an integral part of a national market organisation or are necessary for attainment of the objectives set out in Article 39 of the Treaty. In particular, it shall not apply to agreements, decisions and practices of farmers, farmers' associations, or associations of such associations belonging to a single Member State which concerns the production or sale of agricultural products or the use of joint facilities for the storage, treatment or processing of agricultural products, and under which there is no obligation to charge identical prices, unless the Commission finds that competition is thereby excluded or that the objectives of Article 39 of the Treaty are jeopardised.

The conditions for admission of buyers at these auctions do not qualify for exemption under Article 2(1) of Regulation No 26 for the following reasons:

1. They do not form an integral part of a national market organisation, and in any event a national organisation may no longer exist for fruit and vegetables in France since there is a common organisation of the market governed by Regulation (EEC) No 1035/72.

2. Furthermore they are not essential to the attainment of the objectives of Article 39 of the Treaty. It is clear from the third paragraph of the opening recitals to Regulation No 26 that the second exemption applies only where the application of Article 85(1) would jeopardise the attain-

ment of the objectives of the common agricultural policy in relation to the relevant products, and in any event the means for implementing the objectives of the common agricultural policy as set out in Article 39 of the Treaty are determined, as far as fruit and vegetables are concerned by Regulation (EEC) No 1035/72. Although this Regulation made provision for certain rules being imposed on member producers organisations, it did not make provision for rules applying to persons with whom the producers do business, notably dealers. As the conditions for admission were imposed only on dealers they do not come within Regulation (EEC) No 1035/72. Accordingly the obligation at issue, being imposed only on dealers, cannot be regarded as necessary for the attainment of the objectives of Article 39, nor are they necessary for the proper application of the measures provided for by Regulation (EEC) No 1035/72 in respect of producers organisations, and the removal of these conditions in their present form would in no way affect the smooth operation of the auction held by these organisations. The withdrawal of these obligations, at least in their present form, would in no way impede the smooth functioning of the auction sales. This is abundantly clear at least as regards the requirement for a majority vote in the Board of Directors of the Syndicat des Expéditeurs de Saint-Malo and the obligation to purchase and dispatch only on the dealers own account, since the sole effect of these two restrictions is to reserve the Saint-Malo autumn cauliflower market for dealers already established in the area. The same considerations apply to the exclusive buying obligation and the obligation to have a packing centre in the catchment area of the auctions. These two obligations produce not only the geographical segregation of the three Breton auction centres, which is not necessary for the smooth operation of the auctions themselves, but they also exclude access to other sources of supply outside the area covered by the auctions, which is similarly unnecessary.

3. The conditions for the admission of dealers are imposed either by agreements between growers and dealers, such as the exclusive buying obligation and obligation to have a packing centre, or by decisions of the Syndicat des Expéditeurs de Saint-Malo, in respect of the requirement for a majority vote on the Board of Directors and the obligation on dealers only to buy and dispatch on their own account. They do not form part of the agreements between farmers or decisions of farmers associations within the meaning of the second sentence of Article 2(1) of Regulation No 26, so that the exemption provided for therein does not apply in this case.

*The Commission decided:*

.....

Art. 1. (a) The clauses in the agreements between SICA de Saint-Pol-de Léon and the Union des Expéditeurs de Saint-Pol-de-Léon and between SIPEFEL and the Syndicat des Expéditeurs de Saint-Malo, whereby dealers who obtain supplies at auction sales held at Saint-Pol-de-Léon and Saint-Meloir-des-Ondes are required to accept the obligations:

- to buy exclusively at the auction sales to which they have been admitted and

- to be in possession of a packing centre,

constitute infringements of Article 85(1) of the EEC Treaty.

(b) The decisions taken by the Syndicat des Expéditeurs de Saint-Malo:

- subjecting admission of new buyers to the Saint-Meloir-des-Ondes auctions to a favourable decision by the management bodies set up by the Statutes of the Syndicat, without any reference to fixed and objective conditions of admission, and

- obliging members to buy, pack and dispatch vegetables only on their own account,

constitute infringements of Article 85(1) of the EEC Treaty.

Art. 2. SICA de Saint-Pol-de-Léon, the Union des Expéditeurs, SIPEFEL and the Syndicat des Expéditeurs de Saint-Malo shall forthwith bring to an end the infringements referred to in Article 1.

Art. 3. This Decision is addressed to the following associations of undertakings:

- Société d'Investissements et de Coopération Agricoles, of Saint-Pol-de-Léon,

- Union des Expéditeurs et Exportateurs en Fruits et Légumes du Finistère, of Saint-Pol-de-Léon,

- Société Interprofessionnelle des Producteurs et Expéditeurs de Fruits, Légumes, Bulbes et Fleurs d'Ille et Vilaine SICA-SIPEFEL, of Saint-Méloir-des-Ondes,

- Syndicat des Expéditeurs et Exportateurs en Légumes et Pommes de Terre primeurs de la région Malouine, of Saint-Méloir-des-Ondes.

## V. PUBLIC ENTERPRISE

### (1) S.A.B.A.M. Case (Second Judgment)

For the facts and references see above, page 35.

*The Court held:*

.....

By the third question, this Court is asked to interpret the expression "undertaking entrusted with the operation of services of general economic interest" and to state, in particular, whether this concept implies that the undertaking must have definite privileges which are denied to other undertakings.

By the final question it is asked whether the provisions of Article 90 (2) of the Treaty create rights in respect of private parties which national courts must safeguard.

It emerges from the order for reference that the object of the third question is to ascertain whether an association entrusted by its members with the management of their copyrights can be covered by that expression.

As Article 90(2) is a provision which permits, in certain circumstances derogation from the rules of the Treaty, there must be a strict definition of those undertakings which can take advantage of it.

Private undertakings may come under that provision, but they must be entrusted with the operation of services of general economic interest by an act of the public authority.

This emerges clearly from the fact that the reference to "particular tasks assigned to them" applies also to undertakings having the character of a revenue-producing monopoly.

It is thus the duty of the national court to investigate whether an undertaking which invokes the provisions of Article 90(2) for the purpose of claiming a derogation from the rules of the Treaty has in fact been entrusted by a Member State with the operation of a service of general economic interest.

That is not the position in the case of an undertaking to which the State has not assigned any task and which manages private interests, including intellectual property rights protected by law.

It is, consequently, unnecessary to reply to the final question.

(2) Decision in re GVL

For the facts and references see above, page 67.

*The Commission ruled:*

This Decision concerns the conduct of the Gesellschaft zur Verwertung von Leistungsschutzrechten mbH (hereinafter called 'GVL') towards performing artists who are neither of German nationality nor resident in the Federal Republic of Germany (hereinafter called 'Germany').

I. Organisation of GVL

1. GVL, which has its registered office in Hamburg, is a German collecting society set up to manage rights and claims which are vested pursuant to the German 'Gesetz über Urheberrechte und verwandte Schutzrechte' (Law on copyright and related rights, hereinafter called'Urheberrechtsgesetz' - abbreviated to UrhG) in performing artists, film artists (hereinafter called 'artists'), visual and sound recording manufacturers and promoters or which are assigned to manufacturers and promoters.

GVL is responsible for the exploitation in Germany of 'performers' rights', i.e. rights which arise out of the reproduction of the author's creative work. The activities of such collecting societies are governed by the German 'Gesetz über die Wahrnehmung von Urheberrechten und verwandten Schutzrechten' (Law on the management of copyright and related rights, hereinafter called 'Wahrnehmungsgesetz' - abbreviated to 'WahrnG').

2. GVL was created jointly by the 'Deutsche Orchestervereinigung eV', Hamburg, which represents the interests of performing artists - principally musicians - and the 'Deutsche Landesgruppe der IFPI eV' (International Federation of Producers of Phonograms and Videograms), Hamburg, which represents the interests of sound and visual recording manufac-

turers. The Deutsche Orchestervereinigung eV and the Deutsche Landesgruppe der IFPI eV are the sole members of GVL, which is a limited liability company.

.....

INAPPLICABILITY OF ARTICLE 90 OF THE TREATY

65. Pursuant to Article 90(2), undertakings entrusted with the operation of services of general economic interest shall be subject to the rules contained in the Treaty, and in particular to the rules on competition, only in so far as the application of such rules does not obstruct the performance, in law or in fact, of the particular tasks assigned to them. Private undertakings may also come under that provision where they are entrusted with the operation of services of general economic interest by an act of the public authority (cf. judgment of the Court of Justice in BRT II). Since Article 90(2) permits, in certain circumstances, an arrangement which derogates from the Treaty, the concept of an undertaking which may rely on this provision must, however, be interpreted strictly.

66. GVL is not entrusted, either by an official Act or otherwise, by the public authority with the operation of services. Admittedly, it carries on its activities subject to official authorisation, but no specific task is assigned as a result of this 'precondition of authorisation'. Official authorisation is granted subject merely to a check as to whether the company requesting the authorisation satisfies the preconditions relating to associations for the exploitation of performers' rights laid down in the Wahrnehmungsgesetz.

Such granting of authorisation is, therefore, by its very nature not an assignment of particular tasks, but only a permission to carry on certain activities. Authorisation, which merely overrides a statutory prohibition, has a completely different legal content from the entrusting of a task, whereby specific responsibilities and hence specific obligations are officially conferred upon an undertaking. The necessarily strict interpretation of the concept 'undertaking' contained in Article 90(2), therefore, shows that GVL does not fall under that provision.

67. Even if it were accepted, however, that GVL had been 'entrusted' with the operation of services, such services must be 'of general economic interest'.

68. GVL protects only the private interests of artists. The Court of Justice of the European Communities held in its judgment in BRT II that such a general interest is not protected where an undertaking manages private interests, including property rights protected by law. This also applies to GVL.

*Sequel*

GVL brought an action for annulment before the Court of Justice. The Court upheld the Commission's Decision, also on the point of the interpretation of Article 90.

## (3) Decision in re British Telecommunications

Decision of the Commission of 10 December 1982 in a proceeding under Article 86 of the Treaty in re British Telecommunications. O.J. No L 360, 21 December 1982, p.36; (1983) I CMLR 457; CCH para. 10443; Competition Law CM/M/I/185.

For facts see the Decision below.

*The Commission held:*

A. British Telecommunications

1. British Telecommunications is a public corporation established under the Telecommunications Act 1981, an enactment of the United Kingdom Parliament.

2. British Telecommunications has, under the Telecommunications Act 1981, a statutory duty to provide telecommunication services and a statutory monopoly for the running of telecommunication systems throughout the United Kingdom.

3. During most of the time in which the activities later described took place the telecommunication services now provided by British Telecommunications were provided by the United Kingdom Post Office under the Post Office Act 1969, also an enactment of the United Kingdom Parliament. British Telecommunications assumed the responsibilities of the United Kingdom Post Office for telecommunication services from 1 October 1981 under the Telecommunications Act 1981.

4. The enactment of the Telecommunications Act 1981 formed part of the measures taken by the United Kingdom Government with the intention of encouraging competition in the telecommunication field.

.....

B. Applicability of Article 86 of the EEC Treaty

Article 86 of the EEC Treaty prohibits as incompatible with the common market any abuse by one or more undertakings of a dominant position within the common market, or in a substantial part of it, in so far as such abuse may affect trade between Member States.

(a) *Undertaking in a dominant position*

25. The United Kingdom Post Office and British Telecommunications are public corporations and economic entities carrying on activities of an economic nature. As such they are undertakings within the meaning of Article 86 of the EEC Treaty.

26. British Telecommunications has a statutory monopoly, under the Telecommunications Act 1981, for the running of telecommunications systems throughout the United Kingdom and the Isle of Man. British Telecommunications therefore holds a dominant position in the United Kingdom, which constitutes a substantial part of the common market, for the provision of telex and telephone systems.

27. Under the Telecommunications Act 1981 British Telecommunications became the legal successor of the United Kingdom Post Office in respect

of the statutory monopoly for the running of telecommunication systems throughout the United Kingdom and of all rights and liabilities thereunder. British Telecommunications is therefore the successor to the United Kingdom Post Office for the purposes of this proceeding.
.....

C. Applicability of Article 90(2) of the EEC Treaty

Article 90(2) of the EEC Treaty provides that 'Undertakings entrusted with the operation of services of general economic interest or having the character of a revenue-producing monopoly shall be subject to the rules contained in this Treaty, in particular to the rules on competition, in so far as the application of such rules does not obstruct the performance, in law or in fact, of the particular tasks assigned to them. The development of trade must not be affected to such an extent as would be contrary to the interests of the Community'.

41. Under the Post Office Act 1969 and the Telecommunications Act 1981, BT has been entrusted with the operation of services of general economic interest, namely the provision of telecommunication systems throughout the United Kingdom. The application of the Treaty rules on competition to BT would not and does not obstruct the performance of its duties in an efficient and economic way. For BT to be exempted from compliance with the rules on competition it is not sufficient that such compliance would make performance of its duties more complicated.

42. BT has claimed, but not explained how, it would be obstructed in the performance of its duties. Indeed it would be in BT's interests to allow such traffic. Even if BT were not to experience difficulties with other national telecommunication authorities for not preventing message-forwarding agencies in the United Kingdom from undercutting telex tariffs applied in other countries, such a situation would not 'obstruct' the performance of BT's particular task.

43. The Commission accepts, in its broadest sense, the view held by BT that international cooperation and the honouring of international commitments are essential features in the provision of international communications in an efficient and economic way. However, this cooperation should not go so far as to violate the Treaty rules of competition.

44. For the reasons set out above the restrictions on the use of telex and telephone facilities and services by BT constitute infringements of Article 86 of the EEC Treaty. BT should therefore be required to terminate any of the restrictions that are still in operation.

45. Notwithstanding these infringements, the Commission does not consider that a fine should be imposed on BT in view of the special circumstances of the case and of the matters referred to in paragraph 20 above, and because BT did not enforce the restrictions by disconnecting the facilities of the message-forwarding agencies.

## VI. Crisis Cartels

### A. General

The competition rules and measures to reduce structural overcapacity

As the economic recession persists, problems of overcapacity are appearing in increasingly acute form in individual firms and entire industries. The associated employment problems are particularly worrying at a time of high unemployment in all the Member States. In such circumstances, the Commission must offer guidance as to how far it considers the solutions sought by firms as compatible with Article 85 of the EEC Treaty.

Structural overcapacity exists where over a prolonged period all the undertakings concerned have been experiencing a significant reduction in their rates of capacity utilisation, a drop in output accompanied by substantial operating losses and where the information available does not indicate that any lasting improvement can be expected in this situation in the medium-term.

In a predominantly free market economy such as the Community's, it is up to each undertaking to assess for itself whether and at which point such overcapacity becomes unsustainable and to take the necessary measures to reduce it. However, within a given crisis-struck industry, economic circumstances do not necessarily guarantee a reduction of the least profitable surplus capacity. Undertakings which have failed to make the necessary adjustments may have their losses offset within their groups, to the detriment of healthy undertakings and there may be additional distortion from external subsidies.

Against this background, and in order to combat the structural problems of individual sectors, the Commission may be able to condone agreements in restraint of competition which relate to a sector as a whole, provided they are aimed solely at achieving a coordinated reduction of overcapacity and do not otherwise restrict free decision-making by the firms involved. The necessary structural reorganisation must not be achieved by unsuitable means such as price-fixing or quota agreements, nor should it be hampered by State aids which lead to artificial preservation of suplus capacity.

The Commission will be able however to authorise sectoral agreements where it is satisfied that the other conditions of Article 85(3) of the EEC Treaty are met, notably in the following circumstances:

(i) production can be considered to be improved if the reductions in capacity are likely in the long run to increase profitability and restore competitiveness, and if the coordination of closures helps to mitigate, spread and stagger their impact on employment. For this purpose, the agreement must contain a detailed and binding programme of closures for each production centre, which ensures, on the one hand, that overcapacity is irreversibly dismantled and, on the other, that while the plan is in operation no new capacity is created, except for replacement capacities provided for in the reorganisation programme;

(ii) consumers can be considered to enjoy a fair share of the benefits resulting from the agreement if, at the end of the agreement, they can rely on a competitive and economically healthy structure of supply in the Community, without having been deprived during its operation, despite the effects of the capacity cutbacks, of their freedom of choice or the benefit of continued competition between the participating firms;

(iii) the restrictions of competition which the agreement involves can be considered to be indispensable to the objective of the planned restructuration, if the agreement is concerned solely with reducing surplus capacity and is limited from the outset to the period necessary for the technical implementation of the envisaged programme of cutbacks. The creation of a system of exchanging information to check that promised reductions of capacity are being implemented is admissable provided it does not in any way help to coordinate policy on the utilisation of remaining capacity or to align conditions of sale;

(iv) the parties to the agreement will not be afforded the possibility of eliminating competition eventually for the following reasons: first, since the orderly reduction of excess capacity is only one element, albeit an important one, of the competitive strategy of the participating undertakings, they will not have surrendered all freedom of action in the marketplace, so that a degree of internal competition will be maintained. Secondly, the presence in the market of firms not party to the agreement and the fact that the Community is open to imports from third countries will usually provide a source of external competition. Finally, as the agreement is from the outset to run for a limited period only, the certainty of a return to completely unfettered competition in the near future will prompt the undertakings concerned to take account, in the decisions they make even during the course of the agreement, of the fact that in due course they will again become full competitors.

As an alternative to such sectoral agreements, the Commission can also envisage agreements between a small number of firms providing for reciprocal specialisation which would enable them to close excess capacity.

Whatever type of solution is chosen, the Commission will always have to satisy itself that after the reorganisation programme is completed there will still be a sufficient number of Community manufacturers left to maintain effective competition in the Community. This condition is necessary to ensure that the economy as a whole, and users and consumers in particular, will also benefit from the positive results of the arrangements.

Reorganisation operations should also be such as to stabilise and secure the employment situation within the sector concerned.

(Twelfth Report on Competition Policy 1982, pp. 43-45).

## B. Cases

### (1) Notice on synthetic fibres

Notice of the Commission pursuant to Article 19(3) of Regulation 17/62 concerning a request for application of Article 85(3) of the EEC Treaty, OJ No C314, 14 November 1983, p. 3; Competition Law CM/M/IV/29.

*The Commission stated:*

On 10 November 1982 the companies:
Anicfibre SpA (Italy);
Bayer AG (Federal Republic of Germany);
Courtaulds PLC (United Kingdom);
Enka AG (Federal Republic of Germany);
Enka BV (Netherlands);
Hoechst AG (Federal Republic of Germany);

Imperial Chemical Industries PLC (United Kingdom);
Montefibre SpA (Italy);
Rhône Poulenc SA (France);
Snia Fibre SpA (Italy),
requested the Commission to take a decision applying Article 85(3) of the EEC Treaty to the agreement that they had signed on 21 October 1982.

In its revised version dated 19 July 1983, the agreement provides for a total reduction of the order of 365 000 tonnes in the signatories' production capacities for synthetic fibres (polyamide textile yarn, polyamide carpet yarn, polyester yarn, polyamide staple, polyester staple and acrylic staple). The prolonged recession has led to a serious imbalance between potential supply and actual demand in this sector, causing the signatories to suffer substantial losses and giving rise to the need for capacity reductions.

The parties have undertaken in the agreement to take out certain amounts (on average, 18%) of their production capacity by certain dates determined by the party concerned.

They have agreed to supply full details of their capacity cuts to a trustee body and to allow independent experts onto their premises to check that these are being implemented.

In the event of major developments, such as changes in the behaviour of non-signatory European producers on the European market or in imports from outside Europe or a collapse of export markets, the parties will consult with one another to work out appropriate solutions.

The parties have also undertaken not to sell any of the plant they have agreed to take out to other persons in western Europe or to increase during the currency of the agreement their capacity beyond the level they have determined. Should any party sell any of the capacity fixed under the agreement, he will do his best to get the purchaser, even if not a member, to abide by the general principles of the agreement, except where the capacities are transferred outside western Europe.

All the parties will endeavour to carry out restructuring operations in their plants, whilst as far as possible facilitating the retraining and redeployment of the labour affected and fulfilling their statutory and/or contractual obligations in their respective countries.

The agreement is open to accession by non-signatory companies in the EEC or other western European countries on terms to be determined in each individual case.

Finally, any party failing, except for reasons of force majeure, to carry out the capacity reductions to which he is committed will be required to pay the other parties compensation fixed pursuant to an arbitration procedure applicable to breaches of the agreement.

The agreement will expire on 31 December 1985.

The Commission proposes to take a favourable decision on the agreement summarised above, attaching a condition to ensure that the reporting system established under the agreement does not involve the exchange of information other than that of a purely statistical nature, such as could be the subject, the means or the consequence of horizontal collu-

sion between the parties on output and shipments, whether within the framework of the agreement or through a trustee body or third party.
.....

(2) Communication in re European zinc producers
Press Release of the Commission, 9 January 1984, in re European zinc producers.

The six major Community zinc producers have given up their plans to carry out concerted shutdowns of zinc production capacity and to enter into mutual undertakings not to establish fresh capacity.

In September 1982 the six companies - Australian Mining and Smelting Ltd., Billiton BV, Metallgesellschaft AG, Penarroya SA, Preussag AG and Union Minière SA - notified an agreement to the Commission. This provided that each company would volunteer to close such capacity as it considered advisable, and would refrain from establishing any fresh capacity. Each company cutting capacity was to receive a compensation payment to assist with closure costs, particularly social costs.

In view of the heavy financial losses of the European zinc industry and the fact that the agreement was to last for a set period only, the Commission considered approving the agreement despite its restrictive effects. It did however inform the companies concerned that if there were a sustained improvement in the economic situation of the zinc industry a decision authorising the agreement would not be possible.

In late summer 1983 the zinc market improved and the price situation eased, and in November the firms terminated the agreement. There will now be no concerted capacity shutdowns with compensation paid.

Litterature

Consult theCompetition reports of the Commission up to date nrs. 1-13.
- Gijlstra and Murphy: Distribution systems in EEC Competition Law. The law as it stands. LIEI 1976/1.
- Korah: Group exemptions for exclusive distribution and purchasing in the EEC. (1984) CMLRev. 53-86.
- Chard: The economics of the application of Article 85 to selective distribution systems. (1982) ELRev. 93-102.
- Vadja: Selective distribution in the European Community. (1979) JWTL 409-435.
- Usher: The Belgian (and Luxemburg) Tobacco Case, 1981 JBL 117-122.
- Baden-Fuller: Price variations: The Distributors Case and Article 85 EEC. 1979 ICLQ 128-131.
- Faul: EEC Competition Law checklist. (1980) ELRev. 131-135
- Sharpe: The Commission proposals on crisis cartels.(1980) CMLRev. 75-90.
- Van Gerven: Twelve years EEC competition policy (1962-1973) revisited (1974) CMLRev. 38 .
- Mok: The Cartel policy of the EEC Commission 1962-1969. 1968 CMLRev. 67.

## Chapter Seven

## RELATED PROBLEMS

### I. ARTICLES 30 - 36 EEC TREATY

### A. Industrial Property Rights

#### (1) Consten-Grundig Case

For facts and references see above, page 66 .

*The Court held:*

On the grounds concerning the finding of infringement relating to the agreement on the GINT trademark.

The applicants object that the Commission violated Articles 36, 222 and 234 of the EEC Treaty and furthermore exceeded the limits of its competence by declaring that the agreement on the registration in France of the GINT trademark served to ensure absolute territorial protection in favour of Consten and by excluding thereby, in Article 3 of the dispositif of the attacked decision, the possibility for Consten to enforce the rights deriving from the national trademark law to oppose parallel imports.

The applicants submit more particularly that the effect criticised on the competition level is due not to the agreement but to the registration of the trademark in accordance with French law, which gives rise to an original right to the registrant over the trademark from which the absolute territorial protection derives under national law.

The fact that Consten alone in France disposes of the GINT trademark under the contract, to be used in the same manner in other countries, aims at allowing control and obstacle to parallel imports. Therefore, the agreement by which Grundig, holder of the trademark by virtue of an international registration, has authorised Consten to register it in France in its own name tends to restrict competition. Although Consten, by the registration of the GINT trademark, is regarded as the original holder under French law of the rights relating to that trademark, it is nevertheless by virtue of an agreement with Grundig that it carried out the registration. Therefore the agreement may be struck by the prohibition in Article 85(1). The prohibition would be fruitless if Consten could continue to use the trademark with the same aim as that contained in the agreement recognised as unlawful. Articles 36, 222 and 234 of the Treaty, invoked by the applicants, do not oppose every impact of Community law on the exercise of national industrial property rights. Article 36, which limits the scope of the rules on the liberalisation of trade contained in Title I, Chap. 2 of the Treaty, cannot limit the field of application of Article 85. Article 222 is limited to stating that the 'Treaty shall in no way prejudice existing systems and incidents of ownership' in the Member States. The injunction in Article 3 of the dispositif of the attacked decision not to use national law relating to trademarks to obstruct parallel imports, without touching the grant of those rights, limits their exercise to the extent necessary for the attainment of the prohibition deriving from Article 85(1). The power of the Commission to issue an injunction, provided for in Article 3 of Regulation No 17 of the Council, is compatible with the character of the Community competition system, comprising rules which are immediately effective and which bind individuals directly. Such a system, by reason of the above-mentioned character and its function, does not allow the abusive use of rights deriving from one or another national trademark law in order to defeat the effectiveness of the Community law on restrictive practices. Article 234 has the aim of protecting the rights of third states and is not applicable to the present instance. Therefore the abovementioned grounds must fail.

(2) Deutsche Grammophon Case

See above, page 2, 218 and 254.

(3) Hag Case

Van Zuylen Frères v. Hag AG
Judgment of 3 July 1974, Case 192/73; (1974) ECR 731; (1974) CMLR 127; CCH para. 8230; Competition Law CM/M/III/42.

*Facts:* The company Hag AG was the holder of trademarks in respect of coffees, of which the term "Hag" was the most important element.

In 1927 Hag AG set up a subsidiary in Belgium, Café Hag SA ("Hag/Belgium") which was fully controlled by it. Hag AG's Belgian and Luxembourg trademarks were assigned to Hag/Belgium with effect from May 1935.

Under a Belgain Decree Law of 23 August 1944, all the shares of the capital of Hag/Belgium were placed under sequestration as enemy property. This property was disposed of by the Belgian State by the sale of shares to the Van Oevelen family.

On 18 June 1971, Hag/Belgium assigned its Benelux trademarks, as regards Belgium and Luxembourg, to the Société en commandité Van Zuylen Frères ("VZF"), without however transferring the business. VZF does not itself manufacture decaffeinated coffee, but buys it from Hag/Belgium. That company no longer sells it directly but always to wholesalers.

Hag AG started in 1972 to deliver its coffees to Luxembourg retailers under its German Hag trademark. VZF reacted to this marketing by commencing proceedings for infringement of trademark. On 4 April 1973 VZF brought a second action for the cancellation of Hag AG's trademark registrations effected subsequent to 1945, insofar as Belgium and Luxembourg were concerned. The Tribunal d'Arrondissement of Luxembourg adjourned the proceedings and requested the Court to give a preliminary ruling.

*The Court held:*

.....

6. As a result of the provisions of the Treaty relating to the free movement of goods and in particular of Article 30, quantitative restrictions on imports and all measures having equivalent effect are prohibited between Member States.

7. By Article 36 these provisions shall nevertheless not preclude pro-

hibitions or restrictions on imports justified on grounds of the protection of industrial or commercial property.

8. Nevertheless, it is shown by this very Article, in particular its second sentence, as well as by the context, that whilst the Treaty does not affect the existence of rights recognised by the legislation of a Member State in matters of industrial and commercial property, yet the exercise of these rights may nevertheless, depending on the circumstances, be affected by the prohibition in the Treaty.

9. Inasmuch as it provides an exception to one of the fundamental principles of the Common Market, Article 36 in fact only admits derogations from the free movement of goods to the extent that such derogations are justified for the purpose of safeguarding rights that constitute the specific subject matter of this property.

10. Thus the application of the legislation relating to the protection of trademarks at any rate protects the legitimate holder of the trademark against infringement on the part of persons who lack any legal title.

11. The exercise of a trademark right tends to contribute to the partitioning off of the markets and thus to affect the free movement of goods between Member States, all the more so since - unlike other rights of industrial and commercial property - it is not subject to limitations in point of time.

12. Accordingly, one cannot allow the holder of a trademark to rely upon the exclusiveness of a trademark - which may be the consequence of the territorial limitation of national legislations - with a view to prohibiting the marketing in a Member State of goods legally produced in another Member State under an identical trademark having the same origin.

13. Such a prohibition, which would legitimise the isolation of national markets, would collide with one of the essential objects of the Treaty, which is to unite national markets in a single market.

14. Whilst in such market the indication of origin of a product covered by a trademark is useful, information to the consumers on this point may be ensured by means other than such as would effect the free movement of goods.

15. Accordingly, to prohibit the marketing in a Member State of a product legally bearing a trademark in another Member State for the sole reason that an identical trademark having the same origin exists in the first state, is incompatible with the provisions providing for free movement of goods within the Common Market.

16. In the second question it is asked whether the same would apply if the trading in the trademarked product was carried out not by the holder of the mark in the other Member State but by a third party who had properly acquired the product in that State.

17. While the holder of a trademark in one Member State may himself put the trademarked product on sale in another Member State, the same applies for a third party who has lawfully acquired that product in the first State.

*The Court decided:*

1. To prohibit trading, in one Member State, in a product which lawfully bears a trademark in another Member State, for the sole reason that an identical mark, sharing the same origin, exists in the first State, is incompatible with the provisions laying down the free circulation of goods within the Common Market.

2. While the holder of a trademark in one Member State may himself put the trademarked product on sale in another Member State, the same applies for a third party who has lawfully acquired that product in the first State.

(4) Centrafarm v. Sterling Drug Case

Centrafarm BV and De Peijper v. Sterling Drug Inc.
Preliminary Ruling of 31 October 1974, Case 15/74; (1974) ECR 1147; (1974) CMLR 480; CCH para. 8246; Competition Law CM/M/III/46.

*Facts:* Sterling Drug Inc., a company incorporated according to the law of the State of New York, is the titular holder of national patents in several countries - including the Netherlands and Great Britain - relating to the mode of preparation of a medicament named acidum nalidixicum, for the treatment of infections of the urinary passages. For this product the trademark 'Negram' is the property, in Great Britain of the company Sterling-Winthrop Group Ltd. and, in the Netherlands of a subsidiary of the latter, Winthrop BV.

Centrafarm, of which Mr. De Peijper is a director, imported medicinal preparations manufactured according to the patent method, some of which bore the trademark Negram, without the agreement of Sterling Drug, from England and the Federal Republic of Germany, where they had been put onto the market in a regular manner by subsidiaries of Sterling Drug Inc., into the Netherlands where they were offered for sale.

By importing the goods from Great Britain Centrafarm took advantage of a considerable price differential. It appears that in Great Britain the product is sold for half the price at which it sells in the Netherlands.

On 16 June 1971 Sterling Drug submitted to the President of the Arrondissementsrechtbank at Rotterdam, an application for the immediate adoption of measures of conservation against the actions of Centrafarm and of its director, and requiring them to refrain from any further infringement of the patent belonging to Sterling Drug, together with several subsidiary requests. The President of the court rejected the application on the grounds of an interpretation of the law on patents (Octrooiwet) according to which a product is held to have been put into circulation in a regular manner even if it is put into circulation abroad by the titular holder of a Dutch patent. Sterling Drug thereupon brought an appeal before the Court of Appeal at the Hague, which found in favour of Sterling Drug, with the exception of certain of its subsidiary requests.

Centrafarm and De Peijper brought an appeal on a point of law before the Hoge Raad against the judgment of the Gerechtshof.

Before deciding further, the Hoge Raad stayed the proceedings and requested the Court of Justice, pursuant to Article 177 of the EEC Treaty, to give a preliminary ruling on the following questions:

I. As regards the rules concerning the free movement of goods:

(a) Assuming that: 1. a patentee has parallel patents in several of the countries belonging to the EEC; 2. the products protected by those patents are lawfully marketed in one or more of those countries by undertakings to whom the patentee has granted licences to manufacture and/or sell; 3. those products are subsequently exported by third parties and are marketed and further dealt in in one of those other countries; 4. the patent legislation in the last-mentioned country gives the patentee rights to take legal action to prevent products thus protected by patents from being there marketed by others, even where these products were previously lawfully marketed in another country by the patentee or the patentee's licensee, do the rules of the EEC Treaty concerning free movement of goods, notwithstanding what is stated in Article 36, prevent the patentee from exercising the right under 4 above?

(b) If the rules concerning the free movement of goods do not under all circumstances prevent the patentee exercising the right mentioned under (a) 4 above,

do they however so prevent him if the exercise of that right arises exclusively or partially from an attempt to partition the national markets of the relevant countries from each other for products protected by the patent, or at least has the effect of thus partitioning those markets?

(c) Does it make any difference to the reply to the questions under (a) and (b) above that the patentee and the licensee do or do not belong to the same concern?

(d) Can the patentee successfully rely in justification of the exercise of the above-mentioned right on the fact that the price differences in the relevant countries which make it profitable for third parties to market in one country products originating from another country and give the patentee an interest in taking action against such practices, are the consequence of governmental measures whereby in the exporting country the prices of those goods are kept lower than would have been the case in the absence of those measures?

(e) At any rate where the patent relates to pharmaceutical products, can the patentee successfully rely in justification of the exercise of his patent rights on the fact that the state of affairs described under (a) above prevents him from controlling the distribution of his products, such control being considered by him essential so that measures for the protection of the public can be taken in the event of defects appearing?

(f) Is it a consequence of Article 42 of the Treaty of Accession that, if the rules of the EEC Treaty relating to free movement of goods prevent the exercise of a patent right as before mentioned, those rules cannot be invoked in the Netherlands until 1 January 1975 insofar as the relevant goods originate in the United Kingdom?

II As regards Article 85

(a) Does the fact that a patentee owns parallel patents in different countries belonging to the EEC and that he has in those countries granted to different undertakings associated with the patentee, licences to manufacture and sell (assuming that all the agreements entered into with such licensees are exclusively or in part designed to regulate differently for the different countries the conditions on the market in respect of the goods protected by the patent) mean that this is a case of agreements or concerted practices of the type prohibited by Article 85 of the EEC Treaty, and must an action for infringement as referred to under I(a) above - to the extent that this must be regarded as a result of such agreements or concerted practices - for that reason be held impermissible?

(b) Is Article 85 also applicable if, in connection with the agreements or concerted practices referred to above, it is only undertakings belonging to the same concern that are involved?

*The Court held:*

As regards question I(a)

This question requires the Court to state whether, under the conditions postulated, the rules in the EEC Treaty concerning the free movement of goods prevent the patentee from ensuring that the product protected by the patent is not marketed by others.

As a result of the provisions in the Treaty relating to the free movement of goods and in particular of Article 30, quantitative restrictions on imports and all measures having equivalent effect are prohibited between Member States.

By Article 36 these provisions shall nevertheless not include prohibitions or restrictions on imports justified on grounds of the protection of industrial or commercial property.

Nevertheless, it is clear from this same Article, in particular its second sentence, as well as from the context, that whilst the Treaty does not affect the existence of rights recognised by the legislation of a Member State in matters of industrial and commercial property, yet the exercise of these rights may nevertheless, depending on the circumstances, be effected by the prohibitions of the Treaty.

Inasmuch as it provides for an exception to one of the fundamental principles of the Common Market, Article 36 in fact only admits of derogations from the free movement of goods where such derogations are justified for the purpose of safeguarding rights which constitute the specific subject matter of this property.

In relation to patents, the specific subject matter of the industrial property is the guarantee that the patentee, to reward the creative effort of the inventor, has the exclusive right to use an invention with a view to manufacturing industrial products and putting them into circulation for the first time, either directly or by a grant of licences to third parties, as well as the right to oppose infringements.

An obstacle to the free movement of goods may arise out of the existence, within a national legislation concerning industrial and commercial property, of provisions laying down that a patentee's right is not exhausted when the product protected by the patent is marketed in another Member State, with the result that the patentee can prevent importation of the product into his own Member State when it has been marketed in another Member State.

Whereas an obstacle to the free movement of goods of this kind may be justified on the ground of protection of industrial property where such protection is invoked against a product coming from a Member State where it is not patentable and has been manufactured by third parties without the consent of the patentee and in cases where there exist patents, the original proprietors of which are legally and economically independent, a derogation from the principle of the free movement of goods is not, however, justified where the product has been put onto the market in a legal manner, by the patentee himself or with his consent, in a Member State from which it has been imported, in particular in the case of a proprietor of parallel patents.

In fact, if the patentee could prevent the import of protected products marketed by him or with his consent in another Member State, he would be able to partition off national markets and thereby restrict trade between Member States, in a situation where no such restriction was necessary to guarantee the essence of the exclusive rights flowing from the patent.

The plaintiff in the main action claims, in this connection, that by reasons of divergences between national legislations and practice, truly identical or parallel patents can hardly be said to exist.

It should be noted here that, in spite of the divergences which remain in the absence of any unification of national rules concerning industrial property, the identity of the protected invention is clearly the essential element of the concept of parallel patents which it is for the courts to assess.

The question referred to should therefore be answered to the effect that the exercise, by a patentee, of a right which he enjoys under the legislation of a Member State to prohibit the sale, in that State, of a product protected by the patent which has been marketed in another Member State by the patentee or with his consent is incompatible with the rules of the EEC Treaty concerning the free movement of goods within the Common Market.

As regards question I(b)

This question was referred to cover the possibility that Community rules do not under all circumstances prevent the patentee from exercising the right, under his national law, to prohibit imports of the protected product.

It follows from the answer given to question I(a) above that question I(b) has become devoid of object.

As regards question I(c)

This question requires the Court to state whether it makes any difference to the answer given to question I(a) that the patentee and the licensees do or do not belong to the same concern.

It follows from the answer given to I(a) that the factor which above all else characterises a restriction of trade between Member States is the territorial protection granted to a patentee in one Member State against importation of the product which has been marketed in another Member State by the patentee himself or with his consent.

Therefore the result of the grant of a sales licence in a Member State is that the patentee can no longer prevent the sale of the protected product throughout the Common Market.

Accordingly, it is of no significance to know whether the patentee and the licencee do or do not belong to the same concern.

As regards question I(d)

This question requires the Court to state, in substance, whether the patentee can, notwithstanding the answer given to the first question, prevent importation of the protected product, given the existence of price differentials resulting from governmental measures adopted in the exporting country with a view to controlling the price of that product.

It is part of the Community authorities' task to eliminate factors likely to distort competition between Member States, in particular by the harmonisation of national measures for the control of prices and by the prohibition of aids which are incompatible with the Common Market, in addition to the exercise of their powers in the field of competition.

The existence of factors such as these in a Member State, however, cannot justify the maintenance or introduction by another Member State of measures which are incompatible with the rules concerning the free movement of goods, in particular in the field of industrial and commercial property.

The question referred should therefore be answered in the negative.

As regards question I(e)

This question requires the Court to state whether the patentee is authorised to exercise the rights conferred on him by the patent, notwithstanding Community rules on the free movement of goods, for the purpose of controlling the distribution of a pharmaceutical product with a view to protecting the public against the risks arising from defects therein.

The protection of the public against the risks arising from defective pharmaceutical products is a matter of legitimate concern, and Article 36 of the Treaty authorises the Member States to derogate from the rules concerning the free movement of goods on grounds of the protection of health and life of humans and animals.

Moreover, the specific considerations underlying the protection of industrial and commercial property are distinct from the considerations underlying the protection of the public and any responsibilities which that may imply.

The question referred should therefore be answered in the negative.

As regards question I(f)

This question requires the Court to state whether Article 42 of the Act concerning the Conditions of Accession of the three new Member States implies that the rules of the Treaty concerning the free movement of goods cannot be invoked in the Netherlands until 1 January 1975, insofar as the goods in question originate in the United Kingdom.

Paragraph 1 of Article 42 of the Act of Accession provides that quantitative restrictions on imports and exports shall, from the date of accession, be abolished between the Community as originally constituted and the new Member States.

Under paragraph 2 of the same Article, which is more directly relevant to the question, 'measures having equivalent effect to such restrictions shall be abolished by 1 January 1975 at the latest'.

In this context, the provision can refer only to those measures having an effect equivalent to quantitative restrictions which, as between the original Member States, had to be abolished at the end of the transitional period, pursuant to Article 30 and 32 to 35 of the EEC Treaty.

It therefore appears that Article 42 of the Act of Accession has no effect upon prohibitions on importation arising from national legislation concerning industrial and commercial property.

The case under consideration is therefore subject to the principle enshrined in the Treaty and in the Act of Accession, according to which the provisions of the Treaties establishing the European Communities concerning the free movement of goods and, in particular, Article 30, are applicable, from the date of accession, to the new Member States, save where contrary is expressly stated.

It follows that Article 42 of the Act of Accession cannot be invoked to prevent importation into the Netherlands, even before 1 January 1975, of goods put onto the market in the United Kingdom under the conditions set out above by the patentee or with his consent.

As regards questions II(a) and (b)

These questions require the Court to state whether Article 85 of the Treaty is applicable to agreements and concerted practices between the proprietor of parallel patents in various Member States and his licensees, if the objective of those agreements and concerted practices is to regulate differently for different countries the conditions on the market in respect of the goods protected by the patents.

Although the existence of rights recognised under the industrial property legislation of a Member State is not affected by Article 85 of the Treaty, the conditions under which those rights may be exercised may nevertheless fall within the prohibitions contained in that Article.

This may be the case whenever the existence of such a right appears to be the object, the means or the consequence of an agreement.

Article 85, however, is not concerned with agreements or concerted practices between undertakings belonging to the same concern and having the status of parent company and subsidiary, if the undertakings form an economic unit within which the subsidiary has no real freedom to determine its course of action on the market, and if the agreements or practices are concerned merely with the internal allocation of tasks as between undertakings.

*The Court decided:*

1. The exercise, by a patentee, of the right which he enjoys under the legislation of a Member State to prohibit the sale, in that State, of a product protected by the patent which has been marketed in another Member State by the patentee or with his consent is incompatible with-the rules of the EEC Treaty concerning the free movement of goods with in the Common Market.

2. In this connection, it is of no significance to know whether the patentee and the undertakings to which the latter has granted licences do or do not belong to the same concern.

3. It is also a matter of no significance that there exists, as between the exporting and importing Member States, price differences resulting from governmental measures adopted in the exporting State with a view to controlling the price of the product.

4. The proprietor of a patent relating to a pharmaceutical product cannot avoid the incidence of Community rules concerning the free movement of goods for the purpose of controlling the distribution of the product with a view to protecting the public against defects therein.

5. Article 42 of the Act concerning the Conditions of Accession and the Adjustments to the Treaties cannot be invoked to prevent importation into the Netherlands, even before 1 January 1975, of goods put onto the market in the United Kingdom by the patentee or with his consent.

6. Article 85 is not concerned with agreements or concerted practices between undertakings belonging to the same concern and having the status of parent company and subsidiary, if the undertakings form an economic unit within which the subsidiary has no real freedom to determine its course of action on the market, and if the agreements or practices are concerned merely with the internal allocation of tasks as between undertakings.

*Sequel*

Case 16/74, Centrafarm BV and Adriaan de Peijper v. Winthrop BV concerned a similar subject, this second case dealt however with the right to a trademark. The Court of Justice came to the same conclusion.

In a judgment of 21 February 1975 the Hoge Raad der Nederlanden (the Netherlands Supreme Court) rejected Sterling Drug's and Winthrop's claim for the granting of the relief claimed by the respective companies against Centrafarm and De Peijper. Sterling Drug and Winthrop were ordered to pay the costs of the appeal proceedings.

(5) EMI - CBS United Kingdom Case

EMI Records v. CBS United Kingdom; Case 51/75, Judgment of 15 June 1976; (1976) ECR 811; CCH para. 8350; (1976) 2 CMLR p. 235.

*Facts:* In 1975 three cases, 51, 86 and 96/75 came before the Court by way of reference for preliminary rulings under Article 177 of the EEC Treaty by the Chancery Division of the High Court of Justice of England and Wales, by the Sø-og Handelsretten of Copenhagen and by the Landgericht of Cologne.

In each of them the plaintiff in the proceedings before the national court was EMI Records Ltd., a wholly owned subsidiary of EMI Limited. EMI Records Ltd. amd EMI Limited are both English companies.

The defendent in each case is a locally incorporated subsidiary of CBS Inc., which is an American company. In the English case the defendent is CBS United Kingdom Ltd, in the Danish case it is CBS Records ApS (formerly CBS Grammopon A/S) and in the German case it is CBS Schallplatten GmbH.

The facts may be summarised as follows:

As a result of a number of events and transactions going back to 1894 EMI Records Limited is now in many countries of Europe, Africa, Asia and Australasia the registered proprietor of all trademarks for gramophone records consisting of or including the mark "Columbia". Those countries include every Member State of the Communities except France, where those marks are owned by another subsidiary of EMI Ltd. CBS Inc. is the proprietor of the Columbia Trademarks in the USA, in the other countries of North and South Africa and in a few countries elsewhere.

Both EMI Records Ltd and other subsidiaries of EMI Limited on the one hand and CBS Inc. and its subsidiaries on the other hand manufacture and sell records on a large scale. In other countries where it is entitled to the mark Columbia each group sells records extensively under that mark, but does also under certain other marks. In the countries where it does not own the mark Columbia each group has, until the event giving rise to the present litigation, sold its records under other marks. In particular the CBS group has sold its records in the Community under the mark "CBS".

In some instances, however, the CBS group has imported into the United Kingdom, Denmark and Germany, records manufactured in America and bearing, both on the central label of the record itself and on the sleeve, the mark Columbia. In the case of such imported records, that mark has sometimes been obliterated with a sticker (usually, or so it seems from the exhibits sent to the Court by the Sø-og Handels-retten, a sticker bearing the mark CBS) but on other occasions the mark Columbia has not been obliterated, particularly not from the label on the record itself. It is the sales of such records, with the mark Columbia visible, that have given rise to the litigation.

The defendants contested that the provisions of the Treaty relating to free movement of goods should be interpreted as precluding EMI Records Limited from invoking its rights to the trademark Columbia in the Community for the purposes of preventing imports into the Community from outside of goods bearing that mark.

The defendants' contention was greeted with indignation by EMI Records Ltd. and all seven Member States which intervened in the proceedings and the Commission.

*The Court held:*

(1) With regard to the free movement of goods

Within the framework of the provisions of the Treaty relating to the free movement of goods and in accordance with Article 3(a), Article 30 et seq. on the elimination of quantitative restrictions and of measures having equivalent effect expressly provide that such restrictions and measures shall be prohibited 'between Member States'.

Article 36, in particular, after stipulating that Articles 30 to 34 shall not preclude restrictions on imports, exports or goods in transit justified inter alia on grounds of the protection of industrial and commercial property, states that such restrictions shall in no instance constitute a means of arbitrary discrimination or disguised restriction on trade 'between Member States'.

Consequently the exercise of a trademark right in order to prevent the marketing of products coming from a third country under an identical mark, even if this constitutes a measure having an effect equivalent to a quantitative restriction, does not affect the free movement of goods between Member States and thus does not come under the prohibitions set out in Article 30 et seq. of the Treaty.

In such circumstances the exercise of a trademark right does not in fact jeopardise the unity of the Common Market which Article 30 et seq. are intended to ensure.

Furthermore if the same proprietor holds the trademark right in respect of the same product in all the Member States there are no grounds for examining whether those marks have a common origin with an identical mark recognised in a third country, since that question is relevant in relation only to considering whether within the Community there are opportunities for partitioning the market.

It is impossible to avoid these conclusions by relying on Articles 9 and 10 of the Treaty.

According to Article 10(1) of the Treaty products coming from a third country shall be considered to be in free circulation in a Member State if the import formalities have been complied with and any customs duties or charges having equivalent effect which are payable have been levied in the importing Member State.

According to Article 9(2) of the Treaty the provisions of Chapter 1, Section 1 and Chapter 2 of Title I of Part Two shall apply to products coming from third countries which are in free circulation in Member States.

Since those provisions only refer to the effects of compliance with customs formalities and paying customs duties and charges having equivalent effect, they cannot be interpreted as meaning that it would be sufficient for products bearing a mark applied in a third country and imported into the Community to comply with the customs formalities in the first Member State where they were imported in order to be able then to be marketed in the Common Market as a whole in contravention of the rules relating to the protection of the mark.

Furthermore the provisions of the Treaty on commercial policy do not, in Article 110 et seq., lay down any obligation on the part of the Member States to extend to trade with third countries the binding principles governing the free movement of goods between Member States and in particular the prohibition of measures having an effec: equivalent to quantitative restrictions.

The arrangements concluded by the Community in certain international agreements such as the ACP-EEC Convention of Lomé of 28 February 1975 or the agreements with Sweden and Switzerland of 22 July 1972 form part of such a policy and do not constitute the performance of a duty incumbent on the Member States under the Treaty.

The binding effect of commitments undertaken by the Community with regard to certain countries cannot be extended to others.

Furthermore with regard to the provisions of Regulation No 1439/74 of 4 June 1974 (OJ L 1974, L 159, p. 1) introducing common rules for imports, these provisions relate only to quantitative restrictions to the exclusion of measures having equivalent effect.

It follows that neither the rules of the Treaty on the free movement of goods nor those on the putting into free circulation of products coming from third countries nor, finally, the principles governing the common commercial policy, prohibit the proprietor of a mark in all the Member States of the Community from exercising his right in order to prevent the importation of similar products of the same mark and coming from a third country.

Nor may the provisions of the Treaty on the free movement of goods be invoked for the purposes of prohibiting the proprietor of the mark in the territories of the Member States from exercising his right in order to prevent another proprietor of the same mark in a third country from manufacturing and marketing his product within the Community, either himself or through his subsidiaries established in the Community.

In fact the protection of industrial and commercial property established by Article 36 would be rendered meaningless if an undertaking other than the proprietor of a mark in the Member States could be allowed there to manufacture and market products bearing the same mark since such conduct would amount to an actual infringement of the protected mark.

The steps taken by the proprietor of a mark to prevent a person other than a proprietor of that mark in the Member States from manufacturing and distributing those products bearing the same mark cannot be classified as a means of arbitrary discrimination or as a disguised restriction on trade between Member States within the meaning of Article 36.

<u>(6) Terrapin - Terranova Case</u>

<u>Terrapin Ltd</u> v. <u>Terranova Industrie</u>; Case 19/75; Judgment of 22 June 1976; (1976) ECR 1039; CCH para. 8362; (1976) 2 CMLR 482.

*Facts:* Terranova Industrie has manufactured and marketed for 75 years prepared plaster for facades. It is the proprietor of the following trademarks registered at the German patents office: word-mark 'Terra'; word/device mark 'Terra' with an emblem; word-mark 'Terra Fabrikate';

word/device mark 'Terranova' composed of a name and an emblem and 'Terranova' with a particular arrangement of letters. These marks are registered in respect of a range of building materials and auxiliary building materials. In the trademarks register the objects of the company are given as 'manufacture of dry prepared plaster, construction work and building materials'.

Terrapin (Overseas) Ltd. whose registered office is in England, manufactures and sells prefabricated houses which it markets under the trademark 'Terrapin'. These are generally two-storey buildings which are assembled on site from prefabricated components. In addition it also applies the name 'Terrapin' to units made up of such components and intended for the buildings in question.

In the Federal Republic of Germany Terrapin carries on its business activities itself as well as through its subsidiary company 'Terrapin-Systembau Nordeuropa GmbH', which has its registered office in Cologne.

Terrapin applied in 1961 to have the word-mark 'Terrapin' entered in the register kept by the German patents office. By decision dated 28 December 1962 the latter rejected an opposition by Terranova on the ground that the trademarks 'Terra' and 'Terranova' on the one hand and the trademark 'Terrapin' were not similar.

On appeal by Terranova, the Bundespatentgericht (Federal Patent Court) by order dated 3 February 1967 annulled the decision of the patents office and prohibited the registration of the trademark 'Terrapin'. The products marketed under the trademarks 'Terrapin' and 'Terranova' were said to be similar and the trademark 'Terrapin' gave rise to a risk of confusion with the trademarks 'Terra' and 'Terranova'.

Following this order by the Bundespatentgericht, Terranova brought several actions before German courts against the use of the word 'Terrapin'.

Finally the Bundesgerichtshof stayed the proceedings and referred the following questions for a preliminary ruling by the Court of Justice.

'Is it compatible with the provisions relating to the free movement of goods (Articles 30 and 36 of the EEC Treaty) that an undertaking established in Member State A, by using its commercial name and trademark rights existing there, should prevent the import of similar goods of an undertaking established in Member State B if these goods have been lawfully given a distinguishing name which may be confused with the commercial name and trademark which are protected in State A for the undertaking established there, if there are no relations between the two undertakings, if their national trademark rights arose autonomously and independently of one another (no common origin) and at the present time there exist no economic or legal relations of any kind other than those appertaining to the trademarks between the undertakings?'

*The Court held:* By order dated 31 October 1975, received at the Court registry on the following 5 December, the Bundesgerichtshof referred to the Court for a preliminary ruling under Article 177 of the Treaty the following question on the relation between the provisions of the Treaty on the free movement of goods and the protection given by national laws to the right to a trademark and a commercial name:
(See above).

It appears from the order of reference that the plaintiff in the main action, the respondent to the appeal, is the proprietor in the Federal Republic of Germany of the trademarks 'Terra', 'Terra Fabrikate' and 'Terranova', registered at the German patents office, the last of these names being simultaneously used as a commercial name. The plaintiff manufactures and markets finished plaster for facades and other construction materials under these names. The defendant in the main action and appellant in the appeal is an English company specialising in the production of prefabricated houses and components for the construction of such houses which it sells under the name 'Terrapin', which is at the same time the defendant's commercial name. The defendant applied to the German patents office to register the trademark 'Terrapin', but Terranova lodged an opposition and by order of the Bundespatentgericht of 3 February 1967 registration was refused on the ground of the risk of confusion with the trademarks 'Terra' and 'Terranova'. Subsequently Terranova brought an action before the Landgericht München to prohibit the defendant from using the name Terrapin on its products. This action was dismissed by judgment dated 27 November 1972 since the Landgericht considered that the names in question did not cause any real risk of confusion. Terranova brought an appeal before the Bayerisches Oberlandesgericht, Munich, which reversed the judgment of the Landgericht and by judgment dated 27 September 1973 held that there was a risk of confusion and as a result prohibited the defendant from using the name 'Terrapin' and declared that in principle the defendant was bound to make good any damage caused to the plaintiff by the use of the name in question. Terrapin brought an appeal against this judgment before the Bundesgerichtshof.

The Bundesgerichtshof considers that the first appelate court rightly found similarity between the products of the two parties and risk of confusion between the names in question with the result that according to German law the judgment of the appelate court and the injunction which it issued against Terrapin must be confirmed.

Although this finding has been questioned during the oral procedure the Court does not have to rule on this point since no question has been put to it with regard to the matter. It is right however to stress that the answer given below does not prejudge the question whether an allegation by one undertaking as to the similarity of products originating in different Member States and the risk of confusion of trademarks or commercial names legally protected in these States may perhaps involve the application of Community law with regard in particular to the second sentence of Article 36 of the Treaty. It is for the court of first instance, after considering the similarity of the products and the risk of confusion, to enquire further in the context of this last provision whether the exercise in a particular case of industrial and commercial property rights may or may not constitute a means of arbitrary discrimination or a disguised restriction on trade between Member States. It is for the national court in this respect to ascertain in particular whether the rights in question are in fact exercised by the proprietor with the same strictness whatever the national origin of any possible infringer.

As a result of the provisions in the Treaty relating to free movement of goods and in particular of Article 30, quantitative restrictions on imports and all measures having equivalent effect are prohibited between Member States. By Article 36 these provisions nevertheless do not preclude prohibitions or restrictions on imports justified on grounds of the protection of industrial and commercial property. However, it is clear from that same article, in particular the second sentence, as well as from the context, that whilst the Treaty does not affect the existence of rights recognised by the legislation of a Member State in matters of industrial and commercial property, yet the exercise of those rights may nevertheless, depending on the circumstances, be restricted by the prohibition in the Treaty. Inasmuch as it provides an exception to one of the fundamental principles of the Common Market, Article 36 in fact admits exceptions to the free movement of goods only to the extent to which such exceptions are justified for the purpose of safeguarding rights which constitute the specific subject matter of that property.

It follows from the above that the proprietor of an industrial or commercial property right protected by the law of a Member State cannot rely on that law to prevent the importation of a product which has lawfully been marketed in another Member State by the proprietor himself or with his consent. It is the same when the right relied on is the result of the subdivision, either by voluntary act or as a result of public constraint, of a trademark right which originally belonged to one and the same proprietor. In these cases the basic function of the trademark to guarantee to consumers that the product has the same origin is already undermined by the subdivision of the original right. Even where the rights in question belong to different proprietors the protection given to industrial and commercial property by national law may not be relied on when the exercise of those rights is the purpose, the means or the result of an agreement prohibited by the Treaty. In all these cases the effect of invoking the territorial nature of national laws protecting industrial and commercial property is to legitimise the insulation of national markets without this partitioning within the Common Market being justified by the protection of a legitimate interest on the part of the proprietor of the trademark or business name.

On the other hand in the present state of Community law an industrial or commercial property right legally acquired in a Member State may legally be used to prevent under the first sentence of Article 36 of the Treaty the import of products marketed under a name giving rise to confusion where the rights in question have been acquired by different and independent proprietors under different national law. If in such a case the principle of free movement of goods were to prevail over the protection given by the respective national law, the specific objective of industrial and commercial property rights must be so reconciled that protection is ensured for the legitimate use of rights conferred by national laws, coming within the prohibitions on imports 'justified' within the meaning of Article 36 of the Treaty, but denied on the other hand in respect of any improper exercise of the same rights of such a nature as to maintain or effect artificial partitions within the Common Market.

It is appropriate therefore to reply to the question referred to the Court that it is compatible with the provisions of the EEC Treaty relating to the free movement of goods for an undertaking established in a Member State, by virtue of a right to a trademark and a right to a commercial name which are protected by the legislation of that State, to prevent the importation of products of an undertaking established in another Member State and bearing by virtue of the legislation of that State a name giving rise to confusion with the trademark and commercial name of the first undertaking, provided that there are no agreements restricting competition and no legal or economic ties between the undertakings and that their respective rights have arisen independently of one another.

(7) Hoffmann-La Roche v. Centrafarm Case

Hoffmann-La Roche v. Centrafarm, Case 102/77, (1978) ECR 1139; CCH para. 8466; Competition Law CM/M/III/73.

*Facts:* The plaintiff in the interlocutory action in the national court (hereinafter called the plaintiff) is an independent undertaking forming part of the worldwide organisation known as Roche-SAPAC.

The Roche-SAPAC group has developed, *inter alia*, the psycho-therapeutic product "Valium". The plaintiff manufactures Valium under a licence which it has obtained from Hoffmann-La Roche and Co AG, Basel, and sells it in the Federal Republic of Germany under the name Valium Roche.

Valium and Roche are trademarks protected by international registration and owned by Hoffmann-La Roche and Co, Basel. The proprietory medicinal product has, in accordance with the provisions of the Arzneimittelgesetz (German law on Medicines) been registered in the register of proprietory medicines of the Bundesgesundheitsamt (Federal Public Health Office).

Another subsidiary of the Roche-SAPAC organisation makes Valium in Great Britain under a licence from Hoffmann-La Roche and Co AG, Basel, and puts it on the market in packages containing 100 and 500 tablets. It markets the Valium at prices which are considerably lower than those charged in Germany.

The defendant in the interlocutory action in the national court (hereinafter called 'the defendant') is the legally independent German marketing company of the Netherlands drug undertaking Centrafarm BV, whose objects include, among others, international trade in medicinal products. The defendants purchased Valium Roche from its Netherlands parent company. The latter had in turn purchased it in Great Britain in the original packages put on the British market by the British subsidiary of Hoffmann-La Roche and Co AG. The parent company of the defendant repackaged the products in the Netherlands in batches of 1000 tablets. On the new package it affixed - albeit in an outward presentation different from the presentation on the original package - the names Valium and Roche, the number of the entry on the register of the Bundesgesundheitsamt, together with the name 'Centrafarm' and the words 'Marketed by Centrafarm GmbH 4444 Bentheim-1'. Each package also came with an information leaflet in German which differed only slightly from that of the plaintiff. The leaflet is signed Hoffmann-La Roche and repeats the notice that the medicinal preparation is marketed by the defendant.

The plaintiff, which regards the behaviour of the defendant as an infringement of the trademark rights of the undertaking from which it has obtained a licence, asked the Landgericht Freiburg for an interim order (einstweilige Verfügung) prohibiting the defendant upon a paid penalty:

from using in the course of its business dealings in medical preparations the names Valium and/or Roche as a trademark, except where the use consists of placing on the market or offering for sale the product in the original presentation in which it was put onto the market by a third party with the consent of Hoffmann-La Roche and Co AG, Basel.

The defendant has expressed doubts as to whether its conduct infringes German trademark law. It is also of the opinion that there is some ground for supporting the view that the plaintiff is making improper use of its trademark right in order to abuse its position on the market (Article 86 of the EEC Treaty). In any case, the plaintiff, it is argued, is infringing the rules laid down by the EEC Treaty which secure free competition (Article 30), by abusing the legal provisions concerning trademarks and medicinal preparations in order to partition off national markets, on which there exist unjustified price differentials.

On 31 December 1975 the First Commercial Chamber of the Landgericht Freiburg granted the interim order so requested. It confirmed its order by a judgment of 16 February 1976.

The defendant lodged an appeal against the judgment before the Freiburg Senate of the Oberlandesgericht Karlsruhe.

By order dated 14 October 1976, the Oberlandesgericht stayed its proceedings and referred amongst others the following questions of interpretation to the Court of Justice under Article 177 of the EEC Treaty:

Is the person entitled to a trademark right protected for his benefit both in Member State A and in Member State B empowered under Article 36 of the EEC Treaty, in reliance on this right, to prevent a parallel importer from buying from the proprietor of the mark or with his consent in Member State A of the Community medicinal preparations which have been put on the market with his trademark lawfully affixed thereto and packaged under this trademark, from transferring them into containers of a different size, providing them with new packaging, affixing to such packaging the proprietor's trademark and importing the preparations distinguished in this manner into Member State B?

Is the proprietor of the trademark entitled to do this, or does he thereby infringe provisions of the EEC Treaty - in particular those contained in Article 86 thereof - even if he acquires a dominant position within the market in Member State B with regard to the medicinal preparation in question, when the prohibition on imports of a repacked product to which the proprietor's trademark has been affixed has in actual fact a restrictive effect on the market, because its different sizes of packages are used in countries A and B and because the importation of the product in another manner has not yet in fact made any appreciable progress on the market, and when the actual effect of the prohibition is that between the Member States there is maintained a substantial - in certain circumstances disproportionate - price differential, without its being possible to prove that the owner of the mark is using the prohibition solely or mainly to maintain this price differential?

*The Court ruled:*

.....

1 (a) The proprietor of a trademark right which is protected in two Member States at the same time is justified pursuant to the first sentence of Article 36 of the EEC Treaty in preventing a product to which the trademark has lawfully been applied in one of those States from being marketed in the other Member State after it has been repacked in new packaging to which the trademark has been affixed by a third party.

(b) However, such prevention of marketing constitutes a disguised restriction on trade between Member States within the meaning of the second sentence of Article 36 where:

It is established that the use of the trademark right by the proprietor, having regard to the marketing system which he has adopted, will contribute to the artificial partitioning of the markets between Member States;

It is shown that the repackaging cannot adversely affect the original condition of the product;

The proprietor of the mark receives prior notice of the marketing of the repackaged product; and

It is stated on the new packaging by whom the product has been repackaged.

2. To the extent to which the exercise of a trademark right is lawful in accordance with the provisions of Article 36 of the Treaty, such exercise is not contrary to Article 86 of the Treaty on the sole ground that it is the act of an undertaking occupying a dominant position on the market if the trademark right has not been used as an instrument for the abuse of such a position.

(8) Centrafarm v. American Home Products Case

Centrafarm BV v. American Home Products Corporation, Judgment of 10 October 1978, Case 3/78; (1978) ECR 1823; (1979) 1 CMLR 326; CCH para. 8475; Competition Law CM/M/III/76.

*Facts:* American Home Product Corporation (hereinafter referred to as "AHPC"), the defendant in the main action, is proprietor of the mark Seresta registered in its name in the Benelux trademark register under the head "Préparations médicinales et pharmaceutiques, notamment des préparations tranquillisantes, sédatives et anti-spasmodiques" ("Medicinal and pharmaceutical preparations, in particular tranquilising, sedative and antispasmodic preparations"). In the United Kingdom AHPC is proprietor of the Serenid D mark for the same type of product. Those marks are used to designate a medicament whose active constituent is named oxazepamum. AHPC also owns a patent in the Netherlands and in the United Kingdom for oxazepamum and/or the preparation thereof.

Two undertakings belonging to the AHPC group hold licences in the Netherlands for the Seresta mark and in the United Kingdom for the Serenid D mark.

The therapeutic effects of the Seresta and Serenid tablets are identical. Nevertheless the composition of the two is not quite the same. As far as the consumer is concerned the most obvious difference lies in the taste.

Centrafarm, the plaintiff in the main action, sold oxazepamum tablets in the Netherlands under the Seresta mark. On the packaging there appeared, in addition to the mark, the words "Centrafarm BV Rotterdam, Telephone 010-151411". Centrafarm also used the Seresta mark for such tablets in its price-lists and catalogues. It claims that it bought the said tablets in the United Kingdom where they were put on the market by AHPC under the Serenid D mark and that Centrafarm itself subsequently marketed them in the Netherlands in new packaging.

AHPC disputes that it manufactured all the oxazepamum sold in the

Netherlands by Centrafarm. The court in the main action accepts, however, that the facts as stated by Centrafarm are correct.

The President of the Arrondissementsrechtbank, Rotterdam, made an order on 2 August 1977 in proceedings for the adoption of an interim measure prohibiting Centrafarm from infringing AHPC's rights arising from the Seresta mark.

In the main action before the Arrondissementsrechtbank Centrafarm claimed that the court should rule that it is entitled to place on the market in the Netherlands under the Seresta mark AHPC's oxazepamum lawfully distributed in other countries of the Common Market as a proprietory medicinal product.

AHPC submitted that Centrafarm's claim should be refused and, as a counterclaim, maintained that the Arrondissementsrechtbank should inter alia rule that Centrafarm's conduct infringes AHPC's Seresta trademark rights.

The Arrondissementsrechtbank in its judgment of 19 December 1977 stayed the proceedings and, in accordance with Article 177 of the Treaty, referred the following questions to the Court of Justice:

"I. Assuming that:

1. For a certain product in various States belonging to the EEC one undertaking or various undertakings belonging to the same group is/are entitled to use the trademarks on the understanding that in Member State A only trademark X is registered and in Member State B only trademark Y;

2. Goods bearing the mark X, after being put into circulation in Member State A by the undertaking entitled to the trademark, are exported by third parties which acquire them and imported into Member State B;

3. The person importing the goods into the last-mentioned State removes from them the mark X, affixes the mark Y and subsequently puts the goods into circulation in that State;

4. The legislation relating to trademarks in the last-mentioned State gives the person entitled to the trademark the right to oppose by legal measures the putting into circulation in that country by others of goods bearing the mark Y;

do the rules contained in the EEC Treaty concerning the free movement of goods, notwithstanding the provisions of Article 36, prevent the person entitled to the trademark from making use of the right referred to under 4 supra ?

*The Court held:*

.....

1 (a) The proprietor of a trademark which is protected in one Member State is justified pursuant to the first sentence of Article 36 in preventing a product from being marketed by a third party even if previously that product has been lawfully marketed in another Member State under another mark held in the latter State by the same proprietor.

(b) Nevertheless such prevention may constitute a disguised restriction on trade between Member States within the meaning of the second sentence of Article 36 of the Treaty if it is established that the proprietor of different marks has followed the practice of using such marks for the purpose of artificially partitioning the markets.

2. The provisions on the names under which the proprietary medicinal products may be marketed are irrelevant to the above reply.

.....

In order to judge whether such is the case, it is necessary to take into account not only the rights and obligations arising from the clauses of the agreement, but also the economic and legal context in which the agreement exists and in particular the existence of any similar agreements entered into by the same producer with concessionaires in other Member States.

More particularly, an exclusive agreement is liable to affect trade between Member States, and may have as its effect the impairment of competition, when the concessionaire is able to prevent parallel imports from other Member States in to the territory subject to the concessions by means of a combination of the agreement with the effects of national legislation on unfair competition.

The concessionaire may therefore take advantage of such legislation only if the alleged unfairness in the behaviour of his competitors arises from factors other than the fact that they have carried out parallel imports.

(9) Merck-Stephar-Exler Case

Merck & Co. v. Stephar and Exler, Preliminary ruling of 14 July 1981, Case 187/80; (1981) ECR 2063; (1981) 3 CMLR 463; CCH para. 8707; Competition Law CM/M/III/97.

*Facts:* The plaintiff in the main action, Merck & Co. Inc. (hereinafter referred to as 'Merck') manufactures and markets in all the Member States a drug known as 'Moduretic' intended mainly for the treatment of hypertension. It holds patents for this drug in all the Member States except Luxembourg and Italy and for its manufacturing process in all the Member States except Luxembourg, Italy, Denmark and the Federal Republic of Germany.

.....

Merck expressly stated before the court making the reference without being contradicted by the defendant in the main action that it manufactures Moduretic in the Netherlands and does so in the factory of its wholly owned subsidiary, Merck Sharp & Dohme B.V., Haarlem.

Merck also markets its pharmaceutical product in Italy but has not been able to obtain a patent there, for on 3 October 1962, the date to which the priority right goes back, it was not possible to obtain patents for drugs and their manufacturing process as a result of Article 14(1) of the Italian Patent Law (Royal Decree of 29 June 1939, No 1127). That Article was subsequently declared unconstitutional and therefore inapplicable by a judgment given by the Italian Constitutional Court on 20 March 1978 so that since that date it has been possible to obtain patents in Italy for drugs and their manufacturing process. After that judgment however, Merck could still not obtain a patent because the product no longer fulfilled the legal condition of novelty which is a condition for obtaining a patent. That is no doubt one of the reasons why the drug is cheaper in Italy than in the Netherlands.

The undertaking Stephar B.V., whose business is *inter alia* the import of pharmaceutical products, imports Moduretic from Italy and resells it on the Netherlands market at prices lower than those charged by Merck.

Merck therefore brought summary proceedings before the President of the Arrondissementsrechtbank Rotterdam against Stephar and its director for infringing the patents of which it is the proprietor. The action was based on Article 20 of the Netherlands law on patents (Rijksoctrooiwet) pursuant to which the proprietor of a patent has the exclusive right of manufacturing, using, selling, licensing or putting into circulation the product protected by the patent 'save in and so far as such products have been marketed previously by or with the authority of Merck itself in another Member State of the Community where Merck is the proprietor of the patents' corresponding to the Netherlands patents.

In its application Merck relies on all the facts set out above and further on the fact that it has not been able to obtain patents for its products and their manufacturing process in Italy. It is that latter argument which is challenged by the defendants and which has led the President of the Arrondissmentsrechtbank Rotterdam to make an order dated 2 July 1980 in which it raises the following questions:

'In a case where:

1. an undertaking is the proprietor of a patent in a Member State of the European Communities for a drug and the processes for manufacturing it;

2. by or with the consent of that undertaking that drug is marketed in Italy where the undertaking could not by law acquire a patent for that drug by virtue of Article 14(1) of the Italian Patent Law (Regio Decreto of 29 June 1939 No 1127), later declared unconstitutional by the Italian Constitutional Court in its judgment of 20 March 1978, which prohibited the grant of patents for drugs and processes for manufacturing them;

3. a third party imports the drug referred to in paragraph 2 above from Italy into the Member State referred to in paragraph 1 above and deals in them there;

4. and the patent legislation in that country gives the proprietor of the patent the right to oppose by legal action the marketing there by others of the products protected by the patent even if previously they had been lawfully marketed in another country by or with the consent of the proprietor of the patent,

do the rules contained in the EEC Treaty concerning the free movement of goods, notwithstanding the provisions of Article 36, then prevent the proprietor of the patent from availing himself of the right referred to in paragraph 4 above?'

.....

*The Court held:*

10. That right of first placing a product on the market enables the inventor, by allowing him a monopoly in exploiting his product, to obtain the reward for his creative effort without, however, guaranteeing that he will obtain such a reward in all circumstances.

11. It is for the proprietor of the patent to decide, in the light of all the circumstances, under what conditions he will market his product, including the possibility of marketing it in a Member State where the law does not provide patent protection for the product in question. If he decides to do so he must then accept the consequences of his choice as regards the free movement of the product within the Common Market, which is a fundamental principle forming part of the legal and economic circumstances which must be taken into account by the proprietor of the patent in determining the manner in which his exclusive right will be exercised.

12. That is borne out, moreover, by the statements of the Court in its judgment of 22 June 1976 (*Terrapin*, Case 119/75 (1976) ECR 1039) and 20 January 1981 (*Musik Vertrieb Membran and K-tel*, Joined Cases 55 and 57/80 (1981) ECR 147) inasmuch as 'the proprietor of an industrial or commercial property right protected by the law of a Member State cannot rely on that law to prevent the importation of a product which has been lawfully marketed in another Member State by the proprietor himself or with his consent'.

13. Under those conditions to permit an inventor, or one claiming under him, to invoke a patent held by him in one Member State in order to prevent the importation of the product freely marketed by him in another Member State where that product is not patentable would bring about a partitioning of the national markets which would be contrary to the aims of the Treaty.

14. The reply to the question which has been raised therefore should be that the rules contained in the EEC Treaty concerning the free movement of goods, including the provisions of Article 36, must be interpreted as preventing the proprietor of a patent for a medicinal preparation who sells the preparation in one Member State where patent protection exists, and then markets it himself in another Member State where there is no such protection, from availing himself of the right conferred by the legislation of the first Member State to prevent the marketing in that State of the said preparation imported from the other Member State.

.....

(10) Polydor Case

For facts and references see above, page 54 .

.....

*The Court ruled:*

The enforcement by the proprietor or by persons entitled under him of copyrights protected by the law of a Member State against the importation and marketing of gramophone records lawfully manufactured and placed in the market in the Portuguese Republic by licensees of the proprietor is justified on the ground of the protection of industrial and commercial property within the meaning of Article 23 of the Agreement between the European Economic Community and the Portuguese Republic of

22 July 1972 (Official Journal, English Special Edition 1972 (31 December) (L 301), p. 167) and therefore does not constitute a restriction on trade such as is prohibited by Article 14(2) of that Agreement. Such enforcement does not constitute a means of arbitrary discrimination or a disguised restriction on trade between the Community and Portugal within the meaning of the said Article 23.

(11) Beele Case

Industrie Diensten Groep v. Beele Handelmaatschappij; Preliminary ruling of 2 March 1982, Case 6/81; (1982) ECR 6707; (1982) 3 CMLR 102; CCH. para. 8475; Competition Law CM/M/III/101.

*Facts:* The action pending before the Gerechtshof, The Hague, concerns two cable-duct systems:

(a) MCT (Multi Cable Transit), a Swedish product which is manufactured by AB Lickeaborgs Bruck and has been marketed in the Netherlands since 1963 and since 1973 by J.A. Beele Handelmaatschappij B.V., the respondent in the main action (hereinafter referred to as 'Beele'), as sole importer;

(b) SVT, which is manufactured by System- und Verfahrenstechnik in the Federal Republic of Germany and has been marketed in the Netherlands since 1978 by B.V. Industrie Diensten Groep, the appellant in the main action (hereinafter referred to as 'I.D.G.').

The MCT cable ducts are based on a technique which was patented in the Federal Republic of Germany, the Netherlands and elsewhere. The patents expired in 1975 and System- und Verfahrenstechnik then began to manufacture the SVT cable ducts using the same technique.

In both systens the frame is waterproof, fireproof and gas-tight. It consists of a rectangular frame which may be set into concrete walls, built into walls or welded to metal walls. The frame has a tapped case through which several cables of different thicknesses clasped and secured by means of rubber cable blocks and O-blocks may be passed. In addition both systems have various accessories such as filling blocks, anchorage and press plates and a safety seal.

2. It is common ground that both systems are manufactured in the same sizes and are all but identical insofar as both the frames and other components of the ducts are interchangeable.

3. From the President of the Arrondissementsrechtbank (District Court), The Hague, Beele sought and obtained an interlocutory injunction against I.D.G. restraining I.D.G. from selling SVT cable ducts in the Netherlands upon a penalty of a fine. The President of that court decided that the SVT cable ducts could be made differently without impairing its quality or restricting its application and in his judgment took the provisional view that it was a precise imitation.

I.D.G. appealed against his judgment to the Gerechtshof, The Hague. Relying on an expert's report (whose conclusions are contradicted by another expert instructed by Beele), I.D.G. contended in particular that in order to obtain a product which is technically and commercially equivalent to the MCT system it was necessary for the same dimensions as those used in the MCT system to be used for the frame and accessories. I.D.G. further argued that Beele's application was contrary to Articles

30 to 36 of the EEC Treaty on the ground that the SVT products are manufactured in the Federal Republic of Germany and lawfully marketed in that country.

The Gerechtshof, The Hague, shared the provisional view of the President of the Arrondissementsrechtbank but it reserved its judgment in order to submit the following question to the Court:

'Assuming that:

(a) A trader, A, markets products in the Netherlands which are no longer covered by any patent and which for no compelling reason are practically identical with products which have been marketed for a considerable period of time in the Netherlands by another trader, B, and which are different from similar kinds of articles, and in so doing trader A needlessly causes confusion;

(b) Under Netherlands law trader A is thereby competing unfairly with trader B and acting unlawfully;

(c) Netherlands law gives trader B the right to obtain an injunction on that ground restraining trader A from continuing to market the products in the Netherlands;

(d) The products of trader B are manufactured in Sweden and those of trader A in the Federal Republic of Germany;

(e) Trader A imports his products from the Federal Republic of Germany in which those products are lawfully put on the market by someone other than trader B, the Swedish manufacturer, someone who is associated with one of them or by someone who is authorised to do so by one of them,

do the rules contained in the EEC Treaty on the free movement of goods, notwithstanding the provisions of Article 36 thereof, then prevent trader B from obtaining such an injunction against trader A?'
.....

5. The case-file shows that, just like protection against precise imitation in the law of most other Member States, the rule of Netherlands law to which the question refers has been developed chiefly by the courts. As the Commission has pointed out, no effort has been made hitherto at Community level to harmonise national rules against precise imitation. Therefore an examination of the question whether such protection accords with the rules of the Treaty on the free movement of goods should be confined to the way in which that protection is provided in Netherlands law, as described in the judgment of the Gerechtshof.

6. That judgment shows that, subject to the answer to be given to the question raised, the Gerechtshof is prepared to uphold the injunction against the marketing in the Netherlands of products which it presumes have been lawfully marketed in another Member State.

7. Such an injunction constitutes an obstacle to the free movement of goods between the Member States and in principle is caught by Article 30 which prohibits all measures having an effect equivalent to quantitative restrictions on imports. However, the Court has repeatedly held

(for example, in the judgment of 20 February 1979, in Case 120/1978, the 'Cassis de Dijon' case, (1979) ECR 649 and in the judgment of 17 June 1981 in Case 113/80 *Commission* v *Ireland* (1981) ECR 1625) that in the absence of common rules relating to the production and marketing of products, obstacles to movement within the Community resulting from disparities between national legislation must be accepted in so far as such legislation, applying without discrimination to both domestic and imported products, may be justified as being necessary in order to satisfy mandatory requirements relating in particular to the protection of consumers and fairness in commercial transactions. Therefore the protection against imitation provided in the way described in the judgment making the reference for a preliminary ruling must be examined to determine whether it meets those conditions.

8. Although the main action concerns the protection of a product manufactured in a non-member country against the marketing of a product manufactured in a Member State, according to the national court the application of case-law does not depend on country of origin of the product imitated and country of origin of the imitation. What is more, there is nothing in the judgment of the national court from which it may be inferred that that case-law is applied in a manner adapted to the specific needs of national products thereby putting imported products at a disadvantage. Therefore it must be assumed that the case-law referred to by the national court applies without distinction to national and imported products.

9. National case-law prohibiting the precise imitation of someone else's product which is likely to cause confusion may indeed protect consumers and promote fair trading; these are general interests which, according to the decisions of the Court cited above, may justify the existence of obstacles to movement within the Community resulting from disparities between national laws relating to the marketing of products. That such a rule does meet mandatory requirements is moreover borne out by the fact that it accords with the principle underlying Article 10 bis of the Paris Convention for the Protection of Industrial Property, as last revised on 14 July 1967 at Stockholm, which prohibits *inter alia* all acts of such a nature as to create confusion with the goods of a competitor, and by the fact that this rule is recognised in principle in the case-law of most Member States.

10. In order to answer the question whether case-law such as that described in the judgment of the Gerechtshof is necessary to achieve the afore-said objectives, or whether it goes beyond the limit which they may justify, the manner in which that case-law is applied, as described in the judgment, should be scrutinised.

11. As to that, the very wording of the question submitted shows first that in the provisional view of the national court the products which it intends to prohibit from being marketed are for no compelling reason practically identical to the products imitated and that the appellant in the main action thereby needlessly causes confusion. Furthermore, the judgment of the national court shows that the question whether or not such limitation is necessary was considered not only from the technical point of view, but also from the economic and commercial point of view.

12. Secondly, it is apparent from the wording of the question submitted and from the case-file that there is no indication of an agreement or

of dependence between the Swedish manufacturer of the original product and the German manufacturer of the product which is supposed to be an imitation thereof and the marketing of which in the Netherlands is in dispute.

13. Where the circumstances mentioned by the national court are met a body of case-law prohibiting the precise imitation of someone else's product may not be regarded as exceeding the scope of the mandatory requirements which the protection of consumers and the fairness of commercial transactions constitute.

14. The appellant in the main action has raised before the Court the question of spare parts. It points out that the cable ducts are installed not only in buildings but also in ships and an injunction against the marketing of the German product in the Netherlands would make it necessary to carry out repairs on ships in the Netherlands using spare parts for the Swedish product, even if the ship is fitted with German cable ducts. Since this question has not been raised by the national court and the respondent in the main action has indicated during the procedure before the Court that the injunction which it seeks does not relate to spare parts for the repair of the German cable ducts, it is not necessary to resolve this question for which the foregoing considerations are not necessarily conclusive.

15. The answer to the question submitted by the Gerechtshof, The Hague, must therefore be that the rules of the EEC Treaty on the free movement of goods do not prevent a rule of national law which applies to domestic and imported products alike, from allowing a trader, who for some considerable time in the Member State concerned has marketed a product which differs from similar products, to obtain an injunction against another trader restraining him from continuing to market in that Member State a product coming from another Member State in which it is lawfully marketed but which for no compelling reason is almost identical to the first-mentioned product and thereby needlessly causes confusion between the two products.
.....

(12) Maize Seed Case

Nungesser and Eisele v. Commission, Judgment of 8 June 1982, Case 258/78; (1982) ECR 2015; (1983) 1 CMLR 278; CCH para. 8805; Competition Law CM/M/III/104.

*Facts:* By Decision under Article 85 of the Treaty, the Commission dismissed an application for exemption under Article 85(3) for a set of restrictive practices concerning the production and sale of maize seed for agricultural use. The decision was addressed to the Institut National de la Recherche Agronomique (INRA), Paris, SA Francaise des Semences de Maïs (FRASEMA), Paris, Mr Kurt Eisele, Darmstadt, and L.C. Nungesser KG, Darmstadt.

The Decision concerns:

(1) a contract made on 14 December 1960 whereby INRA transferred its breeders' rights in respect of maize seed for Germany to Mr Eisele;

(2) a contract made on 5 October and notified on 1 November 1965, whereby Mr Eisele received an exclusive licence for the propagation and sale of INRA varieties of maize seed in Germany. The main anti-competitive

clauses of this agreement were the following:

(a) the exclusive rights conferred by the licence, so far as they entailed:

- an obligation upon the licensor not to license other firms to produce or use INRA varieties in Germany and the obligation not to use them there itself;

- the obligation upon the licensor not to license other firms to distribute those varieties in Germany, and the obligation not to distribute them there itself;

- the obligation upon the licensor to prevent third parties from exporting INRA varieties for sale or use in Germany;

- the exercise by Mr Eisele of his own breeders' rights under the contract of 14 December 1960 as a means of preventing imports into Germany by third parties;

(b) the obligation upon the licensor to see that no exports were made to Germany, which entailed an obligation to refrain from exporting to Germany (ban on direct imports) and an obligation to take any necessary measures to prevent third parties from exporting to Germany (ban on indirect imports);

(c) the obligation upon the licensee to refrain from producing or selling maize varieties other than INRA varieties;

(d) the obligation upon the licensee to sell only to establishments offering assurances the assessment of which was a matter for the licensee's discretion;

(e) the obligation upon the two parties to fix selling prices in concert;

(f) the obligation upon the licensee to produce no more than one-third of the quantities required to meet orders in his territory, and to import the other two-thirds from France;

(3) a settlement reached on 14 November 1973 in the action in the German courts between Mr J. Eisele and the firm, L. David was henceforth to import no INRA seeds into Germany.
.....

124. The Commission found that these clauses had as their object and effect an appreciable restriction of competition within the meaning of Article 85(1). Firstly, the exclusive rights clause as applied in practice deprived the licensor of any power to grant other licences in the same territory during the currency of the contract, and of the right to produce or sell the seeds there itself. All third parties and the licensor itself were thereby eliminated from the market as potential suppliers.

Such a restriction is not within the specific subject matter of the breeders' rights. Further, the fact that no third party could import into Germany or export from Germany without Mr Eisele's consent makes for a form of market sharing and deprives German users of any possibility of choosing between potential suppliers. The fact that the transfer of INRA breeders' rights to Mr Eisele by the 1960 contract gives Mr Eisele a secondary right does not suffice to take the 1960 contract itself nor the 1965 contract outside the scope of Article 85 since the transfer of this right and its exercise by Mr Eisele have been used as a means of preventing all imports of original products.

The Commission considered that this arrangement did not qualify for Article 85(3) exemption, not because exclusive licences are automatically excluded from exemption, but because exclusive selling rights can be exempted only where stringent conditions are satisfied, notably when they are necessary for the protection of small- or medium-sized firms penetrating new markets or promoting a new product, and then only if parallel imports are still possible. In the present case the exclusive selling rights and the accompanying export bans did not satisfy the tests for exemption, chiefly because of the absolute territorial protection given to the licensee on his national territory.

The substantial differences between selling prices payable by farmers in recent years as between Germany and France (as much as 70% in 1974) illustrate the consequences that can flow from exclusive licences where they are accompanied by absolute territorial protection.

.....

*The Court held:*

*B. The application of Article 85 of the EEC Treaty to exclusive licenses*

44. By this submission the applicants criticise the Commission for wrongly taking the view that an exclusive license of breeders' rights must by its very nature be treated as an agreement prohibited by Article 85(1) of the Treaty. They submit that the Commission's opinion in that respect is unfounded in so far as the exclusive licence constitutes the sole means, as regards seeds which have been recently developed in a Member State and which have not yet penetrated the market of another Member State, of promoting competition between the new product and comparable products in that other Member State; indeed, no grower or trader would take the risk of launching the new product on a new market if he were not protected against direct competition from the holder of the breeders' rights and from his other licensees.

45. This contention is supported by the German and British Governments and by the Caisse de Gestion des Licences Végétales. In particular, the two Governments claim that the general character of the reasons given for the contested decision is incompatible with the terms of Article 85 of the Treaty and conflicts with a sensible competition policy. The reasons given for the decision are said to be based on the ill-conceived premise that every exclusive licence of an industrial or commercial property right, whatever its nature, must be regarded as an agreement prohibited by Article 85(1) and that it is therefore for the Commission to judge whether, in a given case, the conditions for the grant of an exemption under Article 85(3) are satisfied.

46. During the course of the proceedings objection was made to the use of expression 'exclusive licence' on the ground that, in the present case, the applicants' exclusive right to market the seeds at issue in Germany derived from breeders' rights of which Mr Eisele was the owner in that Member State. Therefore, it was argued, that exclusive right was founded

neither on the grant by INRA of an exclusive right to use, within German territory, industrial or commercial property rights vesting in INRA, nor on the contract of 1965 which appointed Mr Eisele sole distributor of the seeds in question for that territory.

47. However, that argument disregards the fact that, from the point of view of Community law, the contract of 1960 initiating the cooperation between INRA and Mr Eisele, the 'assignments' of breeders' rights in 1961 and the contract of 1965 organising the distribution of INRA seeds in Germany make up an indivisible whole. In economic terms, Mr Eisele's position on the German market was that of an exclusive licensee, since the authorisation given by INRA to Mr Eisele to have registered in his name in Germany breeders' rights of which INRA was the owner in France was due to the fact that the body was not able at that time to have its own breeders' rights registered with the Bundessortenamt and since that operation is to be seen within the context of the grant to Mr Eisele of the exclusive right to organise the sale of INRA seeds in Germany.

48. The statement of reasons on which the decision is based refers to two sets of circumstances in order to justify the application of Article 85(1) to the exclusive licence in question (II, No. 3). The accuracy of the facts thus stated has not been challenged.

49. The first set of circumstances is described as follows:

'By licensing a single undertaking to exploit his breeders' rights in a given territory, the licensor deprives himself for the entire duration of the contract of the ability to issue licences to other undertakings in the same territory..'

(...)

'By undertaking not to produce or market the product himself in the territory covered by the contract the licensor likewise eliminates himself, as well as Frasema and its members, as suppliers in that territory.'

50. Corresponding to that part of the statement of reasons is Article 1(b) of the decision, which in its first and second indents declares the exclusive nature of the licence granted by the 1965 contract to be contrary to Article 85(1) of the Treaty in so far as it imposes:

An obligation upon INRA or those deriving rights through INRA to refrain from having the relevant seeds produced or sold by other licensees in Germany, and

An obligation upon INRA or those deriving rights through INRA to refrain from producing or selling the relevant seeds in Germany themselves.

51. The second set of circumstances referred to in the decision is described as follows:

'The fact that third parties may not import the same seed (namely the seed under licence) from other Community countries into Germany, or export from Germany to other Community countries, leads to market sharing and deprives German farmers of any real room for negotiation since seed is supplied by one supplier and one supplier only'.

52. That part of the statement of reasons is reflected in Article 1(b) of the decision, which in its third and fourth indents declares the exclusive nature of the licence granted by the 1965 contract to be contrary to Article 85(1) of the Treaty insofar as it imposes:

An obligation upon INRA or those deriving rights through INRA to prevent third parties from exporting the relevant seeds to Germany without the licensee's authorisation for use or sale there, and

Mr Eisele's concurrent use of his exclusive contractual rights and his own breeder's rights to prevent all import into Germany or exports to other Member States of the relevant seeds.

53. It should be observed that those two sets of considerations relate to two legal situations which are not necessarily identical. The first case concerns a so-called open exclusive licence or assignment and the exclusivity of the licence relates solely to the contractual relationship between the owner of the right and the licensee, whereby the owner merely undertakes not to grant other licences in respect of the same territory and not to compete himself with the licensee on that territory. On the other hand, the second case involves an exclusive licence or assignement with absolute territorial protection, under which the parties to the contract propose, as regards the products and the territory in question, to eliminate all competition from third parties, such as parallel importers or licensees for other territories.

54. That point having been clarified, it is necessary to examine whether, in the present case, the exclusive nature of the licence, insofar as it is an open licence, has the effect of preventing or distorting competition within the meaning of Article 85(1) of the Treaty.

55. In that respect the government of the Federal Republic of Germany emphasised that the protection of agricultural innovations by means of breeder's rights constitutes a means of encouraging such innovations and the grant of exclusive rights for a limited period, is capable of providing a further incentive to innovative efforts. From that it infers that a total prohibition of every exclusive licence, even an open one, would cause the interest of undertakings in licences to fall away, which would be prejudicial to the dissemination of knowledge and techniques in the Community.

56. The exclusive licence which forms the subject-matter of the contested decision concerns the cultivation and marketing of hybrid maize seeds which were developed by INRA after years of research and experimentation and were unknown to German farmers at the time when the co-operation between INRA and the applicants was taking shape. For that reason the concern shown by the interveners as regards the protection of new technology is justified.

57. In fact, in the case of a licence of breeder's rights over hybrid maize seeds newly developed in one Member State, an undertaking established in another Member State which was not certain that it would not encounter competition from other licensees for the territory granted to it, or from the owner of the right himself, might be deterred from accepting the risk of cultivating and marketing that product; such a result would be damaging to the dissemination of a new technology and would prejudice competition in the Community between the new product and similar existing products.

58. Having regard to the specific nature of the products in question, the Court concludes that, in a case such as the present, the grant of an open exclusive licence, that is to say a licence which does not affect the position of third parties such as parallel importers and licensees for other territories, is not in itself incompatible with Article 85(1) of the Treaty.

59. Part B of the third submission is thus justified to the extent to which it concenrs that aspect of the exclusive nature of the licence.

60. As regard to the position of third parties, the Commission in essence criticises the parties to the contract for having extended the definition of exclusivity to importers who are not bound to the contract, in particular parallel importers. Parallel importers or exporters, such as Louis David KG in Germany and Robert Bomberault in France, who offered INRA seed for sale to German buyers, had found themselves subjected to pressure and legal proceedings by INRA, Frasema and the applicants, the purpose of which was to maintain the exclusive position of the applicants on the German market.

61. The Court has consistently held (cf. Joined Cases 56 and 58/64 *Consten and Grundig v Commission* (1966) ECR 299) that absolute territorial protection granted to a licensee in order to enable parallel imports to be controlled and prevented results in the artificial maintenance of separate national markets, contrary to the Treaty.

62. The Government of the United Kingdom advanced the view that a contract between two undertakings could not impede the freedom of importers to buy seeds in the country of the owner of the breeder's rights with a view to exporting them to the country of the licensee since, according to previous decisions of the Court, a commercial or industrial property right cannot be invoked against the marketing of a product which has been lawfully placed in circulation on the market of another Member State by the owner of that right or with his consent. Therefore such a contract cannot be regarded as an agreement prohibited by Article 85(1) of the Treaty.

63. However, that view fails to take into account the fact that one of the powers of the Commission is to ensure, pursuant to Article 85 of the Treaty and the regulations adopted in implementation thereof, that agreements and concerted practices between undertakings do not have the object or the effect of restricting or distorting competition, and that that power of the Commission is not affected by the fact that persons or undertakings subject to such restrictions are in a position to rely upon the provisions of the Treaty relating to the free movement of goods in order to escape such restrictions.

64. It is clear from the documents in the case that the contracts in question were indeed intended to restrict competition from third parties on the German market. In fact, under Clause 5 of the 1965 contract INRA promises that it and those deriving rights through it will do 'everything in their power to prevent the export' of the varieties of seeds in question to Germany.

65. In the contested decision that clause is interpreted as seeking to prevent third parties who purchase INRA seeds in France from exporting them to Germany (II, No 3(b)). It may be inferred from the obstructions which the parties to the contracts have placed in the way of the efforts

of Louis David KG and Robert Bomberault to sell INRA seeds in Germany that that interpretation is correct.

66. Article 1(b) of the decision expressly refers to Clause 5 of the 1965 contract and to the exercise of breeder's rights by Mr Eisele so as to prevent the marketing of INRA seeds in Germany by third parties. Therefore, to that extent Part B of the third submission is unfounded.

67. An examination of Part B of the third submission therefore leads to the conclusion that that submission is well founded in part and that Article 1(b) of the decision must be declared void to the extent to which it relates to Clause 1 of the 1965 contract and in so far as that contract imposes:

An obligation upon INRA or those deriving rights through INRA to refrain from having the relevant seeds produced or sold by other licensees in Germany, and

An obligation upon INRA or those deriving rights through INRA to refrain from producing or selling the relevant seeds in Germany themselves.

*Fourth submission: The grant of an exemption under Article 85(3) of the EEC Treaty*

68. In support of their fourth submission, the applicants observe that the contested decision refused an exemption under Article 85(3) of the Treaty because there was no question of a new market being penetrated or a new product being launched and because Mr Eisele enjoyed absolute territorial protection in Germany. According to the applicants, those two reasons are incorrect: on the one hand, the very purpose of the 1965 contract, at the time of its notification to the Commission, was to open up a new market and to introduce a new product; secondly, the exclusivity established by that contract did not go beyond what was necessary for the distribution of the varieties which could be grown outside their country of origin and thus for the improvement of the production and distribution of goods.

69. In support of that submission, the Government of the United Kingdom observed that only the benefit of the protection afforded by an exclusive licence is capable of encouraging the licensee to exploit the breeder's rights in question and that that protection thus serves to improve the production and distribution of goods and promote technical and economic progress within the meaning of Article 85(3). It was therefore submitted that the criteria applied by the contested decision were excessively severe.

70. The Caisse de Gestion des Licences Végétales argues that these proceedings concern a fragile and technically advanced product and that in such a case availability of supplies can only be achieved by the establishment of a selective system for planning and stabilising the market. In refusing to grant an exemption the Commission disregarded the specific nature of the contracts in question.

71. It should first be stated that the contested decision left open the assessment under Article 85(3) of the exclusive production and propagation rights granted to Mr Eisele and that it confined itself to stating that the conditions for the exemption of the exclusive selling rights and the accompanying export prohibitions were not

satisfied (III, No 1(b)).

72. It follows that, since Part B of the third submission was partially successful, the Court's appraisal of the refusal to grant an exemption may be confined to an examination of the Commission's arguments relating to the exclusive selling rights in so far as they confer absolute territorial protection.

73. On that point the decision states that Mr Eisele enjoyed absolute territorial protection in respect of the distribution in Germany of the seeds for which he had exclusive rights, and that by its absolute nature the sole and direct consequence of such protection was to prevent all imports through other channels of the original products, namely INRA seeds originating in France, despite a persistent demand for such imports in Germany, which in itself is not capable of contributing to an improvement in the production or distribution of goods within the meaning of Article 85(3) (III, No 1(b), second indent).

74. The Caisse de Gestion des Licences Végétales disputed that reasoning. In its view, the territorial protection enjoyed by the licencee in the present case was rather a relative protection on account of the presence on the market of numerous varieties of maize seed which could be substituted for INRA varieties and which could thus enter into direct competition with those varieties.

75. However, the Commission rightly stated in reply that that view put forward by the Caisse de Gestion Végétales concerns the problem of the demarcation of the market; that is a problem which arises when the Commission has to examine whether an agreement affords 'the possibility of eliminating competition in respect of a substantial part of the products in question' (Article 85(3)(b)) but which is not relevant to the question whether an agreement is capable of improving the production or distribution of goods.

76. It must be remembered that under the terms of Article 85(3) of the Treaty an exemption from the prohibition contained in Article 85(1) may be granted in the case of any agreement between undertakings which contributes to improving the production or distribution of goods or to promoting technical progress, and which does not impose on the undertakings concerned restrictions which are not indispensable to the attainment of those objectives.

77. As it is a question of seeds intended to be used by a large number of farmers for the production of maize, which is an important product for human and animal foodstuffs, absolute territorial protection manifestly goes beyond what is indispensable for the improvement of production or distribution or the promotion of technical progress, as is demonstrated in particular in the present case by the prohibition, agreed to by both parties to the agreement, of any parallel imports of INRA maize seeds into Germany even if those seeds were bred by INRA itself and marketed in France.

78. It follows that the absolute territorial protection conferred on the licensee, as established to exist by the contested decision, constituted a sufficient reason for refusing to grant an exemption under Article 85(3) of the Treaty. It is therefore no longer necessary to examine the other grounds set out in the decision for refusing to grant such an exemption.

79. Therefore the fourth submission must be rejected.

*Fifth submission: The settlement concluded between Louis David KG and Mr Eisele*

80. The fifth submission relates to Article 1(c) of the decision, whereby the Commission declared Clause 1 of the settlement concluded on 14 November 1973 between Louis David KG and Mr Eisele to be contrary to Article 85(1) of the Treaty in so far as it obliged Louis David KG not to sell or place in circulation in Germany seeds of INRA varieties without the authorisation of the German licensee.

81. It appears from the documents before the Court that that settlement was reached in the framework of legal proceedings brought by Mr Eisele before the Landgericht (Regional Court) Bad Kreuznach for infringement of his exclusive rights after Louis David KG had imported from France and resold in Germany, without Mr Eisele's authorisation, a quantity of certified seeds of INRA varieties.

82. The applicants claim that that settlement was a judicial settlement within the meaning of Article 794(1) of the German Code of Civil Procedure concluded between the parties in order to dispose definitively of a dispute before a German court. They submit that such a settlement, which is legally enforceable under the terms of the aforementioned provision, is not an ordinary private contract but amounts to an order of the court.

83. From that the applicants infer that the Commission was not able to declare such a settlement void without encroaching upon the jurisdiction of the German courts; but in view of the automatic nullity decreed by Article 85(2) of the Treaty the Commission did declare the settlement void when it held that a part of it was contrary to Article 85(1).

84. The Commission replies that under German law a settlement concluded for the purpose of disposing of a legal dispute must comply with the requirements of substantive law applicable to every civil contract, and in particular with those deriving from competition law. A judicial settlement is a contract of civil law as well as an act of the court and the nullity of the contract nullifies the whole settlement.

85. The Commission adds that decisions of the German courts, in particular the Bundesgerichtshof (Federal Supreme Court), have confirmed that view. According to those decisions, a party to a judicial settlement may not validly invoke clauses of that settlement which conflict with the German law on monopolies. There is no reason why a settlement which offends against Community rules on competition should be viewed differently.

86. The settlement at issue was submitted to the Court, which was able to find that it was indeed a judicial settlement within the meaning of Article 794(1) of the German Code of Civil Procedure, namely a settlement concluded before a German court in order to dispose of a legal dispute pending before it.

87. Whilst it is true, as the applicants maintain, that the judicial settlement is enforceable, it does not have the authority of *res judicata* under German law and is therefore not effective against other courts, public authorities or third parties. Furthermore, as the

Commission emphasised, the decisions of the German courts are based on the premise that a judicial settlement, to be valid, must comply with the requirements of public policy and *bonos mores* and therefore cannot infringe mandatory rules of competition law.

88. In adjudging the applicants' submissions, it is not however necessary to consider the question whether, and if so to what extent, a judicial settlement reached before a German court may be declared void for infringing Community rules of competition law. The contested decision in fact merely states that the obligation on Louis David KG, arising out of the settlement, no longer to sell or to place in circulation in Germany INRA seeds without Mr Eisele's authorisation conflicts with Article 85(1) of the Treaty.

89. Therefore, the effect of the decision is confined, in this respect, to a prohibition restraining Mr Eisele from relying on Clause 1 of the settlement to prevent the sale or the placing in circulation of INRA seeds in Germany by Louis David KG. Such a prohibition is in conformity with the principle, recognised in German law, according to which a judicial settlement, within the meaning of Article 794(1) of the Code of Civil Procedure, constitutes both an act of the court terminating a legal dispute and a contract of private law which does not allow the parties to disregard mandatory rules of law.

.....

(13) Coditel II Case

Coditel and others v Ciné Vog Films, preliminary ruling of 6 October 1982, Case 262/81; (1982) ECR 3381; (1983) 1 CMLR 49; CCH para. 8865; Competition Law CM/M/III/106.

*Facts:* This case concerns a dispute between three Belgian cable television companies (Coditel) on the one hand and a Belgian film distribution company (Ciné Vog), a French film producing company (Films la Boétie) and other representatives of the film industry on the other hand.

The dispute arose out of the retransmission in Belgium by Coditel through its cable network of a French film dubbed in German which it had picked up by its special television aerials from a German television broadcast. Ciné Vog, which had exclusive distribution rights for this film in Belgium, sued for damages, using the right of action granted to exclusive copyright licensees under Belgian law.

The Court had already been called upon by the Brussels Cour d'Appel to rule on the question of whether Ciné Vog's action was contrary to the Treaty rules on the freedom to provide services (Article 59). The Court held that it was not and in doing so developed its previous case law on intellectual property rights and the free movement of goods by drawing a distinction between on the one hand intellectual property rights incorporated in physical goods and on the other hand intellectual property rights which relate to a right of exhibition or performance (as in a film).

The question which was now referred by the Cour de Cassation was whether the agreement granting Ciné Vog an exclusive right to show the film infringed Article 85; the Cour d'Appel had decided that said Article was not applicable and had not referred this question to the Court of Justice.

*The Court held:*

15. However, the mere fact that the owner of the copyright in a film has granted to a sole licensee the exclusive right to exhibit that film in the territory of a Member State and, consequently, to prohibit, during a specified period, its showing by others, is not sufficient to justify the finding that such a contract must be regarded as the purpose, the means or the result of an agreement, decision or concerted practice prohibited by the Treaty.

16. The characteristics of the cinematographic industry and of its markets in the Community, especially those relating to dubbing and subtitling for the benefit of different language groups, to the possibilities of television broadcasts, and to the system of financing cinematographic production in Europe serve to show that an exclusive exhibition licence is not, in itself, such as to prevent, restrict or distort competition.

17. Although copyright in a film and the right deriving from it, namely that of exhibiting the film, are not, therefore, as such subject to the prohibition contained in Article 85, the exercise of those rights may, none the less, come within the said prohibitions where there are economic or legal circumstances the effect of which is to restrict film distribution to an appreciable degree or to distort competition on the cinematographic market, regard being had to the specific characteristics of that market.

18. Since neither the question referred to the Court nor the file on the case provides any information in this respect, it is for the national court to make such inquiries as may be necessary.

19. It must therefore be stated that it is for national courts, where appropriate, to make such inquiries and in particular to establish whether or not the exercise of the exclusive right to exhibit a cinematographic film creates barriers which are artificial and unjustifiable in terms of the needs of the cinematographic industry, or the possibility of charging fees which exceed a fair return on investment, or an exclusivity the duration of which is disproportionate to those requirements, and whether or not, from a general point of view, such exercise within a given geographic area is such as to prevent, restrict or distort competition within the Common Market.

20. Accordingly, the answer to be given to the question referred to the Court must be that a contract whereby the owner of the copyright in a film grants an exclusive right to exhibit that film for a specific period in the territory of a Member State is not, as such, subject to the prohibitions contained in Article 85 of the Treaty. It is, however where appropriate, for the national court to ascertain whether, in a given case, the manner in which the exclusive right conferred by that contract is exercised is subject to a situation in the economic or legal sphere the object or effect of which is to prevent or restrict the distribution of films or to distort competition within the cinematographic market, regard being had to the specific characteristics of that market.

....

(14) Communication in re BIEM-IFPI

(Communication of the Commission in the Thirteenth Report on Competition

Policy April 1984).

Following moves by the Commission, performing right societies in the Community have amended their agreements with the sound recording industry to bring them into line with the competition rules.

To manufacture and market sound recordings (records, pre-recorded cassettes and tapes) permission of the copyright owner is required. This is granted by performing right societies on payment of a royalty.
According to the case law of the European Court of Justice, Ruling of 20 January 1981 in Cases 55/80, Membran GmbH, K-tel International/Gema, (1981) ECR 147, the importation of sound recordings that have been lawfully placed on the market in another Member State following payment of royalties must not in principle be impeded. The German performing right society GEMA nevertheless opposed such cross-frontier deliveries of records where they took place between companies belonging to the same group, claiming that the records were not yet in free circulation. In some cases manufacturers were given permission to distribute sound recordings in just one Member State.

Furthermore, the performing right societies had agreed among themselves to base the royalties payable by manufacturers on the average retail prices of records in the country of sale, taking into account if necessary the prices charged by competing record manufacturers. This meant that manufacturers had to pay widely differing royalties depending on the country of sale. It also prevented any cost or price advantages that arose in the country of manufacture from being passed on to consumers in the country of sale. Since royalties were based not on the sales revenue of the manufacturer but on the level of retail prices, over which the manufacturer had no direct influence, this system lacked an objective basis of assessment.

After the Commission had instituted proceedings, the parties concerned agreed to put an end to the objectionable practice.

First, they will henceforth not impose any geographical restrictions on the exportation of sound recordings. Sound recordings which are lawfully manufactured in a Member State and are marketable in that State may be sold without restriction anywhere in the Community. This also applies to deliveries between companies within a group. GEMA has already expressly included this in its new agreement with the sound recording industry. Other performing right societies are still in the process of negotiating their agreements.

B. Other national provisions

It is submitted that arguments could be developed to the effect that the principles contained in Articles 30 to 36 of the EEC Treaty are also applicable to private undertakings.

(1) Dassonville Case

Judgment of 11 July 1974, Case 8/74; (1974) ECR 837; (1974) 2 CMLR 436; CCH para. 8276; Competition Law CM/M/III/43.
*Facts:* Belgian law provides that it is prohibited, on pain of penal sanctions, to import, sell, display for sale, have possession of or transport for the purpose of sales or delivery, spirits bearing a designation of origin duly adopted by the Belgian Government when such spirits are not accompanied by any official document certifying their right to such designation.
The designation of origin "Scotch Whiskey" has been duly adopted by the Begian Government.
In 1970 Gustave Dassonville, a wholesaler in business in France, and

his son Benoît Dassonville, who manages a branch of his father's business in Belgium imported into Belgium "Scotch Whiskey" under the brand names "Johnny Walker" and "VAT 69", which Gustave Dassonville had purchased from the French importers and distributors of these two brands of whiskey.

On the bottles, the Dassonvilles affixed, with a view to their sale in Belgium, labels bearing in particular the printed words "British Customs Certificate of Origin", followed by a hand-written note of the number and date of the French excise bond on the permit register. This excise bond constituted the official document which, according to French rules, had to accompany a product bearing a designation of origin. France does not require a certificate of origin for "Scotch Whiskey".

Although the goods were duly imported into Belgium on the basis of the French documents required and cleared for customs purposes as "Community goods", the Belgian authorities considered that these documents did not properly satisfy the objective of the Belgian law.

Following this importation, the Public Prosecutor instituted proceedings against the Dassonvilles before a court of summary jurisdiction. It was alleged that, they:

- committed forgeries or assisted therein in affixing to the bottles the aforementioned labels, with fraudulent intent to induce belief that they were in possession, quod non, of an official document certifying the origin of the whiskey, and made use of forged documents;

- contravened Belgian law by knowingly importing, selling, displaying for sale, holding in their possession or transporting for the purpose of sale and delivery, whiskey bearing a designation duly adopted by the Belgian Governement without causing the whiskey to be accompanied by an official document certifying its right to such designation.

The Dassonvilles claim that the provisions of Belgian law in the way they are interpreted by the Belgian authorities, are incompatible with the prohibition on quantitative restrictions and measures having equivalent effect laid down by Article 30 et seq. of the EEC Treaty.

*The Court held:*

By judgment of 11 January 1974, received at the Registry of the Court on 8 February 1974, the Tribunal de Première Instance of Brussels referred, under Article 177 of the EEC Treaty, two questions on the interpretation of Articles 30, 31, 32, 33, 36 and 85 of the EEC Treaty, relating to the requirement of an official document issued by the government of the exporting country for products bearing a designation of origin.

By the first question it asked whether a national provision prohibiting the import of goods bearing a designation of origin where such goods are not accompanied by an official document issued by the government of the exporting country certifying their right to such designation constitutes a measure having an effect equivalent to a quantitative restriction within the meaning of Article 30 of the EEC Treaty.

This question was raised within the context of criminal proceedings instituted in Belgium against traders who duly acquired a consignment of Scotch whiskey in free circulation in France and imported it into Belgium without being in possession of a certificate of origin from the Britisch Customs Authorities, thereby infringing Belgian rules.

It emerges from the file and from the oral proceedings that a trader, wishing to import into Belgium Scotch whiskey which is already in free circulation in France, can obtain such a certificate only with great difficulty, unlike the importer who imports directly from the producer country.

All trading rules enacted by Member States which are capable of hindering directly or indirectly, actually or potentially, intra-Community trade are to be considered as measures having an effect equivalent to quantitative restrictions.

In the absence of a Community system guaranteeing for consumers the authenticity of a product's designation of origin, if a Member State takes measures to prevent unfair practices in this connection, it is however subject to the condition that these measures should be reasonable and that the means of proof required should not act as a hindrance to trade between Member States and should, in consequence, be accessible to all Community nationals.

Even without having to examine whether or not such measures are covered by Article 36, they must not, in any case, by virtue of the principle expressed in the second sentence of that Article, constitute a means of arbitrary discrimination or a disguised restriction on trade between Member States.

That may be the case with formalities, required by a Member State for the purpose of proving the origin of a product, which only direct importers are really in a position to satisfy without facing serious difficulties.

Consequently, the requirements by a Member State of a certificate of authenticity which is less easily obtainable by importers of an authentic product which has been put into free circulation in a regular manner in another Member State than by importers of the same product coming directly from the country of origin constitutes a measure having an effect equivalent to a quantitative restriction as prohibited by the Treaty.

By the second question it is asked whether an agreement the effect of which is to restrict competition and adversely to affect trade between Member States when taken in conjunction with a national rule with regard to certificates of origin is void when that agreement authorises the exclusive importer to exploit that rule for the purpose of preventing parallel imports or does not prohibit him from doing so. An exclusive dealing agreement falls within the prohibition of Article 85 when it impedes, in law or in fact, the importation of the products in question from other Member States into the protected territory by persons other than the exclusive importer.

More particularly, an exclusive dealing agreement may adversely affect trade between Member States and can have the effect of hindering competition if the concessionaire is able to prevent parallel imports from other Member States into the territory covered by the concession by means of the combined effects of the agreement and a national law requiring the exclusive use of a certain means of proof of authenticity.

For the purpose of judging whether this is the case, account must be taken not only of the rights and obligations flowing from the provisions of the agreement, but also of the legal and economic context in which it is situated and, in particular, the possible existence of similar agreement concluded between the same producer and concessionaires established in other Member States.

In this connection, the maintenance within a Member State of prices appreciably higher than those in force in another Member State may prompt an examination as to whether the exclusive dealing agreement is being used for the purpose of preventing importers from obtaining the means of proof of authenticity of the product in question, required by national rules of the type envisaged by the question.

However, the fact that an agreement merely authorises the concessionaire to exploit such a national rule or does not prohibit him from doing so, does not suffice, in itself, to render the agreement null and void.

*The Court decided:*

1. The requirement of a Member State of a certificate of authenticity which is less easily obtainable by importers of an authentic product which has been put into free circulation in a regular manner in another Member State than by importers of the same product coming directly from the country of origin constitutes a measure having an effect equivalent to a quantitative restriction as prohibited by the Treaty.

2. The fact that an argument merely authorises the concessionaire to exploit such a national rule or does not prohibit him from doing so does not suffice, in itself, to render the agreement null and void.

(2) De Peijper Case

Officier van Justitie v. Adriaan De Peijper, Case 104/75, preliminary ruling of 20 May 1976; (1976) ECR 613; (1976) 2CMLR 271; CCH 8353; Competition Law CM/M/III/58.

*Facts:* In 1973 the company Centrafarm bought from a wholesale dealer established in the United Kingdom several quantities of valium tablets of 5 and 10 mg and imported these into the Netherlands as original valium coming from the British factory of the Hoffmann-La Roche group under the originalworld trademark. Subsequently Centrafarm put the tablets in packages bearing its name and the superscription "Diazepam", generic name of the preparation concerned, and delivered these to various dispensing chemists in the Netherlands.

In respect of these facts the Officier van Justitie (Public Prosecutor) of the District Rotterdam instituted criminal proceedings against Mr. De Peijper, director of Centrafarm, before the district court in Rotterdam.

The requisition contains, among other things, the following statements:

Centrafarm has occupied itself with 'parallel import': it bought notably in the United Kingdom not from the manufacturers of branded medicines, but from the wholesale trade in original branded packages. For the purpose of resale Centrafarm provided the products with a new package with the medicine's generic name, the adhesive label and charge number of Centrafarm, and the superscription 'original make'.

In carrying out these activities Centrafarm has committed the following offences against Dutch law, for which Mr. De Peijper is responsible and which he has in fact admitted:

- The company has made the abovementioned deliveries without having obtained permission to do so as referred to in Para. 3 of the 'B.F.P.' (Besluit Farmaceutische Preparaten = Pharmaceutical Preparations Order)

- It was not in possession of the documents referred to in Para. 6, section 2 of the 'B.F.P.' -

- It was not in possession of the protocols referred to in Para. 14 of the 'B.F.P.', since such documents had not been placed at its disposal by the foreign manufacturer.

Contrary to Mr. De Peijper's objections, the Dutch provisions in question, which apply to both national and to foreign products, are compatible with Article 36 of the EEC Treaty, as they are 'justified in consideration of protection ... of health and life of persons' and 'do not form either a means to arbitrary discrimination or a disguised restriction of the trade between the Member States'. Neither are they in conflict with Directive No. 70/50/EEC of the Commission of 22 December 1969, containing abolition of the measures of similar effect as quantitative import restrictions, not referred to in other provisions laid down in virtue of the EEC Treaty (P.B. No. L 13 of 19 January 1970, page 29), in particular with Para. 3 reading:

'This directive also bears on the measures containing a regulation of marketing products ... the influence whereof on the free trade of goods than what was aimed at by a trade regulation. This is notably the case:

1. If the restrictive influence on the free trade of goods is disproportionate to the object aimed at;

2. if the same object can be attained by a different means that is less hampering to commercial traffic'.

With regard to point 1, the provisions concerned are necessary to safeguard the identity and the quantitative and qualitative composition of the product, which, with a view to its therapeutic effect and its harmlessness is of paramount importance.

With regard to point 2, it cannot be demanded, so long as no harmonisation of legislation between the Member States has been effected, that there should be less stringent control-requirements for the imported product than for the national product. This applies in particular when the importer has not bought the product direct from the manufacturer abroad. For in that case there is no guarantee whatever as to the identity and the composition of the product.

The decision of the Court of Justice of 31 October 1974 in the cases 15/74 (Centrafarm BV and De Peijper v. Sterling Drug Inc.) and 16/74 (the same applicants v. Withrop BV) do not lead to different conclusions. The Court then considered, it is true, that certain actions of holders of a patent or trademark form offences against the Community's laws, but it should be noted in the present case that much greater interests are at stake.

The District Court asked for a preliminary ruling.

*The Court decided:*

.....

1. National rules or practices which result in imports being channelled in such a way that only certain traders can effect these imports, whereas others are prevented from doing so, constitute a measure having an effect equivalent to a quantitative restriction within the meaning of Article 30 of the Treaty.

2. Given a factual situation such as that described in the first question national rules of practices which make possible for a manufacturer of the pharmaceutical product in question and his duly appointed representatives, simply by refusing to produce the documents relating to the medicinal preparation in general or to a specific batch of that preparation, to enjoy a monopoly of the importing and marketing of the product, must be regarded as being unnecessarily restrictive and cannot therefore come within the exceptions specified in Article 36 of the Treaty, unless it is clearly proved that any other rules or practices would obviously be beyond the means which can reasonably be expected of an administration operating in a normal manner.

3. It is only if the information or documents to be produced by the manufacturer or his duly appointed importer show that there are several variants of the medicinal preparation and that the differences between these variants have therapeutic effect that there would be any justification for treating the variants as different medicinal preparations, for the purpose of authorising them to be placed on the market and as regards producing the relevant documents, it being understood that the answer to the first question remains valid as regards each of the authorisation procedures which have become necessary.

.....

(3) Cassis de Dijon Case

REWE-Zentral AG v. Bundesmonopolverwaltung für Branntwein, Case 120/78, Preliminary Ruling of 20 February 1979; (1979) ECR 649; (1979) 3 CMLR 494; CCH para. 8543.

*Facts:* The principal activity of Rewe-Zentral AG (hereinafter referred to as Rewe), is the importation of goods from other Member States of the Community. On 14 September 1976 it requested authorisation from the Bundesmonopolverwaltung für Branntwein (Federal Monopoly for Spirits) to import from France, for the purpose of marketing in the Federal Republic of Germany, certain potable spirits, including the liqueur "Cassis de Dijon", containing 15 to 20% by volume of alcohol.

By letter of 17 September 1976 the Bundesmonopolverwaltung informed Rewe that the "Cassis de Dijon" which it intended to import could not be sold in the Federal Republic of Germany, since Article 100(3) of the Branntweinmonopolgesetz provides that only potable spirits having a wine-spirit content of at least 32% may be marketed in that country.

Rewe brought an action against that decision before the Verwaltungsgericht Darmstadt; by order of 27 December 1976 that court referred the case to the Hessische Finanzgericht. The Finanzgericht decided, by order of its Seventh Senate of 28 April 1978, pursuant to Article 177 of the EEC Treaty, to stay the proceedings until the Court of Justice had given a preliminary ruling on the following questions:

1. Must the concept of measures having an effect equivalent to quantitative restrictions on imports contained in Article 30 of the EEC Treaty be understood as meaning that the fixing of a minimum wine-spirit content for potable spirits laid down in the German Branntweinmonopolgesetz, the result of which is that traditional products of other Member States whose wine-spirit content is below the fixed limit cannot be put into circulation in the Federal Republic of Germany, also comes within this concept?

2. May the fixing of such a minimum wine-spirit content come within the concept of "discrimination regarding the conditions under which goods are procured and marketed ... between nationals of Member States" contained in Article 37 of the EEC Treaty?

*The Court held:*

.....

6. The national court is thereby asking for assistance in the matter of interpretation in order to enable it to assess whether the requirement of a minimum alcohol content may be covered either by the prohibition on all measures having an effect equivalent to quantitative restrictions in trade between Member States contained in Article 30 of the Treaty or by the prohibition on all discrimination regarding the conditions under which goods are procured and marketed between nationals of Member States within the meaning of Article 37.

7. It should be noted in this connection that Article 37 relates specifically to State monopolies of a commercial character.

That provision is therefore irrelevant with regard to national provisions which do not concern the exercise by a public monopoly of its specific function - namely, its exclusive rights - but apply in a general manner to the production and marketing of alcoholic beverages, whether or not the latter are covered by the monopoly in question.

That being the case, the effect on intra-Community trade of the measure referred to by the national court must be examined solely in relation to the requirements under Article 30, as referred to by the first question.

8. In the absence of common rules relating to the production and marketing of alcohol - a proposal for a regulation submitted to the Council by the Commission on 7 December 1976 (Official Journal C 309, p. 2) not yet having received the Council's approval - it is for the Member States to regulate all matters relating to the production and marketing of alcohol and alcoholic beverages on their own territory.

Obstacles to movement within the Community resulting from disparities between the national laws relating to the marketing of the products in question must be accepted in so far as those provisions may be recognised as being necessary in order to satisfy mandatory requirements relating in particular to the effectiveness of fiscal supervision, the protection of public health, the fairness of commercial transactions and the defence of the consumer.

9. The Government of the Federal Republic of Germany, intervening in the proceedings, put forward various arguments which, in its view, justify the application of provisions relating to the minimum alcohol content of alcoholic beverages, adducing considerations relating on the one hand to the protection of public health and on the other to the protection of the consumer against unfair commercial practices.

10. As regards the protection of public health the German Government states that the purpose of the fixing of minimum alcohol contents by national legislation is to avoid the proliferation of alcoholic beverages on the national market, in particular alcoholic beverages with a low alcohol content, since, in its view, such products may more easily induce a tolerance towards alcohol than more highly alcoholic beverages.

11. Such considerations are not decisive since the consumer can obtain on the market an extremely wide range of weakly or moderately alcoholic products and furthermore a large proportion of alcoholic beverages with a high alcohol content freely sold on the German market is generally consumed in a diluted form.

12. The German Government also claims that the fixing of a lower limit for the alcohol content of certain liqueurs is designed to protect the consumer against unfair practices on the part of producers and distributors of alcoholic beverages.

This argument is based on the consideration that the lowering of the alcohol content secures a competitive advantage in relation to beverages with a higher alcohol content, since alcohol constitutes by far the most expensive constituent of beverages by reason of the high rate of tax to which it is subject.

Furthermore, according to the German Government, to allow alcoholic products into free circulation wherever, as regards their alcohol content, they comply with the rules laid down in the country of production, would have the effect of imposing as a common standard within the Community the lowest alcohol content permitted in any of the Member States, and even of rendering any requirements in this field inoperative since a lower limit of this nature is foreign to the rules of several Member States.

13. As the Commission rightly observed, the fixing of limits in relation to the alcohol content of beverages may lead to the standardisation of products placed on the market and of their designations, in the interests of a greater transparency of commercial transactions and offers for sale to the public.

However, this line of argument cannot be taken so far as to regard the mandatory fixing of minimum alcohol contents as being an essential guarantee of the fairness of commercial transactions, since it is a simple matter to ensure that suitable information is conveyed to the purchaser by requiring the display of an indication of origin and of the alcohol content on the packaging of products.

14. It is clear from the foregoing that the requirements relating to the minimum alcohol content of alcoholic beverages do not serve a

purpose which is in the general interest and such as to take precedence over the requirements of the free movement of goods, which constitutes one of the fundamental rules of the Community.

In practice, the principle effect of requirements of this nature is to promote alcoholic beverages having a high alcohol content by excluding from the national market products of other Member States which do not answer that description.

It therefore appears that the unilateral requirement imposed by the rules of a Member State of a minimum alcohol content for the purposes of the sale of alcoholic beverages constitutes an obstacle to trade which is incompatible with the provisions of Article 30 of the Treaty.

There is therefore no valid reason why, provided that they have been lawfully produced and marketed in one of the Member States, alcoholic beverages should not be introduced into any other Member State; the sale of such products may not be subject to a legal prohibition on the marketing of beverages with an alcohol content lower than the limit set by the national rules.

15. Consequently, the first question should be answered to the effect that the concept of "measures having an effect equivalent to quantitative restrictions on imports" contained in Article 30 of the Treaty is to be understood to mean that the fixing of a minimum alcohol content for alcoholic beverages intended for human consumption by the legislation of a Member State also falls within the prohibition laid down in that provision where the importation of alcoholic beverages lawfully produced and marketed in another Member State is concerned.
.....

## II. PATENT KNOW-HOW, TRADEMARK AND RELATED LICENCES

### (1) Decision on the Raymond-Nagoya Agreement

Decision of the Commission of 9 June 1972 on an application for a negative clearance under Article 2 of Regulation No 17; J.O. No L 143, 23 June 1972, p. 39; (1972) CMLR D 45; CCH para. 9513; Competition Law CM/M/I/55.

*Facts and Decisions:* This decision concerns a patent know-how and utility models licence granted by the German subsidiary of the French Raymond firm, the biggest firm in its industry in the Common Market, to the Japanese Nagoya Rubber Co., the biggest sub-contractor in the motor industry , controlled by the Toyota motor company. The licensee obtains the right to manufacture in Japan and to sell in the Far East, applying the grantor's technique, plasting fixing components used in motor constructions; the grantor had undertaken to license no other firms in any part of the territory covered by the agreement.

Granting negative clearance, the Commission accepted the argument that the exclusive nature of the licence and the export ban (under which the licensee may sell only in his own territory) do not affect the competitive situation within the Common Market, given the special features of the particular case: the exclusive dealing arrangement has solely for effect to eliminate potential competitors on the Far East market, and because of the nature of the items concerned, their export from Japan to the Common Market is virtually ruled out (they are manufactured only to special order in class and constant association with the firm giving the order; if the items covered by the contract are incorporated into the spare parts or the coachwork of Japanese motor vehicles, they can be exported in this state to any country in the world).

An earlier version of the licensing contract provided that any improvements made by Nagoya to the Raymond technique would become the property of Raymond and that Nagoya was required to grant only to Raymond a licence on the ownership rights covering parallel inventions. However, following the Commission's intervention, the parties adjusted these commitments so that Nagoya is now only required to grant to Raymond a non-exclusive licence on the patents which it would obtain if improvements or changes were to be made to the Raymond technique.

Nagoya's undertaking not to challenge the validity of Raymond's contractual industrial property rights during the lifetime of the agreement was not found incompatible with Article 85(1), since it seems unlikely that the Japanese licensee would challenge the industrial property rights held by his co-contractor in Europe, since there was little or no possibility of such action succeeding. But, in principle, a non-objective clause of this kind involves a restraint of the freedom of action of the licensee which is not covered by the essential substance of the industrial property right: it prevents him from challenging the validity of the contract in order to reduce the royalties and have certain restrictions discontinued, an action which could strengthen competitive position while improving that of his outside undertakings interested in the manufacture of products under licence, and also improve the position of the users.

On the other hand, it must be possible to include quality control and information exchange within the contractual exploitation of the invention and of the know-how. Consequently, they do not constitute a restraint of competition covered by Article 85(1).

(2) Decision in re Davidson Rubber

Decision of the Commission of 9 June 1972 on a proceeding under Article 85 of the Treaty, J.O. No L 143, 23 June 1972, p. 31; (1972) CMLR D 52; CCH para. 9512; Competition Law CM/M/I/54.

*Facts:* In this decision the Commission exempted under Article 85(3) exclusive patent licensing and know-how concession contracts relating to a process for the manufacture of cushions and arm-rests for motor cars concluded by the American Davidson Rubber Company with its licensees in Germany, France and Italy.

In this case, the Commission took the view that the exclusive manufacturing and sales rights conferred by Davidson in its licensees, although tempered by a clause under which the items covered by the contract can be sold freely as between EEC Member States, was caught by the ban of Article 85(1), since curtailing the number of suppliers produces a perceptible effect on the play of competition and the development of trade between the Member States: the process concerned may be considered as the most important process for manufacturing armrests for motor cars, and Davidson's licensees account for about a third of the market in these items within the EEC.

However, the Commission recognised that the restraint of competition which derives from the Davidson's policy of exploiting its inventions by using exclusive licensees in the countries having large motor industries was a restriction without which the favourable objectives of the patent licences and know-how concessions could not possibly be achieved: it would not be reasonable to expect the licensees to agree to develop a new process and adapt it to the European market, setting up production facilities and hiring skilled staff, if they could not be sure that, within the conceded territories, Davidson would not licence competitors.

Although the position held by the licensees within the EEC was an important one, the Commission found that the agreements did not enable them to eliminate competition to a substantial extent, not only because there are other arm-rests and cushion manufacturers in the Common Market also accounting (together) for a third of the total production of these items, but also because the motor manufacturers, who themselves use various arm-rest shaping processes, account for about a third of their needs from their own resources and have a bargaining position in relation with their suppliers strong enough to avoid any one-sided imposition of terms.

Another important factor, in the Commission's assessment was that, even if each licensee normally supplies the firms having their principal places of business in the territory assigned to him, competition between the licensees is not eliminated, since they are not prevented from selling, and since they do in fact make sales of these items outside the territories for which they are more especially responsible.

In the same context, the decision points out that the clause, deleted during the investigation but contained in the original version of the know-how concession contract which one of the licensees had been instructed to conclude with the others, forbidding each party to export the items concerned to the territories of the other, would have stood in the way of exemption under Article 85(3).

Before exempting the agreements, the Commission had also required the deletion of the non-objection clause, which prevented the licensees from availing themselves of the opportunities provided to them by their national laws for escaping, through proceedings for annulment, from commitments to which they were held by their contracts; there was no evidence that the favourable objectives of the contracts could not be achieved without this clause.

*The Commission ruled:*

.....

7. Under Article 85(1) of the Treaty, the following practices shall be prohibited as incompatible with the Common Market: all agreements between undertakings, all decisions by associations of undertakings and all concerted practices which may affect trade between Member States and the object or effect of which is to prevent, restrict or distort competition within the Common Market.

By virtue of the licensing contracts which the Davidson Rubber Company has concluded with Happich GmbH, Gallino SpA and Maglum SA, the Davidson Rubber Company undertook to each of those undertakings to authorise no-one else to exploit its patents and its know-how concerning elbow-rests and cushions for cars in a defined part of the territory of the Common Market.

A patent confers on its holder the exclusive right to exploit the invention covered by it. The holder may cede, by licences, for a given territory, the use of the rights derived from its patent. However, if it undertakes to limit the exploitation of its exclusive right to a single undertaking in a territory and thus confers on that single undertaking the right to exploit the invention and to prevent other undertakings from using it, it thus loses the power to contract with other applicants for a licence. In certain cases such exclusive character of a licence relating to industrial property rights may restrict competition and be covered by the prohibtion set out in Article 85(1).

In the present case, as set out above, the Davidson process is the most important process for manufacture of elbow-rests for cars. The number of competing processes, like the number of manufacturers using them, is limited and the Davidson licensees hold a considerable share of the market in those articles in the EEC, if account is taken of the fact that the car manufactureres themselves manufacture large quantities for their own needs. In those circumstances, although mitigated by the provision that the sale of the contract articles can be freely made between Member States of the EEC, the exclusivity conferred by the Davidson Rubber Company to each of its licensees has the consequence, apart from the restriction of liberty on the Davidson Rubber Company, that the position of third parties, particularly the manufacturers of interior fitments for cars, who may wish to use the process in question is noticeably altered since they are prevented from exploiting this process within the Common Market.

The licensing contracts in question thus have the effect of noticeably restricting competition within the Common Market.

8. The exclusivity conferred by the Davidson Rubber Company on each of its licensees in a given territory within the Common Market prevents it giving third parties, through the grant of other licences, the possibility of also exploiting its patents and know-how in that territory and consequently of making any export from that territory to other parts of the Common Market. That restriction should therefore be considered as capable of affecting trade between Member States since it is such as to imperil directly or indirectly the freedom of trade between Member States in a way which could run counter to the realisation of the objectives of a single market between States.

The agreement in question thus falls within the field of application of Article 85(1) of the Treaty.

On the other hand, the contracts in which Stampaggio Resine Speciali SpA and the Compagnie Industrielle de Méchanismes took part contain no provisions which are capable of noticeably restricting competition within the Common Market and in particular they do not contribute to reinforcing the restriction following from the policy for the exploitation of its invention followed by the Davidson Rubber Company with the assistance of exclusive licensees. Since one of the conditions for the application of Article 85(1) is not met, a negative clearance can be issued in favour of those two contracts.

9. The other provision of the agreements concluded between the Davidson Rubber Company and its licensees Happich GmbH, Gallino SpA and

Maglum SA are not covered by Article 85(1) because they have neither the object nor the effect of noticeably restricting competition within the Common Market. In particular this applies:

(a) to the application on each exclusive licensee to grant the Davidson Rubber Company and its other licensees relating to any improvements which they have made to the Davidson process, given that that obligation is not exclusive and that each licensee thus preserves the possibility of passing on its experience to third parties and that it benefits from all the technical data which the Davidson Rubber Company has or may in the future acquire;

(b) to the obligation on the licensees to grant sub-licences only with the approval of the Davidson Rubber Company since both that obligation is covered by the exclusive right of the licensor and also it is justified by the latter's interest in its know-how not being divulged without its agreement to undertakings other than those which have been authorised to use it;

(c) to the obligation to submit all disputes to arbitration for the reason that the nature of the restriction and the wording of the agreements, which provides in particular that no clause may be invoked to prevent the sale between Member States of the licensing contract articles, do not permit arbitration awards which would alter the judgment of this case.

(3) Decision on the Kabelmetal-Luchaire Agreement

Decision of the Commission of 18 July 1975 on a proceeding under Article 85 of the Treaty; O.J. No L 222, 22 August 1975, p. 34; (1975) 2 CMLR D40; CCH para. 9761; Competition Law CM/M/I/93.

*Facts:* In pursuance of its policy of encouraging the grant of patent and know-how licences where they provide for the transfer of technology under suitable conditions and where the parties remain free to sell throughout the Common Market, the Commission gave exemption to an exclusive patent and know-how licensing agreement between the German firm Kabel- and Metallwerke Gutehoffnungshütte AG (Kabelmetal) and the French firm Ets. Luchaire SA.

The agreement covers the use of Kabel's cold extrustion policy, the main principles of which were covered by secret patents registered in Germany before the war; these have since expired. Under the agreement Kabelmetal gave Luchaire an exclusive licence for the manufacture in France of extruded stell components (pistons, shoch-absorbers, tubes) for the electrical engineering industry in general and the motor industry in particular, coupled with a non-exclusive licence for the sale of hese goods in all Common Market countries.

The Commission exempted the agreement from the prohibition in Article 85 on the grounds that the exclusivity it granted would help to promote technical and economic progress by providing the licensee with an incentive to work on the development of the licensed techniques although this required new investment. The Commission also took account of the fact that the firms concerned had deleted all the other restrictive clauses in the agreement - concerning the licensee's obligation to refrain from exporting to other EEC countries, to assign to the licensor property rights in any improvements to the processes and to refrain from challenging the patents.

The Commission drew particular attention to two provisions of the agreement: the most favoured licensee clause (whereby the licensor undertakes not to grant other licensees better terms than those granted to the first licensee) and the grantback clause (whereby the licensee undertakes to grant the licensor or other licensees in respect of improvements it may make to the basic processes). In certain circumstances, particularly on an oligopolistic market, these clauses might be anti-competitive, but this was not the case here since the clauses could not be regarded as having perceptible effects on market conditions in the EEC.

(4) Decision in re Bronbemaling-Heidemaatschappij Beheer NV

Decision of the Commission on a procedure under Article 85 of the EEC Treaty;
O.J. No. L 244, 25 September 1975, p. 27; (1975) 2 CMLR D67; CCH para. 9776; Competition Law CM/M/I94.

*Facts:* In a provisional Decision under Article 15(6) of Regulation No. 17, the Commission stated that in its opinion a clause in a patent licensing agreement relating to drainage of the water table, whereby the patentholder undertook not to grant additional licences without the prior consent of the majority of the parties - himself and the existing licencees - was caught by the prohibition in Article 85(1) and could not be exempted under Article 85(3).

The Decision was addressed to five Dutch firms in the drainage industry, one of them being the patentholder in question - Heidemaatschappij Beheer NV. The facts were as follows:

In 1965 and 1967 Heidemaatschappij applied to the Dutch Patent Office for the grant of a patent in respect of a process for the installation of a well-point drainage system consisting of filter tubes connected to pumps and of a well-point drainage system installed in this way. The process is designed to lower the water table and is of considerable economic importance, especially in the Netherlands, where both public authorities and private firms awarding contracts often specify that it must be used for major projects extending beyond Dutch frontiers, such as long-distance oil and gas pipelines.

The four other firms had opposed the grant of the patent to Heidemaatschappij on the ground that the process was already in general use. However, Heidemaatschappij reached an agreement with these firms, granting a licence to each of them and also undertaking to issue no further licence to other firms without first obtaining the consent of at least two of the four.

When another Dutch firm applied for a licence in 1971, the licensees withheld consent. The same occurred when a second firm, Zuid-Nederlandsche Bronbemaling, also applied for a licence in 1973.

The Commission's provisional Decision was issued in response to a complaint filed by Bronbemaling.

(5) Decision on the AOIP-Beyrard Agreement

Decision of the Commission of 2 December 1975 on a proceeding under Article 85 of the EEC Treaty; O.J. No. L 6, 13 January 1976, p. 8;

CCH para. 9801; Competition Law CM/M/I/97.

*Facts:* The Commission issued its first 'cease and desist' decision relating to a patent licensing agreement. This prohibits, as incompatible with Article 85, a number of clauses frequently found in patent licensing agreements. Four of the restrictions (no-challenge clause, non-competition clause, automatic extension of the duration of the agreement, payment of royalties even if the patent is not exploited) were held not to be capable of exemption, whereas two others (exclusivity and export ban) might have been exempted in different circumstances.

The Decision concerns a licensing agreement between the Association des Ouvriers en Instruments de Précision (AIOP), the licensee, and an inventor - Mr Beyrard - relating to existing and future patents for a number of liquid variable resistor electrical devices used principally in automatic starters for electric motors.

The agreement contained the following clauses which were regarded as within the prohibtion and unable to qualify for exemption because of their harmful effects on technical progress.

- Every newly lodged improvement patent extended the duration of the agreement. The Commission could not accept an extension of a patent licensing agreement beyond the duration of the most recent patent held at the time of the agreement, if the extension was automatic or was imposed unilaterally. The parties remained free, however, to enter into a subsequent agreement to extend the term of the original licence.

- The licensee was obliged to pay full royalties even after the expiry of the original patent and even if he was not exploiting any of the improvement patents. Litigation was initiated in the French courts on the subject of this clause, for on the expiry of the original patent the licensee decided to cease paying royalties whereas the licensor demanded payment until the expiry of the latest improvement patent. This clause could not be authorised, for its effect was to increase production costs with no economic justification and to weaken the licensee's competitive position. If subsequent improvement patents are exploited after expiry of the original patent, Community law does not prevent national law from recognising the right to a royalty reflecting the economic value of these patents as compared with that of the patents existing at the date of the agreement.

- The licensee was prohibited from challenging the validity of the licensor's patents. The Decision prohibits the no-challenge clause because it deprives the licensee of a means of removing an obstacle to his freedom of action. In any case it is not in the general interest that anyone concerned, including the licensee, be denied the opportunity to challenge patents wrongfully issued.

- The two sides were to refrain from competing with each other in the relevant markets. The Commission regarded this as a brake on technical progress, because the development of new and possibly better manufacturing processes in related areas was thereby made unprofitable.

The agreement contained two more clauses to which the Commission took exception:

- the licensee could not export to countries where the licensor had granted licences or assigned his patents to other firms (export ban);

- the licensor could not issue a manufacturing or sales licence in France (exclusivity).

The Commission considered that the licensor's obligations resulting from the grant of exclusive manufacturing and sales rights to the licensee were not of the essence of the patents and that the exclusive grant was caught by the prohibtion in Article 85(1). However, the Commission has already stated that in certain circumstances this restriction may be granted an exemption under Article 85(3). In two earlier cases, exclusive manufacturing licences were exempted because they assured the licensees of an adequate return on their investment.

In more general terms, an exclusive manufacturing and sales licence of limited duration qualifies for exemption if, for instance, it provides the licensee with an incentive to penetrate a geographic or product market not yet worked by the licensor.

With regard to the export ban, the Commission has reinforced its stand against a growing tendency by declaring that the protection of one licensee against competition from another licensee is not necessary to guarantee the existence of the patent right. Such bans are therefore caught by Article 85(1) and can be let through only if the tests of Article 85(3) are satisfied, as where a licensee is to be temporarily protected against the licensor or against other licensees and this is necessary in order to reduce the risk inherent in initial investments on a new market.

In this case the exclusivity clause and export ban were not allowed through the net because they formed an indivisible part of a set of restrictions which could not be exempted as a whole.

(6) Decision in re Campari

Decision of the Commission of 23 December 1977, O.J. No L 70, 13 March 1978; (1978) 2 CMLR 397, CCH para. 10.035; Competition Law CM/M/I/129.

*Facts and Decision:*

The Commission took a favourable Decision on the agreements whereby Davide Campari-Milano SpA granted an exclusive licence over its Bitter Capari trademark to Ognibeni & Co,Hans Prang, Campari-France SA, Sovinac SA and John M. Klein & Co. in the Netherlands, Germany, France, Belgium and Luxembourg and Denmark respectively. The licensees are required by these agreements to comply scrupulously with the assignor's instructions as to the manufacture of the relevant products, to ensure that the quality of the raw materials used meets the assignor's requirements and to buy from the assignor the herbal mixtures whose composition, a business secret, gives Bitter Campari its characteristic taste.

The Bitter Campari trademark and label were registered for use in most of the Community countries at the Bureau International de Berne at the beginning of this century.

The main point of interest in this decision is that the Commission can extend to exclusive trademark licences the favourable attitude it has taken on exclusive patent licences as in Davidson Rubber and Kabelmetal Luchaire. The Commission draws particular attention to two clauses - the ban on business in competing products by the licensees and the ban on active sales policies by all the parties outside their allotted territories. The Commission noted that these clauses allow the same benefits as can be obtained from exclusive distribution agreements authorised by the block exemption Regulation No 67/67/EEC.

The Decision also imposes obligations enabling the Commission to verify in good time what effects the agreements are having on exports between Community countries. The earlier version of the agreements prohibited exports to EEC countries. In response to Commission representations the parties deleted this clause and instead undertook to do all they could to meet export orders from EEC countries. They also undertake to help customers who wish to export the products to other EEC countries to obtain redemption from excise duties on alcohol where permitted by tax regulations. They are required to report annually to the Commission on this point.

(7) Communication in re Persil

Informal settlement; Seventh Report on Competition Policy 1977, page 108-110.

*Facts and settlement:*

At the Commission's request Henkel KGaA, Dusseldorf, and Unilever NV, Rotterdam, acting for the Unilever Group, stated that they would not prevent the marketing of Persil washing powder manufactured by either of them even in Member States where the Persil trade mark belonged to the other. Henkel holds the Persil trade mark in Germany, Belgium, Luxembourg, the Netherlands, Italy and Denmark. The trade mark is compounded from the words PER(borate) and SIL(icate). The Unilever Group holds the trade mark in the United Kingdom and France, either directly, or indirectly through group subsidiaries.

The British trade mark belonging to Lever Brothers Ltd, a member of the Unilever Group, has the same origin as Henkel's German trade mark. It was registered in 1970 by the company whose name at the time was Henkel & Co. and was assigned to Joseph Crossfield & Sons Ltd in 1911. The latter firm was subsequently taken over by the Unilever Group.

The French Persil trade mark registered by Lever SA, Paris, a member of the Unilever Group, is of dual origin. Henkel & Co registered it in 1907, but since 1906 there had already been a registered trade mark of a very different appearance; it represented a sprig of parsley (persil) in French) with the word Persil accompanying it, rather than just the word Persil on its own. Later the two trade marks came into the hands of a single holder and were assigned to the Unilever Group after the First World War. The first application for renewal of the trade mark in 1923 was based expressly on the two registrations of 1906 and 1907; the appearance of the trade mark in the application for renewal corresponds to the 1907 registration by Henkel & Co. The Commission concluded that the French Persil trade mark has the same origin as the German mark, but this was contested by the Unilever Group. However, the question can, in the meantime, remain unanswered, in view of the statement made by the two firms.

The two firms used their trade marks in order to prevent imports: Henkel KGaA tried, sometimes unsuccessfully, to prevent imports of cheaper Persil from the UK into Germany; the courts before whom the resulting dispute was brought referred sometimes to trademark law and sometimes to the law relating to unfair competition. The Unilever Group for its part tried, again with some success, to prevent imports of Henkel's Persil from Belgium and Luxembourg into France, working through its French subsidiary Lever SA. There was correspondence between the two firms in 1975, and Henkel wrote it would 'do all we can to prevent the sale of these goods from both Belgium and Luxembourg in France'. Unilever replied that 'we have asked our companies in the UK and France to take equally stringent precautions to try to avoid any flow of Persil from their country into those areas of Europe where the trademark belongs to the Henkel company'.

Henkel also obtained written confirmation from a large number of German distributors that they would no longer distribute Persil originating in the UK.

The Commission concluded that geographical market-sharing was therefore being infringed. In the course of the case the two firms agreed to make the statement referred to above.

The two firms have been in contact to discuss the presentation of their respective trademarks. They have reached a solution which will not involve any formal agreement or undertaking. Henkel and its group companies now have the word Persil in red letters with the word Henkel in smaller letters in a red oval. The Unilever group uses a green Persil trademark.

Even if these contacts between Henkel and Unilever were to constitute a concerted practice within the meaning of Article 85(1), the Commission does not believe that the Treaty rules on competition are violated. An agreement on the presentation of certain trademarks aiming to ensure that there can be no confusion in the consumer's mind as to the difference between the relevant goods, which can then be circulated freely throughout the Community with none of the manufacturers being prevented from using his own trademarks, is clearly inspired by the desire to preserve the existence of the trademark and is accordingly outside the prohibition in Article 85(1).

Having received the statement made by the two firms, the Commission terminated the two proceedings that it had initiated. It acknowledges the concern of these firms to reach a solution which is consistent with the constraints of the common market, even in a difficult situation involving a well known brand-name.

(8) Decision in re Penneys

Commission decision in re Penney trademark; Decision of 23 December 1977, O.J. No L 260, 2 February 1978; Competition Law CM/M/I/126.

*Facts and Decision:* In this case the Commission issued a Decision authorising an agreement entered into in February 1976 by J.C. Penney Inc., New York (Penney America), and Penney's Ltd, Dublin (Penney's Ireland), a subsidiary of Associated British Foods (ABF). The object of the agreement is to settle a conflict which arose between the two companies in most of the Community Member States concerning their respective rights to use the name Penney's as a trademark and business name.

The two companies operate large clothing and textile retail shops. Penney America, which is one of the largest distribution firms in the United States, distributes its goods in the Community under the Penneys trademark, notably through the Sarma chain of supermarkets in Belgium and its sales subsidiaries in other Member States. Penney's Ireland is one of the largest textile distributors in Ireland.

Under the agreements all rights to the Penney's trademark in the Community are conferred on Penney's America. Penney's branded products can thus circulate freely throughout the common market. The agreement imposes the following obligations:

(i) Penney's Ireland assigns the French Penney's trademark, already registered, and the Irish Penney's trademark, currently in the process of registration, to Penney America;

(ii) Penney's Ireland will not contest the validity of Penney's trademark registered by Penney America in the Community during the first five years following the date of the agreement;

(iii) Penney's Ireland undertakes to refrain from using the name Penney's either as a business name or as a trademark except in Ireland, and then only as the name of its retail shops;

(iv) Penney America may sell its Penney's branded products in all Member States including Ireland;

(v) Penney America undertakes to pay a determined amount of money to Penneys Ireland.

As a result, the voluminous litigation between the two companies came to an end. Had there been no agreement, Penney's Ireland was likely to have won the battle in Ireland and France whereas Penney America would have been successful in other Member States, as was already the case in England and Wales following an injunction issued by the High Court of England. Each would then have had a reserved territory which the other side's branded products could not have penetrated.

The Commission considers that firms in this sort of position must seek the least restrictive solution so that the free movement of goods in the Community is not hampered.

A contractual obligation upon the parties to assign or renounce their trademark or business name rights, which would entail recreating the goodwill under other names, can have a substantial anti-competitive effect for the purpose of Article 85(1) of the EEC Treaty and therefore must be exempted under Article 85(3) to be valid.

But in the present case the Commission considered that the agreement was not substantially anti-competitive and therefore qualified for negative clearance. The agreement does not require Penney's Ireland to recreate its goodwill under another name, as it was already doing substantial and quite successful business with another trademark, even before the agreement.

<u>(9) Decision in re Toltecs-Dorcet</u>
Commission Decision of 15 December 1982 in re agreement between P.L. Segers & Zonen and BAT Cigaretten-Fabrieken; O.J. No L 379, 31 December 1982, p. 19; (1983) CMLR 412; CCH para. 10459; Competition Law CM/M/I/188.

*The Commission held:*

II. Applicability of Article 85 (1) of the EEC Treaty

1. Article 85(1) of the EEC Treaty prohibits, as incompatible with the Common Market, all agreements between undertakings which may affect trade between Member States and which have as their object or effect the prevention, restriction or distortion of competition within the Common Market.

2. The agreement between Mr Segers and BAT is an agreement between undertakings within the meaning of Article 85(1).

3. The agreement contains clauses which have as their object and effect the restriction of competition within the common market.

A. By virtue of the first half of Clauses 3, 4 and 5 of the agreement, as applied by the parties from the outset onwards, Mr Segers may not without BAT's consent import fine cut tobacco under the Toltecs trade-mark into the Federal Republic of Germany nor market it there.

(a) The agreement thus keeps Mr Segers' fine cut out of the German market or at least so restricts his freedom to compete that his products can be distributed only through an importer acceptable to BAT or subject to further conditions imposed by BAT, e.g. taking over the remaining Toltecs tobacco stocked by Peter Grassmann GmbH. The object of the agreement is therefore a restriction of competition within the meaning of Article 85(1).

This is not refuted by BAT's argument that the agreement must objectively be construed as merely restricting Mr Segers' freedom to advertise and that no other further restrictions on Mr Segers can be inferred from the erroneous legal position adopted by BAT after conclusion of the agreement.

BAT took up this legal position as early as 1976 when Müller-Broder began to distribute Toltecs fine cut. As a result, and in conjunction with the admittedly ambiguous wording of the agreement, Mr Segers was constrained to behave as if the agreement contained the sales ban alleged by BAT. He accordingly had to discontinue the marketing of his fine cut in the Federal Republic of Germany. If he did not want to submit to BAT's conditions or run the risk of becoming involved in costly litigation - which he could not afford - with a firm in a strong financial position like BAT.

Even if in the future the contracts were to be applied only with the meaning that BAT now seeks to attach to it, i.e. that it imposed on Mr Segers only the obligation to refrain from publicising the suitability of his Toltecs fine cut for rolling cigarettes, this would constitute a restriction of Mr Segers' freedom to make use of a feature of importance to competition and would be caught by Article

(b) The agreement also results in a restriction of competition between BAT and third parties. It is not only Mr Segers who is precluded from the unhampered marketing of his product in the Federal Republic of Germany; the restrictions of competition also affect independent trading companies that may wish to sell products bearing the Toltecs mark in the Federal Republic of Germany. This applies in particular to Planta GmbH and Co., Berlin; BAT prevailed upon Planta to forgo distribution of Toltecs fine cut by drawing attention to the agreement with Mr Segers and the alleged confusion between Dorcet and Toltecs marks.

(c) It cannot be argued that Article 85(1) does not apply because the exclusion effected by the agreement could also be achieved by BAT through unilateral assertion of the rights arising from the Dorcet mark with the result that there is no relationship of cause and effect between the agreement and the restriction of competition.

In its judgment in Terrapin v. Terranova, the Court of Justice made it clear that in the present state of Community law claims may be asserted under trade mark law to prevent the import of a product bearing a mark giving rise to confusion, despite the restrictive effect on competition, provided that the respective rights have arisen independently of one another and that the undertakings concerned have no economic or legal ties.

BAT maintains that this principle, which applies to a right arising under legislation, is also applicable to a 'delimitation' agreement under which such a right is in part exercised and in part waived in favour of the other party. BAT did no more, it alleges, than to reserve to itself the right, to which it was entitled in the Federal Republic of Germany where it held the prior mark, to impose the import of fine cut tobacco under the Toltecs mark in certain cases. The agreement was thus in all respects advantageous to Mr Segers, for he could still use the Toltecs mark in the Federal Republic of Germany in certain circumstances; in the final result it promoted competition. In concept this legal assessment is well founded, but is inapplicable here in the light of the particular facts of the case.

(d) In the present state of Community law, in cases where the products are similar, there is a serious likelihood of confusion and the owner of the prior mark is therefore more likely to be in a position to prevent registration and use of the later mark, restrictions on the use of a later mark do not restrict competition within the meaning of Article 85(1), for in accordance with the case law of the Court of Justice the right to prevent marketing relates to the existence of the prior mark.

(e) However, the greater the difference in the products or the less likely the risk of confusion, the more the agreement must take account of the overriding goal of common market unity. Of all the possible solutions to the conflict, the parties therefore have to adopt that which least restricts the use of both marks throughout the whole of the common market. This includes agreements to reproduce the disputed mark only in a certain way (colour, form of lettering, inclusion of trade name, etc.) or possibly to use it for certain products only.

The Commission recognises the latitude that may exist in the appreciation of such cases both as concerns the relevant national law and as concerns the parties; this is a further factor that must be taken into account when Article 85(1) is applied.

(f) In this case, however, in its scrutiny of the agreement pursuant to Article 85, the Commission cannot find any serious risk of confusion between the word mark Dorcet and the word/device mark Toltecs. There is still no serious risk of visual or phonetic confusion if the pictorial component registered and used by Mr Segers (a wooden shovel lying across four tobacco leaves depicted within a distinctively-shaped gold ground) is disregarded, and the words Dorcet and Toltecs are compared. BAT's assertion that the marks sound similar and are therefore likely to be confused does not change this finding.

Contrary to BAT's viewpoint it is not merely national trademark law that underlies the question whether two marks of different origin are likely to be confused. As the Court of Justice stated in Terrapin v. Terranova, the application of Community law (*viz.* the rules on the free movement of goods and on competition) may be involved. The greater the scope of the protection which national law affords to the Dorcet mark, the greater the restriction on the import into the Federal Republic of Germany of goods bearing the Toltecs mark.

B. In the second half of clause 3, Mr Segers undertakes to claim no rights as against BAT arising from his registration and use of the Toltecs mark, not even if BAT does not use its Dorcet mark for more than five years or if it applies again for registration of this mark or a mark capable of being confused with it within the meaning of section 31 of the German trademark law (other than Toltecs Special).

(a) BAT first put forward the view, in its letter to the Commission dated 9 September 1980, that this clause put Mr Segers under a fully comprehensive obligation, admissible in law, to refrain from challenging the Dorcet mark, even after expiry of the five-year period. After receiving the Commission's statement of objections, however, BAT amended its view to concede that the clause would not prevent Mr Segers from having the Dorcet mark cancelled on grounds of non-use.

(b) Yet even under BAT's amended view, the clause serves to reinforce an agreement which restricts competition (see II(3)A) and is caught by Article 85(1). The clause prevents Mr Segers from freely asserting as against BAT the rights which have arisen in the meantime from his Toltecs mark in the event of the Dorcet mark being cancelled on the grounds of non-use. This clause would also restrict Segers' rights if Dorcet were in fact to lose priority over Toltecs as a result of BAT's using the Dorcet mark for the first time after expiry of the five-year period or of a new application for registration. The clause prevents Mr Segers from invoking the priority of his mark Toltecs against the Dorcet mark in the event of the coming into use or being registered again at a later date. Mr Segers has thus abandoned a ground for defence which is much easier to rely upon than a contestation of confusability. Finally, it was made difficult for Mr Segers to release himself from contractual restriction on registration and use of his Toltecs mark and thus to eliminate a barrier to his economic activity in the Federal Republic.

In conjunction with the contractual restriction on the registration and use of his Toltecs mark the object of the no-challenge clause is to prevent for all time legitimate extension of the mark's field of application, thereby strengthening BAT's position under trademark law.

Contrary to the view expressed in BAT's abovementioned letter of 9 September 1980, Mr Segers' contractual renunciation of his right to attack non-use of the Dorcet mark must be disregarded for the purposes of the application of Article 85. The overriding public interest in the cancellation of trademarks that are not used or that can be challenged on other grounds requires that neither Mr Segers nor any third party should be prevented from taking steps to obtain such a cancellation with all its repercussions.

(c) BAT's objection that the user requirement, as for example in the Federal Republic of Germany pursuant to the Law of 4 December 1967 is not yet a concept acknowledged by Community law since it was first provided for in the draft Council Regulation on Community trademarks and is unknown in Danish law, is on factual ground irrelevant. The object of the user requirement is to avoid overloading the trademark register with unused prior marks, in order to facilitate the registration of new marks for new products and their entry into the market. This reflects the fact that there is a mathematical limit to possible combinations of letters of the alphabet for word marks and even then not all the possible combinations are made up of syllables that can be pronounced. As a result of the unlimited maintenance of unused prior marks in many countries, including several Member States, new marks based on letters are no longer available. Within the Community this is true in particular for France, with 301 711 marks registered, for the Federal Republic of Germany with 285 317 marks and for the United Kingdom with 244 100 marks. In contrast, there are only 86 753 registered marks in Denmark. In the light of these circumstances it follows that agreements which hinder the registration and use of new marks in a Member State with a large number of marks are more serious infringements of Article 85 than in Member States with a small number of marks.

4. The abovementioned clauses of the agreement are also apt to affect trade between Member States. They impede free import and export of the goods covered by the agreement from the Netherlands to the Federal Republic of Germany by raising artificial barriers to trade in a manner which jeopardises attainment of the goal of a single market.

The restriction of competition and its direct effect on intra-Community trade are also appreciable. In its Decision 75/297/EEC (Sirdar/Phildar), the Commission has already pointed out that it is problematical, if not impossible on economic grounds, to replace an established mark by another mark, because of the consequent loss of the advertising impact of the established mark and other practical difficulties. In this case the mark Toltecs has been in use for a number of years and almost one third of Mr Segers' export of tobacco products to the Federal Republic of Germany have borne this mark. Since then Mr Segers' production has increased considerably, while his exports to the Federal Republic of Germany have fallen to almost nil, although demand for Dutch fine cut in the Federal Republic of Germany continues to expand.

In view of the structure of the German tobacco market, which is dominated by a few large undertakings, even the restriction of a small supplier from another Member State is particularly serious, all the more so since BAT has entered into numerous similar agreements.

## Literature

Van Empel: Centrafarm revisited: a few comments on cases 102/77 and 3/78. (1979) CMLRev. 251-258.

Leuvenheim: Trademarks and free competition within the European Economic Community.
XXI Anti Trust Bulletin 727.

Waelbroeck: The effect of the Rome Treaty on the exercise of national industrial property rights,
XXI Anti Trust Bulletin 99.

J.D.C. Turner: Competition and the Common Market after Maize Seeds. (April 1983). 103.

Annex I

## REGULATION No 17/62/EEC[1] OF THE COUNCIL

of 6 February 1962

First Regulation implementing Articles 85 and 86 of the Treaty modified and completed by Regulation 59/62/EEC[2], by Regulation 118/63/EEC[3], by Regulation 2822/71/EEC[4] and amended by the Act of Accession[5] and the Act of Accession of the Hellenic Republic[6]

THE COUNCIL OF THE EUROPEAN ECONOMIC COMMUNITY,

Having regard to the Treaty establishing the European Economic Community, and in particular Article 87 thereof;

Having regard to the proposal from the Commission;

Having regard to the Opinion of the Economic and Social Committee;

Having regard to the Opinion of the European Parliament;

Whereas, in order to establish a system ensuring that competition shall not be distorted in the common market, it is necessary to provide for balanced application of Articles 85 and 86 in a uniform manner in the Member States;

Whereas in establishing the rules for applying Articles 85(3) account must be taken of the need to ensure effective supervision and to simplify administration to the greatest possible extent;

Whereas it is accordingly necessary to make it obligatory, as a general principle, for undertakings which seek application of Article 85(3) to notify to the Commission their agreements, decisions and concerted practices;

Whereas, on the one hand, such agreements, decisions and concerted practices are probably very numerous and cannot therefore all be examined at the same time and, on the other hand, some of them have special features which may make them less prejudicial to the development of the common market;

Whereas there is consequently a need to make more flexible arrangements for the time being in respect of certain categories of agreement, decision and concerted practice without prejudging their validity under Article 85;

Whereas it may be in the interest of undertakings to know whether any agreements, decisions or practices to which they are party, or propose to become party, may lead to action on the part of the Commission pursuant to Article 85(1) or Article 86;

Whereas in order to secure uniform application of Articles 85 and 86 in the common market, rules must be made under which the Commission acting in close and constant liaison with the competent authorities of the Member States, may take the requisite measures for applying those Articles;

Whereas for this purpose the Commission must have the co-operation of the competent authorities of the Member States and be empowered throughout the common market, to require such information to be supplied and to undertake such investigations as are necessary to bring to light any agreement, decision or concerted practice prohibited by Article 85(1) or any abuse of a dominant position prohibited by Article 86;

Whereas, in order to carry out its duty of ensuring that the provisions of the Treaty are applied, the Commission must be empowered to address to undertakings or associations of undertakings recommendations and decisions for the purpose of bringing to an end infringements of Articles 85 and 86;

Whereas compliance with Articles 85 and 86 and the fulfilment of obligations imposed on undertakings and associations of undertakings under this Regulation must be enforceable by means of fines and periodic penalty payments;

Whereas undertakings concerned must be accorded the right to be heard by the Commission, third parties whose interests may be affected by a decision must be given the opportunity of submitting their comments beforehand, and it must be ensured that wide publicity is given to decisions taken;

Whereas all decisions taken by the Commission under this Regulation are subject to review by the Court of Justice under the conditions specified in the Treaty; whereas, it is moreover desirable to confer upon the Court of Justice, pursuant to Article 172, unlimited jurisdiction in respect of decisions under which the Commission imposes fines or periodic penalty payments;

Whereas this Regulation may enter into force without prejudice to any other provisions that may hereafter be adopted pursuant to Article 87;

HAS ADOPTED THIS REGULATION:

Art. 1. *Basic provision.* Without prejudice to Articles 6, 7 and 23 of this Regulation, agreements, decisions and concerted practices of the kind described in Article 85(1) of the Treaty and the abuse of a dominant position in the market, within the meaning of Article 86 of the Treaty, shall be prohibited, no prior decision to that effect being required.

Art. 2. *Negative clearance.* Upon application by the undertakings or associations of undertakings concerned, the Commission may certify that, on the basis of the facts in its possession, there are no grounds under Article 85(1) or Article 86 of the Treaty for action on its part in respect of an agreement, decision or practice.

Art. 3. *Termination of Infringements.* 1. Where the Commission, upon application or upon its own intiative, finds that there is infringement of Article 85 or Article 86 of the Treaty, it may by decision require the undertakings or associations of undertakings concerned to bring such infringement to an end.

2. Those entitled to make application are:

(a) Member States;

(b) natural or legal persons who claim a legitimate interest.

3. Without prejudice to the other provisions of this Regulation, the Commission may, before taking a decision under paragraph 1, address to the undertakings or associations of undertakings concerned recommendations for termination of the infringement.

Art. 4. *Notification of new agreements, decisions and practices.*
1. Agreements, decisions and concerted practices of the kind described in Article 85(1) of the Treaty which come into existence after the entry into force of this Regulation and in respect of which the parties seek application of Article 85(3) must be notified to the Commission. Until they have been notified, no decision in application of Article 85(3) may be taken.

2. Paragraph 1 shall not apply to agreements, decisions and[7] concerted practices where:

(1) the only parties thereto are undertakings from one Member State and the agreements, decisions or practices do not relate either to imports or to exports between Member States;

(2) not more than two undertakings are party thereto, and the agreements only:

    (a) restrict the freedom of one party to the contract in determining the prices or conditions of business upon which the goods which he has obtained from the other party to the contract may be resold; or

    (b) impose restrictions on the exercise of the rights of the assignee or user of industrial property rights - in particular patents, utility models, designs or trade marks - or of the person entitled under a contract to the assignment, or grant, of the right to use a method of manufacture or knowledge relating to the use and to the application of industrial processes;

(3) they have as their sole object:

    (a) the development or uniform application of standards or types; or

    (b) joint research and development[8],

    (c) specialisation in the manufacture of products, including agreements necessary for achieving this,

- where the products which are the subject of specialisation do not, in a substantial part of the Common Market, represent more than 15% of the volume of business done in identical products or those considered by consumers to be similar by reason of their characteristics, price and use, and

- where the total annual turnover of the participating undertakings does not exceed 200 million units of account.

These agreements, decisions and practices may be notified to the Commission.[9]

Art. 5. *Notification of existing agreements, decisions and practices.* 1. Agreements, decisions and concerted practices of the kind described in Article 85(1) of the Treaty which are in existence at the date of entry into force of this Regulation and in respect of which the parties seek application of Article 85(3) shall be notified to the Commission before 1 November 1962. However notwithstanding the foregoing provisions any agreements, decisions and concerted practices to which not more than two undertakings are party shall be notified before 1 February 1963.[10]

2. Paragraph 1 shall not apply to agreements, decisions or concerted practices falling within Article 4(2); these may be notified to the Commission.

Art. 6. *Decisions pursuant ot Article 85(3).* 1. Whenever the Commission takes a decision pursuant to Article 85(3) of the Treaty, it shall specify therein the date from which the decision shall take effect. Such date shall not be earlier than the date of notification.

2. The second sentence of paragraph 2 shall not apply to agreements, decisions or concerted practices falling within Article 4(2) and Article 5(2), nor to those falling within Article 5(1) which have been notified within the time limit specified in Article 5(1).

Art. 7. *Special provisions for existing agreements, decisions and practices.* 1. Where agreements, decisions and concerted practices in existence at the date of entry into force of this Regulation and notified within the time limits specified in Article 5(1) do not satisfy the requirements of Article 85(3) of the Treaty and the undertakings or associations of undertakings concerned cease to give effect to them or modify them in such manner that they no longer fall within the prohibition contained in Article 85(1) or that they satisfy the requirements of Article 83(3), the prohibition contained in Article 85(1) shall apply only for a period fixed by the Commission. A decision by the Commission pursuant to the foregoing sentence shall not apply as against undertakings and associations of undertakings which did not expressly consent to the notification.

2. Paragraph 1 shall apply to agreements, decisions and concerted practices falling within Article 4(2) which are in existence at the date of entry into force of this Regulation if they are notified before 1 January 1967.[11]

Art. 8. *Duration and revocation of decisions under Article 85(3).* 1. A decision in application of Article 85(3) of the Treaty shall be issued for a specified period and conditions and obligations may be attached thereto.

2. A decision may on application be renewed if the requirements of Article 85(3) of the Treaty continue to be satisfied.

3. The Commission may revoke or amend its decision or prohibit specified acts by the parties:

(a) where there had been a change in any of the facts which were basic to the making of the decision;

(b) where the parties commit a breach of any obligation attached to the decision;

(c) where the decision is based on incorrect information or was induced by deceit;

(d) where the parties abuse the exemption from the provisions of the Treaty granted to them by the decision.

In cases to which subparagraphs (b), (c) or (d) apply, the decision may be revoked with retroactive effect.

Art. 9. *Powers.* 1. Subject to review of its decisions by the Court of Justice, the Commission shall have sole power to declare Article 85(1) inapplicable pursuant to Article 85(3) of the Treaty.

2. The Commission shall have power to apply Article 85(1) and Article 86 of the Treaty; this power may be exercised notwithstanding that the time limits specified in Article 5(1) and in Article 7(2) relating to notification have not expired.

3. As long as the Commission has not initiated any procedure under Articles 2, 3 or 6, the authorities of the Member States shall remain competent to apply Article 85(1) and Article 86 in accordance with Article 88 of the Treaty; they shall remain competent in this respect notwithstanding that the time limits specified in Article 5(1) and in Article 7(2) relating to notification have not expired.

Art. 10. *Liaison with the authorities of the Member States.*
1. The Commission shall forthwith transmit to the competent authorities of the Member States a copy of the applications and notifications together with copies of most of the most important documents lodged with the Commission for the purpose of establishing the existence of infringements of Articles 85 or 86 of the Treaty or of obtaining negative clearance or a decision in application of Article 85(3).

2. The Commission shall carry out the procedure set out in paragraph 1 in close and constant liaison with the competent authorities of the Member States; such authorities shall have the right to express their views upon that procedure.

3. An Advisory Committee on Restrictive Practices and Monopolies shall be consulted prior to the taking of any decision following upon a procedure under paragraph 1, and of any decision concerning the renewal, amendment or revocation of a decision pursuant to Article 85(3) of the Treaty.

4. The Advisory Committee shall be composed of officials competent in the matter of restrictive practices and monopolies. Each Member State shall appoint an official to represent it who, if prevented from attending, may be replaced by another official.

5. The consultation shall take place at a joint meeting convened by the Commission; such meeting shall be held not earlier than fourteen days after dispatch of the notice convening it. The notice shall, in respect of each case to be examined, be accompanied by a summary of the case together with an indication of the most important documents, and a preliminary draft decision.

6. The Advisory Committee may deliver an opinion notwithstanding that some of its members or their alternates are not present. A report of the outcome of the consultative proceedings shall be annexed to the draft decision. It shall not be made public.

Art. 11. *Requests for information.* 1. In carrying out the duties assigned to it in Article 89 and by provisions adopted under Article 87 of the Treaty, the Commission may obtain all necessary information from the Governments and competent authorities of the Member States and from undertakings and associations of undertakings.

2. When sending a request for information to an undertaking or association of undertakings, the Commission shall at the same time forward a copy of the request to the competent authority of the Member State in whose territory the seat of the undertaking or association of undertakings is situated.

3. In its request the Commission shall state the legal basis and the purpose of the request and also the penalties provided for in Article 15(1)(b) for supplying incorrect information.

4. The owners of the undertakings or their representatives and, in the case of legal persons, companies or firms, or of associations having no legal personality, the persons authorised to represent them by law or by their constitution shall supply the information requested.

5. Where an undertaking or association of undertakings does not supply the information requested within the time limit fixed by the Commission, or supplies incomplete information, the Commission shall by decision require the information to be supplied. The decision shall specify what information is required, fix an appropriate time limit within which it is to be supplied and indicate the penalties provided for in Article 15(1)(b) and Article 16(1)(c) and the right to have the decision reviewed by the Court of Justice.

6. The Commission shall at the same time forward a copy of its decision to the competent authority of the Member State in whose territory the seat of the undertaking or association of undertakings is situated.

Art. 12. *Inquiry into sectors of the economy.* 1. If in any sector of the economy the trend of trade between Member States, price movements, inflexibility of prices or other circumstances suggest that in the economic sector concerned competition is being restricted or distorted within the common market, the Commission may decide to conduct a general inquiry into that economic sector and in the course thereof may request undertakings in the sector concerned to supply the information necessary for giving effect to the principles formulated in Article 85 and 86 of the Treaty and for carrying out the duties entrusted to the Commission.

2. The Commission may in particular request every undertaking or association of undertakings in the economic sector concerned to communicate to it all agreements, decisions and concerted practices which are exempt from notification by virtue of Article 4(2) and Article 5(2).

3. When making enquiries pursuant to paragraph 2, the Commission shall also request undertakings or groups of undertakings whose size suggests that they occupy a dominant position within the common market or a substantial part thereof to supply to the Commission such particulars of the structure of the undertakings and of their behaviour as are requisite to an appraisal of their position in the light of Article 86 of the Treaty.

4. Article 10(3) to (6) and Articles 11, 13 and 14 shall apply correspondingly.

Art. 13. *Investigations by the authorities of the Member States.*
1. At the request of the Commission, the competent authorities of the Member States shall undertake the investigations which the Commission considers to be necessary under Article 14(1), or which it has ordered by decision pursuant to Article 14(3). The officials of the competent authorities of the Member States responsible for conducting these investigations shall exercise their powers upon production of an authorisation in writing issued by the competent authority of the Member State in whose territory the investigation is to be made. Such authorisation shall specify the subject matter and purpose of the investigation.

2. If so requested by the Commission or by the competent authority of the Member State in whose territory the investigation is to be made, the officials of the Commission may assist the officials of such authorities in carrying out their duties.

Art. 14. *Investigating powers of the Commission.* 1. In carrying out the duties assigned to it by Article 89 and by provisions adopted under Article 87 of the Treaty, the Commission may undertake all necessary investigations into undertakings into undertakings and associations of undertakings. To this end the officials authorised by the Commission are empowered:

(a) to examine the books and other business records;

(b) to take copies of or extracts from the books and business records;

(c) to ask for oral explanations on the spot;

(d) to enter any premises, land and means of transport of undertakings.

2. The officials of the Commission authorised for the purpose of these investigations shall exercise their powers upon production of an authorisation in writing specifying the subject matter and purpose of the investigation and the penalties provided for in Article 15(1)(c) in cases where production of the required books or other business records is incomplete. In good time before the investigation, the Commission shall inform the competent authority of the Member State in whose territory the same is to be made of the investigation and of the identity of the authorised officials.

3. Undertakings and associations of undertakings shall submit to investigations ordered by decision of the Commission.The decision shall specify the subject matter and purpose of the investigation, appoint the date on which it is to begin and indicate the penalties provided for in Article 15(1)(c) and Article 16(1)(d) and the right to have the decision reviewed by the Court of Justice.

4. The Commission shall take decisions referred to in paragraph 3 after consultation with the competent authority of the Member State in whose territory the investigation is to be made.

5. Officials of the competent authority of the Member State in whose territory the investigation is to be made may, at the request of such authority or of the Commission, assist the officials of the Commission in carrying out their duties.

6. Where an undertaking opposes an investigation ordered pursuant to this Article, the Member State concerned shall afford the necessary assistance to the officials authorised by the Commission to enable them to make their investigation. Member States shall, after consultation with the Commission, take the necessary measures to this end beofre 1 October 1962.

Art. 15. *Fines*. 1. The Commission may by decision impose on undertakings or associations of undertakings fines of from 100 to 5 000 units of account where, intentionally or negligently:

(a) they supply incorrect or misleading information in an application pursuant to Article 2 or in a notification pursuant to Articles 4 or 5; or

(b) they supply incorrect information in response to a request made pursuant to Article 11(3) or (5) or to Article 12, or do not supply information within the time limit fixed by a decision taken under Article 11(5); or

(c) they produce the required books or other business records in incomplete form during investigations under Article 13 or 14, or refuse to submit to an investigation ordered by decision issued in implementation of Article 14(3).

2. The Commission may by decision impose on undertakings or associations of undertakings fines of from 1 000 to 1 000 000 units of account, or a sum in excess thereof but not exceeding 10% of the turnover in the preceding business year of each of the undertakings participating in the infringement where, either intentionally or negligently:

(a) they infringe Article 85(1) or Article 86 of the Treaty; or

(b) they commit a breach of any obligation imposed pursuant to Article 8(1).

In fixing the amount of the fine, regard shall be had both to the gravity and to the duration of the infringement.

3. Article 10(3) to (6) shall apply.

4. Decisions taken pursuant to paragraphs 1 and 2 shall not be of a

criminal law nature.

5. The fines provided for in paragraph 2(a) shall not be imposed in respect of acts taking place:

(a) after notification to the Commission and before its decision in application of Article 85(3) of the Treaty, provided they fall within the limits of the activity described in the notification;

(b) before notification and in the course of agreements, decisions or concerted practices in existence at the date of entry into force of this Regulation, provided that notification was effected within the time limits specified in Article 5(1) and Article 7(2).

6. Paragraph shall not have effect where the Commission has informed the undertakings concerned that after preliminary examination it is of opinion that Article 85(1) of the Treaty applies and that application of Article 85(3) is not justified.

Art. 16. *Periodic penalty payments.* 1. The Commission may by decision impose on undertakings or associations of undertakings periodic penalty payments of from 50 to 1 000 units of account per day, calculated from the date appointed by the decision, in order to compel them:

(a) to put an end to an infringement of Article 85 or 86 of the Treaty, in accordance with a decision taken pursuant to Article 3 of this Regulation;

(b) to refrain from any act prohibited under Article 8(3);

(c) to supply complete and correct information which it has requested by decision taken pursuant to Article 11(5);

(d) to submit to an investigation which it has ordered by decision taken pursuant to Article 14(3).

2. Where the undertakings or associations of undertakings have satisfied the obligation which it was the purpose of the periodic penalty payment to enforce, the Commission may fix the total amount of the periodic penalty payment at a lower figure than that which would arise under the original decision.

3. Article 10(3) to (6) shall apply.

Art. 17. *Review by the Court of Justice.* The Court of Justice shall have unlimited jurisdiction within the meaning of Article 172 of the Treaty to review decisions whereby the Commission has fixed a fine or periodic penalty payment; it may cancel, reduce or increase the fine or periodic penalty payment imposed.

Art. 18. *Unit of account.* For the purposes of applying Articles 15 to 17 the unit of account shall be that adopted in drawing up the budget of the Community in accordance with Articles 207 and 209 of the Treaty.

Art. 19. *Hearing of the parties and of third persons.* 1. Before taking decisions as provided for in Articles 2, 3, 6, 7, 8, 15 and 16, the Commission shall give the undertakings or associations of undertakings concerned the opportunity of being heard on the matters to which the Commission has taken objection.

2. If the Commission or the competent authorities of the Member State consider it necessary, they may also hear other natural or legal persons. Applications to be heard on the part of such persons shall, where they show a sufficient interest, be granted.

3. Where the Commission intends to give negative clearance pursuant to Article 2 or take a decision in application of Article 85(3) of the Treaty, it shall publish a summary of the relevant application or notification and invite all interested third parties to submit their observations within a time limit which it shall fix being not less than one month. Publication shall have regard to the legitimate interest of undertakings in the protection of their business secrets.

Art. 20. *Professional secrecy*. 1. Information acquired as a result of the application of Articles 11, 12, 13 and 14 shall be used only for the purpose of the relevant request or investigation.

2. Without prejudice to the provisions of Articles 19 and 21, the Commission and the competent authorities of the Member States, their officials and other servants shall not disclose information acquired by them as a result of the application of this Regulation and of the kind covered by the obligation of professional secrecy.

3. The provisions of paragraphs 1 and 2 shall not prevent publication of generla information or surveys which do not contain information relating to particular undertakings or associations of undertakings.

Art. 21. *Publication of decisions*. 1. The Commission shall publish the decisions which it takes pursuant to Articles 2, 3, 6, 7 and 8.

2. The publication shall state the names of the parties and the main content of the decision; it shall have regard to the legitimate interest of undertakings in the protection of their business secrets.

Art. 22. *Special provisions*. 1. The Commission shall submit to the Council proposals for making certain categories of agreement, decision and concerted practice falling within Article 4(2) or Article 5(2) compulsorily notifiable under Article 4 or 5.

2. Within one year from the date of entry into force of this Regulation, the Council shall examine, on a proposal from the Commission, what special provisions might be made for exempting from the provisions of this Regulation agreements, decisions and concerted practices falling within Article 4(2) or Article 5(2)

Art. 23. *Transitional provisions applicable to decisions of authorities of the Member States*. 1. Agreements, decisions and concerted practices of the kind described in Article 85(1) of the Treaty to which, before the entry into force of this Regulation, the competent authority of a Member State has declared Article 85(1) to be inapplicable pursuant to Article 85(3) shall not be subject to compulsory notification under Article 5. The decision of the competent authority of the Member State shall be deemed to be a decision within the meaning of Article 6; it shall cease to be valid upon expiration of the period fixed by such authority but in any event not more than three years after the entry into force of this Regulation. Article 8(3) shall apply.

2. Applications for the renewal of decisions of the kind described in paragraph 1 shall be decided upon by the Commission in accordance with Article 8(2).

Art. 24. *Implementing provisions*. The Commission shall have power to adopt implementing provisions concerning the form, content and other details of applications pursuant to Articles 2 and 3 and of notifications pursuant to Articles 4 and 5, and concerning hearings pursuant to Article 19(1) and (2).

Art. 25. 1. As regards agreements, decisions and concerted practices to which Article 85 of the Treaty applies by virtue of accession, the date of accession shall be substituted for the date of entry into force of this Regulation in every place where reference is made in this Regulation to this latter date.

2. Agreements, decisions and concerted practices existing at the date of accession to which Article 85 of the Treaty applies by virtue of accession shall be notified pursuant to Article 5(1) or Article 7(1) and (2) within six months from the date of accession.

3. Fines under Article 15(2)(a) shall not be imposed in respect of any act prior to notification of the agreements, decisions and practices to which paragraph 2 applies and which have been notified within the period therein specified.

4. New Member States shall take the measures referred to in Article 14 (6) within six months from the date of accession after consulting the Commission.[12]

The provisions of paragraphs 1 to 4 above still apply in the same way in the case of the accession of the Hellenic Republic.[13]

This Regulation shall be binding in its entirety and directly applicable in all Member States.

Done at Brussels, 6 February 1962.

*For the Council*

*The President*

M. COUVE de MURVILLE

1. J.O. No 13, 21 February 1962, p. 204; O.J. (Special Edition 1959-1962) p. 87.

2. J.O. No 58, 10 July 1962, p. 1655; O.J. (Special Edition 1959-1962) p. 249.

3. J.O. No 162, 7 November 1963, p. 2696.

4. J.O. No L 285, 20 December 1971, p. 49; O.J. (Special Edition 1971

III) p. 1035.

5. Annex I v. 1 of the Act of Accession, signed at Brussels 22 January 1972.

6. Act concerning the conditions of accession of the Hellenic Republic, signed at Athens 28 May 1979, O.J. No L 291, 19 November 1979.

7. Amended by Regulation 2822/71/EEC.

8. Previous text applying till 18 January 1972 'joint research for improvement of techniques, provided the results are accessible to all the parties thereto and may be used by each of them'.

9. Supplemented by Regulation 2822/71/EEC.

10. Amended by Regulation 59/62/EEC.

11. Amended by Regulation 118/63/EEC.

12. Supplemented by the Act of Accession.

13. Supplemented by the Act of Accession of the Hellenic Republic.

Annex II

REGULATION No 27/62/EEC[1] OF THE COMMISSION

of 3 May 1962

First Regulation implementing Council Regulation No 17 of 6 February 1962. Amended by Regulation 1133/68/EEC[2] of 26 July 1968 and Regulation 1699/75/EEC[3] and the Act of Accession of the Hellenic Republic[4] (Form, content and other details concerning applications and notifications)

THE COMMISSION OF THE EUROPEAN ECONOMIC COMMUNITY,

Having regard to the provisions of the Treaty establishing the European Economic Community, and in particular Articles 87 and 155 thereof;

Having regard to Article 24 of Council Regulation No 17 of 6 February 1962 (First Regulation implementing Articles 85 and 86 of the Treaty);

Whereas under Article 24 of Council Regulation No 17 the Commission is authorised to adopt implementing provisions concerning the form, content and other details of applications under Articles 2 and 3 and of notifications under Articles 4 and 5 of that Regulation;

Whereas the submission of such applications and notifications may have important legal consequences for each of the undertakings which is party to an agreement, decision or concerted practice; whereas every undertaking should accordingly have the right to submit an application or a notification to the Commission; whereas, furthermore, an undertaking exercising this right must inform the other undertakings which are parties to the agreement, decision or concerted practice in order to enable them to protect their interests;

Whereas it is for the undertakings and associations of undertakings to transmit to the Commission information as to facts and circumstances in support of applications under Article 2 and of notifications under Articles 4 and 5;

Whereas it is desirable to prescribe forms for use in applications for negative clearance relating to implementation of Article 85(1) and for notifications relating to implementation of Article 85(3) of the Treaty, in order to simplify and accelerate consideration by the competent departments, in the interests of all concerned;

HAS ADOPTED THIS REGULATION:

Art. 1. *Persons entitled to submit applications and notifications.*
1. Any undertaking which is party to agreements, decisions or practices of the kind described in Articles 85 and 86 of the Treaty may submit an application under Article 2 or a notification under Articles 4

and 5 of Regulation No 17. Where the application or notification is submitted by some, but not all, of the undertakings concerned, they shall give notice to the others.

2. Where applications and notifications under Articles 2, 3(1), 3(2) (b), 4 and 5 of Regulation No 17 are signed by representatives of undertakings, associations of undertakings, or natural or legal persons, such representatives shall produce written proof that they are authorised to act.

3. Where a joint application or notification is submitted, a joint representative should be appointed.

Art. 2. *Submission of applications and notifications.* 1. Eleven[5] copies of each application and notification and of the supporting documents shall be submitted to the Commission.

2. The supporting documents shall be either originals or copies. Copies must be certified as true copies of the original.

3. Applications and notifications shall be in one of the official languages of the Community. Supporting documents shall be submitted in their original language. Where the original language is not one of the official languages, a translation in one of the official languages shall be attached.

Art. 3. *Effective date of submission of applications and registrations.* The date of submission of an application or notification shall be the date on which it is received by the Commission. Where, however, the application or notification is sent by registered post, it shall be deemed to have been received on the date shown on the postmark of the place of posting.

Art. 4. *Content of applications and notifications.* 1. Applications under Article 2 of Regulation No 17 relating to the applicability of Article 85(1) of the Treaty and notifications under Article 4 or Article 5(2) of Regulation No 17 shall be submitted on Form A/B as shown in the Annex to this Regulation.

2. Applications and notifications shall contain the information asked for in Form A/B.

3. Several participating undertakings may submit an application or notification on a single form.

4. Applications under Article 2 of Regulation No 17 relating to the applicability of Article 86 of the Treaty shall contain a full statement of the facts, specifying, in particular, the practice concerned and the position of the undertaking or undertakings within the Common Market or a substantial part thereof in regard to products or services to which the practice relates.[6]

Art. 5. *Transitional provisions.* 1. Applications and notifications submitted prior to the date of entry into force of this Regulation otherwise than on the prescribed forms shall be deemed to comply with Article 4 of this Regulation.

2. The Commission may require a duly completed form to be submitted to it within such time as it shall appoint. In that event, applications and notifications shall be treated as properly made only if the forms are submitted within the prescribed period and in accordance with the provisions of this Regulation.

Art. 6. This Regulation shall enter into force on the day following its publication in the Official Journal of the European Communities.

This Regulation shall be binding in its entirety and directly applicable in all Member States.

Done at Brussels, 3 May 1962.

*For the Commission*

*The President*

W. HALLSTEIN

1. J.O. No 35, 10 May 1962, p. 1118; O.J. (Special Edition 1959-1962) p. 132.

2. J.O. No L 189, 1 August 1968, p. 1; O.J. (Special Edition 1968 II) p. 400.

3. O.J. No L 172, 3 July 1975, p. 11.

4. Act concerning the conditions of accession of the Hellenic Republic, signed at Athens 28 May 1979, O.J. No L 291, 19 November 1979.

5. Amended by the Act of Accession of the Hellenic Republic, earlier amended by Regulation 1699/75/EEC.

6. Amended by Regulation 1133/68/EEC.

Annex III

REGULATION No 99/63/EEC[1] OF THE COMMISSION

of 25 July 1963

on the hearings provided for in Article 19 (1) and (2) of Council Regulation No 17[2]

THE COMMISSION OF THE EUROPEAN ECONOMIC COMMUNITY,

Having regard to the Treaty establishing the European Economic Community, and in particular Articles 87 and 155 thereof;

Having regard to Article 24 of Council Regulation No 17[2] of 6 February 1962 (First Regulation implementing Articles 85 and 86 of the Treaty);

Whereas the Commission has power under Article 24 of Council Regulation No 17 to lay down implementing provisions concerning the hearings provided for in Article 19(1) and (2) of that Regulation;

Whereas in most cases the Commission will in the course of its inquiries already be in close touch with the undertakings or associations of undertakings which are the subject thereof and they will accordingly have the opportunity of making known their views regarding the objections raised against them;

Whereas, however, in accordance with Article 19(1) of Regulation No 17 and with the rights of defence, the undertakings and associations of undertakings concerned must have the right on conclusion of the inquiry to submit their comments on the whole of the objections raised against them which the Commission proposes to deal with in its decisions;

Whereas persons other than the undertakings or associations of undertakings which are the subject of the inquiry may have an interest in being heard; whereas, by the second sentence of Article 19(2) of Regulation No 17, such persons must have the opportunity of being heard if they apply and show that they have a sufficient interest;

Whereas it is desirable to enable persons who, pursuant to Article 3(2) of Regulation No 17, have applied for an infringement to be terminated to submit their comments where the Commission considers that on the basis of the information in its possession there are sufficient grounds for granting the application;

Whereas the various persons entitled to submit comments must do so in writing, both in their own interest and in the interests of good administration, without prejudice to oral procedure where appropriate to supplement the written evidence;

Whereas it is necessary to define the rights of persons who are to be heard, and in particular the conditions upon which they may be represented or assisted and the setting and calculation of time limits;

Whereas the Advisory Committee on Restrictive Practices and Monopolies delivers its Opinion on the basis of a preliminary draft decision; whereas it must therefore be consulted concerning a case after the inquiry in respect thereof has been completed; whereas such consultation does not prevent the Commission from re-opening an inquiry if need be;

HAS ADOPTED THIS REGULATION:

Art. 1. Before consulting the Advisory Committee on Restrictive Practices and Monopolies, the Commission shall hold a hearing pursuant to Article 19(1) of Regulation No 17.

Art. 2. 1. The Commission shall inform undertakings and associations of undertakings in writing of the objections raised against them. The communication shall be addressed to each of them or to a joint agent appointed by them.

2. The Commission may inform the parties by giving notice in the *Official Journal of the European Communities*, if from the circumstances of the case this appears appropriate, in particular where notice is to be given to a number of undertakings but no joint agent has been appointed. The notice shall have regard to the legitimate interest of the undertakings in the protection of their business secrets.

3. A fine or a periodic penalty payment may be imposed on an undertaking or association of undertakings only if the objections were notified in the manner provided for in paragraph 1.

4. The Commission shall when giving notice of objections fix a time limit up to which the undertakings and associations of undertakings may inform the Commission of their views.

Art. 3. 1. Undertakings and associations of undertakings shall, within the appointed time limit, make known in writing their views concerning the objections raised against them.

2. They may in their written comments set out all matters relevant to their defence.

3. They may attach any relevant documents in proof of the facts set out. They may also propose that the Commission hear persons who may corroborate those facts.

Art. 4. The Commission shall in its decisions deal only with those objections raised against undertakings and associations of undertakings in respect of which they have been afforded the opportunity of making known their views.

Art. 5. If natural or legal persons showing a sufficient interest apply to be heard pursuant to Article 19(2) of Regulation No 17, the Commission shall afford them the opportunity of making known their views in writing within such time limit as it shall fix.

Art. 6. Where the Commission, having received an application pursuant to Article 3(2) of Regulation No 17, considers that on the basis of the information in its possession there are insufficient grounds for granting the application, it shall inform the applicants of its reasons and fix a time limit for them to submit any further comments in writing.

Art. 7. 1. The Commission shall afford to persons who have so requested in their written comments the opportunity to put forward their arguments orally, if those persons show a sufficient interest or if the Commission proposes to impose on them a fine or periodic penalty payment.

2. The Commission may likewise afford to any other person the opportunity of orally expressing his views.

Art. 8. 1. The Commission shall summon the persons to be heard to attend on such date as it shall appoint.

2. It shall forthwith transmit a copy of the summons to the competent authorities of the Member States, who may appoint an official to take art in the hearing.

Art. 9. 1. Hearings shall be conducted by the persons appointed by the Commission for that purpose.

2. Persons summoned to attend shall appear either in person or be represented by legal representatives or by representatives authorised by their constitution. Undertakings and associations of undertakings may moreover be represented by a duly authorised agent appointed from among their permanent staff.

Persons heard by the Commission may be assisted by lawyers or university teachers who are entitled to plead before the Court of Justice of the European Communities in accordance with Article 17 of the Protocol on the Statute of the Court, or by other qualified persons.

3. Hearings shall not be public. Persons shall be heard separately or in the presence of other persons summoned to attend. In the latter case, regard shall be had to the legitimate interest of the undertakings in the protection of their business secrets.

4. The essential content of the statements made by each person heard shall be recorded in minutes which shall be read and approved by him.

Art. 10. Without prejudice to Article 2(2), information and summonses from the Commission shall be sent to the addressees by registered letter with acknowledgement of receipt, or shall be delivered by hand against receipt.

Art. 11. 1. In fixing the time limits provided for in Articles 2, 5 and 6, the Commission shall have regard both to the time required for preparation of comments and to the urgency of the case. The time limit shall be not less than two weeks; it may be extended.

2. Time limits shall run from the day following receipt of a communication or delivery thereof by hand.

3. Written comments must reach the Commission or be dispatched by registered letter before expiry of the time limit. Where the time limit would expire on a Sunday or public holiday, it shall be extended up to the end of the next following working day. For the purpose of calculating this

extension, public holidays shall, in cases where the relevant date is the date of receipt of written comments, be those set out in the Annex to this Regulation, and in cases where the relevant date is the date of dispatch, those appointed by law in the country of dispatch.

This Regulation shall be binding in its entirety and directly applicable in all Member States.

Done at Brussels, 25 July 1963.

*For the Commission*

*The President*

Walter HALLSTEIN

1. J.O. No 127, 20 August 1962, p. 2268; O.J. (Special Edition 1963-1964) p. 47.

2. J.O. No 13, 21 February 1962, p. 204; O.J. (Special Edition 1959-1962) p. 87.

Annex IV

## REGULATION No 26/62/EEC[1] OF THE COUNCIL

### of 4 April 1962

applying certain rules of competition to production of and trade in agricultural products as amended by Council Regulation 49/62/EEC of 29 June 1962[2]

THE COUNCIL OF THE EUROPEAN ECONOMIC COMMUNITY,

Having regard to the Treaty establishing the European Economic Community, and in particular Articles 42 and 43 thereof;

Having regard to the proposal from the Commission;

Having regard to the Opinion of the European Parliament;

Whereas by virtue of Article 42 of the Treaty one of the matters to be decided under the common agricultural policy is whether the rules on competition laid down in the Treaty are to apply to production of and trade in agricultural products, and accordingly the provisions hereinafter contained will have to be supplemented in the light of developments in that policy;

Whereas the proposals submitted by the Commission for the formulation and implementation of the common agricultural policy show that certain rules on competition must forthwith be made applicable to production of and trade in agricultural products in order to eliminate practices contrary to the principles of the common market and prejudicial to attainment of the objectives set out in Article 39 of the Treaty and in order to provide a basis for the future establishment of a system of competition adapted to the development of the common agricultural policy;

Whereas special attention is warranted in the case of farmers' organisations which are particularly concerned with the joint production or marketing of agricultural products or the use of joint facilities, unless such joint action excludes competition or jeopardises attainment of the objectives of Article 39 of the Treaty;

Whereas, in order both to avoid compromising the development of a common agricultural policy and to ensure certainly in the law and non-discriminatory treatment of the undertakings concerned, the Commission must have sole power, subject to review by the Court of Justice, to determine whether the conditions provided for in the two preceding recitals are fulfilled as regards the agreements, decisions and practices referred to in Article 85 of the Treaty;

Whereas, in order to enable the specific provisions of the Treaty regarding agriculture, and in particular those of Article 39 thereof, to be taken into consideration, the Commission must, in questions of dumping, assess all the causes of the practices complained of and in particular the price level at which products from other sources are imported into the market in question; whereas it must, in the light of its assessment, make recommendations and authorise protective measures as provided in Article 91(1) of the Treaty;

Whereas, in order to implement, as part of the development of the common agricultural policy, the rules on aids for production of or trade in agricultural products, the Commission should be in a position to draw up a list of existing, new or proposed aids, to make appropriate observations to the Member States and to propose suitable measures to them;

HAS ADOPTED THIS REGULATION:

Art. 1. From the entry into force of this Regulation, Articles 85 to 90 of the Treaty and provisions made in implementation thereof shall, subject to Article 2 below, apply to all agreements, decisions and practices referred to in Articles 85(1) and 86 of the Treaty which relate to production of or trade in the products listed in Annex II to the Treaty;

Art. 2. 1. Article 85(1) of the Treaty shall not apply to such of the agreements, decisions and practices referred to in the preceding Article as form an integral part of a national market organisation or are necessary for attainment of the objectives set out in Article 39 of the Treaty. In particular, it shall not apply to agreements, decision and practices of farmers, farmers' associations, or associations of such associations belonging to a single Member State which concern the production or sale of agricultural products, and under which there is no obligation to charge identical prices, unless the Commission finds that competition is thereby excluded or that the objectives of Article 39 of the Treaty are jeopardised.

2. After consulting the Member States and hearing the undertakings or associations of undertakings concerned and any other natural or legal person that it considers appropriate, the Commission shall have sole power, subject to review by the Court of Justice, to determine, by decision which shall be published, which agreements, decisions and practices fulfil the conditions specified in paragraph 1.

3. The Commission shall undertake such determination either on its own initiative or at the request of a competent authority of a Member State or of an interested undertaking or association of undertakings.

4. The publication shall state the names of the parties and the main content of the decision; it shall have regard to the legitimate interest of undertakings in the protection of their business secrets.

Art. 3. 1. Without prejudice to Article 46 of the Treaty, Article 91(1) thereof shall apply to trade in the products listed in Annex II to the Treaty.

2. With due regard for the provisions of the Treaty relating to agriculture, and in particular those of Article 39, the Commission shall assess all the causes of the practices complained of, in particular the price level at which products from other sources are imported into the market in question.

In the light of its assessment, it shall make recommendations and authorise protective measures as provided in Article 91(1) of the Treaty.

Art. 4. The provisions of Article 93(1) and of the first sentence of Article 93(3) of the Treaty shall apply to aids granted for the production of or trade in the products listed in Annex II to the Treaty.

Art. 5. This Regulations shall enter into force on the day following its publication in the *Official Journal of the European Communities*, with the exception of Articles 1 to 3, which shall enter into force on 1 July 1962.

This Regulation shall be binding in its entirety and directly applicable in all Member States.

Done at Brussels, 4 April 1962.

*For the Council*

*The President*

M. COUVE de MURVILLE

1. J.O. No 30, 20 April 1962, p. 993; O.J. (Special Edition 1959-1962, p. 129).

2. J.O. No 53, p. 129, 1 July 1962, p. 1571. (Rec. D.O. No 65, 27 July 1962, p. 1855).

Annex V

## REGULATION No 2988/74/EEC OF THE COUNCIL

of 26 November 1974

concerning limitation periods in proceedings and the enforcement of sanctions under the rules of the European Economic Community relating to transport and competition[1]

THE COUNCIL OF THE EUROPEAN COMMUNITIES,

Having regard to the Treaty establishing the European Economic Community, and in particular Articles 75, 79 and 87 thereof;

Having regard to the proposal from the Commission;

Having regard to the Opinion of the European Parliament[2];

Having regard to the Opinion of the Economic and Social Committee[3];

Whereas under the rules of the European Economic Community relating to transport and competition the Commission has the power to impose fines, penalties and periodic penalty payments on undertakings or associations of undertakings which infringe Community law relating to information or investigation, or to the prohibition on discrimination, restrictive practices and abuse of dominant position; whereas those rules make no provision for any limitation period;

Whereas it is necessary in the interests of legal certainty that the principle of limitation be introduced and that implementing rules be laid down; whereas, for the matter to be covered fully, it is necessary that provision for limitation be made not only as regards the power to impose fines or penalties, but also as regards the power to enforce decisions, imposing fines, penalties or periodic penalty payments; whereas such provisions should specify the length of limitation periods, the date on which time starts to run and the events which have the effect of interrupting or suspending the limitation period; whereas in this respect the interests of undertakings and associations of undertakings on the one hand, and the requirements imposed by administrative practice, on the other hand, should be taken into account;

Whereas this Regulation must apply to the relevant provisions of Regulation No 11 concerning the abolition of discrimination in transport rates and conditions, in implementation of Article 79(3) of the Treaty[4] establishing the European Economic Community, of Regulation No 17[5]: first Regulation implementing Articles 85 and 86 of the Treaty, and of Council Regulation (EEC) No 1017/68[6] of 19 July 1968 applying rules of competition to transport by rail, road and inland waterway; whereas it must also apply to the relevant provisions of future regulations in the fields of European Economic Community law relating to transport and competition,

HAS ADOPTED THIS REGULATION:

Art. 1. *Limitation periods in proceedings.* 1. The power of the Commission to impose fines or penalties for infringements of the rules of the European Economic Community relating to transport or competition shall be subject to the following limitation periods:

(a) three years in the case of infringements of provisions concerning applications or notifications of undertakings or associations of undertakings, requests for information, or the carrying out of investigations;

(b) five years in the case of all other infringements.

2. Time shall begin to run upon the day on which the infringement is committed. However, in the case of continuing or repeated infringements, time shall begin to run on the day on which the infringement ceases.

Art. 2. *Interruption of the limitation period in proceedings.*
1. Any action taken by the Commission, or by any Member State, acting at the request of the Commission, for the purpose of the preliminary investigation or proceedings in respect of an infringement shall interrupt the limitation period in proceedings. The limitation period shall be interrupted with effect from the date on which the action is notified to at least one undertaking or association of undertakings which have participated in the infringement.

Actions which interrupt the running of the period shall include in particular the following:

(a) written requests for information by the Commission, or by the competent authority of a Member State acting at the request of the Commission; or a Commission decision requiring the requested information;

(b) written authorisations to carry out investigations issued to their officials by the Commission or by the competent authority of any Member State at the request of the Commission; or a Commission decision ordering an investigation;

(c) the commencement of proceedings by the Commission;

(d) notification of the Commission's statement of objections.

2. The interruption of the limitation period shall apply for all the undertakings or associations of undertakings which have participated in the infringement.

3. Each interruption shall start time running afresh. However, the limitation period shall expire at the latest on the day on which a period equal to twice the limitation period has elapsed without the Commission having imposed a fine or a penalty; that period shall be extended by the time during which limitation is suspended pursuant to Article 3.

Art. 3. *Suspension of the limitation period in proceedings.* The limitation period in proceedings shall be suspended for as long as the decision of the Commission is the subject of proceedings pending before the Court of Justice of the European Communities.

Art. 4. *Limitation period for the enforcement of sanctions.* 1. The power of the Commission to enforce decisions imposing fines, penalties or periodic payments for infringements of the rules of the European Economic Community relating to transport or competition shall be subject to a limitation period of five years.

2. Time shall begin to run on the day on which the decision becomes final.

Art. 5. *Interruption of the limitation period for the enforcement of sanctions.* 1. The limitation period for the enforcement of sanctions shall be interrupted:

(a) by notification of a decision varying the original amount of the fine, penalty or periodic penalty payments or refusing an application for variation;

(b) by any action of the Commission, or of a Member State at the request of the Commission, for the purpose of enforcing payments of a fine, penalty or periodic penalty payment.

2. Each interruption shall start time running afresh.

Art. 6. *Suspension of the limitation period for the enforcement of sanctions.* The limitation period for the enforcement of sanctions shall be suspended for so long as:

(a) time to pay is allowed; or

(b) enforcement of payment is suspended pursuant to a decision of the Court of Justice of the European Communities.

Art. 7. *Application to transitional cases.* This Regulation shall also apply in respect of infringements committed before it enters into force.

Art. 8. *Entry into force.* This Regulation shall enter into force on 1 January 1975.

This Regulation shall be binding in its entirety and directly applicable in all Member States.

1. O.J. L 319, 29 November 1974, p. 1.
2. J.O. C 129, 11 November 1972, p. 10.
3. J.O. C 89, 23 August 1972, p. 21.
4. J.O. No 52, 16 August 1960, p. 1121, O.J. (Special Edition 1959-1962) p. 60.
5. J.O. No 13, 21 February 1962, p. 204; O.J. (Special Edition 1959-1962) p. 87.
6. J.O. No L 175, 23 July 1968, p. 1; O.J. (Special Edition 1968 I) p. 302.

Annex VI

# REGULATION No 19/65/EEC[1] OF THE COUNCIL

of 2 March 1965

on application of Article 85 (3) of the Treaty to certain categories of agreements and concerted practices as amended by the Act of Accession[2] and the Act of Accession of the Hellenic Republic[3]

THE COUNCIL OF THE EUROPEAN ECONOMIC COMMUNITY,

Having regard to the Treaty establishing the European Economic Community, and in particular Article 87 thereof;

Having regard to the proposal from the Commission;

Having regard to the Opinion of the European Parliament[4];

Having regard to the Opinion of the Economic and Social Committee[5];

Whereas Article 85(1) of the Treaty may in accordance with Article 85 (3) be declared inapplicable to certain categories of agreements, decisions and concerted practices which fulfil the conditions contained in Article 85(3);

Whereas the provisions for implementation of Article 85(3) must be adopted by way of regulation pursuant to Article 87;

Whereas in view of the large number of notifications submitted in pursuance of Regulation No 17[6] it is desirable that in order to facilitate the task of the Commission it should be enabled to declare by way of regulation that the provisions of Article 85(1) do not apply to certain categories of agreements and concerted practices;

Whereas it should be laid down under what conditions the Commission, in close and constant liaison with the competent authorities of the Member States, may exercise such powers after sufficient experience has been gained in the light of individual decisions and it becomes possible to define categories of agreements and concerted practices in respect of which the conditions of Article 85(3) may be considered as being fulfilled;

Whereas the Commission has indicated by the action it has taken, in particular by Regulation No 153[7], that there can be no easing of the procedures prescribed by Regulation No 17 in respect of certain types of agreements and concerted practices that are particularly liable to distort competition in the common market;

Whereas under Article 6 of Regulation No 17 the Commission may provide that a decision taken pursuant to Article 85(3) of the Treaty shall apply with retroactive effect; whereas it is desirable that the Commission be also empowered to adopt, by regulation, provisions to the like effect;

Whereas under Article 7 of Regulation No 17 agreements, decisions and concerted practices may, by decision of the Commission, be exempted from prohibition in particular if they are modified in such a manner that they satisfy the requirements of Article 85(3); whereas it is desirable that the Commission be enabled to grant like exemption by regulation to such agreements and concerted practices if they are modified in such manner as to fall within a category defined in an exempting regulation;

Whereas, since there can be no exemption if the conditions set out in Article 85(3) are not satisfied, the Commission must have power to lay down by decision the conditions that must be satisfied by an agreement or concerted practice which owing to special circumstances has certain effects incompatible with Article 85(3);

HAS ADOPTED THIS REGULATION:

Art. 1. 1. Without prejudice to the application of Council Regulation No 17 and in accordance with Article 85(3) of the Treaty the Commission may by regulation declare that Article 85(1) shall not apply to categories of agreements to which only two undertakings are party and:

(a) - whereby one party agrees with the other to supply only to that other certain goods for resale within a defined area of the common market; or

- whereby one party agrees with the other to purchase only from that other certain goods for resale; or

- whereby the two undertakings have entered into obligations, as in the two preceding subparagraphs, with each other in respect of exclusive supply and purchase for resale;

(b) which include restrictions imposed in relation to the acquisition or use of industrial property rights - in particular of patents, utility models, designs or trade marks - or to the rights arising out of contracts for assignment of, or the right to use, a method of manufacture or knowledge relating to the use or to the application of industrial processes.

2. The regulation shall define the categories of agreements to which it applies and shall specify in particular:

(a) the restrictions or clauses which must not be contained in the agreements;

(b) the clauses which must be contained in the agreements, or the other conditions which must be satisfied.

3. Paragraphs 1 and 2 shall apply by analogy to categories of concerted practices to which only two undertakings are party.

Art. 2. 1. A regulation pursuant to Article 1 shall be made for a specified period.

2. It may be repealed or amended where circumstances have changed with respect to any factor which was basic to its being made; in such case, a period shall be fixed for modification of the agreements and concerted practices to which the earlier regulation applies.

Art. 3. A regulation pursuant to Article 1 may stipulate that it shall apply with retroactive effect to agreements and concerted practices to which, at the date of entry into force of that regulation, a decision issued with retroactive effect in pursuance of Article 6 of Regulation No 17 would have applied.

Art. 4. 1. A regulation pursuant to Article 1 may stipulate that the prohibition contained in Article 85(1) of the Treaty shall not apply, for such period as shall be fixed by that regulation, to agreements and concerted practices already in existence on 13 March 1962 which do not satisfy the conditions of Article 85(3), and a regulation pursuant to Article 1 may stipulate that the prohobition contained in Article 85(1) of the Treaty shall not apply, for such period as shall be fixed by that regulation, to agreements and concerted practices already in existence at the date of accession to which Article 85 applies by virtue of accession and which do not satisfy the conditions of Article 85(3), where[8]

- within three months from the entry into force of the Regulation, they are so modified as to satisfy the said conditions in accordance with the provisions of the regulation; and

- the modifications are brought to the notice of the Commission within the time limit fixed by the regulation. The provisions of the preceding subparagraph shall apply in the same way in the case of the accession of the Hellenic Republic.[9]

2. Paragraph 1 shall apply to agreements and concerted practices which had to be notified before 1 February 1963, in accordance with Article 5 of Regulation No 17, only where they have been so notified before that date.

Paragraph 1 shall not apply to agreements and concerted practices to which Article 85(1) of the Treaty applies by virtue of accession and which must be notified before 1 July 1973, in accordance with Articles 5 and 25 of Regulation No 17, unless they have been so notified before that date.[10]

Paragraph 1 shall not apply to agreements and concerted practices to which Article 85(1) of the Treaty applies by virtue of the accession of the Hellenic Republic and which must be notified before 1 July 1981 in accordance with Articles 5 and 25 of Regulation No 17, unless they have been so notified before that date.[11]

3. The benefit of the provisions laid down pursuant to paragraph 1 may not be claimed in actions pending at the date of entry into force of a regulation adopted pursuant to Article 1; neither may it be relied on as grounds for claims for damages against third parties.

Art. 5. Before adopting a regulation, the Commission shall publish a draft thereof and invite all persons concerned to submit their comments within such a time limit, being not less than one month, as the Commission shall fix.

Art. 6. 1. The Commission shall consult the Advisory Committee on Restrictive Practices and Monopolies:

(a) before publishing a draft regulation;

(b) before adopting a regulation.

2. Article 10(5) and (6) of Regulation No 17, relating to consultation with the Advisory Committee, shall apply by analogy, it being understood that joint meetings with the Commission shall take place not earlier than one month after dispatch of the notice convening them.

Art. 7. Where the Commission, either on its own initiative or at the request of a Member State or of natural or legal persons claiming a legitimate interest, finds that in any particular case agreements or concerted practices to which a regulation adopted pursuant to Article 1 of this Regulation applies have nevertheless certain effects which are incompatible with the conditions laid down in Article 85(3) of the Treaty, it may withdraw the benefit of application of that regulation and issue a decision in accordance with Articles 6 and 8 of Regulation No 17, without any notification under Article 4(1) of Regulation No 17 being required.

Art. 8. The Commission shall, before 1 January 1970, submit to the Council a proposal for a Regulation for such amendment of this Regulation as may prove necessary in the light of experience.

This Regulation shall be binding in its entirety and directly applicable in all Member States.

Done at Brussels, 2 March 1965.

*For the Council*

*The President*

M. COUVE DE MURVILLE

1. J.O. No 36, 6 March 1965, p. 533; O.J. (Special Edition 1965-1966) p. 35.

2. Annex I. V. 2 of the Act of Accession, signed at Brussels 22 January 1972.

3. Act concerning the conditions of accession of the Hellenic Republic, signed at Athens, 28 May 1979. O.J. No L 291, 19 November 1979.

4. J.O. No 81, 27 May 1964, p. 1275.

5. J.O. No 197, 30 November 1964, p. 3320.

6. J.O. No 13, 21 February 1962, p. 204; O.J. (Special Edition 1959-1962) p. 87.

7. J.O. No 139, 24 December 1962, p. 2918.

8. Supplemented by the Act of Accession.

9. Supplemented by the Act of Accession of the Hellenic Republic.

10. Supplemented by the Act of Accession.

11. Supplemented by the Act of Accession of the Hellenic Republic.

Annex VII

# COMMISSION REGULATION (EEC) No 1983/83

of 22 June 1983

on the application of Article 85 (3) of the Treaty to catogories of exclusive distributicn agreements

THE COMMISSION OF THE EUROPEAN COMMUNITIES,

Having regard to the Treaty establishing the European Economic Community, and in particular Article 87 thereof,

Having regard to Council Regulation No 19/65/EEC of 2 March 1965 on the application of Article 85(3) of the Treaty to certain categories of agreements and concerted practices ([1]), as last amended by the Act of Accession of Greece, and in particular Article 1 thereof,

Having published a draft of this Regulation ([2]),

Having consulted the Advisory Committee on Restrictive Practices and Dominant Positions,

(1) Whereas Regulation No 19/65/EEC empowers the Commission to apply Article 85(3) of the Treaty by regulation to certain categories of bilateral exclusive distribution agreements and analogous concerted practices falling within Article 85(1);

(2) Whereas experience to date makes it possible to define a category of agreements and concerted practices which can be regarded as normally satisfying the conditions laid down in Article 85(3);

(3) Whereas exclusive distribution agreements of the category defined in Article 1 of this Regulation may fall within the prohibition contained in Article 85(1) of the Treaty; whereas this will apply only in exceptional cases to exclusive agreements of this kind to which only undertakings from one Member State are party and which concern the resale of goods within that Member State; whereas, however, to the extent that such agreements may affect trade between Member States and also satisfy all the requirements set out in this Regulation there is no reason to withhold from them the benefit of the exemption by category;

(4) Whereas it is not necessary expressly to exclude from the defined category those agreements which do not fulfil the conditions of Article 85(1) of the Treaty;

(5) Whereas exclusive distribution agreements lead in general to an improvement in distribution because the uncertaking is able to concentrate its sales activities, does not need to maintain numerous business relations with a larger number of dealers and is able, by dealing with only one dealer, to overcome more easily distribution

difficulties in international trade resulting from linguistic, legal and other differences;

(6) Whereas exclusive distribution agreements facilitate the promotion of sales of a product and lead to intensive marketing and to continuity of supplies while at the same time rationalising distribution; whereas they stimulate competition between the products of different manufacturers; whereas the appointment of an exclusive distributor who will take over sales promotion, customer services and carrying of stocks is often the most effective way, and sometimes indeed the only way, for the manufacturer to enter a market and compete with other manufacturers already present; whereas this is particularly so in the case of small and medium-sized undertakings; whereas it must be left to the contracting parties to decide whether and to what extent they consider it desirable to incorporate in the agreements terms providing for the promotion of sales;

(7) Whereas, as a rule, such exclusive distribution agreements also allow consumers a fair share of the resulting benefit as they gain directly from the improvement in distribution, and their economic and supply position is improved as they can obtain products manufactured in particular in other countries more quickly and more easily;

(8) Whereas this Regulation must define the obligations restricting competition which may be included in exclusive distribution agreements; whereas the other restrictions on competition allowed under this Regulation in addition to the exclusive supply obligation produce a clear division of functions between the parties and compel the exclusive distributor to concentrate his sales efforts on the contract goods and the contract territory; whereas they are, where they are agreed only for the duration of the agreement, generally necessary in order to attain the improvement in the distribution of goods sought through exclusive distribution; whereas it may be left to the contracting parties to decide which of these obligations they include in their agreements; whereas further restrictive obligations and in particular those which limit the exclusive distributor's choice of customers or his freedom to determine his prices and conditions of sale cannot be exempted under this Regulation;

(9) Whereas the exemption by category should be reserved for agreements for which it can be assumed with sufficient certainty that they satisfy the conditions of Article 85(3) of the Treaty;

(10) Whereas it is not possible, in the absence of a case-by-case examination, to consider that adequate improvements in distribution occur where a manufacturer entrusts the distribution of his goods to another manufacturer with whom he is in competition; whereas such agreements should, therefore, be excluded from the exemption by category; whereas certain derogations from this rule in favour of small and medium-sized undertakings can be allowed;

(11) Whereas consumers will be assured of a fair share of the benefits resulting from exclusive distribution only if parallel imports remain possible; whereas agreements relating to goods which the user can obtain only from the exclusive distributor should therefore be excluded from the exemption by category? whereas the parties cannot be allowed to abuse industrial property rights or other rights in order

to create absolute territorial protection; whereas this does not prejudice the relationship between competition law and industrial property rights, since the sole object here is to determine the conditions for exemption by category;

(12) Whereas, since competition at the distribution stage is ensured by the possibility of parallel imports, the exclusive distribution agreements covered by this Regulation will not normally afford any possibility of eliminating competition in respect of a substantial part of the products in question; whereas this is also true of agreements that allot to the exclusive distributor a contract territory covering the whole of the common market;

(13) Whereas, in particular cases in which agreements or concerted practices satisfying the requirements of this Regulation nevertheless have effects incompatible with Article 85(3) of the Treaty, the Commission may withdraw the benefit of the exemption by category from the undertakings party to them;

(14) Whereas agreements and concerted practices which satisfy the conditions set out in this Regulation need not be notified; whereas an undertaking may nonetheless in a particular case where real doubt exists, request the Commission to declare whether its agreements comply with this Regulation;

(15) Whereas this Regulation does not affect the applicability of Commission Regulation (EEC) No 3604/82 of 23 December 1982 on the application of Article 85(3) of the Treaty to categories of specialisation agreements (3); whereas it does not exclude the application of Article 86 of the Treaty,

HAS ADOPTED THIS REGULATION:

*Article 1*

Pursuant to Article 85(3) of the Treaty and subject to the provisions of this Regulation, it is hereby declared that Article 85(1) of the Treaty shall not apply to agreements to which only two undertakings are party and whereby one party agrees with the other to supply certain goods for resale within the whole or a defined area of the common market only to that other.

*Article 2*

1. Apart from the obligation referred to in Article 1 no restriction on competition shall be imposed on the supplier other than the obligation not to supply the contract goods to users in the contract territory.

2. No restriction on competition shall be imposed on the exclusive distributor other than:

(a) the obligation not to manufacture or distribute goods which compete with the contract goods;

(b) the obligation to obtain the contract goods for resale only from the other party;

(c) the obligation to refrain, outside the contract territory and in relation to the contract goods, from seeking customers, from establishing any branch, and from maintaining any distribution depot.

3. Article 1 shall apply notwithstanding that the exclusive distributor undertakes all or any of the following obligations:

(a) to purchase complete ranges of goods or minimum quantities;

(b) to sell the contract goods under trademarks, or packed and presented as specified by the other party;

(c) to take measures for promotion of sales, in particular:

- to advertise,

- to maintain a sales network or stock of goods,

- to provide customer and guarantee services,

- to employ staff having specialised or technical training.

*Article 3*

Article 1 shall not apply where:

(a) manufacturers of identical goods or of goods which are considered by users as equivalent in view of their characteristics, price and intended use enter into reciprocal exclusive distribution agreements between themselves in respect of such goods;

(b) manufacturers of identical goods or of goods which are considered by users as equivalent in view of their characteristics, price and intended use enter into a non-reciprocal exclusive distribution agreement between themselves in respect of such goods unless at least one of them has a total annual turnover of no more than 100 million ECU;

(c) users can obtain the contract goods in the contract territory only from the exclusive distributor and have no alternative source of supply outside the contract territory;

(d) one or both of the parties makes it difficult for intermediaries or users to obtain the contract goods from other dealers inside the common market or, in so far as no alternative source of supply is available there, from outside the common market, in particular where one or both of them:

1. exercises industrial property rights so as to prevent dealers or users from obtaining outside, or from selling in, the contract territory properly marked or otherwise properly marketed contract goods;

2. exercises other rights or take other measures so as to prevent dealers or users from obtaining outside, or from selling in, the contract territory contract goods.

*Article 4*

1. Article 3(a) and (b) shall also apply where the goods there referred to are manufactured by an undertaking connected with a party to the agreement.

2. Connected undertakings are:

(a) undertakings in which a party to the agreement, directly or indirectly:

- owns more than half the capital or business assets, or

- has the power to exercise more than half the voting rights, or

- has the power to appoint more than half the members of the supervisory board, board of directors or bodies legally representing the undertaking, or

- has the right to manage the affairs;

(b) undertakings which directly or indirectly have in or over a party to the agreement the rights or powers listed in (a);

(c) undertakings in which an undertaking referred to in (b) directly or indirectly has the rights or powers listed in (a).

3. Undertakings in which the parties to the agreement or undertakings connected with them jointly have the rights or powers set out in paragraph 2(a) shall be considered to be connected with each of the parties to the agreement.

*Article 5*

1. For the purpose of Article 3(b), the ECU is the unit of account used for drawing up the budget of the Community pursuant to Articles 207 and 209 of the Treaty.

2. Article 1 shall remain applicable where during any period of two consecutive financial years the total turnover referred to in Article 3(b) is exceeded by no more than 10%.

3. For the purpose of calculating total turnover within the meaning of Aeticle 3(b), the turnovers achieved during the last financial year by the party to the agreement and connected undertakings in respect of all goods and services, excluding all taxes and other duties, shall be added together. For this purpose, no account shall be taken of dealings between these undertakings and undertakings connected with them or between the connected undertakings.

*Article 6*

The Commission may withdraw the benefit of this Regulation, pursuant to Article 7 of Regulation No 19/65/EEC, when it finds in a particular case that an agreement is exempted by this Regulation nevertheless has certain effects which are incompatible with the conditions set out in Article 85 (3) of the Treaty, and in particular where:

(a) the contract goods are not subject, in the contract territory, to effective competition from identical goods or goods considered by users as equivalent in view of their characteristics, price and intended use;

(b) access by other suppliers to the different stages of distribution within the contract territory is made difficult to a significant extent;

(c) for reasons other than those referred to in Article 3(c) and (d) it is not possible for intermediaries or users to obtain supplies of the contract goods from dealers outside the contract territory on the terms there customary;

(d) the exclusive distributor:

1. without any objectively justified reason refuses to supply in the contract territory categories of purchasers who cannot obtain contract goods elsewhere on suitable terms or applies to them differing prices or conditions of sale;

2. sells the contract goods at excessively high prices.

*Article 7*

In the period 1 July 1983 to 31 December 1986, the prohibition in Article 85(1) of the Treaty shall not apply to agreements which were in force on 1 July 1983 or entered into force between 1 July and 31 December 1983 and which satisfy the exemption conditions of Regulation No 67/67/EEC ([4]).

*Article 8*

This Regulation shall not apply to agreements entered into for the resale of drinks in premises used for the sale and consumption of beer or for the resale of petroleum products in service stations.

*Article 9*

This Regulation shall apply *mutatis mutandis* to concerted practices of the type defined in Article 1.

*Article 10*

This Regulation shall enter into force on 1 July 1983.

It shall expire on 31 December 1997.

This Regulation shall be binding in its entirety and directly applicable in all Member States.

Done at Brussels, 22 June 1983.

*For the Commission*
Frans ANDRIESSEN
*Member of the Commission*

(1) OJ No 36, 6.3.1965, p. 533/65.
(2) OJ No C 172, 10.7.1982, p. 3.
(3) OJ No L 376, 31.12.1982, p. 33.
(4) OJ No 57, 25.3.1967, p. 848/67.

Annex VIII

# COMMISSION REGULATION (EEC) No 1984/83

of 22 June 1983

on the application of Article 85 (3) of the Treaty to categories of exclusive purchasing agreements

THE COMMISSION OF THE EUROPEAN COMMUNITIES,

Having regard to the Treaty establishing the European Economic Community,

Having regard to Council Regulation No 19/65/EEC of 2 March 1965 on the application of Article 85(3) of the Treaty to certain categories of agreements and concerted practices ([1]), as last amended by the Act of Accession of Greece, and in particular Article 1 thereof,

Having published a draft of this Regulation ([2]),

Having consulted the Advisory Committee on Restrictive Practices and Dominant Positions,

(1) Whereas Regulation No 19/65/EEC empowers the Commission to apply Article 85(3) of the Treaty by regulation to certain categories of bilateral exclusive purchasing agreements entered into for the purpose of the resale of goods and corresponding concerted practices falling within Article 85 ([1]);

(2) Whereas experience to date makes it possible to define three categories of agreements and concerted practices which can be regarded as normally satisfying the conditions laid down in Article 85(3); whereas the first category comprises exclusive purchasing agreements of short and medium duration in all sectors of the economy; whereas the other two categories comprise long-term exclusive purchasing agreements entered into for the resale of beer in premises used for the sale and consumption (beer supply agreements) and of petroleum products in filling stations (service station agreements);

(3) Whereas exclusive purchasing agreements of the categories defined in this Regulation may fall within the prohibition contained in Article 85(1) of the Treaty; whereas this will often be the case with agreements concluded between undertakings from different Member States; whereas an exclusive purchasing agreement to which undertakings from only one Member State are party and which concerns the resale of goods within that Member State may also be caught by the prohibition; whereas this is in particular the case where it is one of a number of similar agreements which together may affect trade between Member States;

(4) Whereas it is not necessary expressly to exclude from the defined categories those agreements which do not fulfil the conditions of Article 85(1) of the Treaty;

(5) Whereas the exclusive purchasing agreements defined in this Regulation lead in general to an improvement in distribution; whereas they enable the supplier to plan the sales of his goods with greater precision and for a longer period and ensure that the reseller's requirements will be met on a regular basis for the duration of the agreement; whereas this allows the parties to limit the risk to them of variations in market conditions and to lower distribution costs;

(6) Whereas such agreements also facilitate the promotion of the sales of a product and lead to intensive marketing because the supplier, in consideration for the exclusive purchasing obligation, is as a rule under an obligation to contribute to the improvement of the structure of the distribution network, the quality of the promotional effort or the sales success; whereas, at the same time, they stimulate competition between the products of different manufacturers; whereas the appointment of several resellers, who are bound to purchase exclusively from the manufacturer and who take over sales promotion, customer services and carrying of stock, is often the most effective way, and sometimes the only way, for the manufacturer to penetrate a market and compete with other manufacturers already present; whereas this is particularly so in the case of small and medium-sized undertakings; whereas it must be left to the contracting parties to decide whether and to what extent they consider it desirable to incorporate in their agreements terms concerning the promotion of sales;

(7) Whereas, as a rule, exclusive purchasing agreements between suppliers and sellers also allow consumers a fair share of the resulting benefit as they gain the advantages of regular supply and are able to obtain the contract goods more quickly and more easily;

(8) Whereas this Regulation must define the obligations restricting competition which may be included in an exclusive purchasing agreement; whereas the other restrictions of competition allowed under this Regulation in addition to the exclusive purchasing obligation lead to a clear division of functions between the parties and compel the reseller to concentrate his sales efforts on the contract goods; whereas they are, where they are agreed only for the duration of the agreement, generally necessary in order to attain the improvement in the distribution of goods sought through exclusive purchasing; whereas further restrictive obligations and in particular those which limit the reseller's choice of customers or his freedom to determine his prices and conditions of sale cannot be exempted under this Regulation;

(9) Whereas the exemption by categories should be reserved for agreements for which it can be assumed with sufficient certainty that they satisfy the conditions of Article 85(3) of the Treaty;

(10) Whereas it is not possible, in the absence of a case-by-case examination, to consider that adequate improvements in distribution occur where a manufacturer imposes an exclusive purchasing obligation with respect to his goods on a manufacturer with whom he is in competition; whereas such agreements should, therefore, be excluded from the exemption by categories; whereas certain derogations from this rule in favour of small and medium-sized undertakings can be allowed;

(11) Whereas certain conditions must be attached to the exemption by categories so that access by other undertakings to the different stages of distribution can be ensured; whereas, to this end, limits must be set to the scope and to the duration of the exclusive purchasing obligation; whereas it appears appropriate as a general rule to grant the benefit of a general exemption from the prohibition on restrictive agreements only to exclusive purchasing agreements which are concluded for a specified product or range of products and for not more than five years;

(12) Whereas, in the case of beer supply agreements and service-station agreements, different rules should be laid down which take account of the particularities of the markets in question;

(13) Whereas these agreements are generally distinguished by the fact that, on the one hand, the supplier confers on the reseller special commercial or financial advantages by contributing to his financing, granting him or obtaining for him a loan on favourable terms, equipping him with a site or premises for conducting his business, providing him with equipment or fittings, or undertaking other investments for his benefit and that, on the other hand, the reseller enters into a long-term exclusive purchasing obligation which in most cases is accompanied by a ban on dealing in competing products;

(14) Whereas beer supply and service-station agreements, like the other exclusive purchasing agreements dealt with in this Regulation, normally produce an appreciable improvement in distribution in which consumers are allowed a fair share of the resulting benefit;

(15) Whereas the commercial and financial advantages conferred by the supplier on the reseller make it significantly easier to establish, modernise, maintain and operate premises used for the sale and consumption of drinks and service stations; whereas the exclusive purchasing obligation and the ban on dealing in competing products imposed on the reseller incite the reseller to devote all the resources at his disposal to the sale of the contract goods; whereas such agreements lead to durable cooperation between the parties allowing them to improve or maintain the quality of the contract goods and of the services to the customer and sales efforts of the reseller; whereas they allow long-term planning of sales and consequently a cost effective organisation of production and distribution; whereas the pressure of competition between products of different makes obliges the undertakings involved to determine the number and character of premises used for sale and consumption of drinks and service stations, in accordance with the wishes of the customer;

(16) Whereas consumers benefit from the improvements described, in particular because they are ensured supplies of goods of satisfactory quality at fair prices and conditions while being able to choose between the products of different manufacturers;

(17) Whereas the advantages produced by beer supply agreements and service station agreements cannot otherwise be secured to the same extent and with the same degree of certainty; whereas the exclusive purchasing obligation on the reseller and the non-competition clause imposed on him are essential components of such agreements and thus usually indispensable for the attainment of these

advantages; whereas, however, this is true only as long as the reseller's obligation to purchase from the supplier is confined in the case of premises used for the sale and consumption of drinks to beers and other drinks of the types offered by the supplier, and in the case of service stations to petroleum-based fuel for motor vehicles and other petroleum-based fuels; whereas the exclusive purchasing obligation for lubricants and related petroleum-based products can be accepted only on condition that the supplier provides for the reseller or finances the procurement of specific equipment for the carrying out of lubrication work; whereas this obligation should only relate to products intended for use within the service station;

(18) Whereas, in order to maintain the reseller's commercial freedom and to ensure access to the retail level of distribution on the part of other suppliers, not only the scope but also the duration of the exclusive purchasing obligation must be limited; whereas it appears appropriate to allow drinks suppliers a choice between a medium-term exclusive purchasing agreement covering a range of drinks and a long-term exclusive purchasing agreement for beer; whereas it is necessary to provide special rules for those premises used for the sale and consumption of drinks which the supplier lets to the reseller; whereas, in this case, the reseller must have the right to obtain, under the conditions specified in this Regulation, other drinks, except beer, supplied under the agreement or of the same type but bearing a different trademark; whereas a uniform maximum duration should be provided for service-station agreements, with the exception of tenancy agreements between the supplier and the reseller, which takes account of the long-term character of the relationship between the parties;

(19) Whereas to the extent that Member States provide, by law or administrative measures, for the same upper limit of duration for the exclusive purchasing obligation upon the reseller as in service-station agreements laid down in this Regulation but provide for a permissable duration which varies in proportion to the consideration provided by the supplier or generally provide for a shorter duration than that permitted by this Regulation, such laws or measures are not contrary to the objectives of this Regulation which, in this respect, merely sets an upper limit to the duration of service-station agreements; whereas the application and enforcement of such national laws or measures must therefore be regarded as compatible with the provisions of this Regulation;

(20) Whereas the limitations and conditions provided for in this Regulation are such as to guarantee effective competition on the markets in question; whereas, therefore, the agreements to which the exemption by category applies do not normally enable the participating undertakings to eliminate competition for a substantial part of the products in question;

(21) Whereas, in particular cases in which agreements or concerted practices satisfying the conditions of this Regulation nevertheless have effects incompatible with Article 85(3) of the Treaty, the Commission may withdraw the benefit of the exemption by category from the undertakings party thereto;

(22) Whereas agreements and concerted practices which satisfy the conditions set out in this Regulation need not be notified; whereas an undertaking may nonetheless, in a particular case where real doubt exists, request the Commission to declare whether its agreements comply with this Regulation;

(23) Whereas this Regulation does not affect the applicability of Commission Regulation (EEC) No 3604/82 of 23 December 1982 on the application of Article 85(3) of the Treaty to categories of specialisation agreements (3); whereas it does not exclude the application of Article 86 of the Treaty,

HAS ADOPTED THIS REGULATION:

## TITLE I

## General provisions

*Article 1*

Pursuant to Article 85(3) of the Treaty, and subject to the conditions set out in Articles 2 to 5 of this Regulation, it is hereby declared that Article 85(1) of the Treaty shall not apply to agreements to which only two undertakings are party and whereby one party, the reseller, agrees with the other, the supplier, to purchase certain goods specified in the agreement for resale only from the supplier or from a connected undertaking or from another undertaking which the supplier has entrusted with the sale of his goods.

*Article 2*

1. No other restrictions of competition shall be imposed on the supplier than the obligation not to distribute the contract goods or goods which compete with the contract goods in the reseller's principal sales area and at the reseller's level of distribution.

2. Apart from the obligation described in Article 1, no other restriction of competition shall be imposed on the reseller than the obligation not to manufacture or distribute goods which compete with the contract goods.

3. Article 1 shall apply notwithstanding that the reseller undertakes any or all of the following obligations:

(a) to purchase complete ranges of goods;

(b) to purchase minimum quantities of goods which are subject to the exclusive purchasing obligation;

(c) to sell the contract goods under trademarks, or packed and presented as specified by the supplier;

(d) to take measures for the promotion of sales, in particular:

- to advertise,

- to maintain a sales network or stock of goods,

- to provide customer and guarantee services,

- to employ staff having specialised or technical training.

*Article 3*

Article 1 shall not apply where:

(a) manufacturers of identical goods or of goods which are considered by users as equivalent in view of their characteristics, price and intended use enter into reprocal exclusive purchasing agreements between themselves in respect of such goods;

(b) manufacturers of identical goods or of goods which are considered by users as equivalent in view of their characteristics, price and intended use enter into a non-reciprocal exclusive purchasing agreement between themselves in respect of such goods, unless at least one of them has a total annual turnover of no more then 100 million ECU;

(c) the exclusive purchasing obligation is agreed for more than one type of goods where these are neither by their nature nor according to commercial usage connected to each other;

(d) the agreement is concluded for an indefinite duration or for a period of more than five years.

*Article 4*

1. Article 3(a) and (b) shall also apply where the goods there referred to are manufactured by an undertaking connected with a party to the agreement.

2. Connected undertakings are:

(a) undertakings in which a party to the agreement, directly or indirectly:

- owns more than half the capital or business assets, or

- has the power to exercise more than half the voting rights, or

- has the power to appoint more than half the members of the supervisory board, board of directors or bodies legally representing the undertaking, or

- has the right to manage the affairs;

(b) undertakings which directly or indirectly have in or over a party to the agreement the rights or powers listed in (a);

(c) undertakings in which an undertaking referred to in (b) directly or indirectly has the rights or powers listed in (a).

3. Undertakings in which the parties to the agreement or undertakings connected with them jointly have the rights or powers set out in para-

graph 2(a) shall be considered to be connected with each of the parties to the agreement.

*Article 5*

1. For the purpose of Article 3(b), the ECU is the unit of account used for drawing up the budget of the Community pursuant to Articles 207 and 209 of the Treaty.

2. Article 1 shall remain applicable where during any period of two consecutive financial years the total turnover referred to in Article 3(b) is exceeded by no more than 10%.

3. For the purpose of calculating total turnover within the meaning of Article 3(b), the turnovers achieved during the last financial year by the party to the agreement and connected undertakings in respect of all goods and services, excluding all taxes and other duties, shall be added together. For this purpose no account shall be taken of dealings between the parties to the agreement or between these undertakings and undertakings connected with them or between the connected undertakings.

## TITLE II

## Special provisions for beer supply agreements

*Article 6*

1. Pursuant to Article 85(3) of the Treaty, and subject to Articles 7 to 9 of this Regulation, it is hereby declared that Article 85(1) of the Treaty shall not apply to agreements to which only two undertakings are party and whereby one party, the reseller, agrees with the other, the supplier, in consideration for according special commercial or financial advantages, to purchase only from the supplier, an undertaking connected with the supplier or another undertaking entrusted by the supplier with the distribution of his goods, certain beers, or certain beers and certain other drinks, specified in the agreement for resale in premises used for the sale and consumption of drinks and designated in the agreement.

2. The declaration in paragraph 1 shall also apply where exclusive purchasing obligations of the kind described in paragraph 1 are imposed on the reseller in favour of the supplier by another undertaking which is itself not a supplier.

*Article 7*

1. Apart from the obligation referred to in Article 6, no restriction on competition shall be imposed on the reseller other than:

(a) the obligation not to sell beers and other drinks which are supplied by other undertakings and which are of the same type as the beers or other drinks supplied under the agreement in the premises designated in the agreement;

(b) the obligation, in the event that the reseller sells in the premises designated in the agreement beers which are supplied by other undertakings and which are of a different type from the beers supplied under the agreement, to sell such beers only in bottles, cans or other small packages, unless the sale of such beers in draught form is customary or is necessary to satisfy a sufficient demand from consumers;

(c) the obligation to advertise goods supplied by other undertakings within or outside the premises designated in the agreements only in proportion to the share of these goods in the total turnover realised in the premises.

2. Beers or other drinks of the same type are those which are not clearly distinguishable in view of their composition, appearance and taste.

*Article 8*

1. Article 6 shall not apply where:

(a) the supplier or a connected undertaking imposes on the reseller exclusive purchasing obligations for goods other than drinks or for services;

(b) the supplier restricts the freedom of the reseller to obtain from an undertaking of his choice either services or goods for which neither an exclusive purchasing obligation nor a ban on dealing in competing products may be imposed;

(c) the agreement is concluded for an indefinite duration or for a period of more than five years and the exclusive purchasing obligation relates to specified beers and other drinks;

(d) the agreement is concluded for an indefinite duration or for a period of more then ten years and the exclusive purchasing obligation relates only to specified beers;

(e) the supplier obliges the reseller to impose the exclusive purchasing obligation on his successor for a longer period than the reseller would himself remain tied to the supplier.

2. Where the agreement relates to premises which the supplier lets to the reseller or allows the reseller to occupy on some other basis in law or in fact, the following provisions shall also apply:

(a) notwithstanding paragraphs (1)(c) and (d), the exclusive purchasing obligations and bans on dealing in competing products specified in this Title may be imposed on the reseller for the whole period for which the reseller in fact operates the premises;

(b) the agreement must provide for the reseller to have the right to obtain:

- drinks, except beer, supplied under the agreement from other undertakings where these undertakings offer them on more favourable conditions which the supplier does not meet,
- drinks, except beer, which are of the same type as those supplied under the agreement but which bear different trademarks, from other undertakings where the supplier does not offer them.

*Article 9*

Articles 2(1) and (3), 3(a) and (b), 4 and 5 shall apply *mutatis mutandis*.

## TITLE III

### Special provisions for service-station agreements

*Article 10*

Pursuant to Article 85(3) of the Treaty and subject to Articles 11 to 13 of this Regulation, it is hereby declared that Article 85(1) of the Treaty shall not apply to agreements to which only two undertakings are party and whereby one party, the reseller, agrees with the other, the supplier, in consideration for the according of special commercial or financial advantages, to purchase only from the supplier, an undertaking connected with the supplier or another undertaking entrusted with the distribution of his goods, certain petroleum-based motor-vehicle fuels or certain petroleum-based motor-vehicle and other fuels specified in the agreement for resale in a service station designated in the agreement.

*Article 11*

Apart from the obligation referred to in Article 10, no restriction on competition shall be imposed on the reseller other than:

(a) the obligation not to sell motor-vehicle fuel and other fules which are supplied by other undertakings in the service station designated in the agreement;

(b) the obligation not to use lubricants or related petroleum-based products which are supplied by other undertakings within the service station designated in the agreement where the supplier or a connected undertaking has made available to the reseller, or financed, a lubrication bay or other motor-vehicle lubrication equipment;

(c) the obligation to advertise goods supplied by other undertakings within or outside the service station designated in the agreement only in proportion to the share of these goods in the total turnover realised in the service station;

(d) the obligation to have equipment owned by the supplier or a connected undertaking or financed by the supplier or a connected undertaking serviced by the supplier or an undertaking designated by him.

*Article 12*

1. Article 10 shall not apply where:

(a) the supplier or a connected undertaking imposes on the reseller exclusive purchasing obligations for goods other than motor-vehicle and other fuels or for services, except in the case of the obligations referred to in Article 11(b) and (d);

(b) the supplier restricts the freedom of the reseller to obtain, from an undertaking of his choice, goods or services, for which under the provisions of this Title neither an exclusive purchasing obligation nor a ban on dealing in competing products may be imposed;

(c) the agreement is concluded for an indefinite duration or for a period of more than ten years;

(d) the supplier obliges the reseller to impose the eclusive purchasing obligation on his successor for a longer period than the reseller would himself remain tied to the supplier.

2. Where the agreement relates to a service station which the supplier lets to the reseller, or allows the reseller to occupy on some other basis, in law or in facts, exclusive purchasing obligations or prohibitions of competition indicated in this Title may, notwithstanding paragraph 1(c), be imposed on the reseller for the whole period for which the reseller in fact operates the premises.

*Article 13*

Articles 2(1) and (3), 3(a) and (b), 4 and 5 of this Regulation shall apply *mutatis mutandis*.

## TITLE IV

### Miscellaneous provisions

*Article 14*

The Commission may withdraw the benefit of this Regulation, pursuant to Article 7 of Regulation No 19/65/EEC, when it finds in a particular case that an agreement which is exempted by this Regulation nevertheless has certain effects which are incompatible with the conditions set out in Article 85(3) of the Treaty, and in particular where:

(a) the contract goods are not subject, in a substantial part of the common market, to effective competition from identical goods or goods considered by users as equivalent in view of their characteristics, price and intended use;

(b) access by of other suppliers to the dufferent stages of distribution in a substantial part of the common market is made difficult to a significant extent;

(c) the supplier without any objectively justified reason:

1. refuses to supply categories of resellers who cannot obtain the contract goods elsewhere on suitable terms or applies to them differing prices or conditions of sale;

2. applies less favourable prices or conditions of sale to resellers bound by an exclusive purchasing obligation as compared with other resellers at the same level of distribution.

*Article 15*

1. In the period 1 July 1983 to 31 December 1986, the prohibition in Article 85(1) of the Treaty shall not apply to agreements of the kind described in Article 1 which either were in force on 1 July 1983 or entered into force between 1 July and 31 December 1983 and which satisfy the exemption conditions under Regulation No 67/67/EEC[4].

2. In the period 1 July 1983 to 31 December 1988, the prohibition in Article 85(1) of the Treaty shall not apply to agreements of the kind described in Articles 6 and 10 which either were in force on 1 July 1983 or entered into force between 1 July and 31 December 1983 and which satisfy the exemption conditions of Regulation No 67/67/EEC.

3. In the case of agreements of the kinds described in Articles 6 and 10, which were in force on 1 July 1983 and which expire after 31 December 1988, the prohibition in Article 85(1) of the Treaty shall not apply in the period from 1 January 1989 to the expiry of the agreement but at the latest to the expiry of this Regulation to the extent that the supplier releases the reseller, before 1 January 1989, from all obligations which would prevent the application of the exemption under Titles II and III.

*Article 16*

This Regulation shall not apply to agreements by which the supplier undertakes with the reseller to supply only to the reseller certain goods for resale, in the whole or in a defined part of the Community, and the reseller undertakes with the supplier to purchase these goods only from the supplier.

*Article 17*

This Regulation shall not apply where the parties or connected undertakings, for the purpose of resale in one and the same premises used for the sale and consumption of drinks or service station, enter into agreements both of the kind referred to in Title I and of a kind referred to in Title II or III.

*Article 18*

This Regulation shall apply *mutatis mutandis* to the categories of concerted practices defined in Articles 1, 6 and 10.

*Article 19*

This Regulation shall enter into force on 1 July 1983.

It shall expire on 31 December 1997.

This Regulations shall be binding in its entirety and directly applicable in all Member States.

Done at Brussels, 22 June 1983.

*For the Commission*

Frans ANDRIESSEN

*Member of the Commission*

(1) O.J. No 36, 6.3.1965, p. 533/65.

(2) O.J. No C 172, 10.7.1982, p. 7.

(3) O.J. No L 376, 31.12.1982, p. 33.

(4) O.J. No 57, 25.3.1967, p. 849/67.

Annex IX

## REGULATION No 2821/71/EEC[1] OF THE COUNCIL

of 20 December 1971

on application of Article 85(3) of the Treaty to categories of agreements, decisions and concerted practices as amended by Regulation No 2743/72/EEC[2] and the Act of Accession of the Hellenic Republic[3]

THE COUNCIL OF THE EUROPEAN COMMUNITIES,

Having regard to the Treaty establishing the European Economic Community, and in particular Article 87 thereof;

Having regard to the proposal from the Commission;

Having regard to the Opinion of the European Parliament;

Having regard to the Opinion of the Economic and Social Committee;

Whereas Article 85(1) of the Treaty may in accordance with Article 85 (3) be declared inapplicable to categories of agreements, decisions and concerted practices which fulfil the conditions contained in Article 85(3);

Whereas the provisions for implementation of Article 85(3) must be adopted by way of regulation pursuant to Article 87;

Whereas the creation of a common market requires that undertakings be adapted to the conditions of the enlarged market and whereas cooperation between undertakings can be a suitable means of achieving this;

Whereas agreements, decisions and concerted practices for cooperation between undertakings which enable the undertakings to work more rationally and adapt their productivity and competitiveness to the enlarged market may, in so far as they fall within the prohibition contained in Article 85(1), be exempted therefrom under certain conditions; whereas this measure is necessary in particular as regards agreements, decisions and concerted practices relating to the application of standards and types, research and development of products or processes up to the stage of industrial application, exploitation of the results thereof and specialisation;

Whereas it is desirable that the Commission be enabled to declare by way of regulation that the provisions of Article 85(1) do not apply to those categories of agreements, decisions and concerted practices, in order to make it easier for undertakings to cooperate in ways which are economically desirable and without adverse effect from the point of view of competition policy;

Whereas it should be laid down under what conditions the Commission, in close and constant liaison with the competent authorities of the Member States, may exercise such powers;

Whereas under Article 6 of Regulation No 17[4] the Commission may provide that a decision taken in accordance with Article 85(3) of the Treaty shall apply with retroactive effect; whereas it is desirable that the Commission be empowered to issue regulations whose provisions are to the like effect;

Whereas under Article 7 of Regulation No 17 agreements, decisions and concerted practices may by decision of the Commission be exempted from prohibition, in particular if they are modified in such a manner that Article 85(3) applies to them; whereas it is desirable that the Commission be enabled to grant by regulation like exemption to such agreements, decisions and concerted practices if they are modified in such manner as to fall within a category defined in an exempting regulation;

Whereas the possibility cannot be excluded that, in a specific case, the conditions set out in Article 85(3) may not be fulfilled; whereas the Commission must have power to regulate such a case in pursuance of Regulation No 17 by way of decision having effect for the future;

HAS ADOPTED THIS REGULATION:

Art. 1. 1. Without prejudice to the application of Regulation No 17 the Commission may, by regulation and in accordance with Article 85(3) of the Treaty, declare that Article 1 shall not apply to categories of agreements between undertakings, decisions of associations of undertakings and concerted practices which have as their object:

(a) the application of standards or types;

(b) the research and development of products or processes up to the stage of industrial application, and exploitation of the results, including provisions regarding industrial property rights and confidential technical knowledge;

(c) specialisation, including agreements necessary for achieving it.

2. Such regulation shall define the categories of agreements, decisions and concerted practices to which it applies and shall specify in particular:

(a) the restrictions or clauses which may, or may not, appear in the agreements, decisions and concerted practices;

(b) the clauses which must be contained in the agreements, decisions and concerted practices or the other conditions which must be satisfied.

Art. 2. 1. Any regulation pursuant to Article 1 shall be made for a special period.

2. It may be repealed or amended where circumstances have changed with

respect to any of the facts which were basic to its being made; in such case, a period shall be fixed for modification of the agreements, decisions and concerted practices to which the earlier regulation applies.

Art. 3. A regulation pursuant to Article 1 may provide that it shall apply with retroactive effect to agreements, decisions and concerted practices to which, at the date of entry into force of that regulation, a decision issued with retroactive effect in pursuance of Article 6 of Regulation No 17 would have applied.

Art. 4. 1. A regulation pursuant to Article 1 may provide that the prohibition contained in Article 85(1) of the Treaty shall not apply, for such period as shall be fixed by that regulation, to agreements, decisions and concerted practices already in existence on 13 March 1962 which do not satisfy the conditions of Article 85(3), where:

- within six months of the entry into force of the regulation, they are so modified as to satisfy the said conditions in accordance with the provisions of the regulation; and

- the modifications are brought to the notice of the Commission within the time limit fixed by the regulation.

A Regulation adopted pursuant to Article 1 may lay down that the prohibition referred to in Article 85(1) of the Treaty shall not apply, for the period fixed in the same Regulation, to agreements and concerted practices which existed at the date of accession and which, by virtue of accession, come within the scope of Article 85 and do not fulfil the conditions set out in Article 85(3).[5]

The provisions of the preceding subparagraph shall apply in the same way as the case of the accession of the Hellenic Republic.

2. Paragraph 1 shall apply to agreements, decisions and concerted practices which had to be notified before 1 February 1963, in accordance with Article 5 of Regulation No 17, only where they have been so notified before that date.

Paragraph 1 shall be applicable to those agreements and concerted practices which, by virtue of the accession, come within the scope of Article 85(1) of the Treaty and for which notification before 1 July 1973 is mandatory, in accordance with Articles 5 and 25 of Regulation No 17, only if notification was given before that date.[5]

Paragraph 1 shall not apply to agreements and concerted practices to which Article 85(1) of the Treaty applies by virtue of the accession of the Hellenic Republic and which must be notified before 1 July 1981, in accordance with Articles 5 and 25 of Regulation No 17, unless they have been so notified before that date.[6]

3. The benefit of the provisions laid down pursuant to paragraph 1 may not be claimed in actions pending at the date of entry into force of a regulation adopted pursuant to Article 1; neither may it be relied on as grounds for claims for damages against third parties.

Art. 5. Before making a regulation, the Commission shall publish a draft thereof to enable all persons and organisations concerned to submit their comments within such time limit, being not less than one month, as the Commission shall fix.

Art. 6. 1. The Commission shall consult the Advisory Committee on Restrictive Practices and Monopolies:

(a) before publishing the draft regulation;

(b) before making a regulation.

2. Paragraphs 5 and 6 of Article 10 of Regulation No 17, relating to consultation with the Advisory Committee, shall apply by analogy, it being understood that joint meetings with the Commission shall take place not earlier than one month after dispatch of the notice convening them.

Art. 7. Where the Commission, either on its own initiative or at the request of a Member State or of natural or legal persons claiming a legitimate interest, finds that in any particular case agreements, decisions or concerted practices to which a regulation made pursuant to Article 1 of this Regulation applies have nevertheless certain effects which are incompatible with the conditions laid down in Article 85(3) of the Treaty, it may withdraw the benefit of application of that regulation and take a decision in accordance with Articles 6 and 8 of Regulation No 17, without any notification under Article 4(1) of Regulation No 17 being required.

This Regulation shall be binding in its entirety and directly applicable in all Member States.

Done at Brussels, 20 December 1971.

*For the Council*

*The President*

M. PEDINI

1. J.O. No L 285, 29 December 1971, p. 46; O.J. (Special Edition 1971 III) p. 1022.

2. J.O. No L 291, 28 December 1972, p. 144; O.J. (Special Edition 1972 28-30 December) p. 60.

3. Act concerning the conditions of accession of the Hellenic Republic, signed at Athens 28 May 1979. O.J. No L 291, 19 November 1979.

4. J.O. No 13, 21 February 1962, p. 204; O.J. (Special Edition 1959-1962) p. 87.

5. Amended by Regulation 2743/72/EEC.

6. Amended by the Act of Accession of the Hellenic Republic.

Annex X

COMMISSION REGULATION (EEC) No 3604/82

of 23 December 1982[1]

on the application of Article 85 (3) of the Treaty to categories of specialisation agreements

THE COMMISSION OF THE EUROPEAN COMMUNITIES,

Having regard to the Treaty establishing the European Economic Community, and in particular Article 87 thereof;

Having regard to Council Regulation (EEC) No 2821/71 of 20 December 1971 on the application of Article 85(3) of the Treaty to categories of agreements, decisions and concerted practices[2] as amended by Regulation (EEC) No 2743/72[3] and by the Acts concerning the conditions of accession and the adjustments to the Treaties of 1979[4] and in particular Article 1 thereof,

Having published the draft of this Regulation,

Having consulted the Advisory Committee on Restrictive Practices and Dominant Positions,

1. Whereas Regulation (EEC) No 2821/71 empowers the Commission to apply Article 85(3) of the Treaty by Regulation to certain categories of agreements, decisions and concerted practices concerning specialisation, including agreements necessary for achieving it, which fall within Article 85(1);

2. Whereas agreements for the specialisation of present or future production may fall within the prohibition contained in Article 85(1);

3. Whereas agreements for the specialisation of production lead in general to an improvement in the production or distribution of goods, because the undertakings can concentrate on the manufacture of certain products, thus operate on a more rational basis and offer these products at more favourable prices; whereas it is to be anticipated that, with effective competition, consumers will receive a fair share of the profit resulting therefrom;

4. Whereas these advantages arise in the same way out of agreements whereby each participant gives up manufacture of certain products in favour of another as out of agreements whereby participants undertake to only manufacture or have manufactured certain products jointly;

5. Whereas this Regulation must determine what restrictions on competition may be included in a specialisation agreement; whereas the restrictions on competition, going beyond reciprocal giving up of manufacture, which are thus permitted are normally essential for the entering into,

and implementation of, the agreement; whereas these restrictions are therefore in general indispensable for the purpose of ensuring that the desired benefits accrue to undertakings and consumers; whereas it may be left to the contracting parties to decide which of these provisions they include in their agreements;

6. Whereas, in order to ensure that competition is not eliminated in respect of a substantial part of the goods in question, this Regulation applies only if the share of the market held by the participating undertakings and the size of the undertakings themselves do not exceed a specified limit;

7. Whereas in order to facilitate the conclusion of long-term specialisation agreements, which can have an impact on the structure of the participating undertakings, it is appropriate to fix the period of validity of the Regulation at 15 years; whereas, if the circumstances on the basis of which this Regulation was adopted should change within this period, the Commission will undertake the necessary amendments;

8. Whereas agreements, decisions and concerted practices which satisfy the conditions set out in this Regulation need not be notified; whereas an undertaking may nonetheless in a particular case, where justified doubt exists, require the Commission to declare whether its agreements comply with this Regulation;

HAS ADOPTED THIS REGULATION:

Art. 1. Pursuant to Article 85(3) of the Treaty and subject to the provisions of this Regulation, it is hereby declared that Article 85(1) of the Treaty shall not apply to any agreement whereby, with the object of specialisation and for the duration of the agreement, undertakings mutuqlly undertake either:

(a) not to manufacture themselves, or to have manufactured by other undertakings, certain products and to leave to other contracting parties the task of manufacturing, or of having manufactured, such products; or

(b) to only manufacture or have manufactured certain products jointly.

Art. 2. 1. Apart from the obligation referred to in Article 1, no restriction on competition shall be imposed on the contracting parties other than:

(a) the obligation not to conclude with other undertakings specialisation agreements relating to identical products or to products considered by users to be similar by reason of their characteristics, price or use, except with the consent of the other contracting parties;

(b) the obligation to supply the other contracting parties with the the products which are the subject of specialisation, and in so doing to observe minimum standards of quality;

(c) the obligation to purchase products, which are the subject of specialisation, solely from another contracting party or from an undertaking which the contracting parties jointly charged with the manufacture, except where more favourable terms of purchase are available elsewhere and the other contracting party, or the undertaking charged with the manufacture, are not prepared to offer the same terms;

(d) the obligation to grant to other contracting parties the exclusive right to distribute the products which are the subject of specialisation provided that intermediaries and users can also obtain these products from other suppliers and that the contracting parties do not render it difficult for intermediaries or users to thus obtain the products.

2. Article 1 shall apply notwithstanding that the following obligations are imposed:

(a) the obligation to maintain minimum stocks of the product which are the subject of the specialisation and the replacement parts for them;

(b) the obligation to supply customer and guarantee services for the products which are the subject of the specialisation.

Art. 3. Article 1 shall apply only:

(a) if the products which are the subject of the specialisation and other products of the participating undertakings considered by users to be similar by reason of their characteristics, price or use do not represent, in a substantial part of the common market, more than 15% of the market for all such products; and

(b) if the total annual turnover of the participating undertakings does not exceed 300 million ECU.

Art. 4. 1. For the purposes of Article 3(b) of this Regulation, the ECU is the unit of account used for drawing up the budget of the Community pursuant to Articles 207 and 209 of the Treaty.

2. Article 1 of this Regulation shall remain applicable where during any period of two consecutive financial years the share of the market or the turnover referred to in Article 3 is exceeded by no more than 10%.

3. For the pupose of calculating total annual turnover within the meaning of Article 3(b), the turnovers achieved during the last financial year by the participating undertakings in respect of all goods and services excluding all taxes and duties shall be added together. In this connection no account shall be taken of dealings between the participating undertakings or between these undertakings and the undertakings charged with manufacture.

Art. 5. For the puposes of Articles 3(1)(a) and (b) and 4(3), participating undertakings are:

(a) the undertakings party to the agreement;

(b) undertakings in which a party to the agreement, directly or indirectly:

- owns more than half the capital or business assets, or

- has more than half the voting rights, or

- is able to appoint at least half the members of the supervisory board, board of management or bodies legally representing the undertaking, or

- is able to manage the affairs;

(c) undertakings which directly or ondirectly have in or over the undertakings party to the agreement, the rights or powers listed in (b);

(d) undertakings in which an undertaking referred to in (c) directly or indirectly has the rights or powers listed in (b).

Art. 6. The Commission may withdraw the benefit of this Regulation pursuant to Article 7 of Regulation (EEC) No 2821/71 when it finds in a particular case that an agreement exempted by this Regulation nevertheless has effects which are incompatible with the conditions set out in Article 85(3) of the Treaty and in particular where the specialisation is not yet yielding significant results or that consumers are not receiving a fair share of the resulting profit.

Art. 7. This Regulation shall apply by analogy to the categories of decisions of associations of undertakings and concerted practices defined in Article 1.

Art. 8. This Regulation shall enter into force on 1 January 1983.

It shall apply until 31 December 1997.

This Regulation shall be binding in its entirety and directly applicable in all Member States.

Done at Brussels, 23 December 1982.

*For the Commission*

Frans ANDRIESSEN

*Member of the Commission*

1. O.J. No L 376, 31 December 1982, p. 33.

2. O.J. No L 285, 29 December 1971, p. 46; O.J. (Special Edition 1971 III) p. 1022, CM/L/II/13.

3. J.O. No L 291, 28 December 1972, p. 144; O.J. (Special Edition 1972, 28-30, December) p. 60.

4. O.J. No L 291, 19 November 1979, p. 94.

ANNEX XI

# PROPOSAL FOR A COMMISSION REGULATION (EEC) ON THE APPLICATION OF ARTICLE 85 (3) OF THE TREATY TO CERTAIN CATEGORIES OF PATENT LICENSING AGREEMENTS[1]

THE COMMISSION OF THE EUROPEAN COMMUNITIES,

Having regard to the Treaty establishing the European Economic Community, and in particular Articles 87 and 155 thereof,

Having regard to Council Regulation No 19/65/EEC of 2 March 1965 on the application of Article 85(3) of the Treaty to certain categories of agreements and concerted practices[2],

Having published the draft of this Regulation in accordance with Article 5 of Regulation No 19/65/EEC[3],

Having consulted the Advisory Committee on Retsrictive Practices and Dominant Positions in accordance with Article 6 of Regulation No 19/65/EEC,

WHEREAS:

Under Regulation No 19/65/EEC the Commission is competent to apply Article 85(3) of the Treaty by regulation to certain categories of agreements to which only two undertakings are party, which fall within the scope of Article 85(1) and which include restrictions imposed in relation to the assignment or use of industrial property rights, in particular patents, utility models, designs or trade marks, or to the rights arising out of contracts for assignment of, or the right to use, a method of manufacture or knowledge relating to the use or to the application of industrial processes.

Patent licensing agreements are agreements whereby one undertaking, the holder of a patent (the licensor), permits another undertaking (the licensee) to exploit the patented invention.

On the basis of experience so far gained in the light of individual decisions, Article 1 of this Regulation defines a category of patent licensing agreements which fall under the prohibition in Article 85(1), but in respect of which the conditions of Article 85(3) can normally be regarded as fulfilled.

It is not necessary to exclude explicitly from this category agreements which do not satisfy the tests of Article 85(1) of the Treaty. Nevertheless it is useful, with a view to legal certainty in the interests of the undertakings concerned, to list in Article 2 of this Regulation obligations that are commonly included in patent licensing agreements and whose anti-competitive effects may be open to question. This list is not exhaustive. Article 2(1)(1) takes account of the case law of the Court of Justice of the European Communities[4] on the circumstances in which obligations undertaken by a licensor not to operate in his licensee's territory and not to grant further licences there do not fall within the scope of Article 85(1). These circumstances obtain where such obligations are necessary for the introduction and protection of a new technology in the licensed territory, in particular in view of the importance of the research carried out and the risk run in manufacturing and selling a product unfamiliar to consumers in the licensed territory at the time the agreement is entered into.

In so far as the abovementioned obligations do not satisfy the tests established by the Court and are accordingly caught by Article 85(1), it is appropriate to include them in Article 1 so that they may benefit from this Regulation.

Patent licensing agreements to which undertakings in only one Member State are party and which concern patents in that State only are also covered by this Regulation to the extent that they may affect trade between Member States.

It is appropriate to extend this Regulation to patent licensing agreements containing provisions concerning the assignment of, or the right to use, secret methods of manufacture or secret knowledge relating to the use or application of industrial processes, which are communicated to the licensee for the purpose of manufacturing the patented product or using the patented process. This is because such mixed agreements are very common. However, for the purposes of this Regulation such agreements can be regarded as fulfilling the conditions of Article 85(3) only if the methods or knowhow disclosed are secret and contribute to a certain extent to the enhancement of technical knowledge, though without necessarily involving the inventive steps required for patentable inventions (Article 1(1)(6). However, the Regulation covers agreements relating to knowhow for so long only as one licensed patent at least remains in force.

It is also appropriate to extend this Regulation to patent licensing agreements containing ancillary provisions on trade marks. In doing this it must be ensured that the licensing of trade marks is not used to extend the effects of the patent licence beyond the life of the patent (Articles 1(1)(7) and 3(5)).

Each of the obligations listed in Articles 1 and 2 generally contributes to improving the production of goods and to promoting technical progress; in particular they make patentees more willing to grant licences and other undertakings more inclined to run the risk of investing capital to manufacture, use and distribute a new product or to use a new process. Undertakings other than the patentee thereby acquire the possibility of manufacturing their products with the aid of the latest techniques and of developing those techniques further. In this way the number of production facilities and the quantity and quality of goods produced in the common market are increased.

This expansion of production using more advanced techniques represents a benefit in which consumers as a rule share by reason of the increase in the range and quality of goods on the market.

It must, however, be ensured that patent licensing agreements do not contain restrictions that are not indispensable to the attainment of these objectives and do not afford the possibility of eliminating competition in respect of a substantial part of the products in question.

These conditions are fulfilled as a rule in the case if exclusive manufacturing licences for the whole common market, since cases are rare in which a dominant position is founded on the legal monopoly arising from a patent, and in such cases it is exceptional for the patentee to grant exclusive licences. Where such a case arises, and it is found that the patent licensing agreement has led to the elimination of competition in respect of a substantial part of the products in question, the Commission will apply Article 7 of Regulation No 19/65/EEC.

On the other hand, territorial protection afforded by restrictions on imports and exports can be permitted only if it is necessary for securing an improvement in the production of goods and the promotion of technical progress. Very large undertakings cannot be assumed, for the purposes of a block exemption regulation, to require such protection against risks to their investment, in view of their considerable financial capacity. Such financial capacity is determined by reference to a high turnover (Article 1(2)(a)); this is the only criterion by which third parties can assess whether export bans are permissible. The turnover limit of 100 million ECU[5] will allow most independent firms in the Community that grant or take licences to enjoy territorial protection, even if the other party is over the turnover limit.

Turnover means the worldwide turnover of a contracting party and of all undertakings connected with that party (Article 14(3)). Connected undertakings are defined in Article 13. For the purposes of this Regulation it is assumed that in the cases there envisaged a contracting party can benefit from the financial capacity of the group as a whole.

Subject to this limit on the size of the undertaking, territorial protection may be granted for the full life of all patents existing in the areas protected by import restrictions at the time the agreement is made (Article 1(2)(b)). Further, the protection can be allowed only for products in which there is independent trade (Article 1(2)(c)). Lastly, the Regulation requires that the undertaking protected by import restrictions itself assumes the risk of manufacturing the licensed product (Article 1(2)(d)). It therefore does not apply to mere sales licences, they are subject to the provisions of Commission Regulation (EEC) No 1983/83 of 22 June 1983 on the application of Article 85(3) of the Treaty to categories of exclusive distribution agreements[6].

The Regulation specifies the obligations in restraint of competition that may be contained in a patent licensing agreement. It may be left to the contracting parties to decide which of these obligations they specifically include in the patent licensing agreements so as best to achieve the desired advantages.

The Regulation must also specify the restrictions or clauses that may not be included in the patent licensing agreements to which it applies. The restrictions listed in Article 3 of the Regulation generally fall under the prohibition in Article 85(1); in their case there can be no general assumption that they will lead to the positive effects required by Article 85(3), as would be necessary for the granting of a block exemption by regulation. Their exemption must consequently be subject to an examination of the individual circumstances of the case on the basis of a notification.

Such restrictions include clauses whereby the licensee is held to his obligations despite possible doubt as to the patentability of the invention (Article 3(1)) or despite the fact that the licensed patents are not being used or are no longer in force (Article 3(4)(a)), or which impede one of the parties in exploiting the licensed product or process in areas where there is no patent protection (Article 3(12)).

They also include restrictions on the parties' freedom to determine independently the prices of the licensed products (Article 3(7)), their use and in particular their marketing arrangements (Article 3(8)), and the quantities of them manufactured or sold (Article 3(6)), since restrictions of the latter type can have the same effects as export bans.

They include, further, restrictions on the parties' freedom to take an interest in techniques other than those licensed, particularly in the same field as the patent, because possible technical advances would thereby be prevented (Article 3(3)), and restrictions imposed by virtue of a patent that extend beyond the patent's normal life (Article 3(2)).

Finally, they include restrictions to which the licensee submits at the time the agreement is made because he wishes to obtain the licence, but which give the licensor an unjustified competitive advantage, such as an obligation to assign to the licensor any improvements the licensee may make to the invention (Article 3(11)), or to accept other licences or goods and services that the licensee does not want from the licensor (Article 3(9)).

Methods of manufacture or knowledge relating to the application of industrial processes can be of considerable economic value, especially if they are secret and of some technical importance. The value of such know-how depends above all on its secrecy; it is consequently protected against industrial espionage. For this reason, licensees can be obliged under the Regulation to keep secret any know-how disclosed to them (Article 2(6)). Yet know-how does not have the same legal standing as a patent. Patent protection is justified because of the patent's limited life and the fact that the state of the art is advanced for the public benefit by the disclosures made in the patent application. This is not the case with know-how that is kept secret. Consequently, no restrictions may be placed on the licensee's freedom to continue to use lawfully acquired know-how after the agreement has expired (Article 3(10)).

Similarly, licensees may not be obliged to make further payments for the use of know-how that has entered into the public domain, since they are thereby placed at a disadvantage in relation to their competitors (Article 3(4)(b)).

Article 4 provides a simplified procedure whereby the parties ti agreements which do not come within the terms of Articles 1 and 2 and yet do not contain any of the restrictions of competition listed in Article 3 can establish, after notification but without a formal decision, the validity of their agreements and thus attain legal certainty.

The obligation in Article 5 to inform the Commission forthwith of arbitration awards relating to patent licensing agreements is justified because arbitration awards are not given publicity and it is consequently difficult to scrutinise the interpretation or application of the agreements in question relating to this Regulation and Articles 85 and

86 of the Treaty, which form part of the Community's public policy.

Since individual decisions issued so far have not yet provided adequate experience, this Regulation does not apply to patent pools, licensing agreements entered into in connection with joint ventures, reciprocal licensing or sales agreements or licensing agreements relating to plant breeding (Article 6).

This Regulation applies only to licences issued in respect of national patents of the Member States, Community[7] and European patents[8] granted for Member States and rights of a similar nature in the common market (Article 11(1)), and to licences in respect of inventions for which a patent application is made within one year (Article 11(2)).

The Regulation also applies to the assignement and acquisition of such rights where the risk associated with commercial exploitation continues to be with the assignor and the agreement has as its object or effect restrictions of competition equivalent to those listed in Articles 1 to 4 of this Regulation (Article 12(2)); likewise it applies to patent licensing agreements in which the licensor is not the patentee but is authorised by the patentee to grant licences, in particular, therefore, to sublicences (Article 12(1)) and to patent licensing agreements in which the parties' rights or obligations are assumed by connected undertakings (Article 12(3)).

Articles 7 to 9 regulate the retroactive exemption of certain patent licensing agreements in existence when this Regulation comes into force where such agreements already fulfil the conditions for application of this Regulation or are modified so as to do so. These provisions are based on Articles 3 and 4 of Council Regulation No 19/65/EEC, Articles 4 to 7 of Council Regulation No 17, Article 29 of the Act concerning the Conditions of Accession and the Adjustments to the Treaties of 22 January 1972 together with its Annex I, Part V, paragraph 2[9], and Article 21 of the Act concerning the Conditions of Accession and the Adjustments to the Treaties of 28 May 1979 together with its Annex I, Part V, paragraph 3[10]. Under Article 4(3) of Regulation No 19/65/EEC, the benefit of these provisions may not be claimed in actions pending at the date of entry into force of this Regulation, nor may it be relied on as grounds for claims for damages against third parties.

Agreements which satisfy the tests of Articles 1 and 2 of this Regulation and which have neither the object nor the effect of restricting competition in any other way need no longer be notified. Nevertheless, undertakings will still have the right to apply in individual cases for negative clearance under Article 2 of Regulation No 17[11] or for a declaration from the Commission under Article 85(3) of the Treaty.

Art. 1. (1) Pursuant to Article 85(3) of the Treaty abd subject to the conditions set out in this Regulation, it is hereby declared that until 31 December 1994 Article 85(1) of the Treaty shall not apply to patent licensing agreements to which only two undertakings are party and which include one or more of the following obligations:

1. without prejudice to Article 2(1)(1), restrictions on the imports or exports of the patented product or a product manufactured using the patented process (licensed product) made by the contracting parties within the common market;

2. without prejudice to Article 2(1)(1), the obligation on the part of the licensor not to manufacture or use the licensed product or use the patented process within the whole of the common market or a defined area thereof (licensed territory) or not to authorise other undertakings to do so;

3. the obligation on the part of the licensee not to manufacture or use the licensed product or use the patented process outside his licensed territory;

4. the obligation on the part of the licensee to procure goods or services from the licensor or from an undertaking designated by the licensor, in so far and for so long as this obligation is indispensable in the interests of a technically unobjectionable exploitation of the invention;

5. the obligation on the part of the licensee to pay a minimum royalty or to produce a minimum quantity of the licensed products or to carry out a minimum number of operations employing the patented invention;

6. obligations on the parties equivalent to those in subparagraphs (1) to (5) above relating to methods of manufacture or information on other technical matters communicated by the licensor, which are secret and contribute to the enhancement of technical knowledge (know-how) and have a close connection with the exploitation of one or more of the licensed patents; this exemption shall cease when all relevant licensed patents existing at the time when the agreement was entered into are no longer in force;

7. the obligation on the part of the licensee to use a trade mark or get-up determined by the licensor as the exclusive distinguishing mark on the licensed product, provided that this obligation can be terminated by the licensee at least three years before expiry of the licensed patents existing at the time when the agreement was entered into.

(2) Import and export restrictions shall be exempted pursuant to paragraph 1(1) and (6) only:

a) where the total annual turnover of the licensor or licensee whose sales territory within the common market is to be protected by import restrictions on the other party or on another licensee does not exceed 100 million ECU;

b) if import and export restrictions in favour of the licensee are agreed for a period not exceeding the duration of the licensed patents existing at the time when the agreement was entered into and the import and export restrictions

- in favour of the licensor do not exceed the duration of the parallel patents existing in the licensor's sales territory within the common market at the time when the agreement was entered into,

- in favour of another licensee do not exceed the duration of the licensed patents existing in his licensed territory at the time when the agreement for that territory was entered into;

this period may not be extended in respect of such obligations by licensing agreements in respect of patents for new applications or improvements or by agreements relating to know-how; and

c) if the licensed product may be sold within the common market by dealers who are not connected with the licensor or the licensee; and

d) if the undertaking whose sales territory within the common market is to be protected by import and export restrictions either manufactures the licensed product itself or has it manufactured by a subcontractor.

Art. 2. (1) Article 1 shall apply notwothstabding the presence of any of the following obligations:

1. the obligation on the part of the licensor not to manufacture, use or sell the licensed product or use the patented process in the licensed territory or not to authorise otherundertakings established there to do so, provided that such obligations are necessary for the introduction and protection of a new technology in the licensed territory, in view of the importance of the research carried out and the risk incurred in manufacturing and selling a product unfamiliar to consumers in the licensed territory when the agreement was entered into;

2. the obligation on the part of the licensee to restrict his utilisation of the patented invention and any know-how communicated for that purpose to one or more distinct technical fields of application covered by the licensed patent;

3. the obligation on the part of the licensee not to exploit the patent after expiry of the agreement, where the patent is still in force;

4. the obligation on the part of the licensee not to grant sublicences or assign the licence to a third party;

5. the obligation on the part of the licensee to mark the licensed product with an indication of the patentee's name, the licensed patent or the patent licensing agreement;

6. the obligation on the part of the licensee not to divulge know-how communicated by the licensor; the licensee may also be bound by this obligation after the agreements has expired;

7. the obligation:

   a) to inform the licensor of infringements of the patent;

   b) to take legal action against an infringer;

   c) to assist the other party in any action against an infringer;

   provided that this obligation is without prejudice to the licensee's right to challenge the validity of the licensed patent;

8. the obligation on thepart of the licensee to observe specifications concerning the minimum quality of the licensed product, provided that such specifications are indispensable in the interests of a techni-

cally unobjectionable exploitation of the invention, and to allow the licensor to carry out appropriate checks, provided that this obligation does not give rise to differentiation as between the products of the licensor, the licensee or other licensees;

9. the obligation on the parties to pass on to each other any experience gained in working the invention and to grant each other licences in respect of inventions relating to improvements and new applications, provided that this obligation is non-exclusive;

10. the obligation on the part of the licensor to grant the licensee any more favourable terms that the licensor may grant to another licensee after the agreement was entered into.

(2) The exemption granted in Article 1(1) shall apply also to agreements containing obligations listed in paragraph 1 of this Article, in so far as such obligations fall within the scope of Article 85(1) of the Treaty, even if they are undertaken otherwise than in conjunction with one or more of the restrictions of competition exempted by Article 1.

Art. 3. Articles 1 and 2(2) shall not apply where -

1. the licensee is prohibited from challenging the validity of the licensed patent or other industrial or commercial property within the common market belonging to the licensor or any undertaking connected with the licensor; impeding such a challenge shall be equated with prohibiting it. The right of the licensor to terminate the licensing agreement in the event of such a challenge is unaffected;

2. without prejudice to the second sentence of paragraph 10 of this Article, the duration of the agreement extends beyond the expiry of the licensed patents existing at the time when the agreement was entered into, unless each party is entitled after such expiry to terminate the agreement at least yearly;

3. without prejudice to Article 1(1)(1) to (3) and (6), one party is restricted from competing with the other party or with undertakings connected with the other party or with other undertakings in respect of research and development, manufacture, use or sales. An obligation on the part of the licensee to use his best endeavours to exploit the licensed invention is unaffected;

4. the licensee,

   a) without prejudice to Article 1(1)(5), is obliged to pay royalties on products that are not at least partly covered by a licensed patent;

   b) is obliged to make payments for the use of know-how communicated under the licence after such know-how has entered into the public domain, unless entry into the public domain is attributable to some default on the part of the licensee or an undertaking connected with the licensee;

5. the licensee is obliged to pay the full royalties stipulated by the licence for the contemporaneous exploitation of patents and a trade mark, even where the licensed patents are no longer in force;

6. one party is restricted as to the maximum quantity of the licensed product manufactured or sold or as to the maximum number of operations employing the patented invention;

7. one party is restricted in the determination of prices, price components or rebates;

8. without prejudice to Article 1(1)(1) to (3), (6) and (7), one party is restricted as to uses of the licensed products, particularly as regards the way in which and the customers to whom the products may be sold, and the restriction is not covered by the licensed patent;

9. without prejudice to Article 1(1)(4), one party was induced when entering into the agreement to accept further licenses he did not want or agree to be supplied with goods or services he did not want;

10. the licensee is prohibited from using after the expiry of the agreement know-how communicated by the licensor, unless the agreement is terminated prematurely because of some default on the part of the licensee or an undertaking connected with the licensee. Subject to subparagraph 4(b), the right of the licensor to require appropriate payments for the use of such know-how for not more than five years after the expiry of the agreement is unaffected;

11. the licensee is obliged to assign wholly or partly to the licensor rights in or rights to patents for improvements or new applications of the licensed patents;

12. without prejudice to Article 1(2), one party is impeded by the other party or an undertaking connected with that other party in respect of the manufacture, use or sale of the licensed product in areas of the common market where neither the licensor nor any undertaking connected with him holds a parallel patent. The right of the licensor, in the event of such manufacture, to require appropriate payments for the use of his know-how is unaffected.

Art. 4

1. Patent licensing agreements containing obligations which are equivalent in their nature or effects to those listed in Articles 1 or 2 and do not fall under Article 3 shall be exempted under this Regulation from the end of the sixth month following notification to the Commission, unless the Commission opposes exemption within this period.

2. The Commission shall oppose exemption if it receives a reasoned request to do so from a Member State within four months of the notification.

3. Paragraph 1 shall apply only if:

   a) express reference is made to this Article in the notification or in a communication accompanying it; and

b) the notification is complete in accordance with Commission Regulation No 27(11); and
c) the conditions set out in Article 1(2) are fulfilled.

4. The benefit of paragraph 1 may be claimed for agreements notified before the entry into force of this Regulation by submitting a communication to the Commission referring expressly to this Article and to the notification. The period specified in paragraph 1 shall run from the date of submission of the Communication within the meaning of Article 3 of Regulation No 27. Subparagraphs 3(b) and (c) shall apply by analogy.

5. The opposition may be withdrawn at any time.

   a) If the opposition is withdrawn because the undertakings concerned have dispelled doubts as to the applicability of Article 85(3), the exemption shall take effect from the date provided for in paragraph 1.
   b) If the opposition is withdrawn because the undertakings concerned have amended the agreement so as to eliminate the grounds therefore, the exemption shall take effect from the date when the parties are notified of the withdrawal of the opposition, of from the date provided for in paragraph 1, whichever is the later.

6. If the Commission opposes exemption and the opposition is not withdrawn, the effects of the notification shall be regulated by Article 4 of Regulation No 17.

Art. 5

Where disputes on the interpretation or application of patent licensing agreements to which Articles 1, 3 or 4 of this Regulation apply are settled by arbitration, the parties to the agreement shall communicate the terms of the award forthwith to the Commission together with the licensing agreement.

Art. 6

This Regulation shall not apply:

1. to agreements between members of a patent pool which relate to the pooled patents;
2. to patent licensing agreements between competitors who hold interests in a joint venture or between one of them and the joint venture if the licensing agreements relate to the activities of the joint venture;
3. without prejudice to Article 2(1)(9), to agreements under which the parties, albeit in separate agreements or through connected undertakings, grant each other patent or trade mark licences or exchange know-how, where the parties are competitors in relation to the licensed products; this shall apply by analogy where one party is allowed to sell the other's unprotected products;
4. to licensing agreements relating to plant breeding.

Art. 7

1. As regards agreements existing on 13 March 1962 and notified before 1 February 1963 and agreements (whether notified or not) falling under Article 4(2)(2)(b) of Regulation No 17, the declaration of inappblicability of Article 85(1) of the Treaty contained in this Regulation shall apply retrospectively from the time at which the conditions for application of this Regulation were fulfilled.

2. As regards all other agreements notified before this Regulation entered into force, the declaration of inapplicability of Article 85(1) of the Treaty contained in this Regulation shall apply retrospectively from the time at which the conditions for application of this Regulation were fulfilled, or from the date of notification, whichever is the later.

Art. 8

If agreements existing on 13 March 1962 and notified before 1 February 1963 or agreements falling under Article 4(2)(2)(b) of Regulation No 17 and notified before 1 January 1967 are amended before 1 July 1984 so as to fulfil the conditions for application of this Regulation, and if the amendment is communicated to the Commission before 1 August 1984, the prohibition in Article 85(1) of the Treaty shall not apply in respect of the period prior to the amendment. The communication shall take effect from the time of its receipt by the Commission. Where the communication is sent by registered post, it shall take effect from the date shows on the postmark of the place of posting.

Art. 9

1. As regards agreements to which Article 85 of the Treaty applies as a result of the accession of the United Kingdom, Ireland and Denmark, Articles 7 and 8 shall apply except that the relevant dates shall be 1 January 1973 instead of 13 March 1962 and 1 July 1973 instead of 1 February 1963 and 1 January 1967.

2. As regards agreements to which Article 85 of the Treaty applies as a result of the accession of Greece, Articles 7 and 8 shall apply except that the relevant dates shall be 1 January 1981 instead of 13 March 1962 and 1 July 1981 instead of 1 February 1963 and 1 January 1967.

Art. 10

The Commission shall examine whether Article 7 of Regulation No 19/65/EEC is applicable in any individual case, in particular where:

1. it appears likely that the licensed products or services resulting from a patented process have no competition from products or services considered by consumers to be similar by reason of their characteristics, intended use or price;

2. the licensor does not have the right to terminate exclusivity of manufacture or use (Article 1(1)(2)) within five years from the date when the agreement was entered into and at least yearly thereafter, should the licensee have failed to exploit a patent

or have done so inadequately;

3. the licensee does not have the right to terminate his obligation to pay a minimum royalty, to produce a minimum quantity of products or to carry out a minimum number of operations employing the patented invention (Article 1(1)(5)) within five years from the date when the agreement was entered into and at least yearly thereafter, subject to this giving up any exclusivity he may have;

4. a substantial competitive disadvantage arises for the licensee because he is obliged to pay the full royalty after an economically important part of the licensed patents is no longer in force or an economically important part of the know-how communicated by the licensor has fallen into the public domain;

5. one party is impeded from promoting the licensed prodct in trade journals or at fairs or exhibitions anywhere in the common market; an obligation on the party to draw attention to restrictions upon him of the type referred to in Article 1(1)(1) shall not be regarded as impeding him;

6. Article 5 is infringed or an arbitration award communicated under that Article does not state the reasons on which it is based.

Art. 11

1. This Regulation shall apply to:

   a) patent applications;

   b) utility models;

   c) applications for registration of utility models;

   d) "certificates d'utilité" and "certificats d'addition" under French law; and

   e) applications for "certificats d'utilité" and "certificats d'addition" under French law;

   in the same way as it applies to patents.

2. This Regulation shall also apply to agreements relating to the exploitation of an invention if an application within the meaning of paragraph 1 is made in respect of the invention for the licensed territory within one year from the date when the agreement was entered into.

Art. 12

This Regulation shall also apply to:

1. a patent licensing agreement where the licensor is not the patentee but is autorized by the patentee to grant a licence or a sublicence;

2. assignments of a patent or of a right to a patent where the sum payable in consideration of the assignment is dependent upon the turnover attained by the assignee in respect of the patented products on the quantity of such products manufactured or on the number of

operations carried out emplouing the patented invention;

3. patent licensing agreemenets in which rights or obligations of the licensor or the licensee are assumed by undertakings connected with them.

Art. 13

1. For the purposes of this Regulation connected undertakings are:

   a) undertakings in which a party to the agreement, directly or indirectly:

      - owns more than half the capital or business assets, or

      - has the power to exercise more than half the voting rights, or

      - has the power to appoint more than half the members of the supervisory board, board of directors or bodies legally representing the undertaking, or

      - has the right to manage their affairs;

   b) undertakings which directly or indirectly have in or over a party to the agreement the rights or pwers listed in a);

   c) undertakings in which an undertaking referred to in b) directly or indirectly has the rights or powers listed in a).

2. Undertakings in which the parties to the agreement or undertakings connected with them jointly have the rights or powers set out in paragraph 1 a) shall be considered to be connected with each of the parties to the agreement.

Art. 14

1. For the purpose of Article (12)(a), the ECU is the unit of account used for drawing up the budget of the Community pursuant to Articles 207 en 209 of the Treaty.

2. Article 1 shall remain applicable during any period of two consecutive financial years the total turnover referred to in in Article 1(2)(a) is exceeded by no more than 10%.

3. For the purpose of calculating total turnover, the turnovers achieved during the last financial year by the party to the agreement and connected undertakings in respect of all goods and services, before any taxes and other duties, shall be added together. For this purpose, no account shall be taken of dealings between a party to the agreement and undertakings connected with him or between yhe connected undertakings.

This Regulation shall enter into force on 1 July 1984.

This Regulation shall be binding in its entirety and directly applicable in all Member States.

1. (This text is reproduced from a Commission working document which has not yet been published.)

2. OJ No 36, 6.3.1965, p. 533

3. OJ No C 58, 3.3.1979, p. 12 et seq. and C 110, 3.5.1979, p. 10

4. Case 258/78 Nungesser v Commission 1982 ECR 2015.

5. OJ No L 345, 20.12.1980, p. 1.

6. OJ L 173, 30.6.1983, p. 1.

7. Convention for the European Patent for the common market (Community Patent Convention) of 15 December 1975, OJ No L 17, 26.1.1976.

8. Convention on the Grant of European Patents of 5 October 1973.

9. OJ No L 73, 27.3.1972, p. 20.

10. OJ No L 291, 19.11.1979, p. 21.

11. OJ No 13, 21.2.1962, p. 204.

12. OJ No 35, 10.5.1962, p. 1118, as amended by Regulation (EEC) No 1133/68/EEC, OJ L 189, 1.8.1968, p. 1.

ANNEX XII

## DRAFT COMMISSION REGULATION ON THE APPLICATION OF ARTICLE 85 (3) OF THE TREATY TO CERTAIN CATEGORIES OF MOTOR VEHICLE DISTRIBUTION AND SERVICING AGREEMENTS[1]

THE COMMISSION OF THE EUROPEAN COMMUNITIES.

Having regard to the Treaty establishing the European Economic Community, and in particular Article 87 thereof,

Having regard to Regulation No 19/65/EEC of 2 March 1965 on the application of Article 85 (3) of the Treaty to certain categories of agreements and concerted practices[2],

Having consulted the Advisory Committee on Restrictive Practices and Dominant Positions, pursuant to Article 6 of Regulation No 19/65/EEC,

Having published the draft of this Regulation, pursuant to Article 5 of Regulation No 19/65/EEC,

WHEREAS:

1. Under Council Regulation No 19/65/EEC the Commission is empowered to declare by means of a regulation that Article 85 (3) of the Treaty applies to certain categories of agreements falling within Article 85 (1) and to which only two undertakings are parties and by which one party undertakes to supply the other alone with certain goods for resale within a defined territory of the common market. In the light of experience since Commission Decision 75/73/EEC[3], distribution and service agreements in the motor vehicle industry can be defined as a category of agreements which can be accepted as satisfying the conditions laid down in Regulation No19/65/EEC. The block exemption applies to those distribution and service agreements which cover motor vehicles for use on public roads and having three or more road wheels, together with spare and replacement parts therefor. In many cases the agreements are concluded according to specified principles, mostly on the basis of standard contracts drawn up by or with the approval of a motor vehicle manufacturer. Inasmuch as the motor vehicle manufacturer selects principally dealers who distribute new cars only of that manufacturer's marque, the dealers usually form a group which equally attempts to influence the terms of the standard agreement. Such dealer agreements meet the requirements of the first indent of Article 1 (1) (a) of Regulation No 19/65/EEC because one undertaking thereby entrusts another with the task of promoting the distribution and servicing of certain products of the motor vehicle industry in a defined area while agreeing to supply products for resale only to the dealer, or only to a limited number of undertakings besides the dealer, within that area.

2. Articles 1 to 4 of this Regulation set out obligations which are entered into, in the exercise of their freedom of contract and in

individual cases, by undertakings engaged in the distribution of motor vehicles. The form and combination of the clauses used in the distribution networks of individual motor vehicle manufacturers are different, depending on the sales policy pursued by the manufacturer for the constitution of his network. In the countries of the common market the distribution and servicing of the products of a motor vehicle manufacturer are for the most part governed by agreements with clauses restricting competition in the same or similar manner. A large number of distribution and servicing agreements have been notified to the Commission pursuant to Articles 4 and 5 of Council Regulation No 17[4].

3. Notwithstanding that the obligations imposed by distribution and servicing agreements which are listed in Articles 1 to 3 of this Regulation normally have as their object or effect the prevention, restriction of distortion of competition within the common market and are normally apt to affect trade between Member States, the prohibition in Article 85 (1) of the Treaty may nevertheless be declared inapplicable to these agreements by virtue of Article 85 (3), albeit only under certain restrictive conditions. The obligations listed in Article 4 (1) of this Regulation have been included in this exemption as a matter of precaution, since in particular circumstances they may also fall within the scope of Article 85 (1) (Article 4 (2)).

4. The applicability of Article 85 (1) of the Treaty to distribution and servicing agreements in the motor vehicle industry stems from the fact that restrictions same or similar form throughout the common market for the products supplied within the distribution system of a particular manufacturer. The motor vehicle manufacturers cover the whole common market or substantial parts of it by means of a cluster of agreements with similar restrictions on competition and affect in this way not only distribution and servicing in each Member State but also trade between Member States.

5. The restrictions in the distribution networks of motor vehicle manufacturers throughout the common market lead in particular to the following restrictions of competition:
As a result of the exclusive distribution clauses (Article 1 and Article 2, No 1), the resellers in the contract territory who do not benefit from a distribution agreement for the contract goods are excluded from direct supply by the manufacturer or importer, whether or not those resellers' business meet the qualitative conditions (Article 4). Final consumers can no longer obtain contact goods direct from the manufacturer or importer (Article 2, No 2).
At alle levels of distribution only those undertakings selected by or with the approval of the manufacturer and fullfilling certain qualifying conditions have access to the manufacturer's distribution and servicing network (Article 3, No 6 and Article 4 (1). Other undertakings are unable purchase and resell the contract goods (Article 3, No 9). Since in most cases the dealers are subject to a ban on dealing in competing products (Article 3, Nos 3 to 5), the number of intermediaries available to all manufacturers of vehicles and spare parts is limited.
A prohibition of certain distribution activities outside their allotted areas imposed on the selected dealers (Article 3, Nos 7 and 8) has the effect of reducing the intensity of competition throughout the common market both with distribution networks and between them.

6. Motor vehicle industry distribution and servicing agreements will nevertheless satisfy the requirements of Article 85 (3) of the Treaty where they meet the conditions laid down in this Regulation. Such agreements contribute to improving the production and distribution of goods and to promoting technical and economic progress; it may also be taken that the restrictions are indispensable to the attainment of these objectives; they do not afford the possibility of eliminating competition in respect of a substantial part of the products in question; and in particular, consumers are allowed a fair share of the resulting benefit.
The Commission's administrative practise, based on its Decision 75/73/EEC, and the experience gained since then, have confirmed that the special circumstances of the motor vehicle industry justify a block exemption.

7. The exclusive and selective distribution clauses can be regarded as indispensable measures of rationalization in the motor vehicle industry because motor vehicles are consumer durables which at both regular and irregular intervals require expert maintenance and repair, not always in the same place. Motor vehicle manufacturers cooperate with the selected dealers and repairers who may also carry out servicing in order to provide for specialized servicing for the product. On grounds of capacity and efficiency alone, such a form of cooperation cannot be extended to an unlimited number of dealers and service stations. The linking of servicing and distribution must be regarded as more efficient than a separation between a distribution organisation for new vehicles on the one hand and a servicing organization which would also distribute spare parts on the other, particularly as, before a new vehicle is delivered to the final consumer, it must undergo a technical inspection by the distribution and servicing undertaking supplying it.

8. However, obligatory recourse to the authorized network is not all respects indispensable for efficient distribution. The exceptions to the block exemption provide that the sale of contract goods to dealers may not be prohibited where the dealers:

- belong to the same distribution network (Article 3, No 9 (a));

- are authorized by final consumers to purchase amd take delivery of products in order to take advantage of favourable purchasing conditions in the common market (b); or

- require space, exchange or replacement parts for repair purposes, i.e. parts to be fitted by the dealers themselves in the course of repairs carried out by them (c).

9. It should be possible to bar wholesalers not belonging to the distribution network from reselling parts originating from motor vehicle manufacturers. The dealers and repairers belonging to the motor vehicle manufacturer's distribution network are normally obliged to keep a wide range of spare and replacement parts, specified in the contract programme, in stock (Article 4 (1), (c). The nature and extent of the obligation depends on the distribution and stockholding function (wholesale or retail) and on the rate of turnover of the parts. Wholesalers outside the distribution network have no obligation to keep any particular level of stocks. They are able to concentrate on the lower-cost distribution of parts with a rapid turnover, and can

deal in several marques. In comparison, dealers and service stations belonging to the distribution network are placed at a competative disadvantage, as they are obliged to carry stocks of parts specified in the contract programme, including some with a low turnover, and have to bear the higher costs accruing in consequence. It must be supposed that this system of rapid availability of spare parts across the whole contract programme, which is beneficial to the consumer, could not be maintained without obligatory recourse to the authorized network.

10. The ban on dealing in competing products may in principle be extempted, because it contributes to a position where the undertakings in the distribution network concentrate their efforts on the products constructed and assembled by the vehicle manufacturer or supplied by him, and thus ensures distribution and servicing appropriate for that manufacturer's vehicles. The ban provides an incentive for the undertaking to develop sales and servicing of the contract goods and thus to promote competetion in the supply of those products as well as between those products and competing products.

11. However, bans on dealing in competing products cannot be regarded as indispensable in all circumstances to rational distribution. There are two groups of cases in which such a ban should not be exempted. Dealers and repairers must be free to obtain from third parties supplies of parts which match the quality of those offered by the other contracting party, for example where the parts are produced by a subcontracting manufacturer who also supplies the motor vehicle manufacturer who also supplies the motor vehicle manufacturer, and to use and sell them. Such undertakings must also keep their freedom to choose parts which are usable in vehicles covered by the agreement and which not only match but exceed the quality standard. Such a limit on the ban on dealing in competing products takes account of the importance of vehicle safety and of the maintenance of effective competition in the market for motor vehicle parts and repairs (Article 3, No 4). Where the vehicles to be repaired or equipped are not covered by the sealer agreement, an obligation on the dealer not to obtain, use or sell parts which compete with the contract goods cannot be regarded as indispnesable, if only by reason of the undertaking's own secondhand trade.

12. The restrictions imposed on the dealer's activities outside its allotted area lead to more intensive distribution and servicing efforts in an easily supervised area, to market knowledge based on closer contact with consumers, and to more demand-oriented supply (Article 3, Nos 7 and 8). On the other hand, demand for contract goods must remain flexible and should not be limited on a regional basis. Dealers must not be confined to satisfying the demand for contract goods within their contract territories, but must also be able to meet demand from persons and undertakings in other areas of the common market. Dealers should not be prevented from advertising in a wider area than the allotted one where such advertisement is also directed to customers in the contract territory, because advertising of this kind does not run counter to the primary obligation to promote sales within the contract territory.

13. The obligations listed in Article 4 (1) relate to minimum standards in distribution and Services (a), ordering procedures (b), stocks (c), sales efforts within the contract territory (d) and guarantees and

service (e). They are directly related to the obligations in Articles 1 to 3, and influence their restrictive effect. In some cases they may themselves have the object or effect of restricting competition. This is indeed normally the case of stockholding going beyond short-term needs. under No. 3. Where the obligations described in Article 4 (1) are to be passed on to the subsequent level of distribution, and therefore have a restrictive character, they are exempted by Article 3, No.6. The requirements for exempting the obligations listed under Article 4 (1), where they might in individual cases be caught by the prohibition of Article 85 (1) of the reaty, are also satisfied because of their direct relationship with one or more of the obligations exempted by Articles 1 to 3 (Article 4 (2).

14. Obligations imposed on the dealer to purchase supplies of the contract goods exclusively from the other contracting -arty cannot be exempted in an exclusive and selective distribution system, because they unreasonably restrict competition in the products between the limited number of selected dealers (Article 6, No.3). However, clauses wich fix the dates by which orders must be placed (Article 4(1), (b) do not restrict competition provided that they do not have the effect of obliging the dealer to purchase supplies only from the other contracting party for relatively long periods. Clauses relating to the rationalization of orders for contract goods do not affect free competitions so long as it is still possible to purchase contract goods from other dealers who are also authorized to distribute contract goods within the distribution network. It can be assumed that this possibility will normally be possible where the interval for ordering referred to in Article 4 (1) (b) is not exceeded.

15. According to Article 1(2) (b) of Regulation No 19/65/EEC, the declaration of inapplicability made in this regulation must be made subject to conditions.

16. Under Article 1 and Article 2 only dealer agreements which provide either that one dealer shall have the exclusive right within the contract territory to receive direct supplies from the contractual supllier or that such a right is to be extended only to a few other dealers in the contract territory besides the undertaking entrusted with distribution and servicing are exempted. Where several dealers are appointed in one contract territory, Article 5, No 1 provides that each dealer must undertake to promote sales and service throughout that territory . Where several dealers are appointed, the authority conferred by Regulation No 19/65/EEC operates because the contract territory is stated to be a factor in the obligation to promote sales and service and the dealers selected for that territory shall be in active competition with each other.

17. Article 5, No 2(a) provides that restrictions of the kind described in Articles 3 and 4 imposed on a dealer are only exempted where they are offset by an exclusive dealing obligation imposed on the other contracting party. This limitation on the exemption granted is necessary in order to comply with the terms of Regulation No 19/65/EEC, which relates to exclusive supply or purchase obligations. It is also required in order to prevent a situation airising in which a dealer who is norminally free to engage in competitive activity might abstain from doing so because it might jeopardize the interests of the motor vehicle manufacturer or of another undertaking in the distribution net-

work. The risk of such inaction stems from the dealers' economic dependence on the supplier; obligations of the kind described in Articles 3 and 4 will normally create such dependence. These obligations prompt the dealer to adapt his business and investments to the particular need for cooperation with the supplier, so that he cannot make short-term changes without damaging his commercial interests. If these obligations are offset by an exclusive dealing obligation on the part of the supplier, the balance of rights and duties between the parties become more equitable, the dealer's unilateral dependence is reduced, and the latter's capacity to compete is increased. The supplier may, however, reserve the right to appoint further dealers in the contract territory if this is indispensable to overall sales planning (Article 5, No (2) (a)). In cases where the dealer breaches fundamental obligations of the agreement, an appropriate further limitation on the exclusive dealing obligation imposed on the contractual supplier is to be provided for (Article 5, No (2) (b)).

18. Art. 5 No 2 (c) is directed against the conclusion and application of bans on dealing in competing products which are too wide. Clauses delt with in Article 3, Nos 3, 5 and 6 must be subject to the general reservation that the ban may not be invoked without objectively valid reason. Whether or not such a reason exists in an individual case will depend in particular on the extent to which the contract goods are in competition with other such products and whether the promotion of the distribution or servicing of contract goods may be adversely affected if a competing product is distributed.

19. Article 5, No 2 (d) obliges the supplier not to use its power to determine the dealer's obligations, as defined in Article 4 (1), in a discriminatory way. The need for this provision arises in particular because there is usually a no-competition clause.

20. Article 5, No 3 makes it a condition of exemption that the distribution and servicing undertaling shall honour the minimum warranty and provide the minimum free servicing laid down by the manufacturer of with its consent, irrespective of where in the common market the vehicle was purchased. A dealer within the distribution system is not, however, obliged to honour warranties and give free service for a vehicle which he has not supplied to a greater extent than would follow from his obligations in relation to his own sales or from those od the dealer within the distribution system who sold the vehicle (a). It is a further condition that the obligation shall be extended to all the stages of distribution which provide servicing (b). The provisions are intended to prevent the consumer's freedom to buy anywhere in the common market from being limited.

21. In view of the extent of the obligations which may, under Articles 3 and 4 be imposed on the dealer, and their considerable restricting effects, Article 5, No 4 lays down minimum requirements for the duration and termination of agreements which impose a ban on dealing in competing products as described in Article 3, No 3 or 5, and thus make the dealer economically dependent on the supplier.

22. In declaring that certain systems of discount based on total quantities and amounts are not compatible with the exemption, Article 5, No 5 is intended to counterbalance the tendency of the dealer to

concentrate his demand on the other contracting party. The purpose of this provision is to allow suppliers of motor vehicle parts and accessories which do not offer as wide a range of goods as a manufacturer to compete on equal terms for sales to distribution and servicing undertakes belonging to the manufacturer's network.

23. Article 5, No 6 makes exemption subject to the condition that customers in the common market are able to purchase anywhere in the common market a motor vehicle manufactured in series with the specifications appropriate for their place of residence or where the vehicle is to be registered. This does not, however, apply where the corresponding model is not supplied by the manufacturer or his importer through the local dealer at all. This provision averts the danger that motor vehicle manufacturers might apply market partitioning between national markets by means of product differentiation as between parts of the common market in association with deliberate refusals to supply in certain parts.

24. Article 1 (2) (a) of Regulation No 19/65/EEC provides that the restrictions or clauses which must not be contained in dealer agreements shall be specified if the declaration of inapplicability of Article 85 (1) by this Regulation is not valid.

25. Because of their far-reaching effects on competition, agreements by which one motor vehicle manufacturer entrusts another such manufacturer with the distribution of his products cannot benefit from the block exemption provided for in this Regulation (Article 6, No 1).

26. Resale price maintenance precludes exemption under this Regulation (Article 6, No 2).

27. The exemption does not apply where the parties to the agreement negotiate obligations which would be admissible under the combination of obligations which is exempted by Commission Regulation No 67/67/EEC of 22 March 1967 on the application of Article 85 (3) of the Treaty to certain categories of exclusive distribution agreements[5], but which go beyond the scope of obligations exempted by this Regulation (Article 6, No 3). This is particularly necessary in the case of exclusive purchase obligations (Article 1 (1) (b) and (c) of Regulation No 67/67/EEC and of unqualified bans on dealing in competing products (Article 2 (1) (a) of Regulation No 67/67/EEC).

28. A ban of the kind described in Article 3, No 9, which prohibits the sale to dealers of products covered by the agreement, must be excluded from the exemption in two cases (Article 7 (1)).

29. It may generally be concluded from observation of imports of motor vehicles through distribution channels other than those established by the manufacturer (parallel imports) that the incentive to engage in parallel imports within the common market increases rapidly where recommendations in different Member State produce price variations of more than about 12% of the lowest price. Parallel imports grow faster the further recommended prices diverge. Article 7, No 1 is aimed at preventing any abuse of the exemption of obligatory recourse to the authorized network. There is evidence of such an abuse where the manufacturer or importer can by recommending different prices, influence, for a considerable period and differently as between Member

States. In the interests of effective competition, demand from dealers who do not belong to the distribution network for contract goods should therefore be admitted. Price comparisons are to be made in terms of the ECU, the currency unit[6] (Article 7 (2)). In two cases, the public interest does not require that the legal protection given by Article 7 (1) be automatically withheld from clauses in distribution agreements which exclude independent traders from dealing in new motor vehicles (Article 7 (3)). It cannot be ruled out that the pricing of new motor vehicles in a Member State is subject to conditions quite different from those in most other Member States, if those who buy them must pay exceptionally high taxes, duties or fees or if prices and margins are fixed or prescribed by regulations over a considerable period.

30. Where a motor vehicle manufaturer applies delivery periods in respect of the products covered by the agreement which vary considerably within the common market, or causes such delivery periods to be applied by a third party, the same considerations apply as in the case of price variations (Article 7 (1), No 2).

31. Article 8 defines certain terms such as manufacturer, importer and connected undertaking.

32. Article 9 determines the duration of the exemption and its retroactive effect on certain distribution and servicing agreements existing when this Regulation enters into force which either satisfy the terms of the Regulation already or are mended accordingly. Article 2 (1) of Regulation No 19/65/EEC requires that the exemption provided for in this Regulation be granted for a specified period. A period running to 31 December 1993 seems appropriate, because overall plans for distribution networks in the motor vehicle industry have to be settled years in advance. The other provisions of Article 9 are based on Articles 3 and 4 of Regulation No 19/65/EEC, Articles 4 to 7 of Regulation No 17, Article 29 and Annex I (V.2) of the Act concerning the conditions of accession and the adjustments to the Treaties of 22 January 1972[7], and Article 21 and Annex I (V.3) of the Act concerning the conditions of accession and the adjustments to the Treaties of 24 May 1979[8].

33. Article 10 restates, for the purposes of this Regulation, the Commission's powers under Article 7 of Regulation No 19/65/EEC to withdraw the benefit of the exemption declared by this Regulation or to alter its scope in individual cases, and lists several important examples of such cases (paragraph 2). The cases concerned are those of an absence of effective competition (Nos 1 and 2), hindrances of the acquisition of contract goods not covered by the exemption (No 3), substantial differences in price and conditions as between Member States (No 4) and the fixinf of prices and conditions for specifications for export to other Member States which are not objectively valid (No 5).

34. Distribution and servicing agreements can be exempted, subject to the conditions laid down in Articles 5 to 7, so long as effective competition exists within the common market. As regards the categories of products set out in Article 1, which include passenger cars including estate cars, motor buses and goods vehicles including competition in trade between Member States, may be taken to exist at present. The advantages of this competition are thus generally avail-

able to Community consumers.

35, It is to the parties to a distribution and servicing agreement to determine the extent to which they wish to enter into restrictions of competition of the kind exempted by this Regulation. The exemption granted by this Regulation merely sets the limits within which undertakings are free to conclude agreements without infringing Article 85 (1) and (2) of the Treaty.

HAS ADOPTED THIS REGULATION:

Art. 1. Pursuant to Article 85 (3) of the Treaty it is hereby declared that Article 85 (1) of the Treaty shall not apply to distribution and servicing agreements to which only two undertakers are parties and in which one contracting party agrees to supply motor vehicles for use on public roads and having three or more road wheels, and spare, exchange and replacement parts (contract goods) for resale within a defined territory of the common market (the contract territory):
- only to the other party; or
- only to the other party and to a limited number of other undertakings, and which impose on a contracting party or connected undertakings one or more of the obligations mentioned in Articles 2 and 3 below.

Art. 2. The exemption referred to in Article 1 shall apply to an obligation under which the contracting party supplying the products (the supplier) agrees:
1. not to conclude distribution and servicing agreements in respect of contract goods with other undertakings operating within the contract territory;
2. not to sell contract goods to final customers in the contract territory nor to provide them with service.

Art. 3. The exemption referred to in Article 1 shall apply to any obligation imposed on the contracting party entrusted with distribution and servicing (the dealer):
1. not to modify contract goods;
2. not to manufacture products which compete with contract goods;
3. not to sell new motor vehicles which compete with contract goods;
4. for repair of contract goods, not to use or sell motor vehicle parts which compete with contract goods and do not match the quality of contract goods;
5. not to conclude distribution and servicing agreements with third parties in respect with products which compete with contract goods;
6. not to conclude without the supplier's consent distribution and servicing agreements concerning goods and embodying obligations referred to in Articles 1 to 4 with undertakings operating in the contract territory and neither to alter nor to terminate such agreements;
7. outside the contract territory:
(a) not to maintain branches or depots for the distribution of contract goods;
(b) not to seek customers for contract goods, except by means of an advertising medium which operates within the contract territory but extends beyond such territory,
8. not to entrust third parties with the sale or servicing of contract

goods outside the contract territory;

9. not to sell contract goods to dealers; unless

(a) the dealer is also authorized, on the basis of a distribution and servicing agreement relating to contract goods, to sell such goods or provide servicing for them,

(b) the dealer has been authorized by a final consumer to purchase and and take delivery of the contract goods, or

(c) the transaction concerns the sale of spare, exchange or replacement parts for the purposes of repair.

10. to observe the obligations referred to in the numbers 1 and 7 to 9 above and in Article 4 (1) (e) on termination of the agreement, for as long as such party still has stocks of contract goods but no longer than one year after termination of the agreement.

Art. 4. 1. Articles 1 to 3 shall apply notwithstanding any obligation imposed on the dealer to:

(a) observe, for distribution and service, minimum standards which in particular relate to:
- the equipment of the business premises and the technical facilities for servicing available;
- the specialized and technical training of staff;
- advertising methods;
- the collection, storage and delivery to customers of contract goods and servicing relating to them;

(b) order contract goods from the supplier at certain times only or within certain periods, provided that the interval between the dates when products may be ordered does not exceed three months;

(c) maintain a minimum stock of contract goods and demonstration vehicles from the contract programme, in such quantities as may be agreed by the contracting parties or, in the absence of such an agreement, determined by the supplier on the basis of estimates;

(d) endeavour to sell, within the contract terrritory and within specified periods, such minimum quantity of contract goods as may be agreed by the contracting parties or, in the absence of such an agreement, determined by the supplier on the basis of estimates;

(e) provide, on the resale of the contract goods, a guarantee corresponding at least to that given by the supplier and provide final consumers with free servicing to a specified extent.

2. The exemption referred to in Article 1 shall also apply to obligations of the kind referred to in 1 above where such obligations fall in individual cases fall under the prohibition contained in Article 85 (1) of the Treaty.

Art. 5. Articles 1 to 4 shall apply provided that:

1. if several dealers are appointed for one contract territory (Article 1 and Article 2, No 1), each such dealer has undertaken to promote sales of and servicing for contract goods throughout the contract territory;

2. the supplier,

(a) agrees to conclude distribution and servicing agreements in respect of contract goods with other undertakings operating within the contract territory only with the consent of the dealer (Article 2, No 1), except where there are objectively valid reasons for the appointment of other distribution and service undertakings and the dealer has agreed to grant its consent thereto in such a case;

(b) in the event of the failure of the dealer to comply with obligations imposed by the agreement, will only be released from the obligations referred to in Article 2 where the obligation breached is a fundamental one and the dealer has continued to be in breach thereof despite reasonable notice to cease such breach;

(c) agrees to release the dealer from the obligation referred to in Article 3, Nos 3, 5 (no competition clause) and 6 (restrictions on subcontracting) where there are objectively valid reasons for such release;

(d) in the cases referred to in Article 4 (1), lays down the minimum standards and criteria for estimates and applies them in such a way that the dealer is not treated, without objectively valid reasons, in a discriminatory or unreasonable manner;

3. the dealer assumes an obligation:

(a) to honour the guarantee and provide free servicing for motor vehicles sold by the manufacturer, one of the latter's importers or by another of the manufacturer's or importers' dealers in the common market, at least to the extent which corresponds with the dealer's obligation referred to in Article 4 (1) (e) to provide guarantees and give free servicing in connection with his own sales but not to a greater extent than results from the obligation imposed on the selling dealer and referred to in Article 4 (1) (e) or the extent agreed between the selling manufacturer or importer and the final consumer; and

(b) to impose upon any other undertakings operating within the contract territory under an agreement made with the consent of the supplier which relates to the distribution and servicing of contract goods referred to in Article 3, No 6 the obligation to provide a guarantee and free servicing at least as comprehensive as the obligation imposed on the dealer (Article 4 (1) (e) and Article 5, No 3 (a);

4. where the obligations referred to in Article 3, No 3 or 5 (no-competition clause) are entered into, the duration of the distribution and servicing agreement is at least five years, or, if for an indefinite period, the period of notice for terminating the agreement is at least two years for both contracting parties or the party terminating the agreement has to pay appropriate compensation;

5. where discounts are granted by the supplier to a dealer and based on the quantity or value of purchases of contract goods, such discounts are calculated not by reference to total purchases, but by reference to purchases which at least distinguish between,
   - motor vehicles,
   - spare, exchange and replacement parts and accessories bearing exclusively a trade mark of the manufacturer or of the importer or of a connected undertaking, and
   - other spare, exchange and replacement parts and accessories;

6. the dealer can obtain from the supplier, for the purpose of performance of a contract of sale concluded with a customer in the common market, a motor vehicle produced in series and covered by the contract programme which is intended to be registered in a specified Member State outside the contract territory and is marketed by the manufacturer or with the latter's consent in that Member State, with the specifications:

(a) which under the regulation in force in that Member State are indispensable for the registration of a motor vehicle,

(b) which are marketed by the manufacturer or with the latter's consent in that Member State, so that the motor vehicle shall comply with the regulations governing its use on public roads, and

(c) which are otherwise marketed either to the dealer by the supplier for resale within the contract territory or by the manufacturer or or with the latter's consent in that Member State.

Art. 6. Articles 1 to 4 shall not apply where:
1. both parties to the agreement or their connected undertakings are motor vehicle manufacturers;
2. the supplier restricts the dealer in his freedom to set prices when reselling contract goods; or
3. obligations of the kind described in Articles 1 and 2 of Commission Regulation No 67/67/EEC are imposed on one party to the agreement and such obligations relate to motor vehicles having three or more road wheels or spare and replacement parts therefor and exceed the scope of the obligations declared exempt by this Regulation.

Art. 7. 1. Article 1 shall not apply to obligations not to sell contract goods to dealers referred to in Article 3, No 9, where the motor vehicle manufaturer, or any undertaking with the manufacturer's consent
(a) recommends, for the resale of comparable motor vehicles to consumers in the common market, prices such that the price recommended to resellers in another Member State exceed that recommended to the dealer for a motor vehicle in the contract programme by more than 12% from the latter for a period of more than six months, or
(b) applies delivery periods for comparable motor vehicles for consumers in the common market such that the delivery period envisaged for resellers in another Member State exceeds the delivery period envisaged for the dealer in relation to a vehicle in the contract programme by more than six months.

2. The differences referred to in 1 above apply to the prices generally recommended in a Member State (list price) and delivery periods announced for motor vehicles in the manufacturer's or importer's delivery programme which are identical or have essentially the same specifications. The price comparison shall not take account of the duties, taxes and fees due on the sale of the products to the final consumer or on first use. The comparison shall be made in currency units (ECUs). The ECU is the unit of account whose equivalent in national currencies is regularly determined by the Commission and published in the Official Journal of the European Communities.

3. For the purposes of price comparison, recommendations relating to resale in Member States:
- in which consumers must pay duties, taxes and fees which together exceed in amount the net price of the motor vehicle; or
- in which the freedom of fixing prices or profit margins in trade in motor vehicles is restricted by virtue of national regulatory measures and such restriction has not operated for longer than one year;

shall not be taken into account.

Art. 8. For the purpose of this Regulation the following terms shall have the following meanings.
1. A 'manufacturer' is an undertaking:
(a) which maufacturers motor vehicles having three or more road wheels and intended for use on public roads, and spare and replacement parts therefor; or
(b) which is connected with such an undertaking.
2. An 'importer' is an undertaking entrusted by a manufacturer with the distribution of the latter's goods imported from other countries or connected with such an undertaking.

3. 'Connected undertakings' are:
(a) undertakings one of which directly or indirectly,
- holds more than half the capital of business assets of another, or
- has the power to exercise more than half the voting rights in another, or
- has the power to appoint more than half the members of the supervisory board,
board of directors or bodies legally representing another, or
- has the right to manage the affairs of the other;
(b) undertakings in relation to which a third undertaking is able directly or indirectly to exercise such rights or powers as are mentioned in (a) above.

Art. 9. 1. The declaration of inapplicability of Article 85 (1) of the Treaty contained in this Regulation shall apply until 31 December 1993.

2. As it relates to agreements which were notified to the commission before 1 January 1984, the declaration shall have retroactive effect from the time when the conditions of application of this Regulation were fulfilled, but not earlier than the day of notification.

3. As it relates to agreements to which undertakings from one Member State only are parties and which do not relate either to imports or to exports between Member States, the declaration shall have retroactive effect from the time when the conditions of application of this Regulation were fulfilled.

4. As it relates to agreements which were in existence on 13 March 1962 and were notified to the Commission before 1 February 1963, the declaration shall have retroactive effect from the time when the conditions of application of this Regulation were fulfilled.

5. As it relates to distribution and servicing agreements concerning goods of the kind described in Article 1 which were in existence on 13 March 1962, and which:
- were notified to the Commission before 1 February 1963; and
- were amended before 1 April 1984 so as to fulfil the conditions of application of this Regulation, such amendment being notified to the Commission before 1 May 1984, the declaration shall have retroactive effect in respect of the period prior to the amendment.

6. As it relates to distribution and servicing agreements concerning goods of the kind described in Article 1 which were in existence on 13 March 1962, to which undertakings from one Member State only are parties and which do not relate either to imports or to exports between Member States, and which:
- were notified to the Commission before 1 January 1967; and
- were amended before 1 April 1984 so as to fulfil the conditions of application of this Regulation, such amendment being notified to the Commission before 1 May 1984;

the declaration shall have retroactive effect in respect of the period prior to the amendment.

7. In respect of agreements which fall within the scope of Article 85 of the Treaty in consequence of the accession of the United Kingdom, Ireland and Denmark, paragraphs 4 to 6 of this Article shall apply with the proviso that the date 13 March 1962 shall be replaced by the date 1 January 1973 and the dates 1 February 1963 and 1 January 1967 shall be replaced by the date 1 July 1973.

8. In respect of agreements which fall within the scope of Article 85 of the Treaty in consequence of the accession of Greece, paragraphs 4 to 6 of this Article shall apply with the proviso that the date 13 March 1962 shall be replaced by the date 1 January 1981

and the dates 1 February 1963 and 1 January 1967 shall be replaced by the date 1 July 1981.

9. Notification of amendments pursuant to paragraph 6 of this Article shall take effect from the time of receipt thereof by the Commission. Where the notification is sent by registered post, it shall take effect from the date of the postmark of the place of dispatch.

Art. 10. 1. Where the Commission, upon its own initiative or upon application by a Member State or by a person or association of persons demonstrating a sufficient interest, finds that in an individual case agreements or concerted practices which fall within the scope of this Regulation but nevertheless have effects which are incompatible with the provisions of Article 85 (3) of the Treaty, the Commission may, with a view to withdrawing the benefit of the application of this Regulation, issue a declaration pursuant to Articles 6 and 8 of Regulation No 17, without necessaty of notification pursuant to Article 4 (1) of Regulation No 17.

2. The Commission shall adopt decisons pursuant to paragraph 1 in particular,

(a) where, in the common market or a substantial part thereof, contract goods are not subject to competition from products considered by consumers as similar by reason of their characteristics, price and intended use,
(b) where other manufacturers cannot sell similar products in the contract territory or where their doing so is subject to appreciable difficulties,
(c) where a contracting party has abused the exemption by making it more difficult, in a manner which goes beyond the obligations imposed in the distribution and servicing agreement, for persons or undertakings to obtain contract goods from other dealers within the common market or to obtain servicing from them for contract goods,
(d) where prices or conditions of supply for contract goods and for the same manufacturer's comparable goods are recommended or applied within the common market which differ appreciably as between Member States,
(e) where, in agreements concerning the supply to the dealer of vehicles intended to be registered in another Member State and require different specifications (Article 5, No 6) prices and conditions are applied which differ, without objectively valid reasons, from those applied in agreements concerning the supply to the dealer of corresponding vehicles in the contract programme.

Art. 11. This Regulation shall enter into force on 1 January 1984. This Regulation shall be binding in its entirety and directly applicable in all Member States.

1. O.J. No. C 165, 24 June 1983, p. 2.
2. J.O. No. 36, 6 March 1965, p. 533; O.J. (Special Edition 1965-1966) p. 35. CM/L/II/8.
3. O.J. No. L. 29, 3 February 1975, p. 1.
4. O.J. No. 13, 21 February 1962, p. 204/62, as last amended by Regulation (EEC) No. 2822/71, O.J. L 285, 29 December 1971, p. 49. O.J. Special Edition 1959-1962, November 1972, p. 87; CM/L/II/1.
5. O.J. Special Edition No. 57, 25 March 1967, p. 849; last amended by Commission Regulation (EEC) No. 3577/82, 23 December 1982, O.J. No. L 373, 31 December 1982, p. 58.
6. O.J. No. L 345, 20 December 1980, p. 1.
7. O.J. No. L 73, 27 March 1972, pp. 20 and 92.
8. O.J. No. L 291, 19 November 1979, pp. 21 and 94.

ANNEX XIII

Draft Commission Regulation (EEC) on the application of Article 85 (3) of the Treaty to categories of research and development cooperation agreements[1]

THE COMMISSION OF THE EUROPEAN COMMUNITIES,

Having regard to the Treaty establishing the European Economic Community,

Having regard to Council Regulation (EEC) No 2821/71 of 20 December 1971 on the application of Article 85 (3) of the Treaty to categories of agreements, decisions and concerted practices as last amended by the Act of Accession of Greece, and in particular Article 1 thereof,

Having published the draft of this Regulation,

Having consulted the Advisory Committee on Restrictive Practices and Dominant Positions,

1. Whereas Regulation (EEC) No 2821/71 empowers the Commission to apply Article 85 (3) of the Treaty by Regulation to certain categories of agreements, decisions and concerted practices which have as their object the research and development of products or processes up to the stage of industrial application, and exploitation of the results, including provisions regarding industrial property rights and confidential technical knowledge;

2. Whereas the categories of agreements described in this Regulation may fall under the prohibition contained in Article 85 (1) of the Treaty either because the parties give op existing or potential competitive advantages over other parties, who are also competitors, arising out of past or future individual research and development activities, or because they take account of the interests of the other parties when they individually and as competitors produce and sell the jointly developed products, or because the joint ownership of the complementary nature of the technical knowledge gives rise to a licensing policy which renders its dissemination to undertakings which are not parties more difficult;

3. Whereas an appreciable restriction of competition will often occur where the parties are large undertakings with significant market shares, where competition in research and development plays an important role in the competitive performance of undertakings, where the research and development cooperation is particularly long in duration or extensive in scope; whereas it will also usually occur where the parties enter into agreements, or act in concert, in relation to the production or application of the jointly developed products or processes or to any other form of exploitation of the results of the research and development activity, in particular the grant of licences to undertakings not party to the agreement;

4. Whereas it is nog necessary to expressly exclude from the categories of agreements described in this Regulation those agreements which do not fall under Article 85 (1) of the Treaty;

5. Whereas cooperation in research and development generally promotes technical and economic progress by increasing the dissemination of technical knowledge between the parties, avoiding duplication of research and development work so reducing costs and stimulating new advances by permitting the exchange of complementary knowledge; whereas this can only be ensured where the research and development programme and its objectives are clearly defined and limited and where each of the parties is under an obligation to make available for exploitation the whole of the results of the research and development and existing technical knowledge necessary for the effi-ient exploitation of the results to each of the other parties;

6. Whereas the extension of cooperation into production is often necessary in the case of small and medium-sized undertakings in order to enable them economically to produce the new or improved products or apply the new or improved processes resulting from the research and development;

7. Whereas consumers can generally be expected to benefit from the increased volume and effectiveness of research and development effort through the introduction of new or improved products or the reduction of prices brought about by new or improved processes;

8. Whereas, since agreements exempted pursuant to this Regulation must not contain any restrictions which are not indispensable for the attainment of the advantages described above, it is necessary to limit the restrictions of competition which may be included in such agreements to those which are necessary to enable the research and development cooperation to be carried out and to protect the parties' legitimate interests in existing technical knowledge and results of the research and development; whereas it may be left to the parties to decide which of these restrictions to include in their agreements;

9. Whereas, in order to ensure that agreements exempted pursuant to this Regulation do not afford the undertakings in question the possibility of eliminating competition in respect of a substantial part of the products in question, unconditional exemption should be confined to agreements in which not more than one of the actually or potentially leading undertakings in the sector to which the research and development relates are parties and, in the case of cooperation extending into production, to agreements where the aggregate annual turnover of the undertakings party to the agreement does not exceed a specified limit;

10. Whereas agreements which are excluded from unconditional exemption because of the size and importance of the undertakings involved, or because they include provisions which are not expressly exempted in the Regulation but are comparable to provisions which are, may nonetheless often fulfil the conditions of Article 85 (3); whereas it will be possible for the Commission rapidly to establish whether this is the case, especially where the agreements implement projects of common European interest which are already known to it; whereas, therefore, there is no reason to deny the benefit of the exemption provided for in this Regulation to such agreements where they are notified to the Commission and the Commission does not oppose the application of the exemption within a specified period of time;

11. Whereas, since research and development cooperation agreements are often of a long-term nature especially where the cooperation extends into production, it is appropriate to fix the period of validity of this Regulation at 12 years; whereas, if the circumstances on the basis of which this Regulation was adopted should change within this period, the Commission will undertake the necessary amendments;

12. Whereas agreements, decisions and concerted practices which are unconditionally exempted pursuant to this Regulation need not be notified; whereas an undertaking may nonetheless in a particular case, where justified doubt exists, require the Commission to declare whether this is so,

HAS ADOPTED THIS REGULATION:

Article 1

1. Pursuant to Article 85 (3) of the Treaty, and subject to the provisions of this Regulation, it is hereby declared that Article 85 (1) of the Treaty shall not apply to any agreement whereby, for the purpose of cooperating in a specified research and development programme, not including industrial application, undertakings enter into any of the obligations listed in Article 2 (1) of this Regulation.

2. Pursuant to Article 85 (3) of the Treaty, and subject to the provisions of this Regulation, it is hereby declared that Article 85 (1) of the Treaty shall not apply to any agreement whereby undertakings extend the cooperation exempted pursuant to paragraph 1 into the production of products or the application of processes arising out of the research and development by entering into any of the obligations listed in Article 2 (2) of this Regulation.

3. Without prejudice to Articles 5 and 6 of this Regulation:
   (a) paragraphs 1 and 2 of this Article shall only apply on the condition that not more than one of the three actually or potentially leading undertakings in the sector to which the research and development programme relates at the conclusion of the agreement is a party to the agreement; and
   (b) paragraph 2 of this Article shall only apply on the condition that the aggregate annual turnover of the undertakings party to the agreement does not exceed (599) million ECU.

Article 2

1. The exemption referred to in Article 1 (1) shall apply only to the following obligations restrictive of competition:
   (a) the obligation not to carry out independently, or in cooperation with undertakings which are not parties to the agreement, research and development in the same field or a closely connected field to that to which the agreement relates or in a field allocated to another party to the agreement;
   (b) the obligation to make available to parties to the agreement the results of the research and development programme or any part of it;
   (c) the obligation to allow the other parties to the agreement to exploit the results of the research and development programme and, to the extent necessary for the efficient exploitation of

such results, existing technical knowledge communicated pursuant to an onbligation permitted under this Regulation, in both cases whether protected by intellectual property rights or not;

(d) the obligation imposed for a period of no more than two years, from the time when the whole or part of the results of the research and development are capable of exploitation, not to allow undertakings which are not parties to the agreement to use such results of the research and development programme whether these are protected by intellectual property rights or not;

(e) the obligation imposed for a period not exceeding five years not to terminate the cooperation;

(f) the obligation to give notice not exceeding one year prior to termination of the cooperation.

2. The exemption referred to in Article 1 (2) shall apply to the following obligations restrictive of competition:

(a) the obligation imposed on each of the parties to the agreement, with the object of specialization, to undertake only certain aspects of the production;

(b) the obligation to carry out the whole or any part of production in jointly-owned facilities or to entrust the whole or any part of the production to a jointly-controlled undertaking;

(c) the obligation to entrust the whole or any part of the production to an undertaking not party to the agreement;

(d) the obligation not to conclude with undertakings which are not parties to the agreement cooperation agreements relating to the production of identical products or products considered by users to be equivalent in view of their characteristics, price or intended use, to those produced pursuant to the cooperation except with the consent of the other parties to the agreement;

(e) the obligation to supply other parties to the agreement with products which are produced pursuant to the cooperation, and in so doing to observe minimum standards of quality;

(f) the obligation to purchase products, which are produced pursuant to the cooperation, solely from another party to the agreement or from an undertaking which the parties to the agreement have jointly charged with production, except where more favourable terms of purchase are available elsewhere and the other party or undertaking is not prepared to offer the same terms;

(g) the obligation to grant to other parties to the agreement the exclusive right to distribute the products which are produced pursuant to the cooperation provided that intermediaries or users can also obtain these products from other suppliers and that the parties do not render it difficult for intermediaries or users to thus obtain the products.

3. Article 1 of this Regulation shall apply notwithstanding the following obligations:

(a) the obligation to set up and entrust the execution of the whole or any part of the research and development programme to a joint team or to a jointly-controlled undertaking;

(b) the obligation to entrust the execution of the whole or any part of the research and development programme to a jointly selected undertaking or other organization not party to the agreement;

(c) the obligation to communicate to the other parties to the agreement existing technical knowledge, whether protected by intellectual property rights or not, relevant to the research and development programme;
(d) the obligation to obtain and maintain in force intellectual property rights protecting existing technical knowledge communicated or licensed to the other parties to the agreement;
(e) the obligation to preserve the confidential nature of any technical know-how which either results from the research and development programme or has been communicated pursuant to an obligation permitted under this Regulation;
(f) the obligation to obtain and maintain in force intellectual property rights to protect the results of the research and development programme where these results are capable of such protection;
(g) the obligation:
   (i) to inform other parties to the agreement of infringements of intellectual property rights,
   (ii) to take legal action against infringers, and
   (iii) to assist in or share the cost of such legal action with other parties to the agreement;
(h) the obligation to pay royalties to other parties to the agreement to compensate for unequal contributions;
(i) the obligation to share with other parties to the agreement royalty payments, received from undertakings which are not parties to the agreement;
(j) the obligation to maintain minimum stocks of the products which are produced pursuant to the cooperation and of replacement parts for them;
(k) the obligation to provide customer and guarantee services for the products which are produced pursuant to the cooperation.

Article 3

1. The provisions of this Regulation shall apply to a connected undertaking in the same way as they apply to a party to the agreement.

2. Connected undertakings for the purposes of this Regulation means:
(a) undertakings in which a party to the agreement directly or indirectly:
   - owns more than half the capital or business assets, or
   - has the power to exercise more than half the voting rights, or
   - has the power to appoint more than half the members of the supervisory board, board of the directors or bodies legally representing the undertaking, or
   - has the right to manage the affairs;
(b) undertakings which directly or indirectly have in or over a party to the agreement the rights or powers listed in (a);
(c) undertakings in which an undertaking referred to in (b) drectly or indirectly has the rights or powers listed in (a).

3. Undertakings in which the parties to the agreement or undertakings connected with them jointly have the rights or powers set out in paragraph 2 (a) shall be considered to be connected with each of the parties to the agreement.

Article 4

1. For the purpose of Articles 1 (2) and 6 of this Regulation, the ECU is the unit of account used for drawing up the budget of the Communities pursuant to Articles 207 and 209 of the Treaty.

1. O.J. No. C 16, 21 January 1984, p. 3.

Annex XIV

## NOTICE ON EXCLUSIVE DEALING CONTRACTS WITH COMMERCIAL AGENTS
(J.O. No 139, 24 December 1962, p. 2921)

I. The Commission considers that contracts made with commercial agents in which those agents undertake, for a specified part of the territory of the Common Market,

- to negotiate transactions on behalf of an enterprise,or

- to conclude transactions in the name and on behalf of an enterprise, or

- to conclude transactions in their own name and on behalf of this enterprise,

do not fall under the prohibition in Article 85(1) of the Treaty.

It is essential in this case that the contracting party, described as a commercial agent, should, in fact, be such, by the nature of his functions, and that he should neither undertake nor engage in activities proper to an independent trader in the course of commercial operations. The Commission regards as the decisive criterion, which distinguishes the commercial agent from the independent trader, the agreement - express or implied - which deals with responsibility for the financial risks bound up with the sale or with the performance of the contract. Thus the Commission's assessment is not governed by the name used to describe the representative. Except for the usual *del credere* guarantee, a commercial agent must not by the nature of his functions assume any risk resulting from the transaction. If he does assume such risks, his function becomes economically akin to that of an independent trader and he must therefore be treated as such for the purposes of the rules of competition. In such a situation, the exclusive dealing contracts must be regarded as agreements made with independent traders.

The Commission considers that there is particular reason to assume that the function performed is that of an independent trader where the contracting party described as a commercial agent:

- is required to keep or does in fact keep, as his own property, a considerable stock of the products covered by the contract, or

- is required to organise maintain or ensure at his own expense a substantial service to customers free of charge, or does in fact organise, maintain or ensure such a service, or

- can determine or does in fact determine prices or terms of business.

II. Unlike the contracts with commercial agents covered here, exclusive dealing contracts with independent traders may well fall within Article 85(1). In the case of such exclusive contracts the restriction of competition lies either in the limitation of supply, when the vendor undertakes to supply a given product to one purchaser only, or in the limitation of demand, when the purchaser undertakes to obtain a given product from only one vendor. Where there are reciprocal undertakings competition is being restricted by both parties. The question whether a restriction of competition of this nature may affect trade between Member States depends on the circumstances of the particular case.

On the other hand, the Commission takes the view that the test for prohibition under Article 85(1) is not met by exclusive dealing contracts with commercial agents, since these contracts have neither the object nor the effect of preventing, restricting or distorting competition within the Common Market. The commercial agent only performs an auxiliary function in the market for goods. In that market he acts on the instructions and in the interest of the enterprise on whose behalf he is operating. Unlike the independent trader, he himself is neither a purchaser nor a vendor, but seeks purchasers or vendors in the interest of the other party to the contract, who is the person doing the buying or selling. In this type of exclusive dealing contract, the selling or buying enterprise does not cease to be a competitor; it merely uses an auxiliary, i.e. the commercial agent, to distribute or acquire products on the market.

The legal status of commercial agents is determined, more or less uniformly, by statute law in most of the Member States and by case law in others. The characteristic feature which all commercial agents have in common is their function as auxiliaries in the transaction of business. The powers of commercial agents are subject to the civil law provisions of agency. Within the limits of these provisions, the other party to the contract - who is the person selling or buying - is free to decide the product and the territory in respect of which he is willing to give these powers to his agent.

In addition to the competitive situation on the markets where the commercial agent functions as an auxiliary for the other party to the contract, the particular market on which the commercial agents offer their services for the negotiation or conclusion of transactions has to be considered. The obligation assumed by the agent - to work exclusively for one principal for a certain period of time - entails a limitation of supply on that market; the obligation assumed by the other party to the contract - to appoint him sole agent for a given territory - involves a limitation of demand on the market. Nevertheless, the Commission views these restrictions as a result of the special obligation between the commercial agent and his principal to protect each other's interests and therefore considers that they involve no restriction of competition.

The object of this Notice is to give enterprises some indication of the considerations by which the Commission will be guided when interpreting Article 85(1) of the Treaty and applying it to exclusive dealing contracts with commercial agents. The situation having thus been clarified, it will as a general rule no longer be useful for enterprises to obtain negative clearance for the agreements mentioned, nor will it be necessary to have the legal position established through a Commission decision on an individual case; this also means that notification will no longer be necessary for agreements of this type. This Notice is without prejudice to any interpretation that may be given by other competent authorities and in particular by the courts.

Annex XV

## NOTICE CONCERNING AGREEMENTS, DECISIONS AND CONCERTED PRACTICES IN THE FIELD OF COOPERATION BETWEEN ENTERPRISES[1]

Questions are frequently put to the Commission of the European Communities on the attitude it intends to take up, for purposes of implementation of the competition rules contained in the Treaties of Rome and Paris, with regard to cooperation between enterprises.

In this Notice, it endeavours to provide guidance which, though it cannot be exhaustive, may prove useful to enterprises in the correct interpretation, in particular, of Article 85(1) of the EEC Treaty and Article 65(1) of the ECSC Treaty.

1. The Commission welcomes cooperation among small and medium-sized enterprises where such cooperation enables them to work more efficiently and increase their productivity and competitiveness on a larger market. While considering that its duty is to facilitate cooperation among small and medium-sized enterprises in particular, the Commission recognises that cooperation among large enterprises, too, can be economically desirable without presenting difficulties from the angle of competition policy.

Article 85(1) of the Treaty establishing the European Economic Community (EEC Treaty) and Article 65(1) of the Treaty establishing the European Coal and Steel Community (ECSC Treaty) provide that all agreements, decisions and concerted practices (hereafter referred to as 'agreements') which have as their object or effect the prevention, restriction or distortion of competition within the Common Market (hereafter referred to as 'restraints of competition') are prohibited as incompatible with the Common Market; under Article 85(1) of the EEC Treaty this applies, however, only if such agreements may affect trade between Member States.

The Commission feels that, in the interests of the small and medium-sized enterprises in particular, it should give some indication of the considerations by which it will be guided when interpreting Article 85(1) of the EEC Treaty and Article 65(1) of the ECSC Treaty and applying them to certain cooperation arrangements between enterprises, and should indicate which of these arrangements in its opinion do not come under these provisions. This Notice applies to all enterprises, irrespective of their size.

There may also be forms of cooperation between enterprises other than those listed below which are not prohibited by Article 85(1) of the EEC Treaty and Article 65(1) of the ECSC Treaty. This applies in particular if the market position of the enterprises cooperating with each other is in the aggregate too weak for the cooperation agreement between them to lead to an appreciable restraint of competition in the

Common Market and - where the agreements fall within the scope of Article 85 of the EEC Treaty - to affect trade between Member States.

It is also pointed out that other forms of cooperation between enterprises or agreements containing additional clauses, to which the rules of competition of the Treaties apply, can be exempted pursuant to Article 85(3) of the EEC Treaty or be authorised pursuant to Article 65 (2) of the ECSC Treaty.

The Commission intends to clarify rapidly, by means of suitable decisions in individual cases or by general notices, the status of the various forms of cooperation in accordance with the provisions of the Treaties.

No general statement can be made at this stage on the application of Article 86 of the EEC Treaty on the abuse of dominant positions within the Common Market or in a part of it. The same applies to Article 66 (7) of the ECSC Treaty.

As a result of this Notice, as a general rule, it should no longer be useful for enterprises to obtain negative clearance, as defined by Article 2 of Regulation No 17, for the agreements listed, nor should it be necessary to have the legal position established through a Commission decision on an individual case. This also means that notification with this end in view will no longer be necessary for agreements of this type. However, if it is doubtful whether in an individual case an agreement between enterprises restricts competition or if other forms of cooperation between enterprises which, in the view of the enterprises, do not restrict competition are not listed here, the enterprises are free to apply, where the matter comes under Article 85(1) of the EEC Treaty, for negative clearance, or to file as a precautionary measure, where Article 65(1) of the ECSC Treaty is the relevant provision, an application on the basis of Article 65(2) of that Treaty.

This Notice is without prejudice to any interpretation to be given by the Court of Justice of the European Communities.

II. The Commission takes the view that the following agreements do not restrict competition.

1. *Agreements having as their sole object:*
   (a) *An exchange of opinion or experience,*

   (b) *Joint market research,*

   (c) *The joint carrying out of comparative studies of enterprises or industries,*

   (d) *The joint preparation of statistics and calculation models.*

Agreements whose sole purpose is the joint procurement of information which the various enterprises need to determine their future market behaviour freely and independently, or the use by each of the enterprises of a joint advisory body, do not have as their object or effect the restriction of competition. But if the freedom of action of the enterprises is restricted or if their market behaviour is coordinated either expressly or through concerted practices, there may be restraint of competition. This is in particular the case where concrete recommendations are made or where conclusions are given such a form that they induce at least some of the participating enterprises to behave in an identical manner on the market.

The exchange of information may take place between the enterprises themselves or through a body acting as an intermediary. It is, however, particularly difficult to distinguish between information which has no bearing on competition on the one hand and behaviour in restraint of competition on the other, if there are special bodies which have to register orders, turnover figures, investments and prices, so that it can as a rule not be automatically assumed that Article 85(1) of the EEC Treaty or Article 65(1) of the ECSC Treaty do not apply to them. A restraint of competition may occur in particular on an oligopolistic market for homogeneous products.

In the absence of more far-reaching cooperation between the participating enterprises, joint market research and comparative studies of different enterprises and industries to collect information and ascertain facts and market conditions do not in themselves affect competition. Other arrangements of this type, as for instance the joint establishment of economic and structural analyses, so obviously do not affect competition that there is no need to mention them specifically.

Calculation models containing specified rates of calculation must be regarded as recommendations that may lead to restraints of competition.

2. *Agreements having as their sole object:*

(a) *Cooperation in accounting matters,*

(b) *Joint provision of credit guarantees,*

(c) *Joint debt-collecting associations,*

(d) *Joint business or tax consultant agencies.*

In such cases, the cooperation involved covers fields that are not concerned with the supply of goods and services or the economic decisions of the enterprises taking part, and thus does not lead to restraints of competition.

Cooperation in accounting matters is neutral from the point of view of competition as it only assists in the technical handling of the accounting work. Nor is the creation of credit guarantee associations affected by the competition rules, since it does not modify the relationship between supply and demand.

Joint debt-collecting associations whose work is not confined to the collection of outstanding payments in line with intentions and conditions of the participating enterprises, or which fix prices or exert in any other way an influence on price formation, may restrict competition. Application of uniform terms by all participating firms may constitute a concerted practice, and the making of joint price comparisons may have the same result. In this connection, no objection can be raised against the use of standardised printed forms; their use must, however, not be combined with an understanding or tacit agreement on uniform prices, rebates or conditions of sale.

3. *Agreements having as their sole object:*

   (a) *The joint implementation of research and development projects,*

   (b) *The joint placing of research and development contracts,*

   (c) *The sharing out of research and development projects among participating enterprises.*

In the field of research, too, the mere exchange of experience and results serves for information only and does not restrict competition. It therefore need not be mentioned expressly.

Agreements on the joint execution of research work or the joint development of the results of research up to the stage of industrial application do not affect the competitive position of the parties. This also applies to the sharing of research fields and development work if the results are available to all participating enterprises.

However, if the enterprises enter into commitments which restrict their own research and development activity or the utilisation of the results of joint work so that they do not have a free hand with regard to their own research and development outside the joint projects, this may constitute an infringement of the Treaties' rules of competition. Where firms do not carry out joint research work, any contractual obligations or concerted practices binding them to refrain from research work of their own either completely or in certain sectors may result in a restraint of competition.

The sharing out of sectors of research without an understanding providing for mutual access to the results is to be regarded as a case of specialisation that may restrict competition.

There may also be a restraint of competition if agreements are concluded or corresponding concerted practices applied with regard to the practical exploitation of the results of research and development work carried out jointly, particularly if the participating enterprises undertake or agree to manufacture only the products or types of product developed jointly or to share out future production among themselves.

It is of the essence of joint research that the results should be exploited by the participating enterprises in proportion to their participation. If the participation of certain enterprises is confined to a specific sector of the joint research project or to the provision of only limited financial assistance, there is no restraint of competition - in so far as there has been any joint research at all - if the results of research are made available to these enterprises only in relation with the degree of their participation. There may, however, be a restraint of competition if certain participating enterprises are excluded from exploitation of the results, either entirely or to an extent not commensurate with their participation.

If the granting of licences to third parties is expressly or tacitly excluded, there may be a restraint of competition. However, the fact that research is carried out jointly warrants arrangements binding the enterprises to grant licences to third parties only by common agreement or by majority decision.

For the assessment of the compatibility of the agreement with the rules of competition, the legal status of the joint research and development work is immaterial.

4. *Agreements which have as their sole object the joint use of production facilities and storing and transport equipment*

These forms of cooperation do not restrict competition because they are confined to organisation and technical arrangements for the use of the facilities. There may be a restraint of competition if the enterprises involved do not bear the cost of utilisation of the installation or equipment themselves or if agreements are concluded or concerted practices applied regarding joint production or the sharing out of production or the establishment or running of a joint enterprise.

5. *Agreements having as their sole object the setting up of consortia for the joint execution of orders, where the participating enterprises do not compete with each other as regards the work to be done or where each of them by itself is unable to execute the orders*

Where enterprises do not compete with each other they cannot restrict competition between them by setting up consortia. This applies in particular to enterprises belonging to different industries but also to firms in the same industry to the extent that their contribution under the consortium consists only of goods or services which cannot be supplied by the other participating enterprises. It is not a question of whether the enterprises compete with each other in other sectors so much as whether in the light of the concrete circumstances of a particular case there is a possibility that in the foreseeable future they may compete with each other with regard to the products or services involved. If the absence of competition between the enterprises and the maintenance of this situation are based on agreements or concerted practices, there may be a restraint of competition.

But even in the case of consortia formed be enterprises which normally compete with each other there is no restraint of competition if the participating enterprises cannot execute a specific order by themselves. This applies in particular if, for lack of experience, specialised knowledge, capacity or financial resources, these enterprises, when working alone, have no chance of success or cannot finish the work within the required time-limit or cannot bear the financial risk.

Nor is there a restraint of competition if it is only by the setting up of a consortium that the enterprises are put in a position to make an attractive offer. There may, however, be a restraint of competition if the enterprises undertake to work solely in the framework of a consortium.

6. *Agreements having as their sole object:*

(a) *Joint selling arrangements,*

(b) *Joint after-sales and repairs service, provided the participa-*

*ting enterprises are not competitors with regard to the products or services covered by the agreement.*

As already explained in detail under heading 5, cooperation between enterprises cannot restrict competition if the firms are not in competition with each other.

Very often joint selling by small or medium-sized enterprises - even if they are competing with each other - does not entail an appreciable restraint of competition; it is, however, impossible to establish in this Notice any general criteria or to specify what enterprises may be deemed 'small or medium-sized'.

There is no joint after-sales and repair service if several manufacturers, without acting in concert with each other, arrange for an after-sales and repair service for their products to be provided by an enterprise which is independent of them. In such a case there is no restraint of competition even if the manufacturers are competitors.

7. *Agreements having joint advertising as their sole object.*

Joint advertising is designed to draw the buyers' attention to the products of an industry or to a common brand; as such it does not restrict competition between the participating enterprises. However, if the participating enterprises are partly or wholly prevented, by agreements or concerted practices, from themselves advertising or if they are subjected to other restriction, there may be a restraint of competition.

8. *Agreements having as their sole object the use of a common label to designate a certain quality, where the label is available to all competitors on the same conditions.*

Such associations for the joint use of a quality label do not restrict competition if other competitors, whose products objectively meet the stipulated quality requirements, can use the label on the same conditions as the members. Nor do the obligations to accept quality control of the products provided with the label, to issue in uniform instructions for use, or to use the label for the products meeting the quality standards constitute restraints of competition. But there may be restraint of competition if the right to use the label is linked to obligations regarding production, marketing, price formation or obligations of any other type, as is for instance the case when the participating enterprises are obliged to manufacture or sell only products of guaranteed quality.

1. J.O. No C 75, 29 July 1968, p. 3, corrected by J.O. No C 84, 28 August 1968, p. 14.

Annex XVI

## COMMISSION NOTICE[1] OF 19 DECEMBER 1977 CONCERNING AGREEMENTS OF MINOR IMPORTANCE WHICH DO NOT FALL UNDER ARTICLE 85(1) OF THE TREATY ESTABLISHING THE EUROPEAN ECONOMIC COMMUNITY[2]

1. On several occasions the Commission has made clear that it considers it important to promote cooperation between undertakings where such cooperation is economically desirable without presenting difficulties from the point of view of competition policy; in particular, it wishes to facilitate cooperation between small- and medium-sized undertakings. To this end it published the 'Notice concerning agreements, decisions and concerted practices in the field of cooperation between undertakings'[3] (hereinafter referred to as 'agreements') listing a number of agreements that by their nature cannot be regarded as being restraints of competition. By issuing the present notice, the Commission is taking a further step towards defining the field of application of Article 85(1) of the Treaty establishing the European Economic Community, in order to promote cooperation between small- and medium-sized undertakings.

In the Commission's opinion, agreements, whose effects on trade between Member States and on competition are negligible, do not fall within the prohibition on restrictive agreements in Article 85(1) of the EEC Treaty. Only those agreements are prohibited which have an appreciable impact on market conditions, in that they appreciably alter the market position, i.e. the sales outlets and supply possibilities, of non-participating undertakings and of consumers.

In the present Notice the Commission has given a sufficiently concrete meaning to the term 'appreciable' for undertakings to be able to judge for themselves whether the agreements they have concluded with other undertakings, being of minor importance, do not fall under Article 85 (1). The quantitative definition of 'appreciable' given by the Commission is, however, no absolute yardstick; in fact, it is quite possible that, in individual cases, even agreements between undertakings which exceed the limits mentioned below may well have only a negligible effect on trade between Member States and on competition and are therefore not caught by Article 85(1).

As a result of this notice, there should no longer be any point in undertakings obtaining negative clearance, as defined by Article 2 of Regulation No 17, for the agreements covered, nor should it be necessary to have the legal position established through Commission decisions on individual cases; notification for this purpose will therefore no longer be necessary for agreements of this type. However, where it is doubtful whether in an individual case an agreement appreciably restricts trade between Member States or competition, the undertakings are free to apply for negative clearance or to notify the agreement.

This notice is without prejudice to any interpretation which may be given by the Court of Justice of the European Communities.

II. The Commission holds the view that agreements between undertakings engaged in the production or distribution of goods do not fall under the prohibition of Article 85(1) of the EEC Treaty if:

- the products which are the subject of the agreement and other products of the participating undertakings considered by consumers to be similar by reason of their characteristics, price or use do not represent in a substantial part of the common market more than 5% of the total market for such products, and

- the aggregate annual turnover of the participating undertakings does not exceed 50 million units of account.

The Commission also holds the view that the said agreements do not fall within the prohibition of Article 85(1) even if the abovementioned market share and turnover are exceeded by up to 10% within two successive financial years.

For the purpose of this notice the participating undertakings are:

1. The undertakings which are parties to the agreement.

2. Undertakings in which the undertakings which are parties to the agreement hold:

    - at least 25% of the capital or of the working capital whether directly or indirectly, or

    - at least half the voting rights, or

    - the power to appoint at least half of the members of the supervisory board, the board of management or the bodies legally representing the undertaking, or

    - the right to manage the affairs of the undertaking.

3. Undertakings which hold in an undertaking which is party to the agreement:

    - at least 25% of the capital or working capital whether directly or indirectly, or

    - at least half of the voting rights, or

    - the power to appoint at least half of the members of the supervisory board, the board of management or the bodies legally representing the undertaking party to the agreement, or

    - the right to manage the affairs of the undertaking.

The aggregate turnover shall include the turnover in all goods and services achieved during the last financial year by the participating undertakings. The aggregate turnover shall not include dealings between undertakings which are parties to the agreement.

1. J.O. No C 313, 29 December 1977, p. 3.

2. This notice replaces the notice of 27 May 1970 published in J.O. No C 64, 2 June 1970, p. 1.

3. J.O. No C 75, 29 July 1968, p. 3. French and Dutch version as amended in J.O. No C 84, 29 August 1968, German and Italian as amended in O.J. No C 93, 18 August 1968; CM/L/III/3, at page CM. L. III-7.

## COMMISSION

## OPINION CONCERNING THE APPLICABILITY OF THE TREATY OF ROME TO THE IMPORTATION OF JAPANESE PRODUCTS INTO THE COMMUNITY[1]

In recent years and with increasing frequency, cases have occurred in which Japanese industries prepare measures, partly autonomously and partly in concentration with corresponding European industries, that are designed to limit imports of Japanese products into the Community or to control them in another manner, from the point of view of quantities, prices, quality or in any other respect.

The Commission considers it necessary to draw the attention of those concerned to the fact that, by virtue of Article 85 paragraph 1 of the Treaty establishing the European Economic Community, all agreements between enterprises, all decisions of associations of enterprises and all concerted practices which may affect trade between Member States and which have as their object or effect the prevention, restriction or distortion of competition within the common market are prohibited as incompatible with the Common Market. The fact that several or all of the participating enterprises have their head offices outside the Community does not prevent the application of this provision, in so far as the effects of these agreements, decisions or concerted practices extend to the territory of the Common Market.

The Commission recommends that those concerned notify in good time such agreements, decisions and practices, as stipulated by Regulation 17 of the Council concerning the implementation of Articles 85 and 86 of the Treaty.[1] The Commission will proceed to examine these agreements, decisions and practices in order to determine whether they can be considered compatible with the Community provisions on competition. At the same time, the Commission will closely follow the development of the sectors concerned and will, where necessary, propose appropriate measures of commercial policy with a view to rectifying the problems in question.

1. J.O. No C 111, 21 October 1972, p. 13.

Annex XVIII

# COMMISSION NOTICE OF 18 DECEMBER 1978 CONCERNING ITS ASSESSMENT OF CERTAIN SUBCONTRACTING AGREEMENTS IN RELATION TO ARTICLE 85(1) OF THE EEC TREATY

1. In this notice the Commission of the European Communities gives its view as to subcontracting agreements in relation to Article 85(1) of the Treaty establishing the European Economic Community. This class of agreement is at the present time a form of work distribution which concerns firms of all sizes, but which offers opportunities for development in particular to small and medium sized firms.

The Commission considers that agreements under which one firm, called 'the contractor', whether or not in consequence of a prior order from a third party, entrusts to another, called 'the subcontractor', the manufacture of goods, the supply of services or the performance of work under the contractor's instructions, to be provided to the contractor or performed on his behalf, are not of themselves caught by the prohibition in Article 85(1).

To carry out certain subcontracting agreements in accordance with the contractor's instructions, the subcontractor may have to make use of particular technology or equipment which the contractor will have to provide. In order to protect the economic value of such technology or equipment, the contractor may wish to restrict their use by the subcontractor to whatever is necessary for the purpose of the agreement. The question arises whether such restrictions are caught by Article 85(1). They are assessed in this notice with due regard to the purpose of such agreements, which distinguishes them from ordinary patent and know-how licensing agreements.

2. In the Commission's view, Article 85(1) does not apply to clauses whereby:

- technology or equipment provided by the contractor may not be used except for the purposes of the subcontracting agreement,

- technology or equipment provided by the contractor may not be made available to third parties,

- the goods, services or work resulting from the use of such technology or equipment may be supplied only to the contractor or performed on his behalf,

provided that and in so far as this technology or equipment is necessary to enable the subcontractor under reasonable conditions to manufacture the goods, to supply the services or to carry out the work in accordance with the contractor's instructions. To that extent the subcontractor is providing goods, services or work in respect of which he is not an independent supplier in the market.

The above proviso is satisfied where performance of the subcontracting agreement makes necessary the use by the subcontractor of:

- industrial property rights of the contractor or at his disposal, in the form of patents, utility models, designs protected by copyright, registered designs or other rights, or

- secret knowledge or manufacturing processes(know-how) of the contractor or at his disposal, or of

- studies, plans or documents accompanying the information given which have been prepared by or for the contractor, or

- dies, patterns or tools, and accessory equipment that are distinctively the contractor's,

which, even though not covered by industrial property rights nor containing any element of secrecy, permit the manufacture of goods which differ in form, function or composition from other goods manufactured or supplied on the market.

However, the restrictions mentioned above are not justifiable where the subcontractor has at his disposal or could under reasonable conditions obtain access to the technology and equipment needed to produce the goods, provide the services or carry out the work. Generally, this is the case when the contractor provides no more than general information which merely describes the work to be done. In such circumstances the restrictions could deprive the subcontractor of the possibility of developing his own business in the fields covered by the agreement.

3. The following restrictions in connection with the provision of technology by the contractor may in the Commission's view also be imposed by subcontracting agreements without giving grounds for objection under Article 85(1):

- an undertaking by either of the parties not to reveal manufacturing processes or other know-how of a secret character, or confidential information given by the other party during the negotiation and performance of the agreement, as long as the know-how or information in question has not become public knowledge,

- an undertaking by the subcontractor not to make use, even after expiry of the agreement, of manufacturing processes or other know-how of a secret character received by him during the currency of the agreement, as long as they have not become public knowledge,

- an undertaking by the subcontractor to pass on to the contractor on a non-exclusive basis any technical improvements which he has made during the currency of the agreement, or, where a patentable invention has been discovered by the subcontractor, to grant non-exclusive licences in respect of inventions relating to improvements and new applications of the original invention to the contractor for the term of the patent held by the latter.

This undertaking by the subcontractor may be exclusive in favour of the contractor in so far as improvements and inventions made by the subcontractor during the currency of the agreement are incapable of being used independently of the contractor's secret know-how or patent, since this does not constitute an appreciable restriciton of competition.

However, any undertaking by the subcontractor regarding the right to dispose of the results of his own research and development work may restrain competition, where such results are capable of being used independently. In such circumstances, the subcontracting relationship is not sufficient to displace the ordinary competition rules on the disposal of industrial property rights or secret know-how.

4. Where the subcontractor is authorised by a subcontracting agreement to use a specified trade mark, trade name or get up, the contractor may at the same time forbid such use by the subcontractor in the case of goods, services or work which are not to be supplied to the contractor.

5. Although this notice should in general obviate the need for firms to obtain a ruling on the legal position by an individual Commission Decision, it does not affect the right of the firms concerned to apply for negative clearance as defined by Article 2 of Regulation No 17 or to notify the agreement to the Commission under Article 4(1) of that Regulation[1]

The 1968 notice on cooperation between enterprises[2], which lists a number of agreements that by their nature are not to be regarded as anti-competitive, is thus supplemented in the subcontracting field. The Commission also reminds firms that, in order to promote cooperation between small and medium sized businesses, it has published a notice concerning agreements of minor importance which do not fall under Article 85(1) of the Treaty establishing the European Economic Community.[3]

This notice is without prejudice to the view that may be taken of subcontracting agreements by the Court of Justice of the European Communities.

1. First Regulation implementing Articles 85 and 86 of the EEC Treaty (O.J. No 13, 21 February 1962, p. 204/62)

2. Notice concerning agreements, decisions and concerted practices relating to cooperation between enterprises(O.J. No C 75, 29 July 1968, p. 3).

3. O.J. No C 313, 29 December 1977, p. 3.

## ANNEX XIX

### NOTICE ON HEARING OFFICER AND HIS TERMS OF REFERENCE (1)

1. In its Eleventh Report on Competition policy the Commission announced that it envisaged creating the post of Hearing Officer; it has now taken the decision to do so.
To ensure his independence in the performance of his duties, the Hearing Officer will have the right of direct access to the Member of the Commission with special responsibility for competition policy. Administratively he will belong to the Directorate-General for Competition.
The Hearing Officer's task will be to ensure that the hearing is properly conducted and thus to contribute to the objectivity of the hearing itself and of any decision taken subsequently. He will seek to ensure in particular that in the preparation of draft Commission decisions in competition cases due account is taken of all relevant facts, whether favourable or unfavourable to the parties concerned. In performing his duties he is to see to it that the rights of the defence are respected, while taking account of the need for effective application of the competition rules in accordance with the regulations in force and the principles laid down by the Court of Justice.

2. Mr Roland Mussard, an official in Grade A 3, has been appointed Hearing Officer with effect from 1 September 1982.

### TERMS OF REFERENCE OF THE HEARING OFFICER (2)

Art. 1. A post of Adviser is hereby created, in connection with procedures for the application of Articles 85 and 86 of the EEC Treaty and Articles 65 and 66 of the ECSC Treaty; this Adviser, the Hearing Officer, shall chair hearings held pursuant to Articles 9 (1) of Commission Regulation No 99/63/EEC and Article 36 of the ECSC Treaty.
Administratively the Hearing Officer shall belong to the Directorate-General for Competition. To ensure his independence in the performance of his duties, he shall have the right of direct access, as defined in Article 6 below, to the Member of the Commission with special responsibility for competition.
Where the Hearing Officer is unable to act, the Director-General, in concert with the Hearing Officer, shall designate another official, who is in the same grade and is not involved in the case in question, to carry out the duties described herein.

Art. 2. The Hearing Officer shall ensure that the hearing is properly conducted and thus contribute to the objectivity of the hearing itself and of any decision taken subsequently. He shall seek to ensure in particular that in the preparation of draft Commission decisions in competition cases due account is taken of all the relevant facts, whether favourable or unfavourable to the parties concerned.
In performing his duties he shall see to it that the rights of the defence are respected, while taking account of the need for effective

application of the competition rules in accordance with the regulations in force and the principles laid down by the Court of Justice.

Art. 3. Where appropriate in view of the need to ensure that the hearing is properly prepared, and particularly that questions of fact are clarified as far as possible, the Hearing Officer may, after consulting the appropriate Director, supply in advance to the forms concerned a list of the questions on which he wishes them to explain their point of view.
For this purpose, after consulting the Director responsible for investigating the case which is the subject of the hearing, he may hold a meeting with the parties concerned, and, where appropriate, the Commission staff, in order to prepare for the hearing itself.
For the same purpose he may ask for prior written notification of the essential contents of the intended statements of persons whom the undertakings concerned have proposed for hearing pursuant to Article 3 (3) of Commission Regulation No 99/63/EEC.

Art. 4. After consulting the Director responsible, the Hearing Officer shall determine the date, the duration and the place of the hearing, and, where a postponement is requested, he shall decide whether or not to allow it.
He shall be fully responsible for the conduct of the hearing.
In this regard, he shall decide whether fresh documents should be admitted during the hearing, whether persons should be heard pursuant to Articles 3 (3) and 7 (2) of Commission Regulation No 99/63/EEC, and whether the persons concerned should be heard separately or in the presence of other persons summoned to attend.
He shall ensure that, in accordance with Article 9 (4) of the same Regulation, the essential content of the statement made by each person heard shall be recorded in minutes which shall be read and approved by that person.

Art. 5. The Hearing Officer shall report to the Director-General for Competition on the hearing and the conclusions he draws from it. He may make observations on the further progress of the proceedings. Such observations may relate among other things to the need for further information, the withdrawal of certain objections, or the formulation of further objections.

Art. 6. In performing the duties defined in Article 2 above, the Hearing Officer may, if he deems it appropriate, refer his observations direct to the Member of the Commission with special responsibility for competition, at the time when the preliminary draft decision is submitted to the latter for reference to the Advisory Committee on Restrictive Practices and Dominant Positions.

Art. 7. Where appropriate, the Member of the Commission with special responsibility for competition may decide, at the Hearing Officer's request, to attach the Hearing Officer's final report to the draft decision submitted to the Commission, in order to ensure that when it reaches a decision on an individual case it is fully apprised of all relevant information.

1. O.J. No. C 251, 25 September 1982, p. 2.
2. Thirteenth Competition Report 1983 (April 1984).

## ANNEX XX

### NOTICE FROM THE COMMISSION ON PROCEDURES CONCERNING NOTIFICATIONS PURSUANT TO ARTICLE 4 OF COUNCIL REGULATION NO 17/62 (1)

In publishing this notice, it is the intention of the Commission to open the way for a more flexible administrative practice in assessing notifications under Article 4 of Regulation No 17/62 in the light of its past experience in this area. This has shown that in certain cases a provisional letter sent by the Commission's Directorate-General for Competition would be an appropriate response to a notification made for the purposes of obtaining an Article 85 (3) Decision. However, in order to enhance the declaratory value of such a letter, and without prejudice to the possibility of terminating the procedure by a formal Decision, the Commission will now publish the essential content of such agreements pursuant to Article 19 (3) of Regulation No 17/62, so as to give interested third parties an opportunity to make known their views. In the light of the comments received after publication, it would then be possible, in appropriate cases, to send a provisional letter, so as to simplify and shorten the procedure. Such letters will not have the status of Decisions and will therefore not be capable of appeal to the Court of Justice. They will state that the Directorate-General for Competition, in agreement with the undertakings concerned, does not consider it necessary to pursue the formal procedure through to the adoption of a Decision under Article 85 (3) in accordance with Article 6 of Regulation No 17/62.
A list of the cases dealt with by dispatch of provisional letters following publication will be appended to the Report on Competition Policy.

1. O.J. No. C 295, 2 November 1983, p. 6.

ANNEX XXI

NOTICE FROM THE COMMISSION ON PROCEDURES CONCERNING APPLICATIONS FOR NEGATIVE CLEARANCE PURSUANT TO ARTICLE 2 OF COUNCIL REGULATION NO 17/62 (1)

In publishing the notice below, it is the intention of the Commission to open the way for a more flexible administrative practice in assessing applications for negative clearance under Article 2 of Regulation No 17/62, which empowers the Commission to certify that Article 85 (1) of the EEC Treaty does not apply to an agreement. Experience has, indeed, shown that in certain cases a 'comfort letter' closing the procedure sent by the Commission's Directorate-General for Competition was an appropriate respons to an application for negative clearance. However, in order to enhance the declatory value of such a letter, and without prejudice to the possibility of terminating the procedure by a formal decision, the Commission is now publishing the essential content of such agreements pursuant to Article 19 (3) of Regulation No 17/62, so as to give interested parties an opportunity to make known their views. In appropriate cases, it would be possible to send a comfort letter closing the procedure after publication, so as to simplify and shorten the procedure.
Cases closed by a comfort letter following publication will be brought to the intention of interested third parties by the subsequent publication of a notice in the Official Journal of the European Communities.

1. O.J. No. C 343, 31 December 1982, p. 4.

## ANNEX XXII

### EXPLANATORY NOTE TO AUTHORIZATION TO INVESTIGATE UNDER ARTICLE 14 (2) OF REGULATION NO 17/62 ([1])

This note is for information only and is without prejudice to any formal interpretation of the Commission's powers of enquiry.

1. The officials of the Commission authorized for the purpose of carrying out an investigation under Article 14 (2) of Regulation No 17 exercise their powers upon production of an authorization in writing. They prove their identity by means of their staff card.

2. Before starting the investigation the Commission officials shall, at the undertaking's request, provide explanations on the subject matter and purpose of the proposed investigation and also on procedural matters, particularly confidentiality. These explanations cannot modify the authorization and may not compromise the purpose of, nor unduly delay, the investigation.

3. The authorization, not being in execution of a Commission decision under Article 14 (3), does not oblige the undertaking to submit to the investigation. The undertaking may accordingly refuse the investigation. The Commission officials shall minute this refusal, no particular form being required. The undertaking shall receive a copy of the minute if it so wishes.

4. Where the undertaking is prepared to submit to the investigation, the Commission officials are empowered, pursuant to Article 14 (1) of Regulation No 17:
(a) to examine the books and other business records,
(b) to take copies of or extracts from the books and business records,
(c) to ask for oral explanations on the spot,
(d) to enter any premises, land and means of transport of undertakings.

5. Officials of the competent authority of the Member State in whose territory the investigation is made are entitled to be present at the investigation to assist the officials of the Commission in carrying out their duties. They shall prove their identity in accordance with the relevant national rules.

6. The undertaking may consult a legal adviser during the investigation. However, the presence of a lawyer is not a legal condition for the validity of the investigation, nor must it unduly delay or impede it. Any delay pending a lawyer's arrival must be kept to the strict minimum, and shall be allowed only when the management of the undertaking simultaneously undertakes to ensure that the business records will remain in the place and state they were in when the Commission offical s arrived. The officials' acceptance of delay is also conditional upon their not being hindered from entering into and remaining in occupation of offices of their choice. If the undertaking has an in-house legal service, Commission officals are instructed not to delay the investigation by awaiting the arrival of an external legal adviser.

7. Where the undertaking gives oral explanations on the spot on the subject matter of the investigation at the request of the Commission officials, the explanations may be minuted at the request of the undertaking or of the Commission officials. The undertaking shall receive a copy of the minute if it so wishes.

8. The Commission officials are entitled to take copies of or extracts from books and business records. The undertaking may request a signed inventory of the copies and extracts taken by the Commission officials during the investigation. Where the undertaking makes available photocopies of documents at the request of the Commission officials, the Commission shall, at the request of the undertaking, reimburse the cost of the photocopies.

9. In addition to the documents requested by the Commission officials, the undertaking is entitled to draw attention to other documents or information where it considers this necessary for the purpose of protecting its legitimate interest in a complete and objective clarification of the matters raised provided that the investigation is not thereby unduly delayed.

1. Thirteenth Competition Report 1983 (April 1984).

ANNEX XXIII

EXPLANATORY NOTE TO AUTHORIZATION TO INVESTIGATE IN EXECUTION OF A COMMISSION DECISION UNDER ARTICLE 14 (3) OF REGULATION NO 17/62 ([1])

This note is for information only and is without prejudice to any formal interpretation of the Commission's powers of enquiry.

1. Enterprises are legally obliged to submit to an investigation ordered by decision of the Commission under Article 14 (3) of Regulation No 17. Written authorizations serve to name the officials charged with the execution of the decision. They prove their identity by means of their staff card.

2. Officials cannot be required to enlarge upon the subject matter as set out in the decision or to justify in any way the taking of the decision. They may however explain procedural matters, particularly confidentiality, and the possible consequences of a refusal to submit.

3. A certified copy of the decision is to be handed to the undertaking. The minute of notification of service serves only to certify delivery and its signature by the recipient does not imply submission.

4. The Commission officials are empowered, pursuant to Article 14(1) of Regulation No 17:
(a) to examine the books and other business records,
(b) to take copies of or extracts from the books and business records,
(c) to enter any premises, land and means of transport of undertakings.

5. Officials of the competent authority of the Member State in whose territory the investigation is made are entitled to be present at the investigation to assist the officials of the Commission in carrying out their duties. They shall prove their identity in accordance with the relevant national rules.

6. The undertaking may consult a legal adviser during the investigation. However, the presence of a lawyer is not a legal condition for the validity of the investigation, nor must it unduly delay or impede it. Any delay pending a lawyer's arrival must be kept to the strict minimum, and shall be allowed only where the management of the undertaking simultaneously undertakes to ensure that the business records will remain in the place and state they were in when the Commission officials arrived. The official's acceptance of delay is also conditional upon their not being hindered from entering into and remaining in occupation of offices of their choice. If the undertaking has an in-house legal service, Commission officials are instructed not to delay the investigation by awaiting the arrival of an external legal adviser.

7. Where the undertaking gives oral explanations on the spot on the subject matter of the investigation at the request of the Commission officials, the explanations may be minuted at the request of the undertaking or of the Commission officials. The undertaking shall receive a copy of the minute if it so wishes.

8. The Commission officials are entitled to take copies of or extracts from books and business records. The undertaking may request a signed inventory of the copies and extracts taken by the Commission officials during the investigation. Where the undertaking makes available photocopies of documents at the request of the Commission officials, the Commission shall, at the request of the undertaking, reimburse the cost of the photocopies.

9. In addition to the documents requested by the Commission officials, the undertaking is entitled to draw attention to other documents or information where it considers this necessary for the purpose of protecting its legitimate interest in a complete and objective clarification of the matters raised provided that the investigation is not thereby unduly delayed.

1. Thirteenth Competition Report 1983 (April 1984).

Annex XXIV

## AGREEMENT[1] BETWEEN THE EUROPEAN ECONOMIC COMMUNITY AND THE REPUBLIC OF AUSTRIA

22 July 1972[2]

...

Art. 20. The Agreement shall not preclude prohibitions or restrictions on imports, exports or goods in transit justified on grounds of public morality, law and order or public security, the protection of life and health of humans, animals or plants, the protection of national treasures of artistic, historic or archaeological value, the protection of industrial and commercial property, or rules relating to gold or silver. Such prohibitions or restrictions must not, however, constitute a means of arbitrary discrimination or a disguised restriction on trade between the Contracting Parties.

...

Art. 22. 1. The Contracting Parties shall refrain from any measure likely to jeopardise the fulfilment of the objectives of the Agreement.

2. They shall take any general or specific measures required to fulfil their obligations under the Agreement.

If either Contracting Party considers that the other Contracting Party has failed to fulfil an obligation under the Agreement, it may take appropriate measures under the conditions and in accordance with the procedures laid down in Article 27.

Art. 23. 1. The following are incompatible with the proper functioning of the Agreement in so far as they may affect trade between the Community and Austria:

(i) all agreements between undertakings, decisions by associations of undertakings and concerted practices between undertakings which have as their object or effect the prevention, restriction or distortion of competition as regards the production of or trade in goods;

(ii) abuse by one or more undertakings of a dominant position in the territories of the Contracting Parties as a whole or in a substantial part thereof;

(iii) any public aid which distorts or threatens to distort competition by favouring certain undertakings or the production of certain goods.

2. Should a Contracting Party consider that a given practice is incompatible with this Article, it may take appropriate measures under the conditions and in accordance with the procedures laid down in Article

...
Art. 27. 1. In the event of a Contracting Party subjecting imports of products liable to give rise to the difficulties referred to in Articles 24 and 26 to an administrative procedure, the purpose of which is to provide rapid information on the trend of trade flows, it shall inform the other Contracting Party.

2. In the cases specified in Articles 22 to 26, before taking the measures provided for therein or, in cases to which paragraph 3(d) applies, as soon as possible, the Contracting Party in question shall supply the Joint Committee with all relevant information required for a thorough examination of the situation with a view to seeking a solution acceptable to the Contracting Parties.

In the selection of measures, priority must be given to those which least disturb the functioning of the Agreement.

The safeguard measures shall be notified immediately to the Joint Committee and shall be the subject of periodical consultations within the Committee, particularly with a view to their abolition as soon as circumstances permit.

3. For the implementation of paragraph 2, the following provisions shall apply:

(a) As regards Article 23, either Contracting Party may refer the matter to the Joint Committee if it considers that a given practice is incompatible with the proper functioning of the Agreement within the meaning of Article 23(1).

The Contracting Parties shall provide the Joint Committee with all relevant information and shall give it the assistance it requires in order to examine the case and, where appropriate, to eliminate the practice objected to.

If the Contracting Party in question fails to put an end to the practice objected to within the period fixed by the Joint Committee, or in the absence of agreement in the Joint Committee within three months of the matter being referred to it, the Contracting Party concerned may adopt any safeguard measures it considers necessary to deal with the serious difficulties resulting from the practices in question; in particular it may withdraw tariff concessions.

(b) As regards Article 24 the difficulties arising from the situation referred to in that Article shall be referred for examination to the Joint Committee, which may take any decision needed to put an end to such difficulties.

If the Joint Committee or the exporting Contracting Party has not taken a decision putting an end to the difficulties within thirty days of the matter being referred, the importing Contracting Party is authorised to levy a compensatory charge on the product imported.

The compensatory charge shall be calculated according to the incidence on the value of the goods in question of the tariff disparities in respect of the raw materials or intermediate products incorporated therein.

(c) As regards Article 25, consultation in the Joint Committee shall take place before the Contracting Party concerned takes the appropriate measures.

(d) Where exceptional circumstances requiring immediate action make prior examination impossible, the Contracting Party concerned may, in the situations specified in Articles 24, 25 and 26 and also in the case of export aids having a direct and immediate incidence on trade, apply forthwith the precautionary measures strictly necessary to deal with the situation.

...

Art. 29. 1. A Joint Committee is hereby established, which shall be responsible for the administration of the Agreement and shall ensure its proper implementation. For this purpose, it shall make recommendations and take decisions in the cases provided for in the Agreement. These decisions shall be put into effect by the Contracting Parties in accordance with their own rules.

2. For the purpose of the proper implementation of the Agreement the Contracting Parties shall exchange information and, at the request of either Party, shall hold consultations within the Joint Committee.

3. The Joint Committee shall adopt its own rules of procedure.

Art. 30. 1. The Joint Committee shall consist of representatives of the Community, on the one hand, and of representatives of Austria, on the other.

2. The Joint Committee shall act by mutual agreement.

Art. 31. 1. Each Contracting Party shall preside in turn over the Joint Committee, in accordance with the arrangements to be laid down in its rules of procedure.

2. The Chairman shall convene meetings of the Joint Committee at least once a year in order to review the general functioning of the Agreement.

The Joint Committee shall, in addition, meet whenever special circumstances so require, at the request of either Contracting Party, in accordance with the conditions to be laid down in its rules of procedure.

3. The Joint Committee may decide to set up any working party that can assist it in carrying out its duties.

...

Declaration by the European Economic Community concerning Article 23(1) of the Agreement

The European Economic Community declares that in the context of the autonomous implementation of Article 23(1) of the Agreement which is incumbent on the Contracting Parties, it will assess any practices contrary to that Article on the basis of criteria arising from the application of the rules of Articles 85, 86, 90 and 92 of the Treaty establishing the European Economic Community.

Declaration by the European Economic Community concerning the regional application of certain provisions of the Agreement.

The European Economic Community declares that the application of any measures it may take under Articles 23, 24, 25 or 26 of the Agreement, in accordance with the procedure and under the arrangements set out in Article 27, or under Article 28, may be limited to one of its regions by virtue of Community rules.

1. J.O. L 300, 31 December 1972, p. 2. O.J. (Special Edition 1972) 31 December, p. 4.

2. This Agreement entered into force on 1 January 1973.

## TABLE OF DECISIONS AND COMMUNICATIONS - ALPHABETICAL

## TABLE OF DECISIONS AND COMMUNICATIONS - CHRONOLOGICAL

| | References | Also reported |
|---|---|---|
| KEWA (23 December 1975) | p. 62 | |
| Hoffmann-La Roche (Vitamins) (9 June 1976) | p. 53 | p. 253, 254, 258 |
| Centraal Stikstof Verkoopkantoor (CSV) I (25 June 1976) | p. 292 | |
| Reuter-BASF (26 July 1976) | p. 97 | |
| Miller International Schallplatten (1 December 1976) | p. 362 | |
| Junghans (21 December 1976) | p. 86 | p. 430 |
| Theal-Watts (21 December 1976) | p. 292 | |
| GERO Fabriek (22 December 1976) | p. 433 | |
| Vacuum Interruptors I(20 January 1977) | p. 119 | |
| De Laval-Stork (25 July 1977) | p. 124 | |
| GEC-WEIR-Sodium Circulators (20 December 1977) | p. 129 | |
| Cauliflowers (2 December 1977) | p. 139 | p. 477 |
| Deutsche Freiformschmieden (8 December 1977) | p. 299 | p. 271 |
| Hugin-Liptons (8 December 1977) | p. 53 | p. 89, 238, 254, 258, 348 |
| Distillers (20 December 1977) | p. 349 | p. 435 |
| Penneys (23 December 1977) | p. 545 | |
| Jaz-Peter II (23 December 1977) | p. 464 | |
| Campari (23 December 1977) | p. 543 | |
| Persil (April 1978) | p. 544 | |
| RAI-Unitel (26 May 1978) | p. 98 | p. 296 |
| SNPE-LEL (12 June 1978) | p. 99 | p. 388 |
| Centraal Stikstof Verkoopkantoor (CSV) II (20 July 1978) | p. 392 | |
| Belgian Tobacco Cartel (Fedetab) (28 July 1978) | p. 141 | |
| ICI-WANO-Blackpowder (20 October 1978) | p. 135 | |
| VEB Pentacon (23 October 1978) | p. 51 | |
| Zanussi (23 October 1978) | p. 447 | |
| White Lead (12 December 1978) | p. 407 | |
| Kawasaki (12 December 1978) | p. 178 | |
| BP Kemi/DDSF (5 September 1979) | p. 452 | |
| Vacuum Interruptors II (11 December 1980) | p. 67 | |
| Michelin-Actor (April 1979) | p. 266 | |
| Michelin-Netherlands (October 1981) | p. 92 | p. 258 |
| GVL (29 October 1981) | p. 67 | p. 483 |
| Telos (25 November 1981) | p. 297 | |
| Fire Insurance (9 December 1981) | p. 59 | |
| Hasselblad (2 December 1981) | p. 424 | |
| VBVB/VBBB (25 November 1981) | p. 202 | |
| AEG-Telefunken (6 January 1982) | p. 443 | |
| Stichting Sigaretten Industrie (15 July 1982) | p. 59 | |
| Federation de la Chaussure (27 October 1982) | p. 367 | |
| Vimpoltu (13 July 1983) | p. 83 | |
| British Telecommunications (10 December 1982) | p. 485 | |
| Toltecs-Dorcet (15 December 1982) | p. 547 | |
| Synthetic Fibres (14 November 1983) | p. 488 | |

| | References | Also reported |
|---|---|---|
| European Zinc Producers (9 January 1984) | p. 490 | |
| BIEM-IFPI (April 1984) | p. 527 | |

TABLE OF CASES - ALPHABETICAL

| | References | Also Reported |
|---|---|---|
| ACF-Chemiefarma Case (Case 41/69 | p. 109 | p. 316, 323, 330, 331, 332. |
| AEG-Telefunken Case (Case 107/82) | p. 446 | |
| AM & S Case (Case 155/79) | p. 311 | |
| ANSEAU/NAVEWA Cases (Cases 96-102, 104, 105, 108-110/69) | p. 146 | p. 370 |
| BASF Case (Case 49/69) | p. 351 | |
| Bayer Case (Case 51/69) | p. 317 | p. 351 |
| Beele Case (Case 6/81) | p. 514 | |
| Béguelin Case (Case 22/71) | p. 177 | |
| Bloos v. Bouyer Case (Case 59/77) | p. 186 | p. 278 |
| Boehringer Case, First (Case 45/69) | p. 271 | |
| Boehringer Case, Second (Case 7/72) | p. 377 | |
| Bosch Case (case 13/61) | p. 63 | p. 34, 420 |
| Brasserie de Haecht Case, First (Case 45/69) | p. 165 | p. 452 |
| Brasserie de Haecht Case, Second (case 48/73) | p. 183 | p. 185, 269, 278, 282 |
| Camera Care Case (Case 792/79 R) | p. 337 | |
| Cassis de Dijon Case (Case 120/78) | p. 533 | |
| Cement Convention Cases (Cases 8-11/66) | p. 379 | p. 332 |
| Centrafarm v. American Home Products Case (Case 3/78) | p. 509 | |
| Ciments et beton v. Kerpen Case (Case 319/82) | p. 184 | |
| Coditel II Case (Case 262/81) | p. 526 | |
| Commercial Solvents Case (Case 6-7/73) | p. 14 | p. 48, 67, 86, 226, 246, 255, 346 |
| Consten-Grundig Case (Case 56 & 58/64) | p. 66 | p. 108, 164, 167, 170, 192, 193, 345, 420, 424, 491 |
| Continental Can Case (Case 6/72) | p. 10 | p. 243, 265, 318, 324,330 |
| Costa-ENEL Case (Case 6/64) | p. 24 | |
| Dassonville Case (Case 8/74) | p. 528 | |
| Distillers Case (Case 30/78) | p. 179 | p. 271, 281 |
| Demo-Studio Schmidt Case (Case 210/81) | p. 290 | |
| Deutsche Grammophon Case (Case 78/70) | p. 2 | p. 218, 254, 492 |
| EMI Cases (Cases 51, 86 and 96/75) | p. 500 | |
| Fedetab Cases (Cases 209-215/78 & 218/78) | p. 80 | p. 147 |
| Fonderies Case (Case 63/75) | p. 283 | p. 62 |
| Ford Interim Case (Case 228-229/82) | p. 340 | |
| Frubo Case (Case 71/74) | p. 115 | p. 322, 475 |
| Geigy Case (Case 52/69) | p. 318 | p. 321 |
| GEMA Case (Case 125/78) | p. 286 | |
| Van Gend en Loos Case (Case 26/62) | | p. 34 |
| General Motors Case (Case 26/75) | p. 227 | p. 257 |

| | References | Also reported |
|---|---|---|
| Group Exemption Regulation Case (Case 32/65) | p. 210 | p. 268, 420 |
| Hag Case (Case 192/73) | p. 492 | |
| Hoffmann-La Roche Case (Case 85/76) | p. 334 | |
| Hoffmann-La Roche v. Centrafarm Case (Case 102/77) | p. 507 | |
| Hasselblad Case (Case 86/82) | p. 428 | p. 371 |
| Hugin Case (Case 22/78) | p. 90 | p. 241 |
| IBM Case, First (Case 60/81) | p. 269 | p. 320 |
| ICI Case (Case 48/69) | p. 44 | p. 70, 149 329 |
| Kali und Salz-Kali Chemie Case (Case 19-20/74) | p. 170 | |
| Lancome Case (Case 99/79) | p. 188 | |
| Lauder Case (Case 37/79) | p. 38 | |
| Maize Seed Case (Case 258/78) | p. 517 | |
| LTM v. MBU Case (Case 56/65) | p. 69 | p. 108, 163, 192, 420 |
| Merck-Stephar-Exler Case (Case 187/80) | p. 511 | |
| Miller International Schallplatten Case (Case 19/77) | p. 363 | |
| Michelin-Netherlands Case (Case 262/81) | p. 263 | |
| Metro Case (Case 26/76) | p. 18 | p. 382 |
| National Panasonic Case (Case 136/79) | p. 301 | |
| ANSEAU/NAVEWA Cases (Cases 96-102, 104, 105, 108-110/82) | p. 146 | p. 370 |
| L'Oreal Case (Case 31/80) | p. 441 | |
| Papiers Peints de Belgique Case (Case 73/74) | p. 78 | |
| Perfumes Cases (Cases 253/78 and 1-3/79) | p. 29 | |
| De Peijper Case (Case 104/75) | p. 531 | |
| Pioneer Cases (Cases 100-103/80) | p. 364 | p. 424 |
| Polydor Case (Case 270/80) | p. 54 | p. 52, 513 |
| SABAM Case (Case 127/73) First Judgment | p. 35 | p. 269 |
| Second Judgment | p. 35 | p. 255, 482 |
| Simmenthal II Case (Case 106/77) | p. 25 | |
| Sirena-Eda Case (Case 40/70) | p. 63 | |
| Sucrière Cases (Cases 41, 43 and 44/73) | p. 356 | |
| Sugar Cases (Cases 40-47, 50, 54-55, 111, 113-114/73) | p. 94 | p. 157, 252, 319, 330, 422 |
| Terrapin-Terranova Case (Case 19/75) | p. 503 | |
| Transmarine Paint Association Case (Case 17/74) | p. 324 | p. 202 |
| United Brands Case (Case 27/76) | p. 247 | p. 254, 333 |
| VBBB-Eldi Case (Case 106/79) | p. 278 | |
| VBVB-VBBB Cases (Cases 43-63/83) | p. 208 | |
| VCH Case (Case 8/72) | p. 75 | |
| Völk-Vervaecke Case (Case 5/69) | p. 174 | |
| Walt Wilhelm Case (Case 14/68) | p. 6 | p. 27, 371 |
| Züchner Case (Case 172/80) | p. 161 | p. 218, 60 |

TABLE OF CASES - BY CASE NUMBER